RESEARCH IN ECONOMIC ANTHROPOLOGY

Volume 19 • 1998

RESEARCH IN ECONOMIC ANTHROPOLOGY

Editor: BARRY L. ISAAC
Department of Anthropology
University of Cincinnati

VOLUME 19 • 1998

 JAI PRESS INC.

Stamford, Connecticut   London, England

Copyright © 1998 JAI PRESS INC.
100 Prospect Street
Stamford, Connecticut 06901-1640

JAI PRESS LTD.
38 Tavistock Street
Covent Garden
London WC2E 7PB
England

All rights reserved. No part of this publication may be reproduced, stored on a retrieval system, or transmitted in any form or by any means, electronic, mechanical, photocopying, filming, recording, or otherwise, without prior permission in writing from the publisher.

ISBN: 0-7623-0446-4
ISSN: 0190-1281

Manufactured in the United States of America

CONTENTS

LIST OF CONTRIBUTORS

E. Anne Beal

Department of Anthropology
University of Chicago

Rudi Colloredo-Mansfeld

Department of Anthropology
University of Iowa-Iowa City

Andrew C. Fortier

Illinois Transportation Archaeological
    Research Program
University of Illinois-Urbana

Jon L. Gibson

Department of Sociology and
    Anthropology
University of Southwestern Louisiana
Lafayette, LA

Roberto J. González

Department of Anthropology
University of California-Berkeley

James B. Greenberg

Bureau of Applied Research in
    Anthropology
University of Arizona-Tucson

Barry L. Isaac

Department of Anthropology
University of Cincinnati

Lynn A. Meisch

Department of Anthropology and
    Sociology
Saint Mary's College of California
Moraga, CA

Elizabeth Marberry Rogers

Department of Anthropology
University of Wisconsin-Madison

Dorothea E. Schulz

Institut für Ethnologie
Freie Universität Berlin

Susan Vincent

Department of Sociology and
  Anthropology
Mount Allison University
Sackville, New Brunswick

John P. Ziker

Department of Anthropology
University of California-Santa Barbara

INTRODUCTION

Barry L. Isaac

Much of the effort that otherwise would have gone into the writing of a lengthy introduction to this volume, following usual practice, instead was devoted to my chapter in Part IV. Accordingly, my commentary on this volume's contents is somewhat shorter than is customary.

THE ETHNOLOGICAL PAPERS (PARTS I-IV)

Studies of Otavalo, Ecuador

The three papers in Part I are united by several themes, including their common concern with Otavalo, a market town of 26,000 persons in northern Ecuador. All three papers also portray the dynamic interaction of local and extralocal forces that give rise to and define not only the local agrarian-artisan economy but also both local and translocal identity with community and ethnicity. Interesting comparative materials concerning economic-political-ethnic dynamics can be found in the recent special issue of *Ethnology* on Bolivia (Albro 1998), another heavily indigenous Andean country. The recent volume on property edited by Robert Hunt and Antonio Gilman (1998) also provides interesting comparative material for the third paper in this section.

Research in Economic Anthropology, Volume 19, pages 1-7.
Copyright © 1998 by JAI Press Inc.
All rights of reproduction in any form reserved.
ISBN: 0-7623-0446-4

LYNN A. MEISCH examines indigenous ("Indian") Otavalo economic gains in the years since the abolition of debt servitude in 1964. "By the 1990s, indigenous identity in Otavalo was no longer synonymous with serfdom, poverty, or social and political subordination." In a nutshell, once they were freed from servitude, thousands of Otavaleños have become prosperous from the sale of traditional weavings, as some 140,000 foreign tourists visit the Otavalo market annually and as Otavalo weavings are shipped elsewhere in Ecuador and abroad. As musicians, hundreds of young Otavalo males now play music on the streets of Europe and the United States, making their living directly from their audience or from the sale of their tapes or CDs.

RUDI COLLOREDO-MANSFELD examines the Otavaleños' "global archipelago," with "its scattered 'islands'...[of] peasant farming communities, provincial craft markets, urban construction sites, and touristic pedestrian malls in Latin America, Europe, and North American [U.S.] cities." This modern Otavalo archipelago is quite different from the Inka vertical archipelago familiar to most anthropologists (see Murra 1980). Markets and trading—the very institutions by-passed by Inka administrators through their state redistribution system—are the heart of the Otavalo economy. "In the global archipelago, most of the islands are complementary market niches ultimately yielding the same thing—cash—not ecological niches yielding different crops." COLLOREDO-MANSFELD focusses on the ways Otavaleños solve two problems: (1) maintaining the household bond "in a translocal world" and (2) forming interhousehold linkages through *compadrazgo* (ritual co-parenthood).

ELIZABETH MARBERRY ROGERS examines three court cases about land which "center on attempts to control the privatization of communal landholdings in the Otavalo Valley in the early 1900s." Two of these cases involve "intra-community [indigenous] factionalism in which both sides claim to be the legitimate representatives of the community who, as such, have the right to decide the fate of [its] lands." The third case involves indigenous defendants and white plaintiffs; the latter claim that, as members of the community, they also have private rights in its communal lands. ROGERS shows that land disputes involving the privatization (parcelization) of lands belonging to indigenous communities cannot be understood through the hoary linked dichotomies of indigenous-mestizo (white)/communalistic-individualistic, nor can all instances of privatization be attributed "to the rejection of the 'traditional' by particularly 'progressive' community members." In fact, indigenous communities may seek to protect their communal lands from outside predation by means of dividing them into individually-titled parcels that are easier to defend in the court system. Furthermore, the privatization of communal pasture lands may be vigorously opposed within indigenous communities that do not oppose the privatization of communal agricultural lands.

Commoditization

The two papers in Part II continue the theme of local/extralocal dynamics. DOROTHEA SCHULZ studies what happens when Malian praise-singers, whose functions traditionally were embedded in strictly localized and intimate patron-client relationships with the rich and powerful, come to offer their praise services to anyone who can pay for them. Indeed, their music has so transcended local sociocultural contexts that it "is rapidly becoming emblematic of Malian national culture." In short, local-particularistic-noncommercial has become national-universalistic-commercial as the result of modern broadcast and performance media. It has not necessarily been "globalized" in the usual sense of that term, even though a few of these commercialized praise-singers have achieved international renown, but it certainly has become *translocalized* and *metaculturalized* as it has entered Malian national culture. Readers who enjoy SCHULZ's article will also appreciate Meenakshi Chakraverti's account of the ways in which local *patrimoine* and local identity have become objectified and commoditized for the tourist trade in Le Puy-en-Velay, France (Chakraverti 1997; also see Cameron & Gatewood 1994, Pryor 1989, García C. 1995).

JAMES B. GREENBERG's article in Part II examines the twin processes of territorialization and globalization with regard to the destruction of the Colorado River delta. Territorialization both "carves up ecosystems piecemeal among administrative entities"—in this case, the United States and Mexico, with their respective multi-layered bureaucracies—and fractures ecosystems into separable commodities ("natural resources"), which are then subject to market-driven "competition over their current human utility," independently of their biotic importance in the localized ecosystem. In the case of the Colorado River delta, the result was what GREENBERG calls "the tragedy of commoditization."

Women as Consumers and Producers

E. ANNE BEAL has studied shopping among the upper class of Amman, Jordan, where "the association of...shopping with women is a critical component in the construction of the female gender role." Despite the fact that this association is not strictly true, it is made by both sexes, "as is the denigration of this activity as essentially trivial." In the course of her research on shopping for the home, BEAL was "surprised at the extent to which men were involved in the details of consumption decisions, determining the style and color of a sofa or table, for example." This unexpected finding led her to conclude that the public/private distinction, in which the home is represented as a "private and feminine sphere in opposition to a public and masculine sphere," misrepresents "the nuances of consumption practices." In fact, elite Jordanian husbands proudly dominated consumption decisions regarding the "less familiar spaces of the home (mainly, guest rooms and dining rooms)"—boasting of having selected the furnishings for these spaces, even against the tastes of their wives (or daughters-in-law)—while wives dominated the furnishing and decor of "the most familiar spaces (usually kitchens, bedrooms, and family baths)." In practice, then, it is not shopping per se that determines the evaluation of that activity, but the sex of the shopper. "Women's consumption is construed as emblematic of women's relative insignificance within the culture, while men's consumption is taken as evidence of men's power and authority."

SUSAN VINCENT presents "the very different stories of two women's partnerships with men"; the two women "are from the same Peruvian peasant village but are some 50 years apart in age," the elder having been born around 1915. The contrast is instructive of the ways in which "Peruvian family structures have changed because of capitalism." VINCENT's aim is to help us rethink the concepts of household, family, and community—and their interrelations. Among the questions she poses are: "What social or market relation can [could] replace the material component of a husband, wife, sister, brother, parent, or child?"; and, "Why are some [kin] relations more expendable, more problematic, or more necessary than others?"

I suggest that these two papers be read in conjunction with the three papers in Part III of R.E.A. Volume 18 (1997). There, María Quiñones (1997) examines the issues of consumption and identity with respect of Barbadian women "suitcase traders," while Katherine Browne (1997) and Judy Brink (1997) examine women's work in Martinique and Egypt, respectively, with regard to questions of opportunities, structural constraints, and ideology.

Subsistence and Market Production: Siberia, Mexico, Sierra Leone

Part IV returns to the theme of economic translocalization, with emphasis on the tension between subsistence provisioning and production for the market. JOHN P. ZIKER's paper is the result of 18 months of field work, from late 1995 through 1997, in northern Siberia among the Dolgan and Nganasan. Traditionally mobile hunters-fishers-trappers, these groups were sedentized under the Soviets and were encouraged to hunt, fish, and trap for a government hunting enterprise, which brokered their products to the extralocal market. ZIKER "discusses how [these] aboriginal Siberians are dealing with the dissolution of state socialism and subsequent economic collapse."

ROBERTO J. GONZÁLEZ writes about coffee production in a Zapotec village in Oaxaca, Mexico. His paper "is an effort to link global processes with local history, to consider the ways in which recently-introduced commodities can rapidly become 'traditional,' and to compare the hegemonic and counter-hegemonic uses of such crops." Although coffee "has historically been wielded as a hegemonic tool by plantation owners, regional strongmen, and transnational corporations," GONZÁLEZ argues that this very crop also "holds the potential of making a positive impact" to both "the historical transformation of ethnic identities" and "environmentally sustainable economic projects."

My own article, which closes Part IV, deals with the introduction and spread of coffee and cocoa as cash crops among the Mende of Eastern Province, Sierra Leone, West Africa. More specifically, it concerns the question of why subsistence-oriented cultivators abandon or modify their self-provisioning tradition to take up market-oriented production of non-edible crops.

THE ARCHAEOLOGICAL PAPERS (PART V)

Part V consists of archaeological studies of complex prehistoric economies in Louisiana and Illinois. JON L. GIBSON presents a fresh analysis of the political and economic relationships between core and peripheral occupations at Poverty Point (ca. 1730-1350 B.C.) in northeastern Louisiana. The main core consists of six concentrically arranged earthen rings (1.0m to 1.5m in height) that form a crescent-shaped figure in which the opposing ends of the outermost ring are some 1,200m apart. For two reasons, Poverty Point's impressive earthworks are of great interest to students of the political-economic evolution of native North America: first, because they were built by hunter-gatherers rather than agriculturalists; second, because they were long thought to be the oldest such earthworks in what is now the United States. Recent work at Watson Brake, another northeast Louisiana site constructed by hunter-gatherers, has revealed its earthworks to be some 1,900 years older than Poverty Point's, however (Saunders et al. 1997). Because Watson Brake is also older than comparable developments in Olmec, prehistoric Mexico's supposed "mother civilization," the long-running argument about possible Mesoamerican influence upon the evolution of prehistoric Southeastern U.S. may now take a new direction. Returning to JON GIBSON's chapter in this volume, it seems fair to warn that his examination of the raw data of core and peripheral components will interest mainly archaeologists; ethnologists may want to skim through those sections (pp. 291-318) and begin serious reading with "Articulation of Components" (pp. 319-328). The section on "The Corporate Character of Political Economy" (pp. 328-331) will interest anthropologists of all stripes, though, as will the near poetic penultimate section, "Growing the Political Economy: A Hypothetical Saga" (331-335).

The other paper in Part V is by ANDREW C. FORTIER, who writes in a style readily accessible to ethnologists as well as archaeologists. He presents a masterful synthesis of the pre-Mississippian (3000 B.C.-A.D. 1050) economies of the American Bottom, an 80-mile strip of floodplain near the confluence of the Mississippi, Missouri, and Illinois rivers. Among the important benchmarks established by the more than 100 years of archaeological research in this area are: (1) a "horticultural revolution"—*not* based on maize, incidentally—in the 50 B.C.-150 A.D. period, together with a multi-tiered settlement system and trade in such exotic materials as obsidian, mica, copper, and fluorite; (2) the abrupt abandonment of the American Bottom in A.D. 300-350 and its reoccupation ca. A.D. 400

by a "completely distinct" people who eventually gave rise to the American Bottom cultural core; (3) a "second economic transformation" in A.D. 650-850 involving intensified production of both wild and domesticated foodstuffs (but still without significant occurrence of maize) and intensified processing (including both new storage and cooking practices), and a great increase in community ceremonialism (including the beginnings of the renewal ceremonies—with their sacred fires, ballgames, harvest festivals, and potlatch-like giveaways—for which the native Southeast is known in the historic period); (4) the further intensification of the foregoing patterns with a significant commitment to maize production after A.D. 850; and (5) the rapid appearance ca. A.D. 1050 of "controlling polities," especially Cahokia, "where we can see the visible mortuary remains of elites and retainers, exotic goods, figurines reflecting a complex cosmology..., large palisaded enclosures, observatories, and...massive earth-moving projects." Cahokia, the ruins of which are a tourist attraction near St. Louis, Missouri, is arguably the largest and politically strongest prehistoric polity ever to have existed in what is now the United States.

THE *R.E.A.* SERIES

One of my goals as editor of R.E.A. since 1983 has been to encourage the participation of archaeologists and ethnologists (sociocultural anthropologists) on an equal footing in economic anthropology. Most of the annual volumes published under my editorship (Volumes 6-19) have included a mixture of papers from the two subfields. Some readers of the annual volumes may still not be aware, though, of the R.E.A. Supplements, which are devoted entirely to archaeological (and, occasionally, ethnohistorical) papers, and each of which is devoted to a particular prehistoric topic or region. The Supplements published to date are:

- Supplement 7 (1993), *Economic Aspects of Water Management in the Prehispanic New World* (Vernon L. Scarborough & Barry L. Isaac, eds.)
- Supplement 6 (1992), *Long-Term Subsistence Change in Prehistoric North America* (Dale R. Croes, Rebecca A. Hawkins & Barry L. Isaac, eds.)
- Supplement 5 (1990), *Early Paleoindian Economies of Eastern North America* (Kenneth B. Tankersley & Barry L. Isaac, eds.)
- Supplement 4 (1989), *Prehistoric Maya Economies of Belice* (Patricia A. McAnany & Barry L. Isaac, eds.)
- Supplement 3 (1988), *Prehistoric Economies of the Pacific Northwest Coast* (Barry L. Isaac, ed.)
- Supplement 2 (1986), *Economic Aspects of Prehispanic Highland Mexico* (Barry L. Isaac, ed.)
- Supplement 1 (1980), *The Economic Organization of the Inka State* (John V. Murra, author; George Dalton, series ed.).

REFERENCES

Albro, Robert, ed. (1998) *Relocating Bolivia: Popular Political Perspectives* (*Ethnology* 37:2:Special Issue). Pittsburgh, PA: University of Pittsburgh.

Brink, Judy (1997) "The Effect of Employment and Education on the Status of Peasant Wives in Egypt." Pp. 217-229 in *Research in Economic Anthropology, Vol. 18*. Greenwich, CT: JAI Press Inc.

Browne, Katherine E. (1997) "The Economic Immobility of Women in Martinique: Structural Patterns, Risk, Opportunity, and Ideology." Pp. 183-216 in *Research in Economic Anthropology, Vol. 18*. Greenwich, CT: JAI Press Inc.

Cameron, Catherine M., and John B. Gatewood (1994) "The Authentic Interior: Questing *Gemeinschaft* in Post-Industrial Society." *Human Organization* 53:21-32.

Chakraverti, Meenakshi (1997) "Money and Beyond: Local Identity and Individualism in Le Puy-en-Velay, France." Pp. 35-62 in *Research in Economic Anthropology, Vol. 18*. Greenwich, CT: JAI Press Inc.

García Canclini, Néstor (1993) *Transforming Modernity: Popular Culture in Mexico* (trans. Lidia Lozano). Austin: University of Texas Press.

Hunt, Robert C., and Antonio Gilman (1998) *Property in Economic Context*. Lanham, MD: University Press of America, Monographs in Economic Anthropology, No. 14.

Murra, John (1980) *The Economic Organization of the Inka State [Supplement 1, Research in Economic Anthropology]*. Greenwich, CT: JAI Press Inc.

Pryor, John (1989) "Market Forces in the Creation of Pomo Basketry Style and Pomo Ethnicity." Pp. 181-216 in *Research in Economic Anthropology, Vol. 11*. Greenwich, CT: JAI Press Inc.

Quiñones, María I. (1997) "Looking Smart: Consumption, Cultural History, and Identity among Barbadian 'Suitcase Traders'." Pp. 167-182 in *Research in Economic Anthropology, Vol. 18*. Greenwich, CT: JAI Press Inc.

Saunders, Joe W., et al. (1997) "A Mound Complex in Louisiana at 5400-5000 Years Before the Present." *Science* 277:1796-1799.

PART I

STUDIES OF OTAVALO, ECUADOR

THE RECONQUEST OF OTAVALO, ECUADOR:
INDIGENOUS ECONOMIC GAINS AND NEW POWER RELATIONS

Lynn A. Meisch

INTRODUCTION

This paper examines the profound changes in ethnic and power relations between people traditionally defined as indigenous (S. *indígena*)[1] and those of the dominant population (S. *mestizos*) and whites (S. *blancos*) in the Otavalo valley of northern Ecuador (see Figure 1). I use the term "power" in the classic Weberian sense, as the ability to impose one's will and realize one's goals even against the opposition and resistance of others. I argue that the changes in ethnic and power relations discussed below, which have significantly altered the sociopolitical landscape of the region, are a direct result of the economic boom in the valley beginning in the mid-1970s, which was fueled by indigenous household-based textile production. The economic growth was precipitated by several factors: (1) the abolition of debt serfdom (Q. *wasipungu*, also spelled *huasipungo*) in 1964, (2) the

Research in Economic Anthropology, Volume 19, pages 11-30.
Copyright © 1998 by JAI Press Inc.
All rights of reproduction in any form reserved.
ISBN: 0-7623-0446-4

Figure 1.   Map of Ecuador

growth of international tourism to the Otavalo Saturday market beginning in the 1970s, (3) the rise of textile exports, and (4) the transnational migration of Otavalo indígenas in the 1990s to countries on six continents to sell textiles and play Andean music.

In the colonial era, a number of polities or ethnic groups in the region amalgamated and were named Otavalos after a local *ayllu* (Q. land-based descent group). Today, Otavalo refers to the market town of 26,000 persons, the *cantón* (S. equivalent of country) of Otavalo in the intermontane valley in which the town is located, and the approximately 60,000 indígenas who live in 75 small communities throughout the valley, in Otavalo town, and in cities and towns elsewhere in Ecuador and abroad.

During the current decade, the high (9,203[1]), green Otavalo valley became the favorite research destination of many social scientists for various reasons. Researchers flocked to Ecuador during the height (1982-1992) of the dirty war in

Peru between Sendero Luminoso and the Peruvian government, when research in Peru was restricted. Otavalo is easily accessible, located only two hours by bus north of Quito on the paved Pan-American highway. The Otavalos[2] are open to outsiders because of their extensive dealings with tourists and exporters; and finally, the global presence of Otavalo street vendors and musicians attracted the interest of researchers formerly unaware of the region.

On a more profound level, there are compelling reasons to study the Otavalos. Written documentation of the Otavalo valley for every century dating back to shortly after the Spanish conquest of the region in A.D. 1534 affords unparalleled opportunities for historical comparisons; without such documentation, this paper would be impossible. The Otavalos also offer researchers an opportunity to grapple with many current theoretical concerns in the social sciences: ethnic identity, indigenous minorities and their relation to the nation-state, gender and power, economic and cultural globalization and their effects on small-scale societies, transnational migration, the politics of representation, and the nature of postmodernity (see Colloredo-Mansfield, this volume).

THE HISTORY OF TEXTILE PRODUCTION IN THE VALLEY

Long before the Incas of Peru arrived in what is now northern Ecuador in the late 15th century, intent on adding this rich region to their empire, the indígenas of the Otavalo region were known as weavers and traveling merchants (Salomon 1981:434, 1986:102-106). This historical "entrepreneurial ethic" (Chavez 1982) is congruent with participation in cash economics, and the Otavalos challenge the concept of indigenous peoples as uninterested in the marketplace and a drag on the economy. This attitude is common in Ecuadorian discourse about "the Indian problem" and was expressed in a 1992 editorial in *El Comercio*, in which the author observed that "the aim of our Catholic bishops [in declaring November 15th-22nd the week of the Indian and sponsoring programs on indigenous affairs] is to awaken our indígenas from their epoch of semi-vegetative inertia" (Andrade Reimers 1992).

Within a year after the Spanish conquest of northern Ecuador, *encomiendas* (S.) in the Otavalo region were parceled out to Spanish Conquistadors. An encomienda was not a land grant per se, but the right to extract tribute and labor from the indigenous population of a defined region in return for Christianizing them. Among the tribute owed every six months by Otavalos in 1551 to their *encomiendero*, Rodrigo de Salazar, were quantities of traditional textiles, including hundreds of men's and women's shoulder wraps, men's tunics, and women's body wraps. Other textiles owed were European: 3 tablecloths, 3 medium-sized awnings, and 50 1.1 lb balls of cotton yarn for banner, canopy, or tent fabric (Espinosa Soriano 1988, Vol. II:130, Vol. III:12-16). At this early date, Otavalos were not only producing traditional textiles that they themselves used, but non-traditional textiles for outsiders, a pattern which obtains to this day. In other words, for 450 years it has been traditional for Otavalos to produce non-traditional cloth.

Because Ecuador lacked the extensive mineral wealth of Peru and Bolivia and because the existing mines played out in the early colonial era, the Spanish soon established textile sweatshops (S. *obrajes*) which brutally exploited indigenous labor. The Spanish introduced the fiber (sheep's wool) and tools (European treadle looms, spinning wheels, and hand carders) to increase production: these tools form the technological basis of the modern industry. Spaniards also introduced the concept of production weaving, the fabrication of large quantities of textiles for commercial purposes. The labor tax (Q. *mita*) that indígenas paid by working on colonial haciendas and in obrajes ultimately evolved into various systems of permanent servitude on local haciendas in return for the right to farm a plot of land or pasture their animals: "Almost all the people of Carabuela worked on the hacienda [Pinsaquí] as *yanaperos* (Q. helpers). They worked two days a week in return for access to pasture for their animals and firewood from the woods. There were also huasipungueros who had to work for the patrón all week. For their work they did not receive pay, but were only given a tiny piece of land to work" (Korovkin et al. 1994:18; my translation).

By 1900, control of prime valley land by large haciendas and demographic pressure on the land available for indigenous small-farming in parts of the valley resulted in temporary and permanent out-migration by Otavalo indígenas. Among the first to leave were families from Quinchuquí (a small community a few miles from Otavalo) involved in the meat and cattle trade, who moved north to Ibarra. By the 1930s, there were families permanently living in Ibarra, and some had moved farther north to Tulcán on the Ecuadorian-Colombian border (Males 1985:7-8, 45, 79). Rather than assimilate, however, these families retained their Otavalo identity as expressed in a distinctive dress, customs, and the Quichua language, and they maintained their ties with their Otavalo communities of origin. Otavalo textile merchants were soon plying their trade in Tulcán and Colombia, as well as in Quito and other Ecuadorian cities and towns.

The reconstruction of Otavalo textile history itself is an arena where power relations are contested. Rappaport (1990:15) notes that "history is a question of power in the present, and not of detached reflection upon the past. It can serve to maintain power, or can become a vehicle for empowerment." Several early accounts of the rise of the modern industry in Otavalo, written by a foreigner (Parsons 1945) or by a foreigner and a local non-indigenous elite (Collier & Buitrón 1949), credit the owner of the Hacienda Cusín with the introduction of *casimir* (S. cashmere, woolen tweeds): "About forty years ago the Spanish loom began to be taken over by the Indians. José Cajas of Quinchuquí is said to have been the first to use it, at the suggestion of a gentleman of Quito" (Parsons 1945:25). A footnote says that her source was: "F. A. Uribe. Señor Uribe is the son-in-law of the haciendada of Cusín. He told me that in 1917 his prospective mother-in-law presented him with a poncho beautifully woven by José Cajas, and it occurred to him to set up José Cajas with a Spanish loom, supply samples of casimir to be copied, and afford the weaver a Quito market" (ibid.) The authors of *The Awakening Valley* (Collier & Buitrón 1949:160) make a similar claim:

> Thirty years ago a white landlord asked an Indian near Otavalo to weave him a length of woolen cloth for a suit. The Indian, who had never woven anything but ponchos and native woolens, set up his loom and with great skill copied a sample of English tweed. The white man was delighted. Now he would not have to send all the way to London for material for his suits. He told his friends. They, too, ordered cloth. The original weaver shared his orders with a friend, and the foundation for a new enterprise was laid.

According to the story, the trade took off from there and casimir became an important Otavalo product. Since twill weaves or tweeds called *jerga* (S.) had been made since the early colonial era, the José Caja story raises several questions. How did casimir differ from the usual twills? Did Uribe introduce something special? Or is the story an example of whites-mestizos claiming credit for what the Otavalos were already doing? (Two extremely successful contemporary products, tapestries and sweaters, were introduced by outsiders; the Otavalos then applied their textile production and marketing skills to turn these textiles into major sources of income.)

Peguche indígenas have another version of the introduction of casimir (Korovkin et al. 1994:20; my translation):

> The hacienda of Peguche had a textile obraje where children and adults worked almost like slaves. The owner brought samples of English cashmere from Colombia. He locked up two weavers from Peguche on his property in Tabacundo to copy the samples. He said, if you make it you will leave safe and sound and if not, you will disappear. The weavers began to copy the samples, but they did not leave safe and sound as the owner said. Enclosed in the basement of the hacienda of Peguche they had to teach other weavers how to make casimir.

It is entirely possible that both versions are correct, that the weaving of casimir was introduced in several ways, both benign and oppressive, but the indigenous side has not been heard until now, and it changes considerably our understanding of the origin of the casimir industry. There is at least one more possibility for the introduction of casimir, which is that Otavalos in Tulcán or elsewhere obtained English cashmere from Colombia and copied it. The date 1917, mentioned by Parsons (1945:25n), is significant, because World War I had been underway for three years in Europe. German U-boats had made serious inroads on allied shipping, resulting in a scarcity of English products in Ecuador. The casimir produced in Otavalo was intended for the Ecuadorian white-mestizo market in the absence of the English cloth.

Following WWII, however, casimir became less competitive with European- or American-made woolens, but the decline of this market coincided with the arrival of Andean Mission, International Labor Organization, and Peace Corps development programs as well as with the growth of mass tourism in the 1960s, all of which helped move Otavalo textile production in new directions to meet the demands of outsiders. Otavalos made scarves, ponchos, shawls, belts, and other clothing for the local indigenous and white-mestizo markets as well as for tourists and adopted such new products as tapestries and, later, daypacks and duffel bags, to mention just a few items. Otavalos became active as intermediaries in the hand-knitted sweater trade and then began to knit and then weave sweaters themselves.

THE GROWTH OF THE TEXTILE AND TOURISM INDUSTRIES SINCE 1970

The economic growth in the Otavalo valley over the past three decades is nothing short of phenomenal. The abolition of debt serfdom in 1964 permitted former wasipungeros to weave and sell for themselves, rather than working for the local haciendas. The growth of mass tourism worldwide coincided locally with the paving of the Pan-American highway between the Colombian frontier and Quito, making Otavalo only a two-hour bus ride from the capital, and with the construction of concrete kiosks in the Poncho Plaza for the crafts market, a Dutch development project that was completed in 1973. The Organization of American States (OAS) declared 1972 "Tourism Year of the Americas" and actively promoted tourism throughout the hemisphere. Partly as a result of this activity, the Dutch airline KLM inaugurated flights to Quito, "thus making the European tourist market available to the country" (OAS General Secretariat 1973:17). The OAS, in its section on Ecuador, noted that, if the visitor had enough time, the city of Cuenca, "and Otavalo, famous for its colorful Indian fair, are worth visiting" (ibid.).

At the same time, population growth and land shortages in the Otavalo region in the 1970s and 1980s resulted in increased out-migration from numerous rural communities to urban Otavalo and to cities and towns elsewhere in Ecuador, as well as to Colombia, Venezuela, Brazil, Spain, and the United States. The Otavalos in these locales set up weaving workshops, opened stores, and usually maintained ties with their Otavalo valley communities, often returning for the fiesta of San Juan in June or for such family occasions as baptisms, confirmations, weddings, and funerals. The 1970s also saw the blossoming of full-time commercial weaving or merchandising as alternative occupations to farming or to farming and weaving (Chavez 1982). Otavalos now have a range of occupations, from strictly farming to farming and weaving to just weaving or selling, with incomes increasing as families move away from agriculture and toward merchandising. It is no longer possible to say, as it was in the 1940s, "The Otavalo Indian, like all the Indians of the inter-Andean plateau, is above all a farmer" (Collier & Buitrón 1949:49). Today, Otavalo indígenas are above all textile producers and merchants, even though most families still plant corn, squash, haba beans, and potatoes for family consumption on the small plots of land available to them.

The Saturday weekly market was the main tourist attraction, although a few tourists managed to visit the much smaller Wednesday wholesale textile market in the Poncho Plaza. Older Otavalos recall the late 1960s, when two or three foreigners visited the Saturday market, which began about 5:30 a.m. and ended by nine or ten. By the end of the 1970s, the market still began early but ran until noon to take advantage of the tour buses arriving from Quito, and several hundred European and North American tourists visited on a typical Saturday during the height of the tourist season from May through September (Meisch 1980:26). The numbers have gone up each year, with several thousand tourists attending each weekly Saturday fair this decade during the high season. Canny Otavalos began staying until 5 p.m. on Saturdays when they realized that many tourists arrived in the afternoon or had lunch and came back for a second round of shopping. Vendors began filling spaces in the Poncho Plaza with additional kiosks and tables and spreading down the side streets of the town.

The market continued to expand temporally as well as physically. Beginning in January 1989, indígenas began holding a Sunday market in the Poncho Plaza, which by August of that year was three-fourths full of vendors and goods. In 1991, some vendors began to sell in the Poncho Plaza on Fridays as well as Saturdays, Sundays, and Wednesdays. By 1992, vendors were selling in the Poncho Plaza every day of the week.

By March 1991, the Saturday market had expanded so much that the Municipality of Otavalo painted numbered spaces on some of the east-west streets, completely closing them to vehicular traffic. In 1993, the market continued to expand in an east-west direction, with the jewelry booths on Calle Salinas crossing Jaramillo and extending half-way to 31 de Octubre (see Figure 2). *Artesanías* (S. crafts) stands also spread into Calle Sucre on both sides along the Poncho Plaza, almost displacing the pottery vendors who have occupied the space for years. The kiosks began creeping north, entirely lining the street between Calles Quiroga and Quito by 1993, and intermittently occupying space north a number of blocks on Calle Pasaje. By June 1996, the two main plazas in town, the Parque Bolívar and the Poncho Plaza, were entirely connected by kiosks on Calle Sucre.

Ecuador had a record 482,000 foreign tourists in 1994 (*Hoy*, martes 25 de julio de 1995:6-A), up 2.34 percent from the previous year. The country received 455,000 tourists in 1995, who spent 260 million dollars (*El Comercio, Martes Económico*, 27 de agosto de 1996:6). These numbers probably held steady or increased slightly in 1996 and 1997. No one keeps statistics on the number of foreign visitors to the Otavalo Saturday market, although an article using CETUR (the Ecuadorian Tourist Commission) data in *Crucero, Hoy's* tourism supplement, listed Imbabura Province as the third most visited locale in the country (29.10%), after Quito (visited by 69.51% of foreign tourists) and Guayaquil (44.59%) ("En números," *Crucero*, 28 de septiembre de 1994:6). Quito and Guayaquil lead because they are the sites of the country's two international airports. It is safe to assume that a visit to Imbabura Province includes Otavalo, which means that, in

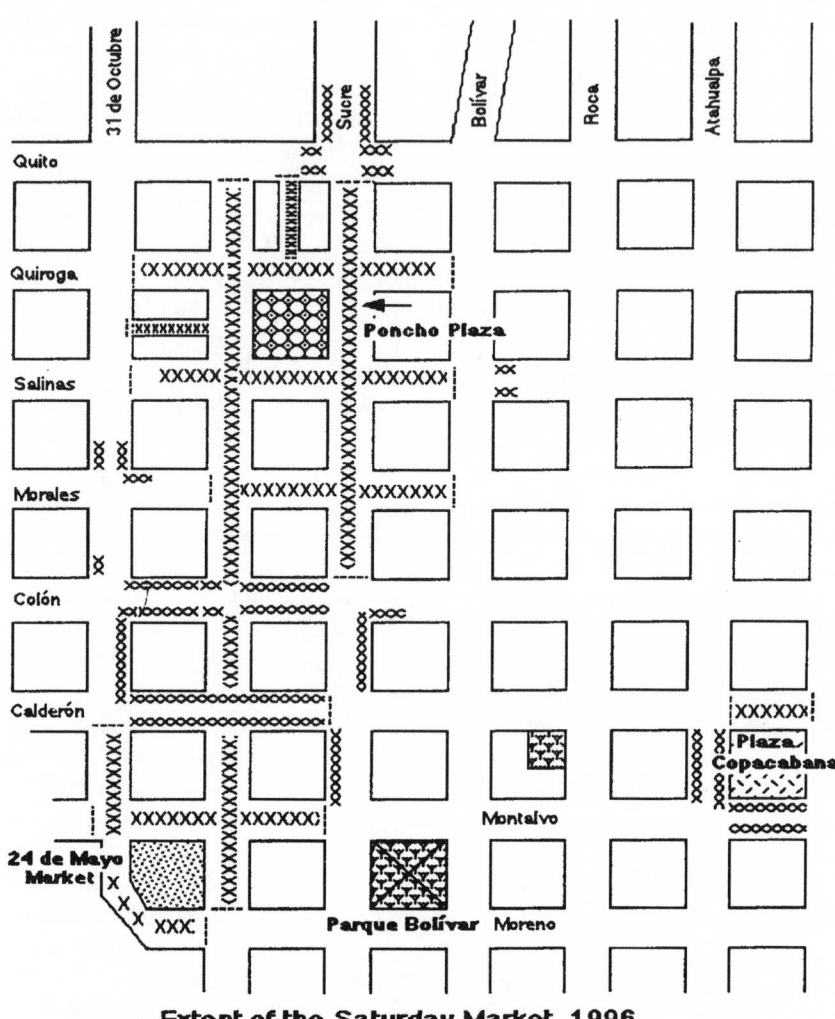

Extent of the Saturday Market, 1996

XXX xxx = vendors in the street, two and sometimes three rows of stands
xxx = one row of stands   ---- = street closed to vehicles

Figure 2.   Extent of the Otavalo Saturday Market in 1996

1994, the town received 29.10 percent of the 482,000 visitors to Ecuador, or
140,262 tourists.

There are no statistics on the amounts tourists spend on artesanías made or sold
in Otavalo or on food, lodging, and transportation, but CETUR broke down the

general expenses of visitors to Ecuador (all visitors, including tourists, business people, attendees at congresses and conventions, and people visiting their families). In 1991, 33.40 percent of visitors' expenses went for lodging, 33.06 percent for food, 15.11 percent for transport, 7.79 percent for recreation, 6.67 percent for purchases (S. *"compras"*), and 3.9 percent for other (*Hoy, Crucero,* supplement, miércoles 19 de octubre de 1994:6). This means that visitors spent $12,606,300 on purchases in 1991. Assuming that the percentages have held steady, the amount was $15,341,000 in 1993, given the increase in tourism and travel to Ecuador. But how much was spent in Otavalo or on Otavalo-produced goods in Cuenca, Quito, or Guayaquil? My best estimate is that a good 75 percent, or approximately U.S. $9,454,725 in 1991, and $11,505,750 in 1993, was spent on artesanías made in northern Imbabura and southern Carchi provinces or sold at the Otavalo market. The other 25 percent went for goods, including artesanías, produced and sold elsewhere in Ecuador, including such Cuenca-area crafts as "Panama" hats, ceramics, sweaters, and ikat textiles; *shigras* (Q. netted bags) from the central sierra, and balsa wood carvings and ceramics from the Orient. These figures do not include expenditures by foreign exporters, which are equal to or greater than the amounts spent by tourists.

For example, if 2,500 tourists spend an average of U.S. $50 apiece on crafts per Saturday during the three months of the summer high season (and that figure is probably low, the cost of just two sweaters and two tapestries), they would enrich the artisans by U.S. $1,500,000 (2,500 x $50 x 12). If they average $100 apiece in the market, then the amount is U.S. $3,000,000. This figure, of course, does not include purchases by tourists shopping outside Otavalo, by townspeople, or by other Ecuadorian visitors to the crafts market, by Otavalo merchants for sale elsewhere in Ecuador or abroad, or by foreign exporters, nor does it include tourist purchases made during the other nine months of the year.

The infrastructure of the town has increased each decade to meet the needs of the two separate but closely related industries: exports and tourism. An archaeologist who visited the Otavalo market in 1969 when he was a Peace Corps volunteer recalled, "There were no decent places to stay in Otavalo; we stayed in Ibarra [a half-hour north] and got on the bus with the Indians in the cold and dark. What stands out most is that the market was devoted to selling wool—raw wool and yarn. There were no sweaters or clothing, maybe a few tapestries" (Stephen Athens, pers. comm.). By 1980, there were 15 hotels, residences, and pensions listed in the *1981 South American Handbook* (Brooks 1981:569). By January 1995, there were 37 such establishments. All are locally owned and operated, at least six or seven by indígenas and one by resident expatriate Americans. There are no chain hotels or multinationally-owned hotels anywhere in the region. In addition, there are two indígena-owned and -operated hotels in the nearby community of Peguche.

In the 1970s and 1980s, indígenas also opened restaurants, folk music clubs (S. *peñas folklóricas*), bus lines, and other businesses in Otavalo, and began buying or renting property in the town—until the northern half of Otavalo became 65 percent to 75 percent indigenous. The number of stores selling crafts climbed from"several" in the early 1960s (Cooper 1965) to at least 150 by the summer of 1997, most of them indígena-owned and operated.

Some services arrived relatively late. The first tourist agency, Zulaytur, opened in 1986 and involved a partnership between an Otavaleña, Zulay Saravino of Quinchuquí, and a white-mestizo, Rodrigo Mora of Otavalo, which foundered amidst mutual recriminations and lawsuits. The white-mestizo retained rights to the name "Zulaytur," and Zulay opened here own travel agency directly across the street from Mora's with the name "Zulay, Diceny Viajes, Inc."

Inti Express, which offers airline bookings and tickets on credit and "Indian Village tours," money changing, FAX facilities, horseback tours, postcards, and air freight, opened at the end of 1988. Inti Pungo opened right across the street in March1990, and suddenly there was a cluster of four tourist agencies on Calle Sucre near the corner of Colón. As the decade advanced, agencies began sprouting like mushrooms, until there were nine by late 1995. These agencies exist as much for Otavalos as they do for tourists, with their various services including help with Ecuadorian documents and selling tickets on credit because the first half of the 1990s witnessed substantial movement abroad, both permanent and temporary emigration to every continent except Antarctica. This exodus was fueled by demographic pressure and land shortages in the valley and the search for new textile markets. "*Demasiada competencia*" (S. too much competition) is the Otavalo mantra of the 1990s.

Although sales to other tourists and Ecuadorians at local markets and in stores throughout the country are important, sales to foreign exporters constitute another large market. An Otavaleño with stores in Quito and Otavalo, who makes silk-screened and batiked T-shirts, estimated that 10 percent of his business was local and 90 percent was for the export market. I estimated that, in the mid-1980s, foreign exporters of Otavalo region crafts poured at least U.S. $2 million into the textile economy of Imbabura province (Meisch 1987-88), and many exporters thought that figure was low. At that time, there were no air cargo or shipping agencies of any kind in Otavalo; exporters had to hire cabs or trucks to haul their merchandise to Quito. In 1994, I again interviewed all the foreign exporters I could find, who probably constituted no more than half of the exporters who passed through town. Based on interviews with this group, I estimate that exporters invested about U.S. $12 million in merchandise in northern Ecuador that year (Meisch 1997:129). In the summer of 1997, I talked with exporters from the United States and Canada who routinely spend a quarter of a million dollars annually on artesanías produced in Imbabura Province, and they estimated that exports by foreigners accounted for U.S. $50 million annually. I think this figure is high unless *all* exports by Otavalos, other Ecuadorians, and foreigners are factored in.

With exports of this magnitude, the establishment of air cargo companies in Otavalo served an obvious need. The first air cargo company in town, Panatlantic, opened in 1988. In 1993, there were seven air cargo agencies in Otavalo, most clustered around the Poncho Plaza. By the beginning of 1994, there were ten: U.N.A.I.M.C.O., Mundo Export, and Runa Marca on Calle Quiroga, Inti Express (which is also a travel agency), Ecuador Cargo (also a travel agency), and Panatlantic on Calle Surce, Transchryver on Calle Salinas, M.S. Exportación/Importación on Calle Jaramillo, Roman Cargo on Calle Calderón, and SADECOM on Calle Ordoñez. Later in 1994, U.N.A.I.M.C.O. discontinued its air cargo services, but another office, Intertrafic, opened in 1995, giving the town ten air cargo companies. By the summer of 1996, there were 14 air cargo companies in Otavalo. Thirteen of these companies are located in the north-central end of town, close to the Poncho Plaza, and one is located near the Instituto Otavaleño de Anthropología in the Ciudadela Imbaya. According to an American expatriate hotel owner in Otavalo, another agency (Pachakutik) opened in 1997, which is owned and operated primarily by indígenas (Margaret Goodhart, pers. comm.). The agencies provide boxes, pack goods, haul the merchandise to the Quito air freight offices at the airport, and handle all the paperwork, including the shipping papers and export taxes payable to the Bano Central del Ecuador.

At the end of 1994, I interviewed the nine existing air cargo companies about the kinds and quantities of artesanías they shipped that year, and to where and to whom. Among them, they shipped at least 1,500 tons of artesanías abroad that year. I did not repeat a detailed survey the summer of 1997, but every air cargo agency worker with whom I spoke said exports were up.

Although the town of Otavalo has always had indigenous inhabitants dating back to the days of the colonial obrajes, indígenas were socially invisible and politically powerless; they "knew their place." Today, they are at least half the population of the town and the most prosperous half, at that. A 1995 newspaper article estimated that Otavalo was 70 percent indígena (i.e., 17,500 persons), and the author observed that, "Otavalo was reconquered by the Indians" (Frank 1995:B-7; my translation). If only the northern *half* of Otavalo was 70 percent indígena in 1995, it meant an urban indigenous population of roughly 8,750. Zulay Saravino, an Otavaleña who is owner of the tourist agency Zulay Diceny Viajes, Inc., estimated that more than half the population of Otavalo as a whole was indígena, meaning 12,500 indigenous residents. Zulay called it "*un cambio total*" (S. a complete change) and said, "*Los otavaleños son dueños de Otavalo*" (S. The Otavaleños are owners of Otavalo). The "total change" includes new indigenous-owned concrete-block apartment buildings and artesanías stores, as well as a number of support industries for the textile trade, including air freight companies, yarn stores, and other services, many of which are indigenous-owned and -operated.

The textile and tourism industries have benefited whites-mestizos as well as indígenas. Many town residents operate or work in grocery stores, clothing or furniture shops, restaurants, hotels, travel agencies, and air cargo companies, or they drive taxis and buses, knit sweaters, make jewelry, or sell in the market. Some seek employment from indígenas as salespersons or sew labels on clothes. Several larger-scale artesanías operations are run by Americans married to Ecuadorians, including Miller Herrera in Cotacachi and Harrington's in Ibarra. Both concerns employ hundreds of local workers, mainly whites-mestizos.

There is no doubt that many of the wealthiest people in the valley are now indígenas who operate larger-scale artesanías producing or merchandising ventures. An Otavalo sweater wholesaler can make a minimum profit of U.S. $1 per sweater, and many make twice that amount. Indigenous families are selling anywhere from 5,000 to 250,000 sweaters annually. This is impressive in a country where the average annual per capita income has hovered around U.S. $1,000 since the end of the 1980s, according to World Bank statistics. By way of comparison, in 1990 the GNP per capita for Ecuador was U.S. $1,117; for the United States, U.S. $19,789 (MacGlobe 1991).

For example, Luis Alfonso Morales, originally of Agato, now lives in Otavalo. "Morales had only one year of schooling....Yet at 50, he is one of the two or three wealthiest men in Otavalo. Using a score of electric looms to produce 25,000 sweaters and ponchos a year, he nets the equivalent of a six-figure dollar income, mostly from sales abroad" (Kandell 1993:32). Because of the new indigenous wealth and the disparities in wealth within and among local ethnic groups, inter- and intra-ethnic relations in the Otavalo valley are now so complex that they merit a brief discussion of their own below.

OTAVALO ETHNIC AND POWER RELATIONS IN HISTORICAL PERSPECTIVE

Today, Otavalos and a smaller indigenous group constitute approximately 70 to 75 percent of the population of Imbabura. The province is also populated by blancos-mestizos, African- and Asian-Ecuadorians, and foreigners. Although it has been said before, it is worth repeating that the concept of "Indian" is a result of the Spanish Conquest. Aboriginal inhabitants of the Americas had their own names for themselves, which usually translate as "the people." Furthermore, historically each group has had preferred self-referential terms for itself and disparaging appellations used by outsiders, some of whom considered these divisions based on heredity (race or caste) and others, on culture (ethnicity). As one researcher noted, "it is not possible to find one true way of describing Andean social divisions," and both perspectives need to be taken into account (Colloredo-Mansfield n.d.).

By the time *wasipungu* (Q. debt serfdom) was abolished in 1964, there were five basic categories to describe the major groups in the Otavalo valley. These categories resembled a pyramid with social, political, and economic power accruing to the top, *blancos* (S. whites). Beneath them were *mestizos* (S. mixed bloods), then *cholos* (S. indígenas who were acculturating), with indígenas (S. indigenous people) generally called by the pejorative term, "*indios*" (S.) or worse, and African-Ecuadorians (negroes, morenos) at the bottom. Indígenas constituted the largest, most visible population in the Otavalo valley, and many still remember how they were regarded: "We do not speak Spanish so that was their excuse when they called us '*indio sucio*' (S. dirty Indian) and '*ignorante*' (S. ignoramus). We did not know what 'ignorante' meant but it hurt and saddened us greatly" (Korovkin et al. 1994:10, my translation). When I first arrived in Otavalo in 1973, older indígenas knelt down and kissed the hands of whites and addressed them as *patrón* (S. patron) or *mi amo* (S. my lord), a legacy of colonialism and serfdom that many of us found highly disconcerting.

It is difficult to imagine the situation of indígenas until the abolition of wasipungu: "Before, in Otavalo there was much abuse on the part of the authorities and mestizos, and they took advantage of indígenas in the plazas, in the offices, in transport, and in the schools" (Lema A. 1995:136; my translation from Spanish). The indígenas of the community of Cachimuel explained, "In daily life the community was dominated by the town of San Rafael. As in the case of other communities, the people of Cachimuel was obliged to sweep the streets and do other work in San Rafael. As in other communities, the church continued to charge tithes and first fruits" (Korovkin et al. 1994:56; my translation).

Other Otavalos have told me of "being forced off the sidewalk to make way for the people with neckties;" of having their hats and ponchos confiscated by the police when they walked to Otavalo and held until they finished forced labor cleaning the streets or repairing roads; of being sent to the back of the bus or made to stand so whites-mestizos could have their seats; of brutality and beatings when they were *wasipungeros* (S. serfs); of all the humiliations of socially and legally enforced subservience. Walter, among other authors, pointed out that 15 years ago (i.e., in 1966) in the Otavalo valley, "For Indians without land or crafts, shedding at least the external symbols of their ethnic category may be a better strategy than accepting the menial, low-paying jobs reserved for Indians" (Walter 1981). A researcher who focused on indígena ethnic identity and identity change in Otavalo noted that indígenas "change their ethnic status when they cannot be successful as indígena" (Butler 1981:81). Such change enables them to "escape discriminatory treatment in anonymous interaction with non-indígena" (ibid.:vii).

The categories in effect through the early 1970s were social constructions, mutable, and far less dependent on phenotype than on lifestyle, including dress, language, place of residence, occupation, and self-identification. Because of the disadvantages of indigenous identity, some individuals and families chose to change their identity by abandoning indigenous dress and, for some, by outmigration in addition to costume change. An article titled, "When *Indios* become *Cholos*: Some Consequences of the Changing Ecuadorian Haciendas" (Crespi 1973), illustrates this process. People in the middle categories tended to identify up, while those around them often placed them in a category lower than their self-identified one (Crespi 1981:486-497, Stark 1981:398). As Lema A. (1995:27; my translation) noted, "Those in charge of the haciendas were mestizos, but in those times, although they hardly wore shoes they believed they were whites, looking down on and mistreating the *runas* (Q. the people, indígenas). They might have had mostly indigenous roots but nonetheless they tended to negate their indigenous aspect."

Although it was advantageous to be identifiable as an Otavalo when selling textiles in Ecuador or abroad, overall, it was not advantageous to be indigenous in Ecuador. The most extreme social strictures outlasted wasipungu by a decade. As late as 1978, indígenas were not allowed to each in many Quito restaurants or to stay at most hotels, and many Ecuadorians remain deeply prejudiced against the indigenous population. The Ecuadorian government, for its part, considered the indígenas a "problem" that could be solved by their assimilation, a policy of *mestizaje* which held that indígenas would cease to be a problem when they all became white and accepted the goals of national culture (Stutzman 1981). This ideology was accepted by some Ecuadorians of all backgrounds and firmly rejected by others, for varying reasons. Some whites-mestizos believe the various groups constitute distinct races, with the indigenous "race" being inherently inferior, and they therefore deny (in some cases, probably correctly) that they have any indigenous heredity. Others simply do not pay much attention to the concept of race or caste but consider indígenas inferior by virtue of their culture. Most indígenas reject mestizaje, seeing no reason why they should assimilate, and for many Otavalos, indigenous identity now has many advantages, which I will discuss below.

Otavalo economic gains in the 33 years since the abolition of wasipungu (Q. debt servitude) have been beyond the wildest dreams and predictions of even the most prescient Otavalos or outsiders. These gains are a result of adaptability and hard work, including the willingness to invest in textile cottage industry instead of agriculture when land shortages developed, and an ability to change production and go with national and global fashion trends. The necessity for large numbers of Otavalos to migrate to look for markets is causing stresses within families and communities as those left at home take over tasks previously performed by absent family members or when absent family members establish romantic or sexual liaisons with foreigners. The increasing reliance on export markets for Otavalo textiles makes the community vulnerable to global economic upheavals and changes in consumption patterns.

Increased indigenous wealth has altered ethnic and power relations in the valley in a number of ways and by various direct and indirect means. By the 1990s, indigenous identity in Otavalo was no longer synonymous with serfdom, poverty, or social and political subordination. The crucial question is how and why did Otavalo wealth change local social relations, from indígenas on their knees before whites in the 1960s, to indígenas owning the town and flying off to England or France in 1998?

In a capitalist society, wealth often correlates with power. Because the Ecuadorian justice system runs on money and connections, many Otavalos no longer find themselves at a disadvantage in disputes. They are able to hire good lawyers and to make the payments (what we would call bribes) necessary to move papers through the system. Indígenas have been able to educate their children through the university level and beyond to professional training in law and medicine. Some young indígenas, through their increased contacts with the outside world, have been able to obtain scholarships to study abroad. As part of the shift in power relations, which includes access to education at every level, indígenas are writing their own ethnographies and articles (Conejo 1995, Conejo Maldonado 1995, Lema A. 1995, Males 1985), recording local history in high school honors theses (C. Conterón Córdova n.d., L. Conterón n.d.), and being included in oral histories (Korovkin et al. 1994). In short, educated indígenas are no longer at the mercy of whites-mestizos in the courts or government bureaucracies. They can represent themselves in every sense of the word: in courts of law, in the political system, in the writing of history, and in the wording of tourism publicity.

New Otavalo wealth has altered power relations in other ways. Even a casual visitor to the valley can notice a palpable feeling of prosperity and confidence among Otavalo indígenas. There is nothing like running a successful weaving enterprise in Peguche, buying a new Chevy Trooper, and owning an apartment building in Otavalo to induce a sense of well-being, not to mention the daughter at Catholic University in Quito, another daughter happily married and with a new baby and running the Quito store, a son helping out in the Otavalo market kiosk, and another son playing music with a band in Europe and selling the group's CD. It sounds like the middle-class dream, and it is, and until recently it was beyond the dreams of most indígenas.

The old hierarchy, in which indígenas were generally socially, economically, and often legally subordinate to whites and mestizos and accepted it (at least in their public dealings with whites and mestizos), is crumbling. Indígenas are now, for the most part, no longer in this subordinate position, and members of all ethnicities know it. Some white-mestizos have begun treating Otavalos better through sheer economic self-interest. Otavalos are not only a majority in the region, but they are now purchasers of big-ticket merchandise including cars, trucks, stoves, refrigerators, video cameras, stereo and CD systems, and furniture. White-mestizos merchants who might have disdained or been rude to Otavalos now do so at their peril: Otavalos will take their considerable business elsewhere. Many whites-mestizos also depend on indígenas as landlords and employers, and therefore are generally more polite to them, despite their own private feelings on the matter. The building boom in Otavalo is primarily indígena-financed and -owned; whites-mestizos compete with their own group and with other indígenas for housing. Nasty behavior can mean losing out on a rental. Mario Conejo said, "In the indígena, including up to the present, the feeling of inferiority is alive. Acquiring confidence has been a long process. Today we are proud to be Otavalo Indians" (Ortiz de Rozas 1994:D10; my translation).

Music has also brought both prosperity and status to Otavalo. The success of Otavalo music groups in Europe, the most famous being Charijayac, composed of young members of the Otavalo expatriate community in Barcelona, Spain, led hundreds of young Otavalo males to form bands and try their luck playing music on the streets of Europe and the United States. Many musicians record tape cassettes and CDs to sell, and many combine music with textile merchandising. The recording locations printed on Otavalo music CDs offer a glimpse of the extent of Otavalo wanderings: Amsterdam, Munich, Rome, Barcelona, Ottawa, Toronto, Philadelphia, Minneapolis, Seattle, Lima, Bogota. The musicians' and merchants' remittances to Otavalo often constitute important contributions to their families' economic well-being. Because most Otavalo families own land, looms, and houses, the young musicians are able to secure loans or to buy their tickets to Europe on credit, eliminating the need for large savings to cover start-up costs.

Rather than "indios becoming cholos," there are now whites-mestizos becoming indígenas (by wearing traditional dress) in order to improve sales in the market, play in Otavalo Andean music groups, attract foreign women, marry a prosperous spouse, or obtain the benefits of development projects. Young white-mestizo men who choose to identify as Otavaleños usually wear the old-style dress whites daily, just to make sure everyone gets the point. A number of Otavalo bands have members who have chosen indigenous identity, perhaps temporarily, perhaps permanently. Indígenas who changed their dress to white-mestizo clothing or whose parents raised them as white-mestizo, are now reverting to indigenous identity. One member of the Grupo Ali Shungu has Otavalo indigenous parents, but he was raised white-mestizo with short hair and Euro-American-style dress. He grew his hair long and wears dress whites when he plays music with the group in Otavalo and Europe.

Even Peruvians are becoming Otavalos. One member of the Otavalo music group Inti Raymi, which plays in the United States, is a Peruvian who grew his hair long and wears Otavalo dress whites to play with the group. Occasionally, he even wears a hat. In a photo shown to me by anthropologist Linda Belote, I could not distinguish him from the "real" Otavalos.

In addition, some young Otavalos are reclaiming or rehabilitating the term "indio," as in Terán's article (1991) about "Indios Plásticos," a critique of costume change by young Otavaleños. A young Otavaleño from Peguche told me, "We are reclaiming this word." Just as the preferred self-referential term for African-Americans in the United States has changed in the past 50 years from Colored to Negro to Black to African-American, the self-referential terms for indígenas are changing. I have heard Otavalos refer to themselves as indígenas, runa, naturales, and indios. Most Otavalos, however, prefer that foreigners or whites-mestizos use the word indígena, because indio still carries disparaging connotations.

In October 1995, Margaret Goodhart, co-owner of the Hotel Ali Shungu in Otavalo, wrote me, "Mestizo girls are actually dressing up like indigenous to get indigenous boyfriends and there are more than a few of these couples. This tells me that Indigenous are now DESIRABLE" (pers. comm.). In June 1996, and Ilumán comadre told me that a "mestiza from Agato" married an indígena, wears Otavaleña dress, and "speaks Quichua better than he does." She and her sisters added that lots of local whites and mestizas want an indígena husband "because they see them driving around in their cars." Ethnic categories have become increasingly fluid, resembling two amoebas dancing the lambada rather than a pyramid with the bottom labeled "indígena" and the top labeled "white."

In addition, indígenas are now occupying positions in Otavalo formerly reserved for whites. In 1994, the Banco del Pichincha in Otavalo had three young women clerks sitting behind desks with computers. One was white-mestiza and the other two were Otavaleñas in traditional dress. In this same bank, the "supervisor," sitting behind a large, impressive desk, was an Otavaleño wearing his dress whites. The white-mestizo owned Vaz money exchange employs white-mestizo and indígena clerks, and indígenas now hold political offices in Imbabura formerly considered beyond their reach. For example, an Otaveleño, Auki Tituaña, was elected mayor of Cotacachi in 1996, and in that same election another Otavaleño, Mario Conejo, narrowly lost the race for mayor of Otavalo.

In 1970, there were five ethnic categories in use. In 1990, there were only two main categories (indígenas and whites-mestizos), as identities moved toward the poles, plus that for African-Ecuadorians. The names of the categories have also changed. In the past 25 years, the mestizo category has blended with white, and cholo has dropped out altogether, as dress styles also tended to move toward the poles: either indigenous or Euro-American. The African-Ecuadorian category conflates ethnic and racial identity, but people of African biological heritage may self-identify and be identified by others as members of other ethnicities, depending partly on dress and partly on phenotype.

If the only indicator of or criterion for social status were economic, indígenas would be at the top of the pyramid, but residual colonial prejudices rank whites-mestizos above indígenas overall, partly because the former group still controls politics in the valley despite recent indigenous gains. Mario Conejo, an Otavalo sociologist and artisan, predicated that this will change: "Ten years from now Indians will control political power" (Ortiz de Rojas 1994:D-10; my translation). It is important to note that indigenous wealth is unevenly distributed and that many families struggle to make ends meet. It is equally important, however, to note that the economic advances have improved social and political conditions for indígenas across the board.

The emerging social and political power relations do not mean an absence of ethnic tensions. Indígenas insist that many whites-mestizos are "*envidiosos*" (S. envious). Racist graffiti still appear on walls in Otavalo, and some whites-mestizos still use demeaning terms of address for indígenas in public. Nonetheless, change there has been—brought about, as I have argued, by indigenous economic ascendancy. Nearly 50 years ago, Collier & Buitrón (1949) named the Otavalo region, "The Awakening Valley." To use their metaphor, the indígenas of the valley have indeed awakened, disrupting the white-mestizo dream of continued economic, social, and political dominance of the region.

ACKNOWLEDGMENTS

My interest in the Otavalo valley began with trips to the region in 1973 and 1974, shortly after the new kiosks in the Poncho Plaza were built, and I've been following the growth of the region ever since. My early research in southern Ecuador and in the Otavalo region in 1977-1979 was funded by a Fulbright Fellowship and a grant for film expenses from the Institute for Intercultural Studies. I returned to Otavalo throughout the 1980s, which enabled me to track the growth of the textile economy. In the summer of 1990, Andrew W. Mellon Foundation and Josephine Knott Knowles fellowships (administered by the Center for Latin American Studies at Stanford University) allowed me to pursue pre-dissertation research in Otavalo. My 27 months of fieldwork between September 1992 and February 1995, were funded by the Institute for International Studies at Stanford, the Wenner-Gren Foundation for Anthropological Research (Predoctoral Grant No. 5483), and the National Science Foundation (Doctoral Dissertation Grant No. NSF DBS-9216489). I also returned to Otavalo during the summer of 1996 as part of a group project Fulbright sponsored by the University of Wisconsin-Madison under the direction of Frank Salomon and Carmen Chuquín. My recent visit in the summer of 1997 was funded by a grant from the Stanford Center on Conflict and Negotiation. The support of the people affiliated with the above institutions, and the help of hundreds of residents of the Otavalo region, made this paper possible and I am greatly indebted to them. I owe additional thanks to Barry Isaac, Rudi Colloredo-Mansfield, and Linda and Jim Belote for providing thoughtful critiques of the first draft of this article.

NOTES

1.   Spanish and Quichua (the indigenous language) terms are defined the first time they are used and identified by S. for Spanish and Q. for Quichua. Because Quichua was not a written language until the arrival of Europeans, there is considerable disagreement about its spelling.

2.   The Otavalo indígenas generally refer to their group as Otavalos, although the term Otavaleños is also used. In this article, Otavaleño refers to a male Otavalo and Otavaleña to a female Otavalo, following local usage.

REFERENCES

Andrade Reimers, Luis (1992) "Nuestros indígenas y la Iglesia Católica" ("Our Indigenous and the Catholic Church"). *El Comercio,* Miércoles, 25 de noviembre de 1992.

Brooks, John, ed. (1981) *The 1981 South American Handbook* (57th annual ed.). Bath, ENG: Trade & Travel Publications.

Butler, Barbara Y. (1981) *Indígena Ethnic Identity Change in the Ecuadorian Sierra.* Ph.D. dissertation, Department of Anthropology, University of Rochester.

Chavez, Leo Ralph (1982) *Commercial Weaving and the Entrepreneurial Ethic: Otavalo Indian Views of the Self and the World.* Ph.D. dissertation, Department of Anthropology, Stanford University.

Collier, John Jr., and Aníbel Buitrón (1949) *The Awakening Valley.* Chicago: University of Chicago Press.

Colloredo-Mansfield, Rudi (n.d.) "Dirty Indians, Rich Natives, and the Problem of Social Difference in Modern Ecuador." *Bulletin of Latin American Research,* in press.

Conejo, Mario (1995) "Los mindalas que migraron" ("The Mindalas Who Migrated"). *Azul* (Revista Quincenal, No. 8). Otavalo, 26 de agosto de 1995, p. 9.

Conejo Maldonado, Mario (1995) "El indígena Otavaleño urbana" ("The Urban Otavalo Indigenous"). Pp. 157-185 in José Almeida Vinueza (coordinator) *Identidades indias en el Ecuador contemporáneo (Indian Identities in Contemporary Ecuador)*. Quito: Ediciones Abya-Yala, Serie Pueblos del Ecuador, 4.

Conterón Córdova, Carlos (1994) *El tejido de la faja, una indumentaria indispensable de la mujer otavaleña (The Weaving of the Sash, Indispensable Clothing for the Otavalo Woman)*. Tesis, Ciencias Sociales, Año Lectivo 1993-1994. Otavalo, Ecuador: Colegio a Distancia "31 de Octubre."

Conterón, Laura (1985) *Comercialización de tejidos en Ilumán (Commercialization of Weaving in Ilumán)*. Tesis, Sexto Curso Commercial, Año Lectivo 1984-1985. Otavalo, Ecuador: Colegio Nacional de Señoritas "República del Ecuador."

Cooper, Jed Authur (1965) *The School in Otavalo Society*. Tucson, AZ: Panguitch Publications.

Crespi, Muriel (1973) "When *Indios* become *Cholos*: Some Consequences of the Changing Ecuadorian Hacienda." Pp. 146-166 in John W. Bennett (ed.) *The New Ethnicity, Perspectives from Ethnology*. St. Paul, MN: West Publishing, American Ethnological Society Proceedings.

———— (1981) "St. John the Baptist: The Ritual Looking Glass of Hacienda Indian Ethnic and Power Relations." Pp. 477-505 in Norman E. Whitten, Jr. (ed.), *infra*.

El Comercio (various dates) Daily newspaper. Quito, Ecuador.

Espinosa, Soriano, Waldemar (1988) *Los Cayambes y Carangues: Siglos XV-XVI, El Testimonio de la Etnohistoria, 3 Vols. (The Cayambes and Carangues: 15th-16 Centuries, The Testimony of Ethnohistory, 3 Vols.)*. Otavalo: Instituto Otavaleño de Anthropologia.

Frank, Florian (1995) "Otavalo: entre el telar y el dólar" ("Otavalo: Between the Loom and the Dollar"). *El Comercio*, 4 de enero de 1995, p. B-7.

Hoy (various dates) Daily newspaper, Quito and Guayaquil, Ecuador.

Kandell, Jonathan (1993) "Shuttle Capitalism." *Los Angeles Times Magazine*, November 14, 1993, pp. 30-34, 46-48.

Korovkin, Tanya, Vidal Sánchez and José Isama, coordinadores [co-authored by 102 persons from the communities of Cachimuel, Carabuela, Cutambi, Gualsaquí, Ilumán, Peguche, Pijal, Rinconada, San Agustín de Cajas, San Francisco de Cajas, Tocagon, González Suárez and San Rafael] (1994) *Nuestras comunidades ayer y hoy: HIstoria de las comunidades indígenas de Otavalo, Ñucanchic aillu llactacuna ñaupa, cunan pachapash (Our Communities Yesterday and Today: History of the Indigenous Communities of Otavalo)*. Luz María del la Torre, trans. Spanish to Quichua. Quito: Abya-Yala.

Lema A., Germán Patricio (1995) *Los Otavalos: Cultura y tradición milenarias (The Otavalos: Millenarian Culture and Tradition)*. Quito: Ediciones Abya-Yala.

MacGlobe (version 1.0) (1991) Computer program. Copyright 1991 P.C. Globe, Inc., Tempe, AZ.

Males, Antonio (1985) *Villamanta ayllucunapac punta casual: Historia oral de los Imbaya de Quinchuquí-Otavalo, 1900-1960 (Oral History of the Imbaya of Quinchuquí-Otavalo, 1900-1960)*. Quito: Ediciones Abya-Yala.

Meisch, Lynn A. (1980) "The Weavers of Otavalo." *Pacific Discovery* (California Academy of Sciences) XXXIII:6:November-December:21-29.

———— (1987) *Otavalo: Weaving, Costume and the Market*. Quito: Ediciones Libri Mundi.

———— (1997) *Traditional Communities, Transnational Lives: Coping with Globalization in Otavalo, Ecuador*. Ph.D. dissertation, Department of Anthropology, Stanford University.

OAS General Secretariat (1973) *Tourism in the Americas: Road to a Better Life*. Washington, DC: Organization of American States, Department of Information and Public Affairs.

Ortiz de Rozas, Marilu (1994) "Otavalo, Centro Indígena y Capitalista" ("Otavalo, Indigenous and Capitalist Center"). *El Mercurio* (daily newspaper, Santiago, Chile).

Parsons, Elsie Clews (1945) *Peguche: A Study of Andean Indians*. Chicago: University of Chicago Press.

Rappaport, Joanne R. (1990) *The Politics of Memory: Native Historical Interpretation in the Colombian Andes*. Cambridge, ENG: Cambridge University Press.

Salomon, Frank (1981) "Weavers of Otavalo." Pp. 420-449 in Norman E. Whitten, Jr. (ed.), *infra*.

_____ (1986) *Native Lords of Quito in th Age of the Incas: The Political Economy of North Andean Chiefdoms*. Cambridge, ENG: Cambridge University Press.

Stark, Louisa R. (1981) "Folk Models of Stratification and Ethnicity in the Highlands of Northern Ecuador." Pp. 387-401 in Norman E. Whitten, Jr. (ed.), *infra*.

Stutzman, Ronald (1981) "El Mestizaje: An All-Inclusive Ideology of Exclusion." Pp. 45-94 in Norman E. Whitten, Jr. (ed.), *infra*.

Terán, Benjamín (1991) "Indios Plásticos" ("Plastic Indians"). *Shimishitachi*, Vol. 9, diciembre, pp. 20-22.

Walter, Lynn (1981) "Otavaleño Development, Ethnicity and National Integration." *América Indígena* 41:319-337.

Whitten, Jr., Norman E., ed. (1981) *Cultural Transformations and Ethnicity in Modern Ecuador*. Urbana: University of Illinois Press.

THE HANDICRAFT ARCHIPELAGO:
CONSUMPTION, MIGRATION, AND THE SOCIAL ORGANIZATION OF A TRANSNATIONAL ANDEAN ETHNIC GROUP

Rudi Colloredo-Mansfeld

The transnational peasant has arrived. She runs her handicraft business in a store-front boutique owned by a Japanese-American woman in California. Occasion-ally, she returns to San Jerónimo in the Mixteca region of Oaxaca to help her father-in-law plant, cultivate, and harvest the land that one day will be inherited by her husband (Kearney 1996). In Washington, DC, migrant "peasants" from Cabanaconde in Peru's remote Colca Valley work as mechanics, lab technicians, and hairdressers. In 1992, some members of this expatriate community spent much of their savings on the annual saint's day fiesta back in the Andes (Gelles & Martinez 1993). Meanwhile, in the rural hamlets around Cuenca in southern Ecua-dor, the cement-block, multi-story homes cropping up amid the maize fields signal remittances from New York, not the agricultural earnings of Andean farmers (Miles 1997). Surveying such changes, Kearney (1996) declares the traditional peasant dead. He musters a new vocabulary of "postpeasants," "polybians," "retic-ula," and "Oaxacalifornia" to describe the fragmented communities and hybrid identities of agrarian Latin America.

Research in Economic Anthropology, Volume 19, pages 31-67.
Copyright © 1998 by JAI Press Inc.
All rights of reproduction in any form reserved.
ISBN: 0-7623-0446-4

Ethnographers in the Otavalo region of Ecuador's northern Andes note a similar transnationalization of a rural society. Discussing the dispersion of Otavaleño craftspeople, Buitrón (1962:319; my trans.) writes:

> The radius of action of the Indians has been extended year after year. Until recently, one could count on one's fingers the Indians who had traveled outside the Cantón [county of Otavalo]. Currently, they are numerous, those who have traveled outside the Cantón, outside the Province, and outside the country.

> One frequently encounters the merchants from Otavalo in the airports and the hotels of Lima, Bogotá, Caracas and Panama. A few indigenous families have settled with their small textile workshops in Colombia, Venezuela, Brazil, and Uruguay.

Note that this quotation dates not from 1992, but from 1962. In comparison to other native peasant groups, Otavaleño weavers and merchants have had at least a five-decade head start on journeys to and settlement in foreign countries. While the extent of their travel attracts the attention of anthropologists (as well as travel agents and migration authorities), their conservative values impress white-mestizo Ecuadorians and secure Otavaleños' reputation as the "authentic" native group of the nation (see, e.g., Whitten 1985:222). Most Otavaleños speak Quichua as their first language, wear traditional clothing, work in the handicraft business, farm, and participate in the new and ancient fiestas of the region. This dynamic cultural homeland contrasts with other rural parishes, where the exodus of men or entire households diminishes the economy and community social life. In short, despite generations of migration, the center has held. Otavalo's homes, markets, plazas, and fields remain the site of cultural identity and authority.

In this article, I present two arguments for Otavalo's success—one about structure and the other about mechanisms. First, combating the social splintering induced by migration, Otavaleño society has taken the form of an intercontinental "archipelago." Its scattered "islands" include peasant farming communities, provincial craft markets, urban construction sites, and touristic pedestrian malls in Latin American, European, and North American cities. Unlike some migrant or trade diasporas that have been profoundly displaced from their native territory, Otavaleños stay connected with both their distant homeland and the other expatriate communities. A nested social organization of households bound by dyadic ties works against the centrifugal pressures of spatial and economic mobility. These social ties also preserve a measure of self-sufficiency. Supplementing (and now replacing) the subsistence security of agriculture, Otavaleño household economies integrate capital, products, and information from multiple places. Taking advantage of these resources, Otavaleños have made themselves into the national middlemen of the handicraft weaving business.

Second, I argue that Otavaleños depend on culturally defined "institutional consumption" to maintain their social relations. That is, they use consumer goods to accomplish three critical tasks in the formation of households and family networks: to define shared purposes, to organize members' activities, and to legitimize the group's existence. The first two speak to the practical side of consuming. A spacious new house or efficient gas stove brings personal satisfaction and social status to owners while making possible a new allocation of time and resources among family members. The third task is less tangible but no less important. Consumption decisions can reaffirm the legitimacy of subsistence work in a profit-driven economy or affirm parents' authority in the eyes of migrant children. Also, in a society in which members are scattered through at least a half dozen more or less permanent communities in the Americas and Europe, material practices socialize people of all ages and diverse locales into a common set of ideals. These expensive fiestas marking baptisms, confirmations, and weddings indoctrinate the younger generation and long absent family members in the habits of reciprocity that have long structured the relations among Otavalo's peasant farmers and artisans.

Below, I describe the social bonds and consumer practices of Otavalo's global archipelago. I begin with a brief introduction on Otavaleños, the recent history of the craft trade, and a description of a migrant's career. I go on to examine the archipelago metaphor as it has been construed in previous discussions of Andean dispersion and political organization, using this past research to point out the continuities, innovations, and paradoxes of Otavalo's case. Next, I focus on how consumption practices address two critical problems of social organization: managing the formation of new households and restoring trust and balance to the dyadic bonds used (and misused) in business ventures. Finally, describing the recent changes in both the regional economy and consumption practices, I explain how Otavalo's handicraft archipelago is transforming itself, becoming more fragmentary and stratified.

OTAVALO, HANDICRAFT TRADING, AND LONG-DISTANCE TRAVEL

Otavaleños number about 70,000 and are one of many ethnically distinct, Quichua-speaking groups of the Ecuadorian Andes. As with other native, highland peoples, the basic social and economic unit of Otavaleño society is a household, formed around a single nuclear family. With very low per capita incomes, high illiteracy rates, and a large proportion of households farming holdings of less than 1 ha, the periphery of the Cantón (county) of Otavalo suffers the poverty and underdevelopment that plagues much of the Andes. Rural families depend on subsistence crops—primarily, maize—grown on inherited plots. While men and women devote much less effort to agriculture than to commercial or social activities (Figure 1), the food they cultivate forms the core of their diet. It also hedges against the uncertainty of other work, which may include positions as maids, construction workers, market porters, or other low-paying jobs in cities.

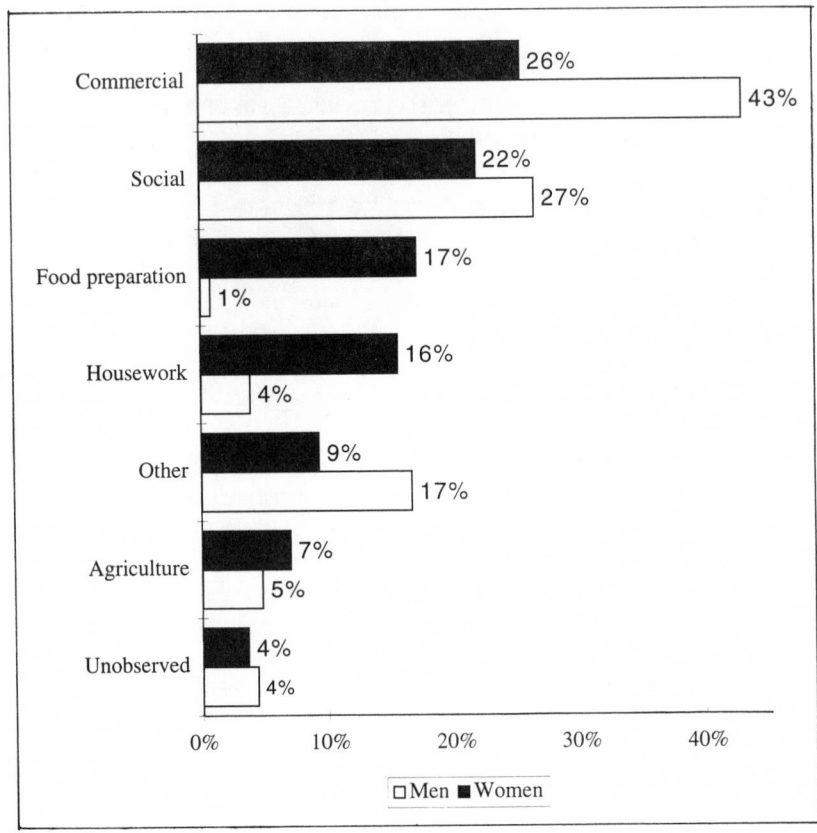

Figure 1. Time Allocation among Primary Activities in Ariasucu, 7:00 AM-
6:00 PM, February-November 1994 (Percentages are based on 1,298
observations of 49 women aged 18-39 and 1,026 observations of 37 men
aged 18-60. Sampling time slots and subjects were selected at random.)

In spite of these similarities to many other Andean communities, three things distinguish Otavaleños from other native groups: geography, dress, and the handicraft
textile economy.[1] The majority live in the farm communities and suburbs of
Otavalo, a market town in the province of Imbabura, lying 80 km north of Quito.
Additionally, Meisch (1987) estimates that 5,000 Otavaleños now live in urban
communities in Quito, Guayaquil, Bogotá, Caracas, Amsterdam, New York, and
elsewhere. No other Ecuadorian native group has dispersed as widely. Wherever
they live, their appearance marks their identity. Men wear their hair long—in either
a single braid or a ponytail—and don a traditional outfit of white pants, white shirt,

and blue poncho for formal business and social occasions. Most of the time, though, they wear Western clothes, preferring baggy jeans, thick-soled leather shoes, bright print shirts, and stiff, narrow-brimmed fedoras. Women dress more conservatively, wearing dark *anakus* (wrap around straight skirts), white polyester blouses that are embroidered with colored thread and shawls as the basis of their daily outfit.

The distinctiveness of their clothing and the beauty of the region has caused pictures of Otavaleños to be featured on billboards in Ecuador (Harrison 1989) and in travel sections of newspapers across the United States, drawing crowds of both national and foreign tourists to the textile market in Otavalo. The current expansion of local craft production, however, had its start back in the 1920s, before the rise of ethnic tourism. At that time, British textile imports dominated the market for quality cloth. In response to the popularity of imports, native weavers in the communities began to weave fine, imitation tweed fabric to sell to urban consumers (Parsons 1945, Korovkin et al. 1994). The market for this cloth, called *casimir*, not only increased incomes but also provided a direct connection between Otavaleño artisans and Quito markets.

In the 1940s, market forces caused artisans to change their weavings. Demand for handmade Otavaleño *casimires* dwindled, causing manufacturers to refocus their efforts on the nascent market for ethnic arts. While more and more tourists made the trip to Otavalo, indigenous merchants did not depend on this traffic as the sole outlet for their goods. Long-distance sales trips have been a central feature of the craft economy since its inception. Already in 1947, Buitrón (1947:48-49; my trans.) reported that some of the residents of Peguche "travel continually within and outside the country," while other Otavaleño merchants "travel from Carchi [Ecuador's northern most province] to Loja [the southern most], selling ponchos and *chalinas* [shawls], which they buy in the Otavalo market" (Buitrón 1947:48-49).

Over the next two decades, Otavaleño merchants traveled further, stayed away longer, and established residences in remote cities. As noted in the passage cited above, Buitrón (1962) recorded that weavers lived in major cities throughout Latin America by the early 1960s. Further, Otavaleño trading practices were extending simultaneously in two directions. Not only did merchants expand into new foreign territory, but commercial activities drew new participants from the more remote rural sectors within the Cantón. Thus, in the early 1960s, the first handicraft dealers from neighborhoods on the rural fringes of Otavalo—places such as Ariasucu, where I have done much of my research—got their start in international travel and sales. Galo Ajala[2] was one of the pioneers from this sector.[3] His story bears repeating, as it illustrates the vulnerability of native migrants' careers and the material dimensions of their successes.

GALO AJALA AND THE MIGRANT'S CAREER

On most days, Galo smiles at the approach of strangers. He flashes them a wide grin of gold-repaired teeth and asks them where they are from and where they are going. Galo's good humor is sincere; it is also conditioned by having lived and sold handicrafts in towns throughout Ecuador and Colombia since he was a boy. His father died when he was two, leaving his mother, Mamá Rosa, to provide for her four children (two of whom survived to adulthood) by supplementing the crops of their fields with sales of wool and sheep. Galo, the youngest, attended an evangelical Protestant elementary school for two years before dropping out to help his mother with her flock. In 1961, an older cousin visited Mamá Rosa and convinced her and Galo that he should go to Quito and learn how to sell *artesanías* (handicrafts). Thus, at the age of 12, Galo embarked upon a long career in textile dealing.

After spending his teenage years selling in both Quito and Ecuador's third largest city, Cuenca, Galo took his career in a new direction. He left with another cousin to sell in Colombia. Residing in the Caribbean port city of Cartagena, Galo marketed crafts to Asian seamen, played soccer with local Colombians, and doubled his inventory. Misfortune then struck in the form of customs inspectors who, after ignoring him for a year, confiscated his goods. Escaping back to Otavalo with the remainder of his earnings, he spent his savings on a plot of land below his mother's house. He stayed home for a while, in part to earn money with his loom and in part to court Mónica Quilla, who lived just over the *wayku* (gully) in Agato. They wed in 1973. Not long after, they moved to Cuenca with their infant daughter, Clara.

There, Galo sold sweaters while Mónica split her time between caring for Clara and their second child, Celestina, working with Galo, and selling lunches to other vendors. Gradually, their inventory grew and Galo had to rent space in a storeroom to guard it at night. In another catastrophe, the storeroom burned down. The young couple packed up their cooking utensils, small chairs, and tables and went back to live with their parents in Ariasucu. In the late 1970s, they tried their luck again, moving up to Tulcan, on the Colombian border, with four young children. In yet another mishap, they lost their sweater inventory to a robber in 1984. Returning to Ariasucu, they finally left their parents' houses and built a new home (the second cement block house in the sector) on the plot Galo bought years before. Since the mid-1980s, they have stayed put. Galo weaves; Mónica runs a small store; and, now that their children are older, they are sponsoring them in their efforts to travel and work in the textile business.

While the handicraft trade underwrote Galo and Mónica's travels, many of the next generation of Otavaleño migrants have pursued other opportunities. In the 1970s, a dramatic increase in the exploitation of Ecuador's petroleum reserves spawned a construction boom in Quito. Otavaleño men came to the city to mix concrete, plaster walls, and lay floors. Women arrived either to work as cooks and maids or find jobs vending in Quito's markets and streets.

The combination of the textile trade and urban wage migration have now made dispersion a fact of life for many Otavaleño families. In 1994, I surveyed a small sample of 33 married couples[4] to see who had close family members (defined as a sibling, parent, uncle, aunt, or child) living outside the province. Only 6 did not

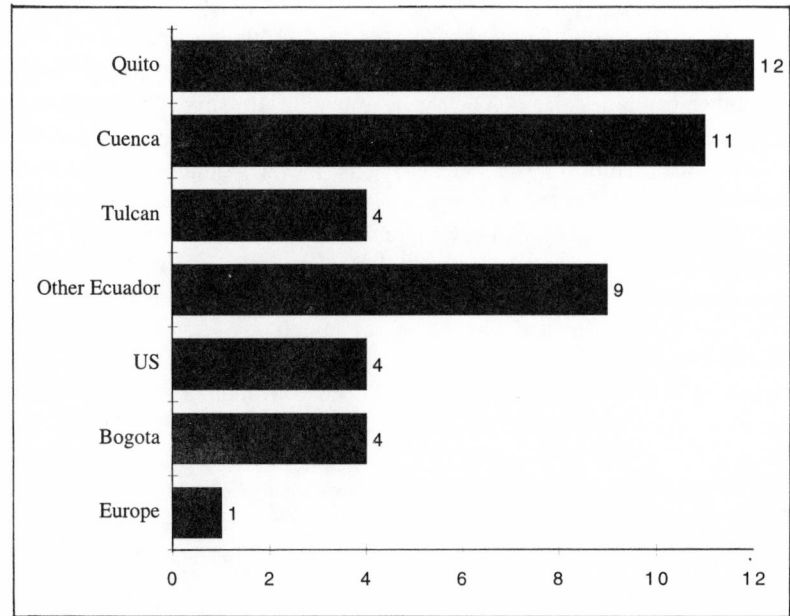

Figure 2.   Location of Migrant Family Members (N=45) of
33 Ariasucu Households, 1994

have such a contact. Many had family members living in more than one place. While the most common place for a relative was Quito (with 12 of the 33 families having someone living there), some had connections in the United States, Colombia, and Europe (Figure 2). Thus, after nearly a century of trade and migration, many Otavaleños live like Galo did—developing a career, finding a mate, forming a household, and achieving the respect of their peers while moving back and forth between Otavalo and cities throughout Ecuador, Colombia, and elsewhere.

FROM RURAL-TO-URBAN MIGRATION TO ARCHIPELAGOES

In the 1970s, research into Latin American migration modified the stereotype of the migrant as a destitute peasant fleeing a failing agricultural sector. Presenting a more complex picture, social scientists showed that migrants often enjoyed higher incomes, more extensive social networks, or some other advantage over their peers. That is, internal migration related to local enterprise, not stagnation (Roberts 1975, 1978). Indeed, Otavaleños offer a classic example of peasant entrepreneurs who developed connections to the city in order to advance businesses and careers already begun in the provinces. Their arrival in town is not a blind flight from rural desperation, but planned with some prior contact and information and dependent on resources amassed before the move (cf. Roberts 1978). Such migration can, in fact, raise the importance of the countryside's economy.

In the Andean nations, city and county exist in a dynamic relationship (Isbell 1974, Roberts 1974). Cycles of economic booms and busts and the accompanying failures of the labor market compel migrants to fall back on subsistence agriculture for survival (de Janvry 1987, Nash 1994). Nor is adversity the only cause for the continued connection to the land. In Ecuador, positive developments—including the agrarian reform and expanding urban job markets in the 1960s and 1970s—decreased the level of permanent migration from rural areas in the Sierra while increasing temporary migration (Peck 1982). With more economic opportunities, many peasants found work in the cities while keeping their homes on the land.

Otavaleño migration, however, cannot be modeled solely in terms of these bilateral links between urban and rural economies. At least since the 1960s, migrants have dispersed to scattered destinations, melding multiple incomes: subsistence grains grown in the province of Imbabura, wages earned in Quito, revenue from wholesale sweater selling on the Colombian border, and profits from general craft sales in foreign tourist destinations. The earnings from one niche can complement the seasonality of others and raise the value of marginal resources such as a remote maize field, since "the value of each form of total household income is a product of its being in relation to other forms of income" (K. Friedman 1984:46). To earn the money and launch a trading career, therefore, people must learn to handle the spatial diversification of resources.

Otavaleños are not the first Andean people to make a living in an economy spread over varied and distant locales. In his study of the Inka, for example, Murra (1972, 1985a) argued that southern Andean polities exploited discrete ecological niches dispersed by altitude: a vertical archipelago. Anticipating some aspects of current studies of diaspora and migration, Murra (1985b) wrote that Andean archipelagoes had the following characteristics: (1) ethnic groups sought to control the maximum number of niches, (2) economic relations of the archipelago were governed by principles of reciprocity and redistribution, (3) peripheral "islands" may have been shared with other ethnic groups, (4) with the creation of states, peripheral islands were located in more distant areas, and (5) these archipelagoes maintained a clear political and social center in the high, dry regions of the altiplano. Most Andean research has focused on the ecological aspects of this model (Masuda et al. 1985, Knapp 1991, Brush 1977). In analyzing mountain micro-environments, ethnologists and archaeologists describe the agricultural potential of different zones and analyze the social mechanisms linking them.

Enrique Mayer (1985), however, argues that Murra's model is fundamentally political. Pointing out that agricultural production zones are man-made things, he writes that managing these zones across space and time requires the integration of three nested social levels: the household, the community of local groups exploiting common resources, and the ethnic group capable of mobilizing local groups. This dense, interlocking organization exacts a social price. The material interests of individuals and households run up against communal efforts to preserve and distribute resources. Reconciling private ambition with collective obligations can cause conflicts.

Archipelago forms of economic organization have another social cost. Coordinating a population to integrate resources from dispersed zones through reciprocal exchanges among bounded social units leads to those units' isolation from other ethnic groups. In his analysis of the Inka conquest of the northern Andes, Salomon (1986) argues that the Inka imposition of an archipelago economic model on the region broke the pre-existing horizontal ties among regional polities. He writes, "The 'archipelago' was inherently a radical measure, a true revolution from above. It substituted for the premises of interdependency and complex alliance, typical of the aboriginal world, flatly contrary principles of economic closure and trans-zonal self sufficiency" (p. 200). The archipelago reinforced the economic power of the center—and often of the elites who lived there—not links with outsiders (Van Buren 1996). The outlying members of the archipelago sacrificed their bonds with nearby peoples to achieve this goal.

The economic practices and political organization of modern Otavalo significantly differ from the Inka vertical archipelago. Markets and trading are the heart of the Otavalo economy, while they are just what the Inka administrators by-passed through their system of redistribution. Cash and commodity exchange, not reciprocal exchange, dominate the flow of goods. In the global archipelago, most of the islands are complementary market niches ultimately yielding the same thing—cash—not ecological niches yielding different crops. Nonetheless, the archipelago model of integrated complementarity still helps us address a key question: How has an indigenous Andean ethnic group expanded its handicraft industry into urban areas while preserving cultural and social institutions tied to a relatively remote rural region?[5]

Despite its deviations from the Inka model, Otavalo's global, market-oriented economy exhibits features of an archipelago organization. First, the niches complement each other, stretching from maize fields and weaving porches on Mount Imbabura to market stalls and craft showrooms in Germany. Second, for most Otavaleños, access to remote opportunities depends on kinship connections. Many handicraft transactions take place among *compadres* (one's child's godparents) who share enduring moral obligations to grant favors to each other; reciprocity still directs economic activity. Third, the networks of urban communities, trade associations, extended families, and ritual kin afford a degree of self-sufficiency. Turning to their own institutions, Otavaleños control growing levels of capital and information—enough to increase the productivity and geographic range of their textile industry. This self-reliance bears the same consequences that Salomon (1986) identified with pre-Hispanic archipelagoes. It reinforces other external factors—from ethnic discrimination to Otavaleños' frequent status as undocumented immigrants—which isolate them from the wider societies in which they operate. Finally, although they lack political sovereignty, Otavaleños' ritual and economic centralization nevertheless channels the movement of people and resources through their homeland.

In order to grasp how this "global archipelago" functions, I follow Mayer's (1985) lead and investigate nested levels of social organization. In particular, I am interested in how Otavaleños solve two problems. The first relates to the developmental cycle of households. Like Heyman (1990), I argue that consumption issues gain urgency when a younger generation prepares to leave the natal household. As they being to develop urban incomes and tastes, adolescents can threaten the continuity of household 'relations in particular and the reproduction of community social relations more generally. Studying the United States-Mexican border, Heyman (1990) records how Sonoran migrants have cut themselves off from the parents' social relations and strategies by focusing on urban goods and the skills needed to get them. In Otavalo, however, the consumption and inter-generational commitments of commercial migrants have followed a different trajectory. Both parents' and offspring's spending has largely kept up rural hearths and extended family networks. Facing substantially different risks and rewards than Mexico's transnational proletariats, Otavalo's merchants have acquired and used goods to recreate a vital, rural center for their migratory careers.

The second problem concerns how to form *compadrazgo* (ritual co-parenthood of parents-godparents) relationships, which are based on a morality of mutual assistance, and turn them towards the business of making profits without rupturing those relationships. Compadres, or networks of compadres, often hold the key to business success by offering resources needed to operate in transnational, commercial trading niches. Studying related cases of collective action among individuals in complex, urban society, Adrian Mayer (1966) describes such groups of cooperating persons as "action sets."[6] His term highlights the transitory nature of a group defined primarily by temporary pursuit of a shared goal. Otavaleño merchants develop action sets of their ritual kin to set up potentially profitable deals or international sales trips. The entanglement of kin and commerce, though, produces tensions that compadres must learn to mitigate if they are not to fracture these relationships irretrievably. In the remainder of the article, I describe the social, ritual, and material mechanisms that hold Otavalo's family-based institutions together.

OTAVALEÑO HOUSEHOLDS IN
A TRANSLOCAL WORLD

Of Galo and Mónica's children, Celestina, their second daughter, has become the most dedicated textile dealer. In 1992, at age 15, she went to live and work with

Mónica's sister and brother-in-law up in Tulcan. I visited her then and was struck by her poise and competence. Whether she wrestled large bundles of sweaters onto the sidewalk in front of the store or stood by to answer the brusque questions of Colombian merchants, she calmly took care of business. As her father had done, she saved her commissions from the sales she made for her uncle and aunt and reinvested them in her own wares. She hoped to be operating on her own by her 18th birthday.

Later, when my wife, Chesca, and I moved to Ariasucu, I learned that Celestina's life in Tulcan was not as independent as it had seemed. Even as she sat watching TV and waiting for customers amid stacks of sweaters in Tulcan, she remained an important member of the household back home. This membership, however, could not be taken for granted. Celestina had arrived at a critical juncture in her life. Old enough to offer substantial resources to her old home, she also had the inventory and skills to stay in Tulcan to build her business. Galo and Mónica had to work diligently to maintain their claims on her visits, labor, or earnings.

The ambiguous position of older, unmarried children is not unique to families split by migration or to Otavaleños in general. In many peasant cultures, coping with autonomy of young adults and formation of new households from existing ones is perhaps the most critical phase in the household development cycle (Goody 1962). Weismantel (1989b) has described how indigenous Zumbaguans in the province of Cotopaxi, Ecuador, stretch out the formation of new, independent domestic units from established ones. Older children begin to separate themselves from their parents and younger siblings by taking up residence in an out-building removed from the main house. Upon marriage, the young couple may sleep apart, but they continue to cook with the parents of either the bride or the groom. Only after the third generation is born do they set up a second hearth. This model of slow development describes those Otavaleño households that live and work mainly within the province.

The migration of adolescents to distant cities, in contrast, pushes the development cycle in two opposing directions. On the one hand, the textile trade may speed the exodus of children from the household. As they became teenagers, both Galo and, later, his daughter moved not just into a different building, but to a different province. On the other hand, the frequent movement from city to city in pursuit of better markets may delay a young couple's effort to establish an independent hearth. Galo and Mónica returned repeatedly to their parents' home for periods ranging from six months and two years when they were not away selling. The current generation of textile dealers similarly seems destined to trek back and forth between cramped urban apartments and their parents' households, until they are close to 30 years old, before building their own house.

A child's early exit from home and his or her delayed effort to set up his or her own house, therefore, prolongs a critical phase of independent earnings coupled with few social attachments that could rival parental claims. Precisely during this period, "archipelago households" have their greatest opportunity. Families can take advantage of the growing inventory, cash reserves, or market contacts of a member in a remote locale and use them to expand weaving ventures, textile inventories, or the physical plant of the household in Otavalo.

Parents cannot, however, automatically claim their offsprings' earnings. As research has shown in rural Ecuador and elsewhere, few households fit Sahlin's (1972) model of a domestic unit in which all members pool their incomes and enjoy equal rights to all resources (Weismantel 1988; Netting & Wilk 1984; Wilk 1989a, 1992). Rather, men, women, and their children usually control their own earnings and may have limited access to those of other household members. Teenagers, in particular, often keep their earnings for themselves. Young Otavaleño males, for example, may spend their cash on shoes with Nike swooshes and baseball caps embroidered with the logos of the Charlotte Hornets, snarling tigers of Gambling State, or some other team. Teenage girls typically buy new, shiny polyester blouses or perhaps even imported Italian woolen cloth for their *anakus* (wrap around skirts). Few boys or girls spend their money on common possessions for the household. As they get older, both boys and girls may change tacks and reinvest their earnings in handicrafts and other ventures to earn money.

Faced with their children's priorities, parents can tap into their offspring's income only sporadically. Economic resources thus typically pass among household members and across distance in the form of concrete transactions, not generalized reciprocity. A household member may provide money for others to acquire designated commodities: cones of thread, pig feed, sacks of sugar for the family store, woven sweaters, or a truckload of cement blocks. Even if cash is changing hands, parents or children often quickly purchase the specified object, and people track their money through these goods, using them to reckon who owes what to whom.

I became aware of the materialized nature of the flow of resources when Chesca and I joined forces with Galo and Mónica to add a room onto their home to use as our own residence in Ariasucu in 1994. We had decided to divide the costs. Chesca and I would pay for the cement blocks, doors, windows, reinforcement bar, and sacks of concrete; Galo and Mónica would buy the tiles, beams, and wooden runners for the roof. To meet their end of the deal, Galo and Mónica had to do a lot of last minute, creative financing. When it came time to frame the roof, Galo complained that the price of the narrow wooden tile runners had risen sharply and that he could not afford them. He then declared, "It is fine, it is fine, my José [his 16-year-old son] will buy the runners—with the money he made as a piece-rate commercial *faja* (sash) weaver. Next Galo claimed that he could not pay for the tiles. Reversing himself later in the week, he proudly said that his daughter, Celestina, would loan the money to complete the roof. After the red tiles had been delivered to the patio, he gestured to them, reminding me, "These tiles, these tiles are from my Celestina."

In this way, commodities and consumer goods put a public face on intra-family transactions. Such spending symbolically ratifies the bonds of a family split by migration and economically connects them through shared material assets. Noting a similar situation among the Kekchi Maya of Belize. Wilk (1989b) argues that the family's greatest tool in its struggle against members' competing economic agendas is the house itself. By allocating income to furnishings and building materials, the whole family can listen to the radio, walk on the concrete floors, and share in the envy of the neighbors. He (Wilk 1989b:311) writes that

> this sharing is a potent device, on the part of the parents, in the struggle to keep children attached to the household after they marry. It is a demonstrable fact that the income they donate to the household is not going to be wasted on rum for the father or clothes for the mother, but instead it will be spent on permanent improvements that the whole family can use for many years to come, and which add materially to the family's assets.

By allocating their loans to specific goods, family members have more confidence that their funds are not being squandered. In Ariasucu, one man receives remittances in the form of cash wired to Otavalo from his 35-year-old sister, who works at a medical supply factory in Chicago. The cash comes with no specific instructions except that he should use it to help their mother. Not surprisingly, these funds have caused tension and distrust among mother, brother, and sister. Mother and cousins alike whisper that the brother is misappropriating the cash. By promptly using the money for specific, agreed upon purchases, even consumable items such as animal feed, other families keep their finances out in the open and minimize strife.

In contrast to the Kekchi households, however, Otavaleño spending is not seen in strictly communal terms; people borrow and loan more than they share. In their own way, though, such actions, when mediated through the material world, can help solidify family bonds. The runners and tiles that sheltered Chesca and me for a year represented an obligation that Galo and Mónica had to pay back. The roof called for a future transaction with their mobile and absent children, perpetuating a cycle of favors and exchanges. That these economic actions took a specified physical form only enhanced their social impact. For Galo, the runners bespoke "my José," and the tiles, "my Celestina." These goods made their presence felt at home and served as a bridge to them as they pursued their lives among the sweater merchants of Tulcan.

CONSUMPTION IN THE FORMATION OF ARCHIPELAGO HOUSEHOLDS

As Wilk (1989) and others document, consumer decisions have become important for migrant family stability in native and peasant societies throughout Latin America. Weismantel (1989a) has shown how provisioning a household in the parish of Zumbagua has become culturally and politically changed. Struggles over cuisine—when to serve homegrown gains and when to serve commoditized food such as bread or rice—bring home gendered conflicts between indigenous subsistence values and the urban, ethnically white commodity economy. Similarly, in the northern Mexican border state of Sonora, the adoption of manufactured consumer goods by migrants has sped up the region's connections with the world economic system. Heyman (1994) describes the new capitalist mode of consuming as a "flow-through household economy" in which domestic groups have experienced the "delocalization" of basic consumer goods.

Both these and other cases support Orlove and Rutz's (1989) contention that consumption is not an individualistic act passively completing a cycle of production and exchange. Rather, consuming entails the investment of time and energy and the reproduction of social relationships. In their explorations of consumption, some anthropologists focus on how consumer goods substantiate cultural categories (Douglas & Isherwood 1979). Others concentrate on the creation of identities (Friedman 1994). Still others detail how consumption marks the broad historical shifts of capitalism and industrial society (McKendrick et al. 1982) or the transition to modernity (Miller 1994, 1995; Orlove & Rutz 1989). In contrast to scholarship that has focused either on individuals or global changes, the approach I take here is an institutional one that plumbs the sociological middle ground between individual and over-arching society.

Although not explicitly concerned with institutional economics, I share the economists' concern with the rules and processes that stabilize relationships and constrain individual behavior (North 1990). In the case of Otavaleño migration, I focus on three dimensions of institutions—purpose, organization, and legitimacy—and show how consumption strengthens each one. Wilk's (1989b) analysis of Maya spending captures the complexity of the household's shared purposes. The purchases illustrate not only concern with joint subsistence security but also a desire for economic advancement and the status that comes with it. Consumption is both an end in itself and a means to achieve these other social purposes. In terms of organization, consumer practices help define and commit people to core economic and social practices. Purchases of land and tools for farming or time-saving appliances for the kitchen not only map out a household's potential economic activities but also help members divide their time according to changing priorities.

Finally, at an institutional level, consumption's importance goes beyond these practical and economic issues to problems of legitimacy and ideology. For any social group to function without an undue level of conflict and tension, people must accept a set of standards that define appropriate behavior under a variety of circumstances (Colson 1974). Such acceptance comes hard in societies such as Otavalo. Some have grown up farming, weaving, and rarely venturing outside the province, while others have lived abroad, acquiring a flair for risky textile deals and a taste for hip-hop clothing fashions, sharing few of the interests and skills of their rural kin. Consumption, thus, provides migrants and non-migrants alike with a framework for reasserting common values. That is, in their acquisition and use of goods, people "materialize" their ideals and make them a tangible part of social interactions and negotiations of power (DeMarrais et al. 1996).

For young travelers, the institutional power of goods arises not only when they commit resources to their parents' households, but also when they try to initiate their own. Migrant men and women acquire everything from spinning wheels to soup cauldrons in order to organize their lives for greater independence and to make clear their commitment to Otavaleño domestic ideals. Celestina, for example, signaled her impending break with her family by spending heavily on furniture about four months before she got married. At the time, she had been embroiled in a simmering argument with her parents over her boyfriend in Tulcan. Galo and Mónica kept warning her of the dangers of "walking with" this young man named Pedro, whose parents lived in Peguche (a wealthy community below Ariasucu)—of how she would ruin her reputation. They pleaded with her not to get married too young (barely 18 years old). She, however, was convinced of Pedro's love for her and was ready to be on her own. In the midst of their discussions, she announced that she was going to buy a new double bed and combination dresser-wardrobe to replace he old single bed and wooden chest. Not long afterward, Galo dropped in on us and said he now believed she would get married.

Like Celestina, many young men on the verge of marriage spend soberly on the home. In the late 1980s and early 1990s, Ariasucu experienced a small surge in

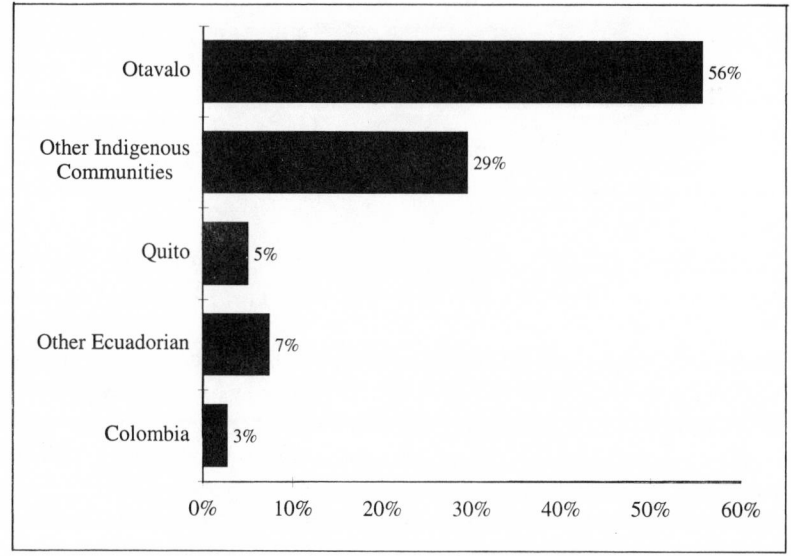

Figure 3. Place of Origin of 1,171 Possessions Found in 33 Ariasucu Homes in 1994 (Both Otavalo and "other Indigenous Communities" are located in the province of Imbabura, along with Ariasucu.)

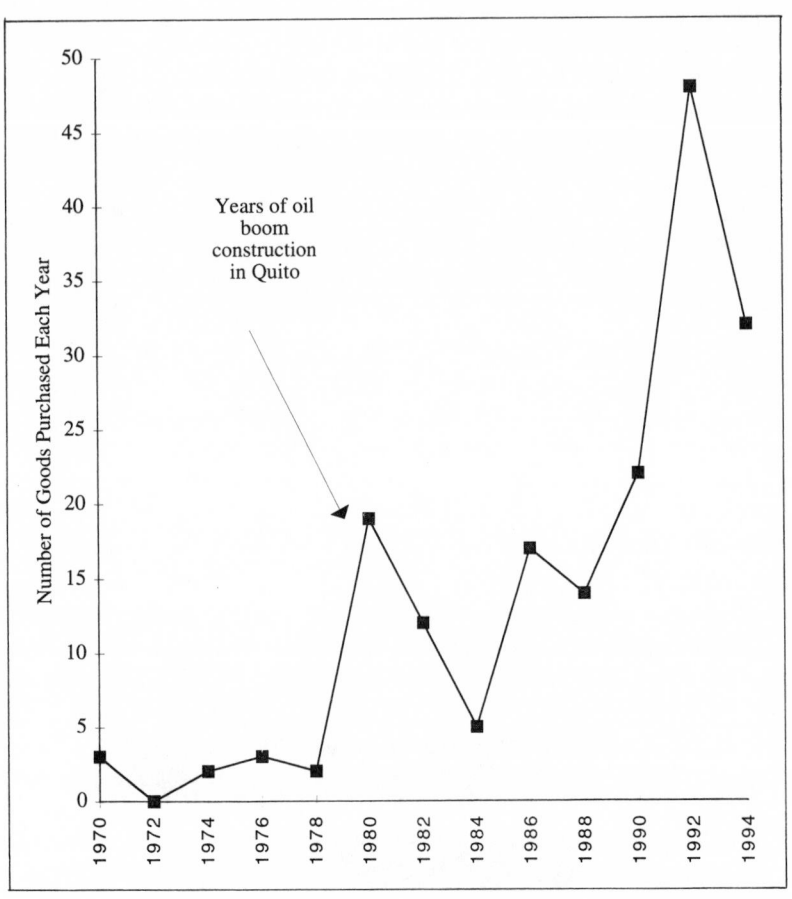

Figure 4.   Growth in Out-of-Province Purchases by 33 Ariasucu
Households, 1970-1994 (Projected for 1994, based on first half of the year.)

out-migration as a new cadre of young men left to sell handicrafts in Quito,
Cuenca, Cañar, and other Ecuadorian cities. Staying away for up to two years, they
spent more conservatively than their peers who stayed at home to weave. Instead
of getting a dirt bike or color TV, these migrants came back with extra-large soup
cauldrons, plastic buckets and, in two cases, gas stoves. Despite being single
males, they all worked to equip the feminine world of the hearth. I asked one of
these migrants why he had purchased a gas stove when he was 18 years old. He
paused, opened his mouth to say something, stopped, shrugged, and smiled while
his wife blurted out, "To catch a woman." When young merchants' thoughts turn
towards love, their money goes towards the kitchen.

The practice of outfitting the house in advance of marriage and from afar has been gaining momentum in recent years. Historically, Otavaleños have acquired the furnishings of their homes locally. Doing inventories of 32 houses, I learned that the majority (56%) of possessions were purchased in Otavlao, while much (29%) of the rest of the tables, hoes, kitchen pots, and weaving equipment were locally made or inherited from relatives who live in Ariasucu or other indigenous communities. Put another way, 85 percent of the 1,171 items that I catalogued came from within the province, while 15 percent had been acquired outside (Figure 3). This low number of externally-acquired goods, though, masks a new trend.

Since the late 1970s, the number of goods that have traveled back to Otavalo with their owners has grown, although not evenly. Extra-provincial purchases expanded in the early 1980s, with the growth in the Quito oil economy, then declined through the middle of the decade, during Ecuador's deep economic recession. These purchases climbed again with a new spurt in textile dealing, only to tail off in the mid-1990s as over-competition began to cut off some trading careers (Figure 4). Like the small chairs and stools bought by Galo and Mónica in Cuenca, some of these goods joined the inventories of established households. In most cases, however, young people acquire these non-local goods just before or after they get married.

These objects confirm Otavaleños' peripatetic existence, bringing the reality of the textile archipelago into the home. Signaling local dependence on distant markets, the furniture and appliances memorialize people's entanglement with the regional and national economies. Questioning people about their goods, I found myself doing an archaeology of how international economic cycles change the character of a home. The "strata" of black-and-white TVs, small cassette players, and two-burner gas stoves reveal the flush times of the oil economy in 1981 and 1982; a "layer" of boom boxes, blankets, and four burner stoves bears witnesses to the money that was being made selling textiles to tourists in the early 1990s; and collections of patched-up cooking pots and repaired farm tools testify to the intermediate phases of low incomes and missing opportunities.

Juxtaposed against the humble possessions of farm life, the remotely-purchased products remind Otavaleños of the reasons to travel, symbolize the potential payoffs of crafts markets, and verify this indigenous people's worldliness. Common possessions such as chairs, cooking pots, and even hammers or hoes become exotic (see Figure 5). Dealers even joke about a radio as "a souvenir of Bogotá" (*un recuerdo de Bogotá*) or a house as "a souvenir of Italy," inverting the standard of Otavaleño roles of tourist and local. Most of these migrants made their money selling souvenir handicrafts to foreign tourists. Inserting themselves into the place of the casual traveler, Otavaleños display new appliances and furniture as tokens of trips in alien lands.

Otavaleño "souvenirs," however, differ in one key respect from the sweaters and tapestries that they sell to others. While their mementos may remind them of Bogotá or Cuenca, they buy these goods not because they represent a foreign cul-

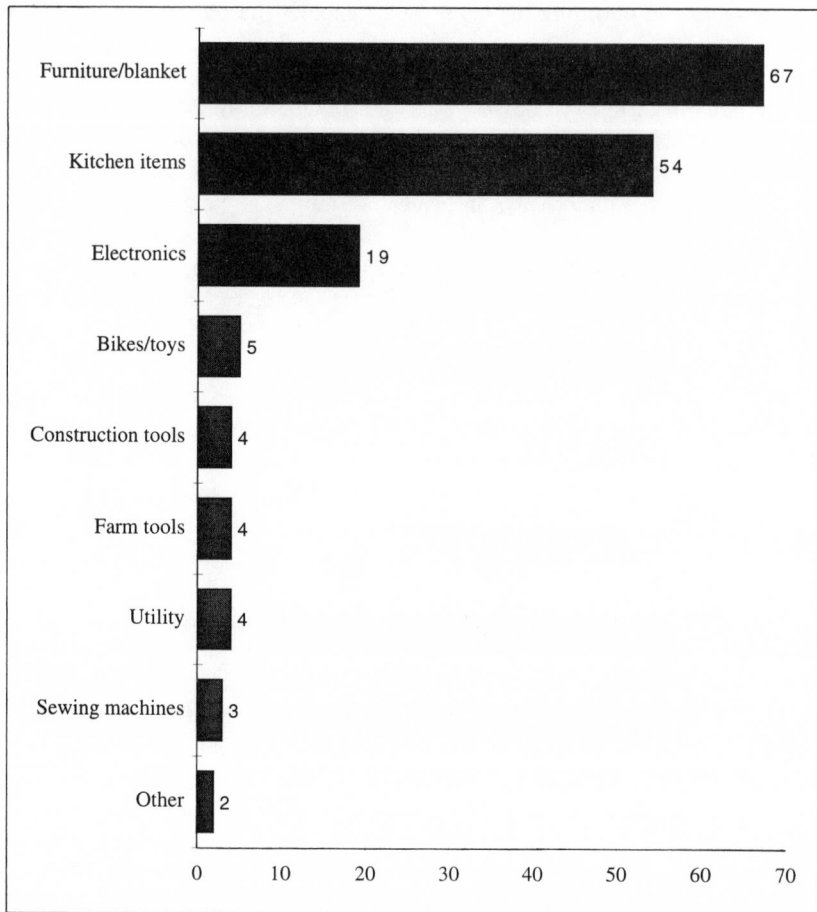

Figure 5.   Number and Types of Possessions Brought Back to Ariasucu by
Migrants from 33 households, 1970-1994

ture, but because they fit within their own in Otavalo. The top four out-of-town
goods include blankets, grain mills, gas stoves, and radios and stereos (Figure 6).
Some of these items are clearly needed for life in the small rented spaces in the cities
where migrants work, but others—such as grain mills, hoes, and water jugs—have
no immediate urban use. Indeed, half of the grain mills in the Otavalo homes that
I inventoried were purchased out of the province—a clear sign of the investment
young couples are making in rural life and products even as they live in the cities.

By buying the implements of country life, migrants' consumption habits build
up their economic incentives to return home and realize the value of their goods.
Even the purchase of a TV, radio, or other electronic appliances can abet the pro-

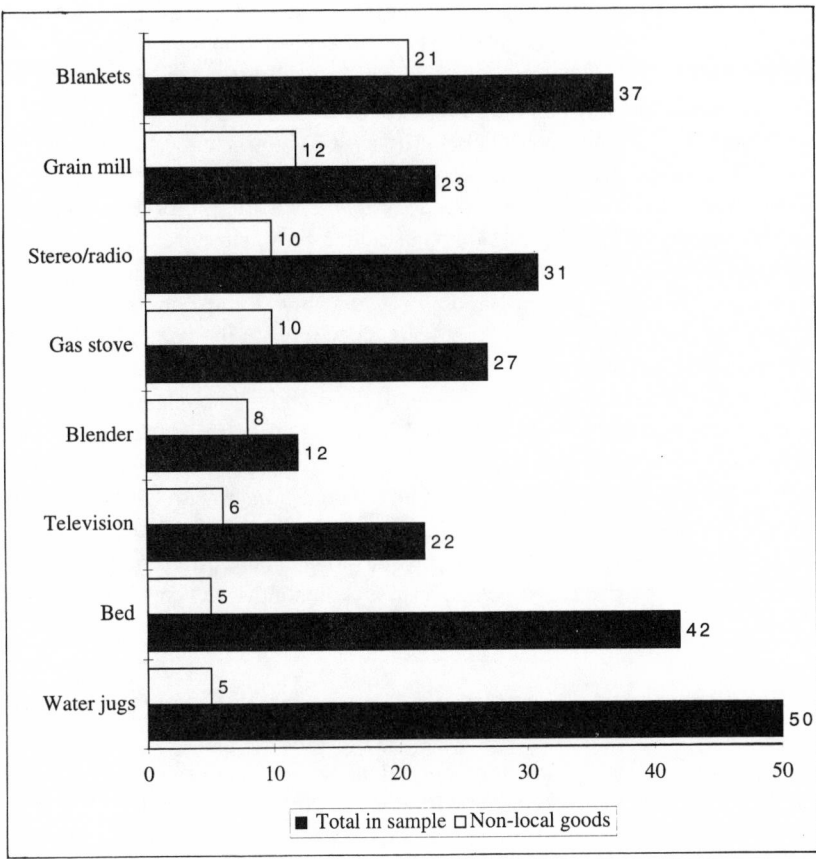

Figure 6. The Eight Most Popular Nonlocal Goods Found in a Sample of 33 Ariasucu Houses

ductive practices of a weaving/farming household. As I discuss elsewhere (Colloredo-Mansfield n.d.), consumer electronics make long hours at the loom more palatable—"TVs make the afternoons happy," in the words of a dedicated *faja* (sash) weaver. By conceiving their needs in terms of the productive routines of Ariasucu, rather than as an unlimited demand for cash, some young merchants place a clear limit on their participation in urban handicraft markets.

Beyond economic reasons, buying agrarian goods in urban settings affirms Otavaleño cultural ideals. McCracken (1988) has argued that singular, "out-of-context" purchases—as in the case of the Otavaleño man who bought a spinning wheel in Bogotá (when better, cheaper ones were to be had back home)— help people to recapture "displaced meanings." He writes that people often locate their cherished values—such as the Otavaleño ideal of "having one's own work in one's own home"—within mythical or remote times and places: a golden past, utopic future, or distant land (McCracken 1988:104). Goods provide symbolic bridges to these realms, allowing people to recapture displaced meanings, without having to take immediate responsibility for them.

For some, these bridges are quickly crossed. Gas stoves and cauldrons bought in Cuenca are used later that year to cook a *caldo* (broth) soup of fresh *choclo* (maize) back in Ariasucu. For others, the bridge is wistful, preserving a link to a life away from polluted cities, fickle construction jobs, and indifferent tourists. I once spent and evening with a young couple and their two children in a one-room apartment in the tourist town of Baños. They had hung drying cobs of maize from the beams of their small loft and kept some farm tools in the corner by their TV. For much of the time I was with them, we talked about how they wanted to move back to Imbabura and buy some land. For all their talking, though, they had yet to sink their tools into the fields of rich, black soil that they described for me. Indeed, they had no concrete plans to return. As with some of the richest Otavaleño merchants, this couple's possessions seem both to connect them with Otavalo's agrarian traditions and to make those traditions seem more romantic than real. The ambiguous meaning of farm tools raises questions about current migrants' economic dependence on the archipelago's rural center, an issue taken up in the last section.

FROM HOUSEHOLDS TO COMPADRE ACTION SETS

Strong relationships *within* the household alone do not insure success in an international, handicraft, textile economy. Rather, the connections *among* households enable young dealers to get into new markets or allow established merchants to strike risky deals using new products. These inter-household links grow out of kinship, community ties, or friendship. Whatever the initial reason for the bond, people formalize it through the rituals of *compadrazgo*, or ritual co-parenthood.[7] At their core, these relationships revolve around Catholic (and now, some Protestant) church rites that involve the sponsorship of a child's baptism, confirmation, or marriage. *Compadrazgo* changes a person's social relations in two ways. First, it intensifies existing family relations when people choose their siblings, parents, and even older children to baptize younger ones. Second, co-parenthood extends social networks as they recruit richer, non-related neighbors, white-mestizos, and foreigners to baptize their children (Figure 7). Mingling bonds of affection with periodic economic assistance, compadres can both comfort each other with loyal support and vex each other with burdensome requests for favors.

In the 1960s, anthropologists predicted that institutionalized, personal obligations would decline in social and economic importance in Latin American peasant communities. They observed both falling participation in religious saints' days festivals and rising efforts to keep *compadrazgo* obligations from interfering with

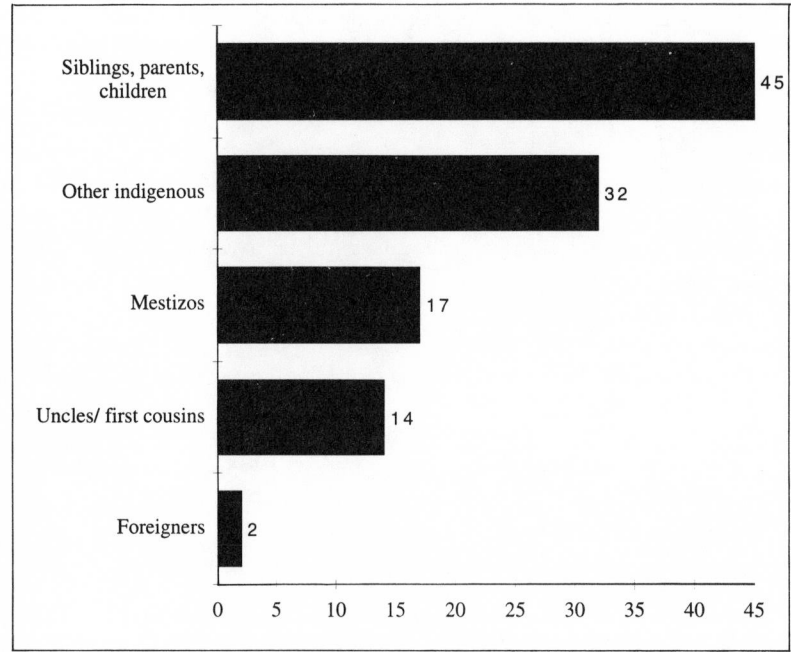

Figure 7.   Kinship and Ethnic Identities of Baptismal Compadres (N=110
Baptisms), 1965-1994

business ventures (Belote & Belote 1977). Base on this evidence, some researchers argued that, as other economic opportunities rose, heavy public investment in
social obligations would decline (Wolf 1966, Smith 1977). In northern Ecuador,
for instance, Walter (1981) said that, with the development of the Otavaleño handicraft tourist industry, wealthier community members' sons no longer spent
money on fiesta obligations and compadre bonds. She (Walter 1981:183) wrote of
young men that, as they "choose to explore new options in the textile sector, they
abandon not only the elaborate, expensive community festivals, but also the elaborate, expensive family festivals associated with *compadrazgo* initiations."

In Otavalo and other parts of the Andes, however, capitalist expansion has not
squeezed out *compadrazgo*. Instead, migration has kept dyadic ties vital, providing
more resources to celebrate these bonds and new reasons to pursue them (see Long
& Roberts 1978, 1984). Both the generic risks of markets and the marginal position
of Otavaleño traders combine to perpetuate compadre bonds. Handicraft markets
shift unpredictably, foreign ones in known cities especially so. In 1995, for example,
Ecuador's short war with Peru resulted in the closure of the border with Colombia,

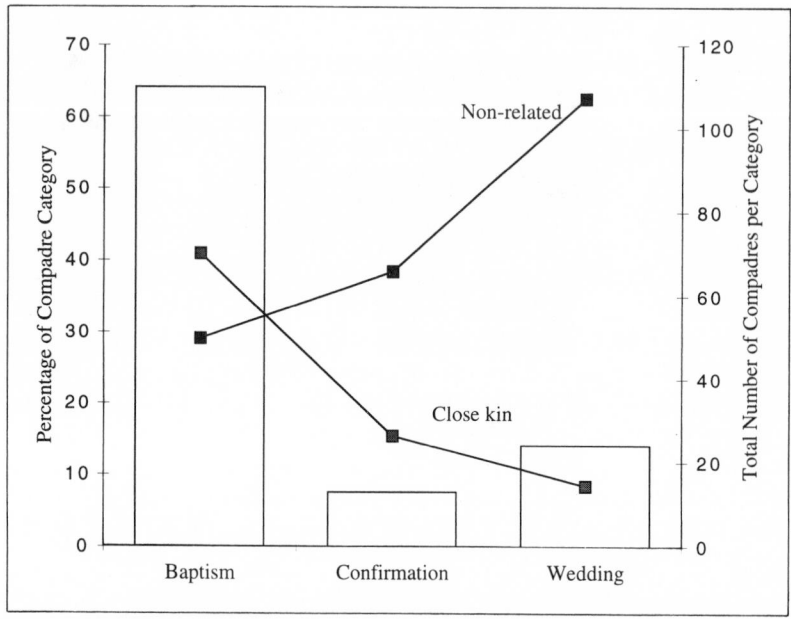

Figure 8.   Kinship Identities of Compadres for Baptisms, Confirmations,
and Weddings in a Sample of 33 Ariasucu Households, 1965-1994
(Histogram bars represent total numbers of compadres per category.)

cutting off craft supplies to Bogotá and the flow of Colombian tourists to Tulcan.
Such fluctuations can wipe out a dealer's earnings and assets. The most experienced
(and, usually, the wealthiest) operators can arrange loans from development agencies in times of hardship; most, however, must protect themselves through personal
ties. For the average dealer, compadres prove to be consistent customers, flexible
creditors, and reliable informants about the state of the market.

Trends in the selection of compadres indicate the way people extend their social
networks as they become older and more involved in the handicraft business.
Some ambitious traders find new, powerful compadres in every town or business
venture they enter into. Reaching out to sweater factory owners, transport operators, and shopkeepers, they turn their children's later rites of confirmation and
wedding to business use (Figure 8). While the numbers of new confirmation and
wedding compadres in the sample are small—because baptismal compadres often
serve for confirmation rites, as well, and because my generally young sample did
not have many weddings yet—they document the power of wealthier native merchants. Many of these *compadrazgo* alliances with non-related *indígenas* (native
peasants) are "vertical" ones between patrons and clients rather than "horizontal"

ones between equal partners. As Mintz and Wolf (1950) have pointed out, dyadic bonds have long flourished in stratified societies with weak central institutions, conditions that exist in Otavalo's handicraft archipelago.

CONSUMPTION AND THE MAINTENANCE OF SOCIAL NETWORKS

Both Galo in his time and Celestina and her husband, Pedro, in the 1990s have depended on extensive networks of kin and fictive kin (*compadrazgo*) to undertake their sales trips. Again, the construction of our home demonstrated how compadre bonds and commercial networks develop out of important consumption activities. Other families now add rooms to their homes with a minimum of social effort by hiring sufficient skilled and unskilled labor to do the work. In contrast, Galo and Mónica hired a master carpenter, a *maestro*, and then by serving him extra food and giving him buckets of *chicha* (home-brewed corn beer) to distribute to others who came to help, they elevated his status from technical expert to a social master of ceremonies. With the *maestro* "officializing" (Bourdieu 1977:40) both the construction and house-warming party, the work's social importance expanded to encompass the widest circle of family and neighbors.

Excluding the *maestro*, the immediate family, and Chesca and me, Galo and Mónica recruited 11 people to volunteer approximately 33 days of work to the addition. The helpers were not just local neighbors, but several of Ariasucu's most prosperous textile dealers. Drawing from outside Ariasucu, Galo and Mónica received support from one cousin who worked in Quito; from another one, named Francisco, who exported sweaters out of Otavalo; and from Galo's sister and brother-in-law, who had lived in Medellin for almost a decade. To deepen their friendship with these compadres, Galo and Mónica held a proper inaugural meal. Although the celebration lasted only a day-and-a-half and involved about 30 people—modest by local standards—Galo secured the participation of his prosperous kin. His cousin Francisco and wife Zoila, for example, arrived early, driving up in their Toyota truck from Otavalo. Their clothes and gifts signaled their respect for the occasion. He wore traditional *alpargata* shoes (white cloth sandals) and formal white pants with a sharp crease and a spotless leather jacket, and he carried a case of Pepsi. Zoila, dressed in a clean, new *anaku* (skirt), followed with a sack of eggs.

Galo's happiness at their arrival dimmed when he saw his sister's son hop out of another cousin's Suzuki hatchback. His nephew Miguel, age 15, was reared mostly in Colombia. He was readjusting awkwardly to rural life in Otavalo and seemed to want a way back to the city as soon as possible. With the exception of his long hair, he conceded little to Otavaleño styles. He wore an earring. His hair was pulled tightly back across his head into a braid and covered by a black Duke baseball cap worn backwards so that the word "Devils" arched neatly over his brow. He had an oversized purple shirt; its dark color accentuated the silver chains and razor blade medallions hanging from his neck. Sagging jeans and brown leather shoes completed the outfit. The style mixed trends introduced by young musicians coming back from Europe as well as personal tastes that he had picked up in Colombia. Galo hated it. Miguel flaunted it, reciprocating Galo's displeasure by acting like he was being held hostage at this event.

The guests took their places in the new room. Galo found his special folding chair for Francisco; Zoila arranged herself on the mats. Mónica gave soup to all the guests. Returning several times, she delivered to Zoila six more bowls, a generous but not unusual amount. Zoila thanked Mónica for the platters around her. Not having brought a pot, though, she could not take the soup home with her as the others were doing. She ate some spoonfuls, then seemed to lose interest. A few minutes later, she plucked a potato out of the congealed skin forming on top of the soup and threw the white lump to a small dog.

I thought Galo would be upset about his cousins' aloof behavior. On the contrary, he was pleased with the way things went. When I asked him the next day what they thought about the house, Galo beamed. He reported that Francisco had said, "It is very beautiful. The roof is good. These runners are very good. The round one [cheaper, unmilled poles] are worthless." Galo was able to shrug off his nephew's eccentricities and Zoila's boredom, to declare the party a success. Within a few months, he would have them all back to celebrate Celestins's wedding.

Although these parties are not hosted with specific business ventures in mind, sales trips and new business ventures among compadres draw on the goodwill they generate. In Pedro and Celestina's case, for example, Pedro's trip to Europe, which he embarked upon in 1996, became possible with the help of the people who came to the new house party and wedding. For airfare, spending money, and inventory purchases, they received cash loans totaling close to U.S. $4,000 from their closest compadres. From others, such as Francisco, Celestina sought a good deal on a bulk purchase of sweaters, and she and her father used the offices of yet another compadre to package handicrafts for shipment to Pedro after he got to Amsterdam. Most of the help was not free, but rather was subject to the terms of regular business transactions. Deals between compadres, thus, do not require the sacrifice of profits and financial gain. The point of these exchanges is not that they are charity, but rather that they make it possible for a newly married couple in their early 20s to enter into such risky transactions at al.

The scale, intensity, and geographic spread of Otavalo social networks create a competitive advantage for them that is not shared by other indigenous artisans in Ecuador. The relative self-sufficiency of Otavaleño traders, though, raises a paradox. As Salomon (1986) points out, the precolumbian precedents to today's northern Andean dealers, the "merchant Indians" known as *mindaláes*, helped to link independent political and economic units. For ethnic traders like to Otavaleños, though, commerce may not lead to lasting connections between merchants and their host communities. While they may develop lasting personal relationships, perhaps even finding compadres or spouses in their adopted cities, Otavaleño expatriates frequently turn to Imbabura to further their economic or social careers. Despite traveling extensively and settling widely, their occupation, products, and social lives consistently reproduce the boundaries between themselves and other groups.

This isolation relates to historic problems of class inequality and ethnic discrimination that go beyond individual social strategies and economic decisions. Galo's uneven career illustrates the most obvious barriers indigenous people face. As a boy, he had no access to proper schools; the two years he spent attending the missionaries' classroom made him literate but did not lead to remunerative employment in the formal sector. For members of his generation, Ecuador's educational system worked more to undermine the values of native culture than to prepare indigenous people for professional careers. Turning to the most promising chance for economic advancement outside the formal economy, Galo became a craft dealer. He developed his trade without the support of official economic or even civic institutions (with the exception of a few public marketplaces). Indeed, he considered it folly to turn to officials for help. Despite the chronic danger thieves posed to his business, experience taught him that authorities often brought more problems than they solved.

Otavaleños add to their institutional isolation as they commit time and money to the restricted networks of their own economic "safety nets." After 50 years, textile deals are still largely a matter for friends, compadres, and patrons. Favors and reciprocal obligations, not formal contracts, structure the region's multi-million dollar, transnational industry. To gain access to this business world, merchants learn the nuances of gift-giving, participate in the fiestas of other prospering dealers, and keep a high social profile around Otavalo. In contrast to earlier predictions made by anthropologists, Otavaleños have not abandoned church sanctioned family celebrations for more formal opportunities. Instead, they pour money into the baptisms and weddings that they host in their home province of Imbabura.

CONSUMPTION RITUALS AND RECIPROCITY

When we lived in Ariasucu, the neighborhood rang with the amplified music of baptisms, weddings, confirmations, and new house parties. The festivities frequently precluded the possibility of a good night's sleep, as the music pounded on until 1 AM and the dogs barked mercilessly at drunken revelers staggering home for hours afterwards. The salsa-tinged pop songs, soap opera ballads, and regional melodies provided a soundtrack to Otavalo's prosperity. All the labor and time invested in the tedious work of minding distant market stalls blossomed in the piercing melodies and food and drink of these gatherings.

Galo and Mónica's plans for Celestina's wedding illustrated for me how much goes into these events. They had recruited us to be the *padrinos* (godparents).

Pleased to be asked, we calculated that our responsibilities—buying a gift for the bride and groom, paying for the band, and maybe buying some clothes—would take up most of our monthly stipend. It would be expensive, but we thought we could afford it. We were wrong. In addition to what we planned to spend, Galo and Mónica wanted to double the paved area of their patio to accommodate the dancing, to hire the band for two days, and to serve a special dish of roasted pork to the guests.

They hoped to (and eventually did) host the kind of party that showed that, "although Galo has had all those disasters, he has had success," as his neighbor put it. The fuss Mónica made about expanding their party and improving the house reflected a desire to show themselves to be well off. But the meaning of the event cannot be reduced to mere "conspicuous consumption" or to the tactical exchanges that sustain the networks of dealers discussed in the previous section. For all their significance for activating social ties and building reputations, these parties are also great fun—drunken bashes in which people eat and drink their fill and dance for days on end.

Beyond this fleeting festive dimension, there is also an enduring ideological one. Long-distance textile dealing eats away at the trust and respect of friendships; commerce breeds misunderstandings between relatives and compadres. During long absences, rumors often circulate about a dealer misspending earnings or exploiting junior family members. When I asked one man about how his son was faring in a town called Cañar, where he had gone with his maternal uncle, the man had a hard time containing his anger. He felt his son had been working too hard and that his brother-in-law had kept all the profits. He said, bitterly, "More distant people are better. One has friendships with non-family. With family, you fight. It is better to work for others." For his part, the brother-in-law complained about the hassles of being obligated to take on his inexperienced nephews as apprentices. As long as Otavaleños strive for handicraft profits by turning to family and compadres, these tensions will dog their relationships.

Amid this volatile mix of commerce, compadres, and travel, fiestas afford a way to restore trust and balance to relationships. The flow of gifts, food, and drink and the continual servings of soup, soda, and beer reaffirm relationships in a "succession of rights and duties to consume and reciprocate" (Mauss 1990:14). Even more than the relatively expensive crates of soda and sacks of potatoes that participants present as gifts at the start of the party, the basic exchanges embedded in acts of consumption sustain goodwill within and beyond the event itself. Food at new house parties or weddings is not indiscriminately handed out to guests who gather within the family's patio and corredor. Rather, hosts monitor the status of each participant so that they can present the right amount of each dish in its proper order.

These festive meals often begin with *buda*, a thick soup of milled maize colored a deep reddish-brown with achiote, delivered when guests arrive—which can occur at any time during the course of the event. Then hosts serve a *caldo*, a clear broth of chicken and potatoes, followed later by helpings of the *midianu*, a festive meal of boiled potatoes, roasted guinea pigs, and chicken. The servers take care to catch up late comers, typically feeding them *buda*, even when others are eating *caldo*, then moving quickly on to the other dishes. Beyond observing sequence, hosts also vary quantity by gender and status. By carefully presenting six or eight bowls of soup to a single compadre, a woman can scale her servings to acknowledge past generosity or to elevate the current relationship to a new level of admiration or friendliness.

At a party where up to 200 people come and leave at irregular intervals, tracking guests can be difficult and stressful. At Celestina and Pedro's wedding, for instance, Mónica's father, Papasu, spent hour after hour trying to match the work in the kitchen to the traffic of guests. Mónica, her daughter Clara, her sister, he mother-in-law Mamá Rosa, and a *comadre* (one's child godmother) crowded each other in the kitchen over-heated by two smoky cooking fires and three black, soot-covered cauldrons bubbling with *buda* and *caldo*. For ten hours a day, two days in a row, Papasu worked long shifts and *tayta servicio* (Master of Service), cajoling, commanding, and pleading for more and more bowls of soup. The compadre in the courtyard handed each one out to the designated receiver—with spoons for men and without for women, who did not eat theirs but rather took it home. Guests promptly handed empty bowls back to servers so they could get food out to others. In this unceasing traffic of soup and bowls flowed the soul of the fiesta. The dense mass of resources assembled from all the compadres and guests diffuses into myriad ritual acts of service.

The region's new wealth and consumption habits have made these serving rituals, if anything, even more complex. Richer families have used their money not only to increase the number of compadres and padrinos they must honor but also to elaborate the types of food served at *compadrazgo* fiestas. Thus, tracking the status of individual guests has become even more important. With their costly new dishes, hosts stand ever vigilant to insure that all participants get generous helpings of a thick, smoky-flavored *buda*; then of the tender dark meat of the slow-roasted *kuchi* (pig), presented with thick kernels of boiled *choclo* (sweet corn), chopped lettuce, and cool, sweet tomatoes; and then of more *buda* soup served with gristly chunks of beef. With the range of dishes, the deft motions of ladies and knives in the kitchen, and swift passage of bowls in the patio, families give substance and form to the ideals and relationships that have sustained them during their absence from Otavalo.

Compadres, fiestas, and reciprocal bonds feature as critical elements of indigenous societies throughout the Andes, not just in Otavalo. Allen (1988), for example, eloquently describes the place of reciprocity in the daily life and ritual practices of Sonqo, and Quechua community in the Peruvian Andes near Cuzco. "Reciprocity," she writes, "is like a pump at the heart of Andean life." Men and women, house and field, people and the earth bind themselves together in webs of dependence and opposition. The careful exchange of *k'intus* (small offerings of coca leaves) back and forth among neighbors gathered to harvest a field or mourners standing at a graveside is a frequent and "tangible expression of their social and moral relationships" (Allen 1988:128). As with other Andean ethnographers (see, e.g., Isbell 1978), she explains how the exchange of food, drink and coca ritually constructs shared values basic to interactions. Allen's book on coca and the symbolic practice of Sonqo thus fits a broader anthropological tradition which interprets ritual as "an ideal version of the social structure. It is a model of how people suppose their relations to be organized" (Leach 1964:286).

As in Sonqo, the flow of gifts at family gatherings in Otavalo expresses the ideals underlying social relations. The problem for transnational Otavaleños, however, is to go from these expressions—from producing "ideal versions" of social relations with bowls of soup—to insuring that sweater deals or sales apprenticeships in distant cities fit those ideals. Approaching her uncle for a loan, Celestina has to find a way to fit her requests into the cycles of favors and support that are symbolized at these parties. Casting handicraft deals in terms of reciprocity depends both on following the rules of etiquette spelled out in the rituals and on something less tangible. Participants structure commercial exchanges to yield the same "feel" that the serving of soup or exchange of drinks has. They build upon the sense of dependability that results from both the history of exchange among a pair of compadres and the experiential details of ritualized, reciprocal transactions—the habits of prestation, counter-prestation, and responsiveness that inhere in the very movement of a plate of food or a cup of beer.

Consumption ritual, in other words, do more than express ideals of reciprocity. The transform abstract cultural ideals into a referential experience (Maquet 1986). What the ideal of reciprocity "means" for compadre relations thus becomes tantamount to how it "feels" at these events. Through the patterned acts of consumption at family rituals, Otavaleños learn reciprocity as a discipline of the body so that a movement, comment, or offer does not feel right without a complimentary reaction. The intricacies of drinking shots of chicha, Coca-Cola, or *trago* (cane alcohol) illustrate how rituals boil reciprocity down to simple gestures and implicit expectations.

Beverages at a fiesta flow in patterns of dyadic interactions. To serve drinks, the host grabs a bottle and approaches a guest and offers him or her a drink. When it is accepted, the host hands over the bottle, receives a shot in return, and then that participant serves the rest. As the individual with the bottle makes the rounds, he or she drinks only when recipients insist that the server drink in tandem with them, saying "*salud*" (health) or "*ishcandi nishun*" (the two of us will drink). Furthermore, he or she must remain until the whole bottle of *trago* or case of beer has been served, one measure at a time.

The server's duty to minister to the guests and drink with those who request it supersedes all other responsibilities. Frequently, the server must stand by, waiting for a distracted drinker to break another conversation, and hand back an empty shot glass. Disrupting a promise to drink together, drinkers may temporarily abandon servers to whom they have said "*salud*" because a second server has moved in to try to force a drink on a popular (or prolific) drinker. In these cases, the original server holds his or her ground, carefully protecting a brimming shot glass from nearby dancers, biding the time until the drinker returns to the original cycle, which must be completed after the other servers are dispensed with. Taking a drink is, thus, always bundled in a moment of discourse that subordinates other social acts to the necessity of maintaining a cycle of give and take.

As these rituals of service and consumption play out over several days, the action routinizes reciprocal values into mannerisms and bodily etiquette. The commands of reciprocity—"*salud*," "*ishcandi nishun*"—fade into a short wave of the hand, a nod, or sometimes the more explicit revolving of one hand over another to indicate that the recipient will follow the server. People learn to insist on the completion of a cycle simply by standing there, their silent body bringing about a close to the transaction.

Bourdieu (1977:94, his emphasis) has argued that this transformation of principles into conventional etiquette and unconscious habits protects a culture's most basic ideals:

> If all societies...set such store on the seemingly most insignificant details of *dress, bearing, physical and verbal manners*, the reason is that treating the body as a memory, they entrust to it in abbreviated and practical, i.e. mnemonic, form the fundamental principals of the arbitrary content of culture...Nothing seems more ineffable, more incommunicable, more inimitable, and therefore, more precious, than the values given body, made body by the transubstantiation achieved by the hidden persuasion of an implicit pedagogy.

Bourdieu, however, construes this "hidden persuasion" as a limited phenomena. Describing the symbolic patterning of the Kabyle home, he argues that the children raised in these culturally ordered spaces learn the habits of their culture's practical logic and meanings. The house serves as an exclusive tool for "incorporat[ing] beliefs beyond the reach of consciousness" (Bourdieu 1977:69). In his Algerian case study, no other setting seems to offer the same possibilities for implicit pedagogy. The fiestas of Otavalo, however, illustrate that such socialization extends beyond childhood and the architecture of a traditional house.

For migrants who occupy a fragmented social world, the totality of consumption elevates the importance of these periodic family gatherings to a crucial period of socialization. Consuming together both reinforces values learned when growing up in Otavalo and teaches the community's etiquette to those who grew up elsewhere, such as the rebellious Miguel. By turning ideals into habits, shared consumption practices help create an experiential frame capable of adapting commerce to a morality of reciprocity. The ideological consequences of heavy spending on communal consumption in Otavalo, thus, are borne in the bodies, gestures, and demeanors of migrants selling in the islands of the handicraft archipelago.

FROM ARCHIPELAGO TO DIASPORA:
STRATIFICATION AND DISPLACEMENT IN THE 1990s

In recent years, a rising class of merchants have challenged the very practices that stabilize the handicraft archipelago. Young dealers have given up on subsistence agriculture, while older, richer migrants have begun to change the way the celebrate family rituals. Under the pressure of these changes, the centralization that distinguishes Otavalo's handicraft merchants from the long-term transnational migration of other Ecuadorian peasants (Miles 1997) gives way. Otavaleño society now threatens to fragment socially as well as spatially, with rich migrants circulating in a trade diaspora defined by multiple urban communities in Quito, Cuenca, and Tulcan as well as central Otavalo. Meanwhile, poorer families from remote sectors have had a more difficult time breaking into the textile business. While I do not have the space to examine fully these transformations, I shall briefly review two obvious changes: the new architecture of the richest merchants and the shortened schedules of their family fiestas.

In recent years, the wealthiest return migrants have broadcast their rising incomes in the two- and three-story modern houses they build throughout the rural sectors.[8] These homes often take years to build as owners return annually to add new stories, a garage, tinted windows, and other details. The men and women who construct them talk of providing a secure asset for their families, of the desire for a nice place in which to retire, and the need for a sturdy house in an earthquake. Most of their neighbors attribute to these owners and ulterior motive: the desire to show at home the cash they earn abroad.

In a narrow sense, the conspicuous consumers themselves would agree. They see their construction projects as symbols of their commitment to their community. According to one migrant, this commitment is what distinguishes indigenous from mestizo migration. This *indígena* (indigenous person) divided his time between the large, East Coast cities of the United States and his home in Ariasucu. "Mestizos," he said, "go and stay [a board], go and stay, go and stay. Indigenous people always come back." He cited his house as proof of his own willingness to return. He had been working on it for five years. Compared to the other migrants' houses, it was small—one story divided into four rooms. However, the owner had invested in accessories: a double set of glass doors in the front entrance, full gas stove, a broad cement patio, and a wide stone and cement path leading to the main path.

Another migrant couple, who lived in Bogotá where their young children went to elementary school, similarly explained that they built a house in the country because "this is what indigenous people do." Although they return for only two weeks a year, they spend most of that time overseeing the construction of a double home built around a wide courtyard decorated with two fruit trees. Two hundred yards away, a young neighbor of theirs had displaced his parents' livestock pen with construction of a new home designed with an attached garage.

These migrants' commitment to their homeland, however, evaporates under close scrutiny. The same houses that anchor them to the Otavaleño countryside repudiate its priorities. These are vacation homes, not the productive hearths of agricultural households (cf. Fletcher 1997). The traveler who pointed out to me that indigenous people always come home did not even put a kitchen in his new house. His design is not unique. Frequently the new architecture does not incorporate an open hearth, a *corredor* (open porch) for milling corn and preparing grains for storage, or even a space primarily dedicated to cooking. When migrants return home, they improvise by placing a small gas stove somewhere inside the house. If they have to stay for more than a month, they often build a cooking shed out back.[9] In short, their houses reveal their indifference, if not disdain, toward the subsistence activities of rural communities.

The wealthy migrants' festive consumption shows a reordering of ideals. Upon his return from a sales trip to Europe, for example, the ex-president of Ariasucu built a substantial two-story addition to his home. Unlike Galo and Mónica, he contracted with laborers to finish the work as quickly as possible. With its completion, the man and his wife hired a band and hosted a new house party. Going beyond normal fare for such events—*buda, caldo*, and perhaps a mutton soup— they also served a roast pig. Remarkably, given all they had invested, the party lasted only a day. Rather than serving multiple cycles of food and drink, the hosts had condensed the event to the presentation of the most expensive dishes.

Similarly, a married couple who spent much of their time in Cuenca cut short their participation in a wedding for which they were the padrinos. The day-and-a-half spent with the newlyweds did not signal their lack of generosity. In fact, they gave more kitchen wares than most padrinos give to their wedding godchildren. Rather, the truncated fiesta signaled the sponsor's desire not to lose too much selling time, not a rejection of *compadrazgo*. The brevity of the event, however, undermined its value as a period for the padrinos and godparents to deepen their relationship. Perhaps not coincidentally, interchanges between the two couples became fraught with misunderstandings.

Six months after the wedding, the padrino returned from Cuenca and asked his new godchild/"compadre" (the two were very close in age and called each other "compadre") for help in preparing materials for his *faja* (belt) looms. At first, the godson seemed pleased to help his padrino. However, as the day wore on, he became irritated as the padrino kept sending over his daughter to ask for more work, as if the godson were a paid laborer.[10] Failing to make the requests personally, not sharing in a few rounds of drinks, and minimizing the food served during this work day, the padrino turned his back on the standard compadre etiquette. Having declined to invest his time and presence in the rituals of family and fictive kin, this family and other local elites now jeopardize their dyadic ties through bad manners. Their expensive foods and gifts preserve the forms of *compadrazgo* but do not maintain the feel of the relationships. Consequently, they fray the bonds that have given the regional economy its strength, variety, and flexibility.

CONCLUSION

Galo, Mónica, Celestina, Pedro, and others illustrate the combination of debt, misfortune, optimism, and earnings that the transnational handicraft textile industry has brought to the Imbabura countryside. While the history of *casimires* and the cuisine of family rituals may make Otavaleños unique, the general experience of becoming mobile artisans and laborers on the fringe of the world economy unites them with peoples from other regions of Ecuador and the Andes. As other scholars have noted, the changing realities of rural Latin America means that "the new emerging postpeasant subject often has a transnational identity" (Kearney 1996:8). This transnationalism has already impacted Otavaleño household development, compadre obligations, and consumption priorities for close to half a century.

To describe the structure of Otavalo's migration, I have borrowed from the metaphor of the "vertical archipelago." The model highlights key economic features and social practices: the complementarity of resources from different market and subsistence niches, the importance of reciprocal relations, the isolation of Otavaleños from their host countries and, above all, the centrality of Otavalo as the place of social authority mediating access to opportunities in the expatriate "islands" of the archipelago.

In appropriating Murra's metaphor, however, I am less interested in rigidly establishing a new category of transnational social organization. Rather, I am concerned with processes of archipelago formation—and dissolution. What Salomon (1985) argues for pre-Hispanic archipelago organization applies with equal validity to today's transnational society. The complentarity, reciprocity, and centralization of Otavalo's social economy should not be understood as a permanent essence of indigenous culture, "but a collective project, continually renewed through processes of adjustment, mobilization, innovation, and conflict" (Salomon 1985:521). In Otavalo, these processes gain their greatest power in material forms. Institutional consumption establishes the goals of migrants and serves households and compadres as a practical mechanism for both defining ideals and framing interactions in terms of those ideals.

Otavaleños' involvement in international markets means that adjustment and innovation are a constant part of life. The organization of the archipelago intensifies or weakens with broader economic cycles. Oil booms, rising demand for handicrafts, or the economic stagnation brought on by border conflicts between Ecuador and Peru have all impacted the flow of migrants and the connections among Otavalo's dispersed communities. The economic developments of the 1980s and 1990s have specifically augmented the forces of class formation within indigenous society. The growing gaps between rich and poor compound the problems of extended absences and reduce the common cultural ground of Imbabura communities.

As prosperous migrants have accumulated new houses, larger inventories, and substantial savings, they have moved away from the values of subsistence production. While still nominally committed to the forms of traditional Otavaleño society, their new consumption practices ironically diminish the cultural power of rural hearths and institutional friendships. The new elites, however, have not yet displaced the practices that give weight and gravity to Otavalo as the center of a thriving trade archipelago. Rather, they have defined a new phase in its development. In their struggle to direct this development, all Otavaleños assemble their commitments and aspirations out of the material world; they serve rich soups, wear flashy baseball hats, hold onto inherited spinning wheels, and shop for new bedroom furniture. In so doing, they stake their claims on each other and point the way to the future.

ACKNOWLEDGMENTS

Funding for research was provided with awards from the National Science Foundation (#9318289), Fulbright Hayes/IIE program, UCLA Latin America Center Small Grants Program, and the UCLA Department of Anthropology. For their generosity and inclusion of me in the celebrations of their lives, I thank my compadres Luis Antonio Castañeda, Elena Chiza, Zoila Arias, and Pedro Vásquez. I am also grateful for the advice and insights offered by Chesca Colloredo-Mansfield, Susan Philips, Nancy Levine, Alessandro Duranti, Tim Earle, and Mary Weismantel. A portion of this paper was presented at the panel "Traditional Communities, Transnational Contexts: Andean Societies in the Global Arena" at the 1995 meeting of the American Anthropological Association, Washington, DC.

NOTES

1. Since the 1940s, numerous researchers have stressed the cultural and political importance of textiles in Otavalo. Buitrón (1947, 1956) provides interesting regional, quantitative data. Parsons (1945) complements his work with the study of Peguche, perhaps the wealthiest indigenous community in Ecuador. Salomon (1981), Casagrande (1981), and Rubio Orbe (1956) describe how indigenous culture developed through the 1950s and 1960s, partly on the strength of the weaving business. Walter (1981) and Chavez (1985) document the growing self-confidence of the wealthiest weavers in the 1970s, as do Meisch (1987) and D'Amico (1993) for the 1980s and 1990s.

2. All proper names used in this article are pseudonyms.

3. I know of only one man from Ariasucu who seems to have preceded Galo in international handicraft selling. He told me (with a laugh) that he and a friend traveled through Cali and Bogotá in the late 1950s selling green papier maché dogs. He sold these and other objects for two or three years until switching to more local forms of trading. He now barters soap, salt, and cooking oil for raw pelts of wool in the most rural communities around Imbabura. In a further rejection of his old occupation, he seems to have forgotten all his Spanish or, at any rate, chooses only to speak Quichua.

4. The sample was determined as part of a larger investigation into a group of belt weaving specialists (Colloredo-Mansfeld 1996:Ch. 5). It includes 17 households specialized in textile manufacture and 16 households drawn at random from the rest of the community. Although not specifically designed to address migration, the sample is not unduly biased by its heavy concentration of weavers, since their overall careers can and often do include lengthy periods of general handicraft selling.

5. This question borrows from Murra's (1985a:3) original inquiry into the organization of the Inka state. As he wrote, "Given the scattered geographical distribution of Andean polities, how does one explain that for centuries, and perhaps millennia the seat of power and the highest demographic density in the pre-European Andes are found at altitudes above 3400 meters?"

6. Brush's (1977) analysis of action sets in agricultural production in the Peruvian Andes drew my attention to Mayer's concept.

7. See Mintz and Wolf (1950) for a general description of compadrazgo in Latin America. Martínez (1963), Long (1971) have also written usefully on the economic, personal, and social importance of compadres in an Andean context.

8. In another article (Colloredo-Mansfeld 1994), I explore how architectural styles and materials mediate between economic changes and the social authority still vested in subsistence resources.

9. Ironically, those families forced by circumstances to return for extended periods often find themselves living primarily in an improvised structure behind their impressive new homes. These crude, functional shacks, which they intended as short-term supplements to their vision of a modern life, wind up betraying that vision, as returning families spend their time clustered in a building inferior to those of most of their neighbors who had stayed more connected to their fields and the community.

10. I think he found it particularly irksome that she would make the requests in Spanish rather than Quichua/*Runa Shimi* (the people's tongue), which would be the language compadres use with each other. In fact, he often responded to her in Quichua.

REFERENCES

Allen, Catherine (1988) *The Hold Life Has: Coca and Cultural Identity in an Andean Community.* Washington, DC: Smithsonian Institution Press.

Belote, Jim, and Linda Belote (1977) "The Limitation of Obligation in Saraguro Kinship." Pp. 106-116 in Ralph Bolton & Enrique Mayer (eds.), *infra.*

Bolton, Ralph, and Enrique Mayer, eds. (1977) *Andean Kinship and Marriage.* Washington, DC: American Anthropological Association, Special Publ. No. 7.

Bourdieu, Pierre (1977) *Outline of a Theory of Practice.* Cambridge, ENG: Cambridge University Press.

Brush, Stephen (1977) "Kinship and Land Use In a Northern Sierra Community." Pp. 136-152 in Ralph Bolton & Enrique Mayer (eds.), *supra.*

Buitrón, Aníbal (1947) "Situación económica y social del indio otavaleño." *América Indígena* 7:45-67.

_____ (1956) "La tecnificacíon de la industria textil manual de los indios del Ecuador." Pp. 287-295 in Eusebio Dávalos Hurtado & Ignacio Bernal (eds.) *Estudios Anthropológicos en Homenaje al Dr. Manuel Gamio.* Mexico, DF: Universidad Nacional Autónoma de México.

_____ (1962) "Panorama de la aculturación en Otavalo, Ecuador." *América Indígena* 26:53-79.

Casagrande, Joseph B. (1981) "Strategies for Survival: The Indians of Highland Ecuador." Pp. 260-277 in Norman E. Whitten, Jr. (ed.) *Cultural Transformations and Ethnicity in Modern Ecuador.* Urbana: University of Illinois Press.

Chavez, Leo Ralph (1985) "'To Get Ahead': The Entrepreneurial Ethic and Political Behavior among Commercial Weavers in Otavalo." Pp. 159-189 in Jeffrey Ehrenreich (ed.) *The Political Anthropology of Ecuador: Perspectives from Indigenous Cultures.* Albany: State University of New York at Albany and the Society for Latin American Anthropology, Center for Caribbean and Latin America.

Clifford, James (1994) "Diasporas." *Cultural Anthropology* 9:302-338.

Colloredo-Mansfeld, Rudolf (1994) "Architectural Conspicuous Consumption and Economic Change in the Andes." *American Anthropologist* 96:845-865.

_____ (1996) *Farmers, Weavers, and Textile Dealers: Material Culture, Economic Change, and the Making of an Indigenous Social World in the Ecuadorian Andes.* Ph.D. dissertation, University of California, Los Angeles.

_____ (n.d.) "Rethinking Cultural Hybrids: Social Agency and Craft Production in the Andes." MS, 1997.

Colson, Elizabeth (1974) *Tradition and Contract: The Problem of Order.* Chicago: Aldine.

D'Amico, Linda (1993) *Expressivity, Ethnicity, and Renaissance in Otavalo.* Ph.D. dissertation, University of Indiana.

Dávilo, Mario (1971) "Compadrazgo: Fictive Kinship in Latin America." Pp. 396-406 in Nelson Graburn (ed.) *Readings in Kinship and Social Structure.* New York: Harper & Row.

de Janvry, Alain (1987) "Latin American Peasants." Pp. 391-404 in T. Shanin (ed.) *Peasants and Peasant Societies: Selected Readings.* Oxford, ENG: Blackwell.

DeMarrais, Elizabeth, Luis Jaime Castillo, and Timothy K. Earle (1996) "Ideology, Materialization and Power Strategies." *Current Anthropology* 37:15-31.

Douglas, Mary, and Baron Isherwood (1979) *The World of Goods.* New York: Basic Books.

Fletcher, Peri (1997) "Building from Migration: Imported Design and Everyday Use of Migrant Houses in Mexico." Pp. 185-202 in Benjamin Orlove (ed.) *The Allure of the Foreign: Imported Goods in Post Colonial Latin America.* Ann Arbor: University of Michigan Press.

Friedman, Jonathan, ed. (1994) *Consumption and Identity.* Chur, SWITZ: Harwood Academic Publishers.

Friedman, Kathie (1984) "Households as Income Pooling Units." Pp. 37-55 in Joan Smith & Immanuel Wallerstein (eds.) *Households and the World Economy.* Beverly Hills, CA: Sage.

Gelles, Paul, and Wilton Martinez (1993) *Transnational Fiesta 1992.* Berkeley, CA: Center for Media and Independent Learning.

Goody, Jack (1962) *The Development Cycle of Domestic Groups.* Cambridge, ENG: Cambridge University Press.

Harrison, Regina (1989) *Songs, Signs, and Memory in the Andes: Translating Quechua Language and Custom.* Austin: University of Texas Press.

Heyman, Josiah (1990) "The Emergence of the Waged Life Course on the United States-Mexican Border." *American Ethnologist* 17:348-359.

_____ (1994) "The Organizational Logic of Capitalist Consumption on the Mexico-United States Border." Pp. 175-238 in Barry L. Isaac (ed.) *Research in Economic Anthropology, Vol. 15.* Greenwich, CT: JAI Press.

Isabell, Billie Jean (1974) "The Influence of Migrants upon Traditional Social and Political Concept: A Peruvian Case Study." Pp. 237-262 in Wayne Cornelius & Feliciana Trueblood (eds.) *Latin America Urban Research, 4.* Beverly Hills, CA: Sage.

_____ (1978) *To Defend Ourselves: Ecology and Ritual in an Andean Village.* Austin: University of Texas, Institute of Latin American Studies.

Kearney, Michael (1996) *Reconceptualizing the Peasantry: Anthropology in Global Perspective.* Boulder, CO: Westview Press.

Knapp, Gregory (1991) *Andean Ecology: Adaptive Dynamics in Ecuador.* Boulder, CO: Westview Press.

Korovkin, Tanya, Vidal Sánchez, and José Isama, eds. (1994) *Nuestras communidades ayer y hoy: Historica de las comidades indígenas de Otavalo. Ñucanchic aillu llactacuna ñaupa, cunan pachapash.* Quito: Abya-Yala.

Leach, Edmund (1964) *Political Systems of Highland Burma: A Study of Kachin Social Structure.* London: The Athlone Press.

Long, Norman (1977) "Commerce and Kinship in the Peruvian Highlands." Pp. 153-176 in Ralph Bolton & Enrique Mayer (eds.), *supra.*

Long, Norman, and Brian Roberts, eds. (1978) *Peasant Co-operation and Capitalist Expansion in Central Peru.* Austin: University of Texas, Institute of Latin American Studies.

_____ (1984) *Mines, Peasants, and Entrepreneurs: Regional Development in the Central Highlands of Peru*. Cambridge, ENG: Cambridge University Press.

Maquet, Jacques (1986) *The Aesthetic Experience: An Anthropologist Looks at the Visual Arts*. New Haven, CT: Yale University Press.

Martínez, Hector (1963) "Compadrazgo en una comunidad indígena altiplánica." *América Indígena* 23:127-139.

Masuda, Shozo, Izumi Shimada, and Craig Morris, eds. (1985) *Andean Ecology and Civilization*. Tokyo: University of Tokyo Press.

Mauss, Marcel (1990) *The Gift: The Form and Reason for Exchange in Archaic Societies*. New York: W.W. Norton.

Mayer, Adrian (1966) "The Significance of Quasi-groups in the Study of Complex Societies." Pp. 97-122 in M. Banton (ed.) *The Social Anthropolgy of Complex Societies*. London: Tavistock Publications, ASA Monographs No. 4.

Mayer, Enrique (1985) "Production Zones." Pp. 45-84 in Shozo Masuda et al. (eds.), *supra*.

McCracken, Grant (1988) *Culture and Consumption: New Approaches to the Symbolic Character of Consumer Goods and Activities*. Bloomington: Indiana University Press.

McKendric, Neil, John Brewer, and J.H. Plumb (1982) *The Birth of a Consumer Society: The Commercialization of Eighteenth-Century England*. London: Hutchinson.

Meisch, Lynn (1987) *Otavalo: Weaving, Costume and the Market*. Quito: Ediciones Libri Mundi.

Miles, Ann (1997) "The High Cost of Leaving: Illegal Emigration from Cuenca, Ecuador, and Family Separation." Pp. 55-75 in Ann Miles & Hans Buechler (eds.) *Women and Economic Change: Andean Perspectives*. Washington, DC: The American Anthropological Association, Society for Latin American Anthropology Publication Series, 14.

Miller, Daniel (1994) *Modernity: An Ethnographic Approach*. New York: Berg Publishers.

_____ (1995) *Acknowledging Consumption*. New York: Routledge.

Mintz, Sidney W., and Eric R. Wolf (1950) "An Analysis of Ritual Co-Parenthood (Compradrazgo)." *Southwest Journal of Anthropology* 6:341-368.

Murra, John V. (1985a) "'El Archipiélago Vertical' Revisited." Pp. 3-14 in Shozo Masuda et al. (eds.), *supra*.

_____ (1985b) "The Limits and Limitations of the Vertical Archipelago." Pp. 15-20 in Shozo Masuda et al. (eds.), *supra*.

Nash, June (1994) "Global Integration and Subsistence Insecurity." *American Anthropologist* 96:7-30.

Netting, Robert, Richard Wilk, and E. Arnould (1984) *Households: Comparative and Historical Studies of the Domestic Group*. Berkeley: University of California Press.

North, Douglass C. (1990) *Institutions, Institutional Changes, and Economic Performance*. Cambridge, ENG: Cambridge University Press.

Orlove, Benjamin, and Henry Rutz (1989) "Thinking about Consumption: A Social Economy Approch." Pp. 1-58 in H. Rutz & B. Orlov (eds.), *infra*.

Parsons, Elsie Clews (1945) *Peguche: A Study of Andean Indians*. Chicago: University of Chicago Press.

Peek, Peter (1982) "Agrarian Change and Labour Migration in the Sierra of Ecuador." Pp. 121-146 in Peter Peek & Guy Standing (eds.) *State Policies and Migration*. London: Croom Helm.

Roberts, Bryan (1974) "The Interrelationships of City and Provinces in Peru and Guatemala." Pp. 207-236 in Wayne Cornelius & Feliciana Trueblood (eds.) *Latin America Urban Research, 4*. Beverly Hills, CA: Sage.

_____ (1975) "Center and Periphery in the Development Process: The Case of Peru." Pp. 77-108 in Wayne Cornelius & Feliciana Trueblood (eds.) *Latin America Urban Research, 5*. Beverly Hills, CA: Sage.

_____ (1978) *Cities of Peasants: The Political Economy of Urbanization in the Third World*. Beverly Hills, CA: Sage.

Rubio Orbe, Gonzalo (1956) *Punyaro, estudio de antopología social y cultural de una comunidad indígena y mestiza.* Quito: Casa de la Cultura Ecuatoriana.

Rutz, Henry, and Benjamin Orlove, eds. (1989) *The Social Economy of Consumption.* Lanham, NJ: University Press of America.

Sahlins, Marshall (1972) *Stone Age Economics.* Chicago: Aldine.

Salomon, Frank (1981) "Weavers of Otavalo." Pp. 420-449 in Norman E. Whitten, Jr. (ed.) *Cultural Transformations and Ethnicity in Modern Ecuador.* Urbana: University of Illinois Press.

_____ (1985) "The Dynamic Potential of the Complementarity Concept." Pp. 511-531 in Shozo Masuda et al. (eds.), *supra.*

_____(1986) *Ethnic Lords of Quito.* Cambridge, ENG: Cambridge University Press.

Smith, Waldemar (1977) *The Fiesta System and Economic Change.* New York: Columbia University Press.

Van Buren, Mary (1996) "Rethinking the Vertical Archipelago: Ethnicity, Exchange, and History in the South Central Andes." *American Anthropologist* 96:338-351.

Walter, Lynn (1981) "Social Strategies and the Fiesta Complex in an Otavaleño Community." *American Ethnologist* 8:172-185.

Weismantel, Mary (1988) *Food, Gender, and Poverty in the Ecuadorian Andes.* Philadelphia: University of Pennsylvania Press.

_____ (1989a) "The Children Cry for Bread: Hegemony and the Transformation of Consumption." Pp. 85-100 in H. Rutz & B. Orlove (eds.), *supra.*

_____ (1989b) "Making Breakfast and Raising Babies." Pp. 55-72 in Richard Wilk (ed.) *The Household Economy: Reconsidering the Domestic Mode of Production.* Boulder, CO: Westview Press.

Whitten, Norman, Jr. (1985) *Sicuanga Runa: The Other Side of Development in Amazonian Ecuador.* Urbana: University of Illinois Press.

Wilk, Richard (1989a) "Beyond the Black Box." Pp. 23-52 in Richard Wilk (ed.) *The Household Economy: Reconsidering the Domestic Mode of Production.* Boulder, CO: Westview Press.

_____ (1989b) "Houses as Consumer Goods: Social Processes and Allocation Decisions." Pp. 297-322 in H. Rutz & B. Orlove (eds.), *supra.*

_____ (1992) *Household Ecology, Economic Change and Domestic Life among the Kekchi Maya in Belize.* Tucson: University of Arizona Press.

Wolf, Eric (1966) *Peasants.* Englewood Cliffs, NJ: Prentice-Hall.

ETHNICITY, PROPERTY AND THE STATE:
LEGAL RHETORIC AND THE POLITICS OF COMMUNITY IN OTAVALO, ECUADOR

Elizabeth Marberry Rogers

INTRODUCTION

The post-colonial indigenous struggle for land in the Americas has been expressed through a myriad of forms as indigenous peoples have fought in the courts, on the ground, and now increasingly through media representations to retrieve lands that they perceive as rightfully their own. Within Ecuador, the "recuperation" of indigenous lands now plays a central role in what has become a pan-indigenous political movement capable of mobilizing large-scale public demonstrations, such as the Levantamiento Nacional Indígena (National Indian Uprising) of June 1990, an impressive display of protest involving tens of thousands of Indians and spanning multiple provinces (Ibarra 1991, Sawyer 1997, Zamosc 1994; see Albó 1991). Specifically intended to establish continuity with indigenous insurrections of the past, the *levantamiento* differed from the uprisings of the colonial period and 19th

Research in Economic Anthropology, Volume 19, pages 69-113.
Copyright © 1998 by JAI Press Inc.
All rights of reproduction in any form reserved.
ISBN: 0-7623-0446-4

century in its ability to bring national and international attention to a list of popular grievances among the nation's Indians, grievances that included the resolution of a number of local land conflicts (Zamosc 1994).

Although protests such as the *levantamiento* are remarkable in their level of organization, many indigenous people in Ecuador have chosen not to participate in such official displays of "ethnic resurgence." Indeed, within the Otavalo region of highland Ecuador, there are many *indígenas* (indigenous people) who actively contest the images and discourses of Indianness, "community," and property rights adopted and promoted by local groups affiliated with the indigenous political movement. This opposition has perhaps most recently been expressed in the Otavalo area in local conflicts taking place between and within the region's indigenous communities over rights to hacienda lands expropriated in the mid-1980s.

What are we to make of such opposition? How do we explain conflict that occurs *within* indigenous (or peasant) communities over access and control of land? It might be tempting to discount such conflict altogether, recognizing it simply as an anomaly or, maybe, to explain it as a product of socioeconomic divisions within these communities (i.e., a product of capitalist penetration). One could even, perhaps, attribute this type of conflict to the rejection of the "traditional" by particularly "progressive" community members. In this article, however, I suggest that it is possible to move away from overly structuralist interpretations or analyses that rely upon an idealized image of indigenous communalism in explaining the emergence and expression of conflict in general and the articulation of subaltern resistance in particular. Specifically, I argue that an alternative interpretation of intra-communal land conflict can be suggested based on the analysis of the particular instances in which individualism and communalism are variously appealed to in encounters between *comuneros* (indigenous community members) and intrusive "outsiders," as well as among *comuneros* themselves.

This article examines three different land conflicts, all of which center on attempts to control the privatization of communal landholdings and all of which took place in the Otavalo Valley in the early 1900s. Two of these cases involve members of the same indigenous communities, La Compañía-Camuendo and Imbaquí-Agato-Maldonado. More specifically, they are examples of intra-community factionalism in which both sides claim to be the legitimate representatives of the community who, as such, have the right to decide the fate of lands designated as belonging to it. The third case occurs between indigenous defendants and white plaintiffs, the latter of whom argue for their own rights, as *comuneros* (community members), to lands belonging to the community of Gualacata. Together, these disputes reveal the appropriation of state power by Otavaleños (*indígenas* from the area), in their defense of both individual and shared rights to communal lands, from three categories of individuals: local state representatives, expansionist elite landowners and, even, fellow members of their communities.

An examination of these disputes discloses the means by which Otavaleños were able to accomplish this feat: the strategic manipulation of a shared legal discursive framework (see Roseberry 1994, Seligmann 1993, G. Smith 1989). Specifically, in this article, I argue that Otavaleños engaged and negotiated particular legal categories and discourses endowed with state authority in order to defend communal control of pastoral lands from three figures, in particular—the state, encroaching hacienda owners, and fellow community members—while simultaneously protecting their individual rights to communal lands used for agricultural purposes. Otavaleños at the turn of the century can especially be seen to take advantage of the disparity between the reality of how communal lands were actually used and administered and the ideological understanding underlying the legal differentiation between individual- and communal-based rights to land.

Close analysis of the three land conflicts presented here reveals that both Indians and "elite" whites employed arguments based on discursive strategies commonly considered to be "traditional"—e.g., statements of ancestral rights to land, of ownership and possession since "time immemorial," of rights to communal lands based on community membership—in order to capitalize on existing forms of legitimacy co-constructed in an arena defined in part by state policies regarding the conservation and protection of communal lands. Similarly, indigenous community members also sought to privatize specific extensions of land recognized by the state as communal through recourse to the legal protection of individual rights to exclusively owned property.

Contrary to what might be expected, however, I suggest that the choice of alternative strategies elaborating "communalistic" or "individualistic" principles by the Otavaleños involved in these land disputes cannot be attributed to the emergence of class divisions within these communities or to the articulation of ethnic differentiation. Rather, the choices made by indigenous community members and the intra-communal conflicts incurred by them were informed by the application of common but distinct social constructions of communal property (i.e., the designated and accepted use of the land in question), as well as legal criteria established by the state. This article thus argues that indigenous recourse to strategies that propose apparently contradictory understandings of rights to communal properties in the early 20th century did not represent a shift in the basis of property rights from communal to individual (see Nugent & Alonso 1994). Instead, maneuvering within conduits opened by ambiguities and tensions within republican legislation, Otavaleños were able to focus attention on specific but common aspects of communal rights to property through which access and possession were validated in their attempt to concretize, and have recognized by the state, both individual and communal ownership rights.

CONFLICT, "COMMUNITY," AND LAND RIGHTS

This article offers a critical perspective on common paradigms found in studies of agrarian conflict and subaltern resistance by challenging two implicit assumptions that unite them, namely, the inherent opposition of subaltern "communities" to the nation-state and the penetration of capitalism (see Nugent 1998) and, consequently, the emergence of "resistance" out of an essentialized tradition of communalism. Increasingly, these assumptions are being critiqued. In particular, a number of scholars (see, e.g., Joseph & Alonso 1994, Nugent 1998, Poole 1994a, Seligmann 1995) are questioning the image of an overwhelming and homogenizing nation-state that is resisted by local collectivities stubbornly or heroically maintaining particularistic institutions, identities, and moral codes often identified as "traditional." The work of these scholars shows us how, contrary to that scenario, subaltern peoples have envisioned such "forces" as the nation-state, modernity, and the market as potentially liberating rather than as threatening and, thus, to be resisted at all costs.

While the focus has shifted from the dominant to the subaltern, from colonial elite to peasant *indígenas*, from the state to the local community in studies of state-building and subaltern political activity, David Nugent (1994), in particular, has noted how both components continue to appear as essential, fixed, and bounded, with the latter term consistently portrayed as resisting the expanding, absorbing former term. The land disputes examined in this article, however, undermine such an oppositional model in their illustration of the ways in which the "community" in general and indigenous communities in particular are constantly being redefined and reproduced through negotiations and even appropriations of state power (see Seligmann 1993). Specifically, these disputes highlight the ways in which the "community" and its rights—legally and/or collectively formulated—are invoked to justify individual actions and claims, actions that can be merely assertive or even overtly hostile. Indeed, the legitimacy conferred on the "community" and actions undertaken on its behalf by the state augments its efficacy as an image that can be deployed to explain and legitimize behavior and motivations by individuals seeking to justify their rights to resources via a rhetoric of communal values, rights, and forms of organization. Thus, while conflict might be articulated by the individuals involved via symbolic constructions of "community," these concrete examples illustrate how conflict is decidedly not coterminous with the disintegration of a stable, harmonious, essentialized community.

Subaltern Resistance and Agrarian Conflict

The study of subaltern "resistance" to domination, with its focus on both rebellion and everyday acts of subversion, provided a much needed improvement on the previous academic tradition of eliding the role of indigenous peoples and peasants in the transformation of agrarian structures altogether. Within Andean studies, in the 1970s and 1980s a number of scholars, intent on combating the implied passivity of indigenous peasants found in "elite-driven" models of change (see, e.g., Baraona 1965, Barraclough 1973, Barsky 1978, Guerrero 1978, Lambert 1971), turned in a direction commonly associated with James Scott's (1985) study of everyday peasant resistance in Southeast Asia. Specifically, Andeanist studies of domination and conflict shifted towards an examination of multiple forms of indigenous response to structures of inequality, ranging from overt organized protest and rebellion to "everyday" strategies of subsistence and survival rooted in "traditional" Andean forms of communal labor and reciprocity (see, e.g., Crain 1988, Guerrero 1991a, Harris 1989, Klein 1982, Larson 1988, Moreno 1978, Silverblatt 1987, Spalding 1984, Stern 1982, Thurner 1993).

Studies of resistance have, without question, increased our awareness and understanding of subaltern engagement of processes of colonialism and neocolonism. Attentive to the ways in which marginalized people have actively responded to oppression and the need to position focal communities within broader political and economic histories, these studies provide fascinating and insightful accounts of the myriad ways in which indigenous peoples have creatively and strategically engaged structures of domination. Despite their contributions, however, resistance studies have often neglected key aspects of indigenous political engagement and agrarian transformation in their equation of resistance with collective unity and solidarity (G. Smith 1989) and in their assumption of the opposition of indigenous peasants to the spread of capitalist relations and integration into colonial systems and the nation-state. Because *indígenas* and peasants are construed as invariably resisting "external" forces such as the market, the state, and capitalism, their degree of incorporation or integration into these monolithic entities is presented as patterning both their political responses and the form they will take. Striving to explain the refusal or failure of some Indians or peasants to mobilize against these forces, internal differences motivating people's political choices are frequently reduced to an articulation of socioeconomic differentiation.

Implicit in this construction of resistance is an acceptance of the notion that social life is ideally harmonious, an affirmation of humans' mutual interdependence based on reciprocal cooperation. Accordingly, order is construed as the ideal norm and, conversely, conflict is seen as the result of a breakdown in the normative social control that is enforced by and within the community, a harmonious, consensual collectivity (see, e.g., Beals 1964, Gluckman 1967, Gulliver 1979, Siegel & Beals 1960, Turner 1957). In turn, the emergence of conflict is commonly attributed to factors and forces that introduce or contribute to the disintegration of this idealized state of harmonious coexistence, commonly glossed as "community," namely, change (often in the form of "modernization"), factionalism, and individualism.

Despite the apparent persuasiveness of such a model, I suggest that the ensuing dichotomies—cooperation vs. conflict, traditional vs. modern or progressive, and collectivism vs. individualism—are misleading. Conflict, in any of its forms, cannot be defined simply as the dissolution of normative, rule-governed order, nor can "community" be implicitly equated with the absence of factionalism and of "modern," individualistic forms, practices, and motives. Individuals, regardless of their religion, ethnic identity, or class, frequently combine supposedly contradictory interests, practices, and values. Rather than explaining away their articulation and interplay within indigenous and peasant communities as a result of the spread of capitalist relations, we need to address specifically just these processes.

Resistance, the "Community," and Individualism

As Deborah Poole (1994b:22) has recently remarked, for many scholars of Andean conflict and resistance, the actions and strategies of individuals upon whom they focus are often rooted in an enduring Andean Indian identity that is equated with "corporatist ideas of community, ethnicity and class." In some studies of indigenous political engagement, resistance itself is presented as an artifact of a uniform and homogenous Andean cultural tradition. For the authors of such texts, an objectified "community" that has returned to or reactivated the "traditional" communalistic moorings of Andean society is commonly identified as the mobilizing actor (Findji 1992, Rosero 1991). For others, particularly those informed by class-based analyses, resistance is manifested in critiques of imposed capitalist relations of production (see, e.g., Crain 1991, Nash 1979, Taussig 1980) or successful integrations of "traditional," pre-capitalist structures and practices with more "modern" capitalist strategies within the context of colonial or state projects of unification through conformity (see, e.g., Larson 1988, Guerrero 1991b).

In both types of analysis, however, "community" is endowed with the responsibility and capacity of regulating both individual and communal behavior. In turn, the strength of communal institutions, specifically those regulating organized, unified activity, is perceived to determine peasant or indigenous political response to intruding outside forces which threaten such means of survival as access to land (Wolf 1957). With the erosion of "community" through such processes as the emergence of social and economic differentiation and the introduction of transformative elements, indigenous peasants are perceived to increasingly turn to individualistic, rather than communalistic, strategies (see, e.g., Mallon 1983, Wolf 1969). Indexed by the degree of incorporation into the capitalist market, resistance becomes, in effect, associated with a homogeneity that rests on the suppression of "possessive individualism" or, more accurately, "individualism of the kind associated with the rise and establishment of western capitalism" (G. Smith 1989:28).

Within this framework, the maintenance of communal property—or, more specifically, property jointly-administered, exploited, and owned—is both evidence of community solidarity and organization and a motivation for mobilization.[1] Conversely, the privatization of communal land is linked with its commodification and, concomitantly, communal relationships based on exchange (Mallon 1983, Turner 1993). Privatization thus comes to constitute a historical marker, a moment of conversion, after which Andean Indians experience not only a physical alienation and displacement from their lands but also a spiritual decentering due to their dislocation from the communal land base necessary for their subsistence and reproduction.[2] Its perpetrators, consequently, are frequently identified as agents of a modernizing state and unscrupulous or encroaching white-*mestizos* or, if indigenous, elite community leaders who reject traditional communal values, having been co-opted by external forces (e.g., bribed by white landowners, manipulated by lawyers) (see Cevallos 1993, Guerrero 1989).

Theoretically, then, the privatization and "communalization" of landholdings are diametrically opposed, each representative of a discrete and irreconcilable system of land tenure that is "determined by the type of community and the orientation of the economic system toward subsistence or market production" (Brush & Guillet 1985:25). Studies that adopt such dichotomies as explanatory devices often interpret agrarian conflict and internal factionalism, in particular, as emerging out of a clash between two competing and contradictory systems of land tenure, the one "traditional" and ancestral, and the other, "modern" and capitalist, with the degree of capitalist penetration determining the adoption of one over the other (Roseberry 1993, Stern 1987). This opposition, in turn, organizes lesser-level oppositions. Individual-based rights are commonly juxtaposed against community-based rights. Similarly, rights based on purchase and title are opposed to rights based on kinship and community membership, just as permanent-use rights (i.e., rights of full ownership) are posed against usufruct rights based on occupation and possession. Privatization of communal lands thus connotes the displacement of a systems of usufruct land rights based on ancestral custom and its replacement by a system of land tenure codified by an externally-imposed system of law that privileges the individual ownership of private landholdings (Guerrero 1989, Turner 1993).

Yet, even proponents of this idealized system of land tenure admit that "usufructory rights in many communities have become permanent-use rights that are inheritable and may be exchanged within the community" (Brush & Guillet 1985:25). Other scholars working in the Andes have pointed out, as Gose (1994:15) does, that

> notions of communal property often amount to little more than private agricultural use-rights validated by *ayni* [an egalitarian mutual aid relation] within the community, and by the community paying a collective labour tribute to the state. This property is communal only in the way it is worked and legitimated, not at the level of rights to the product.

Within the Otavalo area, there are numerous examples of indigenous community members transferring their usufruct rights to particular areas within territories recognized as belonging to the community by bequeathing them to their heirs, lending their rights to these lands as collateral for loans, and even permanently foregoing them through sales (Guerrero 1989; see G. Smith 1989).

The examination of local-level discourses of property, property rights, and community found within the three land disputes discussed in this article, in particular, undermines the notion of an overarching, collective indigenous notion of communally-based land rights that can easily be contrasted with individually-based rights and claims (Hale 1994). The privatization by Otavaleños of lands recognized by the state as communal at the turn of the 20th century, I argue, was not evidence of their recent conversion into individualistic capitalists or the disintegration of their communities and "communal values." Indeed, these purportedly two distinct types of systems of rights can be seen as aspects of an overarching system of tenure which integrates both "individualistic" and "communalistic" ideas of access, use, and control. I, thus, contend that the partition and privatization of specific communal lands—namely, agricultural—by Otavaleños did not represent a fundamental change in their understanding of and meanings ascribed to land rights. In other words, it did not represent a shift in the basis of property rights from communal to individual (Nugent & Alonso 1994).

The disputes examined in this article certainly challenge the assumption of a unilinear continuum that runs from the premodern, cooperative community to the modern, individualist and factionalized state. As evidenced in the legal actions that comprise these conflicts, well before the purported penetration of capitalism in the area (see, e.g., Collier & Buitrón 1949, Meier 1984, Walter 1981), Otavaleños were articulating their rights to communal lands through discursive strategies that promoted principles of both individualism and communalism. The indigenous members of communities mentioned here, like all members of communities, were not solely individuals *or* community members, but were both simultaneously. It was in both of these capacities that Otavaleños sought to defend individual- and communal-based rights to lands recognized by the state as belonging to the community from threats originating both within and outside of the "community."

Contrary to prevalent interpretations, in this article I argue that privatization of communal land does not necessarily constitute the replacement of a traditional system of land tenure by a capitalist one that is imposed by an outside, "colonizing" force and adopted by modernizing Indians. Instead, the privatization of communal lands by *indígenas* can be approached as an act of strategic recourse to national legislation by individuals seeking to concretize property rights that are part of a common cultural framework of meaning which includes complex notions of use, control, and ownership of resources. Consequently, this article suggests that land conflicts *within* communities are not simply the result of competing discrete conceptualizations of property rights which purportedly correspond to degrees of capitalist penetration. Nor, I argue, can these processes be reduced to conflicts between "traditional" and "modern" Indians. Instead, these disputes serve as a reminder of the need to be attentive to the cultural conceptions and social constructions of community and property rights that provide meaning and incentive to the articulation of conflicting strategies within communities and broader, encompassing structures of power such as the state.

EARLY ECUADORIAN LAND LEGISLATION

While the recent "resurgence" of ethnicity in Ecuador has highlighted the indigenous negotiation between national and ethnic identities, Ecuadorian Indians have long been caught in the tension between rights to state-administered resources and cultural autonomy (Bebbington 1992, Clark 1998, Guerrero 1997; see Platt 1982). Indeed, the contradiction between integration into a culturally white national society (*mestizaje*) as equally protected citizens and the maintenance of ethnic difference that conferred special rights as well as obligations has characterized *indígenas'* relations with the Ecuadorian state since its inception.[3] It is this tension—between being both Ecuadorian and Indian—which has served as the backdrop for indigenous negotiation of individual and communal rights to land in general since the early 19th century.

Encouraged and influenced by the revolutions of France and the United States, early legislators of the republics of Gran Colombia and Ecuador embraced an ideologically liberal project designed to override racial and ethnic differences and transform "*los indios*" into citizens (R. Smith 1982). Elite nationalists endeavored specifically to redefine and incorporate Indians into the emerging nation-state as "equal" private-property owners and "free" laborers, in an effort to both modernize and "civilize" Ecuador.[4] As part of this project, early legislation focused on the transformation of lands held jointly by members of indigenous communities--"*resguardos*," or simply, "*tierras de la comunidad*"—into private landholdings that could be "rationally" exploited by their owners (Ibarra 1991, Moscoso 1991; see Yambert 1980). Within this group of early decrees, perhaps the most decisive statements on indigenous land tenure were laws passed in 1828, 1865, and 1867.

The Law of 1828, the Law of Empty Lands (1865), and the Law of 1867

Ostensibly, the Law of 1828 outlined the terms of the reinstitution and regulation of the "*contribución personal de indígenas de 18 a 50 años*," a head tax imposed on male *indígenas* aged 18 to 50 years old in specie or marketable goods. It also outlined the processes by which communal lands could be privatized (Rubio Orbe 1954). Passed in part as an attempt to protect communal lands from their "rapid and exploitative alienation" following Independence (Thurner 1996:306), the decree stipulated the allocation of plots of land to families already in possession of them for their own private use and cultivation, and established the right to rent communal lands considered as "surplus" ("*sobrante de tierras*"). Although this law may theoretically have facilitated the privatization of communal lands, it also denied the vast majority of newly-propertied indigenous owners a fundamental right associated with equal citizenship—namely, the right to sell their property—in its stipulation that only new owners who were literate in Spanish could alienate their lands (Thurner 1996).

The tension between the incorporation of Indians into the nation-state as equal citizens and the maintenance of their ethnic and administrative separation through a denial of the full rights and responsibilities that citizenship and private owner-ship conferred would characterize later republican land legislation, as well. Spe-cifically, in the 1860s, this tension can be seen in elite attempts to simultaneously promote the privatization of communal lands and lands in the "public domain," yet conserve their communal possession and ownership. Caught between the premises of a founding liberal ideology and the demands of highland hacienda owners seek-ing to consolidate large-scale landholdings and increase their livestock production (Clark 1998), legislators passed two laws, in particular, that exemplified the para-dox of protecting individual property rights while maintaining the integrity of communal lands jointly worked by community members.

In 1865, the *Ley de Terrenos Baldíos* (Law of Empty Lands) was passed. As sug-gested by its title, this piece of legislation focused on the adjudication and titling procedures of *terrenos baldíos*, or lands within the boundaries of the Republic not used or owned by individuals, corporations, or communities.[5] This law, however, also addressed ownership rights to lands constituting *"tierras de resguardo o reversión"*—lands comprising sites forming indigenous villages (*"pueblos y reducciones"*) destined for indigenous collective or private use (*"uso común o par-ticular de la raza indígena"*) (Rubio Orbe 1954). Specifically, it stipulated that *tierras de resguardo* or *reversión* being worked by *indígenas "en comunidad"* (collectively) would continue to be designated *"para su uso común"* (for their common use) (Rubio Orbe 1954). Communal lands that had previously been dis-tributed for individual, private use, however, were to stay in *"pleno dominio"*—a term meaning literally "in absolute control" but also signifying the legal recogni-tion of rights of absolute ownership—of those who were currently in possession of them (Art. 15). In 1867, a related law was passed admonishing "possessors" of *tierras baldías* to register at the cantonal level their ownership of lands possessed "without contradiction."

Like previous laws dealing with the "indigenous problem," the Laws of 1865 and 1867 attempted to straddle the divide between the rights of indigenous indi-viduals as individuals and their rights as community members, their rights as prop-ertied citizens and their rights as members of distinct groups with distinct rights—often to fail.[6] In neglecting to codify the different forms or local interpretations of communal rights to property, both laws provided the means by which these very lands could be recognized by the state as privately owned. Despite facilitating the transformation of indigenous *comuneros* into private-property owners, however, these laws did not fully ensure the integration of Indians into the nation-state as homogenous citizens. These laws, in vesting land rights in the name of indigenous communities, also provided the means by which *"comuneros"* (community mem-bers) benefited from identifying themselves as Indians and, thus, aided in the reproduction of the category of *"indio"* (see Schryer 1993). Thus, ironically, leg-islators in effect aided in the reproduction of both communal lands (or, at least, the reproduction of particular forms of communal property) and Indian communities in their continuation of the category of *"terrenos comunales"* and the identification of communities implicitly defined as indigenous as their owners.

Ecuadorian Nation-State Formation and Indigenous Engagement of "the Law"

The internalization of competing and often contradictory inclinations by Ecuador's early land legislation aptly demonstrates a conclusion already reached by many others: although elite enactments of liberal republican ideology are intentionally meant to be monolithic and totalizing, the project of nation-state formation is, in fact, neither. Instead, state-building embodies "competing agendas for using power, competing strategies for maintaining control, and doubts about the legitimacy of the venture" (Cooper & Stoler 1991:609). Within Ecuador, this problematic unity of the nation—the tension between cultural integration and ethnic difference, and between national affiliation and its collective expression and social, cultural, and historical distinction—is a tension that is mirrored in the competing dispositions not only of white-*mestizo* elites and Indians, but also of the individuals within these divisions. Thus, while independence from Spain may have put a legal end to the separation of *"indios"* and *"blancos-mestizos,"* throughout Ecuador's first hundred years, *indígenas* found themselves the focus of competing elite factions that sought to use them in a variety of not always compatible ways (see Sider 1993).

More specifically, in Ecuador in the 19th and early 20th centuries, the contradiction between the dualistic processes of incorporation and segregation of *indígenas* was mirrored in the political and socioeconomic dissension between the two principal political parties—the Liberals and the Conservatives. While these two groups were by no means internally uniform, they can be approached as representative of the conflicting interests of two factions: coastal agro-exporters specializing in cacao production, who were predominantly anticlerical (Liberals), and staunchly Catholic highland *hacendados* (Conservatives) (Arcos 1984, Crain 1990, Silva 1990, Marchán 1983). While both parties were motivated by a need to ensure a continual supply of labor, the Liberals, on one hand, can be identified as promoting the intensification of export-oriented production by means of legislation that advocated a contractual individualism favorable to capitalist development. The Conservatives, on the other hand, can be seen as focusing on production for internal, specifically regional consumption and, accordingly, supporting measures that advanced the expansion and consolidation of the hacienda as well as guaranteed the supply of a predominantly indigenous labor force for hacienda production (Almeida 1990, Fuentealba 1990, Quintero 1986).[7]

It is within such an arena, however, that Ecuadorian *indígenas* were able to negotiate and even manipulate the images and discourses through which republican indigenous policies were elaborated (see Seligmann 1994). As Mark Thurner

(1996: 298) has recently remarked, "It is not, as was once the fashion to claim, that these dictatorial decrees and the politico-military events that accompanied them meant nothing to the Andean majorities. The problem, rather, is that they could mean several things at once, some of them rather unanticipated by their architects." This multiplicity of meanings meant that the explicit intentions of the nation-state could be transformed and even distorted in the interpretation and application of state legislation, policies, and projects at the local level (Collier 1989, Starr & Collier 1989a). Indeed, the interplay between competing interests of Ecuador's political and economic elite arguably created spaces in which indigenous individuals could maneuver through complexly structured fields of power (Clark 1994, Roseberry 1993, Sider 1987, Stern 1987). The three land disputes examined in this article illustrate, in particular, how Otavaleños have adroitly adopted different facets of the various images of Indian advanced by the state— e.g., an object of manipulation or condescension in need of protection, a naïve "other" (Guerrero 1997, Ibarra 1991); a member of a collectivity with special rights to cultural and material autonomy; a propertied citizen with the equal rights of all citizens—for their own use in their defense of both individual and shared rights to communal lands with the court system.

LOCAL NEGOTIATIONS OF PROPERTY RIGHTS AND "COMMUNITY"

The three disputes examined in this article all involve legal contestations over the division and distribution of lands recognized as "belonging to the community." More specifically, all three cases center on attempts by Otavalan *indígenas* to gain state recognition of individual possession and, consequently, ownership of designated communal lands. In the first two conflicts discussed, groups of *indígenas* belonging to two different communities in the Otavalo Valley—"La Compañía-Camuendo" and "Imbaquí-Agato-Maldonado"—confront one another over the rights of community members to claim exclusive ownership of certain communal areas and distribute plots in these areas among themselves for individual use. In the third dispute, a group of *indígenas* from the village of Caluquí attempt to prove and, thus, defend their ownership of individually-possessed plots of communal lands against the encroachment of a group of local whites.

Together, these three cases demonstrate the partition of a large area of communal land in the Otavalo area, in general, and their privatization by Otavalan *indígenas*, in particular.[8] The communal lands under contention in the first and most complicated case are identified as the "leftovers" of a state-regulated parcelization of land belonging to La Compañía-Camuendo executed in 1900 at the request of a select group of the community's members. This partition stipulated the distribution of plots located in the "lower" section of the community's lands among a portion of the community's members, namely, those *comuneros* who claimed a long history of having "worked" (i.e., cultivated and built houses on) the land in this area. Other community members, namely, those excluded from this process, challenged what they perceived to be the unequal distribution of plots dictated by the area's division. Unsuccessful in the attempt to legally invalidate the partitioning, the group initiated the distribution and cultivation of plots located in an area of communal land immediately above the contested area, the "upper" region. Unlike the "lower" region, the "upper" section did not have a history of being cultivated. Instead, it had been traditionally exploited by all members of the community as pasture and woodlands. It is the legality and moral acceptability of the second partitioning of communal lands, that of lands located in the "upper" region, that is the focus of three lawsuits that comprise the first case.

In the second land dispute, a group of members of the indigenous community Imbaquí-Agato-Maldonado attempt to privatize a section of lands, located on the flanks of Mount Imbabura, that belongs to the community. The group initiates this legal action, based on the argument that the introduction of agricultural production in the area will increase the productivity of the land and, therefore, benefit the well-being of the community as a whole. Although the group's legal attempt to create and distribute plots in the area meets with initial success, in a subsequent petition, its request for the parcelization of the area is rejected on the grounds that rights of the group do not include the right to dispose of or alienate communal properties.

In the last dispute discussed in this article, a group of *indígenas* from the community of Caluquí oppose the invasion of a section of communal lands they are already cultivating by a group of whites. Both parties agree that these lands, recognized as belonging to two communities, Caluquí and Gualacata, were divided and distributed some 40 years previously among members of the two communities. They do not agree, however, upon the legitimacy of the original partition or the claim that the whites are members of Gualacata and, based on this identity and their performance of acts of co-possession, have rights to its communal lands.

Of these three disputes, the first two, in particular, do not simply expose the division and distribution of communal lands by Otavaleños. Indeed, the first two land disputes serve to illustrate two processes that are central to the emergence and articulation of intra-communal conflicts over the privatization of communal property: (1) the application of two separate but shared categories of communal land by the *indígenas* involved, and (2) the deployment of specific legal rhetorical strategies that implicate distinct definitions of community and individual and communal property rights promoted by the state. Upon closer inspection, the first two cases discussed in this article reveal that not all communal land was considered available for privatization by the *indígenas* who comprised the communities involved in these disputes. The parcelization of communally-exploited grasslands and woodlands, in particular, was passionately opposed within these indigenous communities. Alternatively, the privatization of communal lands that had a long history of individual cultivation was not opposed. In short, the two cases convey widespread indigenous acceptance of the concretization of what, in effect, are individually-based rights to communal lands through legal privatization, but the rejection of the transformation of communally-exploited grasslands and woodlands into individually-possessed cultivated plots.

Although the third case explored in this article confirms this conclusion, it speaks more specifically to a second process that structures these disputes—namely, the deployment of rhetorical strategies that play off an ambivalence in Ecuadorian land legislation concerning the rights of propertied citizens (i.e., individuals) and the rights of members of collectivities sharing in joint possession and ownership (i.e., community members). This ambivalence is internalized in a set of laws that simultaneously base rights of co-ownership on exclusive possession for a period of time ranging anywhere from one year to "since time immemorial" and recognize proof of ownership as the legal basis for their privatization. The opposition between rights based on community membership and/or the working of lands (*posesión*, or possession), and rights based on private ownership and having title (*dominio*, or dominion) implicit in this equation, in turn, provided a framework within which opposing parties formulated their arguments in an effort to capitalize on recognized forms of land ownership.[9] The third case, in particular, illustrates how not only indigenous but white-*mestizo* groups negotiated claims to communal lands through recourse to the ambiguous or seemingly contradictory legal categories that encapsulated these paradoxes.

More specifically, the inconclusiveness of exactly who a community's members were and what constituted "*uso de común*" (collective use) and "possession" frequently supplied both plaintiffs and defendants with the bases of their arguments. Not surprisingly, then, the legal strategies of claimants and their opponents in all three cases incorporate similar arguments with regard to community membership, the rights of *comuneros*, and the performance of acts of co-possession. In addition, the recognition of "possession" and the persuasiveness of proof of "*prescripción extraordinaria*"—tranquil and uninterrupted possession for more than 30 years—in authenticating ownership for many judges informed the frequent use of particular, formulaic phrases by a variety of parties attempting to legally secure their rights to land. One of these phrases is "*desde tiempo inmemorial*" (since time immemorial), a phrase most commonly used by *indígenas* attempting to assert long-standing possession.[10] Yet, in all three of these disputes, individuals, including the white defendants of the third dispute, seek to prove and defend their right to communal lands, based on their rights as *comuneros* and rights of co-ownership instantiated by their exclusive co-possession "since time immemorial." The adoption of such an approach merely affirms the viability of a variety of discursive strategies for a diverse body of individuals, even those for whom such protectionist legislation was not originally designed.

CASE ONE: THE EROSION OF LA COMPAÑÍA-CAMUENDO'S COMMUNAL LANDS

The specifics of the La Compañía-Camuendo land dispute are found in documents associated with three interrelated lawsuits that appeared before the First Court of the Canton of Otavalo in 1910, 1914, and 1915, respectively.[11] All three suits involve the same parties and revolve around the same expanse of communal land. This region is actually part of a larger area that was the focus of several legal cases that took place before the onset of these three particular suits. In these earlier lawsuits, the "community of Camuendo" successfully defended its right to sections of this larger region against two individuals: the first, an indigenous community member, who based his claim on his and his grandfather's possession of certain lands since 1878; the second, the owner of the hacienda La Compañía, who accused members of the community of the violent appropriation of one particular area within this region.

It was after the "community" won this latter case (and, with it, the recognition of their legal rights to an area of communal land measuring some 1,043,818 square meters, or 1,238,354 square varas) that a number of community members petitioned the state for the partition of the "lower" part of this large area. More specifically, a number of *comuneros* requested and received state assistance in the division of a portion of communal lands into 136 plots and their distribution among these individual *comuneros* with their titles. The "upper" portion of this area—a section composed of *páramo* (high pasture lands traditionally used for pasture and the collection of straw and firewood)—was left undivided, to be used by all community members.

The first lawsuit, in particular, arose as a legal response to the reactions of one particular group of *comuneros* to the partitioning of this "lower" section of La Compañía-Camuendo communal lands. Initially, after the division of this area but prior to the actual onset of the first trial in 1910, a number of community members, led by Juan Potosí, petitioned the Governor of Ibarra (the provincial capital) for annulment of the partition, based on their contention that they had been denied plots within this area. Their request was denied. Refusing to give up, in 1900 Potosí and his companions filed a lawsuit against the group of community members who had been adjudicated plots, demanding the nullification of the partition. Surprisingly, perhaps, they did not argue their case on the illegality of alienating recognized communal lands. Instead, citing the shared rights of community members to communal property (Art. 2287 of the Civil Code) and their joint possession of this area since "time immemorial," they requested the annulment of the partition based on their claim that not all "co-owners or possessors" of the area had agreed to its division.

Their opponents, represented by Abelino Cañamar, in a seeming contradiction of prior declarations made by members of this group in the case against the owner of the hacienda La Compañía, contested the very grounds on which Potosí and other "co-owners" had based their argument. They asserted that the lands "had never belonged to the community" (ff. 70v-71). The divided area, they claimed, belonged exclusively to themselves, the area's "co-owners." Were there not houses on the land, they asked, and had they not been the only ones to have ever cultivated and used these lands? Lands belonging to the community, they contended, lands to which all community members had a right, remained available for all to use as pasture. Their ownership ("*dominio*") of the section below these communal lands, maintained the defendants, was established "by *prescripción* for more than fifty years of lawsuits" and "by inheritance" (ff. 70v-71).[12] Their ownership never in doubt, they requested only the partition of this area in order to formally "recognize the property of each one" of the defendants (ff. 73-74).

Some six years after the initiation of this suit, in 1906, the judge ruled that there were no grounds for the annulment of the division and distribution of lands, based on his finding that Potosí and the other plaintiffs had failed to prove that they had ever been in possession of the particular section of land. In 1909, a year prior to the first trial and their opponents' accusation that they had committed *despojo* (unlawful appropriation), Potosí and 60 other *comuneros* again petitioned the provincial governor for his help. They took a different tact than before, however, asking for the "equal distribution" among members of the group of a small area of communal land within the "upper" region that "since time immemorial (*tiempo inmemorial*) [has] belonged to everyone" (ff. 20-20v). This time, they were successful.[13] As a result, despite the vigorous opposition of a number of their fellow community members, in February 1910 members of the group led by Potosí were adjudicated plots totaling some 435,000 square varas within an area comprised of "lands that actually are communal."

The Alleged Appropriation of Communal Lands in the Upper Region

Shortly after the distribution of plots within the upper section of La Compañía-Camuendo's communal lands to Potosí and his companions, the group was accused of their *despojo* (unlawful appropriation) by individual owners of plots in the lower section. Surprisingly, early in the proceedings of this trial, the defendants admit to having appropriated the lands in question with the intention of dividing and distributing them among themselves. Potosí and his colleagues contend, however, that their actions did not constitute an act of *despojo*, based on their claim that the partition of a section of lands within the upper region was performed by an agreed-upon outside expert, was approved of by all, and left untouched all of the *páramo* and some of the wooded area. More importantly, they argue for their right to divide and distribute this area of land on the grounds that they, like their accusers, have a right to plots comprised on land identified as belonging to the community. They claim this right as descendants of earlier *comuneros* at one time in possession of these lands and as community members.

The plaintiffs, represented by Abelino Cañamar and Joaquín Castañeda, attempt to undermine any claim of the defendants to these lands—lands that they, too, recognize and identify as communal—through a two-pronged approach. First, they attempt to prove that the defendants, unlike themselves, are not actually members of the community to which the lands belong and, thus, do not have rights to them. Community membership, according to the testimony of the plaintiffs' and defendants' witnesses, is revealed to be based on both kinship—i.e., being related to other, recognized or identified, community members—and village residence. Cañamar and Castañeda thus deny under questioning that certain defendants are family members of specific individuals they recognize as community members, including themselves. In addition, they, as well as other witnesses called by their lawyer, refuse to acknowledge that the defendants even live in the same village as themselves. They defendants, they claim, are from La Compañía, a distinct and separate community from that of Camuendo, their own community, with distinct and separate communal lands from those of Camuendo. Second, the plaintiffs deny any possession on the part of the defendants prior to their purported act of *despojo*.[14] Thus, they claim that

> we, the *indígenas* who form and compose the real community of 'Camuendo Compañía', have maintained [possession] not just one immediately prior continuous year, but more than thirty years, exercising acts of possession for which only dominion gives the right; such as the cutting of straw and firewood in the mountainous and wooded section of the said lands, for the domestic needs of the Community; sowing and harvesting on these said lands, and pasturing our animals (6-Aug-1910; ff. 4-5).

Potosí and his group's defense relies upon proving that they, as "part of that community and [...] descendants of the same ancestors to whom was adjudicated the portion of land referred to by the plaintiffs," also exercised the "same acts of possession that the actors say that they have executed" (f. 10). To this effect, all their witnesses, all of whom are monolingual-Quichua speakers from the community, identify them as community members who used the land in question for collecting firewood, gathering straw, and pasturing their animals. These same witnesses, however, recognize Potosí and the other co-defendants as having begun to "work" these lands only since Carnival.

In February 1913, the 1910 trial reached it final stages. Reviewing the points of the defendants, the judge concluded that, while there was plenty of evidence that the defendants did indeed belong to the same community as the plaintiffs, the defendants had not proved that all community members were in agreement about the distribution of plots located in the upper area. This upper area, in turn, the judge recounts in his decision, was designated for the "common enjoyment of all *indígenas* of the community" (ff. 116-117v). Accordingly, both plaintiffs and defendants had rights of joint ownership or dominion. In a seeming twist of logic, however, the judge declared the claim of the plaintiffs to be without merit, based on two conclusions: (1) that the plaintiffs had failed to prove that the defendants were in "co-possession" of the lands purportedly dispossessed from the plaintiffs, and (2) that they had failed to prove that the defendants had performed the alleged acts of possession together; instead, based on a visual inspection, they had been found to be individually working their own plots within the area in question. Thus, the judge appeared to uphold a premise that formed the basis of the plaintiffs' distribution of individual plots in the lower section, namely, that individual cultivation of specific areas transforms land once designated as communally-owned into privately-owned plots.

Not surprisingly, the plaintiffs appealed the decision, but in 1914 a judge on the Superior Court of Quito provided his own confirmation of the lower court's decision: "the actors have not possessed communal lands that are the subject of this lawsuit in exclusion of the defendants, but that, on the contrary, they have demonstrated with a larger number of witnesses that they have exercised different acts of ownership on these same lands" (f. 123). Not satisfied with this finding, the plaintiffs again appealed the finding, this time to the Supreme Court, only to drop it shortly thereafter.

The Petition to Partition the Upper Section

Additional legal action was taken in 1914 in Otavalo Canton's First Court. This time, a large group of "*indígenas* of the community of 'Camuendo'" demanded the division of cultivable lands in the "upper section" and their distribution to "all the community" (f. 1-1v). This group, led by eight men identified as the "principal leaders" of Camuendo, is listed in the documents as comprising some 237 married and single indigenous men and women. Representing these persons, all of whom are to receive equal plots of land measuring 33 varas by 50 varas, is Manuel Chávez, the very same man who served as the lawyer for the plaintiffs in the 1910 lawsuit. In fact, in a later lawsuit, it is claimed that this group of community members includes some of the plaintiffs from the previous trial. The listed leaders, as recompense for their efforts, are to receive plots of land from an area measuring 343 varas by 50 varas (approximately 17 square varas) in addition to the plot each will receive as a community member. No opposition to this petition is cited, and arrangements are made for the lands to be divided and titles to be granted.

The Demand for the Return of the "Usurped" Communal Lands of the Upper Region

Shortly after the legal partition of this "upper" portion of the communal lands, Abelino Cañamar and a number of his fellow *comuneros* renewed their attempt to legally force Juan Potosí and others to relinquish this area. Specifically, in 1915 they filed a complaint with the cantonal court of Otavalo accusing Potosí and others of having "usurped in an illegitimate, arbitrary and unjust mode" this area (ff. 134-137) and demanding its return. This third litigation, as opposed to the previous two legal actions, centers on the question of whether or not the plaintiffs' purported possession of the land satisfies the criteria established for an "*acción reivindicatoria*," or a lawsuit demanding the return of property to its rightful owner(s) by the individual(s) in possession of it. In particular, the plaintiffs must prove that their possession of the land is "regular" and that the lawsuit has not been brought against its actual owner or someone who has equal or greater rights to the property. The land in question must also be recognized as "*una cosa singular*," or something which is determinable, concrete, and circumscribed under boundaries which are defined absolutely.

In filing this type of suit, the plaintiffs explicitly adopt a new strategy. Here, they allege that the land "usurped" by Potosí and his co-defendants actually composes part of a larger, singular expanse of communal land that includes both upper and lower regions and of which they are the exclusive owners. This area is glossed by their lawyer as "lands of cultivation, pasture, and a mountainous portion known by the name of *páramo*," and they cite to their possession of a 1701 title that covers this expanse of land as proof of their ownership. As before, Cañamar and the other plaintiffs base their right to this region on "*prescripción extraordinaria*," asserting that, as community members, they performed acts of possession on these communal lands. "[S]ince time immemorial, a lot more than thirty years," their lawyer claims, "my clients have occupied, used, and had at their disposal the referred to land without having had anyone interrupt their possession and as absolute owners" (ff. 134-137).

The joint possession of the "usurped" lands by community members prior to their division and distribution is not a point of contention for the defendants. Witnesses appearing on behalf of the defendants, all of whom were adjudicated plots in this area, concur in their testimony that the area had been used jointly by all members of the community for pasturing animals and collecting firewood, wood, and straw since, several state, "the time when my parents lived" or "I was a child" (ff. 114-117).[15] Testimony reveals, however, that since the partition of a portion of this area and the cultivation of specific plots within it, some members have been "specified a portion of the lands" in this area, resulting in the exclusion of others (ff. 122v-124).

The defendants contest the purported distinction between the two communities of Camuendo and La Compañía made by the plaintiffs, as well as the claim that the area in question belongs to one community and not the other. Both these claims, as well as others made by the plaintiffs in this lawsuit, the defendants point out, were ruled upon in the earlier trial accusing them of *despojo*. In that lawsuit, they remind the court, it was found that the plaintiffs have never been the exclusive owners of the lands they are cultivating but, instead, have only shared in rights of co-ownership along with other community members. They also note that the plaintiffs have never been able to produce the said title and that the land the plaintiffs seek to recover is neither a property unto itself, instead being part of a larger area, nor is it the area demarcated in their claim.

After an interval of several years, this lawsuit finally came to a close in 1921. In his ruling, the cantonal judge found that the area under dispute did constitute "*una cosa singular*," thus establishing the grounds on which the plaintiffs argued the recognition of their rights of ownership. In his ruling, the judge points out that the defendants themselves as well as the witnesses recognize the co-ownership of the plaintiffs of this land "since time immemorial," or more than 30 years. In addition, the visual inspection performed late in the trial, he concludes, demonstrated that the plaintiffs were in possession of the land in question. He also finds that the defendants have not furnished evidence proving their own right to the co-owner-ship of the *páramo* land or their co-ownership or co-possession of the other sections of the entire expanse of land under dispute. Based on these considerations, the judge rules in favor of the plaintiffs, declaring that they are the owners of the disputed land and ordering the defendants to return immediately to the plaintiffs the part of the *páramo* in their possession (ff. 237-239v).

Handwritten notes that dot the pages of this trial reveal additional consider-ations underlying the judge's decision. For the judge, the fact that the plaintiffs were the recognized exclusive owners of the lower section appeared to lend cre-dence to their argument rather than highlighting the parity of the defendants' actions. The judge interprets the earlier acknowledgment of Potosí and others that they had been excluded in the first distribution of lands and the judicial decision to uphold the partition in 1910 as proof of their lack of possession prior to the act of *despojo*.[16]

The cantonal court's ruling in this case was quickly overturned by the Superior Court. The Superior Court judge based his ruling principally on two conclusions: (1) that the plaintiffs had not clearly and definitively defined which lands they were demanding be returned to them and which lands the defendants were in pos-session of, and (2) that, if the boundaries of the disputed area were as the plaintiffs contended, they would monopolize not only this particular region but, in effect, the "whole zone which forms the community of 'Camuendo'"(f. 240v).

CASE TWO: THE DIVISION OF IMBAQUÍ-AGATO-MALDONADO'S COMMUNAL LANDHOLDINGS

The second dispute to be examined, like the first, involves multiple related litiga-tions that center on the division and distribution of expanses of land claimed to be or recognized as communally-owned: (1) "Second petition. The partition of the land Mortiños-Tola,"[17] and (2) "Partition of the lands Imbaquí, Agato, and Mal-donado."[18] In the first lawsuit, a group of 26 *indígenas* of the community "Mortiños Tola Imbaquí Agato" request in 1920 the division and distribution of land that "since time immemorial more than thirty years they have possessed, used, and enjoyed" (f. 2). In addition to "*prescripción extraordinaria*," the group bases its right to divide the land on its possession of an 1809 document that purportedly proves the community's ownership of the land in question.[19]

The group's request is opposed by a number of their fellow *comuneros*, who argue that the land in question belongs to the community as a whole and not just to the few members who have requested its division. In arguing against such a partition, these individuals point out that the land in question was the focus of a trial that took place 20 years earlier. In that trial, members of the group that now seeks the partition requested the annulment of the division and distribution of this same extension of land and won on the grounds that the land did not belong to people "as individuals of the community Imbaquí-Agato, but as members of this community" (f. 13v). Opposition to the 1920 division is blocked, however, based on a legal technicality: its opponents, as a "third party" attempting to intervene, are excluded from the proceedings. Thus, their claims have no standing.

In the second, related trial, in 1924, 50 members of the community, led by Cornelio Maldonado, petition the first cantonal judge for the division of "a plot of cultivable land which forms part of the lands belonging to the community." This partition is designed to extend the area of land under production into the *páramo* grasslands lying to the east of the community. The division of this high-lying area—identified by the group as unexploited and wasted due to the "unqualified apathy of [our community's] members"—and the cultivation of the newly-formed plots, the group claims, will increase the land's productivity and, in the end, benefit the social well-being of the community as a whole (ff. 1-1v).

Other members of the community, however, disapprove of the distribution of plots in this area. Specifically, Juan Males and 32 other community members reject the validity of the claimants' request. Their basis for doing so is not new: they assert that a number of the plaintiffs, Cornelio Maldonado in particular, are not community members of Imbaquí-Agato-Maldonado, as they claim, but of the village of Santellán. Maldonado's party thus has no right to request legal action that involves recognized communal lands. They, on the other hand, and their ancestors have always been members of the community of Imbaquí-Agato-Maldonado and, as such, have performed "acts of possession," specifically the pasturing of animals and the collection of firewood and straw, on these lands.

Maldonado, on behalf of his companions, responds to this opposition on two fronts. He seeks to provide a legal foundation for his right to engage in legal proceedings that involve the entire community, based on his irrefutable standing as a community member. He argues, in fact, that his own identity as a community member is actually more certain than Males', due to his own standing as a descendant of a lineage with a longer history of community membership and authority: he is, he alleges, the grandson of Tomás Mirapuento Maldonado, "the Cacique of the lands of Agato or the village of Imbaquí-Agato-Maldonado" (f. 19v). It is in this capacity that Maldonado introduces into evidence an 1814 copy of two documents, both dated 1750, in defense of his and his fellow *comuneros'* right to divide the lands covered within these colonial texts.[20]

Maldonado also defends the rights of his group to divide communal lands by accusing his antagonists of ignoring the existence of the Laws of 1865 and 1867. These laws, he reminds the court, explicitly state that title to lands on which indigenous villages are located (*tierras de reversión*), and which are destined for indigenous collective or private use, are to be adjudicated to their possessors. As the possessors, he and his colleagues thus have rights of co-ownership to the section of the community's land under contention. As co-owners of this land, Maldonado and his colleagues, in turn, demand the recognition of their right to divide it, based on provisions within the Civil Code and the Political Constitution.

The judge's ruling on the petitioners' request challenges their attempt to privatize Imbaquí-Agato-Maldonado's communal lands as well as the interpretation of the rights of community members to communal lands, upon which it is based. Specifically, the judge finds that lands belonging to a community "do not belong to any one of its individuals, nor do they belong to all the individuals within a community which exist at a certain time" (f. 116). Accordingly, the rights of individual community members "[do] not consist of the right to dispose of or alienate communal properties" (f. 116-116v). The petitioners, as *comuneros* who hold no unique individual or private right to these lands, are thus denied the division of communal lands that they solicit.

CASE THREE: INTER-ETHNIC CONFLICT OVER COMMUNAL LANDS OF CALUQUÍ AND GUALACATA

In the last land dispute to be examined, "Ignacio Rivera and others against Daniel Méndez and other, for possession" (1924),[21] a group of *indígenas* from the parish of González Suárez attempt to maintain their possession of an expanse of recognized communal lands when it is "interrupted" by a group of "*blancos*" (whites) from the same parish. In particular, the whites are accused of initiating plowing within a particular area, known locally as Urumbilla, in February 1924, two months before the suit was filed. At the heart of the dispute are two competing versions of the partition of this expanse of land some 30-40 years previously. This land is recognized by both parties, as well as local authorities, as belonging to two communities, Caluquí and Gualacata, located in the González Suárez parish.

In one version, that of the whites, the defendants identify the partition as resulting in the demarcation of two separate plotted regions—Urumbilla and another expanse of land located within Urumbilla, known as Habas cucho. Plots situated in Urumbilla, the defendants argue, were adjudicated exclusively to Indians from the community of Caluquí. Plots located in Habas cucho, however, were adjudicated exclusively to themselves as members of the community of Gualacata. Although the defendants admit that one of the indigenous plaintiffs bought and owns several plots located in Habas cucho, the remainder of this section, they contend, has been left undivided and has remained in the exclusion possession of whites from Gualacata since the partition, or for 32 years (ff. 27-29). Indians from Caluquí or Gualacata, they insist, have never even exercised "acts of ownership" in this area.

In the other version, that of the indigenous plaintiffs, although a partition of Urumbilla is acknowledged as having taken place some 40 years previously, it is argued that the individuals who performed the act of division and distribution had no authority to do so.[22] The plaintiffs also reject the premise that the partition delineated two separate areas that were adjudicated to two different groups of individuals, whites from Gualacata and Indians from Caluquí. Testimony of several plaintiffs reveals their understanding that control of Habas cucho was handed over by the Reverend Superior of the Augustines to their "grandfathers" and leaders of the community Caluquí. As proof of their ownership of the area as a whole, they seek confirmation of the existence of visible signs of their sole possession (e.g., houses that they have built, cultivated fields) "for more than forty years or for a time immemorial"(ff. 3-3v) and their transformation of the area into cultivated space at the time of the partition. The defendants, they contend, unlike themselves, do not live in the area or have animals pastured there, nor are they even familiar with the lands in question. More significantly, the indigenous plaintiffs assert that the whites are members of neither Caluquí nor Gualacata and, thus, have no rights to lands belonging to either community.

The two parties' competing versions and claims take center stage during a visual inspection of the area. While outside consultants are unable to discern which group planted the plots located in the region and, thus, are their definitive owners, whites or *indígenas*, they do discover the existence of sharecropping arrangements between members of these two parties. Specifically, they observe planted fields belonging to white defendants "*en partido con*" indigenous plaintiffs (ff. 58-59).[23] In turn, they find that the inspected plots of land have been planted by *indígenas* in their capacities as both "*dueños propios*" (the rightful owners), in accordance with what they themselves have claimed, and "*partidarios de los blancos*" (sharecroppers of the whites), in accordance with what the defendants have alleged.

In 1926, the Otavalan Second Court's judge came to a conclusion. He threw the case out. He based his finding on several considerations: that the defendants' lawyer proved that the plaintiffs' claim of ownership based on *prescripción extraordinaria* was false; that the inspection demonstrated that the performance of acts of possession by the plaintiffs, upon which such a claim was founded, was uncertain; and that the legitimacy and disinterested nature of the witnesses providing information was challenged.

DEPLOYING INDIVIDUALISM, PROMOTING COMMUNALISM: AN INTERPRETATION OF THE THREE LAND DISPUTES

Given the early goals of the Ecuadorian nation-state and elite political factions within it, there is little doubt that the integrity of Indian-held communal lands especially vulnerable during the early republican period. Based on the three examined disputes, it appears that, in the Otavalo area, extensive sections of communal lands were the focus of parcelization and privatization attempts in the last quarter of the 19th century, in particular. Indeed, all three land conflicts can be traced back to privatization projects originating between 1878 and the early 1900s, often at the behest of indigenous community members themselves.

The three discussed disputes also reveal another pattern, however. Only a particular category of communal land is targeted for privatization by indigenous community members, namely, land that they have been "administering, planting on, cultivating, and exclusively utilizing its products as the sole owners" (EP/J, 2a [1924; 1747], Caja 105, ff. 3-3v). In fact, in none of these cases do Otavaleños contest the principle of privatization itself. Nor do *indígenas* in these cases appear to challenge the recognition of the right to specific "production zones" (Mayer 1985) of individual *comuneros* who have a history of working a particular area. What the different indigenous parties to these lawsuits do contest is limited and specific to several aspects of communal land tenure: the unequal distribution of individual plots of communal lands, the negation of *de facto* ownership rights to communal land that has been cultivated for many years and on which houses are built, and the parcelization of lands designated by the community to be exploited for their provision of straw, pasture, and firewood.

These two patterns, I argue, converge in a way to suggest an explanation for the deployment of particular rhetorical strategies that appeal to specific ideals— the "individualistic" argument for the privatization of state-recognized communal lands and the "communalistic" demand for their maintenance as communally-possessed and -owned—by the different parties involved in these disputes. For Otavaleños, I suggest that privatization was perceived as an acceptable and recognized means of successfully defending and concretizing long-standing rights of access and control to a specific category of communal land—namely, agricultural—against three figures: the state (as represented by local, cantonal, and parish officials), encroaching *hacendados*, and fellow community members. These three conflicts, of course, also demonstrate that joint rights of ownership and possession to lands designated as belonging to indigenous communities were also vigorously defended against these figures. Such rights, however, are consistently identified in these conflicts as pertaining to pastoral, as opposed to agricultural, communal lands. With this in mind, three factors can be suggested as informing the choices made by indigenous *comuneros* in their defense of individual or communal rights to communal lands: the particular category of communal land in question, the source of threat to its conservation, and the legal criteria established by the state and applied at the local level.

Otavaleño Constructions of Communal Property and Judicial Interpretation

The dispute over the communal lands of La Compañía-Camuendo, the first conflict examined in this article, speaks most directly to the construction of two categories of communal lands, each with its own type of use rights. Throughout the materials presented in this dispute, usufruct rights to pastoral communal lands (i.e., lands designated for pasturing and collecting firewood) are identified as contingent upon community membership, to be enjoyed equally by all community members. Although rights to these lands may be based on descent and community residence, it does not appear that the right to access or exploit a specific area within pasture and woodlands is inherited or otherwise transferred. With the introduction of agricultural production into pastoral areas, however, rights appear to be converted into individually-based rights, held by the family transforming the land into cultivated space. Rights to cultivated communal lands in this and the other two conflicts are commonly glossed as rights to particular plots that are held by individual community members which can be inherited and bequeathed, loaned out, or even sold. Complete rights to the fruits of their labor appear to be held by individual families. While the community presumably has some control over the administration and transmission of these plots, these disputes bear out the suggestion made with regard to other areas within the Andes that "the more intensively land can be worked (i.e., the longer it can be cultivated in a more permanent way), the more independence farmers want to have over production decisions" (Mayer 1985:61).

Ostensibly, the rights to both categories of communal property—individually-held agricultural lands and communally-exploited pastoral lands—are lodged in community membership and residence, with rights to neither category emanating from legal title. Consequently, I do not want to suggest that cultivated communal lands constitute some sort of "capitalist property" owned by individualist entrepreneurs (see Nugent & Alonso 1994). But neither are they strictly "communally- or community-based" in the common sense of the term. Instead, the two folk classifications of communal property outlined here can be seen as dual facets of an overarching system of property rights, based on community membership and the completion of acts of possession, which is authorized by "tradition" and the "community" but which does not exclude the recognition of individually-based rights.

Such a typology would help explain a focal point of contention in the first dispute: the exclusion of a number of *comuneros*, all of whom lived in an area previously recognized by the community solely as grasslands and woodlands (i.e., the upper section), from an earlier partition of the "lower" extension of land. Despite the fact that the entire area had been recognized earlier by the state as lands belonging to the community, only a select number of community members actually lived on and cultivated the lands comprising this lower section. Arguably, these individuals did not conceive their rights to these lands as based solely on communal membership but, rather, on their and their ancestors' exclusive use of them. Parcelization and/or privatization can thus be seen as an attempt on the part of these individuals to legally concretize long-standing use rights to these plots and gain complete individual control. Rights to the "upper section," however, were consistently identified by both parties as based on communal usage by all community members. In opposing the initiation of agricultural production within the upper region, members who had previously argued for their rights to apportion out communal lands can thus be interpreted as defending the rights of the community against members who attempt to bypass communal restrictions imposed on the use of jointly-possessed *páramo* lands.

The conversion of communally-based rights to land into individually-based rights through long-term possession helps explain, in part, the oppositional nature of the versions presented by the two parties in the third dispute discussed above. Based on both versions, it can be supposed that a group of whites were adjudicated plots within an area recognized as belonging to the communities of Gualacata and Caluquí some 30-40 years earlier (i.e., in the 1880s or 1890s).[24] Reticent to provide their own labor, the group engaged local *indígenas* to work these lands in exchange for access to them. In turn, the plaintiffs began to think of this land as their own, based on several different factors: their conversion of this area into a cultivated, lived-in space, particularly if, as they claim, they have been the exclusive users of the products harvested from these fields; their perception of the illegitimacy of the original act of partition; and the use of parts of this land by their ancestors and themselves as resources for pasture, firewood, and wood. In effect, the *indígenas* can be seen to argue for their transformation from *partidarios* to owners, a contention rejected by the court, which, in the end, deferred to the authority of the previous, state-administered partition.

The co-existence of differently-constructed usufruct rights that vary according to the specific productive resources whose exploitation they regulate (i.e., "production zones") has been noted before, perhaps most prominently by Enrique Mayer (1985). It is in making this observation that Mayer (1985: 58) cautions us to "ask who has the right to use what portions of land for specific productive purposes, rather than who has rights over land as property." Although we, as scholars, should certainly heed this advice, early Ecuadorian legislators did not make any such distinction. More specifically, the exact nature of rights of individuals to different types of communal lands, variously based on possession, succession or inheritance, and agreements of contracted reciprocity, were not explicitly addressed in early land legislation (Guerrero 1989). Instead, elite legislators grouped distinct production zones under the common umbrella of "*tierras de resguardo* or *reversión.*" This gloss, coupled with the identification of "*posesión extraordinaria*" as a privileged means of proving ownership, in turn provided indigenous community members with the means of privatizing not only agricultural but pastoral communal lands, as well.

The Modernization of Highland Agrarian Structure and the Threat to Communal Lands

Regardless of early attempts to safeguard against the sale of communal lands (e.g., the decree of 1843), vast expanses of communal lands, specifically those of the highest quality, slowly underwent privatization in the early republican period, as both indigenous and non-indigenous persons claimed tracts for their individual use (Almeida 1990, Fuentealba 1990, Ibarra 1991, Moscoso 1991, Ramón 1991a-b). Within the Otavalo area, I argue, this process of erosion was facilitated at the turn of the 20th century, in particular by the promulgation of national policies designed to promote economic development and modernization and a concomitant move toward the expansion of production on the part of elite highland landowners (see Grieshaber 1989, Yambert 1980).

Ecuador's national economy at the turn of the 20th century has been characterized as shaped by the same struggle for power between highland hacienda owners (Conservatives) and lowland agro-exporters (Liberals) that defined much of the previous century. Beginning with the second cacao boom in the late 19th century and climaxing with the "Liberal Revolution" of 1895, a shift in power occurred, from Conservative to Liberal predominance (Arcos 1984, Yambert 1980). This transition was marked by the passage of legislation that attempted to ensure three related goals, all aimed at disrupting "pre-capitalist" relations and all designed to support Ecuador's growing participation in the cacao, sugar, and rice markets of the world: (1) the establishment of "free" land and labor markets, (2) the undermining of the Church's monopolization of vast landholdings, and (3) the liberation of Indians from particularly exploitative forms of labor and tenancy arrangements (Clark 1998, Costales & Peñaherrera 1964, Marchán 1983, Thurner 1989).[25]

In promoting such aims, however, these measures also equipped local state authorities with the means to violate the rights of communities and individuals to their landholdings. In particular, while the termination of the "*contribución territorial y del trabajo subsidiario*" in 1895 may have abolished a tax applied to the landless and small-scale property holders, the explicit intentions of this act were mitigated by aspects of the law itself and its local application. Specifically, the second article allowed municipalities to recruit local labor for the construction of municipal public works such as schools, plazas, and public buildings (Clark 1998). In addition, in the Otavalo area, there is evidence of numerous lawsuits that appeared before local tribunals in which indigenous property owners contested the municipal requisition of lands on which these works were to be built. Such acts of dispossession were not new to Otavaleños. Beginning in 1833, legislation was passed promoting the establishment of schools for *indígenas* designed to teach them the fundamentals of Catholic religion and the Ecuadorian constitution, as well as literacy skills. These schools were to be funded from revenues garnered by the renting of communal lands that were identified as "surplus" by cantonal authorities (Rubio Orbe 1954).

Threat to communal landholdings came from an additional source. In response to Liberal measures, a number of prominent highland hacienda owners, most of whom came from the northern Ecuadorian provinces of Carchi, Imbabura, Pichincha and Cotopaxi, began to strongly advocate the restructuration of agrarian production in the Sierra (Cevallos 1993, Clark 1998).[26] Modernization took on added importance in the face of increasing competition for a primarily indigenous labor force between themselves and coastal agro-exporters and the emergence of new internal markets with the expansion of commercial exchange between coastal and highland regions and with increased urbanization. Elite highland landowners thus sought to expand agricultural and livestock production, often at the expense of neighboring indigenous communities, as well as streamline production through such means as the sale of land lots—typically, the uppermost, more eroded lands—to indigenous peasants (Cevallos 1993, Clark 1998, Ramón 1991a).

The elite initiative to transform highland agrarian structure at the turn of the century was extended by a more general, state-sponsored movement toward modernization witnessed in the 1920s. In particular, after a cacao crisis, there emerged a prominent call for legislation that would effectively modernize the state's infrastructure and national economy. In response, Ecuador witnessed the passage of legislation in the 1920s designed specifically to realize the "decomposition" of the most "backward" sectors of highland agriculture, the promotion of "capitalist forms of production" in the rural sector, and the support of industrialization (Cevallos 1993:232). Prominent among the group of laws passed at this time are the *Ley de Patrimonio Territorial del Estado* (Law of National Territorial Patrimony),[27] decreed in 1927, and legislation passed in 1928 that stipulated the establishment of rural public schools designed to promote indigenous and peasant education and encourage the formation of a free, educated working class (Cevallos 1993, Rubio Orbe 1954).[28]

While there is ample evidence of the encroachment of elite landowners, municipal officials, and even white small-scale property holders upon communal lands in the Otavalo area, ascertaining the exact role of "the state" and certain of its representatives in facilitating the erosion of communal lands is made more difficult by conclusions drawn from these disputes. A complex pattern of judicial interpretation emerges from the rulings on the legal actions comprising them. These rulings, in particular, reveal the difficulties entailed by the state's ambivalence in recognizing *indígenas* as propertied citizens, while advocating individually-held rights to private property. In their application of laws and legal precedent regarding land tenure issues, local judges are seen to recognize communally-based rights to land but also to use the notion of such rights as the basis of decisions that recognize the private ownership of individually-possessed communal lands. The legislation's overt protection of indigenous communal lands, thus, was undermined by the discrepancies between particular laws, as well as the conflict between the use and local administration of "communal lands" and that implied within indigenous legislation.

On the one hand, these contradictions allowed *indígenas* to formalize their essentially private possession of some communal areas and to have it legally and not just locally recognized as tantamount to ownership. Theoretically, of course, the possible conflict between the claims of individual owners of plots of communal lands and corporate members of the community was attenuated not only in the state's recognition of individual community members as exclusive owners of plots of communal lands but in its refusal to recognize the rights of these very same individuals to sell these plots of land. Yet, both the first and third cases examined in this article provide evidence of individuals in receipt of such plots doing just that, selling them. Thus, despite the fact that communal lands were legally protected, their conservation presumably insured, early republican measures also made possible their privatization by the very people who presumably benefited from their joint possession, namely, indigenous community members.

On the other hand, the decisions reached by the judges in the legal cases analyzed here belie the seemingly obvious conclusion that the state, through its judicial system, unambiguously aided in the privatization and erosion of communal lands. There is an overwhelming reluctance by these representatives of the state to accept the privatization and potential alienation of communal lands, particularly, it would appear, when it is *indígenas* who solicit the right to do so.[29] This reluctance was clearly evidenced in the judge's rejection of the request to partition communal lands of Imbaquí-Agato-Maldonado (Case Two).

An Appeal to Communalism and the Defense of "Community"

It is within this local and national politico-economic context that the three disputes must be situated. Faced with the dual threats of a modernizing state and expansionist white landowners, Otavaleños involved in these conflicts can be interpreted as "resisting" state and *hacendado* encroachment through the deployment of particular legal arguments formulated in dialogue with national and local officials.[30] Against such adversaries, I argue, appeals to "community" and communalism, regardless of the exact designated use of the communal land in question, were frequently adopted by Otavaleño *comuneros* seeking to protect their landholdings and, at the same time, defend communal autonomy. For example, as witnessed in the La Compañía-Camuendo dispute (Case One), a group of indigenous community members took on the owner of a nearby hacienda, arguing for their right to an extension of land based on their joint possession of it "since time immemorial" in their capacity as community members collectively exploiting the area. This group did so, however, presumably with the explicit intention of formally dividing and distributing the land among its members, once the community's right to the land had been upheld. Similarly, in Case Three, *indígenas* of Caluquí argued for the recognition of their rights to an area of communal lands that they had been individually cultivating, based, in part, on their and their ancestors' collective possession of constitutive grasslands and woodlands.

Yet, Case One and Case Two also illustrate how fellow indigenous community members could threaten the joint or individual possession of communal landholdings through attempts to distribute jointly-held lands or impede the legal recognition of already-partitioned individual plots. With regard to the former category, these cases reveal that attempts to privatize *pastoral* communal lands, in particular, are opposed by other *comuneros,* on the grounds that the partition of these lands constitutes a breach in community control and unity. In Case One, opposition to the distribution and cultivation of the community's pastoral lands by a group of community members seeking parity arises from the very same *comuneros* who had previously requested the partition of the "lower" section. Within the courts, this group supports its position through appeals to the integrity of both the community and its landholdings. More specifically, by attempting to discredit their opponents' assertion that they are community members, the members of this group imply that the "community" wants neither this partition nor the intrusion of outsiders into the area.

Case Two also demonstrates how community members successfully invoke the image of "community" and principles of communalism in their contestation of the introduction of agriculture and parcelization of pastoral communal lands. They are in possession of these lands, they claim, as members of the community of Imbaquí-Agato-Maldonado, not as individuals, an argument that foreshadows the judge's ruling. These *comuneros* also call upon images of egalitarianism and harmony central to the prevailing construct of community (and, most likely, indigenous society)[31] in arguing for the need for all community members to be in agreement with decisions made with regard to communal lands.

Such appeals to communalism and community, thus, cannot be correlated in any simple way to the defense of communalistic land tenure practices by *indígenas,* nor to their protection of communal landholdings solely from white-*mestizos* or the state. Indeed, appeals to joint possession "since time immemorial" and community integrity can be made at the service of protecting individually-held lands and in land disputes against expansionist white-*mestizos* or organized indigenous *comuneros* (see Nader 1989). Instead, Otavaleños appear to deploy communalistic discursive tactics against different figures for different transgressions. Against the encroachment of white-*mestizos,* they appear to use such rhetorical strategies to defend individually-held, as well as jointly-held communal lands. They also promote principles of communalism and the ideal of community, however, against the organized attempts of fellow indigenous *comuneros* to privatize jointly-held pastoral lands.

This pattern suggests that the use of such rhetorical strategies by Otavaleños is not an articulation of an essentialized tradition of communalism. Rather, their use, I argue, is evidence of the effectiveness of Otavaleños at manipulating legal constructs defined in relation to particular images of *"el indio"* and community before the Ecuadorian judicial system, in particular (cf. Nader 1989, Starr & Collier 1989b). The deployment of these same strategies by whites from the González

Suárez parish only reinforces the idea that such discursive tactics should not be interpreted unquestioningly as an affirmation of "traditional" or authentic Indianness or indigenous practice. Instead, the development of strategies based on "traditional" land tenure and "ancestral property rights" by a variety of individuals indicates the need to recognize such strategies as enacted instances of a "norm of the communicative code" required by the state of its interlocutors (Guerrero 1997).

Yet, despite the fact that this communicative code may be demanded and even established by the state, the meanings attributed to its constitutive signs are never entirely dictated by any one actor—neither the state's representatives nor the litigants or their mediators. As witnessed in the three cases discussed above, core constructs such as "community," "communal land," and the property rights of *comuneros* are remarkably labile in the meanings ascribed them by the plaintiffs, defendants, their legal representatives, and judges of these cases (G. Smith 1991). As concrete groupings, communities are being continually redefined and reconstituted in particular contexts and in interaction with the nation-state and elite ideologies (see G. Smith 1989). As symbolic tropes, metaphors of community not only serve as glosses for united groups of individuals who may be engaged in conflict, but they also contribute to the construction and reproduction of those very groups. This flexibility and lability of "community" is, therefore, simultaneously the source of its ideological potency and, ironically, its anti-essentialist nature. In short, the consensualism of "community" is neither primordial nor determined by a single-causal variable, but is, rather, a processual achievement that is reproduced or reformulated in the multi-layered interactions of the local, regional, and national within particular historical, political, and sociocultural contexts.

The Deployment of Individualism, Privatization, and the Protection of Communal Lands

Whereas strategies grounded in a discourse of communalism may be addressed against both intruding outsiders and transgressing insiders, indigenous deployment (or, more accurately, acceptable use) of principles of individualism appears to be limited to attempts to legally formalize individual control of agricultural lands within indigenous communities. In Case One, a group of *indígenas* from La Compañía-Camuendo, in spite of their self-identification as joint owners of the "lower" section, are able to successfully lobby for an interpretation of a specific area as essentially comprising private and individual landholdings. Houses have not been built on these lands by all families but only by particular families within the community. These lands, they claim, have not been cultivated by all families but only by the families of the defendants and their ancestors.

In arguing for their right to divide and distribute the area in question, this group of *indígenas* from La Compañía-Camuendo both advocate their co-ownership to this area and assert their individual rights to the lands within it. In so doing, they assume a role—that of joint owners without individual title but with corporate rights to communal lands—which conforms to state constructions of indigenous land tenure (i.e., joint possession of communal lands) and allows them to effectively argue for the legal recognition of their rights to this area. At the same time, however, they are arguing for the legal recognition of their individual rights to particular areas of communal lands, namely, sections that are and were worked by themselves and past family members, rights which will be concretized and legitimized by the state through the act of formal partition. But, while opposition to this partition does arise within the community, it is not the parcelization of the "lower" section that is contested as much as the exclusion of a number of *comuneros* from the process. Similarly, in Case Two, it is not the principle of privatization that appears to be opposed by one group of *comuneros*. Rather, they seek to prevent their adversaries from expanding agricultural production into pastoral communal land, particularly after an earlier unsuccessful attempt of their own fathers to partition this area.

Ironically, these disputes also suggest that Otavaleños successfully defended jointly-possessed pastoral communal lands against the attempts of *comuneros* to divide and distribute them through the deployment of "individualistic" principles. Such is the case of *comuneros* of La Compañía-Camuendo (Case One) who, on the local cantonal level, successfully accused others of having appropriated communal lands located within an area that they and only they exclusively owned. In effect, their establishment of the right to divide and distribute communal lands— in effect, to pave the way toward their privatization—provided the basis for later claims of exclusive ownership. This claim, in turn, served as the legal foundation for denying other community members the ability to partition pastoral communal lands.

CONCLUSION

Within the northern Andes, members of indigenous communities have found themselves fighting against encroaching haciendas and white-*mestizos* for their communal lands since as early as the late 1700s (Ramón 1991a, 1991b). Based on the cases explored in this article, it would appear that, in the 1890s, extensive sections of communal land in the Otavalo Valley underwent a period of intensive division and distribution. By the mid-1930s, communal lands in this area were scarce enough to draw comment by outside observers, who noted that much of what had once been communal was now owned and controlled by haciendas or individual indigenous and *mestizo* owners (García 1935). For Otavalan indigenous villages such as Agato, La Compañía, Peguche, and Quinchuquí (all located to the northeast of San Pablo Lake and on the skirts of Mount Imbabura), lands that remained in the control of the community were principally those of the high regions of Mount Imbabura, used almost exclusively as pasture and woodlands, and certainly were not cultivated collectively (García 1935, Parsons 1945). Cultivated plots that did exist in these areas were identified as owned by the individual families planting them (García 1935:35).

But, while there is little doubt that communal lands in Ecuador have been privatized over the course of the past two centuries, there is some question as to the sources of this transformation. Based on the examination of three local land disputes, no longer can we limit agents of privatization to a particular set of white-*mestizo* figures, namely, unscrupulous white hacienda owners, lawyers, and "land speculators" (Cevallos 1993; see Langer 1990).[32] Indeed, these three land disputes indicate that a variety of *indígenas*, not just rogue community leaders co-opted by external forces (see, e.g., Guerrero 1989), were active participants in the partition and eventual privatization of lands belonging to indigenous communities.

I argue that this process of transformation, at least when deemed acceptable within indigenous communities, pertained specifically to individually-possessed agricultural lands. It was through the partition of such lands, I suggest, that Otavaleños positioned themselves to be able to successfully claim exclusive ownership before local and national authorities, and, in so doing, made the communal lands they possessed, as well as themselves, less vulnerable to the needs of expansionist hacienda owners and "modernizing" state representatives (see Nugent & Alonso 1994).

The three cases analyzed in this article, in particular, demonstrate how Otavaleños at the turn of the century skillfully negotiated inherent contradictions and ambiguities in republican legislation to protect both communal and individual rights to lands recognized by the state as belonging to indigenous communities. Ironically, then, the right to cultural and material autonomy so frequently argued by Ecuadorian *indígenas* within arenas such as the court system was facilitated by the very body of legislation that sought to transform them. At the same time, however, in legally concretizing their individual rights through state-recognized acts of division and distribution, indigenous *comuneros* advanced their individual autonomy in the administration and transmission of these plot from the community as a whole. While this move could be met with opposition from within the community, the basis of disapproval appears to be the perception of inequity rather than a refusal to recognize individual rights to these lands.

Conversely, the privatization of communal pastoral lands was rigorously opposed by the *indígenas* involved in these land disputes. This pattern—the simultaneous antagonism toward the partition of communally-possessed grasslands and woodlands and acceptance of the division and distribution of cultivated lands— challenges one notion commonly present in studies of indigenous resistance: that the privatization of communal lands constituted the dislocation of one system of "traditional," strictly communalistic tenure by another, more individualistic one. When attempts to partition pastoral lands are made in these disputes, intra-communal conflict does inevitably arise. Such attempts, however, are interpreted by *comuneros* as evidence of a blatant disregard of shared social precepts and practices, namely, equal access for all community members to lands designated by the community as strictly pastoral. Transgression of this common right, these disputes show us, constitutes grounds for communal sanction, hostility, and divisiveness.

Nevertheless, while these disputes might reflect the conflict and contention that can arise both within indigenous communities and between them and other social collectivities over the privatization and appropriation of communal lands, they do not, I argue, provide evidence of the erosion of communal values or a breakdown of a purported indigenous "community." Interestingly, aspects of these conflicts suggest just the opposite, i.e., that the partition of communal lands—presumably a representation of the adoption of an individualistic ethic—was used to successfully stem the privatization of communally-possessed pastoral lands. Indeed, Otavaleños in these disputes can be seen to defend communal lands through recourse to both individualistic and communalistic discursive strategies constructed in dialogue with their lawyers, local and regional court officials, and the criteria of national land legislation.

Interestingly, their choice of strategies does not appear to correlate with socio-economic divisions within the community or to the maintenance of "traditional" or the adoption of "modern" land tenure practices. Instead, choices regarding the deployment of individualism or the promotion of communalism are informed by a combination of several factors: the designated use within the community of the communal land in question, the parties involved in the dispute, and particular legal categories and constructs established by the state. Consequently, these strategies can be viewed more as different articulations of long-standing, collectively-held constructions of property and property rights within particular legal and political arenas (see Roseman 1996) than as indicators of traditionalism or market insertion.

These three disputes demonstrate, in particular, how Otavaleños have worked within the parameters of Ecuadorian land legislation in formulating their claims to communally-administered lands and resources. In so doing, they give rise to an admonition: No longer can the texts elaborating such disputes be approached simply as transparent representations of indigenous social, cultural, and political reality. Clearly, the legal arguments and testimonies of the *indígenas* found within these documents are constructed in interactions occurring between such diverse actors as indigenous plaintiffs and defendants, indigenous community leaders responsible for representing the interests of their fellow community members, white-*mestizo* representatives and mediating agents (e.g., interpreters and lawyers), and other court officials (e.g., surveyors, judges, and outside consultants). Accordingly, the legal strategies of the participants in these cases are most accurately approached as the mediated products of varied and sometimes competing interests, social practices and schemas, legal constructs, and indigenous narrated accounts that are predominantly articulated by persons (e.g., lawyers, *tinterillos*,[33] and indigenous authority figures) authorized to perform within particular arenas such as the court system.

In revealing the complex negotiations which underlie the local interpretation and application of Ecuadorian law and land tenure policies, the analysis presented here suggests a need to reevaluate scholarly representations of indigenous political engagement of structures and processes of domination. In these land conflicts, Otavaleños are seen to use a variety of legal strategies to defend their rights to communal landholdings from state and elite encroachment, as well as members of their own communities. Yet neither "resistance," with its implication of mono-lithic and univocal response, nor "accommodation," with its suggestion of acqui-escence, seem to adequately capture the simultaneous manipulation and reproduction of legal categories and constructs that takes place in the formulation and employment of these strategies.

This article has centered on the ways in which Otavaleños or, more generally, Indians have used law and the legal system as resources to defend cultural and material autonomy from the state and local elites, while, at the same time, assert-ing personal and individual independence within their communities. In framing the article in this way, I have implicitly supported William Roseberry (1994:363-364) in his assertion that "the form and languages of protest or resis-tance must adopt the forms and languages of domination in order to be registered or heard." Yet, one might well ask, What does the adoption of "the forms and lan-guages of domination" mean for the individuals who appropriate the terms, for-mulae, and constructs of a legal discursive field that both enforces and endows unequal social relationships with legitimacy? Certainly, legal categories and iden-tities, as well as the social relationships that they simultaneously represent and constrain, can be and are subverted by individuals engaged in their elaboration (Lazarus-Black & Hirsch 1994). However, while law undoubtedly constitutes a resource that can be used in ways which can defy the power relationships and nat-uralized images of a social order legitimized by it, law also "maintains power rela-tions by defining categories and systems of meaning" (Merry 1992:362), both of which, in turn, shape subjective consciousness and identity.

The disputes discussed in this article suggest that, although legislation might have opened paths for the advancement of their claims, *indígenas* did not assert their individual and communal rights to the exclusion of integration into the nation. Indeed, in basing rights to "communal lands" on community membership, early land legislation also reaffirmed the reverse proposition: community member-ship—or, more specifically, membership within indigenous communities—was defined, in part, by the possession of lands designated as "communal." In this affirmation, such laws can be seen to effectively implement the nationalist vision of binding a nation's members to a particular territory, namely, a "community" and lands that had been demarcated and recognized by the state as belonging to it (A.D. Smith 1994). While it is not the intent of this article to resolve these broader questions, this corollary problem—namely, how images and metaphors of Indian, indigenousness, and community affect the construction and representation of identity and the practices that purportedly embody it by the *indígenas* engaged in the deployment of these constructs—points to one direction that others interested in these issues might go.

ACKNOWLEDGMENTS

I want to thank Jane Collins, Linda Seligmann, Mark Rogers, and Barry Isaac, in particular, for their array of thoughtful, penetrating and, in the end, very helpful comments on an earlier version of this article. I would also like to express my gratitude to the staff at the Otavalan Institute of Anthropology and especially to Drs. Carlos Coba and Hernán Jaramillo, who were particularly supportive of my work in the archives housed there. The research on which this article is based was supported by a Fulbright-IIE grant and the Wenner Gren Foundation.

NOTES

1. This position has its roots in a body of Andeanist studies that have been criticized (see, e.g., Starn 1991, 1994) for their representation of local communities as embodying an homogeneous Andean culture that is static and resistant to change and characterized by social and economic reciprocity, ritual communalism, and ecological adaptability, legacies of the pre-Columbian, Incan tradition (see, e.g., Bastien 1978, Brush 1977, Isbell 1977).

2. The point at which the transformation of "traditional" indigenous peasants into individualistic, private-property-owning capitalists presumably takes place is remarkably variable in the literature. For the Otavalo Valley, the penetration of a capitalist system has been fixed at dates ranging as far back as the early republican period and as recent as the 1960s (Collier & Buitrón 1949, Herrera 1909, Meier 1984, Walter 1981). Certainly, there is little doubt about the long history of indigenous involvement in the market in the Otavalo region, and it has been suggested that Otavaleños have been active as merchants since the precolonial era, combining agricultural and artesanal production with commerce for centuries (Caillavet 1981, Salomon 1973). Many argue for the initiation of internal social differentiation and class formation, however, in the late 1950s and early 1960s with the introduction of new production techniques and materials such as the power loom, the expansion of Otavalan entrepreneurial activities, and the Ecuadorian state's explicit promotion of tourism in the area (see, e.g., Meier 1984, Walter 1981). The variability of these dates and the partition of communal lands by Otavaleños as early as the mid-19th century certainly call into question the simple assumption that internal differentiation determined choices regarding the conservation or distribution communal lands.

3. Technically, Gran Colombia became independent from Spain in 1821. Ecuador later separated from Gran Colombia, achieving national sovereignty in 1830.

4. The literature that has addressed the enactment of early Ecuadorian legislation and nationalist attempts to forge an "imagined political community" (Anderson 1983) has focused primarily on the measures taken to ensure labor and monies necessary for the development of state infrastructure (e.g., the expediting of the construction of a "redemptive" national railroad linking the coast and highlands), the regulation of the collection of tribute (*contribución personal* and *diezmos*), and the building of municipal public works (Clark 1998, Ibarra 1991, Moscoso 1989).

5. Specifically, the law decreed that such lands be legally awarded to "*indígenas y personas miserables*" in possession of them (Art. 14). While this phrase can be translated as "indigenes and miserable persons," the assumption, of course, is that, while *indígenas* are miserable persons or members of

a miserable race, miserable persons can also include individuals who are not indigenous. Both these categories, identified as such, are implicitly recognized as in need of state protection (see also Guerrero 1997, Ibarra 1991).

6.   This tension was further exacerbated by additional legislation regulating individual property rights that directly contradicted some of the more explicit aims of these two laws. For example, at least since the early 20th century, Ecuador's Civil Code and Political Constitution have assigned co-owners the right to request at any time the division of their jointly-held property.

7.   Ecuadorian historian Rafael Quintero (1986: 413) breaks down early republican legislation that sought to ensure the legitimization of these regionally-based factions into three types: (1) laws intended to secure the economic subjugation of the peasantry, which prohibited "vagrancy" and limited freedom of movement (*"libre tránsito"*), (2) decrees directed toward the impoverishment of small-scale indigenous and peasant property holders, and (3) laws that favored the monopolization of land.

8.   By law, such lands were not to be sold or transferred out of the hands of the community. Despite these constraints, in the Otavalo area, individual plots were often bequeathed to members of one's family and loaned out to acquaintances (e.g., *compadres*, or members of a family's fictive kin network), or even sometimes sold or offered as collateral for loans, to be subsequently transferred in the event of failure to repay (see Grieshaber 1989 for comparable sales in Bolivia). Thus, regardless of the fact that title was to remain in the name of the community, the partition of communal lands, in fact, corresponded with their transformation into private landholdings.

9.   Both legal categories were recognized by the courts as potentially constituting ownership. Dominion, "the actual right in a corporal thing, to enjoy and dispose of arbitrarily" (Civil Code, Art. 880), was proved through such means as legal title to the lands. Possession, on the other hand, could be recognized as rightful ownership if an individual or group of individuals could prove that acts of possession (e.g., cultivation) had been performed "tranquilly" and uninterrupted for at least a year prior to the trial. If lands had been in possession for more than 30 years, this type of holding—tranquil and without interruption, yet bolstered by no title—was identified as *"prescripción extraordinaria"*; if for less than that period of time, as *prescripción*. Complications could and did arise, of course, when competing parties maintained contradictory positions (e.g., suits classified as an *"acción reivindicatoria o de dominio,"* whereby property was purportedly in the "dominion" of one party but in the "possession" of another).

10.   This phrase invokes rights to land that are recognized within indigenous communities by its members as well as by the state. In one sense, it is an invocation of rights of inheritance that are predicated on the possession of lands by one's ancestors and their devolution to his or her heirs. The phrase also plays on and is sometimes used interchangeably with the legal category of *"posesión inmemorial,"* defined in 1881 by a lawyer, quoting the Dictionary of Legislation, as "that which exceeds the memory of the most elderly men, so that there is no one that has knowledge of its origins" (The National Historical Archives, Quito [ANH/Q]: [Ti 10-V-1881, Caja 275]). The dictionary fixes "elderly" at 70 years of age.

11.   The three trials are: (1) "The *indígenas* of the community (*parcialidad*) of La Compañía-Camuendo against other *indígenas* of the same community, for the dispossession (*despojo*) of lands," Otavalan Institute of Anthropology: EP/J, 1a, (1907-10; 2241), Caja 91; (2) "The *indígenas* of the community of 'Camuendo', regarding a partition of lands," Otavalan Institute of Anthropology: EP/J, 1a (1914; 2350), Caja 95; and (3) "Continued by Abelino Cañamar and others against Juan Potosí and others for the demand for the return of an expanse of land," Otavalan Institute of Anthropology: EP/J, 1a (1915; 2365), Caja 96.

12.   The allegation of 50 years would place the beginning of conflicts surrounding this area in the middle of the 1800s or around the time of the passage of the Law of Empty Lands.

13.   The local political lieutenant who provided the report that led to this favorable ruling supported his finding that "there would be nothing more just than to have an equitable distribution among the sixty indians"(ff. 20v-21) with an accusation: he claimed that Miguel Castañeda, whom he identi-

fied as a head of the community, had been selling some of the plots in the "lower" section to whites, in particular, Manuel Chávez of Otavalo, Castañeda's lawyer in the 1900 annulment case.

14.　Later in the case, they also support their general allegation with the contention that the Governor, in authorizing the partition, was acting out of his jurisdiction.

15.　Similarly, witnesses variously set the time of the inauguration of their own rights to perform such acts of possession at their own infancy or childhood or at the birth of their parents. To a person, though, they understand themselves as "possessing" these lands via such acts.

16.　Handwritten comments also suggest that the judge interpreted Castañeda's refusal to take part in an earlier meeting to discuss the redistribution of lands as evidence that, contrary to what the defendants had argued, not all actors were in agreement with this course of action (ff. 23v-24).

17.　Otavalan Institute of Anthropology: EP/J, 2a (1920; 1574), Caja 99.

18.　Otavalan Institute of Anthropology: EP/J, 2a (1924; 1766), Caja 105.

19.　This document was originally presented by community representatives on behalf of "*el comun de Yndios de Anejo de Ymvaji, y Agato*" (the community of Indians of the Annex of Imbaquí and Agato) who requested the return of common lands allegedly appropriated by the current renter of an adjacent hacienda, the hacienda Quinchuquí.

20.　The documents themselves reveal that "*Casique principal* don Thomas Mirapuento Maldonado" and "*el Comun de Yndios de dicha parcialidad*" (the Cacique and Indians of the community of Imbaquí-Maldonado) were granted title to 5 *caballerías* (probably about 480 acres) of land located in the *páramo* area of the Mount Imbabura in 1723 and 1747. This land was designated explicitly for pasturing animals. In 1750, 18 *caballerías* of the community's lands were divided by Don José de Astorga y Oballe in preparation for their sale through auction, apparently an act of land-grabbing perpetuated, in part, by the owner of the adjacent hacienda Quinchuquí. Indigenous members of the community, however, were able to retain possession of the 5 *caballerías* due to their possession of the title previously granted to them. Although his opponents do not challenge the legitimacy of the documents or their applicability in proving rights of co-ownership in general, they do question the legality of the manner in which they were introduced into the trial, as well as the relatedness of the plaintiffs to those *comuneros* mentioned in the submitted texts.

21.　Otavalan Institute of Anthropology: EP/J, 2a (1924; 1747), Caja 105.

22.　There is the implication in several statements that this partition came about after the loss of a lawsuit by the communities of Caluquí and Gualacata.

23.　Currently in the Otavalo area, this particular type of labor arrangement entails an exchange between the land's *dueño* (owner) and its *partidario* (sharecropper tenant) in which the tenant receives usufruct rights for half or a portion of the harvested crop. The owner of the land is also responsible for supplying the seed, while the tenant is responsible for supplying all necessary labor or costs of labor (e.g., tractor fees, payment of peons) involved in preparing and planting the field and harvesting the crop.

24.　Whether or not this partition was legitimate is questionable; the indigenous plaintiffs certainly challenge the validity of the distribution of what they perceive of as the lands of indigenous communities.

25.　The Liberal reforms of President Eloy Alfaro perhaps best exemplify this legislation. As part of this Liberal project, the collection of *diezmo* (tithe), a 10 percent tax placed on agricultural and livestock products whose proceeds were divided between the State and the Church, was terminated in 1883 (Fuentealba 1990), and a new land tax (30 *centavos* a year for every 100 *sucres* of "*valor real de los predios rústicos*," excluding Church and State properties) and tax of exported cacao were substituted in its place (Costales & Peñaherrera 1964). In 1895, legislators abolished the "*contribución territorial y del trabajo subsidiario*" for "*la raza india.*" In 1908, the confiscation and rental of the Church's landholdings was authorized, based on the passage of the *Ley de Manos Muertos* (Law of Mortmain).

26.　In particular, in 1918 highland hacienda owners suffered a setback with the legal suppression of debt imprisonment and, consequently, the undermining of the legal underpinnings of the institution of *concertaje*, a labor arrangement in which "*conciertos*" contracted with hacienda owners to receive a monthly salary (which would be given in anticipation of the fulfillment of the contract), a small plot of land, and usufructory rights to such hacienda resources as pasture, roads, firewood, and water in exchange for their labor (Guerrero 1991c, Moscoso 1991). Its abolition did not eradicate exploitative forms of labor relations, however, as other insecure tenancy arrangements came into popular use, most notably *huasipungaje*, a labor arrangement in which the worker exchanged his labor for a small-subsistence plot, a low wage, and usufructory rights to the *hacienda's* resources such as water and firewood. In addition, Indians from nearby villages (i.e., *peones sueltos*, or *libres*) also worked on the *haciendas* in exchange for money but without access to its resources.

27.   In general terms, the Law of National Territorial Patrimony stipulated the review of property titles of all lands adjudicated as "*baldías*" (vacant) in 1865, the return to the state of all untitled private properties as well as properties which had not been cultivated for a certain period of time, and the creation of national land reserves. Not surprisingly, it was opposed by both sierran and coastal large-scale landowners, who thought that it violated a sacrosanct right to property.

28.   Despite such measures, it has been suggested that the cacao crisis actually reinforced the use of "traditional" exploitative labor and land tenure arrangements such as *concertaje* and *huasipungaje*. In particular, highland *terratenientes* are envisioned as taking advantage of the "freeing up" of sources of labor—particularly highland migrant laborers—in their efforts to increase production, reduce monetary requirements and, at the same time, ensure a subordinated working force (Cevallos 1993).

29.   This ambivalence toward recognizing indigenous private ownership of plots of communal land is reflected in a 1930 "Report to the Nation" distributed by the Ministry of Agriculture and Social Security. In it, the Minister Francisco Boloña reports that many of the sales of communal lands, if they were to transpire, would not be recognized. While *comuneros* had been declared by judges to be "exclusive owners of their plots," he asserts, in a number of cases these sales would be nullified, "it being well known that he who possesses in common can only obtain the benefits of prescription for all co-possessors [i.e., can only hold the rights held by all other joint holders]" (quoted in Cevallos 1993: 238).

30.   Otavaleños were not unique in their efforts to protect or reclaim lands that had fallen victim to the modernization attempts of elite highland landowners. Indeed, Galo Ramón (1991a) demonstrates that *indígenas* from the Cayambe area of the northern highland province of Pichincha began mobilizing against modernizing *hacendados* in the 1920s in response to elite expansion of cultivation and parcelization of *huasipungos* (plots held by *huasipungueros*). These efforts, he argues, resulted from the delegitimization of landlord-tenant "pacts" in the face of landlord violence during the period of 1921-1947 and were facilitated by alliances between *mestizos* and *indígenas*.

31.   I make this suggestion based, in part, on the particularly strong influence of Mexican agrarian thought and Peruvian *indigenismo* (an intellectual and political movement prominent in the 1920s that embraced "Indianist" models) on Ecuadorian elites in the 1920s and 1930s.

32.   One notable contradiction to this trend is Nancy Forster's (1989) work. In her study of the transformation of *páramo* lands in the Tisaleo area of Tungurahua province, she found that *comuneros* began to cultivate the commons as a means of securing their legal claim, thus removing it from the danger of expropriation under provisions of the agrarian reform laws of 1964 and the early 1970s.

33.   *Tinterillos* perform such duties as interpreting the petitions of indigenous clients and codifying or "translating" them into juridical language. While in the past, they were commonly white or *mestizo*, today bilingual *indígenas* familiar with the courts take on these duties.

REFERENCES

Albó, Xavier (1991) "El retorno del indio" ("The Return of the Indian"). *Revista Andina* 9:299-345.
Almeida Vinueza, José (1990) "Luchas campesinas del siglo XX (primera parte)" ("Peasant Struggles in the 20th Century [first part]"). Pp. 163-186 in E. A. Mora (ed.) *Nueva Historia del Ecuador* (*The New History of Ecuador*). Quito: Corporación Editora Nacional/Grijalba.

Anderson, Benedict (1983) *Imagined Communities*. London: Verso.

Arcos, Carlos (1984) "El espíritu del progreso: Los hacendados en el Ecuador del 1900" ("The Spirit of Progress: Hacienda Owners in Ecuador in 1900"). *Cultura* 7(19):107-134.

Baraona, Rafael (1965) "Una tipología de haciendas en la sierra ecuatoriana" ("A Typology of Haciendas in the Ecuadorian Highlands"). Pp. 688-696 in O. Delgado (ed.) *Reformas Agrarias en la América Latina* (*Agrarian Reforms in Latin America*). México, DF: Fondo de Cultura Económica.

Barraclough, Solon (1973) *Agrarian Structure in Latin America: A Resumé of the CIDA Land Tenure Studies*. Lexington, MA: D.C. Heath & Co.

Barsky, Osvaldo (1978) "Iniciativa terrateniente en la reestructuración de las relaciones sociales en la sierra ecuatoriana" ("Landowner Initiative in the Restructuration of Social Relations in the Ecuadorian Highlands"). *Revista de Ciencias Sociales* 2(5):74-126.

Bastien, Joseph (1978) *Mountain of the Condor: Metaphor and Ritual in an Andean Ayllu*. St. Paul, MN: West.

Beals, Alan (1964) *Gopalpur: A South Indian Village*. New York: Holt, Rinehart & Winston.

Bebbington, Anthony (1992) "Grassroots Perspectives on 'Indigenous' Agricultural Development: Indian Organisations and NGOs in the Central Andes of Ecuador." *European Journal of Development* 4:132-167.

Brush, Stephen (1977) *Mountain, Field, and Family: The Economy and Human Ecology of an Andean Valley*. Philadelphia: University of Pennsylvania Press.

Brush, Stephen, and David Guillet (1985) "Small-Scale Agro-Pastoral Production in the Central Andes." *Mountain Research and Development* 5(1):19-30.

Caillavet, Chantal (1981) "Entre sierra y selva: Las relaciones fronterizas y sus representaciones para las etnias de los Andes septentrionales" ("Between Mountains and Jungle: Frontier Relations and Their Representations for Ethnic Groups of the Northern Andes"). *Anuario de Estudios Americanos* 46:71-91.

Cevallos, Arturo (1993) "Sublevaciones y conflictos indígenas en Chimborazo (1920-1930)" ("Indigenous Uprisings and Conflicts in Chimborazo [1920-1930]"). *Memoria* 3:227-251.

Clark, A. Kim (1994) "Indians, the State and Law: Public Works and the Struggle to Control Labor in Liberal Ecuador." *Journal of Historical Sociology* 7:49-72.

_____ (1998) *The Redemptive Work: Railway and Nation in Ecuador, 1895-1930*. Wilmington, DE: Scholarly Resources, Inc.

Collier, George (1989) "The Impact of Second Republic Labor Reforms in Spain." Pp. 201-222 in J. Starr & J. Collier (eds.) *History and Power in the Study of Law: New Directions in Legal Anthropology*. Ithaca: Cornell University Press.

Collier, John, and Aníbal Buitrón (1949) *The Awakening Valley*. Chicago: University of Chicago Press.

Cooper, Frederick, and Ann Stoler (1991) "Introduction: Tensions of Empire: Colonial Control and Visions of Rule." *American Ethnologist* 16:609-621.

Costales, Alfredo, and Piedad Peñaherrera de Costales, eds. (1964) "Recopilación de leyes sociales indígenas de 1830 a 1918" ("Compilation of Indigenous Social Laws from 1830 to 1918"). *Revista Llacta* 19 (whole issue).

Crain, Mary (1988) "Peasant Ideological Practices and Political Process in the Ecuadorian Highlands: Conflict and Consensus in Agrarian Politics." Pp. 219-238 in J. W. Bennett & J. R. Bowen (eds.) *Production and Autonomy: Anthropological Studies and Critiques of Development*. Lanham, MD: University Presses of America.

_____ (1990) "The Social Construction of National Identity in Highland Ecuador." *Anthropological Quarterly* 63:43-59.

_____ (1991) "Poetics and Politics in the Ecuadorean Andes: Women's Narratives of Death and Devil Possession." *American Ethnologist* 18:67-89.

Findji, María Teresa (1992) "From Resistance to Social Movement: The Indigenous Authorities Movement in Colombia." Pp. 112-133 in A. Escobar & S. Alvarez (eds.) *The Making of Social Movements in Latin America: Identity, Strategy and Democracy.* Boulder, CO: Westview.

Forster, Nancy (1989) "When the State Sidesteps Land Reform: Alternative Peasant Strategies in Tungurahua, Ecuador." University of Wisconsin-Madison, Land Tenure Center, LTC Research Paper 133.

Fuentealba, Gerardo (1990) "La sociedad indígena en las primeras décadas de la Républica: Continuedades coloniales y cambios republicanos" (Indigenous Society in the First Decades of the Republic: Colonial Continuities and Republican Changes"). Pp. 45-73 in E. A. Mora (ed.) *Nueva Historia del Ecuador (The New History of Ecuador).* Quito: Corporación Editora Nacional/Grijalba.

García Ortiz, Humberto (1935) *Breve Exposición de los Resultados Obtenidos en la Investigación Sociológica de Algunas Parcialidades Indígenas de la Provincia de Imbabura (A Brief Exposition of the Results Obtained in the Sociological Investigation of Some Indigenous Communities in Imbabura Province).* Quito: Imprenta de la Universidad Central.

Gluckman, Max (1967) *The Judicial Process among the Barotse of Northern Rhodesia* (2nd ed.). Manchester, ENG: Manchester University Press.

Gose, Peter (1994) *Deathly Waters and Hungry Mountains: Agrarian Ritual and Class Formation in an Andean Town.* Toronto: University of Toronto Press.

Grieshaber, Erwin (n.d.) "Indian Resistance to Communal Land Sales in the Department of La Paz, 1881-1920." Paper presented at the IX Simposio Internacional de Historia Económica CLACSO-FLACSO, Quito, 1989.

Guerrero, Andrés (1978) "Renta diferencial y vias de disolución de la hacienda precapitalist en el Ecuador" ("Differential Rent and Paths of Dissolution of the Precapitalist Hacienda in Ecuador"). *Revista de Ciencias Sociales* 2(5):52-73.

_____ (1989) "Curagas y tenientes políticos: La ley del estado y la ley de la costumbre" ("Curagas and Political Lieutenants: State Law and Customary Law"). *Revista Andina* 7:321-365.

_____ (1991a) "Determinaciones del pasado y mentalidades del presente: Un conflicto entre comuneros" ("Determination of the Past and Mentalities of the Present: A Conflict Among Community Members"). Pp. 149-192 in A. Guerrero (ed.) *De la Economía a las Mentalidades: Cambio Social y Conflicto Agrario en el Ecuador (From Economy to Mentalities: Social Change and Agrarian Conflict in Ecuador).* Quito: Editorial El Conejo.

_____ (1991b) "La hacienda precapitalista y la clase terrateniente serrana" ("The Precapitalist Hacienda and the Highland Landowner Class"). Pp. 9-76 in A. Guerrero (ed.) *De la Economía a las Mentalidades: Cambio Social y Conflicto Agrario en el Ecuador (From Economy to Mentalities: Social Change and Agrarian Conflict in Ecuador).* Quito: Editorial El Conejo.

_____ (1991c) *La Semántica de la Dominación: El Concertaje del Indio (The Semantics of Domination: The Peonage of the Indian).* Quito: Ediciones Libri Mundi.

_____ (1997) "The Construction of a Ventriloquist's Image: Liberal Discourse and the 'Miserable Indian Race' in Late 19th-Century Ecuador." *Journal of Latin American Studies* 29:555-590.

Gulliver, Philip (1979) *Disputes and Negotiations: A Cross-cultural Perspective.* New York: Academic Press.

Hale, Charles R. (1994) "'Wan Tasbaya Dukiara' Contested Notions of Land Rights in Miskitu History." Pp. 67-98 in J. Byarin (ed.) *Remapping Memory: The Politics of TimeSpace.* Minneapolis: University of Minnesota Press.

Harris, Olivia (1989) "The Earth and the State: The Sources and Meanings of Money in Northern Potosí, Bolivia." Pp. 232-268 in J. Parry & M. Bloch (eds.) *Money and Morality of Exchange.* Cambridge, ENG: Cambridge University Press.

Herrera, Amable (1909) *Monografía del Cantón de Otavalo (Monograph of the Canton of Otavalo).* Quito.

Ibarra, Hernán (1988) "Haciendas y concertaje al fin de la época colonial en el Ecuador (Un análysis introductorio)" ("Haciendas and Peonage at the End of the Colonial Era [An Introductory Analysis]"). *Revista Andina* 6:175-200.

_____ (1991) "La identidad devaluada de los 'Modern Indians'" ("The Devalued Identity of the 'Modern Indians'"). Pp. 319-349 in J. Almeida (ed.) *Indios: Una Reflexión Sobre el Levantamiento Indígena de 1990 (Indians: A Reflection About the Indigenous Uprising of 1990).* Quito: ILDIS/El Duende/Abya-Yala.

Isbell, Billie Jean (1977) *To Defend Ourselves: Ecology and Ritual in Andean Community.* Austin: University of Texas Press.

Joseph, G., and Daniel Nugent, eds. (1994) *Everyday Forms of State Formation: Revolution and the Negotiation of Rule in Modern Mexico.* Durham, NC: Duke University Press.

Klein, Herbert (1982) "Peasant Response to the Market and the Land Question in the 18th and 19th Century Bolivia." *Nova Americana* 5:103-133.

Lambert, Jacques (1971) "Responsibility of the Latifundios for Lags in Social Development." Pp. 60-70 in J. Martz (ed.) *The Dynamics of Change in Latin American Politics.* Englewood Cliffs, NJ: Prentice Hall.

Langer, Erick (1990) "Andean Rituals of Revolt: The Chayanta Rebellion of 1927." *Ethnohistory* 37:227-253.

Larson, Brooke (1988) *Colonialism and Agrarian Transformation in Bolivia: Cochabamba, 1550-1900.* Princeton: Princeton University Press.

Lazarus-Black, Mindie, and Susan Hirsch (1994) "Introduction/Performance and Paradox: Exploring Law's Role in Hegemony and Resistance." Pp. 1-31 in M. Lazarus-Black & S. Hirsch (eds.) *Contested States: Law Hegemony and Resistance.* New York: Routledge.

Lopéz-Ocón, Leoncio (1986) "Etnogénesis y rebeldía andina: La sublevación de Fernando Daquilema en la Provincia del Chimborazo en 1871" ("Ethnogenesis and Andean Rebellion: The Revolt of Fernando Daquilema in Chimborazo Province in 1871"). *Boletín Americanista* 36:113-133.

Mallon, Florencia (1983) *The Defense of Community in Peru's Central Highlands: Peasant Struggle and Capitalist Transition, 1860-1940.* Princeton, NJ: Princeton University Press.

Marchán Romero, Carlos (1983) "El panorama agrario de la Sierra centro-norte (1550-1982)" ("The Agrarian Panorama in the Northern-central Highlands [1550-1982]"). In F. Avila Paredes (ed.) *Economía Ecuador: 1830-1980 (Ecuadorian Economy: 1830-1980).* Quito: Corporación Editora Nacional.

Mayer, Enrique (1985) "Production Zones." Pp. 45-84 in S. Masuda, I. Shimada, & C. Morris (eds.) *Andean Ecology and Civilization.* Tokyo: University of Tokyo Press.

Merry, Sally Engle (1992) "Anthropology, Law, and Transnational Processes." *Annual Review of Anthropology* 21:357-379.

Meier, Peter (1984) "Continuity and Change in Peasant Household Production: The Spinners and Knitters of Carabuela, Northern Ecuador." *Canadian Review of Sociology and Anthropology* 21: 431-448.

Meisch, Lynn (1987) *Otavalo: Weaving, Costume and the Market.* Quito: Libri Mundi.

Minchom, Martín (1986) "La evolución demográfica del Ecuador en el siglo XVII" ("The Demographic Evolution of Ecuador in the 17th Century"). *Cultura* 24b:459-479.

Moreno Yánez, Segundo (1978) *Sublevaciones Indígenas en la Audiencia de Quito (Indigenous Rebellions in the Audiencia of Quito).* Quito: Ediciones de la Universidad Católica.

Moscoso, Martha (1989) "Comunidad, autoridad indígena y poder republicano en el siglo XIX" ("Community, Indigenous Authority and Republican Power in the 19th Century"). *Revista Andina* 7:481-499.

_____ (1991) "La tierra: espacio de conflicto y relación entre el Estado y la comunidad en el siglo XIX" (Land: Space of Conflict and Relation between the State and the Community"). Pp. 367-390 in H. Bonilla (ed.) *Los Andes en la Encrucijada: Indios, Comunidades y Estado en el*

Siglo XIX (The Andes at the Crossroads: Indians, Communities, and State in the 19th Century).
Quito: Ediciones Libri Mundi/FLACSO.

Nader, Laura (1989) "The Crown, the Colonists, and the Course of Zapotec Village Law." Pp. 320-344
in J. Starr and J. Collier (eds.) *History and Power in the Study of Law: New Directions in Legal
Anthropology.* Ithaca, NY: Cornell University Press.

Nash, June (1979) *We Eat the Mines and the Mines Eat Us: Dependency and Exploitation in Bolivian
Tin Mines.* New York: Columbia University Press.

Nugent, David (1994) "Building the State, Making the Nation: The Bases and Limits of State Centralization in 'Modern' Peru." *American Anthropologist* 96:333-369.

——— (1998) "The Morality of Modernity and the Travails of Tradition: Nationhood and the Subaltern in Northern Peru." *Critique of Anthropology* 18:7-33.

Nugent, Daniel, and Ana María Alonso (1994) "Multiple Selective Traditions in Agrarian Reform and
Agrarian Struggle: Popular Culture and State Formation in the *Ejido* of Namiquipa, Chihua-
hua." Pp. 209-243 in G. Joseph & D. Nugent (eds.) *Everyday Forms of State Formation: Revolution and the Negotiation of Rule in Modern Mexico.* Durham, NC: Duke University Press.

Palomeque, Silvia (1991) "Estado y comunidad en la región de Cuenca en el siglo XIX: Las autori-
dades indígenas y su relación con el Estado" ("State and Community in the Cuenca Region in
the 19th Century: Indigenous Authorities and Their Relationship with the State"). Pp. 391-417
in H. Bonilla (ed.) *Los Andes en la Encrucijada: Indios, Comunidades, y Estado en el Siglo XIX
(The Andes at the Crossroads: Indians, Communities, and State in the 19th Century).* Quito:
Ediciones Libri Mundi/FLACSO.

Parsons, Elsie Clews (1945) *Peguche, Canton of Otavalo, Province of Imbabura, Ecuador: A Study of
Andean Indians.* Chicago: University of Chicago Press.

Pearse, Andrew (1975) *The Latin American Peasant.* London: Frank Cass.

Platt, Tristan (1982) *Estado boliviano y ayllu andino: Tierra y tributo en el norte de Potosí (The Bolivian State and the Andean Ayllu: Land and Tribute in the North of Potosí).* Lima: Instituto de
Estudios Peruanos.

Poole, Deborah, ed. (1994a) *Unruly Order: Violence, Power, and Cultural Identity in the High Provinces of Southern Peru.* Boulder, CO: Westview.

——— (1994b) "Introduction: Anthropological Perspectives on Violence and Culture--A View from
the Peruvian High Provinces." Pp. 1-30 in D. Poole (ed.) in *Unruly Order: Violence, Power, and
Cultural Identity in the High Provinces of Southern Peru.* Boulder: Westview.

Quintero López, Rafael (1986) "El estado terrateniente del Ecuador (1809-1895)" ("The Landowner
State in Ecuador [1809-1895]"). Pp. 398-417 in J.P. Deler & Y. Saint-Geours (eds.) *Estados y
Naciones en los Andes, Volumen 2 (States and Nations in the Andes, Volume 2).* Lima: IEP/
IFEA.

Ramón, Galo (1986) "Del cacicazgo andino a la hacienda: La transformación del espacio productivo
en Cayambe" ("From Andean Chiefdoms to the Hacienda: The Transformation of Productive
Space in Cayambe"). *Cultura* 8:639-654.

——— (1991a) "Indios, tierra y modernización: Cayambe, Ecuador" ("Indians, Land, and Modernization"). Pp. 157-210 in I. González Aguirre (ed.) *Los Campesinos en el Proceso Latinoamer-
icano de los Años Ochenta y Sus Perspectivas (Peasants in the Latin American Process of the
80s and Their Perspectives).* Cuenca, Ecuador: IDIS.

——— (1991b) "Los indios y la constitución del Estado nacional" ("Indians and the Constitution of
the Nation-State"). Pp. 419-455 in H. Bonilla (ed.) *Los Andes en la Encrucijada: Indios, Comunidades, y Estado en el Siglo XIX (The Andes at the Crossroads: Indians, Communities, and
State in the 19th Century).* Quito: Ediciones Libri Mundi/FLACSO.

Roseberry, William (1993) "Beyond the Agrarian Question in Latin America." Pp. 318-368 in F. Cooper et al. (eds.) *Confronting Historical Paradigms: Peasants, Labor, and the Capitalist World
System in Africa and Latin America.* Madison: University of Wisconsin Press.

_____ (1994) "Hegemony and the Language of Contention." Pp. 355-366 in G. Joseph & D. Nugent (eds.) *Everyday Forms of State Formation: Revolution and the Negotiation of Rule in Modern Mexico*. Durham, NC: Duke University Press.

Roseman, Sharon 1996 "'How We Built the Road': The Politics of Memory in Rural Galicia." *American Ethnologist* 23:836-860.

Rosero Garcés, Fernando (1991) "Defensa y recuperación de la tierra: Campesinado, identidad etnocultural y nación" ("The Defense and Recuperation of the Land: Peasantry, Ethnocultural Identity and the Nation"). Pp. 419-448 in J. Almeida (ed.) *Indios: Una Reflexión Sobre el Levantamiento Indígena de 1990 (Indians: A Reflection on the Indigenous Uprising of 1990)*. Quito: Abya-Yala.

Rubio Orbe, Alfredo (1954) *Legislación Indigenista del Ecuador (Indigenist Legislation of Ecuador)*. Mexico, DF: Instituto Indigenista Interamericano.

Salomon, Frank (1973) "Weavers of Otavalo." Pp. 430-449 in D. Gross (ed.) *Peoples and Cultures of Native South America*. New York: Doubleday/Natural History Press.

Sawyer, Suzana (1997) "The 1992 Indian Mobilization in Lowland Ecuador." *Latin American Perspectives* 24(3):65-82.

Schryer, Frans (1993) "Ethnic Identity and Land Tenure Disputes in Modern Mexico." Pp. 197-214 in J. Kicza (ed.) *The Indian in Latin American History: Resistance, Resilience, and Acculturation*. Wilmington, DE: Scholarly Resources Inc.

Scott, James (1985) *Weapons of the Weak: Everyday Forms of Peasant Resistance*. New Haven, CT: Yale University Press.

Seligmann, Linda (1993) "The Burden of Visions Amidst Reform: Peasant Relations to Law in the Peruvian Andes." *American Ethnologist* 20:25-51.

_____ (1995) *Between Reform & Revolution: Political Struggles in the Peruvian Andes, 1969-1991*. Stanford, CA: Stanford University Press.

Sider, Gerald (1993) *Lumbee Indian Histories: Race, Ethnicity and Indian Identity in the Southern United States*. New York: Cambridge University Press.

Siegel, Bernard and Alan Beals (1960) "Pervasive Factionalism." *American Anthropologist* 62:394-417.

Silva, Erika (1990) "Estado, iglesia e ideología en el siglo XIX" ("State, Church and Ideology in the 19th Century"). Pp. 9-35 in E.A. Mora (ed.) *Nueva Historia del Ecuador (The New History of Ecuador)*. Quito: Corporación Editora Nacional/Grijalbo.

Silverblatt, Irene (1987) *Moon, Sun, and Witches: Gender Ideologies and Class in Inca and Colonial Peru*. Princeton: Princeton University Press.

Smith, Anthony (1994) "The Politics of Culture: Ethnicity and Nationalism." Pp. 706-733 in T. Ingold (ed.) *Companion Encyclopedia of Anthropology*. London: Routledge.

Smith, Gavin (1989) *Livelihood and Resistance: Peasants and the Politics of Land in Peru*. Berkeley: University of California Press.

_____ (1991) "The Production of Culture in Local Rebellion." Pp. 180-207 in J. O'Brien & W. Roseberry (eds.) *Golden Ages, Dark Ages: Imagining the Past in Anthropology and History*. Berkeley: University of California Press.

Smith, Richard (1982) "Liberal Ideology and Indigenous Communities in Post-Independence Peru." *Journal of International Affairs* 36:73-83.

Spalding, Karen (1984) *Huarochirí: An Andean Society Under Inca and Spanish Rule*. Stanford: Stanford University Press.

Starn, Orin (1991) "Missing the Revolution: Anthropologists and the War in Peru." *Cultural Anthropology* 6:63-91.

_____ (1994) "Rethinking the Politics of Anthropology: The Case of the Andes." *Current Anthropology* 35:13-38.

Starr, June and Collier, Jane, eds. (1989a) *History and Power in the Study of Law: New Directions in Legal Anthropology*. Ithaca, NY: Cornell University Press.

_____ (1989b) "Introduction: Dialogues in Legal Anthropology." Pp. 1-28 in J. Starr & J. Collier (eds.) *History and Power in the Study of Law: New Directions in Legal Anthropology.* Ithaca, NY: Cornell University Press.

Stern, Steve (1982) *Peru's Indian Peoples and the Challenge of Spanish Conquest: Huamanga to 1640.* Madison: University of Wisconsin Press.

_____ (1987) "New Approaches to the Study of Peasant Rebellion and Consciousness: Implications of the Andean Experience." Pp. 3-25 in S. Stern (ed.) *Resistance, Rebellion, and Consciousness in the Andean Peasant World, 18th to 20th Centuries.* Madison: University of Wisconsin Press.

Taussig, Michael (1980) *The Devil and Commodity Fetishism in South America.* Chapel Hill: University of North Carolina Press.

Thurner, Mark (1989) "Hacienda Dissolution, Peasant Struggle, and Land Market in Ecuador's Central Highlands (Canton Colta, Chimborazo Province)." University of Wisconsin-Madison, Land Tenure Center, LTC Research Paper 99.

_____ (1993) "Peasant Politics and Andean Haciendas in the Transition to Capitalism: An Ethnographic History." *Latin American Research Review* 28(3):41-82.

_____ (1996) "'*Republicanos*' and '*la Comunidad de Peruanos*': Unimagined Political Communities in Postcolonial Andean Peru." *Journal of Latin American Studies* 27: 291-318.

Turner, Brian (1993) *Community Politics and Peasant-State Relations in Paraguay.* Lanham, MD: University Press of America, Inc.

Turner, Victor (1957) *Schism and Continuity in an African Society: A Study of Ndembu Village Life.* Manchester, ENG: Manchester University Press.

Walter, Lynn (1981) "Otavaleño Development, Ethnicity, and National Integration." *América Indígena* XLI:319-337.

Wolf, Eric (1957) "Closed Corporate Peasant Communities in Mesoamerica and Central Java." *Southwestern Journal of Anthropology* 13:1-18.

_____ (1969) *Peasant Wars of the Twentieth Century.* New York: Harper and Row.

Yambert, Karl (1980) "Thought and Reality: Dialectics of the Andean Community." Pp. 55-78 in B. Orlove & G. Custred (eds.) *Land and Power in Latin America: Agrarian Economies and Social Processes in the Andes.* New York: Holmes and Meier Publishers, Inc.

Yarrington, Doug (1994) "Public Land Settlement, Privatization, and Peasant Protest in Duaca, Venezuela, 1870-1936." *Hispanic American Historical Review* 74:33-61.

Zamosc, Leon (1994) "Agrarian Protest and the Indian Movement in the Ecuadorian Highlands." *Latin American Research Review* 29(3):37-68.

PART II

COMMODITIZATION

MORALS OF PRAISE:
BROADCAST MEDIA AND THE
COMMODITIZATION OF JELI PRAISE
PERFORMANCES IN MALI

Dorothea E. Schulz

INTRODUCTION

The *jelis*[1] of Mali were in the past a professional group of negotiators, praise-sing-ers, genealogists, and historians, one of whose functions was to speak for and to help legitimate a family's predominant position in a locality and the rule of the var-ious chiefs. Since Mali's independence in 1962, the jeli musical performances have been broadcast on national radio and, more recently, on local radio stations. Some of the jelis, most of them women, have become highly successful pop stars of national and even international renown. Strongly supported by governmental cultural policies, jeli music is rapidly becoming emblematic of Malian national culture. Often referred to by their French name, "griots,"[2] the pop stars of jeli ori-gin have received much attention in popular and scholarly literature (Hale 1994, Duran 1995). It might seem paradoxical that these pop stars are commonly por-

Research in Economic Anthropology, Volume 19, pages 117-132.
Copyright © 1998 by JAI Press Inc.
All rights of reproduction in any form reserved.
ISBN: 0-7623-0446-4

trayed, especially by Malian intellectuals and scholars, as the epitomy of the alteration of Malian culture (Diawara 1994, Keita 1995). They have, it is charged, lost the authentic knowledge that their ancestors possessed and guarded, and the praise they now bestow on national or local celebrities is a made-up commercial product, degraded by the exchange of praise for money. This portrayal of jeli pop stars resonates with a common tendency to hold money accountable for the cultural and moral decay of Malian society. Malians from various backgrounds, when asked why Malian society today seems so different than it did only 20 years ago, generally start their accounts with, "It is money that has changed everything."

Given the charges of lacking knowledge and of venality, the high success of these griot pop stars as emblematic figures of Malian traditional culture is all the more remarkable. Even more striking is the fact that their most popular songs are those that deplore the negative effects of monetization, that is, the process from which the singers themselves benefit considerably. Admirers of the pop stars react enthusiastically to the singers' nostalgic evocation of a better past. During live performances, when they hear the griot bemoan that "money has destroyed everything," some members of the audience become very excited. As a sign of admiration, they walk up to the stage and throw bundles of money at the feet of the star.

This article seeks to understand the apparent contradiction between the negative judgments that are commonly passed upon these jeli stars and their high prestige on the market of Malian popular culture as well as their spectacular national and international success. The pop stars in Mali, be they of jeli or other social origin, illustrate what could be called the commoditization of a social service. Combined with technological innovation, jeli praise has been transformed into a commodity, yet it retains some features of gift exchange. The transformation of jeli praise from a routine service into a commodity has more contradictory outcomes than we would expect from the comments of people who experience these changes. Depending on the situation, actors will, to enforce their respective interests, represent the public praise of patrons either as a "gift" and sign of friendship or as an activity that has lost its value by its monetization. Thus, to account for recent changes in the characteristics of the services performed by jeli clients on behalf of patrons, the distinction between gift and commodity exchange has limited explanatory value.

The incongruence between actual transformations and people's accounts of them suggests that the tendency in anthropological literature to oppose commodity to gift exchange is due to the fact that scholars have taken at face value people's accounts of the destructive forces of money. This article proposes to interpret people's assessment of social and economic change in view of the cultural meanings in which their evaluations of money are embedded.

MORALS OF EXCHANGE

There is a striking resemblance between the terms in which many people in Mali today explain and evaluate recent economic and social changes, and two traditions in Western anthropological thought. Over the last 20 years, numerous studies of the influences of global processes and institutions on local cultures have interpreted the local consumption of Western media images as instances of the "Westernization" and, by implication, of the distortion of "traditional" local cultures. Several economically oriented studies followed the Maussian (Mauss 1960) distinction between gift and commodity and portrayed gift exchange and commodity exchange as two opposed, mutually exclusive economies (Mauss 1960, Sahlins 1974, Gregory 1982). Gift exchange is seen as embedded in social relations and associated with a spirit of social cohesion, solidarity, and *Gemeinschaft*. Commodity exchange, on the other hand, is thought to be disconnected from social relations and expectations of trust and obligations. According to this view, the introduction of money necessarily undermines the spirit of community and social cohesion. Monetization is equated with commoditization, and both developments are seen as ultimately leading to the alteration of previous harmonic human relationships.

A number of studies have recently challenged this opposition of gift and commodity as two distinct systems of exchange. One prong of this challenge comes in the form of demystifying the romantic notion of gift as the emanation of a totally harmonious community made up of altruistic individuals. Some critics restate a point already made by Mauss but often neglected in later analyses, namely, that these systems of exchange have crucial constitutive features in common, such as economic calculation as the motivating force of economic transaction (Bourdieu 1977:177, Carrier 1995; also see Appadurai 1986:12).[3]

The other side of the critique comes from authors who claim that it is misleading to assume that impersonal and individualistic strategies of acquisition are characteristic of all monetary forms of transaction. While self-driven strategies of economic transactions do exist in non-monetary societies, money does not necessarily imply impersonal exchange (e.g., Parry 1989; also see Parry & Bloch 1989:12-21). Various authors also take issue with the evolutionary and unidirectional assumptions behind the gift exchange versus commodity and monetary economies contrast. The assumption that monetization necessarily brought commoditization with it served as the conceptual basis of many studies of the impact of capitalist and market production on endogenous economies and led to the view of monetization and commoditization as natural results of capitalist encroachment. Critics of this view assert that monetization and commoditization are genuinely distinct processes that are not necessarily linked to capitalism (cf. Parry & Bloch 1989:16). Finally, Kopytoff (1986) has put forward the highly productive suggestion of looking at the ways in which the same object mediates between people at different times and places. His interest in the "social biography" of things provides a powerful argument against the view of commoditization as an irreversible process; things may move in and out of a commodity status.

In spite of these substantial revisions, blind spots remain in the study of commoditization. Even studies that make people's own accounts of economic change a central concern of their analysis (Taussig 1980, Harris 1989) tend to give a too monolithic a view of that development and to underestimate the contradictory currents that underlie a process of economic change. Authors tend to see people's ambivalent feelings and contradictory explanations as reflective of a period of transition to commoditization, rather than as inherent in any process of transformation. My argument is that it is precisely the diversity and the contradictory nature of people's judgments that will allow us to draw a more realistic picture of the multiple facets of a commodity's "social life" (Appadurai 1986) and "cultural biography" (Kopytoff 1986). The second shortcoming is that most authors focus on *things*-as-commodities and neglect cases where *services* are transformed into commodities. In addition to the exchange of physical objects, we need to consider the provision of services. The exchange of services for money is an important element of social life in West Africa, and it is the focus of this article.

Another body of literature investigates consumption in the context of global institutions (Miller 1987) and "global culture" (Featherstone 1990), yet also focuses exclusively on objects. These studies differ from previous interpretations, though, in that cultural and technological transfers from the West are not seen only as instances of cultural imperialism or the distortion of an authentic culture. Instead, they explore the "globalization" of cultures and identities with a more neutral stance and pay particular attention to the domestication of foreign cultural elements and technologies by way of their incorporation into local cultures.

These studies mark an important departure from previous investigations of goods-as-commodities, because they closely investigate commodities from the perspective of their consumption. They offer fascinating glimpses of what happens to Western goods and elements when they are transplanted elsewhere. Beauty ideals, clothing fashions, dance styles, and musical elements are transformed into new cultural products such as "World Music" (Erlmann 1996) or "la sape" (Friedman 1990) and are displayed and rearranged at beauty contests, concerts, and other public occasions (Miller 1992). A few authors show the dynamics triggered by the interplay between technological transfer and long-standing traditions of cultural production (Barber & Waterman 1995), but in that literature, too, little attention is paid to what happens when services turn into commodities. Services have no physical existence, but they have continuity in time if they are provided again and again by the same group of people in recognizably similar form. Whether their commoditization can also be studied as an event in a biography is a topic that has been little explored.

The purpose of this article is twofold. It accounts for the particular ways in which jeli pop stars appropriate media technologies and the idiom of tradition to secure themselves a position in the new market of praise and popular music. The second purpose is to explore one particular phase in the biography of a service: its transition from being a task provided on a regular basis by a client to that of being a paid service and a commodity. Two questions guide the analysis: (1) How does the transition of jeli praise from a non-monetary routine service to a service paid in money affect its value? and (2) How do people explain and evaluate the changes in the relationship between jelis and their patrons?

The great success of jeli pop stars in Mali suggests that electronic media in Mali create favorable conditions for, and go hand in hand with, the transformation of indigenous culture under the guise of preserving the authenticity and dignity of Malian culture. Some performers use electronic media to transform praise into a highly lucrative profession, while presenting it rhetorically as a traditional expression of friendship and attachment to patrons.

THE TRANSFORMATION OF JELI-PATRON RELATIONS OVER THE PAST 100 YEARS

In late 19th century Mande society, jelis, both men and women, performed important tasks of social mediation, conflict resolution, information management, and political legitimation for the rich and powerful families of their locality[4] by acting as public spokespeople, counselors, praise-singers and family historians. At public events, jeli men evoked in elaborate speeches the prestigious origin and legendary past of their patrons, whom they referred to as their "hosts" (*jatigi*).[5] Praise-songs were a genre in which many jeli women specialized: lauding the accomplishments of eminent family members, they presented their patron family's claim to an outstanding political position in the local power hierarchies as legitimate. To that end, jelis would, if necessary, rearrange local history, omitting the less laudible details of their patron family's history. Depending on their economic standing, patrons remunerated jelis with grain, cattle, slaves, and other occasional gifts. Only rich free families provided their dependent jeli families with all the food and housing they needed. Other jeli families cultivated little plots of land.

The jelis' affiliation with patrons did not preclude their having ambivalent feelings towards them, nor did it prevent open conflicts. The constant threat of disagreement was, of course, nothing particular to relations between jelis and free people; it is a typical feature of patron-client relationships in general (Eisenstadt & Roniger 1984:37-39,166-172). Patrons and jelis constantly sought to define the nature of their "friendship" in their own interest, because the exchange rate of services and gifts was never clearly defined. Many free people considered a jeli's praise a mixed blessing, because they knew that the jelis could always damage their public reputation by alluding during their performances to some skeletons in the patron's family closet. Because differences in political power among families of free descent were not defined by rank, free people felt under constant pressure to prove that their claims to political leadership were well-founded. Free people were aware that they risked loosing their jeli clients if the latter were disappointed about their patrons' lack of "friendship." To demonstrate their capacity of attracting followers, patrons publicly displayed their generosity towards jelis, under the gaze of other people of free birth. Jelis, on the other hand, sought to maintain their reputation as trustworthy and devoted clients.

Members of other free families who listened to the jelis' public acclaim of the patron did not always believe what was claimed about the free origin or the prestigious family history of the patron. Nevertheless, people who listened to a jeli woman's praise-song certainly considered it as a jeli's routine service for her patron and as an appropriate way to prove to the public her gratitude towards her patron. Jeli women and men, and sometimes other *nyamakalas* (see Note 1), were the only people for whom it was appropriate to recount historical events and laud individuals in public, although some people of free birth held considerable knowledge of past events and genealogical connections, as well. The latter were able to check the claims of jeli speakers, especially when they had been living together for some generations with the family on whom the jelis bestowed their praise. Yet, even though they sometimes had strong doubts about the jeli's representation of the local history, they would greatly enjoy listening to the rhetoric and musical performance of a skillful jeli.

It is possible that the patron and other free people did not even expect a jeli to tell the truth. To them, what mattered most in a jeli's praise was that it would impress the audience by the compelling force of the music and the words and, thus, enhance the patron's renown. To jelis, in contrast, it was important to assert their credibility and to sustain their public recognition as knowledgable guardians of the past. In public interaction with patrons, the jelis would base their claims to "truthfulness" on the *longue durée* of their alliance, that is, on the fact that they had been the clients and devotees of the patron's family for generations.

With the abolition of slavery, the pacification of large areas of southern Mali under colonial rule, and the imposition of taxes in money, the families of free birth lost in many localities their political and economic power; they could no longer support their client families. Also, under colonial rule, schooling opened up new opportunities for people, including members of formerly subordinate groups, to occupy positions in the colonial and, later, post-colonial state bureaucracy. Many jelis, in particular those living in urban areas, felt abandoned by their former patrons and sought to affiliate with new patrons among the rich and influential. As a result of the social changes over the 100 years, jelis now pursue a wide array of professional activities that are not related to their birth as jelis. Nevertheless, public praise continues to be a valued service in contemporary Malian society. A considerable number of singers have specialized in publicly praising rich and influential individuals at family feasts and, in rural areas, at most events of public importance. Not all of these singers are of jeli origin. Some of them are from other *nyamakala* groups and some are of free origin. Free people and jelis from rural areas call all musicians who have made praise-singing a profession the "new jelis" (*jeli kura*).

Most relationships between jelis and their "patrons" in the capital, Bamako, and in smaller towns have little in common with jeli clientage relations in rural areas.

In the village, jeli-patron relations are based on long-term affiliation, but in the towns jelis may work for "patrons" they have never seen before. At weddings or circumcision ceremonies, jelis show up without being invited and sing the praise of patrons without knowing their family background and history. In Bamako, during public live and broadcast performances, jelis stars frequently interrupt their songs and insert passages lauding particular patrons and other rich individuals whose generosity they are trying to attract.

With the interaction between urban jelis and patrons being reduced to singular occasions in this manner, one constitutive principle of traditional patronage relations has been eroded: the long-term affiliation between clients and patrons and the feelings of mutual obligation connected to it. In town, the audiences cannot be certain that the rich individual on whom a jeli singer bestows her praise is even of free origin. This situation stands in sharp contrast to that of the village, where a jeli woman, in her praise-song, could never unjustifiably claim the free birth of her patron without exposing herself and the patron to doubt and ridicule. Yet, regardless of these substantial changes in the nature of patronage and sponsorship, the jeli singers refer to the objects of their praise as "patrons" or "hosts" (*jatigi*). They do this not only to flatter the targeted person but also to remind them of their obligations towards the jeli who claims client status.

Another crucial difference between jeli-patron relations in urban areas and the rural "model" is that many jeli services in urban areas are paid in money. In remote rural areas, social mediation and reputation management are considered routine tasks that are not remunerated in money. The patrons occasionally compensate jelis who perform this task in kind—a gesture that they call "to give a gift to the jeli" (*ka jeli sòn*). In town, in contrast, jeli services and public praise in particular are paid in money. Anybody who can pay for it may purchase praise. National radio and television, which started broadcasting in 1957 and 1985, respectively, have reinforced this development, because they established a veritable market for public praise. National radio, television, and cassette productions make praise-songs available to a national and even international audiences. Individuals who rose in social rank thanks to recent political and economic changes[6] find it highly desirable, and easier than ever before, to invest large sums of money in the exaltation of their name before a nationwide audience.

THE DEVALUATION OF DEVOTION

These changes have serious implications for the prestige of jeli singers, as well. The new circumstances affect the contents and the symbolic value of jeli services and, in consequence, the social recognition of the performing jeli as a knowledgeable and faithful client. Free people and jelis from rural areas frame their disapproval of the recent changes as a criticism of the "new jelis'" lack of competence and authenticity. They assert that praise as well as any recitation of family history requires the jeli's thorough acquaintance with the patron family. In town, numerous jelis spontaneously bestow praise on rich individuals whom they meet by chance in the street or at a festive event. The jeli might have never seen the "patron" and won't know his regional provenance. Critics of the "new jelis" often complain that such a jeli will, therefore, fail to render the patron's exact family identity, which is usually locally defined. Gifted singers and speakers will certainly impress their audience with their compelling performances, but the same listeners will often assert that the jelis' lack of knowledge is a serious flaw in their praise performance. People who listen to these new-style praises refer to them as "forged songs" (*donkili karabalen*). In situations when listeners doubt that the performing griot and the patron have met before, they will, in private conversations, express their doubts about the griot's assertion to be a trustworthy and knowledgeable client of the patron. Thus, as praise is carried over to new arenas such as concerts and broadcast performances, the loss of credibility of jeli speech diminishes its value. Listeners often assert that the songs of "these new jelis who shout (for money) in town" (*jeliw min bè 'sorio' kè dugu kònò*) are "useless to us " (*Jeli nègèbòlen de do)*" and "no real jelis" (*Jeli yèrè yèrè tè*).

These scathing judgements indicate that listeners declare the current relations between jelis and patrons as debased and inauthentic. The critics also link this state of affairs to an erosion of ethics. This view resonates strongly with how jelis and patrons experience and explain the radical changes in their relationship. In rural and urban areas, many jelis and people of free descent accuse each other of a corrupted morality and selfishness. A central term used in the comments is "ingratitude" (*wali nyuman donbaliya*). Jelis in rural areas and their urban cousins often complain that today's patrons are "greedy" and "ungrateful" because they refuse to appropriately compensate their clients for their services. Free people, on the other hand, present jelis as "ungrateful" and "unfaithful," and claim that "today's jelis" are ready to desert their patrons once they are no longer able to support their clients economically. People of both jeli and free origin tend to contrast their current relationship to former affiliations, which they depict as a true friendship devoid of self-interest and personal acquisition. Clearly, this representation omits the fact that, already in former times, the relations between jelis and their rich patrons were riven with tension resulting from their unequal political standing and differences in wealth, and also from the fact that the exact rate of exchange of services and goods was never clearly or explicitly defined. It is likely that the term "ingratitude" was used in former times as much as today to enforce the partners' respective claims. The present charges also imply that immoral behavior was nonexistent in 19th-century society and that free people of that time had no reservations about the credibility of jeli praise.

However, to dismiss these comments as nostalgic rememberances of a paradise lost would be misleading. The current disagreements between jelis and free people, and the complaints about the partners' ingratitude, do reflect recent changes in their relationship. The comments express people's feelings of instability, as the near disappearance of long-term relationships renders the fulfillment of mutual obligations less certain. Current relations between jelis and patrons are, even in the more remote rural areas, more prone to disagreement and conflict than ever before. The free people's and jelis' frequent complaints about the loss of the old, selfless friendship relations reveal their perception that a central institutional arrangement is no longer operating. Their retrospective idealization of past patronage affiliations is a way of expressing their dissatisfaction with the monetization of services previously performed under the guise of complementarity and friendship.

It is striking how often free people and jelis identify the spirit of money as the source and driving force of these changes and contrast the former practices of gift exchange to the current forms of compensation, which they call "to give money." People of free birth often assert that "it is money that has changed everything. Money has made people greedy. Nowadays, you cannot even be sure that a jeli will stay with a patron, if this patron cannot pay him." Clearly, money has become a master metaphor of moral corruption.

At first blush, these constant references to money seem to resonate with the long-standing tradition in Western thought that links the process of monetization to the degradation of ethics. However, a closer look at the jelis' and free people's assertion that "money has changed everything" suggests that their complaints make a different point and refer to two specific changes that affect their previous relationship: (1) the impoverishment of the patrons and (2) the loss of long-term obligations. The first of these changes is not a necessary outcome of monetization, even though free people and jelis portray it as such. The second change is indeed related to the monetization of jeli services. With the possibility of remunerating the services immediately, a jeli can no longer expect long-term support from the patron. Conversely, a patron can no longer count on, as free people call it, "a jeli's faithfulness." In this sense, the assertion that "money has changed everything" reflects general feelings of increased instability. Long-term obligations of reciprocity and attachment are no longer assured if the services are paid in money, while consumption goods have to be purchased with money. Money symbolizes the incapacity of patrons to support their clients and the clients' readiness to desert their patrons.

People of free birth, when asked about the relevance of the jelis to contemporary social life, often assert that "the times of the jelis are over" (*jeli ka dinya banna*). Not only do jelis no longer pass on the moral values of the community, the "new jelis" have become emblematic of the monetization of social obligations and of moral degradation. Many jelis living in rural areas hold a similar view of their urban cousins, in particular those who have become successful pop singers on broadcast media. Rural jelis often portray the pop stars, whether they are of jeli or free birth, as egocentric, money-driven, and untrustworthy. This criticism reflects the disappointment of jelis living in rural areas who are excluded from the market of praise and entertainment promoted by broadcast media.[7] Rural jelis often make these charges in the presence of their patrons, to contrast their own devotion to the immorality of the griot pop stars and other "new jelis."

THE MORAL LESSONS OF BROADCAST PRAISE

Given these criticisms of the griot broadcast stars, their high popularity among urban and rural listeners appears as a contradiction. Free people who criticized "those new jelis who sing for everybody and who are useless to us" would in another situation point out to me how much they enjoyed listening to what the pop stars told them in their songs because "they give us moral lessons" (*olu bè an'w ladili*). What, then, are the reasons for the great popularity of these broadcast stars? And why is griot praise, in spite of the allegations of the singers' "corruption," a highly sought out service for which wealthy patrons are ready to pay large sums of money?

One reason for the pop stars' success is that they respond to demands for both entertainment and reputation enhancement on the market created by broadcast media. Their songs preserve formal elements of the praise genre, the *fasa*, that jelis sing in rural areas for their patrons. Listeners usually refer to the pop stars' praise by the same term (*fasa*), but they often observe that there are crucial differences between the "authentic" (*fasa yèrè yèrè*) praise and the songs of the" new jelis" that "have no beginning and no end" (*jeli kura fasa—kun t'a la, kan t'a la*), that is, songs without a meaning. Regardless of the alleged emptyness of the contents of these songs, listeners are moved strongly by the often outstanding musical and performing skills of the pop stars. They will explain their preferences for a particular singer with reference to the artist's knowledge of "our authentic songs and ways of playing" (*an'w ka mara donkili yèrèyèrè, an'w ka foli cògò yèrèyèrè*). This means that listeners prefer to listen to musicians who draw on the rhythm, melodies, instrumentation, and texts of songs typical of the locality or region from which they come.

In conventional praise-songs that are today performed in rural areas, a common method of adulation is to present the patron as an exemplary person whose extraordinary accomplishments and ethical eminence everbody should imitate. This flattery is often combined with some allusions to illustrious events or individuals of the family history. The comparison to famous ancestors is a subtle way of exhorting the patron to accomplish remarkable deeds on behalf of the community. Listening to these accounts of the history of the area, members of the patron family and other people of free birth are often very visibly moved. Their enthusiastic reactions show that these performances carry a meaning for all members of the community which goes far beyond the praise of an individual.

The pop stars of broadcast media similarly frame the exhortation and the aggrandizement of their Maecenas as moral advice. They present the patron as an exemplary figure and as a descendant of illustrious heroes of the Mande past. To many listeners, however, the pop stars' public acclaim comes close to mere flattery, because these genealogical connections to heroes of the past are often of doubtful veracity. Even though boundaries between deserved praise and empty flattery could never be drawn clearly or with certainty, this contemporary rearrangement of praise-songs shows clear signs of mere flattery. The arrangement that would endow the praise with acceptability, namely, a long-term relation between the singer and the patron, is missing.

Despite these reservations, the broadcast praise of a patron enhances his public renown. Listeners might feel that the genealogy presented to them is forged, but the mere display of the praise and, on television, the patron's ostentatious gift-giving gesture magnify the patron's reputation. Most people, if they are mentioned in one of the pop star's songs broadcast on radio and television, feel flattered.

Thus, two concommittant processes—the monetization of jeli services and broadcast technology—have promoted the expansion of the previous market for praise. At the same time, some constitutive features of praise have been altered. It has become a commodity, because it is purchased by anybody who is able to pay for it. Yet, the new market for praise and the possibility of purchasing *renommé* put its consumers in a contradictory position. On the one hand, it is highly desirable for an individual that her name will be publicly linked to illustrious personalities of the past. Such a prestigious genealogical connection is particularly important in the current sociopolitical situation in which the real and imagined past serves as a basis for reinforcing positions in national politics (see Schulz 1997). Reputation management in form of praise-songs can be bought with money and presents, and it is available to those who can pay for it. On the other hand, its "venal" character casts doubt on the content of the praise in the eyes of the public. Spectators who follow a public praise interaction may react enthusiastically to the patron's display of generosity—and only a half-hour later cynically comment that the same patron spent much money for "forged" praise. Therefore, there is a paradox in this development. Public praise makes a good reputation; at the same time, it puts the good reputation at risk.

A second reason for the widespread popularity of these broadcast stars is that they articulate the concerns of many people facing the new forces of urbanization, but fashion a musical arrangement that bears strong resemblance to the "authentic" music from rural areas. The entertainment that pop stars offer in their songs and their praise of particular patrons are dressed up in the cloak of moralizing reflections about the degradation of ethics and morality. This theme is part of a wider current discourse in Mali that deplores the difficulties of present livelihood by contrasting it to a nostalgically remembered past. Pop stars of international renown, such as Ami Koita, Kandia Kouyaté and Oumou Sangare[8] bemoan in their songs that money has undermined any basis of trust and love, and that people have become greedy and selfish.

These complaints about the devastating effects of money are usually followed by the singer's exhortation of the patron to demonstrate his generosity. Radio, television, and concert audiences react with great enthusiasm to what appears to outsiders as profoundly contradictory claims. During live concerts, patrons, their relatives, and other member of the audience will cover the stage with money to encourage the singer to continue with her moralizing reflections on the destructive forces of money.

Thus, the griot pop stars, *bricoleurs* of a sort, turn their musical products on the electronic media into a kind of entertainment recasting the traditional idiom. Many pop stars present their praise under the cover of moral education and earn money moralizing about increasing monetization—from which they benefit more than many other groups of society. They draw on widespread nostalgia for times past and morality lost. In this fashion, nostalgia itself has become a commodity. The griot pop stars thus effect change of the "traditional" idiom, at the same time that they contribute to the persistence of this idiom and of "authentic" performance conventions.

CONCLUSION

This article has explored how people in Mali explain and judge a process in which a task performed by clients as part of a gift exchange becomes a service compensated in money. A second purpose of the discussion has been to understand the ways in which broadcast technology contributed to the transformation of an activity from one performed by clients into a paid service. Therefore, particular attention was paid to the ingenuity of some jelis and other musicians who use media technology to their advantage.

One question that guided the discussion was how to account for the contradiction between the common view of jeli stars as emblematic of moral degradation and their outstanding success as pop singers. Supported by broadcast technology, jeli praise has been turned by some musicians into popular entertainment. Along with this recent career change of jeli praise, a veritable market for praise has emerged. The blessings of public praise are less than before tied to long-term obligations between jelis and patrons. The public enhancement of one's name by famous griot stars has become a commodity because it is available to anybody who can pay for it. Paradoxically, however, the monetization of jeli praise erodes the value of public praise. Public *renommé* can currently be purchased by any rich individual, and this fact undermines the reputation of anybody for whom this praise is performed; the patron's claims to a prestigious family origin and to a free birth are fraught with suspicion.

This paradoxical development of jeli praise illustrates that the transformation of a task performed regularly by clients into a monetized market service implies substantial changes in the nature of the service. At the same time, there is an important continuity between the previous praise activities and the current praise performances: public praise continues to put its receivers in a bind. Praise promises a good name to everybody, but it has to be handled with care, because it can bring ridicule and challenge as well.[9]

The second concern of the analysis has been to explore the relationship between social and economic change and its discursive representations by people who experience the change. One question guiding the discussion was how we should interpret the idioms people construct to judge processes of monetization and commoditization, and whether we might take their assertions about the altering force of money as an indication of the actual distortion of social relationships and of traditional culture.

In Mali, people's contradictory statements about the disappearance of patron-client relations point, first, to their own mixed feelings about these changes. Second, they illustrate that there are countervailing tendencies within what appears to be a triumphant march toward the supremacy of the market. The outcomes, commoditization and monetization of some client services, are as open-ended and inconsistent as people's views on them.

The griot pop stars couch public flattery of rich celebrities in terms of exhortation and moral education. They claim that their praise is a sign of "love" and "friendship" and call its monetary compensation a "gift." Yet, it would be misleading to interpret this rhetoric of friendship and love as a mere extortion strategy. Certainly, jeli praise on electronic media and in public concerts has become a commodity, but it has become such while preserving some features that indeed resemble gift-giving. The enhancement of a patron's reputation is not totally devoid of personal relations and feelings, as is the case in the purchase of a car or a pricy outfit. Mutual obligation between patron and singer is still part of the understanding, at least as a pretense, even in the short-term praise encounters. This finding is consistent with the criticisms of any clear-cut analytical distinction between commodity and gift economies, and it corresponds to Appadurai's (1986:11-12) observation that the exchange of goods-as-commodities may retain some gift-like features.

The high success of griot pop stars in combining a new media technology with a nostalgic idealization of the past shows that technological transfer, instead of inevitably distorting "traditional" culture, offers opportunities to actors to transform their routine tasks into lucrative activities, while presenting them as a matter of cultural authenticity. As a side-effect of the emergence of an entertainment market, the nostalgic idealization of times past has itself become a genre and a lucrative activity. Thus, in the setting created by broadcast technology, nostalgia and praise performances take on a new salience, cultural importance, and monetary value in the cloak of cultural authenticity and tradition.

ACKNOWLEDGMENTS

The research on which this article is based was funded by a grant from the National Science Foundation (grant number 9413360), by a Harry Hochschild Memorial Fellowship granted by the Yale University Center for International and Area Studies, and by the Deutscher Akademischer Austauschdienst, Germany. I wish to thank Mahir Saul and Harold Scheffler for comments on previous versions of this article. The article is based on 22 months of field research conducted between June 1992 and February 1996.

NOTES

1.   The plural form of the Bamanan term *jeli* is *jeliw*. Throughout this article, I am treating all Bamanan terms like English words, adding the English plural suffix -s to Bamanan plural forms (e.g., *jelis*). The jelis are among the *nyamakalas*, one of the three categories of personhood of Malian society. In the 19th century, *nyamakala* families lived together with rich people of "free birth" (*hòròn*) and performed special tasks for them. The third category of people were serfs (*jon*).

2.   Many scholars refer to the entire group as "griots" (e.g., Hale 1994). Using the French gloss risks creating confusion, because it hides the substantial differences that exist between modern praise-singers with respect to their social origin, training, and particular skills. Some of these musicians are of *jeli* origin, that is, they belong to the endogamous group of praise-singers who in the 19th century worked on behalf of rich and powerful patron families. Some singers are of free birth but imitate the *jeli* praise style. In the following analysis, the term "griots" refers to the stars who perform at public concerts in town and on broadcast media, regardless of their social origin. "Jeli," in contrast, designates people of jeli origin who perform their tasks of social mediation and praise while living in a long-term clientage relation.

3.   Thomas (1991:14-15) has pointed out that, because gift and commodity exchange are construed by scholars as opposite models, they define each other dialectically and are, thus, mutually constitutive. Carrier (1995: 87-88) rightly notes that Mauss himself was not fully consistent in his distinction between gift and commodity economies, because he observed that gift relations exist in the industrial societies of the West, even though in a concealed fashion: "Et comme nous constaterons que *cette morale et cette économie fonctionnent encore dans nos sociétés de façon constante et pour ainsi dire sous-jacente*, comme nous croyons avoir *ici trouvé un des rocs humains sur lesquels sont bâties nos sociétés*, nous pourrons en déduire quelques conclusions morales sur quelques problèmes que pose la crise de notre droit et la crise de notre économie et nous nous arrêterons là" (1960:148, italics mine).

4.   In the scholarly literature, people of free birth (*hòròn*) are often referred to as "nobles" who alone were able to hold political office (but see Bazin 1982). Yet, the term "noble" is misleading, because it suggests the existence of an aristocracy in 19th-century Mande society. It posits a rank difference between "free" farmers and "nobles" for which, however, no equivalent expression exists in Bamanankan or Maninkakan, the two dominant Mande languages of Mali. *Hòròn* (from Arabic *hurr*,"free") simply indicates that a person is free and not of slave origin. In the 19th century, free families differed considerably in their economic and political standing, depending on their capacity to mobilize people for both agricultural production and warfare. But their different positions in local power hierarchies were not expressed in terms of rank. Political power was usually in the hands of individuals or families who were able to mobilize the greatest number of men in times of war. These families often claimed to be of free origin (*hòròn*). The wealth of the *hòròn* was dependent on the number of their serfs (*jon*), who cultivated fields for them.

5.   Earlier ethnographic literature on the Mande world refers to jeli and other *nyamakala* as "castes," because they are endogamous and because free people attribute impurity and danger to the transformative powers that the *nyamakalas* are said to control. More recently, some authors have pointed out that the term "caste" does not apply to the Mande context, because it glosses over substantial differences between the Indian castes and the *nyamakalas*. Also, by emphasizing the impure and dangerous dimensions of the *nyamakalas'* activities, this term uncritically adopts the views that free people hold of their clients (Hoffman 1990, Conrad & Frank 1995). I have argued elsewhere (Schulz 1996:177-181, 230-232) that even some recent research on the Mande reflects a tendency to overesti-

mate the importance of the *nyamakalas'* "occult" powers. It is likely that these scholars have been influenced by the assertions of some *nyamakala* informants who, in research situations, sought to convince scholars of *naymakalas'* important position in society.

6. A decisive factor that furthered upward mobility was colonial schooling, which made it possible for people of inferior birth to occupy positions in the lower echelons of the colonial administration (Schulz 1997:472-473).

7. Until the early 1990s, the careers of popular musicians started with their discovery by the agents of the national radio station, and the opportunity to make a recording in the national broadcast station in Bamako. Today, it is still easier for musicians from Bamako to bring their musical skills to the attention of influential people at the broadcast station.

8. Oumou Sangaré, the famous singer from the Wassoulou in southern Mali, is of free birth. But her praise and "educational messages" resemble strongly the rhetoric of jelis. The same applies to Salif Keita who, in the international popular press, has been sometimes described as "the griot of Mali" but who, in fact, was born into a noble family in a village near Bamako.

9. A further continuity between the two forms of praise is that both are presented by the singer as a gift, that is, as an expression of mutual attachment and obligations. However, as the previous analysis has shown, this presentation hides substantial differences between the long-term affiliations of previous times and the current short-term interactions between praise-singer and patron.

REFERENCES

Appadurai, A. (1986) "Introduction: Commodities and the Politics of Value." Pp. 3-63 in his (ed.) *The Social Life of Things: Commodities in Cultural Perspective.* Cambridge, ENG: Cambridge University Press.

Barber, K. and C. Waterman (1995) "Traversing the Global and the Local: *Fuji* Music and Praise Poetry in the Production of Contemporary Yorùbá Popular Culture." Pp. 240-262 in D. Miller (ed.) *Worlds Apart: Modernity through the Prism of the Local.* London: Routledge.

Bazin, J. (1982) "Etat guerrier et guerres d'Etat." Pp. 321-373 in J. Bazin & E. Terray (eds.) *Guerres de lignages et guerres d'Etats en Afrique.* Paris: Editions des Archives Contemporaines.

Bourdieu, P. (1977) *Outline of a Theory of Practice.* Cambridge, ENG: Cambridge University Press.

Carrier, J. (1995) "Maussian Occidentalism: Gift and Commodity Systems." Pp. 85-108 in his (ed.) *Occidentalism. Images of the West.* Oxford, ENG: Clarendon Press.

Conrad, D., and B. Frank, eds. (1995) "Introduction: Nyamakalaya, Contradiction and Ambiguity in Mande Society." Pp. 1-23 in their (eds.) *Status and Identity in West Africa: The Nyamakalaw of Mande.* Bloomington: Indiana University Press.

Diawara, M. (1994) "Production and Reproduction: The Mande Oral Popular Culture Revisited by the Electronic Media." *Passages* 8:13-22.

Duran, L. (1995) "*Jelimusow*: The Superwomen of Mali." Pp.197-207 in G. Furniss & L. Gunner (eds.) *Power, Marginality, and African Oral Literature.* Cambridge, ENG: Cambridge University Press.

Eisenstadt, S., and L. Roniger (1984) *Patrons, Clients, and Friends: Interpersonal Relations and the Structure of Trust in Society.* Cambridge, ENG: Cambridge University Press.

Erlmann, V. (1996) "The Aesthetics of the Global Imagination: Reflections on World Music in the 1990s." *Public Culture* 8:467-487.

Featherstone, M., ed. (1990) *Global Culture.* London: Sage Publications.

Friedman, J. (1990) "Being in the World: Globalization and Localization." Pp. 311-328 in M. Featherstone (ed.), *supra.*

Gregory, C. (1982) *Gifts and Commodities.* London: Academic Press.

Hale, T. (1994) "Griottes: Female Voices from West Africa." *Research in African Literatures* 25:71-91.

Harris, O. (1989) "The Earth and the State: The Sources and Meanings of Money in Northern Potosí, Bolivia." Pp. 232-268 in J. Parry & M. Bloch (eds.), *infra*.

Hoffman, B. (1990) *The Power of Speech: Language and Social Status among Mande Griots and Nobles*. Ph.D. dissertation, Indiana University.

Keita, M. C. (1995) "Jaliya in the Modern World." Pp. 182-195 in D. Conrad & B. Frank (eds.) *Status and Identity in West Africa: The Nyamakalaw of Mande*. Bloomington: Indiana University Press.

Kopytoff, I. (1986) "The Cultural Biography of Things: Commoditization as Process." Pp. 64-94 in A. Appadurai (ed.) *The Social Life of Things: Commodities in Cultural Perspective*. Cambridge, ENG: Cambridge University Press.

Mauss, M. (1960) "Essai sur le don: forme et raison de l'échange dans les sociétés archaiques." Pp. 145-279 in his *Sociologie et Anthropologie* (with an Introduction by C. Lévi-Strauss). Paris: Presses Universitaires de France.

Miller, D. (1987) *Material Culture and Mass Consumption*. Oxford, ENG: Basil Blackwell.

———— (1992) "The Young and the Restless in Trinidad: A Case Study of the Local and Global in Mass Consumption." Pp. 163-183 in R. Silverstone & E. Hirsch (eds.) *Consuming Technologies: Media and Information in Domestic Spaces*. London: Routledge.

Parry, J. (1989) "On the Moral Perils of Exchange." Pp. 64-93 in J. Parry & M. Bloch (eds.), *infra*.

Parry, J., and M. Bloch, eds. (1989) *Money and the Morality of Exchange*. Cambridge, ENG: Cambridge University Press.

Robertson, R. (1995) "Globalization: Time-Space and Homogeneity-Heterogeneity." Pp. 25-44 in M. Featherstone, M., S. Lash, and R. Robertson (eds.) *Global Modernities*. London: Sage Publications.

Sahlins, M. (1974) *Stone Age Economics*. London: Tavistock.

Schulz, D. (1996) *Praise in TImes of Disenchantment: Griots, Radios, and the Politics of Communication in Mali*. Ph.D. dissertation, Yale University.

———— (1997) "Praise without Enchantment: Griots and the Politics of Tradition in Mali." *Africa Today* 44:443-464.

Taussig, M. (1980) *The Devil and Commodity Fetishism in South America*. Chapel Hill: University of North Carolina Press.

Thomas, N. (1991) *Entangled Objects: Exchange, Material Culture and Colonialism in the Pacific*. Cambridge, MA: Harvard University Press.

THE TRAGEDY OF COMMODITIZATION:
POLITICAL ECOLOGY OF THE COLORADO RIVER DELTA'S DESTRUCTION

James B. Greenberg

Driving south along the Lower Colorado River toward its mouth (see Figure 1), a traveler sees a vast, barren delta with few signs of vegetation. Strong tides sweep up the river many miles. As water mixes with desert mirages, it is often difficult to tell if you are seeing water or salt flats. While this vista seems "natural" and blends into the harsh desert and stark mountain ranges that border the river, this landscape is far from "natural." Until the beginning of this century, the Colorado River delta was an exceptionally fertile riparian habitat, covering some 3,325 square miles. The upper reaches held thick stands of willow, poplars, cottonwood, and mesquite, with undergrowth and grasses, covering the several-mile-wide, marshy river bottom (Sykes 1937:3-19). The river fanned out across the delta, through an intricate system of waterways, flood channels, swamps, and bayous, and the vegetation gave way to dense breaks of cane, wild hemp, and cattails. Nearer the Gulf, great sloughs and mud flats were covered with extensive fields of wild rice and carpets of salt grass. This swampy jungle was the feeding grounds

Research in Economic Anthropology, Volume 19, pages 133-149.
Copyright © 1998 by JAI Press Inc.
All rights of reproduction in any form reserved.
ISBN: 0-7623-0446-4

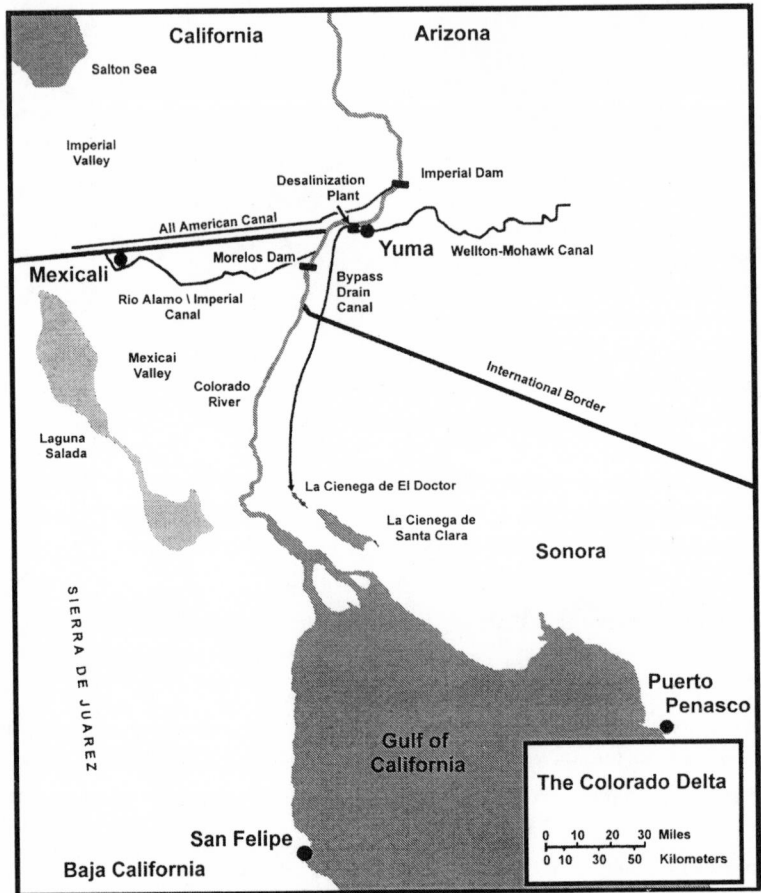

Figure 1.   The Colorado River Delta Area

of many migratory birds, and it supported an abundance of wildlife—javelina, deer, beaver, and species of mountain lion and coyote not found elsewhere (McDougal 1906:10-13).

The story of the destruction of the Colorado River delta's riparian oasis is fairly simple, at least on its surface. The delta was degraded because the Colorado's water was diverted to irrigate agricultural lands and to supply urban consumers. Yet, the history of commodification of the Colorado's water bears careful scrutiny. Its story suggests that destruction of the Colorado's delta cannot be understood in terms of local factors, but must be seen as a consequence of the way the Colorado River is integrated into a larger set of political and economic systems. Ecosystems, in this larger political-ecology, are divided among a hierarchy of territorial entities from local communities to nation-states, and among a variety of local, state, and federal agencies.

While "divide and rule" may be sound statecraft, such gerrymandering of natural ecosystems often leads to poor environmental management. In such political ecologies, poor management is often compounded by the treatment of natural resources as so many individual commodities. The Colorado's history, I shall argue, is the story of what I call the "tragedy of commoditization."

The tragedy of commoditization is driven by a logic very different from that which controls biotic relationships. Market forces put prices on selective parts of the ecosystem without regard to their ecological function or importance, but simply in terms of the demand for such commodities. Moreover, because of the complex ways in which governmental policies and regulations are formulated and enforced, decisions affecting the ecosystem are seldom made by the local populations that have the greatest knowledge and the greatest stake in its preservation. Even when governmental policies and regulatory efforts attempt to strike a balance between the "conservation" of natural resources and the economic interests of various competing groups, these efforts are often either poorly coordinated or have contradictory effects on the ecosystem.

CAPITAL, TERRITORIALIZTION, AND GLOBALIZATION

The political ecology of the lower Colorado River has historically been shaped by dependent forms of capitalism. Dependent capitalism typically relies heavily upon extraction of natural resources to pay for its growth. Because a restricted range of interests drive the bargained transactions in the market, the primary consideration guiding decisions as nature is turned into commodities is a narrow monetary calculus of profits and losses, and not their wider environmental impacts or social costs (McGoodwin 1990:85). Most industrial processes hinge on intensive exploitation of natural resources, and usually they seek quick profits, with little eye to the impact on ecosystems or their capacity to recover (Alvarez López 1988:58). Given this complex picture, we must examine the history of the region's political ecology if we are to understand its current problems. Because such an exposition is demanding, I shall discuss the more general processes of territorialization and globalization of capital and their impact on the environment of modern nation-states (Engel 1989:27, Alvarez Jr. 1994) before tackling specifics.

Territorialization and globalization seem to be opposed concepts. They are, in fact, two halves of the process through which nature is transformed into commodities exchanged in globally integrated market economies. Through the first, states set the "rules of the capitalist game" and attempt to control the assignment of rights to natural resources by imposing administrative and territorial hierarchies (Mann 1993:44-91, Heyman 1994:13-14). This process of territorialization fractures nature into separable commodities and establishes legitimate access and ownership of them.[1] The second process involves the dance of commodities as they enter markets. It is governed not only by the technologies of power imposed by states (Biddick1990:3-4) but, in an increasingly integrated global economy, also by decisions made in distant markets, boardrooms, and halls of power. Since territorialization and globalization are parts of a single process, their effects on local ecosystems are closely related.

Territorialization rarely follows the natural contours of ecosystems. Thus, political entities seldom control all the key elements or parts of ecosystems upon which they depend. As ecosystems are carved up among administrative and territorial units, actions that may be advantageous to one entity may be damaging to another. Where pulverization of an ecosystem is extreme, territorial units may be less and less viable both economically and ecologically. Not only is the physical space of an ecosystem divided among political entities and fractured into kinds of property, the natural resources they contain may even be conceptually divided among various agencies, such that its forests may be controlled by one agency, its wildlife by another, and so forth.

Although agencies attempt to manage their particular resources, the "rational" management of one resource may adversely impact those controlled by others. If territorialization is the first step in the commoditization of nature and is largely a historical product of struggles over scarce resources among contending groups, the second step is globalization of the economy, which ensures that the "capitalist game" is played on a global field (Wallerstein 1974).

Historically, the growing incorporation of local systems into national and world metropoli not only implies growing demands on local resources, but frequently entails a steady loss of local control over natural resources. This process increases the political and economic dependence of local economies on the wider society. Because global capital is constantly searching for higher rates of profit, investments shift from place to place. The result is uneven development in which regions prosper while money is to be made and then are left to languish when profits fall. Globalization also creates a succession of territorializations and reterritorializations as various local, national, and international groups vie to control resources. Exploitation of natural resources, as globalization proceeds, is increasingly driven by the narrow economic calculus of the market or by national economic policies, such as increasing exports to pay off foreign debts. As distant entrepreneurs, powerholders, and even consumers make "rational" economic decisions, little thought may be given to the ecological impact or costs to faraway places.

DEVELOPMENTS AFFECTING THE COLORADO RIVER

A number of events in the mid-19th century opened the door for capitalist development in Mexico and the western United States. U.S. expansion between 1836 and 1856 took vast tracts of territory from Mexico, laying the groundwork for a massive reterritorialization of the west that affected both the Mexican population and many Native American groups.

As pioneers moved west, establishing farms and cattle ranches, capitalist interests moved with them, investing in mining, logging, ranching, and railroads. This process not only created new territorial structures—states and territories, counties and towns—but, because it also created new forms of tenure based on private property with new requirements for title, the land claims and water rights of Mexican and Native American were soon attenuated, reduced, or simply denied. Mexico, beginning in mid-century, also began a massive process of reterritorialization.

Aspiring to foster capitalist development, between 1855 and 1857 the Mexican government passed a series of reform laws to force the privatization of corporately held property belonging to the church and Indian communities. Since few peasants and still fewer Indians had enough money to buy land, rich Mexicans and foreigners bought it at ridiculously low prices when it was put up for sale, creating a new class of large landowners (McHenry 1962:122).

Faced with a foreign invasion, this process went a step further in 1863. To raise money to repulse the French, the government enacted a law to expropriate "empty" lands. Such property was defined as any land not put to public use or not assigned by authorities to an individual or corporation. Using this law, any Mexican citizen could claim up to 2,500 ha of "empty" land in the *municipios* (counties) in which they resided or neighbored (Verdugo Fimbres 1983:15). New legislation was passed in the 1870s and 1880s that further fueled land speculation. In 1875 and 1883, colonization laws were passed to encourage settlement of sparsely populated regions. This legislation granted survey companies large expanses of land in exchange for their services (i.e., surveying land and dividing it into parcels to be sold to settlers). It also promised not only to pay the transportation costs of settlers but to guarantee them the means necessary for their subsistence for one year, if they became naturalized citizens.

During the administration of Porfirio Díaz (1884-1911), survey companies used these laws to take lands from Indian and peasant communities. The result was a radical change in the agrarian structure as small holdings disappeared and large latifundias were created, concentrating most of Mexico's lands into a few hands (Verdugo Fimbres 1983:16-18).

The Díaz administration, disciples of *laissez-faire* and positivism, believed that national economic development could only be achieved by dependence on foreign capital and the feverish exploitation of natural resources. Porfirian development policies not only promoted vast reterritorialization of the landscape but also globalization of the national economy, as foreign capital was encouraged to invest in cattle ranching, agricultural settlement schemes, mining, and railways (Anguiano Téllez 1990:30-31).

Guillermo Andrade, a Mexican living in Los Angeles, California, was among those who took advantage of this legislation. In 1858, he acquired 30,000 ha surrounding the Bay of San Felipe (Equihua Ballesteros 1983:509). In 1874, Andrade formed the Compañía Mexicana Agrícola, Industrial y Colonizadora de Terrenos del Río Colorado (Piñera Ramírez 1983b:334). After passage of the Lerdo colonization law in 1875, Andrade and Thomas H. Blythe, a North American investor, petitioned the Mexican government for land in the Colorado's delta—an area, I should note, that was already inhabited by the Cocopa Indians. The government granted Andrade and Blythe some 136,000 ha in the lower delta.

Following the law, Andrade promised to survey the concession and subdivide it into lots that could be purchased by settlers (Meade 1986:149-151). Andrade obtained concession after concession from the Mexican government over the next 25 years.[2] By 1900, Andrade controlled most of the Mexicali Valley, the Colorado delta from its mouth on the Gulf of California to the international border, and had properties surrounding the Bay of San Felipe and in the Sierra de Juárez in Baja California (Piñera Ramírez 1983b:334).

The key to development of the desert was water. Developers dreamed of turning the Colorado River into the American Nile, and of making the desert bloom. This dream was shared not only by Mexican entrepreneurs like Andrade, but also by American investors who eyed cheap desert lands in California and Arizona.

Dr. Oliver M. Wozencraft, passing through the Imperial Valley in 1849, saw its potential if water from the Colorado River could be diverted to irrigate it. Wozencraft contracted Charles Rockwood, an engineer, to do a feasibility study. Rockwood concluded that it was technically feasible to build a canal on the U.S. side of the border to the Imperial Valley. However, because it would have to cross a long expanse of sand dunes, where an enormous amount of water would be lost, the best option was to construct a canal through Mexican territory and channel the water though the Río Alamo, a natural branch of the Colorado River running parallel to the boundary for some 65 km before reentering the U.S. Wozencraft tried to interest the U.S. Congress and financial institutions in the scheme in 1859, but his efforts amounted to naught (Calleros 1990:7-8).

In 1891, Guillermo Andrade and Manuel Martínez del Río acquired lands along the Sonoran bank of the Colorado and organized the Arizona and Sonora Land and Irrigation Company to irrigate their property. They hired Charles Rockwood to direct the project, and in the winter of 1892-1893, he reconnoitered the district (Verdugo Fimbres 1983:20). The company had difficulties raising capital, however, because of its image as a Mexican-North American company.[3] Rockwood decided, in 1896, to undertake the development of the Imperial Valley on his own. He went into partnership with Andrade, whose land along the Alamo River also would be served by this scheme, and organized the California Development Company (Sykes 1937:110-111, Meade 1986:152-153).

The California Development Company quickly bought up land in the Imperial Valley. By 1898, the California Development Company and its sister company, The Society for Irrigation and Lands of Baja California, respectively petitioned the U.S. and Mexican governments for permission to divert waters from the Colorado River through the Mexicali valley and into the Imperial Valley. They proposed that the diversion canal would have a capacity of 248 m^3 per second and that its waters would be shared equally by both countries.

Although permission was obtained from the U.S. authorities, Mexican officials dragged their feet. Nevertheless, work on the canal began in 1900. Using the old channels of the Alamo River, the canal was completed by the end of the year. By May 1901, some 2400 ha in the Imperial Valley were being irrigated (Anguiano Téllez 1990:37-38). The development of the Imperial Valley went forward rapidly. During 1903, over 600 miles of distributing canals and "laterals" were built, so that by 1904 fully 60,000 ha were being cultivated (Sykes 1937:112). By 1905, over 200,000 ha of land had been opened for cultivation (Anguiano Téllez 1990:43).

The opening of the Río Alamos Canal set off a rush of land speculation and development in Mexico, as well. In 1902, under Mexican law, American investors organized the Colorado River Land Company, which was to dominate the region for the next 40 years (Aguirre Bernal 1983:349). Guillermo Andrade sold his extensive landholdings in the Mexicali Valley to the Colorado River Land Company in 1904. By the end of the year, the Colorado River Land Company and its sister company, the California-Mexico Land and Cattle Company, had acquired some 800,000 ha of land in the Mexicali Valley and lower delta of the Colorado River (Grijalva Larrañaga 1983:350). This land gave the company control over the Río Alamos Canal.

The Mexican government, faced with the canal's de facto existence, granted the Colorado River Land Company the concession to channel waters from the Colorado River through Mexican territory toward the Imperial Valley, and permission to use up to half the water to irrigate its lands in the Mexicali Valley (de la Fuente V. : 1982:76). Between 1904 and 1930, the Colorado River Land Company built some 3,600 miles of levees, canals, and drains to irrigate its Mexican landholdings (Grijalva Larrañaga 1983:357).

The development of the Colorado River was not without problems. In 1905, torrential rains caused a breach in a diversion dike, sending the river's flow through the Alamo River into the Salton valley, creating the Salton Sea (see Figure 1). It required enormous effort to close the breach, badly straining the resources of the California Development Company. The company sought economic aid from the Southern Pacific Railroad, which took it over, and finally managed to return the river to its old course in 1907. Because of the law suits, however, and the financial liabilities involved,[4] the Southern Pacific Railroad allowed the California Development Company to go into receivership in 1909. This receivership was maintained until the Imperial Irrigation District, organized in 1916 under California state law, assumed control (Sykes 1937:119, Meade 1986:155).

Since these events occurred in the midst of the Mexican Revolution (1910-1920), the coordination required by agreements with Mexican holding companies through whose lands the canal passed and the Imperial Irrigation District was fraught with insecurities and difficulties (Sykes 1937:77). As early as 1912, concerns over this awkward arrangement were being voiced by movements in the Imperial Valley that demanded the building of a new, all-American canal across U.S. territory to supply water to the valley (Sykes 1937:121).

Mexico's new Constitution of 1917 served only to heighten these concerns. Article 27 gave the state broad rights to regulate the use of the country's lands, water, and natural resources.[5] This article not only formed the basis for land reform by placing limits on size of property that could be held by individuals or corporations but, just as distressing to U.S. interests, it provided the executive branch the power to nullify contracts and concessions granted by the state after 1875.

Because all the land and irrigation companies formed in Mexico potentially came under Article 27,[6] Americans soon found intolerable the idea that the Imperial Valley was dependent on Mexican water. In the early 1920s, as part of U.S. investigations considering the construction of large storage dams on the Colorado River to control its irregular flow, which threatened agricultural interests, feasibility studies for an all-American (U.S.) canal were also undertaken (de la Fuente V. 1982:77). As a result, when Congress authorized the construction of the Hoover Dam in 1928, it included funds for the All-American Canal as well. The Hoover Dam was completed by 1932, although it was another ten years before the All-American Canal was finished and another two years before it went into operation (Calleros 1990:12-13).

Even before these projects were approved, other political acts were being taken that would affect Mexico's share of Colorado River water. A pact, which is still in effect, was signed in 1922 between upper Colorado River users (Colorado, New Mexico, Utah, and Wyoming) and lower Colorado users (California, Arizona, and Nevada), in which it was agreed that the Colorado's waters would be divided equally among upper and lower users. Mexico was not a party to these negotiations, because relations between the two countries were suspended at the time, so the pact treated the division of the Colorado's waters as an internal matter.

According to this agreement, any water Mexico may be entitled to under international agreement is to be taken from any surplus after its division between upper and lower U.S. users. If this quantity of water proves to be insufficient, equal shares are to be taken from upper and lower users to meet treaty obligations (de la Fuente V. 1982:77-78).

The completion of the All-American Canal forced Mexico to renegotiate its rights to Colorado River water. In 1944, the United States-Mexico Water Treaty was signed, guaranteeing Mexico 1.5 million acre-feet annually, based on the average yearly flow calculated at 15 million acre-feet.

Under the terms of the treaty, the International Boundaries and Waters Commission (IBWC) was given the responsibility to coordinate the river's management. The Commission is composed of two national sections. Each section, headed by a licensed engineer, has an executive staff comprised of two principal engineers, a legal adviser, and a secretary. The commission's responsibilities include regulating boundary demarcation, flood control, water storage, hydroelectric power, drainage works, sanitation and sewage facilities, stream gauging, the diversion of waters, and planning water deliveries according to treaty terms. The commissioners and their executive staff investigate and adjudicate any problems related to these matters. Since these are problems between countries, the commissioners and their executive staff are vested with full diplomatic privileges (Mumme 1993:94-102).

A drought that struck in summer 1945 revealed some weaknesses in the 1944 treaty and put the IBWC to its first test. Although the treaty specified how much water Mexico was entitled to receive, it did not guarantee when it would be delivered. During the drought, following good dam management principles, U.S. dam managers tried to conserve as much water as possible high in the system, and so released only enough water to meet U.S. users' needs. Unfortunately, cutting water off for even short periods can have disastrous consequences for agriculture, and many Mexican farmers in the delta did not get enough water to save their harvests.

When the rains did come, the Hoover dam, already near capacity, released a deluge that flooded thousands of hectares of agricultural lands and ruined thousands more. Because construction of storage dams on the Mexican side was technically difficult, Mexican diplomats returned to the table.

Although this issue was not entirely resolved, an additional agreement was signed between the two countries. This agreement acknowledged that, when annual precipitation falls below 10 cm, any reduction in Mexico's allocation of the Colorado's water makes irrigation of 115,000 ha along the border impossible and damages Mexico's economic interests (Guardarrama 1985:170-71). Because negotiators simply could not agree, another weakness in the 1944 treaty was that it failed to address issues of water quality. Treaty obligations to deliver certain quantities of water were met by mixing Colorado River water with waste waters from agriculture, industry, and urban areas. Over the years, this mixture became not only increasingly saline but increasingly toxic as levels of chemicals and heavy metals rose (Calleros 1990:24).

When the 1944 treaty was signed, the salinity of waters delivered to Mexico was less than 900 parts per million. By the early 1960s, however, because highly saline waters of 6,000 ppm emptied from the Wellton-Mohawk Valley into the Colorado, the salinity of waters delivered to Mexico had risen to more than 2,500 ppm, causing damage to arable lands (Alvarez López 1988:79, de la Fuente V. 1982:79).

The IBWC took up the matter and, in 1965, approved Act 218. In Mexico, waters for irrigation are diverted from the Morelos Dam. Act 218 provided for the construction of a concrete lined, lateral canal, to be built at U.S. expense, that would drain salinated waters from the Wellton-Mohawk Valley in Arizona to a point below the Morelos Dam in Mexico, to reduce salinity to 1300 ppm.

Although the canal reduced the salinity of waters delivered to the Morelos Dam, it did not solve the problem. Mexican farmers and political leaders continued to complain of salinity and damages. The IBWC again took up this issue and, in 1973, signed Act 242. Under this agreement, the salinity of waters delivered to Mexico's Morelos Dam was not exceed an annual average of 121 ppm (de la Fuente V. 1982:97).

To prevent highly saline waters from the Wellton-Mohawk Canal from contaminating subterranean aquifers in the region, the U.S. promised under Act 242 to lengthen the canal from the Morelos Dam to the estuary of Santa Clara, where its saline waters would empty into the Gulf of California. This project was completed in 1977. The U.S. also agreed to build a desalinization plant, the world's largest, with the capacity to treat the 143,000 acre-feet of Wellton-Mohawk water a year (Kishell 1993:709). Under the terms of the agreement, this plant was supposed to go into operation in 1978, but it was not completed until 1992.

Unfortunately, by the time this plant was finished, at a cost of more than 500 million dollars, its expensive method of desalination had become outmoded. Millions more would be required to refit the plant with more cost-efficient equipment. Because the U.S. has been able to meet its treaty obligations by mixing saline waste waters with Colorado River water, the desalinization plant has not been put into operation.

One unintended consequence of lengthening the Wellton-Mohawk Canal was that it created two marshes, La Ciénega de Santa Clara and La Ciénega El Doctor (see Figure 1), where the vegetation native to the delta's wetlands began to flourish, attracting an abundance of wildlife that includes some 80 species of birds and providing some of the few remaining refuges for the endangered desert pup fish (*Cyrinodon macularius macularius*) (Secretaría de Desarrollo Social 1994: 35-40). Conservationists now worry that, if the desalinization plant in Yuma is brought on-line, a torrent of salty brine from Wallton-Mohawk Canal will empty into these marshes and destroy the last remnants of the delta's wetlands.

The problems facing the IBWC suggest that, as ecosystems are increasingly fractured, territorialized, and commoditized, their management becomes not only more complex but more difficult to coordinate, harder to change, and slower to respond. At the international level, management of the Colorado River requires binational agreements. Complex legal and political disputes arise that may involve a host of local, state, and national bureaucracies. For example, in the United States, at the federal level alone, problems affecting the river fall under the Department of Interior. There, they are divided among the Bureau of Reclamations, Fish and Wildlife Service, Bureau of Land Management, National Park Service, Forest Service, Environmental Protection Agency, and even the Bureau of Indian Affairs, where Indian water rights are concerned.

There is a similar host of agencies at the state level with jurisdiction over various aspects of the river. Finally, at the local level, there are a variety of municipalities, counties, irrigation districts, and power companies whose decisions also affect the use of the Colorado's waters. Management in Mexico is equally complex. For instance, at the federal level, jurisdiction over various aspects of the river is shared among the Secretaría de Agricultura y Recursos Hidráulicos (SARH), the Secretaría de Pesca (SEPESCA), the Secretaría de Desarrollo Urbano y Ecología (SEDUE), and even the Secretaría de Marina (Revah & Espejel 1990: 145-147). The solution to ecological problems may require cooperation among local, state, and national governments; as a result, irreversible environmental damage may continue for years despite on-going efforts.

Increasing demands and high costs of the infrastructure and bureaucracy required to divide the Colorado among various users has made its waters a precious commodity. The complex politics decides who gets water for what purpose, when, and for what price—but this is only the half of the story. The other half is the impact on the areas from which water is taken (Waller 1994:16). The hidden cost of taking water from the river has been the drastic metamorphosis of the natural landscape of the lower delta.

DESERT OASIS TO WASTELAND

Since the early 1900s, the ecosystem of the river has been profoundly modified to meet human needs for water, irrigation, and electrical power.[7] The Colorado River over the years has become one of the most regulated rivers in the world. This historic process began with the construction in 1902 of the Morelos Dam to divert waters to the Imperial Valley, and led to the building of the Hoover dam in 1936. A series of other dams have been constructed on the Colorado: Laguna, Imperial, Parker, Davis, and Glen Canyon. In addition, some 117 impoundments have been built on the tributaries of the Colorado in the upper basin alone. These dams and reservoirs have the capacity to store about four times the river's mean annual flow (Andrews 1991:55). In addition, more than 40 diversions systems have been put into operation to export the Colorado's water to adjacent basins (Minckley 1991:141).

As these projects have increased storage or diverted water to other areas, the amount of water flowing in the river has fallen. For example, prior to the construction of the Hoover Dam, the annual average flow measured in Yuma was 15 million acre-feet between 1902 and 1934. After the start of water storage in Lake Mead in 1934, the average annual flow decreased dramatically, to only 4.4 million acre-feet between 1935-1963 (Schreiber 1969:84-85). Because of the extraordinary demand for the Colorado's water in both the United States and Mexico, less than one percent of its virgin flow now reaches its mouth (Minckley 1991:141).

Although choking off the waters flowing through the delta into the sea was a gradual and cumulative process, evidence of ecological changes began to appear early on. Before 1905, the Colorado was a navigable river. Some damage to the willow, poplars, cottonwood, and mesquite groves that lined the river was done by ferry boats, whose steam engines burned wood. In 1905, the entire river flow was accidentally diverted into the Salton basin, where it formed the present Salton Sea. Two years were required to turn the river back to its natural course. In the meantime, silting and plant growth obliterated the former channel, and the river soon ceased to run through a clear-cut channel across the delta (Schreiber 1968:83). By 1909, the erection of diversion weirs at the intake of the Imperial Canal left the bed of the lower Colorado River dry for longer or shorter intervals, depending on the season and the water requirements of the Imperial Valley (Sykes 1937:34).

By the late 1920s, extensive changes were visible in the estuary and tidal flats at the mouth of the river. For example, driftwood from willow, cottonwood, and popular trees that formerly densely covered the flood-plain had disappeared entirely, and "no recently deposited material was found except occasional loose masses of salt-grass, tule roots, and other transitory debris" (Sykes 1937:87). In 1931, a drought struck and dropped river flows far below recorded lows. The Colorado's entire flow was diverted for several months into the Imperial Canal to save the crops in the Imperial Valley. This prolonged action severely affected plant life in the lower delta. Vast areas that usually flooded annually were bare and dry. The wild rice, quelite, and wild flax that normally covered great expanses either failed to germinate or failed to mature. Extensive beds of tules died off. Cottonwoods and other trees perished by the thousands. Even the ribbons of seedling willows that ordinarily line the bars, shoals, and banks of the river were discernably sparse (Sykes 1937:94).

The Treaty of 1944 reduced Mexico's share of the Colorado to 1.5 million acre-feet, leaving little water to flow into the sea. What had been a rich riparian oasis in the lower delta, except for the Ciénega of Santa Clara, became a barren tidal flat and waste land. The delta changed from a positive estuary, with fresh water flowing into the sea, to a negative one with tides carrying saltwater up river from its mouth. Moreover, because of the high rate of evaporation, this tide water becomes increasingly saline as it flows upriver (Hernández-Ayon et al. 1993:593, Barrera Guevara 1992:58, Thomson 1968:106).

The ecological damage to the riparian habitat of the lower delta is but a fraction of the destruction done to riparian systems in the southwest. Damming of the Colorado has led to a process of desertification that has resulted in losses of 90 to 95 percent of riparian habitats throughout the southwest's lowlands (Johnson 1991:189).

Damming the Colorado also affected fauna. The loss of riparian vegetation affected the habitat of many species of wildlife. The delta's peculiar species of mountain lion and coyote disappeared. Of the eight endemic species of freshwater fish found in the Colorado River, four are in danger of extinction. The endangered species of native fish in the Colorado River are the *Gila cypha, Gila elegans, Ptychocheilus lucius,* and *Xyrauchen texanus* (Minckley 1991:131-32). The reasons, however, are not simple. As tempting as it might be to blame the threats to native fish on physical changes in habitat, only two effects of dams seem directly involved: blockage of spawning migrations and depression of summer temperatures of water flowing from deep reservoirs. More important, perhaps, has been the introduction of at least 50 exotic fish that have been either intentionally stocked for sports fishermen by State and Federal agencies or accidentally introduced. Non-native fish have invaded every habitat. These species not only compete with native fish, but some of them feed on their young. Thus, the prognosis for native fish is poor (Minckley 1991:141-149).

The decrease of fresh water flowing into the Gulf of California has also been implicated as a factor threatening the totoaba. Again the story is complex. Totoaba migrate to the mouth of the Colorado annually to breed in its brackish waters, and changes in flow appear to have degraded its spawning and nursery grounds. Between 1942 and 1958, the decline in totoaba catches was correlated with declining, erratic flow of the Colorado River. The relationship between flow and catch for this period suggests some flow-related quality was important to the nursery ground.

Following 1958, though flow varied little, the totoaba catch increased to a secondary peak, but then it crashed. The initial increase was probably due to the establishment in 1955 of a breeding reserve at the mouth of Colorado River. While the reserve offered some temporary relief from exploitation and yielded a fleeting increase in numbers, totoaba continued to be exploited outside the reserve until 1975.

Although there is now a ban on totoaba fishing, poaching continues and endangers the species (Flanagan & Hendrickson 1976:538-540). The schooling of totoaba in the shallow, muddy waters at the mouth of the Colorado River, however, also made them easy prey for fishermen, and overfishing seems to have played a significant role in their decline.

CONCLUSIONS

The destruction of the riparian ecosystem in the Colorado delta cannot be blamed on the local population. The evidence suggests that its demise is the product of a tragedy of commoditization that valued water above all else. Although water might be considered a "common good," this tragedy entails a more complex mismanagement than that envisioned in the "tragedy of the commons" (Hardin 1968).

The problem is not just that some water users have taken more than their share of water, but that the commodification of water made it the basis of the "commons" at the expense of all the less commoditized resources within the ecosystem—fish, wildlife, and trees. Because the price of water does not reflect the costs of the resources sacrificed, consumers do not pay its true costs. In short, cheap water is subsidized by environmental destruction. Such unpriced resources fall outside the sphere of the market and rational calculations of decision-makers interested in water. And, even where such resources fall within an entity's jurisdiction, such as the fish in the river, they are managed independently from its water.

Although damming and diverting the Colorado's water sacrificed its delta's ecosystem to commercial uses, this environmental tragedy is by no means unique. Such tragedies are common wherever the complex processes of territorialization and globalization have wrested control over natural resources away from local communities.

The tragedy, however, is not just that local populations with the greatest stake in local ecosystems are politically marginalized in processes of globalization, but that natural resources are managed not as constituent parts of an ecosystem but as so many separate assets by a host of agencies. The landscape is divided among local, state, and national entities, and control over natural resources is split among various administrative hierarchies in which there is at best little coordination; worse, their policies are often incompatible. What seems rational policy for one resource, often harms another. This kind of mismangement certainly applies to the Colorado River.

If such mismangement were not calamity enough, states are arenas in which competing classes and interests constantly vie for control and, as different groups gain power or influence, policies change constantly. For example, each new administration in Mexico is anxious to make its mark and pay off political debts, each establishes new programs and policies. In the best of all possible worlds, good policies would supplant bad ones. The world being what it is, more often the interests of the powerful are favored over the weak, the rich over the poor, the national over the local, and the short term over the long, without much consideration to environmental consequences.

The process of territorialization that carves up ecosystems piecemeal among administrative entities and divides control over natural resources among a host of agencies is only half of the tragedy of commodity management. The other half lies in the process of globalization as commodities enter markets. Territorialization establishes legitimate access and ownership of natural resources, and thereby transforms them into separable commodities. Once commodities enter the market, they are subject to an alien logic of competition for scarce resources, in which price is not a function of their biotic importance, but simply of competition over their current human utility. For commodities whose price is determined in a local and regional arena, price is closely linked to local supply and demand. By contrast, in larger markets such prices no longer reflect local supplies, but rather the average supply in a national or international market.

This globalization of price fundamentally changes the relationship of the market to the ecosystem. Because commodity price in world markets is no longer tied directly to local demand or supplies, prices are fairly insensitive to local conditions. Moreover, because developing countries need hard currencies to pay foreign debts and buy goods on the international market, they must export their natural resources to earn the required currencies. Because demand for such resources in world markets is seemingly inexhaustible, when world prices are high, there are few incentives to conserve natural resources. The temptation is to make hay while the sun shines. Tragedically, even when world prices are low, because the need for hard currencies is often paramount, developing countries may subsidize and even expand exploitation of natural resources, regardless of the costs to the environment. Unfortunately, as long as natural resources are treated as so many separate commodities rather than as integral parts of ecosystems, tragedies of commoditizaton will remain commonplace.

NOTES

1.   Bundles of rights are entailed in commodities over which the state may exercise control. In the process of territorialization and reterritorialization, the forms of ownership, rights of access, usufruct rights, modalities of transfer, and rights of consumption or destruction may be substantially redefined.

2.   In 1876, Andrade signed a contract with the Mexican government to colonize the Puerto of San Felipe. As part of this effort, he constructed 135 miles of road for the government, running northwest from San Felipe to Real de Castillo (Equhua Ballesteros 1983:509). In 1882, as payment for the road, the government granted Andrade another 205,000 ha along this road (Meade 1986:149-151). In 1891, Andrade and another partner acquired lands on the Sonoran side of the Colorado River. In 1892, the Mexican government granted Andrade yet another concession (Verdugo Fimbres 1983:20).

3.   In 1892, the Arizona and Sonora Land and Irrigation Company changed its name to the Colorado River Irrigation Company, whose goal was to also develop the Colorado Desert of California.

4.   Lawsuits were filed by Imperial Valley farmers who had gone without water and had suffered the loss of crops and income, and by property owners whose lands had been drowned in the Salton Sea.

5.   Article 27 of the Constitution of 1917 established that waters and lands within the territory are the original endowments of the nation. This article not only provided the legal basis for land reform but further laid the legal foundations for environmental planning. It established that the nation has the right at any time to impose upon private property modalities it deems to be in the public interest, such as the regulation of the use of natural resources susceptible to exploitation or appropriation (Alvarez López 1988:67, Gatti et al. 1985:31).

6.   During the administration of Lazaro Cardénas (1934-1940), the lands held by the Colorado Land Company and other companies in the region were expropriated (Murrieta 1985:168). Even so, until 1961 when the Mexican Government finally completed payment for the works constructed by the Colorado Land Company, the Imperial Valley Irrigation District continued to be the owner of the irrigation system in the Mexicali Valley (Calleros 1990:13).

7.   Although the diversion and damming of the Colorado is perhaps the most significant factor that transformed the ecosystem of the lower delta, other human impacts also played a role. For example, during the late 19th century the sternwheelers that plied the river as far north as Yuma cut wood for fuel. In the 1890s, cattlemen also began to run herds in the area, degrading the natural vegetation in the delta and surrounding lands.

REFERENCES

Aguirre Bernal, Celso (1983) "Desarrollo inicial de Mexicali" ("Initial Development of Mexicali"). Pp. 346-349 in David Piñera Ramírez (ed.), 1983a, *infra.*

Alvarez, Robert R., Jr. (n.d.) La Maroma: Chile, Credit and Chance: An Ethnographic Case of Global Finance and Middlemen Entrepreneurs. Manuscript, 1994.

Alvarez López, Juan (1988) *El medio ambiente en el desarrollo económico de la frontera norte de México (The Environment in the Economic Development of the Northern Border of Mexico)*. Tijuana, BC: Universidad Autónoma de Baja California, Facultad de Economía, Cuadernos de Economía, Serie 3, No. 5.

Andrews, Edmund D. (1991) "Sediment Transport in the Colorado River Basin." Pp. 54-74 in *Colorado River Ecology and Dam Management*. (Proceedings of a Symposium, May 24-25, 1990, Santa Fe, New Mexico.) Washington, DC: National Academic Press.

Anguiano Téllez, María Eugenia (1990) "La formación social en el Valle de Mexicali a principios de siglo" ("The Social Formation of the Mexicali Valley at the Beginning of the Century"). Pp. 27-50 in *Historia y Cultura, Vol. VI*. Tijuana, Baja California, Mexico: Colegio de la Frontera Norte y Universidad Autónoma de Ciudad Juárez, 1st Colegio de la Fontera Norte Conference.

Barrera Guevara, J.C. (1992) "The Conservation of Totoaba macdonaldi (Gilbert) (Pisces Sciaenidae) in the Gulf of California, Mexico." *Journal of Fish Biology* 37 (Suppl. A): 201-202.

Biddick, Kathleen (1990) "People and Things: Power in Early English Development." *Comparative Studies in Society and History* 32(1):3-23.

Calleros, Jesús Román (1990) "El revestimiento del canal All-American, una nueva diferencia internacional Mexico-USA" ("The Revetment of the All-American Canal, a New Mexico-USA International Difference"). Pp. 7-39 in *Frontera y medio ambiente, Vol. V (Frontier and Environment, Vol. 5)*. Tijuana, BC: Colegio de la Frontera Norte y Universidad Autónoma de Ciudad Juárez, 1st Colegio de la Frontera Conference.

de la Fuente V., Marco Antonio (1982) "Examen jurídico de algunos problemas de aguas y límites entre México y los Estados Unidos" ("Legal Examination of Some Problems of Water and The Border between Mexico and the United States"). Pp. 59-101 in Gerardo Acevedo Danache & Victor Carlos Garcia Moreno (eds.) *Análisis de algunos problemas fronterizos y bilaterales entre México y los Estados Unidos (Analysis of Some Border and Bilateral Problems between Mexico and the United States)*. Mexico, DF: Universidad Nacional Autónoma de México, Instituto de Investigaciones Jurídicas.

Engel, J. Ronald (1989) "The Symbolic and Ethical Dimension of the Biosphere Reserve Concept." Pp. 21-32 in W. P. Gregg, Jr., et al. (eds.) *Proceedings of the Symposium on Biosphere Reserves, Fourth World Wilderness Congress (Estes Park, Colorado, September 11-18, 1987)*. Atlanta: National Park Service, Science Publications Office.

Equihua Ballesteros, Serafín (1983) "El puerto de San Felipe" ("The Port of San Felipe"). Pp. 507-515 in David Piñera Ramírez (ed.), 1983a, *infra*.

Flanagan, Christine A., and John R. Hendrickson (1976) "Observations on the Commercial Fishery and Reproductive Biology of the Totoaba, Cynoscion Macdonaldi, in the Northern Gulf of California." *Fishery Bulletin* 73(3):531-544.

Gatti, Luis María et al. (1985) *La vida en un lance: Los pescadores de México (A Life of Chance: The Fishermen of Mexico)*. Mexico, DF: Museo Nacional de Culturas Populares, Dirección General de Culturas Populares, SEP Cultura, Secretaría de Pesca.

Grijalva Larrañaga, Edna Aidé (1983) "La Colorado Land Company." Pp. 350-361 in David Piñera Ramírez (ed.), 1983a, *infra*.

Guadarrama, Rocio (1985) "Los proyectos colonizadores" ("Colonization Projects"). Pp. 167-171 in Gerardo Conejo Murrieta (ed.) *Historia general de Sonora: Historia contemporánea de Sonora, 1929-1984, Vol. V (General History of Sonora: Contemporary Historia of Sonora, 1929-1984, Vol. 5)*. Hermosillo: Gobierno del Estado de Sonora.

Hardin, G. (1968) "The Tragedy of the Commons." *Science* 162:1243-1248.

Hernández-Ayon, J. M., et al. (1993) "Nutrient Concentrations are High in the Turbid Waters of the Colorado River Delta." *Estuarine, Coastal and Shelf Science* 37(6):593-602.

Heyman, Josiah (1994) "The Mexico-United States border in Anthropology: A Critique and Reformulation." *Journal of Political Ecology* 1:43-65.

Johnson, R. Roy (1991) "Historic Changes in Vegetation along the Colorado River in the Grand Canyon." Pp. 178-206 in *Colorado River Ecology and Dam Management*. (Proceedings of a Symposium May 24-25, 1990, Santa Fe, New Mexico.) Washington, DC: National Academic Press.

Kishell, Jeffery (1993) "Lining the All-American Canal: Legal Problems and Physical Solutions." *Natural Resources Journal* 33(3):697-726.

Mann, Michael (1993) *The Sources of Social Power, Vol. 2: The Rise of Classes and Nation-States, 1760-1914*. Cambridge, ENG: Cambridge University Press.

McDougal, Daniel Trembly (1906) "The Delta of the Rio Colorado." *Bulletin of the American Geographical Society* 38(1):1-16.

McGoodwin, James R. (1990) *Crisis in the World's Fisheries: People, Problems, and Policies*. Stanford, CA: Stanford University Press.

McHenry, J. Patrick (1962) *A Short History of Mexico*. Garden City, NY: Dolphin Books.

Meade, Adalberto Walther (1986) *El distrito norte de Baja California (The Northern District of Baja California)*. Mexicali, BC: Universidad Autónoma de Baja California.

Minckley, W. L. (1991) "Native Fish of the Grand Canyon Region: An Obituary?" Pp. 124-177 in *Colorado River Ecology and Dam Management*. (Proceedings of a Symposium, May 24-25, 1990, Santa Fe, New Mexico.) Washington, DC: National Academic Press.

Mumme, Stephen (1993) "Innovation and Reform in Transboundary Resource Management: A Critical Look at the International Boundary and Water Commission, United States and Mexico." *Natural Resources Journal* 33 (1):93-120.

Piñera Ramírez, David, ed. (1983a) *Panorama histórico de Baja California (Historical Panorama of Baja California)*. Tijuana, BC: Centro de Investigaciones Históricas, Universidad Nacional Autónoma-Universidad Autónoma de Baja California.

Piñera Ramírez, David (1983b) "Guillermo Andrade." P. 334 in David Piñera Ramírez (ed.), *supra*.

Revah Ojeda, Lina, and Lleana Espejel (1990) "El sistema de áreas naturales protegidas a lo largo de la frontera" ("The System of Protected Natural Areas along the Border"). Pp. 137-163 in *Frontera y medio ambiente, Vol. V (Frontier and Environment, Vol. 5)*. Tijuana, BC: Colegio de la Frontera Norte y Universidad Autónoma de Ciudad Juárez, 1st Colegio de la Frontera Norte Conference.

Schreiber, J. A. Jr. (1969) "Changes in Colorado River Flow." Pp. 83-87 in D. A. Thomson et al. (eds.) *Environmental Impact of Brine Effluents on Gulf of California*. Washington, DC: U.S. Department of the Interior, Office of Saline Water, Resource and Development Program, Report 387.

Secretaría de Desarrollo Social (n.d.) Programa de Manejo de la Reserva de la Biosfera del Alto Golfo de California y Delta del Río Colorado (Program for the Management of the Biosphere Reserve of the Upper Gulf of California and the Colorado River Delta). Mexico, DF: Secretaría de Desarrollo Social. Manuscript, 1994.

Sykes, Godfrey (1937) *Delta, Estuary, and Lower Portion of the Channel of the Colorado River, 1933 to 1935*. Washington, DC: Carnegie Institution of Washington.

Thomson, D.A. (1969) "Resumé of Site Visits to the El Golfo de Santa Clara Region." Pp. 104-109 in D. A. Thomson et al. (eds.) *Environmental Impact of Brine Effluents on Gulf of California*. Washington, DC: U.S. Department of the Interior, Office of Saline Water, Resource and Development Program, Report 387.

Verdugo Fimbres, María Isabel (1983) *Frontera en el desierto: Historia de San Luis Río Colorado (Frontier in the Desert: History of the San Luis Colorado River)*. Hermosillo, Sonora: Instituto Nacional de Antropología e Historia, Centro Regional del Noroeste, Serie de Historias Municipales.

Waller, Tom (1994) "Expertise, Elites, and Resource Management: Resisting Agricultural Water Conservation in California's Imperial Valley." *Journal of Political Ecology* 1:13-42.

Wallerstein, Immanuel (1974) *The Modern World-System I: Capitalist Agriculture and the Origins of the European World-Economy in the Sixteenth Century*. New York: Academic Press.

PART III

WOMEN AS CONSUMERS AND PRODUCERS

CONSUMING WOMEN, PRODUCING MEN:
THE GENDERED CONSTRUCTION OF ELITE JORDANIAN SHOPPERS

E. Anne Beal

Since the early 1970s, which marked the rise of a heightened critical awareness of the importance of gender issues to the study of society and culture, much of the anthropological work on gender relations has been motivated, implicitly or explicitly, by a concern with uncovering the sources and manifestations of what has been frequently depicted as the universal fact of male domination and female subordination. Among the most influential conceptual frameworks for the analysis of gender relations has been that of the separation between the domestic, or private, sphere and the public, or politico-jural domain, with the domestic sphere associated with women, or femininity, and the public sphere associated with men, or masculinity (Rosaldo 1974).

The conceptual separation of men and women into disparate spheres has long occupied a central place in the development of Western political thought as well as in Western definitions of what it means to be a woman. The notion that the private and the public are separate spheres, with each appropriate to a particular sex,

Research in Economic Anthropology, Volume 19, pages 153-178.
Copyright © 1998 by JAI Press Inc.
All rights of reproduction in any form reserved.
ISBN: 0-7623-0446-4

has been of particular salience since the 19th-century development of industrial capitalism and urbanization, which resulted in the increasing separation of men and women in their daily lives, though this separation was never complete, of course, and was most pronounced for the middle classes (McDowell & Pringle 1992:15). The overall idea guiding this imagined separation of spheres is that men govern society, while women govern the homes within it (McDowell & Pringle 1992:15).

Since the early effort of Rosaldo (1974) to introduce the dichotomy of the private/public as a universalizing explanation of sexual asymmetry, the appropriateness of these categories to the analysis of sociocultural life has come under sustained and devastating attack. Early criticisms tended to accept the categories as a valid means of characterizing gender relationships but insisted on the interlocking, rather than the separation, of the two spheres (McDowell & Pringle 1992:16). Other criticisms similarly retained the usefulness of the private/public distinction in sociocultural analysis but emphasized the need to incorporate the historical and cultural specificity of any instance of gender relations under investigation (Rapp 1979:510-511, Rosaldo 1980:400-401).

A later and more damaging category of critiques of the private/public opposition has demonstrated that such divisions are not naturally occurring but are instead socially and culturally constructed (McDowell & Pringle 1992:16). The compelling point raised by these critics is that oppositional categories such as private/public (as well as the related dichotomy of nature/culture) are products of specific Western historical situations and cannot be extrapolated to other settings. What some analysts have taken to be universal categories of sexual asymmetry are historically contingent and, thus, not exportable to all sociocultural contexts (Bloch & Bloch 1980:39, Strathern 1980:179, Yanagisako 1987:104, Yanagisako & Collier 1987:20).

The relevance of the debate over the private/public dichotomy is particularly apparent in turning to the question of gender relations in Islamic societies, where the distinctions between the subordinate world of women and the dominant world of men have been characterized as particularly rigid and pronounced by numerous commentators (Davis 1983:3-5, 171 ff). In her early review of prevailing assumptions about gender in the Middle Eastern anthropological literature, Cynthia Nelson (1974:552) argues that the private realm of women is linked not only with domesticity, but also with narrowness and restriction, while the male world of public activity is associated with politics and expansiveness. Most of the works of Middle Eastern ethnography emerging in the period prior to Nelson's critique employ the conceptual distinction between the social worlds of private women and public men as a major trope (Asad 1970, Barth 1961, Cunnison 1966, Marx 1967, Pehrson 1966). This association of Middle Eastern women with the realm of domestic seclusion is a key component of the invidious stereotyping of Muslim women as essentially passive and obedient to men's demands, whether sexual or otherwise.[1]

Most of the more recent works dealing with Middle Eastern women take as a given the existence within society of women's and men's worlds (Abu-Lughod 1988, 1993; Altorki 1986, Davis 1983, Dwyer 1978, Maher 1974, Makhlouf 1979, Mernissi 1987, Peteet 1991, Sayigh 1994), an unsurprising fact in light of the sharp sexual division of labor and high degree of sexual segregation related to the extreme distinction between private and public that Lila Abu-Lughod (1989: 287-88) notes is popularly associated falsely with the Arab world. Most of these accounts also accept the division of society into private and public spheres of life. The degree of actual spatial segregation of the sexes depicted is highly variable, ranging from the extreme segregation of elite Saudi Arabian urban women (Altorki 1986) to the virtual absence of segregation among the middle class and elite of Lebanon (Joseph 1988:41-42), the crowded lower-class quarters of Cairo (El-Messiri 1978:525), and the middle and upper-class Circassian communities of Amman (Shami 1988).

Yet, while these recent accounts acknowledge the existence of women's and men's worlds, as well as private and public domains, they do not necessarily accept the notion that the private/public distinction is analogous to the opposition between women and men or that the opposition is culturally and historically invariable (Davis 1983:9). Many of these works offer finely nuanced views of gender relations in which the boundaries between men's and women's worlds appear as fluid rather than rigid, demonstrating that the private sphere of women can become highly politicized, particularly in times of war, while the public world of men and politics can become increasingly feminized as more and more women move into public life (Peteet 1991, Sayigh 1994). Other works have demonstrated how women routinely participated in activities of the public sphere, opening up the possibility for exercise of female power in what had previously been taken to be an exclusively male realm (Altorki 1988:63-64, Joseph 1978:541). Other writers have pointed to the importance of women's networks as mechanisms for the exercise of power in a variety of social contexts (Aswad 1974, Maher 1974:22, 48; Makhlouf 1979:43). Within their own solidarity groups, it is argued, women exclude men from a range of contacts which women enjoy among themselves (Abu-Lughod 1985:644, Dwyer 1978, Nelson 1974:559, Makhlouf 1979:25,28).

From this brief discussion, it is evident that there is widespread support among anthropologists that Middle Eastern societies are divided into domestic and public realms, though in culturally and historically specific ways that are always vulnerable to transformation, and that women exert power in both domains. The literature suggests further that a primary source of women's empowerment within the private domain is their ability to exclude men from the domestic world, an argument that is not entirely consistent with the assertion that both sexes participate in both realms. The image of women arising from this literature, in refreshing contrast to the Orientalist conception of Middle Eastern women as passive participants in the structures of their own oppression, is that of strong-willed individuals exerting supreme control over the domestic realm while simultaneously exerting power over many aspects of public social life. At the same time, the most radical critiques of the private/public dichotomy—namely, that the division itself is a product of a historically specific Western European experience and not exportable to the analysis of gender relations in different sociocultural contexts—seem not to have been assimilated within the Middle Eastern ethnographic literature. In other words, quite apart from the fluidity and transformative capacity of the spheres, is the notion of private and public domains necessarily appropriate to the analysis of Middle Eastern gender relations?

Before moving to a discussion of the private/public issue within the context of elite Jordanian consumption practices, some background information about gender roles and assumptions among contemporary Jordanian elites is in order. For the purposes of this paper, I use the terms "elites" and "upper classes" interchangeably to refer to a group of people of either Jordanian or Palestinian heritage living in Amman who possess significant economic resources, typically derived from land ownership, industrial enterprises, commercial ventures, or some combination of these. In general, elites possess significant resources that permit the consumption of luxury items such as villas, exquisite furnishings, copious quantities of clothing and jewelry, private cars, personal computers, satellite dishes, and so forth.

The majority of women, as well as men, whom I queried on the issue of gender relations in Jordan were in agreement with the findings of Jordanian social scientists that indicate an overall strengthening of the social position of women in Jordan in recent years (Barhoum 1987:121). Most agreed that women today participate more actively in social life than did their counterparts of 25 or more years ago, although some elites voiced to me a concern that the increasing prominence of religious fundamentalism in Jordanian life threatened to make inroads on women's rights. Very few of the elite women with whom I worked veiled, and those who did were in their fifties or older. The overwhelming majority of younger women possessed university degrees and in many cases pursued professional careers; most older women, plus a significant number of younger women, devoted their full-time attention to household management. Women of this class enjoyed a great deal of mobility, largely as a result of privately-owned cars, which women of all ages utilized for trips around the city. Sexual segregation was minimal; men and women mixed with relative ease at work as well as in the home and engaged jointly in a variety of leisure activities including restaurant dining, participation in exclusive health clubs, and private parties. In sum, elite women enjoy a great deal of visible independence and autonomy vis-à-vis their male counterparts.

Despite the relative autonomy that elite women enjoy in their daily lives, they nonetheless emphasized to me the fact of female subordination within Jordanian society. The fact of male domination in Jordanian life, from national politics to household interactions, was taken for granted among elite women. Anxiety about male power was often manifested in women as anxiety about harassment and physical assault on the streets of Amman, which could occur "even in the Western neighborhoods." Although not every woman I met voiced strong feelings of resentment toward male authority, the perception of male domination over all aspects of women's lives was a key datum arising from my observations of elite life.

One of the most striking points to emerge out of my discussions with elite women was the absence of a clearly demarcated sense of private and public activity among them with regard to the ubiquity of male domination. In other words, issues of male domination permeated life both within and outside the home; the chronicles of women's confrontations with male authority were presented as forming a seamless whole of social life. Women did not present their experiences to me in terms of bounded spheres, in which the domestic realm, for example, was construed as a realm of relative feminine autonomy in contrast to a public realm of professional and political activity in which their ambitions were frequently challenged by male influence. Rather, all attempts at self-expression and autonomy, whether within the home or the workplace, were viewed as subject to interference by men or women intent on enforcing traditional norms of feminine behavior, necessitating the rigorous and persistent application of hard-headed determination in order to claim one's own right to live according to one's own desires. Thus, the existence of a domestic world in which women exert influence by excluding men, as described in some of the anthropological literature on Middle Eastern women, is not consistent with my findings among elites; men and male influences seemed to be everywhere. The assertion of male authority within the home was taken to be especially galling to women, precisely because of the existence of a prevailing ideology of gender roles within Jordan that suggests that the home constitutes a realm of feminine control.

The second point to be made concerning gender relations among elites is that, although male domination was accepted as a fact of Jordanian life that was unlikely to change anytime in the near future (if ever), the possibilities for resisting this domination were recognized as existing at all levels of society. In other words, the point that women often experience the oppressive forces of male dominion in all spheres of life should not be misconstrued as an indication of passivity on the part of elite women. This point is consistent with much of the literature on Middle Eastern women that emphasizes women's power even within contexts of apparent subjugation. At the same time, the degree of resistance to prevailing gender norms varies widely from one individual to the next; while some women perceive themselves to be involved in a daily struggle for autonomy, others comply with the restrictions imposed on their activities by husbands, fathers, fathers-in-law, and brothers despite their protestations of dissatisfaction with their situation.

Finally, a distinction must be made at times between men and women and male and female roles, even if in the majority of cases biological distinctions coincide with gender roles. Borrowing from Susan Davis' (1983:7) discussion of roles as bundles of rights and obligations associated with particular status positions, I want to suggest that gender roles represent an intersection of the rights and responsibilities deemed appropriate to a particular gender orientation. The male role in Jordan, for example, is popularly associated with the obligation to provide for one's family as well as the right to control the behavior of one's wife and children; the female role is associated with the obligation to defer to male authority as well as the right to have one's material needs provided for. Some men, however, are very open to their wives' assumption of authority both in and outside the home, while some women are particularly resistant to the notion of women's increasing autonomy within Jordanian society, taking steps to brake the professional aspirations of other women. It is evident, then, that neither men nor women always conform to particular gender roles. Some elite women complained quite bitterly to me about the efforts of their mothers to rein in their independent lifestyles, appropriating a form of power (the right to restrain women's behavior) often glossed within Jordan as a prerogative of masculine authority.[2]

The suggestion here that men and women as individuals may or may not conform to masculine or feminine roles is consistent with the findings of researchers working in the fields of sex, gender, and personhood. As Ortner and Whitehead (1981:9) have noted, the axes of gender distinctions are not unique to the domain of gender but are shared with other domains of social life, such that gender distinctions may cross-cut other kinds of identifications, such as those based on sex, creating possibilities for a variety of categories of persons. Recent work on gender and sexuality supports the assumption that the behavior and beliefs that distinguish one as a member of a particular gender category—masculine or feminine— are not the result of biological imperatives but are socially and culturally constructed, so that sex, gender, and person can combine in any configuration (Devor 1989:13). Given the emphasis in recent work on the changing and contextual meanings of sex and gender (Chauncey 1994, Cornwall & Lindisfarne 1994, Tiefer 1995, Lancaster & di Leonardo 1997), it should not appear controversial to suggest here that there are elite Jordanian women who imagine themselves and are construed by others as masculine in their actions and thoughts, just as there are Jordanian men who are identified with feminine roles within the prevailing context of gender assumptions.

I have tried to show in this discussion some of the overarching issues relating to gender roles within Jordanian elite society. Turning now to consumption practices, I will attempt to demonstrate some of the links between consumerism and the construction of gender roles.

CONSUMPTION AND THE CONSTRUCTION OF GENDER

The ideological associations between gender and consumption in Western capitalist societies have been widely recognized. To briefly summarize, capitalist production characterized as "useful, creative, value-producing" and "important" only those activities which took place outside of the home, transforming the ideological construction of the home from a place of productive and worthwhile activity into a sphere of leisure and consumption. The subsequent demarcation of a private sphere of feminine activity in contrast to the masculine domain of public action led to the popular imagination of the home as a place of leisure and consumption, presided over by women whose domestic caretaking responsibilities required little expertise and were of little importance, relative, that is, to the productive activities of men (Firat 1994:207). The denigration of the woman's world of private consumption in popular discourse is amply demonstrated by the devaluation of shopping as a feminine and ultimately insignificant pastime. As Daniel Miller (1993:2) argues, the realm of shopping and the realm of political activity, the latter being taken to represent the pinnacle of important activity within the public sphere, have been opposed in the popular imagination of Western nations as non-overlapping terrains.[3]

The association of consumption and, particularly, the work of shopping with women is a critical component in the construction of the female gender role among Jordanian elites. Elite women, even those who work full-time outside the home, are imagined not only to spend a great deal of their time shopping but to thoroughly enjoy the pursuit of consumer goods.[4] The association of shopping with women and women's work is made by both men and women, as is the denigration of this activity as essentially trivial. Upon learning of the subject of my research, for example, men as well as women often volunteered eagerly the names of individuals whom they viewed as exemplifying the stereotype of the relentless shopper; in all cases, these recommended contacts were women. Moreover, the social stigma attached to the characterization of an individual as an avid shopper, even within the context of elite society in which the possession of copious quantities of consumer goods is evidently of central importance to social life, was apparent in the fact that no one, upon hearing of the thrust of my study, recommended herself or himself as a suitable subject. In addition, none of the allegedly avid female shoppers I interviewed were comfortable with their designation as conspicuous consumers; they either rejected the characterization altogether or acknowledged their proclivity to shop as representative of some personal failure or fault.

It is worth taking a moment here to think a bit more about the question of why shopping is devalued among Jordanian elites. One possibility (though one never volunteered by my informants) is that shopping is particularly tedious, mindless, and time-consuming work. Although shopping is often a bit more difficult to manage in Jordan than among comparable classes in the United States—given that the patchy availability of particular consumer goods frequently transforms shopping into something of a scavenger hunt, with shoppers tracking the city's remaining inventory of a particular item on the basis of tips gleaned from family and friends—shopping is frequently an enjoyable and social activity in which two or three shoppers enjoy a pleasant day of travelling around the city, perhaps stopping for a late lunch of pasta and wine. Moreover, the realm of professional activity contains its fair share of tedium and unpleasantness. It is, thus, hard to imagine why the occasionally tedious aspects of shopping, such as standing in lines, should be singled out for denigration.

The argument advanced earlier linking the denigration of the realm of consumption with the valorization of the realm of production within the context of Western capitalist development appears relevant to the question of why Jordanian elites delegitimize shopping. There is little doubt that the shopping activities of women are degraded at least in part because they are as seen as participating in the realm of leisure activity which is compared negatively to the realm of production, identified primarily as the arena of income-generating activities. The criticism levelled by one husband, for example, against his wife's penchant for shopping was that she did nothing but spend money, without any thought about income replacement; she enjoyed the freedom to fritter her day away in leisurely shopping, he argued, only because of his commitment to the sphere of work. For this man, a Jordanian who owned his own consulting firm, consumption activities were essentially viewed as leisure pursuits, in contrast to his own professional life, which he characterized as demanding and very important, not least of all because he earned a significant income. The creation of income is accorded a higher value than the transformation of that income into the goods and services fundamental to the maintenance of elite status within the community.

Thus, the contrast between income-consuming and income-producing activities forms one component of the ideological construction of shopping as a devalued activity and might even appear primary: after all, isn't it more important to earn money than to spend it? At the same time, however, it is rather obvious that the distinction between earning and spending, and the valorization of the former, is not an adequate framework for the analysis of prevailing views of shopping. Two examples can be marshalled in support of this point. First, many elite women generate income for the household, either through their own professional activities or through the resources they bring to bear as a result of wealthy family connections. Yet, the shopping activities of these income-generating women were generally reviled by their husbands, as well as by other women, in a manner identical to those criticisms made of women who were "only spenders." Second, a variety of resource-depleting activities, such as hunting, yachting, and social drinking in clubs and restaurants, that were often, if not exclusively, associated with men did not carry the same stigma of wasteful unimportance for either men or women as did women's shopping. In other words, the denigration of leisure activities vis-à-vis world of production seemed to apply only for *women's* leisure pursuits.

In general, then, I found that the readily proffered explanations by men and women for the denigration of shopping on the grounds that it was "merely leisure" or that it "wasted money" were not adequate to an understanding of the ideological significance of shopping in elite life. There seems to be nothing intrinsic to the activity of shopping itself that accounts for its negative associations within elite society. What seems to be of greater importance in the ideological construction of shopping among elites is not the activity of shopping itself, but rather the gendered identity of the shopper. In other words, the question of who shops is more important to the analysis of shopping than the question of shopping itself as an undifferentiated practice.

Women's shopping is largely degraded in elite society simply because it is practiced by women. Shopping is deployed within the ideological construction of gender relations among Jordanian elites as one means by which female activity and agency can be subordinated and in some respects denigrated vis-à-vis the valorized sphere of masculine activity and power. As such, shopping and the associations surrounding it constitute a powerful means by which prevailing notions about gender roles and identities are constituted and reinforced throughout the routines of daily life. The ubiquitous smirks and sarcastic remarks directed toward the shopping activities of women by men and women alike reinforce prevailing assumptions about the inferiority and insignificance of the feminine role within elite culture, while the simultaneous dissociation of men from the realm of "mere shopping" reinforces popular notions about male importance and dominion over the "important" realms of life.

As a corollary to Rosaldo's (1974:20-21) trenchant observation—that in all societies some area of activity is always associated either exclusively or predominantly with men and is, therefore, cast as overwhelmingly important—I suggest that those societies that demarcate some sphere of life as exclusively male simultaneously define some arena of activity as overwhelmingly female and trivial. Women's shopping functions precisely as one of the spheres of feminine and unimportant activity which, through its opposition to the sphere of masculine and valorized activity, is critical to the production of gendered meaning within Jordanian elite society.

Moreover, I would argue that the denigration of shopping, which seemed to me, on the basis of casual observation, far less prevalent if not non-existent among lower socioeconomic classes, is peculiarly suited for the reproduction of existing relations of male domination and female subordination among elites in light of elite women's apparent independence and autonomy in relation to women of subordinate classes.[5] As suggested earlier, elite women frequently enjoy a degree of liberty with respect to dress, mobility, and professional autonomy that is lacking among the lower classes. At the same time, however, given the persistence of the ideology of male superiority among the upper classes, the fact of women's successful participation in realms popularly classified as bastions of male power has presented something approximating cognitive dissonance for both male and female elites. To take an extreme but by no means unusual example, how does one continue to construct an ideology of female passivity and subordination in the face of independently wealthy professional elite women who roar about Amman in expensive cars and short skirts on shopping excursions that signal power and status to observers of the social scene? Part of the answer, I am suggesting here, is to label these instances of "power shopping" as nothing more than a manifestation of women's predisposition to trivial indulgence, thus undercutting the significance of elite women's autonomy.

It is worth emphasizing that women as well as men participate in the devaluation of women's shopping. An example of the denigration of the realm of women's shopping by a woman was evidenced in the case of M, an unmarried Jordanian woman in her early thirties who grew up in a wealthy and politically influential family in Amman and spent most of her time managing her newly-formed import company. She frequently complained, during small parties at her minimally-furnished apartment located in a chic West Amman neighborhood, that long hours of work left her little time for any other activities, particularly shopping. "I don't have time to shop," she snapped one evening in response to a friend's tale of the travails of a recent shopping expedition in pursuit of a dress for an upcoming event. "I'm just too busy for that sort of thing. After I work all day, if I have some time in the evening, I'm not going out to look for clothes or things like that." Speaking later with me about her views toward shopping and about consumption more generally, she explained:

> Look, all I heard growing up was shopping. It was so important to look a certain way, for our house to look a certain way....My mother spends the whole day looking for just the right blouse. But, look, I'm not like that, I don't have time for all that silly girl stuff, I want to build my company, be really successful on my own....Look around [the apartment], you don't see a lot of things, just what I need.

M's style of furnishing was quite simple by the standards of elite society. Her living room contained a single small couch and pillows on the floor; her bedroom, only a bed and nightstand. Her dress tended toward understated simplicity; her usual uniform was a pair of khaki pants and a men's type of short-sleeved knit shirt, accented only by a pair of small, gold earrings. At the same time, however, her home's sparse furnishings were supplemented by a CD player, television, microwave oven, and espresso maker, which were not gifts but, rather, items she had purchased herself. Also, her casual clothing style belied her commitment to "quality," which in practice meant that virtually all of her clothes, no matter how casual in appearance, were expensive imports from the United States. It would seem that M, despite her protests to the contrary, managed to find the time to shop within the constraints imposed by her rigorous work schedule. What is of interest here is not the discovery that indeed M participates in the universe of material culture characteristic of her class, but that she characterizes shopping and the consumption of clothing and home furnishings as "silly" and incompatible with the morally significant realm of professional activity.

The stated aversion to the realm of women's shopping by other women was a common sentiment within the upper classes, particularly among unmarried professional women. These women claimed to reject the realm of material goods (despite the fact that they lived extremely comfortably, usually in their parents' elaborately-furnished homes), citing their disdain for elegant and formal dress as a key indicator of their lack of interest in consumer culture. These women, within the context of shopping and consumption, assumed a stereotypical masculine role in their assertion that they were involved with important professional matters and had little time for and even less interest in indulging in leisure shopping. Janeen Costa (1994:6) has suggested that, in societies in which men are primarily responsible for producing outside the home, women who move into the workforce are expected to conform to male ideals of behavior and dress. It appears that some elite professional women's simple cuts of clothing as well as their vehement denunciation of women's shopping and consumption patterns represent a degree of assimilation to prevailing masculine values pertaining to the relative importance of the activities of consumption and production in everyday life.

I have attempted to demonstrate in this section the role that consumption plays in the construction of gender roles among Jordanian elites. The ideological construction of shopping as a manifestation of the relatively trivial nature of women's activities within the private realm occupies a key position in the popular imagination of gender roles. Based on the prevailing assumption that the world of shopping is insignificant and occupied by women, we might expect to find men, as well as those professional women who disparage women's consumption, to be relatively disengaged from the entire world of consumer culture. The example above of M's acquisition of numerous consumer products, despite her disavowal of shopping, suggests that the reality of involvement in consumption is more complicated than popular discourse on the subject might suggest. Perhaps, some might argue, M's propensity to consume clothing and other goods, albeit relatively discreetly, merely goes to prove that all women are, as popular ideology suggests, shoppers at heart. Yet, the images of ubiquitous male domination, even in the allegedly feminine realms of pregnancy and childbearing, that emerged from my discussions with elite women hint at the possibility that the popular characterization of shopping as a realm of feminine authority more or less ignored by men may not correspond to the real-world behavior of men and women. Are elite women in fact able to conduct their shopping trips and make their "trivial" purchases beyond the scrutiny of the male gaze? In other words, although the domain of shopping is a denigrated one, is it at least a domain in which women can exercise some freedom apart from male interference and domination?

MEN'S CONSUMPTION AND THE MYTH OF THE WOMEN'S WORLD

The characterization of the domestic realm as one of relative female autonomy in relation to the ubiquity of male domination that is imagined to exist within the public sphere is a commonplace in the public/private literature. This point is underscored in Rosaldo's (1974:27) original article on the public/private distinction, in which she argues that men avoid the domestic sphere and in so doing avoid "becoming embedded in an intimate, demanding world." Nelson (1974:552), in reference to the public/private distinction within the context of Middle Eastern societies, suggests that, while the home is viewed as the man's property for the purposes of articulating it with the political sphere, the "home is regarded as the woman's for all internal purposes. Her authority in domestic affairs is an established fact." Historically, it is argued, Middle Eastern women have controlled the household (Keddie 1990:91). The basic living comforts of the Middle Eastern home, according to Deniz Kandiyoti (1987:333), are created by women. Women's control of domestic life, regardless of whether or not they are imagined to exert some control over the public arena, is a well-established trope of the anthropological literature pertaining to the Middle East (Altorki 1986:24, Davis 1983:65-66, Shami 1996). Although accounts of male dominion over the material realm of the household, including descriptions of the husband's responsibility for shopping, are not entirely lacking from the literature (El-Messiri 1978:537), the overall thrust of anthropological writings on Middle Eastern domestic life is to underscore the authority of women within the realm of the home.

Given this prevailing view of women as the ultimate power within the household, I fully expected shopping and the consumption of household goods and furnishings to fall within the women's realm, a realm which men would avoid out of sheer indifference. Yet, my experience in the field was at not all consistent with the assumption that Jordanian women control the home and, more specifically, the things in it. I had expected to encounter a private sphere of domesticity in which women reigned supreme; instead, I found a realm better characterized as a site of ongoing struggle between wives and husbands in which opportunities exist for varying degrees of masculine and feminine authority.[6] And far from being an area of relative lack of interest to men, the sphere of household consumption appeared as one in which men frequently asserted their authority.

At one extreme, I encountered elite households in which wives spoke bitterly of their husbands' total control over all consumption decisions. This domination included not only their husbands' careful control over the family finances, but also the selection of the household furnishings in a manner at variance with the wives' own style preferences. N, a Palestinian Christian women in her middle forties, managed a large house filled with Persian carpets, marble floors and, to my eyes, gorgeous dark-wood furniture with elaborate carved designs. Her husband was the prosperous owner of five factories located a short distance from Amman. Upon entering her home for the first time, I commented on the beauty of the things in it. My remark prompted a flood of angry words from N:

> What? This house? Look at the furniture. It's all so dark, I can't see anything in this house, it's like night in the middle of the day. I wanted white furniture, but my husband said, no, we must have black furniture, everything must be dark for his taste. [She sighs heavily.] This is the way things are here. Listen, I'll tell you, the Arab man selects everything for the house, *everything*.

He makes all the decisions in the house. Come, we have a satellite dish, do you want to watch
CNN? Rabin [the Israeli prime minister] is in Petra today!

In another case, S, a Palestinian Muslim woman in her earlier forties who also
managed a large home filled with luxurious things, complained to me that she had
never learned to accept the furnishings that her husband and her father-in-law had
selected for the home, especially the living room sofas and chairs. According to S,
these furnishings were overly ornate and quite "vulgar" in appearance; her own
tastes ran toward "simple things, nicely arranged"—a sharp contrast, she felt, with
the ostentatious furnishings of the men's choosing. But, she continued, there was
nothing to be done about this problem; the man's say in the house is the final one,
and she could do nothing to create a home in a fashion more in keeping with her
own preferences.

These examples of male authority in the realm of household furnishing are suggestive of two points. First, it is apparent that the phenomenon of husbands'
choosing ostentatious furniture over the objections of their wives is hardly consistent with the stereotype of the home as the domain of womanly control. While I
expected to find that men determined the overall amount of money available for
expenditures in homes in which women did not hold salaried positions, providing
their wives with a shopping budget out of the overall household income, I was surprised at the extent to which men were involved in the details of consumption decisions, determining the style and color of a sofa or table, for example.[7] Second, the
image of men shopping for furniture and insisting on certain styles runs counter to
the prevailing ideological association of consumption with the world of women's
trivial activity. Shopping, it would appear, matters very much to men.

In the two cases cited above, it appears that the husbands have predominated in
their efforts to control the material expression of the home, at least from the perspective of their wives, who evince a grudging acceptance of the status quo. This
was hardly the case in all instances of spousal conflict in the consumption realm
that I witnessed in Amman. In many instances, the question of which person was
gaining the upper hand in the struggle to determine the appearance of the household was open; of the myriad battles that occurred within the overall context of
home consumption, some were won by the wife and others by the husband. The
following case study depicts some of the complexities involved in the construction
(both literally and figuratively) of the home by women and men.

THE HOME OF A AND M

Of the many homes I visited during my recent field research, none displayed the
meticulous attention to interior design and decoration more so than the villa of A
and M, a married Jordanian couple in their early forties with two small children.
A, an architect who received her training in Jordan, came from a particularly
wealthy and influential Amman family, while M, an environmental engineer who

received his graduate training in the United States, hailed from a much smaller and much less successful family, described by a mutual acquaintance as rather nondescript—in a city where family name and reputation are important indicators of social status. Popular Western images of Middle Easterners to the contrary, A and M, like so many of their elite compatriots, presented an image of carefully cultivated international chic, sipping tea in casual attire and chatting at ease in fluent English about global politics and their extensive travels abroad.

By any reckoning, the villa was extravagant. The entry was punctuated by an elaborate, hand-carved wooden door, a replica, A explained, of one of the doors of actress Gina Lollabrigida's home, featured in the American semi-popular publication, *Architectural Digest*. The first room, labelled "the stranger guest room" by M, was replete with glittering gilded furniture and served as a sort of holding-tank for visitors who lacked sufficient familiarity to proceed into the interior of the home. Cognizant of my research interest in elite houses, A and M eagerly swept me past the stranger guest room and up the stairs into a series of rooms intended for the eyes of family and intimate friends only. As we proceeded through the house, each room unfolded into a seemingly even more splendid space, adorned with hand-crafted furniture and objects of art. In some instances, the furniture was imported directly from Europe and the United States; in others, the furniture, like the front door, was handcrafted in Amman according to designs featured in *Home and Garden* or other popular Western interior decoration magazines. Throughout the villa, the combined effect of high ceilings and picture windows created light and airy rooms that blurred the boundary between interior and exterior space. Gazing out from the kitchen's floor-to-ceiling windows upon a panoramic view of the hills of Amman, I felt as though I were perched on the side of a cliff, unencumbered by walls or other intervening structures.

Who, I asked, was responsible for the design of this house and for the selection of the great quantity of furnishings in it? "It's her house," said M, pointing to A. "It's not mine. Ninety percent of this house doesn't reflect me." He repeated this last sentence for emphasis, eyeing his wife for her reaction. She smiled at me, as though to say she had heard this all before, but said nothing. M paused briefly and then continued:

> I don't like the things she buys. I like simple things, quality things. She buys and buys, and everything she buys is junk. She would rather buy a plastic dish from Germany for six dinars than a ceramic dish made in Jordan for half a dinar. But we are men ruled by women. I don't care what she does, what she buys. I don't have time to shop. I go to work, I have a busy social life, I am an environmentalist, I have causes that are important to me.

Later, in the car while giving me a ride home, M elaborated on the irrelevance of his wife's consumption. "Women have nothing to do," he explained. "A spends all her time shopping and buying things for the house because she's bored. It gives her something to do with her time. It means nothing to me."

And what did A say to all of this? Yes, she asserted, the design of the house was her own:[8]

> It's my home, I created it. I wanted something light, something with open spaces, so I would always feel that I am outside, in touch with the world. Take the kitchen, for example. When I sit at the table and look out, I feel like I am in a restaurant or a cafe in Europe. A woman spends most of her time at home in the kitchen. And kitchens are usually small and dark, with only a single window over the sink. Here, I am surrounded by windows.

She also agreed that she shopped a lot and enjoyed buying new things:

> It's very boring for a woman here in Amman. After work, I have nothing to do but come home. There are no beaches, no parks. On the weekend in Chicago, don't you go out, go to restaurants, go to cinemas? Most people don't favor those things here. I come home, and I entertain family guests. Sometimes a friend from work. But that's all. It's very boring, a very boring life for a woman. I get bored in my house, so I want new things. This house is not finished, the interior is not complete. But before it is finished, I will change all the furnishings. Because I get very tired of looking at old things.

What should we make of A's consumption habits? On the face of things, A seemed to exemplify the elite stereotype of the unstoppable woman shopper, while M demonstrated the appropriate disregard for the womanly realm of consumption. M's characterization of A's purchases as "junk" (despite the fact that the expensive villa hardly appeared to lack for quality goods) can be interpreted as male contempt for the wasteful expenditure of the family's income on insignificant household goods.

Yet, at the same time, the case of A's shopping raises an intriguing question. A was, after all, a successful businesswoman who enjoyed a great deal of respect within the professional world of "significant" activity; her firm enjoyed a solid reputation for innovative house designs. How was it, then, that a woman who was the owner of a successful architecture firm as well as the mother of two small children, who found time to entertain family visitors as well as colleagues from the office, was characterized both by her husband and in her own words as having "nothing to do" with her time? Reflecting on my own efforts to juggle parenting and graduate work, I couldn't help but gaze upon A with a mixture of admiration and envy for "having it all"—family, friends, and career success. Yet, she asserted that she had nothing to do but shop! In her self-described obsession to purchase newer and newer things, A seemed to exemplify the modern consumer discussed in the academic literature—that perplexing creature of insatiable wants, propelled by the inexplicable and ceaseless quest for new purchases to replace purchases recently made.

Leaving A's professional success aside for the moment, A and M apparently occupied "typical" gender roles within the household: she shopped and arranged the house, and he stayed as far away from the shopping as possible. My initial impressions proved entirely misleading, however. As my conversations with A and M continued, it became apparent that the dynamics between A and M regarding the consumption of home furnishings were significantly more complicated than had first appeared. Despite M's initial protestations that he had no interest in the house, as my tour continued, he increasingly insisted on taking the lead in describing to me key pieces of furniture throughout the villa. Leading me back to the stranger guest room, M pointed to a cabinet and explained, "A wanted American furniture here; she picked it out of a magazine. But I said no. American furniture is junk; it won't last. So I bought this furniture, this Jordanian furniture." Having heard earlier that A bought *everything* in the house, I felt a wave of confusion. "*You* selected this furniture?" I asked M. "Yes, yes," he replied. "It's all good quality. This mirror, for example, it's also by a Jordanian." A interjected, "Yes, but the design is from *Architectural Digest*. I saw the design and I liked it. It's an American design." "Yes, yes, it's an American design, but it's not American," countered M, who seemed somewhat flustered by this tangible assertion of A's own taste in a room whose decoration he now described as completely of his own choosing. "So you didn't buy American furniture for this room, after all," I murmured out loud as I scribbled in my notebook. "Oh, yes I did, I bought it, but I put it in the next room," responded A. "You saw it before. It's very beautiful," she exclaimed. "It's an ugly style," growled M, following us into the adjoining room. "She wanted to furnish the entire house that way, but I put my foot down."

As we moved again through the house, A and M's contests over the acquisition and display of a variety of household objects emerged with clarity. The painting in the living room was something A wanted, not something M liked, and she insisted on buying it because one of her friends knew the artist. The cabinet in the dining room was a gift from M's family, and so it was displayed at M's insistence, but A intended to throw it away. A was planning to buy an imported dining room table, but M went shopping on his own and found something locally-produced that he bought instead. Even the design of the house itself was an issue of contention (although one in which A, as architect, prevailed). "Too many windows," complained M. "Her next house won't have a roof," he remarked curtly, referring to A's penchant for open spaces. "I like windows; they make the house less boring," asserted A. "And, yes," she added, her voice growing shrill, "perhaps my next house will not have a roof!"

"A does all the buying, but I give the OK," M told me later, out of A's presence. Yet, it was clear that he himself did a great deal of the buying, and that in other cases he hadn't approved the purchases that A had made. Far from being a realm of irrelevance which M was happy to leave to the attention of his bored and purposeless wife, the consumption of household consumer goods constituted an arena of ongoing contest between A and M within the context of spousal relations. As I discovered again and again in my interviews of married couples in elite Amman society, the stereotypical view that the woman was in charge of the home while the husband focused on the affairs of the outside world was inaccurate.

It is important to recognize in these struggles over consumption within the home that not all consumption practices are of equal ideological significance within the highly-charged realm of gender contests. A and M viewed their home not as an undifferentiated whole—an entirely private domain, for example—but rather as being spatially segregated according to a scale of familiarity, ranging from those parts of the home deemed suitable for the reception of strangers to those appropriate only for family viewing. While the stranger and the family member represent extreme positions embodying either the absolute lack or absolute totality of familiarity with the residents of the household, degrees of familiarity occupy a continuum rather than rigidly bounded domains, with intermediate possibilities such as that of "friend" existing between the categories of stranger and family. Within A and M's home, the stranger guest room, the most formal room of the home, gave way to guest rooms deemed more familiar and, thus, more appropriate for the entertainment of friends, to the most familiar rooms considered appropriate only for family (or for very close friends who are treated as family). Dinners for business associates and similarly unfamiliar acquaintances were held in the formal dining room, a space identified as more appropriate for "strangers" than for "family," while close friends and family were, according to A, often invited to share a meal in the roomy kitchen, a space deemed more familiar and, thus, more appropriate for intimate gatherings. A and M's bedrooms and the children's bedrooms and playroom, as well as the family's baths, were clearly perceived by A and M as familiar spaces unlikely to be seen by any but the most intimate visitors to the home.[9]

The conceptualization of the home as divided into distinct spaces corresponding to degrees of familiarity was the norm among the elites I knew, with all homes exhibiting formal stranger guest rooms, less formal living rooms, formal as well as casual dining areas, and so forth. Rather than a unitary and private domain, the home is more accurately characterized as a structure of interlocking spaces, with varying degrees of social familiarity.

What is especially interesting about this spatial differentiation of the home from the perspective of gender relations is that the domain of the stranger tends to be identified with men, while the more familiar domains are identified either with both men and women or, in the case of the family realm, almost entirely with women. In A and M's home, it was in the stranger guest room that M initially and most forcefully articulated his determination to decorate in a manner keeping with his preferences. Although A wanted to decorate this room with American-made furniture, M insisted that her furniture be displayed in another room, which was less likely to be viewed by formal visitors to the home. The most heated contests over home decoration between A and M concerned furnishings in those rooms that were the most formal, such as guest rooms or the dining room (where, as mentioned above earlier, M displayed a locally-produced table despite A's preference for an imported one). The overall design of the home, another area of heated debate between the couple, can be viewed as lying within the domain of the unfamiliar, as the house stands in clear view of all passers-by, regardless of their degree of closeness to the family. Conversely, the bedrooms and playroom did not appear to constitute a domain of conflict between M and A. A had decorated these rooms to her own taste, and when I queried M about these rooms, he appeared sincerely indifferent, saying that it was his wife who concerned herself with such matters.

Apparently, then, it was not the fact of A's purchasing any goods for the home that challenged M's authority, but rather the fact of her attempting to control the consumption decisions within those domains of the home identified as masculine that elicited the most strident conflicts. While M apparently imagined himself as the master of the home's "stranger" spaces, A, confident in her own competence as a home designer and decorator as well as a professional broker of style and taste, asserted her own authority in these so-called masculine realms. A's frequent purchases, her preference for styles that offended her husband's sense of aesthetic (not to mention his strong commitment to Jordanian nationalism and, hence, his favoring of locally-produced items over imports) and, most importantly, her determination to display her purchases in rooms of the house in which they would be viewed by all household visitors, both the unfamiliar and familiar, provided an ongoing and tangible reminder to her husband that she was a force to be reckoned with in the home, despite his efforts to relegate her to a realm of irrelevance by denigrating her choice of purchases as "cheap" and "pure junk."

In agreeing with her husband that she really had little to do with her time except shop to ward off boredom, A participated in the prevailing devaluation of her activities, accepting, at some level, the view that, as a woman, her activities were essentially inferior in relationship to the world of masculine professional ambition, social relations, and "causes." Yet, her defiant assertion of her own authority in matters of taste and her corresponding refusal to submit to M's decoration preferences, including his desire for "things that last," clearly indicated that, at the level of practice, she was determined to defy her husband's attempts to place her within a subordinate role. Given her professional stature as an architect, A's assertion of authority in the realm of her own home's design merged with her domain of authority outside the home. Thus, A's and M's efforts to dominate the "stranger" spaces of the home were read by each of them as a struggle over what constituted the appropriate scope of A's authority, both at home and at work. M's irritation with A's power was no doubt heightened by his sense of her superior family connections, although when questioned about their relative family backgrounds, he asserted that her family was not wealthier, only larger.

A and M were by no means exceptional in their conceptualization of the home as constituted by a continuum of domains corresponding with degrees of familiarity. The pattern of male domination of the less familiar spaces of the home (mainly, guest rooms and dining rooms) and female domination of the most familiar spaces (usually kitchens, bedrooms, and family baths) was the norm, with husbands (and often their fathers) selecting furnishings for the "stranger" spaces, despite the opposition of their wives. While women complained bitterly about

their husbands' impositions of decorating taste, it was only rarely that I encountered a woman who stood her ground and rejected her husband's wishes for a particular style of furniture. One exception, an elderly woman who was a successful
writer and shopowner, bragged to me that she made all of the purchasing decisions
within her household without any consultation with her husband, a senior member
of the Jordanian bureaucracy. "I control everything," she beamed proudly as we
walked around her home, her husband remaining in a bedroom because, she
explained, he disliked company. "My husband has a chair, a stool for his feet, and
a television, and that's his entire space in the house—the rest is mine!" she
exclaimed. Upon meeting her husband on another occasion at their home during a
small afternoon party, I observed from his reticence and deference to his wife's
conversation that she clearly appeared the dominant member of the household.
"After all, he's a very thoughtful and quiet man," she explained to me later. "He's
no match for me!"

What conclusions can be reached from these examples in the context of earlier
discussions about the prevalence of the private/public distinction as a framework
for the analysis of gender relations within Middle Eastern societies? As I have suggested through my introduction of the concept of the continuum of familiarity as
an organizing principle of Jordanian elite family life, the dichotomous representation of the home as a wholly private and feminine sphere in opposition to a public
and masculine sphere fails to capture the nuances of consumption practices at
issue here. If we take the home to be private and feminine, how do we explain the
participation of men in the domain of household consumption? The notion that the
division between the private and the public is a valid one but not analogous to the
distinction between male and female, permitting the argument that both men and
women participate in the realm of the home, does not explain a great deal about
the ways in which consumption practices enter into gender contests (Davis
1983:9).

There is yet another reason why we should be wary of employing the private/
public opposition as a framework for interpreting gender relations among Jordanian elites. For Jordanian elites, the notion of the private sphere is associated with
economic activity that takes place outside of the direct control of the Jordanian
state. This realm of relatively autonomous economic activity is imagined primarily as a masculine realm. According, then, to popular usage of the term private
among Jordanian elites, the notion of the private is not at all consistent with a
domain of feminine domination. An interesting comparison can be made here with
Susan Gal's (1997:128) discussion of the oxymoronic rendering of the private
sphere by some Hungarian writers in the 1980's as a celebration of autonomous
male political and economic action, with the key difference between the two case
studies being that the private sphere in Jordan is associated overwhelmingly with
economic and not political activity; the realm of political activity is widely
acknowledged as one of near-absolute control by the regime. The Western concept
of a private domain centered on the home (governed by women) contrasted with a

public domain of political activity (governed by men) is particularly inappropriate to Jordan, where only a handful of people wield political power. If we insist on employing the private/public dichotomy in Jordan, then we would have to say that the monarchy and associated loyalists in positions of political power occupy the public domain, while everyone else, men and women included, occupy the private. This sort of dichotomization, however, will do very little to explain the complexities of consumption practices observed within the households of Jordanian elites. The participation of both men and women in the various domains within the home suggests that a more appropriate way of thinking about gender relations among Jordanian elites is not in terms of the public/private distinction but rather within the context of a continuum of familiarity in which less familiar places and relationships are classified as masculine while more familiar spaces and relationships are classified as feminine.

THE CONSTRUCTION OF THE MASCULINE SHOPPER

Jordanian elite men, as I have shown, are indeed shoppers, yet the world of shopping and home consumption is popularly denigrated by them as a trivial and feminine activity. How, then, do men reconcile their own shopping with the prevailing construction of the activity as feminine within a culture that places a premium upon masculinity? Can Jordanian elite men only occupy the role of consumer, in the words of Nancy Fraser (1989:125), with "conceptual strain and cognitive dissonance"?

The notion that men's shopping is incompatible with the culturally-determined masculine role assumes that there is one predominant cultural image of the shopper—that is, of the shopper as feminine. Yet, there is no reason to assume *a priori* that the image of feminized shopping is the only image available to the members of a culture. Instead, the issue of men's consumption raises the possibility that the construction of the *male* shopper among Jordanian elites is altogether different from that constellation of negative images associated with shopping by women, as suggested by the following case studies.

L, 43 years of age, is an attorney practicing in a law firm in Amman. The daughter of the owner of several luxury hotels in Jordan, L, who is divorced with two children and lives in a house adjoining her parents' home, enjoys a luxurious material lifestyle. Meticulously dressed, typically in designer suits during working hours and chic pant suits in the evenings, she describes herself as obsessed by clothes. Complaining that it is impossible to buy any clothes of quality in Amman, she shops in France or the United States or from catalogues. Yet, despite L's obvious pleasure in selecting and wearing beautiful clothing, she expresses a great deal of ambivalence about her adherence to fashion. She has no choice but to devote so much attention to her appearance, she explains, because she is a woman, and women of her social standing must dress in a certain way in order to avoid gossip. Even her family and her closest friends are continually assessing her appearance; if she went to work one day in jeans, everyone would think she was sick or crazy.

L's consumption of imported clothing is somewhat tarnished, in her own eyes, by her perception of an aspect of compulsion to her purchases. She is, as an elite woman, expected to demonstrate through her dress a relentless attention to quality clothing and current fashion; she perceives very little free choice in this situation. In short, she shops from a position of assumed weakness, of subordination to cultural norms, rather than from a position of power. Her interpretation of her obsession with clothes is rather different from that of the young man in the following example.

B is an unmarried Jordanian man, 27 years old, who works in the Amman office of his father's consulting firm. After receiving his undergraduate degree from an American university, B spent several months in France visiting his sister and "playing around." While living with his sister, he developed a passion for boldly colored French jackets, shirts, and ties. He continues to visit his sister and her family in Paris two or three times a year, taking advantage of these trips to shop for the latest fashions. He enjoys French clothing, he explains, because the patterns are vivid and powerful, unlike the relatively subdued hues preferred by most Jordanian men; when he wears French clothing, everyone recognizes him as someone special. At a large party at the U.S. Embassy in Amman, he revelled in the attention he received from other guests, who commented favorably throughout the night on his flamboyant, rainbow-colored Parisian jacket.

B, it seems, occupies the role of shopper and consumer of expensive imported clothing with little or no "conceptual strain and cognitive dissonance" (after Fraser 1989:125). For B, the consumption of dazzling French clothing represents a tangible assertion of his power and autonomy within the Jordanian social circuit, a far cry from an association of shopping with the trivial world of women's activity. In contrast to women, who were likely to perceive their shopping in negative terms, elite Jordanian men were more likely to construct their personal experience of shopping as an expression of their superior power and social status. This positive valuation of male consumerism is seen within the realm of the consumption of household furnishings, as well, with men such as M (in the extended case study presented earlier) perceiving their participation in the realm of shopping and home decoration as an aspect of their overall superiority vis-à-vis their wives.

In short, the significance of shopping within the context of elite Jordanian society depends very much on the identity of the shopper. *Who* buys and uses goods—and, particularly, the gender identity of that shopper—matters very much in the determination of the cultural valuation of particular instances of consumption. In general, the ideological construction of the shopper is subordinated to dominant assumptions about gender roles within Jordanian society. Women's consumption is construed as emblematic of women's relative insignificance within the culture, while men's consumption is taken as evidence of men's power and authority.

CONCLUSION

We can see, then, from even this brief discussion, the fundamental importance of the explicit incorporation of gender into any analytical framework intended to elucidate the place of consumption within a particular sociocultural context. Consumption plays a critical role in the production of gender ideology and is, thus, intimately bound up with the playing out of relations of power that are implicit in gender roles (Scott 1988:42). Although, as Joan Scott (ibid.) has argued, concepts of gender structure the perception as well as the actual and symbolic organization of all areas of social life, including consumption practices, consumption itself serves to reinforce and at times to contest prevailing gender ideology. The predominant ideology of male domination within Jordanian society identifies women's shopping with the realm of triviality while simultaneously linking men's shopping to power and status. Thus, we see consumption playing a key role in the construction of what it means to be a woman or a man within Jordanian elite society.

Although I have argued that consumption practices are played out within the overall constraints of male hegemony operative within Jordanian society, I have also underscored the fact of contest and opposition surrounding the construction of gender assumptions. I have tried to convey the strength of elite Jordanian women, both in and outside of the home. At the same time, I take issue with the unproblematized link between domestic life and women's power that dominates much of the literature on Middle Eastern women as well as with the assumption that the Middle Eastern social world is comprised of private and public realms corresponding, respectively, to domains of female and male power. Within elite Jordanian society, the home is by no means the special preserve of women, off limits to men who are mostly indifferent to the trivial activities they imagine to occur within.[10] While the experience of elites may be of limited relevance to the exploration of gender issues among other classes, the material presented here suggests a disjuncture between the ideology of feminine domination of the home and the reality of male participation within the household. As a tangible means by which women and men produce and contest gender roles and assumptions, consumption provides a critical window onto the dynamics of gendered struggles for power and domination.

ACKNOWLEDGMENTS

My field research in Amman was supported by a 1995 USIA/NMERTP Pre-Doctoral Fellowship through the American Center of Oriental Research in Amman and by a 1995-96 Fulbright-Hays Doctoral Dissertation Abroad Fellowship. Special thanks are due to Michael Markovitz, whose generous endowment of the Markovitz Dissertation Fellowship at the University of Chicago has provided me financial support during the write-up phase of this project. I also thank Susan Gal for comments on earlier versions of this paper.

NOTES

1. For a provocative discussion of the construction of the Middle Eastern female by the colonial (male) observer, see Malek Alloula's (1986) analysis of French colonial postcards from Algeria for the period from 1900 to 1930.

2. I anticipate, in making the argument that women appropriate masculine roles and vice versa, that I will arouse the ire of readers who interpret my stance as suggesting that I consider the assertion of power, by definition, to be an action associated exclusively within the masculine realm. My point here is not to suggest that power is necessarily masculine (as the image of the dominating matriarch is not alien to the Jordanian cultural landscape, for example) but rather that certain kinds of power (such as that which reins in women's independence) are associated with the masculine role within Jordanian culture. I must note, however, that I consider it a distinct possibility that all forms of power, even those wielded by women, are ultimately glossed as masculine in Jordanian culture, but I leave the development of that argument to another work.

3. The increasingly common linkage between political issues such as environmentalism and social justice and consumer products (consider the Body Shop's environmentally-friendly goods or Benetton's advertisements promoting racial equality, for example) raises the interesting possibility that the barrier between the the realms of consumption and politics is eroding in contemporary capitalist societies. It is also clear that men are increasingly targeted as consumers by marketers. At the same time, however, the overall point that shopping is construed as a trivial and feminine activity continues to occupy a strong position among vast sectors of the Western consuming populations.

4. As Myriam Jansen-Verbeke (1987:73) notes in her analysis of shopping patterns in the Netherlands, it is problematic to classify shopping as a single activity; shopping includes such diverse activities as purchasing goods essential for everyday survival, seeking out a particular consumer item, window shopping, comparing goods on display, and even just strolling around in the shopping area. For the purposes of my discussion, I use the word "shopping" to include the constellation of activities associated with the pursuit of consumer goods and services that for the most part lie outside the orbit of everyday necessities such as basic foodstuffs. Among elites, the responsibility for the provisioning of everyday items is typically relegated to domestic employees.

5. See, for example, Sawsan El-Messiri's (1978) account of the valorization of shopping as a realm of masculine authority among lower-class residents of Cairo. In the case of an upwardly-mobile, lower-middle class couple in Amman with whom I spent many pleasant afternoons, there was not a hint of stigma attached to shopping; both the husband and the wife were pleased to show me their "finds" from shopping expeditions. For a comparative perspective, see Jansen-Verbeke's (1987:84) finding that lower and middle-class shoppers in the Netherlands were more likely to value positively aspects of the shopping experience than were elite shoppers, who were more likely to have negative or indifferent feelings within the same shopping environment.

6. My focus here is on gender struggle within the domain of spousal relations, given the frequency with which I observed struggles between wives and husbands over issues of shopping and home decoration. This is not to deny the existence of other struggles for power occurring within the household. The conflict between parents and their children, for example, provides a rich context for the playing out of relations of power and domination with regard to consumption practices. See, for example, Abu-Lughod's (1990) study of the use of such items as lingerie, bras, cosmetics, and bobby pins by Egyptian Bedouin girls and young women as a means of resisting directly the control of older women as well as indirectly the authority of fathers and uncles.

7. The determination of the overall household budget by the male head of household is well-documented within the Middle Eastern literature (Davis 1983:67). Even those works emphasizing the power and autonomy of women within the home acknowledge the point that it is typically the husband, as the primary wage earner, who determines what percentage of the household income will be available for the wife's purchases. In a description of poorer residents of Amman's squatter settlements, for example, Shami (1996:20) points out that all "good" men turn over to their wives or mothers their

entire earnings, minus a small amount of "cigarette money." The responsibility of running the household on a budget is interpreted as an example of the authority of women within the household realm. Without entering a lengthy discussion of this point, I would like to suggest that ensuring the survival of a household on what remains of the family income after the male wage-earner skims off his personal requirements for luxury expenditures should not automatically be construed as evidence of women's power.

8. Compare the importance A attaches to light and openness, in both an architectural and a social sense (the mixed-sex cafes of Europe compare favorably in her view with those of Amman which are predominantly the preserve of men), with N's preference in the earlier example for light furniture. The opposition of dark and light functions within the home as a metaphor for contrasting notions of constraint and freedom, cast in distinctly gendered terms.

9. Being neither a family member nor a close friend of A and M, I was nonetheless extended the privilege of visiting the entire villa, including areas intended for family viewing only. My status as a foreign researcher, coupled with A and M's interest in my research topic and desire to see their home featured in my writing, undoubtedly contributed to my reception within the home.

10. Many authors have noted the movement over time away from extended family and friendship networks in Middle Eastern social life and the increasing significance of the nuclear family and particularly the conjugal dyad within the context of elite and other "modernizing" populations (Altorki 1986:21-22 and 51, Makhlouf 1979:89, Mernissi 1987:91, Peteet 1991:187). It must be emphasized that the active role of men in the household that I observed during my research may be a consequence of the fact that elite spouses spend more time together at home than is the case in other classes, with the possible consequence that elite women enjoy less autonomy within the home than their less well-off counterparts. My hunch, however, is that male domination of the so-called "stranger" spaces within the home is not limited to elite households but is prevalent throughout all classes of Jordanian society. Given, however, the focus of my research on elite individuals, generalizations about the relationship between social class and gender roles throughout Jordanian society, including the possibility that notions of masculinity and femininity vary according to class position, must await future research.

REFERENCES

Abu-Lughod, Lila (1985) "A Community of Secrets: The Separate World of Bedouin Women." *Signs* 10:637-657.

_____ (1988) *Veiled Sentiments: Honor and Poetry in a Bedouin Society.* Berkeley & Los Angeles: University of California Press.

_____ (1989) "Zones of Theory in the Anthropology of the Arab Word." *Annual Review of Anthropology* 18:267-306.

_____ (1990) "The Romance of Resistance: Tracing Transformations of Power Through Bedouin Women." *American Ethnologist* 17:41-55.

_____ (1993) *Writing Women's Worlds: Bedouin Stories.* Berkeley & Los Angeles: University of California Press.

Alloula, Malek (1986) *The Colonial Harem* (trans. Myrna Godzich & Wlad Godzich). Minneapolis: University of Minnesota.

Altorki, Soraya (1986) *Women in Saudi Arabia: Ideology and Behavior among the Elite.* New York: Columbia University Press.

_____ (1988) "At Home in the Field." Pp. 49-71 in Soraya Altorki & Camillia Fawzi El-Solh (eds.)*Arab Women in the Field: Studying Your Own Society.* Syracuse, NY: Syracuse University Press.

Asad, Talal (1970) *The Kababish Arabs: Power, Authority, and Consent in a Nomadic Tribe.* London: C. Hurst.

Aswad, Barbara C. (1974) "Visiting Patterns among Women of the Elite in a Small Turkish City." *Anthropological Quarterly* 47:9-27.

Barhoum, M.I. (1987) "Divorce and the Status of Women in Jordan." *International Journal of Sociology of the Family* 17:121-142.

Barth, Fredrik (1961) *Nomads of South Persia: Basseri Tribe of the Khameseh Confederacy.* Boston: Little, Brown.

Bloch, Maurice, and Jean Bloch (1980) "Women and the Dialectics of Nature in Eighteenth-Century French Thought." Pp. 25-41 in Carol P. MacCormack (ed.) *Nature, Culture, and Gender.* Cambridge, ENG: Cambridge University Press.

Chauncey, George (1994) *Gay New York: Gender, Urban Culture, and the Makings of the Gay Male World, 1890-1940.* New York: Basic Books.

Cornwall, Andrea, and Nancy Lindisfarne (1994) *Dislocating Masculinity: Comparative Ethnographies.* London: Routledge.

Costa, Janeen Arnold (1994) "Introduction." Pp. 1-10 in Janeen Arnold Costa (ed.) *Gender Issues and Consumer Behavior.* Thousand Oaks, CA: Sage Publications.

Cunnison, Ian (1966) *The Baggara Arabs: Power and Lineage in a Sudanese Nomad Tribe.* Oxford, ENG: Clarendon Press.

Davis, Susan Schaefer (1983) *Women's Lives in a Moroccan Village.* Cambridge, MA: Schenkman Publishing Co.

Devor, Holly (1989) *Gender Blending: Confronting the Limits of Duality.* Bloomington: Indiana University Press.

Dwyer, Daisy Hilse (1978) *Images and Self-Images: Male and Female in Morocco.* New York: Columbia University Press.

El-Messiri, Sawsan (1978) "Self-Images of Traditional Urban Women in Cairo. " Pp. 522-540 in Lois Beck & Nikki Keddie (eds.) *Women in the Muslim World.* Cambridge, MA: Harvard University Press.

Firat, A. Fuat (1994) "Gender and Consumption: Transcending the Feminine?" Pp. 205-228 in Janeen Arnold Costa (ed.) *Gender Issues and Consumer Behavior.* Thousand Oaks, CA: Sage Publications.

Fraser, Nancy (1989) *Unruly Practices: Power, Discourse, and Gender in Contemporary Social Theory.* Minneapolis: University of Minnesota Press.

Gal, Susan (1997) "Gender in the Post-Socialist Transition: The Abortion Debate in Hungary." Pp. 122-133 in Roger N. Lancaster & Micaela di Leonardo (eds.), *infra.*

Jansen-Verbeke, Myriam (1987) "Women, Shopping and Leisure." *Leisure Studies* 6:71-86.

Joseph, Suad (1978) "Women and the Neighborhood Street in Borj Hammoud, Lebanon." Pp. 541-557 in Lois Beck & Nikki Keddie (eds.) *Women in the Muslim World.* Cambridge, MA: Harvard University Press.

―――― (1988) "Feminization, Familism, Self, and Politics: Research as a *Mughtaribi.*" Pp. 25-47 in Soraya Altorki & Camillia Fawzi El-Solh (eds.) *Arab Women in the Field: Studying Your Own Society.* Syracuse, NY: Syracuse University Press.

Kandiyoti, Deniz A. (1987) "Emancipated but Unliberated? Reflections on the Turkish Case." *Feminist Studies* 13:317-338.

Keddi, Nikki R. (1990) "The Past and Present of Women in the Muslim World." *Journal of World History* 1:77-108.

Lancaster, Roger N., and Micaela di Leonardo, eds. (1997) *The Gender/Sexuality Reader.* New York : Routledge.

Maher, Vanessa (1974) *Women and Property in Morocco: Their Changing Relation to the Process of Social Stratification in the Middle Atlas.* Cambridge, ENG: Cambridge University Press.

Makhlouf, Carla (1979) *Changing Veils: Women and Modernisation in North Yemen.* Austin: University of Texas Press.

Marx, Emmanuel (1967) *Bedouin of the Negev.* New York: Praeger.

McDowell, Linda, and Rosemary Pringle (1992) "Defining Public and Private Issues." Pp. 9-17 in Linda McDowell & Rosemary Pringle (eds.) *Defining Women: Social Institutions and Gender Divisions*. Cambridge, MA: Polity Press.

Mernissi, Fatima (1987) *Beyond the Veil* (rev. ed.). Bloomington: Indiana University Press.

Miller, Daniel (n.d.) "Could Shopping Ever Really Matter?" *Consumer Cultures in Global Perspectives*. New Brunswick, Working Papers of the Rutgers Center for Historical Analysis, Series 2, 1993.

Nelson, Cynthia (1974) "Public and Private Politics: Women in the Middle Eastern World." *American Ethnologist* 1:551-563.

Ortner, Sherry B., and Harriet Whitehead (1981) "Introduction: Accounting for Sexual Meanings." Pp. 1-27 in Sherry B. Ortner & Harriet Whitehead (eds.) *Sexual Meanings: The Cultural Construction of Gender and Sexuality*. Cambridge, ENG: Cambridge University Press.

Pehrson, Robert (1966) *The Social Organization of the Marri Baluch*. New York: Viking Fund Publications in Anthropology.

Peteet, Julie M. (1991) *Gender in Crisis: Women and the Palestinian Resistance Movement*. New York: Columbia University Press.

Rapp, Rayna (1979) "Review Essay: Anthropology." *Signs* 4:497-513.

Rosaldo, Michelle Zimbalist (1974) "Woman, Culture, and Society: A Theoretical Overview." Pp. 17-42 in Michelle Z. Rosaldo & Louise Lamphere (eds.) Woman, Culture, and Society. Stanford, CA: Stanford University Press.

_____ (1980) "The Use and Abuse of Anthropology: Reflections on Feminism and Cross-cultural Understanding." *Signs* 5:389-417.

Sayigh, Rosemary (1994) *Too Many Enemies: The Palestinian Experience in Lebanon*. London & Atlantic Highlands, NJ: Zed Books.

Scott, Joan Wallach (1988) *Gender and the Politics of History*. New York: Columbia University Press.

Shami, Seteney (1988) "Studying Your Own: The Complexities of a Shared Culture." Pp. 115-138 in Soraya Altorki & Camillia Fawzi El-Solh (eds.) *Arab Women in the Field: Studying Your Own Society*. Syracuse: Syracuse University Press.

_____ (1996) "Gender, Domestic Space, and Urban Upgrading: A Case Study from Amman." *Gender and Development* 4:17-23.

Strathern, Marilyn (1980) "No Nature, No Culture: The Hagen Case." Pp. 174-219 in Carol P. MacCormack (ed.) *Nature, Culture, and Gender*. Cambridge, ENG: Cambridge University Press.

Tiefer, Leonore (1995) *Sex Is Not a Natural Act and Other Essays*. Boulder & San Francisco: Westview Press.

Yanagisako, Sylvia Junko (1987) "Mixed Metaphors: Native and Anthropological Models of Gender and Kinship Domains." Pp. 86-118 in Sylvia Junko Yanagisako & Jane Fishburne Collier (eds.) *Gender and Kinship: Essays Toward a Unified Analysis*. Stanford, CA: Stanford University Press.

Yanagisako, Sylvia Junko, and Jane Fishburne Collier (1987) "Toward a Unified Analysis of Gender and Kinship." Pp. 14-50 in Sylvia Junko Yanagisako & Jane Fishburne Collier (eds.) *Gender and Kinship: Essays Toward a Unified Analysis*. Stanford, CA: Stanford University Press.

THE FAMILY IN THE HOUSEHOLD:
WOMEN, RELATIONSHIPS, AND ECONOMIC HISTORY IN PERU

Susan Vincent

INTRODUCTION

In this paper, I present the very different stories of two women's partnerships with men and speculate on the reasons for these differences. The women are from the same Peruvian peasant village but are some 50 years apart in age. By the time the younger of the women was a young adult, the social and economic context of the village and the country had changed considerably. These changes allowed her employment opportunities the older woman had never been able to consider and, at the same time, gave her more control over the types of relationships she wished to engage in with men. These case studies suggest ways in which Peruvian family structures have changed because of capitalism. Rather than losing in importance, the family, newly formulated, is maintained as a way of allowing for more flexibility. Relationships with partners, parents, and other kin are qualitatively different. This paper suggests ways in which women choose kin groups of varying composition in accordance with their other livelihood options and their personal preference.

Research in Economic Anthropology, Volume 19, pages 179-187.
Copyright © 1998 by JAI Press Inc.
All rights of reproduction in any form reserved.
ISBN: 0-7623-0446-4

The information presented here invites speculation concerning the materiality of social relations. As people engage in the ways of making a living that are available to them, they also engage in social relations, over which they have varying degrees of control and which are subject to both ideological norms and manipulation. Two concepts that collide here are "household" and "family." There is an extensive literature on each of these concepts separately and on the relationship between them (on households see, e.g., Meillassoux 1981, Hartmann 1981, Folbre 1986, Mackintosh 1989, Smith & Wallerstein 1992; on family see, e.g., Barrett & McIntosh 1982, Segalen 1986, Tilly and Scott 1987, Hareven 1990; on the relationship between them, see, e.g., Yanagisako 1979, Harris 1982, 1984, Wilson & Pahl 1988, Narotzky 1988, Rapp 1991, Lem 1991). While there is a diversity of views over how to define these concepts, and even whether they are analytically useful, Rapp's (1991) characterization of the household as an economic and residential construct, and the family as an ideological one, has been widely accepted. However, as will be shown by the cases below, this stark contrast does not deal adequately with the complexity of the relationship between these two concepts. I will use "household" to refer loosely to an economic grouping for mutual reproduction, and "family" to refer to the socially formed grouping of affinal and consanguineal kin. I make no attempt to provide a rigorous definition of either term and will return to a discussion of the relationship between them at the end of the paper.

THE 1930s AND FARMING

The two cases I will present concern women from the community of Mata Chico in the Peruvian central highlands. Mata Chico has been a legally recognized indigenous/peasant[1] community since 1936. It is located along the central railway and the central highway, about 250 km inland from Lima. Since the turn of the century, there has been a process of increasing involvement with the national capitalist economy, first through male migrant work in the regional mining and rail transport sectors, especially in the period from the 1930s to the 1960s, and then expanding into formal and informal sector work in Lima for both men and women from the 1970s onward. The economy of the 1930s was very different from the economy of the 1980s and 1990s, as I shall outline below.

The first woman whose story I will discuss, Gregoria,[2] was born around 1915. She loved herding the livestock, mostly sheep, when she was a child, skipping out of school to do so. At this time, there were some paid jobs for women as domestic servants. As a young adult, she worked for a family for three months but quit because she did not like to leave her sheep. When she was around 20 years old, she said some old women came to pressure her to marry the man who became her husband. She said she did not like men—"*yo odiaba hombre, mamá*"—she told me. She said she would still be single now if it were not for these women. Gregoria did not feel she had any choice but to marry. Around the late 1930s and early 1940s, Gregoria and her husband lived in Oroya for three years while he worked in the smelter there and she learned to be a midwife. They then returned to Mata Chico, where they lived with his mother, who, according to Gregoria, exploited the two. She went on to have four children and has lived in Mata Chico to the present.

The economic context in which these events took place covered a period of transition from a subsistence peasant economy to dependence on wages from industry. From the turn of the century, the central highlands saw significant foreign capitalist investment in mining and in the railway and, after 1920, in mineral refining. These operations offered jobs to men, who increasingly sought them to earn money to buy the land on which they had previously been sharecroppers.[3] Locally, peasant farming was the focal point of the economy. Some women worked as domestic servants in the homes of the American managers, but most of the women of Mata Chico who went to the work centers at this time did so to provide food and services for fathers or husbands who worked there. Some earned money, as Gregoria did, by providing goods and services to other workers and their families, but this was not their major reason for migrating.

A census of the community taken in 1935 as part of the application for legal indigenous community status emphasizes its agricultural nature. Most of the men are listed as farmers or livestock owners, while there are a few miners, weavers, carpenters, musicians, etc. Given the purpose of the census, it is likely that people deliberately chose to represent themselves as farmers rather than wage workers, but the importance of farming is also evident in the fact that they made such an application. Only unpartnered women were listed on the census. Of these, the vast majority were "*hiladoras,*" or "spinners," a designation for "homemaker." One woman is listed as a cook and another as a domestic servant. Again, it is difficult to place much reliance on the lists of occupations, but it is probably true that there were limited opportunities for women.

THE 1980s: A DIVERSE ECONOMY

If we now move forward in time to the 1980s, the economic context has greatly changed. Ester, the other woman whose story I will present, had very different choices from Gregoria. She went to work as a domestic servant in Lima in the early 1980s and was given extra training in cooking by her employers. With this training and with the contacts she made through her employers, she was able to set herself up as a caterer when they no longer needed her. Eventually, she participated in a land invasion in Lima, and she has a small house there. She has two children by different fathers. Ester says that both men drank too much and she does not want to have to deal with drunkenness. She did have a lover who did not drink, but she discovered he was already married.[4] She does not think she will marry, because she is unwilling to put up with the problems the men she has been involved with have had. Ester leaves her daughters to be cared for by her parents in Mata Chico while she lives and works in Lima.

Ester lives in a much different community from Gregoria's, largely because of different patterns of work migration. Between their two eras, male migrant work reached a peak as a standard part of men's working careers in the 1950s and 1960s, and then fell as the jobs disappeared with the crisis of the late 1970s and 1980s. Through this period, women began to migrate more often to take up informal sector work on their own instead of as a side effect of male migration. Everyone was going more often to Lima rather than staying in the region. Lima offered more work to women in both formal and informal sectors than the local area did.

The period of male migrant work had caused households to withdraw from the community to become more self-reliant. Households with income from migrants had less time for community work and preferred to hire agricultural labor rather than get involved in traditional work exchanges. The help Ester got from her employers indicates the extent to which people could substitute work or other relations for community relations. The result was that interhousehold relations were more often mediated by the market than by the multifaceted demands of the community. Since people no longer depended on the community, the community lacked the power to force a young woman to marry.

The evidence is contradictory as to whether there is a trend against marriage either in Mata Chico or in Peru more generally. On the one hand, Yanaylle (1996) argues that there is still significant pressure on women in Peru to marry. In Mata Chico, women like Ester are still in the minority, and they seem to arouse the resentment of married women because of their "laziness" (an interesting way to articulate what relationships with men are like). As Chaytor (1980) points out for 16th- and 17th-century England, such social disparagement can pressure women to marry even when it is not clearly in their economic interest to do so. However, there is also anecdotal evidence from Mata Chico that indicates that parents often encourage their children to delay marriage in favor of education, more life experiences, or to build a better life for themselves. Further, there are a significant number of unmarried Peruvian women. Thirty-nine percent of Peruvian women aged 12 years old or older are single (Blondet & Montero 1995:112), as are 8.5 percent of the women who are mothers in the department of Junín, in which Mata Chico is situated (Dirección Nacional de Estadísticas Regionales y Locales 1994:40).

Whether or not there is a trend to more unpartnered women is not really the issue here. People make partnership decisions for reasons other than the purely economic, after all. What I am saying is that changes in the economy allow non-economic factors, including personal taste, to be taken into account, leading to more flexibility in relationships. The formation and progression of relationships are, thus, qualitatively different from in the past.

The difference between Gregoria's and Ester's cases tells us something about the changes that have occurred within the family as a result of the change in the mateño peasant economy. In Gregoria's time, farming was the goal of all, old and young, male and female. Waged work was undertaken to support the farm. If Gregoria wanted to be able to stay in the community and raise livestock, and she really had no other choice, then she needed to pay attention to the people who could support her in that goal. Parents as well as other community members had a lot of control over children in this system. There was what I call an "intergenerational community of purpose" (Vincent n.d.) in supporting the peasant farm. In this era, even though sometimes young men and women might be away earning money, they were earning it for the farm to which they ultimately expected to return.

In Ester's time, there was no longer consensus that peasant farming was a desirable goal. There had been significant permanent outmigration in the 1960s, when men's waged work provided a viable alternative, but in the 1970s and 1980s, neither farming nor monetary income-earning activities were sufficient to make a living. Parents and children still helped each other out, but in what I call "intergenerational complementarity": one generation might work on the farm while another would earn money (Vincent n.d.). There was no assumption that everyone wanted to end up farming. Members of a family continued to help one another out, but if children did not need to inherit the land, they had greater independence to make life choices (also see Weyland 1993). Ester was aided in the choices she made by being able to call on her parents to look after her children, and she offered her parents access to money and the various advantages Lima makes available in return. The family is not of any less importance now than in the past; it is simply that different parts of it are important in different ways.

DISCUSSION

I want to consider here why it is important to think about how marriage and the family are constituted in peasant societies and how they relate to the economic institution of the household. In peasant studies, as well as in other analyses of livelihood strategies (see, e.g., Pahl 1984, Whitehead 1984, Mingione 1985, J. Smith 1990), we embraced the concept of "household" as allowing us to talk about the economic reproductive grouping which constituted the peasant economy when aggregated with others. "Household" is a very useful economic term. As I use it, it can cover both coresidents and those away from the principal dwelling who continue to contribute to and benefit from activities for mutual reproduction. The feminist discussions of the late 1970s and early 1980s allow us to see the internal inequalities in it and, therefore, to develop a more sophisticated understanding of household dynamics. Further, many of the analyses of peasant households take account of socioeconomic status (e.g., Sánchez 1987, G. Smith 1989, Deere 1990), or life cycle stage (often Chayanovian) (e.g., Laite 1984, Collins 1986, Stephen 1991).

However, if "household" is an economic term, so is "family." Family is quite clearly important economically for both Gregoria and Ester, although for Gregoria "family" entails getting a husband and for Ester it means a heavy emphasis on her parents and some of her siblings. These formulations of "family," I have argued, are affected by the wider economic structure. In peasant societies, where there are relatively few pure market relations, the language of kinship can permeate the social—and economic—universe.

It is difficult to examine familes without reference to their economic role. Although writing before the development of the concept of "household," Firth et al. (1969) illustrate, along with the range of qualitative ties to various kin among the English middle-class, an important economic basis for kinship, existing apart from state-provided social services (Firth et al. 1969:462):

> It is also recogized that the increasingly protective role of the State in the provision of educational, health and welfare services has tended to reduce the area in which family and kinship provision is required. Studies of English working-class society have indicated that, despite this, kin outside the family have important roles to play. It might be argued that in middle-class circles greater family prosperity would make it less necessary for extra-familial kin to supplement the functions of the State. But as our study has demonstrated, middle-class families too have their areas of social relationships in which neither their own financial prosperity nor the protective intervention of the State can adequately replace the contribution given by kin.

Preferences for partners or consanguineal kin emerge in various cases as economic structures interact with ideas about the family. Weyland (1993) illustrates an opposite relationship preference from Ester's, in that couples are able to distance themselves from dominating parents in Egypt through income from male migration for work. In Stack's classic *All Our Kin* (1974: 109-117), kin ties among women actually militate against marriages as potentially sapping the strength of the women's kin network.[5] Other cases are more similar to Ester's in their implication that it is male partners who are more oppressive. For example, Roldán (1988) shows how marital relations are renegotiated when women contribute significant monetary income to the household in Mexico City. Even more similar is the case of Zinacantecan women, discussed by Flood (1994), who try to avoid excessive dependence on male partners by becoming "self-provisioning," some of which involves engaging in local marketing. Clearly, the process of family construction and that of household construction at least overlap, if they are not more closely related.

Does this evidence mean that the family and the household are indistinguishable? Wilson and Pahl (1988) argue that they are not and that the family remains an important analytical tool. However, they imply a coresidential, nuclear family-based definition of the household, rather than the wider definition I use, which is based on mutual rights and obligations for reproduction. Much of their evidence demonstrates the importance of extended kin precisely in this reproductive economic role. This argument would still seem to imply that the family is constituted only insofar as it can be of use in the household, i.e., that it is formed in each case out of those kin who are useful. Their definition of "family" recognizes its dynamic quality but is conceptually vague in relying on emic definitions (Wilson & Pahl 1988:262-263). Of course, kin are used for social, emotional, and other forms of support besides economic, but household members might also perform these functions.

To make the situation even more complex, Kehoe (1994) argues that it can be misleading to concentrate on either of the household or the family. She maintains that, while both households and family are important to members of an Aymara community, ties of community dominate behavior and provide a material and ideological basis for close mutual aid relations. Thus, the discussion may have to extend beyond households and families to other groupings that can perform the same or similar roles.

CONCLUSION

Families, households, and communities, however they are consituted in a particular society, are all likely to be both ideologically and economically defined. Individuals engage in these groupings according to economic necessity and cultural prescription. In the comparison of Gregoria and Ester, we can see how people might rearrange what has been taken as normative family formation, given alternative economic choices. This situation allows us to ask: What social or market relation can replace the material component of a husband, wife, sister, brother, parent, or child? Can alternative relations make some kin relations entirely dispensable? Why are some relations more expendable, more problematic, or more necessary than others? How do gender roles and ideas about individual freedom affect family formation? Answering these questions will permit a clearer understanding of the role of the family in the household.

We need to consider kin resources in evaluating the socioeconomic condition of households, but we also need to remember that the demands of kinship are different from those of landownership or work relations. Ultimately, the question of how women's relations with men have changed is part of a larger question of the connection between class and kinship.

ACKNOWLEDGMENTS

This paper is based on "'Yo Odiaba Hombre': Women, Work and Relationships," presented at the 1997 American Anthropological Association annual meeting in Washington, DC. It is based on research funded by the Social Sciences and Humanities Research Council of Canada and the Women's Studies Research Unit of the University of Saskatchewan, to both of which I am very grateful. I thank Barry Isaac for his constructive comments. I owe "Gregoria" and "Ester" and others from Mata Chico my very deepest gratitude.

NOTES

1. I include both "indigenous" and "peasant" here as descriptors to reflect the changes in the official terminology, from *comunidades indígenas* (established in the 1920 Constitution) to *comunidades campesinas* (as a result of the 1969 agrarian reform). There is no space here to explore the implications of the meanings of these two concepts.

2. The names have been changed.

3. The community was formed, in terms of land possession, in 1929, when the land was purchased from the Mantaro Valley communities that had controlled the area.

4. This indicates that men are also choosing alternate forms of family formation.

5. Perhaps here a woman might embrace an economic opportunity that would allow her to have a stable relationship with a man and avoid the oppressive kin network.

REFERENCES

Barrett, Michèle, and Mary McIntosh (1982) *The Anti-Social Family*. London: Verso.

Blondet, Cecilia, and Carmen Montero (1995) *La Situación de la Mujer en el Perú, 1980-1994 (The Position of Women in Peru, 1980-1994)*. Lima: Instituto de Estudios Peruanos.

Chaytor, Miranda (1980) "Household and Kinship: Ryton in the Late 16th and Early 17th Centuries." *History Workshop Journal* 10:25-60.

Collins, Jane (1986) "The Household and Relations of Production in Southern Peru." *Comparative Studies in Society and History* 28:651-671.

Deere, Carmen (1990) *Household and Class Relations: Peasants and Landlords in Northern Peru*. Berkeley: University of California Press.

Dirección Nacional de Estadísticas Regionales y Locales (1994) *Compendio Estadistico 1993-94, Departamento Junín*. Lima: Instituto Nacional de Estadistíca e Información.

Firth, Raymond, Jane Hubert, and Anthony Forge (1969) *Families and Their Relatives: Kinship in a Middle-Class Sector of London*. London: Routledge & Kegan Paul.

Flood, Merielle K. (1994) "Changing Gender Relations in Zinacantán, Mexico." Pp. 145-173 in B.L. Isaac (ed.) *Research in Economic Anthropology, Vol. 15*. Greenwich, CT: JAI Press.

Folbre, Nancy (1986) "Cleaning House: New Perspectives on Households and Economic Development." *Journal of Development Economics* 22:5-40.

Hareven, Tamara (1990) "A Complex Relationship: Family Strategies and the Processes of Economic and Social Change." Pp. 215-244 in Roger Friedland & A.F. Robertson (eds.) *Beyond the Marketplace: Rethinking Economy and Society*. New York: Aldine de Gruyter.

Harris, Olivia (1982) "Households and their Boundaries." *History Workshop Journal* 13:143-152.

——— (1984) "Households as Natural Units." Pp. 136-155 in Kate Young, Carol Walkowitz & Roslyn McCullagh (eds.) *Of Marriage and the Market: Women's Subordination Internationally and Its Lessons*. London: Routledge.

Hartmann, Heidi (1981) "The Family as the Locus of Gender, Class, and Political Struggle: The Example of Housework." *Signs* 6:366-394.

Kehoe, Alice (1994) "The Centro de Madres in the Village of Lakaya, Bolivia." Pp. 119-133 in Alice Littlefield & Hill Gates (eds.) *Marxist Approaches in Economic Anthropology*. Lanham, MD: University Press of America and the Society for Economic Anthropology.

Laite, Julian (1984) "Migration and Social Differentiation Amongst Mantaro Valley Peasants." Pp. 107-139 in Norman Long & Bryan Roberts (eds.) *Miners, Peasants and Entrepreneurs: Regional Development in the Central Highlands of Peru*. Cambridge, ENG: Cambridge University Press.

Lem, Winnie (1991) "Gender, Ideology and Petty Commodity Production: Social Reproduction in Languedoc, France." Pp. 103-117 in Alice Littlefield & Hill Gates (eds.) *Marxist Approaches in Economic Anthropology*. Lanham, MD: University Press of America and the Society for Economic Anthropology.

Mackintosh, Maureen (1989) *Gender, Class and Rural Transition: Agribusiness and the Food Crisis in Senegal*. London: Zed Books.

Meillassoux, Claud (1981) *Maidens, Meal and Money: Capitalism and the Domestic Community*. Cambridge: Cambridge University Press.

Mingione, Enzo (1985) "Social Reproduction of the Surplus Labour Force: The Case of Southern Italy." Pp. 14-54 in Nanneke Redclift & Enzo Mingione (eds.) *Beyond Employment: Household, Gender and Subsistence*. Oxford, ENG: Basil Blackwell.

_____ (1994) "Life Strategies and Social Economics in the Postfordist Age." *International Journal of Urban and Regional Research* 18(1):24-45.

Narotzky, Susana (1988) "The Ideological Squeeze: 'Casa,' 'Family' and 'Cooperation' in the Processes of Transition." *Social Science Information* 27(4):559-581.

Pahl, R.E. (1984) *Divisions of Labour*. Oxford: Basil Blackwell.

Rapp, Rayna (1991) "Family and Class in Contemporary America: Notes Towards an Understanding of Ideology." Pp. 197-215 in Elizabeth Jelin (ed.) *Family, Household and Gender Relations in Latin America*. London: Kegan Paul International and UNESCO.

Roldán, Martha (1988) "Renegotiating the Marital Contract: Intrahousehold Patterns of Money Allocation and Women's Subordination Among Domestic Outworkers in Mexico City." Pp. 229-247 in Daisy Dwyer & Judith Bruce (eds.) *A Home Divided: Women and Income in the Third World*. Stanford, CA: Stanford University Press.

Sánchez, Rodrigo (1987) *Organización Andina, Drama y Posibilidad (Andean Organization: Drama and Possibilities)*. Huancayo: Instituto Regional de la Ecología Andina.

Segalen, Martine (1986) *Historical Anthropology of the Family*. Cambridge, ENG: Cambridge University Press.

Smith, Gavin (1989) *Livelihood and Resistance: Peasants and the Politics of Land in Peru*. Berkeley: University of California Press.

Smith, Joan (1990) "All Crises Are Not the Same: Households in the United States during Two Crises." Pp. 128-141 in Jane L. Collins & Martha Gimenez (eds.) *Work without Wages: Domestic Labor and Self-Employment within Capitalism*. Albany: State University of New York Press.

Smith, Joan, and Immanuel Wallerstein, eds. (1992) *Creating and Transforming Households: The Constraints of the World-Economy*. Cambridge, ENG: Cambridge University Press.

Stack, Carol (1974) *All Our Kin: Strategies for Survival in a Black Community*. New York: Harper & Row.

Stephen, Lynn (1991) *Zapotec Women*. Austin: University of Texas Press.

Tilly, Louise, and Joan W. Scott (1987) *Women, Work and Family*. New York: Routledge.

Vincent, Susan (n.d.) "Flexible Families: Capitalist Development and Crisis in Rural Peru." Unpublished paper, 1997.

Weyland, Petra (1993) *Inside the Third World Village*. London: Routledge.

Whitehead, Harriet (1984) "'I'm Hungry Mum': The Politics of Domestic Budgeting." Pp. 93-116 in Kate Young, Carol Walkowitz, & Roslyn McCullagh (eds.) *Of Marriage and the Market: Women's Subordination Internationally and Its Lessons*. London: Routledge.

Wilson, Patricia, and Ray Pahl (1988) "The Changing Sociological Construction of the Family." *Sociological Review* 36(2):233-266.

Yanagisako, Sylvia Junko (1979) "Family and Household: The Analysis of Domestic Groups." *Annual Review of Anthropology* 8:161-205.

Yanaylle, María Elena (1996) "Tiene Veinteocho Años y Aún es Virgen: Femineidad y Esterotipo de la Mujer sin Pareja" ("She's Twenty-Eight and Still a Virgin: Femininity and Stereotype of the Unmarried Woman"). Pp. 73-90 in Patricia Ruiz-Bravo (ed.) *Detrás de la Puerta: Hombres y Mujeres en el Perú de Hoy (Behind the Door: Men and Women in Today's Peru)*. Lima: Pontificia Universidad Católica del Perú.

PART IV

SUBSISTENCE AND MARKET PRODUCTION: SIBERIA, MEXICO, SIERA LEONE

KINSHIP AND EXCHANGE AMONG THE DOLGAN AND NGANASAN OF NORTHERN SIBERIA

John P. Ziker

This paper discusses how aboriginal Siberians are dealing with the dissolution of State socialism and subsequent economic collapse—through formation of family/ clan holdings or maintenance of current employment. From late 1995 through 1997 (18 months), I lived in the Taimyr Autonomous Region of northern Krasno- yarksii Territory (*Krai*) researching this problem. The community of Ust Avam, located in the central Taimyr lowlands, was the focus for 12 months of the research. Two native groups, the Dolgan (*Tehlar*) and the Nganasan (*Nya*), and a minority of non-indigenous people from all over the former Soviet Union populate the Avam tundra and settlement of Ust Avam. This paper documents the transfor- mation of Ust Avam's economy through the last years of Communism to the end of 1997.

Ethnographers in the former Soviet Union have recently observed an explosion of self-interested strategies among a variety of groups and have associated nega- tive social effects with these behaviors. For example, Kuehnast (n.d.) established that the introduction of the market economy in Kyrgyzstan has led to black mar- keting and speculation, while privatization of enterprises has led to a host of other

Research in Economic Anthropology, Volume 19, pages 191-238.
Copyright © 1998 by JAI Press Inc.
All rights of reproduction in any form reserved.
ISBN: 0-7623-0446-4

social problems, such as prostitution, drug trading, begging, and homelessness. Dudwick (n.d.) confirmed that the dissolution of socialism has led to atomization of social and economic life in a variety of rural locations, bringing on mutually reinforcing poverty and isolation.

In Ust Avam, the native mixed economy and sharing networks have not collapsed. A large number of aboriginal Siberians are maintaining social and economic traditions in the face of rapid financial and infrastructure changes. What are these traditional strategies and why are they being employed rather than strategies that are explicitly oriented towards self-interest? These questions go to the crux of debates about hunter/gatherer economics and economic anthropology. Do individual humans by nature maximize calories, status, and profit? Or are they acting according to norms and limits that restrict maximization? Do group norms, in this context, provide an insurance policy against starvation or serve some other risk-minimizing or -reducing function?

ETHNOGRAPHIC INTRODUCTION

The Ust Avam community includes two of the Taimyr Region's native populations along with a minority of individuals from other regions and republics of the former Soviet Union. The settlement's largest population block is the Dolgan community. The Nganasan population in Ust Avam is slightly smaller. Figure 1 shows the relative populations reported to the regional bureau of statistics by the Ust Avam administration for 1993 through 1996. These statistics are somewhat misleading, since approximately one-half of the individuals less than 16 years of age are of mixed marriages. Ethnicity is usually reported to be that of the father unless he is unknown.

The Dolgan of Arctic Siberia are essentially unknown to Western readers and students of anthropology. There is virtually no literature in English on them. There has been a furious debate in the Russian literature about whether or not they are a distinct ethnic group (reviewed and critiqued in Anderson 1995). The Nganasan are somewhat better known in the West because of their shamans and their being used as examples in scientific theories (e.g., Milovskii 1992, Popov 1966, Ingold 1980).

The part of Siberia where the Dolgan and Nganasan live, the Taimyr Autonomous Region, was closely regulated as a border zone for most of the last 70 years. Even Soviet citizens needed special permission to enter and leave. Border troops met passengers on incoming and outgoing vessels to check documentation. Because of past peculiarities of travel to the Taimyr Region, contemporary Western researchers began long-term study only after the breakup of the Soviet Union in 1991.

The Dolgan population traditionally inhabited the band of forest tundra extending across the Taimyr Peninsula from the North Slope of the Central Siberian Pla-

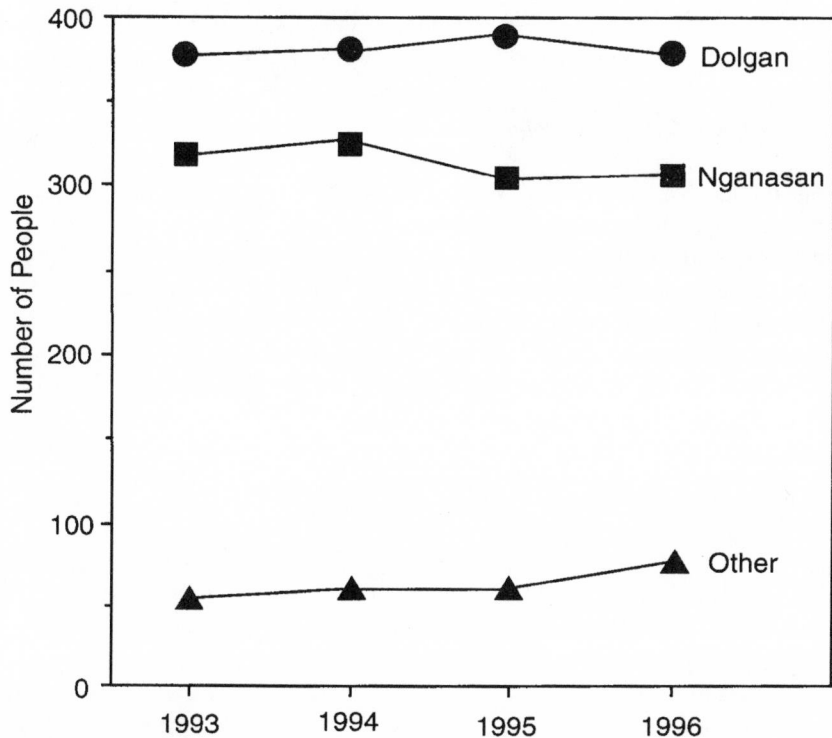

Figure 1. Ethnic Composition of the Ust Avam Community, Settlement Statistics Reported to Taimyr Regional Statistical Bureau

teau to the Dudypta and Kheta rivers. The Dolgan language is classified as a creole. In the 18th and 19th centuries, Yakut was the lingua franca along the reindeer trail from Dudinka to Khatanga. The Dolgan language developed with Yakut grammatical structure and Evenki and Russian vocabulary.[1]

The Nganasans generally inhabited the tundra zones north of the Dudypta and Kheta rivers. Their language is one of the northern Samoyedic languages, with closest affinity to the Nenets and Enets languages. The Samoyedic group of languages is often grouped with the Uralo-Altaic language family. Figure 2 shows the territories of the two groups at the beginning of the 20th century (following Levin & Potopov 1964).

The Ust Avam area was especially critical in the merchant trade, since it was at the Taganari Lakes where one could cross from the Pyasina, Dudypta, and Avam rivers to the Volochanka, Kheta, and Khatanga rivers in the east. The Avam River was, thus, a strategic link in trade caravans from Dudinka to Khatanga, beginning

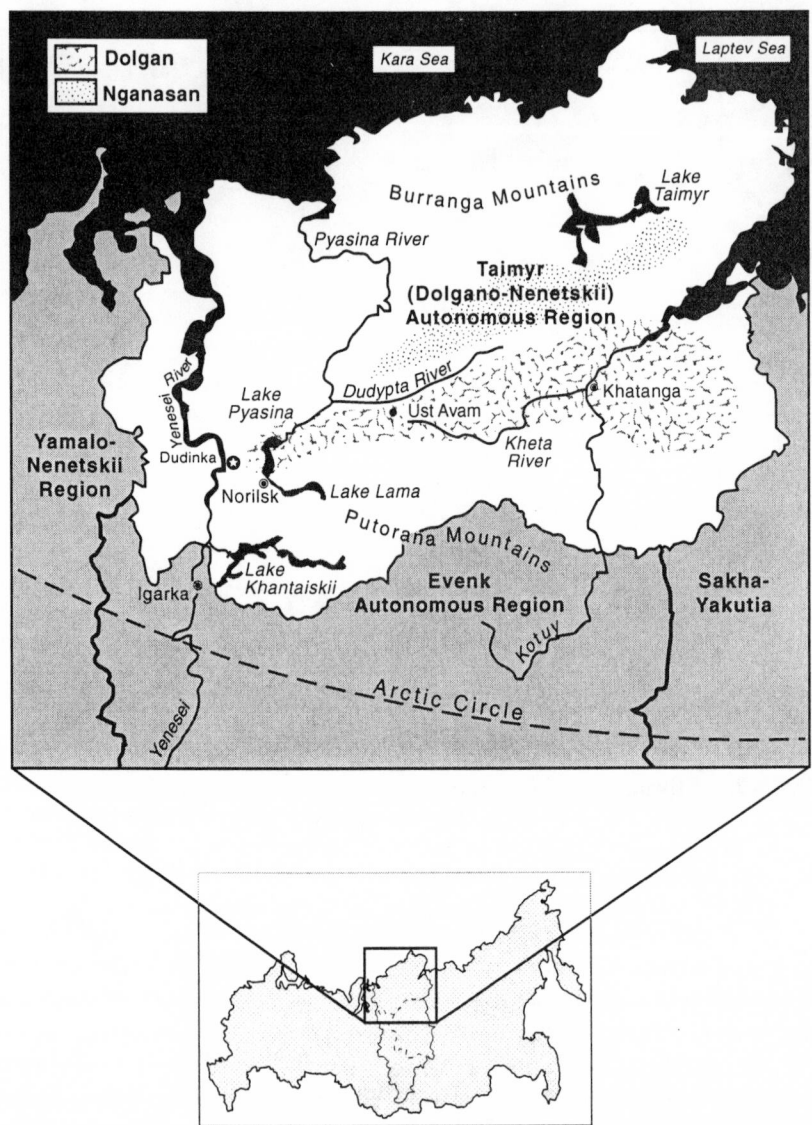

Figure 2.   Map of the Taimyr Region, with Early 20th-Century Territories
of the Dolgan and Nganasan

in the 17th century. A few Dolgan families living in the area were fairly rich and, along with members of poorer families, maintained herds of up to 15,000 reindeer before the 1917 revolution. The larger and richer households traveled widely and practiced some degree of trade themselves. To this day, individuals from the Avam tundra maintain contact with relatives in the Yesei area, several hundred kilometers to the south in the Evenkiskii Autonomous Region.

In contrast to the Dolgans, the Nganasan population had very little contact with the pre-Revolutionary Russian government, church, and merchants. The Nganasans paid tribute to the Czar, but they were never baptized and they generally did not work for merchants. The Nganasans generally inhabited the lands to the north of the main Dudinka-Khatanga reindeer trail, and their wide settlement pattern afforded them a degree of isolation until the collectivization period in the 1930s.

The community of Ust Avam began to take its present form in the late 1950s, when the government closed stations along the Dudinka-Khatanga reindeer trail. At that time, the Dolgan and Nganasan populations in Avam District worked for several collective farms administered out of these government stations. When the government closed these collective farm stations, it moved services such as education and medical care, along with the local administration, to Ust Avam. After several phases of collective farm consolidation in the 1950s and 1960s, the administration of Ust Avam's working population was moved to Volochanka, 90 km east, the center of the then Avam District and Joseph Stalin state farm (*sovkhoz*). In June 1971, 10 million hectares, including Ust Avam, were carved out of the territory of the Volochanka administration. The Soviet of Ministries created the government hunting enterprise, "Taimyrskii" (*gospromkhoz*), with its main office near Norilsk. The Avam tundra population was no stranger to administrative shifts.

The population of Ust Avam and surrounding tundra was sedentized in the 1970s as the state contracted the government hunting enterprise to build housing. Reindeer herding became less viable as children were taken off to boarding school and the population density increased. In this region, however, reindeer herding provided mostly a transportation function, as mentioned above. Caribou hunting, lake and river fishing, and fur-bearing animal trapping were the main traditional sources of sustenance and cash. Despite the loss of domestic reindeer at the time of sedentization, the government encouraged hunting, fishing, and trapping through employment in the rural state enterprise (at various times collective farm, state farm, or government hunting farm). Ust Avam still had 50-60 professional staff hunters at the time of this research. The staff hunters practiced hunting, fishing, and trapping as workers in this large administrative structure.

Families living in the rural villages had fairly equal access to material goods, despite differentiated employment. In the Ust Avam settlement, as in other parts of the former Soviet Union, the state provided standardized housing units. During the 1970s and 1980s, a wide assortment of consumer goods were available in Ust Avam. Before the fall of the Soviet Union, native families in Ust Avam village had a high standard of living. Salaries and pensions were more than adequate. Parents regularly sent their children to summer camp and encouraged secondary education. Before 1991, even pensioners could fly to the city and back, go shopping, and have part of the month's pension left over. Flights to and from the capital were

Table 1.   Source of Income for All Adult Men and Women in Ust Avam,
from the 1997 Administration Registry

Employment or Income Source	Men	Women
State Hunting Enterprise	95	51
Budgetary Organizations (School, Clinic, Post office, Administration)	10	52
Federal Pension/Unemployment	41	49
Store	2	1
TOTAL	148	153

scheduled three times a week. Currently, passenger flights operate once every two weeks.

The main employer in the Avam tundra area, the state hunting enterprise "Taimyrskii," historically provided hunters, trappers, and fishermen with the implements of labor, such as snowmobiles, steel traps, fishnets, gasoline, boats, and outboard motors, as well as a consistent outlet for the products obtained. I surveyed the enterprise's current professional hunters about their history of instruments/materials received. These data are presented below. Historically, the state enterprise gave each hunter a plan for a certain number of caribou, Arctic fox pelts, and fish for each season. Native men received very respectable salaries, depending on how much they produced, plus fuel and modern instruments of labor. (See Appendix A for the exchange records at one hunting brigade.)

Native women also received respectable salaries for piecework they did for the *gospromkhoz* "Taimyrskii," the state hunting enterprise. In the settlement of Ust Avam, the state enterprise had a sewing facility where upwards of 40 women produced beaded sections for caribou fur boots. The boots, called *untaiki*, were put together with rubber soles at the state hunting enterprise's main office in Norilsk, which employs mainly non-natives. In addition, many women were employed in budgetary organizations, such as the school, clinic, and post office. Single mothers received large federal welfare payments through the post office. Table 1 represents the registered income sector for each sex, based on my 1997 census. The information was provided by the Ust Avam settlement administration.

In Ust Avam, there are 143 working-age men (18 to 55 years) and 151 working age women (18 to 50 years). There are many working-age men and women in Ust Avam who do not work and do not receive unemployment benefits; since they were never employed, they are not eligible. There are additional individuals who are effectively unemployed but who have not gone through the bureaucratic steps necessary to receive unemployment benefits.

The federal pension/unemployment figures above do not include the goodly number of women who receive single-mother welfare payments (*mat odinochka*) or supplemental benefits for children (*posobiye dlya detyei*). Most families I interviewed with young children receive the latter. The single-mother benefit depends on the number of children and can be as large as an average worker's salary.

ARCTIC HUNTER-GATHERERS IN RUSSIA'S TRANSITIONAL ECONOMY

Rapidly changing social, political, and macroeconomic conditions provide a unique opportunity to observe evidence for differing individual economic strategies in indigenous communities. The dynamic situation in Russia provides openings for individuals to experiment with strategies that were not allowed or preferred in the past. Two general processes have been proposed for capitalist transition in northern Eurasia:

> When modern factory-produced technological devices, especially those that are motor driven, replace man-powered and animal-powered machines in local production systems, the inevitable and very far-reaching consequence is a *de-localization* of essential energy sources. This creates greatly increased dependencies on the macrocosm of commercial enterprise and political influence outside the local community....As de-localization and technological development proceed, a likely concomitant is an increasing technical and economic differentiation among the individuals and family units seeking to adapt to these changes in their environment (Pelto 1987).

> The build-up of elements of "subsistence economy" in running the economy in Russia, mainly agriculture, has been underway throughout the country. [Our] life itself compels [us] to take this turn, and it should be realized as an historic necessity of the "period of transition" for it has been going on not only in villages but also in big cities. [F]or example, "the belt of vegetable patches" emerging in recent years around Moscow is a sign of "neotraditionalism" just as well. During the painstaking period of transition in places of residence and economic activities of small peoples of the North in national Northern villages, one should not in any way be afraid of, or be opposed to, the growth of elements of subsistence economy, since they have been either directly, or as an intermediary, gradually transforming into live "ethnicity," encouraging preservation and revival of cultural individuality, national traditions of the way of life, economy, and use of natural environment of small peoples (Pika & Prokhorov 1994:189-190).

State enterprises have played a significant role in the social and economic organization of aboriginal Siberian people for the last 30 years (Forsyth 1989). State farm enterprises (*sovkhozy*) employed native Siberians and produced meat, fish, and fur for the larger market. These organizations were government-administered rural enterprises that controlled the local economy, much as a factory in a factory town does. The majority of the working population was dependent on the enterprise for housing, fuel, employment, and the instruments of labor.

The state enterprise system has come under increasing fiscal and political pressure since the collapse of the Soviet Union in 1991 (Abrosimova 1992, Pika & Prokhorov 1994). The small villages where most Siberian native people live have experienced rapid inflation in the costs of capital equipment and transportation.

Additionally, people who work for state enterprises cannot predict when they will be paid or how much the salaries will be worth when they actually get them. These conditions of uncertainty are widespread across the Russian north.

On one hand, the Russian government has explicitly encouraged self-interested strategies in the economic reform of their country (e.g., voucher privatization, commercial banks, and the freely convertible ruble). On the other hand, the government has bowed to political pressures from the native Siberian political associations for economic protection through special budgetary programs and decrees. The motives for the government's position towards native peoples are complex, and I will not attempt to explicate all of them here. Historically, since Count M.M. Speransky's reforms in 1822, the Russian government took a paternalistic stance in the form of protectionist measures regarding Siberian natives. These measures were intensified during the first years after the 1917 Communist revolution. Then, during Joseph Stalin's reign (1922-1953), native people were forcibly integrated into an economy that was the product of socialist construction. After the break-up of the Soviet Union, Russia had to deal with the human rights abuses that resulted from the Stalinist economic revolution.

Russian president Boris Yeltsin issued a decree in April 1992 creating a new form of land use: family/clan holdings for aboriginal people of Siberia in the far north and east. The decree's ostensible goal was to affirm and protect the traditional economic activities and living spaces of aboriginal Siberian peoples. Under this 1992 decree, ministerial councils and administrative organs in the territories (*krai*), regions, and autonomous districts were to work with the regional native associations. Together, they were to define and issue territories as inalienable property for the sectors of indigenous populations. Reindeer pastures and hunting, fishing, and trapping territories were to be issued free of charge to clan communities and families desiring to practice traditional economic activities. In addition, the decree gave priority to aboriginal families and clans in concluding agreements and obtaining licenses for use of renewable resources. The decree stated that no one should expropriate native territories for industrial or any other development. This point is significant, since industrial development in northern territories is a high priority in the Russian economy. In the Taimyr Autonomous Region (see Figure 2) where I conducted this research, the regional administration wrote "Temporary Regulations" following the 1992 decree. Using these regulations, approximately 50 family/clan holdings have been formed.

MODELS OF ECONOMIC TRANSITION

Three Models

Russian ethnographers A.A. Pika and V.V. Prokhorov (1994) recently proposed that the transition to capitalism should dovetail traditional aspects of the northern

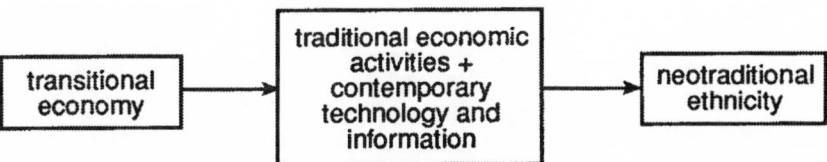

Figure 3. Neotraditionalism Development Flow Chart, Derived from
Pika & Prokhorov (1994)

native mixed economy with modern implements and information. The result
should be a revitalization of northern indigenous ethnicity (ibid.). I have converted
their model of *neotraditionalism* into a flow-chart (Figure 3). Are contemporary
family/clan holdings an example of neotraditionalism? And what are the implications of the vast majority of households' not taking territory as a family/clan holding?

Pertti Pelto (1987) proposed another model of north Eurasian development,
which I have converted into the flow chart in Figure 4. Are family/clan farms an
example of entrepreneurial activity and socioeconomic differentiation?

With the current Russian economic policy virtually abandoning the rural enterprise sector in the north, enterprises in the Taimyr region have had severe budgetary cuts. The high standard of living of the 1980s that was the result of a
delocalized economy has given way to relative poverty and isolation of communities. Instruments of labor supplied by government enterprises until 1992, such as
combustion-powered vehicles and nylon fishnets, are now falling into disrepair.
Professional hunters rarely see new spare parts. Until 1994, every hunter received
a minimum of 1 ton of gasoline every year. In the fall of 1997, each received 170
liters, enough to travel 500 km by snowmobile. Considering that trap lines are
often 25 km in one direction, that hunting cabins are up to 100 km from the village,
and that 5-year-old Russian snowmobiles get 3 km to the liter, 170 liters of gas is
very little.

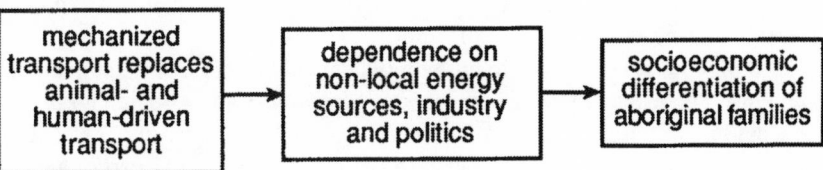

Figure 4. Capitalist Development in Northern Eurasia Flow Chart,
Derived from Pelto (1987)

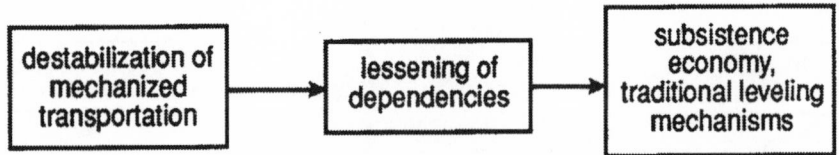

Figure 5.   Subsistence-Oriented Development and Government
Isolation Flow Chart

I have amended Pelto's model to provide an alternative to both his and the neotraditionalism model. The key concept in my model is the decrease in dependencies on the larger economy. In Ust Avam, these decreases in dependencies appear to be a function of changes in access to government and services. Reliance on the local subsistence economy and sharing networks are the result. Exchanges with the larger economy are reduced from previous levels. My model is shown in the flow chart in Figure 5.

Hypotheses and Predictions

   1.   Following Pika & Prokhorov's (1994) model, if the motives for formation of family/clan holdings or maintaining current employment were related to mitigating the uncertainty in Russia's rapidly changing economy, one would expect that the local subsistence economy would gain in importance, along with access to new technologies and information. As part of a growing subsistence economy one should observe generalized reciprocity, delayed returns, other forms of aid, resource husbanding, and communal ownership and use of resources. To the extent that subsistence economies are gaining in importance, one should observe a transformation in Siberians' dependencies on external energy sources. This transformation would occur through a relocalization of energy and raw material sources (Pelto 1987, Bodley 1990). It follows, then, that industrial institutions and formal economic principles should be losing local importance if subsistence economies are expanding. As a result, the capitalist transformation facilitates perpetuation of ethnic traditions. Pika & Prokhorov (1994) call this process neotraditionalism.

   2.   If the motives for formation of family/clan holdings or maintaining current employment were related to the new economic freedoms and the search for profits, one would expect participation in the cash economy to be increasing. One would expect socioeconomic differentiation in the native community. As part of a growing market economy among family/clan farms, one should observe increasing commodity production and intensive utilization of local renewable resources. Use of non-local energy, capital, and wage labor should increase. One would also

expect contractual sales (balanced exchange), competitive consumption of resources within and between family groups along with a concomitant breakdown in cultural traditions. Industrial institutions and formal economic principles should be gaining local importance with imported energy, raw materials, and capital equipment. Proximity to government facilitates access to distribution of territory and capital.

HUNTER-GATHERER SHARING IN A RAPIDLY CHANGING PLURAL SOCIETY

Despite the rather liberal conditions under which family/clan holdings can be obtained, very few families have actually taken the new, that is to say, "traditional," form of land holding in the heart of the tundra. Out of the native population of the Avam Tundra area, over 700 individuals, only four families have taken claim to traditional territories. Most of the family/clan holdings are close to the regional capital, Dudinka, or the industrial city of Norilsk. Why did so few decide to take legal control of ancestral lands? In order to understand the motivations for their not taking family/clan holdings, I also surveyed native families still retaining rights to state enterprise holdings. I characterized and compared the two types of households in terms of land-use, local economy, social organization, and relationships with the macroeconomy. I asked specific questions about types of exchange and the kinds of changes in exchange since the break-up of the Soviet Union. My goal was to find out if individual Siberian hunter-gatherers were pursuing self-interest, minimizing risk, optimizing some other utility, or following mixed strategies with group-determined aspiration levels. A similar range of strategies is also found in the theoretical study of hunter-gatherer exchange and traditional economies.

The Nature of Human Social Exchange: Three Models

One explanation of why fully self-interested strategies might not be spreading among Siberian hunter-gatherers as much as expected can be derived from seemingly unlikely sources—optimal foraging theory and economic anthropology. This section reviews theoretical alternatives to classical microeconomic models of hunter-gatherer exchange with assumptions of self-interest and supply and demand.

Although mainly concerned with production (i.e., foraging decisions), Jochim (1976) looked at a series of general criteria for guiding decision-making processes in hunter-gatherer societies. Jochim's main assumption was that economic choices are deliberative, rational, and based on preferences among consequences. Similarly, rational decision-making is a basic assumption of formal economic theory (Wilk 1996). An apparently contrasting assumption is that hunter-gatherer decisions are made to satisfy a group-determined aspiration level rather than to maximize specific utilities (Jochim 1976). This supposition is similar to key postulates in substantive economic theory (Plattner 1989, Wilk 1996) and Polanyi's institutional approach (Halperin 1994). For example, Jochim (ibid.) also proposes that, for hunter-gatherers, there is an underlying desire to limit effort and a preference or allowance for mixed-strategy solutions. Mixed-strategy solutions entail simultaneous performance of more than one activity, simultaneous exploitation of more than one location or region, and sequential changes of activities and locations utilized (Jochim 1976:7). An example of mixed strategies in hunter-gatherer societies would include local food sharing side by side with long-distance exchange, such as the hxaro that presumably mitigates against hard times among the !Kung (Lee 1984:101-102, Wiessner 1977).

Risk-sensitive foraging models in behavioral ecology postulate conditions (high risk and uncertainty) under which utilities other than energy or profit are optimized. In risk-sensitive foraging models, the relationship between the benefit gained and the energy expended during a given foraging interval is not linear and, therefore, individuals may choose alternatives that do not give the highest mean net gain of energy (McNamara & Houston 1992, McNamara et al. 1991). Similarly, in hunter-gatherer exchange, it is likely that individual decisions do not always lead to the maximizing of energy or profits if the costs and the benefits are not related in a linear manner. Long-term social utilities, such as group norms or the maintenance of a moral code, may be more important than energy or profit. For example, in the native community where I conducted my research, many households regularly gave food and brought firewood to a set of invalid pensioners who had no children to render such assistance. Upon follow-up inquiry, I found that this action was predicated on charity and conformity to group norms. I will discuss similar cases in detail below.

In most evolutionary models of exchange (see Cosmides & Tooby 1992, Smith 1991), individuals are assumed to behave in ways that make sense in terms of observable or hypothesized individual costs and benefits. These models are similar to formal economic models in their assumptions of self-interest and marginal utility. In the debate about why hunter-gatherers share, Hill and Kaplan (1993:701-702) summarize the causal models in evolutionary ecology:

> [R]esources may be relinquished by an acquirer to another individual because (1) kin selection favors altruistic resource transfer, (2) reciprocal altruism favors sharing in order to decrease daily intake variance, (3) food exchanged for another currency (resource or service) is worth more fitness to the acquirer than the food given up, or (4) the cost of defending the food from another individual is greater than the fitness value to the acquirer.... Hawkes' [1993:341-61] discussion assumes that single observations of food redistribution incongruent with one of these four factors constitute evidence that the factor is generally unimportant in explaining the observed food redistribution in that society.... We do not yet see any evidence that will allow us to determine in any human society what fraction of food sharing is attributable to which of the four factors just listed.

Hill and Kaplan (1993:705) call for research that tests the specific predictions derived from these hypothesis. Before detailing these predictions, I shall define the technical terms in each hypothesis. I review each of the hypotheses presented above in their order appearance and outline some problems with comparability.

The first key concept in Hill's and Kaplan's Hypothesis 1 is kin selection, a process by which characteristics are favored due to their beneficial effects on the survival of close relatives, including offspring *and* non-descendant kin (Maynard Smith 1964). The second important concept in Hypothesis 1 is altruism, which implies a benefit to a recipient and a cost to the altruist (Krebs & Davies 1993). The evolutionary conditions under which an altruistic act will spread by kin selection were formalized in Hamilton's (1964) concept of inclusive fitness, the sum of an individual's personal reproductive success and his or her influence upon the fitness of relatives, weighted according to the coefficients of relatedness[2] to each individual. According to Hamilton's Rule (Krebs & Davies 1993:268), altruistic traits can perpetuate benefits by selection through inclusive fitness if the costs to the altruist are less than the benefits to the relative divided by the coefficient of relatedness.

Hypothesis 1 attempts an explanation in terms of ultimate causation, which concerns adaptive, selective, or reproductive significance: kin selection, which operates over evolutionary time, leads to altruistic resource transfer. According to Hamilton's Rule, one would expect, other things being equal, that altruistic resource transfer would be a direct function of genealogical relatedness: where the sum of the coefficient of relatedness times the benefit to the recipient minus the cost to the altruist is greater than zero, altruism can evolve. Thus, inclusive fitness benefits would play a role in the perpetuation of the genotypic substrate of the altuistic characteristic. Obviously, ultimate causation requires more than one generation. Synchronic data showing that altruistic resource transfer to non-descendants correlates with genealogical relatedness is suggestive, but it does not prove that kin selection for altruism is operating. The problem with this hypothesis is that it says nothing about proximate causation, the direct mechanism that brings something about. It is my contention that the motivation underlying kinship cooperation is the proximate mechanism that was shaped by natural selection to promote altruistic resource transfer. I will discuss evidence for this mechanism in the section on kinship and exchange below.

Hypothesis 2 is based on the key concept of reciprocal altruism. Trivers (1971) defined reciprocal altruism to account for cooperation among non-kin when the benefit of the altruistic act to the recipient is greater than the cost of to the actor and when the favor is paid back in the future. Like kin selection, reciprocal altruism is another, ultimate-level explanation to account for cooperation. Reciprocal altruism implies the evolution of proximate mechanisms, such as evaluation of costs and benefits (Axelrod & Hamilton 1981) and cheater detection (Cosmides 1989, Cosmides & Tooby 1992), and certain conditions, such as high probability of future interaction (Axelrod 1984), in order for it to operate. The main difference between Hypothesis 1 and Hypothesis 2 is that, in the second, the altruistic act is paid back directly rather than through inclusive fitness benefits.

It is likely that the proximate mechanisms evolved through reciprocal altruism are different than those evolved from kin selection. Reciprocity, also known in game theory terms as TIT-for-TAT (Axelrod 1984), is a fairly rational strategy. TIT-for-TAT is defined as: start with cooperation, then repeat what the other individual did on the first move. The rationality of reciprocal altruism is often applied historically to the development of human economies (e.g., Hill & Kaplan 1993:701). It is likely that altruism to individuals related genealogically (nepotism and extra-parental nepotism) is a more emotional trait than reciprocity.[3]

A key concept in Hypothesis 3 is fitness. It is unclear in the quote whether the fitness Hill and Kaplan refer to in the hypothesis is inclusive or personal (direct). I assume they mean personal fitness, since inclusive fitness would conflate Hypothesis 3 with Hypothesis 1. Direct fitness is the component of inclusive fitness gained through personal reproductive success. The concept is useful for ultimate explanations of the evolution of traits. In the case of Hypothesis 3, the trait is the ability to weigh costs and benefits in different currencies of exchange.

Unfortunately, Hypothesis 3 mixes ultimate and proximate explanations in its formulation. The hypothesis compares apples (food given up) with oranges (other resource or service) by converting both to pineapples (fitness terms). In people's motivations, not to mention a field study, it is unlikely to directly differentiate the fitness implications of exchanging food for other resources. In addition, Hypothesis 3 does not propose any specialized proximate mechanisms for the ability or motivation to exchange food for another resource or service worth more to the individual.

I propose that Hypothesis 3 is really a special case of Hypothesis 2, where the exchange returns are in different material or social currencies. Hill and Kaplan (1993:701) suggest that reciprocal altruism (Hypothesis 2) is a basis for modern economic phenomenon, such as the monetary system, borrowing and lending, and insurance. When discussing Hypothesis 3, they state that "[e]xchange of resources for some other fitness currency also appears to be common in human societies and is the basis for market exchange in human societies" (ibid.). Similarly, I do not see that Hypotheses 2 and 3 can be differentiated in terms of the ultimate causation (reciprocal altruism). In terms of proximate causation, one might imagine that exchange of food for resources in another currency is practiced to leverage the benefit to the giver (i.e., to accumulate resources by exchange for more durable goods or social and reproductive wealth). The difference between Hypothesis 2 and Hypothesis 3 is in the motive for the greater payoff to the individual exchanging food for other resources. The motivation to accumulate and manipulate surpluses is necessary for the development of the modern economy (Marx 1994, Engels 1972:32).

Hypothesis 4 converts energetic currencies into fitness terms, then weighs the fitness costs and benefits over evolutionary time. Again, the hypothesis mixes ultimate and proximate explanations. What differentiates Hypothesis 4 from the other hypotheses is the unfriendly nature of the exchange: you allow someone to take from you, if the costs of protecting the resource are greater than the benefits of protecting it. On the proximate level, this hypothesis implies specific motivations, such as taking measures to protect resources and judgement of other individuals' relative aggressive formidability or social formidability, as well as the motivation to take resources from others, whether through stealing or begging.

The proximate mechanisms for the hypotheses above need closer examination before specific predictions can be derived. One of the goals of this paper is to ascertain what fraction of food sharing in one society is attributable to the three evolutionary and economic models described above. Whether the proportion of food sharing and exchange through the various strategies is changing is the other question the paper addresses. Evolutionary ecological models have been formulated to show the selective conditions where four exchange strategies can be perpetuated. The direct mechanisms that bring about food sharing and other forms of exchange are discussed in more detail below. Following Jochim's (1976) assumptions of effort limitation and mixed-strategy solutions, one would predict that all four strategies would be present in a subsistence economy, with a preference for altruistic resource transfer and reciprocal altruism. Following risk-averse models, one would expect some sharing to make sense only in terms of local traditions of social welfare.

Exchange Types and the Direction of Change

One of the basic assumptions about the history of human economic and social organization is that our ancestors lived in small groups comprised mainly of kin. Sahlins (1968:85, 1972:193-196) proposed a scheme of reciprocities based on this phylogenetic assumption. He distinguished different kinds of exchange by the immediacy and equivalence of returns, as well as their material and mechanical likeness. Sahlins' types of reciprocity are mapped onto an abstracted social structure of nested spheres of social affiliation and their associated types of reciprocity (1968:85, 1972:199). The main feature differentiating Sahlins' types of reciprocity is "the spirit of exchange, about its disinterestedness or its interestedness, the impersonality, the compassion" (Sahlins 1972:192). Sahlins views his scheme as much a moral as a mechanical typology.

Generalized reciprocity, or "putatively altruistic" transactions of assistance given and, if possible and necessary, returned, occurs generally among close kin, according to Sahlins' model (1972:193-194, 199). At one point, Sahlins (1972:194) distinguishes generalized reciprocity by a "sustained one-way flow" of resources; failure to reciprocate does not cause the giver to stop giving. According to this definition, generalized reciprocity could be formulated into game theory terms as a strategy: "always cooperate." However, Sahlins (1972:194) notes that, while the material transaction is repressed by the social realm, "the expectation of reciprocity is indefinite." In another discussion of reciprocity, Sahlins (1968:88 following Gouldner) states that it entails: (1) helping those that have helped you and (2) not injuring those who have helped you. Thus stated, the "always cooper ate" strategy is not sufficient to characterize generalized reciprocity, since these conditions intercede against endless cooperation (and the costs implied in it).

Balanced reciprocity refers to exchange where the returns are made in the cus tomary equivalent of the thing received (Sahlins 1972:194). According to Sahlins (1972:199) model, balanced reciprocity would be expected between households or villages within recognized bands or tribes. Balanced reciprocity is less persona and more economic than generalized reciprocity. Unlike generalized reciprocity "the relations between people are disrupted by a failure to reciprocate within lim ited time and equivalence leeways" (Sahlins 1972:195). In game theory terms, bal anced reciprocity clearly entails the strategy of "cooperate, then do what the other player did on the previous move." In balanced reciprocity, social relations hinge on material flow, while in generalized reciprocity, the material flow depends or social variables, according to Sahins (ibid.).

And finally, negative reciprocity—"the attempt to get something for nothing with impunity, the several forms of appropriation, as well as transactions opened and conducted to gain net utilitarian advantage" (Sahlins 1972:195)—is expected between strangers or recognized enemies, according to Sahlins' (1972:199) model. Negative reciprocity is the most impersonal form of exchange. Not surpris ingly, negative reciprocity may entail one-way flows, with reciprocation contin gent upon mustering countervailing pressure or guile. On the mild end of negative reciprocity (e.g., barter, haggling, gambling), there is an attempt to cooperate With the more self-interested forms of negative reciprocity (e.g., seizure, theft, violence), the "partner" defects in the first round and there is a return defection when possible. In negative reciprocity, the participants are opposed interests, each looking to maximize at the other's expense in a zero-sum game. Again, the actor is expected to repeat what the other player did on the previous move.

What really differentiates Sahlins' types of reciprocity is the participants' intent in gaining specific benefits at certain costs. Since material flows can be "one-way" for both generalized and negative reciprocity, material flow and expectation of returns are not good distinguishing features. Intent ranges from the putatively altruistic in generalized sharing to the fully self-interested forms of negative reci procity. In balanced reciprocity, self-interests are compromised in a positive-sum game. Describing the proximate causes for exchange in terms of the psychological and moral motivations allows more precise categorization for sharing and exchange.

One problem with Sahlins' model is the static association of the types of reci procity with certain social spheres. In reality, the occurrence of various types of exchange in any given instance is likely to be conditional. Sahlins (1968:85) pro posed that environmental conditions should change the types of reciprocity occur ring in a given person's social sphere. For example, one would expect a prolonged and severe drought to cause increasing levels of negative reciprocity to occur between households after an initial period of generalized reciprocity.

The proximate motivations derived from Sahlins' typology map fairly well onto the (ultimate) evolutionary ecological hypotheses for exchange outlined in the previous section. Generalized reciprocity corresponds with the altruistic resource transfer of Hill and Kaplan's (1993:701) Hypothesis 1. Balanced reciprocity corresponds with exchanges for other currencies (e.g., reduction of intake variance, and other resources or services) in their Hypotheses 2 and 3. Negative reciprocity corresponds with the resource defense and acquisition of Hypothesis 4.

In this paper, I attempt to check preferences for the types of exchange in a hunting-and-gathering community in the Avam tundra. I expected that the exchange types would be changing in a certain direction due to the conditions of transitional stress in Russia: either to an entrepreneurial, self-interested economy or to a neotraditional economy, as defined above. Sahlins' model (1972:194-199) provides additional logic for the expected direction of change. As resources become scarce for extended periods, the costs of sharing increase and the benefits decrease, even among relatives.

In the case studies mentioned at the beginning of the paper (Dudwick n.d., Kuehnast n.d., Ssorin-Chaikov n.d.), it is clear that negative reciprocity has encroached on social spheres that were previously dominated by balanced reciprocity or generalized reciprocity. What has prevented this effect from occurring in large part for aboriginal Siberians? It is my contention that kinship is the key to understanding the unexpected preservation of generalized reciprocity in aboriginal Siberian exchange. I base this claim not on prior theoretical considerations, such as kin selection, but on explicit discussions observed among the Avam community, along with my observation of exchange. I will discuss the role of kinship after presenting the exchange data.

In addition to focussing on Sahlins' (1968, 1972) three types of reciprocity, my research focused on delayed exchange, a form of reciprocity in which an individual aids another person with an expectation of returned aid at some time in the future. Delayed exchange is in some respects a subtype of both generalized and balanced reciprocity. Sahlins (1968:85) and Service (1979:17) included delayed exchange within balanced reciprocity. At any given time, an act of delayed exchange appears unidirectional. However, if the aid is not returned within an agreed upon or expected time frame or equivalency, the exchange partnership ends. In my research in the Avam community, I found that most adults were familiar with delayed exchange (*vzaimno-obratnaya pomoshch*) and had opinions on how it has changed since 1991.

I divide balanced reciprocity into two types of exchange for reasons specific to the field site. The first type of balanced reciprocity is *barter (trade)*, in which one resource is exchanged for another of equal value. The relative value is often times negotiated, and equivalencies may vary, depending on supply and demand conditions. I have documented several instances of price negotiation in barter and will describe them below. Bartering techniques range from good-natured trading to speculation, depending on the good being traded and the partner. With speculation, barter is unsociable and should be classified with negative reciprocity. In most cases, however, barter equivalencies are stable and certain locally produced commodities are used as a currency. With trade, barter should be classed as a form of balanced reciprocity. The second type of balanced exchange is *money purchasing*. Here, resource exchanges are mediated by a universal currency. What happens, then, in indigenous hunter-gatherer societies when the universal currency looses most of its value?

METHODS

The question of whether family/clan farms represent one or another strategy would provide only a narrow picture of current events in northern Siberia. Only a small percentage of the native population has taken the family/clan or community/ clan holdings (*semyeino-rodovoye* or *obshchino-rodovoye khozyaistvo*). Thus, in order to examine the local foraging economy and its relationship to the land and to the larger economy, I had to widen my focus to include those families that had not privatized land. I applied the hypotheses above to the households maintaining employment with the state enterprise.

To evaluate alternative explanations of social and economic change in the aboriginal Siberian communities where I worked, I developed an exchange schedule to document the importance of the subsistence and cash sectors through time. I interviewed participants about income, expenses, and sources of consumer goods, capital equipment, and spare parts. I also asked questions about the relative importance of generalized sharing, delayed returns, other forms of aid, balanced exchange, imported goods, and competitive consumption of those goods prior to and after the break-up of the Soviet Union. Subsequent interviews focused on the informal economy and exchange through time, along with the motives for establishing family and clan farms or for remaining in the state enterprise.

In addition to the above-mentioned structured surveys, I used the techniques of participant observation and informal, unstructured interviews to get an idea of the history of the population and its resource use patterns. I also reviewed archival and statistical data made available by various offices of the Taimyr regional government. To locate family/clan holdings in the region, I spent a few weeks in the spring of 1997 in the Government Archive of the Taimyr Autonomous Region and the Dudinka City Committee of Land Resources. I reviewed 110 acts in which land was taken from or assigned to newly formed holdings. Many of these acts were made for non-native hunting/trapping and fishing holdings. Approximately 50 were family/clan holdings for native households, and most of these were close to the regional capital, Dudinka, or the Norilsk industrial district.

My research was focused in the Avam tundra area of the Taimyr Autonomous region of northern Krasnoyarksii Territory (*Krai*). During the first nine months, I conducted 26 open-ended interviews using my exchange schedule. For the next nine months, I refined my survey, based on the previous experience. The settlement administration cooperated with me on my project and facilitated validity and replicability testing by allowing me to make a complete census of the area, based on their registration book. There were 673 individuals (167 households) registered to live in Ust Avam and the surrounding tundra. The administration of Ust Avam defined households as those individuals living together in one apartment. I interviewed 78 individuals from households that did not participate in previous interview (plus one that had participated). I surveyed a random sample of adults working in the four main income sectors in Ust Avam in order to generate valid and replicable data (Pelto & Pelto 1978:33). The income sectors are: (1) the "Taimyrskii" government hunting enterprise (*gospromkhoz*); (2) budgetary organizations, including the settlement administration, school, health clinic, and post office; (3) federal pensions and unemployment; and (4) the store and bakery. The exchange data presented later are based on this second set of interviews.

ECONOMIC TRANSITION

To get an idea of how the formal economic situation has changed for the native people of the Avam tundra, I generated diachronic data on the cost of living. These data are based on information from the Agricultural Bureau of the Taimyr Autonomous Region and my own interviews of 79 household heads. The data show relative stability in cost of living throughout the 1980s and a small improvement in standard of living in 1988 and 1989. In 1991, rapid inflation in goods and services began, along with the devaluation of the ruble. That year marks the beginning of Russia's transition to market capitalism.

A striking indicator of the economic transition's impact on the native people of the Avam tundra is the cost of bread, an important food item in Russia. During the 1800s, the Czar set up grain reserve stores across the north to prevent starvation. The Soviet government included bakeries along with clinics and schools at the stations established along the Dudinka-Khatanga reindeer trail. Bread remains an important food item in the Avam tundra. It was consumed at almost every meal in which I participated. I have observed a significant increase in the cost of bread since 1991.

Figure 6 shows the cost of a 1 kg bread loaf at the Ust Avam bakery in proportion to the average salary of all rural-enterprise workers. The average salary figures come from the Taimyr Regional Agricultural Bureau's published reports on economic performance. I determined the cost of one loaf of bread from informant interviews as well as my own observations.

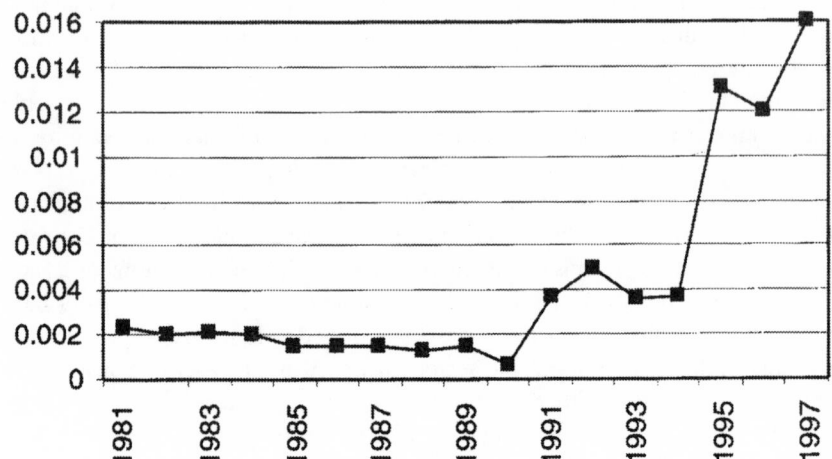

Figure 6.   Cost of One Loaf of Bread (1 kg) as a Proportion of the Average
Salary of All Taimyr Rural Enterprise Workers (1981-1997)

Another striking indicator is the increase in the cost of snowmobiles and spare
parts. Snowmobiles are used in production, mainly for transportation to hunting
cabins but also to check fishnets on distant lakes and trap-lines, and during pursuit
of caribou. During interviews, the professional and sports hunters of the Avam
area often mentioned the rapid increase in the price of snowmobiles and spare
parts since 1991. The most widely used snowmobile in Russia is the Buran
("snowstorm"), produced in the Perm Region.

In the 1970s and 1980s, the government hunting enterprise gave snowmobiles
to professional hunters for five seasons, at the end of which time the machines

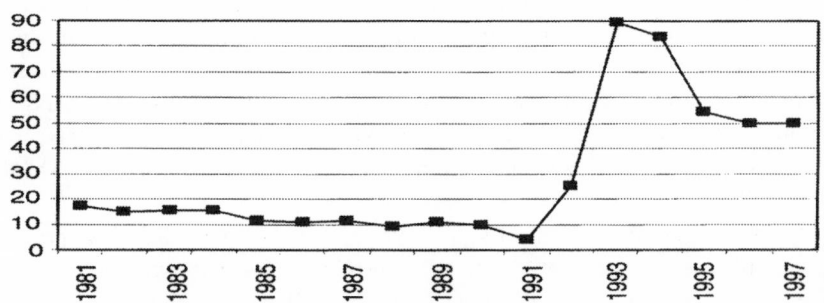

Figure 7.   The Cost of One "Buran" Snowmobile in Terms of the Average
Monthly Salary of All Taimyr Rural Enterprise Workers (1981-1997)

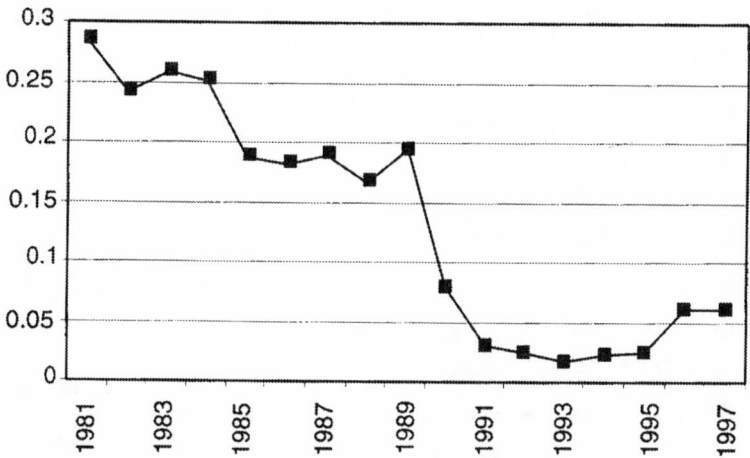

Figure 8.   The Average Value of an Arctic Fox Pelt in Terms of the Average
Monthly Salary of All Taimyr Rural Enterprise Workers (1981-1997)

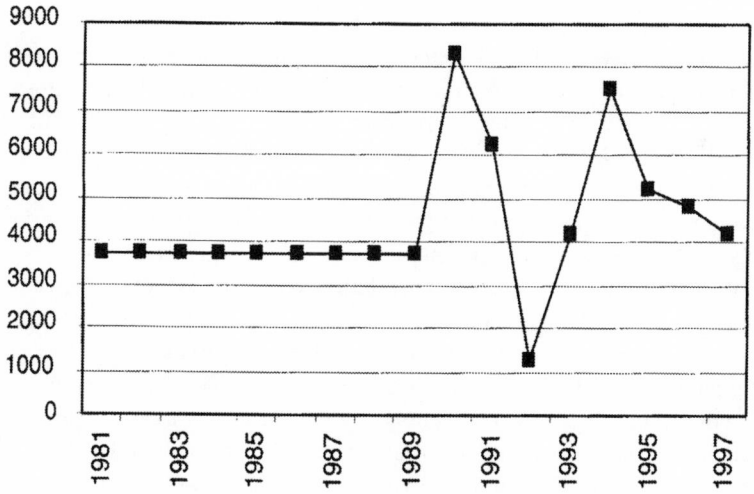

Figure 9.   The Cost of One "Buran" Snowmobile in U.S. Dollars at the
Official Exchange Rate (1981-1997)

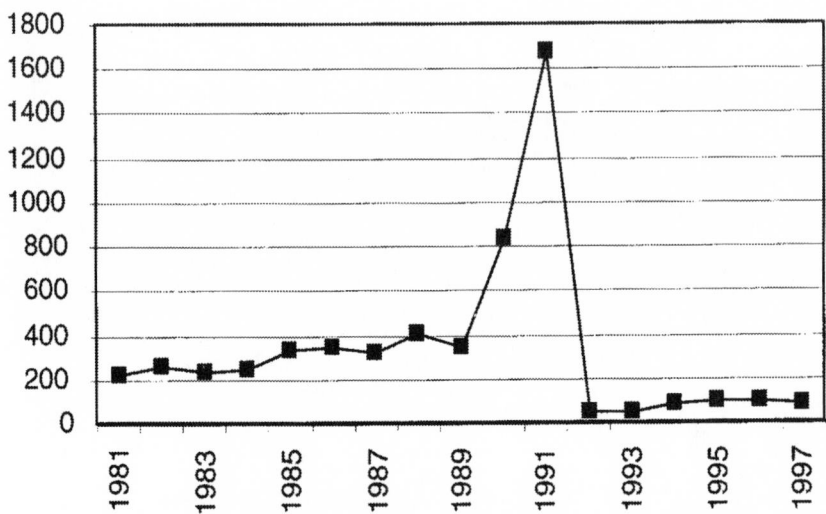

Figure 10. The Average Monthly Salary of All Taimyr Rural Enterprise
Workers, Converted to U.S. Dollars at That Year's Average Official
Exchange Rate (1981-1997)

were written off (*spisany*) the enterprise's balance sheet and became personal
property of the hunters. In addition to these "plan" snowmobiles, before 1991
hunters received snowmobiles as prizes and, in some cases, purchased them with
personal income. I summarize the data on snowmobile cost in Figure 7. Since the
break-up of the Soviet Union, no one in the Ust Avam tundra has purchased a
snowmobile. Spare parts are not regularly available, and those that are ordered or
brought in by speculators are expensive and of dubious quality. Figure 7 shows the
cost of Russian-made snowmobiles in relation to average monthly income. Snowmobiles have gone from less than 10 average monthly salaries to over 50.

As an indicator of the value of the native hunter's contribution to exchange with
the larger economy, I calculated the average price of an Arctic fox pelt in terms of
the average monthly salary of all Taimyr rural enterprise workers. Figure 8 shows
the change in value from 1981 through 1997. The Agricultural Bureau of the
Taimyr Autonomous Region, as above, provided the average salary figures. The
average cost of the Arctic fox pelt was determined from actual receipts kept by
Avam hunters and, in my 1995 through 1997 fieldwork, through informant interviews.

In 1995, Russia introduced a monetary policy, called the ruble "corridor," that
effectively limited devaluation of the ruble. The Russian Central Bank purchases
rubles on the Moscow Inter-Currency Exchange (*MMVB*), using its hard currency

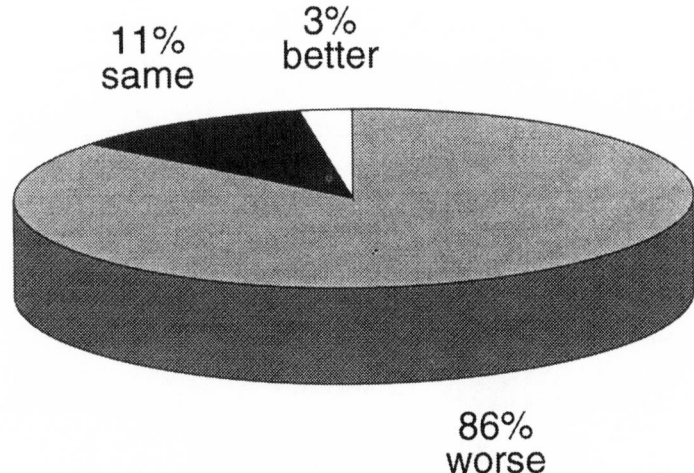

**11%
same**

**3%
better**

**86%
worse**

Figure 11. Survey Results:
Socioeconomic Situation before 1991 and Today
(79 Heads of Households, Avam Tundra, 1997)

reserves to create demand at times when confidence in the ruble is low. Thus, if current prices for goods and services are converted to dollars, the cost roughly approximates that prior to the fall of the Soviet Union. Figure 9 shows the cost in U.S. dollars of the Russian snowmobile from 1981 to 1997.

In urban centers, Russians have been converting rubles to dollars for years and have, thus, limited the negative effects of the ruble devaluation. In Ust Avam, where there is no way to convert rubles to dollars, people must bear the full brunt of the devaluation. In addition, they do not receive wages regularly. For example, in May 1997 salaries for the previous six months were flown in. In effect, salaries have increased 1,000 times and prices 10,000–20,000 times since 1991. A more than 10-fold decrease in purchasing power in six years has quite a powerful effect on the local economy. Figure 10 shows the average salary of all Taimyr rural enterprise workers in U.S. dollars at that year's average official exchange rate.

During interviews of heads of households, I asked, "Do you feel today that you are in a better, similar, or worse socioeconomic situation in comparison to prior to 1991?" The summary results are presented in Figure 11. The 79 representatives of households that participated in the survey included men and women from the four income sectors as defined above. These people were Dolgan, Nganasan, and Russian. The 79 participants also included six heads of family/clan holdings. I feel confidant that these results are representative of the overall position in which people in the Avam tundra feel themselves. These results confirm the seriousness of the effects of economic transition for the native community of Ust Avam, and by

Table 2.   Socioeconomic Situation, Before 1991 and Today: The "Worse"
Responses from 1997 Interview Questionnaire, 79 Households in the
Avam Tundra (Dolgan, Nganasan, and Non-Native)

Response	Number Giving This Response
Worse.	28
Worse, of course.	16
Earlier, of course better.	6
Not better.	4
Even more worse now/every year worse and worse.	3
Very bad.	3
100 times worse/the government could spit on them from a tall bell tower.	2
Worse (money), otherwise the same.	2
Naturally worse.	1
Everything not understandable now.	1
WWII was worse.	1
TOTAL	67

implication, other native communities in the Taimyr, although there was quite a bit of variation in the responses. A more fine-grained breakdown of the "worse" answers is presented in Table 2.

Thus, the overall economic climate for the people living in the Ust Avam tundra has degenerated significantly since the break-up of the Soviet Union. Objectively, purchasing power has decreased by at least an order of magnitude. Subjectively, the vast majority of households have seen a worsening in their socioeconomic situation. How might the transition economy affect the types of exchange? Following Sahlins' (1968) model, the spheres of balanced and negative reciprocity should be impinging on relationships formerly characterized by generalized reciprocity in good times.

CAPITAL DISTRIBUTION

As mentioned above, the professional hunters of the *gospromkhoz* (government hunting enterprise, "Taimyrskii") received capital equipment and supplies as part of their working relationship with that organization. This relationship was embodied in the "plan." In turn, the hunters provided meat, fish, and fur to the larger economy through the *gospromkhoz*.

Below, I present two sets of data to characterize the relationship between the *gospromkhoz* and its professional hunter/fishermen. One of these sets derives from interviews about each hunter's history of capital received. The other set consists of documentation about goods turned in to the *gospromkhoz* and capital received by one hunting brigade (see Appendix A). This documentation provides a concrete history of exchange between worker and employer during the socialist period. After 1991, there was very little documented, formal exchange for this brigade.

In interviews with *gospromkhoz* professional hunters and family/clan holders, I asked specific questions about the history of capital purchased and received from the state. The following information on rifles, shotguns, fishnets, and snowmobiles is based on 28 interviews. Some brigades specialized in caribou hunting and others in fishing and arctic fox trapping. This specialization had to do with differences in geography of the brigade territories in the Avam tundra. These geographical differences were reflected in the plans. Despite differences, most hunters received rifles and some ammunition for protection against predators and for subsistence.

Nineteen of 28 hunters received rifles for the season from the *gospromkhoz* every year they were employed. Three informants from surrounding state farms (*sovkhoz*) reported the same. Only five informants purchased rifles in stores at costs ranging from 2.5 to 7 million rubles (from U.S. $500 to $2000 at various times from 1994 through 1997). Three of those who purchased rifles were family/clan holders; two were employed hunters for the Gospromkhoz. One informant did not have access to a rifle.

The pattern with shotguns is different. Eight informants received shotguns as gifts from fathers, grandfathers, or the *gospromkhoz* (as prizes). Nine hunters reported not owning shotguns (an expected result, considering the difficulties of maintaining registrations in Russia now). Eleven informants purchased shotguns in stores. Most of these purchases were made in the 1970s and 1980s, costing the equivalent of U.S. $100 to $250.

Nineteen informants reported receiving fishnets from the *gospromkhoz*. Seven of them received fishnets every year or for a certain amount of fish caught (usually 200 kg). Four informants stated that they have not received fishnets. Two informants with family/clan holdings bought fishnet material in a store and in trade for fish at the Norilsk fish factory. One informant bought used fishnets, and another inherited his nets.

The pattern with snowmobiles was similar. Eighteen informants received snowmobiles from the government hunting enterprise or state farm. Snowmobiles were given with a 5-year life expectancy, after which they were written off the books and became the hunter's personal property. One informant bought a used snowmobile, and another inherited one from his father. Three informants received government hunting enterprise snowmobiles and also purchased snowmobiles in stores. One professional hunter purchased his only snowmobile in a store in 1986; two family/clan enterprise heads purchased theirs in recent years.

During socialism, the government owned all resources. Thus, hunters and fishermen who produced meat and fish were obliged to turn it all in to the government. Their own food needs were to be met by purchasing meat and fish from the government-owned store or the government hunting enterprise. The political aim of the government was to bring the native people of the north from "primitive communism" to "state socialism" in one step. Providing the instruments of labor and a consistent outlet for production was seen as providing economic motivation for participation in socialist construction. Appendix A provides a chronological summary of receipts documenting goods turned in and supplies received at one hunting brigade.

DISTRIBUTION OF LOCALLY-PRODUCED PROTEIN

I asked 79 heads of households in the Avam tundra about the source of their meat and fish in order to determine protein distribution patterns. Locally hunted and fished protein comprises the bulk of that consumed. In the 1,200 meals I recorded, 96 percent of the meat and fish came from locally hunted sources. The ratio of protein dishes to meals was close to 1:1 for the winter months and 0.8:1 for the summer months. For Arctic populations, daily intake of calories in the form of protein is important. The Avam community is no exception.

Not all heads of households I interviewed were hunter/fishermen or had such a person in the immediate family. Table 3 shows where all 79 households get their meat and fish. The table indicates a heavy reliance upon subsistence hunting and fishing. Close to half (48%) of informants answered that their main source of meat and fish is their own hunting and fishing activities in the tundra (coded "Hunting"). Of the 38 respondents who answered "hunting," 35 were men and 3 were women. "Offspring" were the source of protein for one male and four female respondents. Five women answered that "spouses" were the main source of protein. Two women and two men answered that most of their local protein is from their "purchasing" from the *gospromkhoz* (government hunting enterprise) or directly from hunters. "Other relatives" were the main source for one man and two women. Of those respondents describing single sources of protein, subsistence hunting is the most important, especially since it is likely that "offspring," "spouses," and "other relatives" gain most of their protein through "hunting." Of the respondents who neither hunt nor have a member of the immediate family who hunts, "offspring" and "other relatives" provide protein through regular gifts. "Purchasing" appears to be a supplemental strategy.

Twenty-four respondents (30.4 %) gave multiple answers to the question of where they get their meat and fish (coded "Mixed Sources"). Of these 24, seven were men and 17 were women. Six of the seven men included "hunting" and "purchasing." Of the 17 women, only four noted "hunting." Twelve women included "relatives," and 10 women included "purchasing." Again, with mixed sources the data indicate a heavy reliance upon subsistence hunting and sharing with relatives. "Purchasing" meat and fish from the government hunting enterprise (*gospromkhoz*) or directly from hunters is an option for 20 (25.3 %) of the respondents,

Table 3.   Responses to the Question on Source of Meat and Fish, 1997
           Interview Questionnaire, 79 Household Sample

	Respondents	
Sources of Meat and Fish	N	%
Hunting	38	48.1
Offspring	5	6.3
Spouse	5	6.3
Purchase	4	5.1
Other Relatives	3	3.8
Mixed Sources (n = 24)		
(a) Purchase and gift from kin or friends	6	7.6
(b) Gift from relatives and friends	4	5.1
(c) Hunting plus purchasing from *Gospromkhoz* or hunters	4	5.1
(d) Fishing, purchasing meat	4	5.1
(e) Gifts from consanguineal or affinal relatives	2	2.5
(f) Hunting, gifts or purchasing	1	1.3
(g) Hunting, purchasing fish	1	1.3
(h) Hunting, fish from relatives	1	1.3
(i) Gift from relatives and social security	1	1.3
TOTAL	79	100.0

as all or part of their strategy to get protein (four single-source responses plus 16 mixed-source responses).

Where families get their meat and fish is only part of the local protein distribution picture. The vast majority (93.7 %) of the 79 individuals taking part in the survey give away meat and fish. Table 4 provides rank-order answers to the question, "To whom do you give meat and fish?" Many of the 79 heads of households interviewed provided multiple answers to this question. The most common answer was "relatives" (consanguineal and/or affinal kin). Some people mentioned specific relatives, while others simply stated "relatives" (*rodnya*). When interviewees mentioned two categories of people to whom they gave meat and fish, the category mentioned second most often was "friends."

How much do hunting and fishing households give away relative to their own needs? In other words, how much meat and fish are they investing in the local social system? This information was very hard to determine through direct observation. In 18 months, I observed distribution of meat and fish at irregular intervals. The bulk of meat and fish distribution took place behind closed doors or at inopportune times for observation (such as at the helicopter pad). My direct observations being limited, I asked 79 heads of households during interviews, "How much meat and fish do you require for yourselves and how much do you require for shar-

Table 4. Rank-Ordering of Responses by 79 Heads of Households of the Avam Tundra to the Question, "To Whom Do You Give Meat and Fish?"

	Order Mentioned			
Recipients of Meat and/or Fish	*1st*	*2nd*	*3rd*	*4th*
Relatives (*rodnya*)	49	6	0	0
Friends	5	13	1	0
Affinal Kin	3	0	0	0
Neighbors	2	3	0	0
Pensioners, Single Mothers	7	8	2	1
Other People Who ask	8	7	6	0
Outsiders	0	2	0	0
No One	5	0	0	0

ing with other households?" Most informants could not distinguish between these amounts and stated how much they required in total. Some stated that it is a sin to count such things. Twelve of the 79 household heads gave relative estimates on their own caribou consumption and distribution for the winter (9 months), seven gave estimates on fish, and two gave estimates on fowl.

Five of the 12 who estimated winter caribou requirements indicated they gave away as much as they used themselves, from 2:2 to 20:20 caribou carcasses. One informant stated that the family consumed more than that given away—40 versus 10 caribou carcasses. The remaining six household heads stated that they consumed less than what they gave away. Four households gave away double what they consumed, one gave away triple, and another gave away quadruple their own consumption!

The results with fish are similar. Three household heads estimated they consumed less than they give away. Two informants estimated similar quantities consumed and given away. One family estimated that they consumed more than they give away. The estimates ranged from one to 20 bags consumed and from four to 15 bags (1 bag = 40 kg) given away in one winter.

It is clear from these data that significant portions of the meat and fish that Avam households obtain is given to other households in the community. Most of this protein appears to go to affinal and consanguineal relatives, but friends and neighbors also receive protein, as do pensioners, single mothers, and "other people who ask." The result is that it is rare that any household goes without protein, the major meal component. Even invalids are taken care of.

It was unexpected that people who do not hunt or fish would state that they give meat and fish away to other families. Thirty respondents (38%) answered that their main source of meat and fish was either purchased or given by friends, relatives, and other people. Twenty-seven (or 90%) of these people said that they gave meat and fish to relatives, friends, single mothers, pensioners, affines, and "other people who ask." What kind of benefit do they gain by giving away meat and fish if they themselves have a limited quantity of it?

One widely accepted hypothesis in anthropology, mentioned earlier, is buffering against variability in individual consumption rates—a risk reduction strategy. For exchange to work as a buffering mechanism, present abundance must be converted into a future obligation (Halstead & O'Shea 1989:4).

For certain households, such as the household with four invalid pensioners or the household of a single mother with nine young children, the buffering hypothesis does not make sense, since the receiving household has limited ability to fulfill its return obligation in kind or otherwise. To the contrary, I have documented a sustained, one-way flow of meat and fish from hunting to non-hunting households. According to informants in both households, this flow was maintained for two generations in one case.

The buffering hypothesis appears to work, however, in the cases of two non-hunting households sharing meat at various times. The receiving households can reciprocate when they have meat or fish themselves; their sources of meat and fish are likely to be different than those of the giving household, since everyone has their own set of relatives, friends, and neighbors. It is also likely that the receiving households have money at different times than the giving households if household incomes are from different sectors (*gospromkhoz* versus budgetary organization). The *gospromkhoz* brings salaries on its own helicopter flights, while budgetary organization monies and welfare payments are flown in on the regular passenger flights. Two non-hunting households are likely to have the ability to fulfill their obligation in kind or otherwise, a condition that supports the buffering hypothesis for non-hunting households sharing protein.

The buffering hypothesis also appears to work for non-related, casual hunting partners and their households. During one point in time, hunter A has meat and gives some to hunter B, who does not have meat. They go hunting or fishing together sometimes but not always. At another point in time, hunter A does not have meat but hunter B does; hunter B gives some meat to hunter A. I have documented this kind of exchange for three households.

A traditional aspect of giving and receiving meat and fish in the Avam tundra indicates that sharing is motivationally closer to generalized reciprocity than to reciprocal altruism. When someone gives meat and fish in a bag, the receiver returns the bag with something in it. The rule is: Never return an empty bag. The value of the thing returned is not significant. It can be matches, cigarettes, or some homemade fry bread, for example. This type of return is characteristic of generalized reciprocity. The value of the thing returned or the timing of the return is not what is important, but rather the exchange itself.

Thus, the question of the benefits a household gains by supporting households that cannot fulfill obligations is left open. Alternative hypotheses based on altruistic resource transfer, exchange for another "currency" (such as resources, services, or status), and high cost of defending resources against others in the group need to be checked. I will discuss the issue of kin selection in the final data section.

In the Avam tundra, meat and fish are distributed to relatives, friends, single mothers, pensioners, and other people who ask. Many of these people distribute locally produced protein further, as mentioned above. Thus, the individuals who procure the meat and fish are not directly involved in all the sharing. This practice is similar to other leveling mechanisms (Woodburn 1982) among groups of hunter-gatherers (e.g., !Kung "insulting the meat" [Lee 1984:50] and Mardudjara foodstuffs exchange [Tonkinson 1978:41]). These practices appear to be oriented toward feeding non-household members when there is surplus. Rather than maximizing specific utilities, such as cash or status, the Avam population appears to be conforming to group-determined aspiration levels (Jochim 1976). Over the long term, investing in social utilities, such as the maintenance of a moral code of sharing, may have benefits for individuals in terms of community support. In the Siberian Arctic, support may be needed at any time.

Exchange for another currency, such as status, does not appear to be an operative mechanism in these exchanges. I did not document any signs of heightened status for successful hunting households in terms of their equipment, household appliances, or domicile. In fact, some of the more successful hunters lived in the worst houses and could not sell meat or fish if their lives depended on it. Several hunters complained to me about how people had money for alcohol but not for meat and fish.

Despite the lack of a "market" for locally produced meat and protein, who has meat and fish is important information. The *gospromkhoz's* staff hunters, as well as sports hunters and fishermen, are often observed returning to the village carrying large burlap bags with butchered caribou or fish. Fairly accurate estimates of the amount brought into the village are made. "So-and-so brought six bags in this morning," was a common type of conversation opener.

This subsistence information spreads rapidly. When someone needs meat or fish, they usually know which house to go to. Hawkes's (1993) tolerated theft hypothesis is too strong for this situation, especially for the "other people who ask" category. Outright theft of meat and fish is rare. I documented only two cases. Rather, individuals come to the house and ask for meat or fish. If the hunter/fisher has a surplus of meat or fish, he or she usually gives it. Successful hunters/fishers could be accused of being stingy or greedy if they do not share their catch. The charge of being greedy would carry some cost, and charges made as rumors must be dispelled, even if the accusation is unfounded. Hiding or securing the meat and fish certainly carries a cost in building a secure shed or underground ice-chamber. Preserving meat and fish by smoking or salting carries the most cost, including the processing effort and the highly visible nature of processing in the settlement. Begging by other people who ask for meat and fish is another area where group-determined aspiration levels and effort minimization appear to be operative.

EXCHANGE DATA

Below, I show the results of surveys with family/clan and state enterprise households concerning economic change since 1991. I addressed the following questions to 79 household heads in the Avam Tundra. This number represents approximately 50 percent of the households in the area.

The first question had to do with the sharing economy: "When a hunter returns to the village with catch from the tundra, this catch is often shared. Is this sharing less, the same, or more than prior to1991?" Figure 12 summarizes the answers to this question. Forty respondents (50 %) felt that sharing had decreased since 1991. On follow-up inquiry, asking for explanation, 16 respondents felt that hunting households now were acting more for their own and close relatives' benefit. Twelve felt that hunting households wanted money or alcohol in exchange more often than before. Seven respondents cited fewer caribou in the area, due to changes in caribou migration patterns, as the main cause.[4] Twenty-five respondents (32 %) felt that the sharing of bush products was the same. "Tradition" was the most frequent answer to my follow-up question of

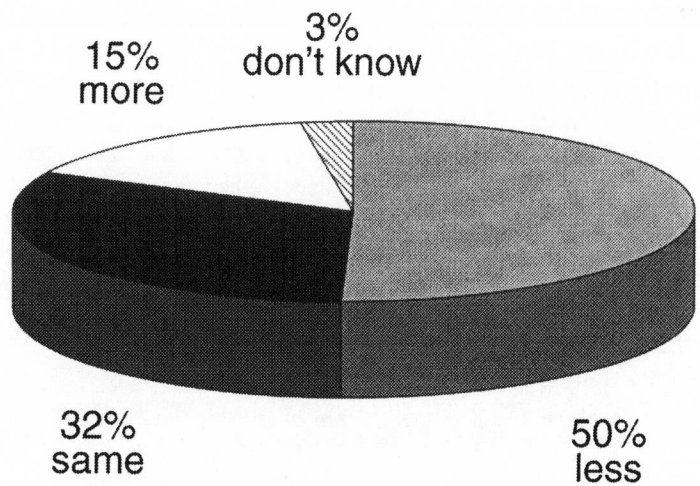

Figure 12. Survey Results:
Generalized Reciprocity before 1991 and Today
(79 Heads of Households, Avam Tundra, 1997)

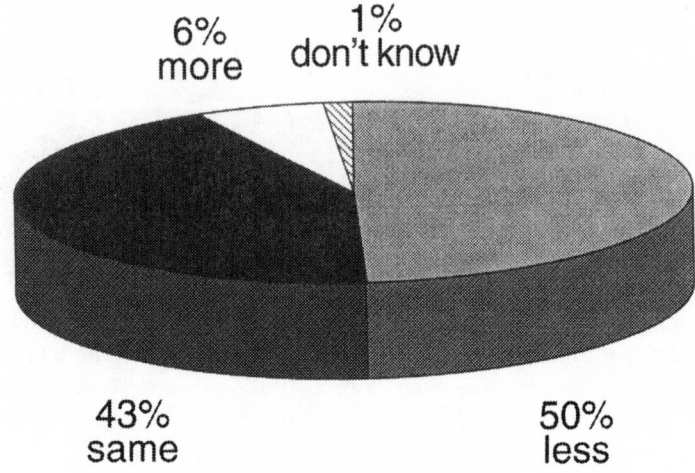

Figure 13. Survey Results:
Delayed Reciprocity before 1991 and Today
(79 Heads of Households, Avam Tundra, 1997)

why generalized reciprocity was the same. Surprisingly, 12 respondents (15 %) felt that generalized sharing had increased. These individuals cited a greater need in the village and fewer people producing food since 1991. Three percent had no opinion or did not know.

The second question had to do with delayed exchange, or mutual-return aid (*vzaimno-obratnaya pomoshch*). In the Russian Arctic, mutual aid has long been documented among native peoples. The state demonized mutual aid, as a sign of primitive communism, during collectivization. Nevertheless, mutual aid remained to mitigate the dangers and rigors of travel and the irregularity of spare-part supply. During interviews I asked, "When you need something, for example, a spare part or groceries, you can ask someone, for example, a relative, a friend or an acquaintance. In the future you promise to help them out with something. Does this kind of mutual-return aid occur more, the same, or less than it did before 1991?" Figure 13 summarizes the results of the question on delayed exchange.

Thirty-nine of 79 heads of households (50 %) felt that delayed reciprocity had decreased since 1991. Upon follow-up, ten of these individuals felt that people had changed and become greedier. Nine felt that things, such as spare parts, had become rare and expensive. Five felt that they had nothing with which to help others.

Thirty-four of 79 heads of households (43 %) felt that delayed reciprocity was the same as it had been before 1991. Having close social relationships (proxim-

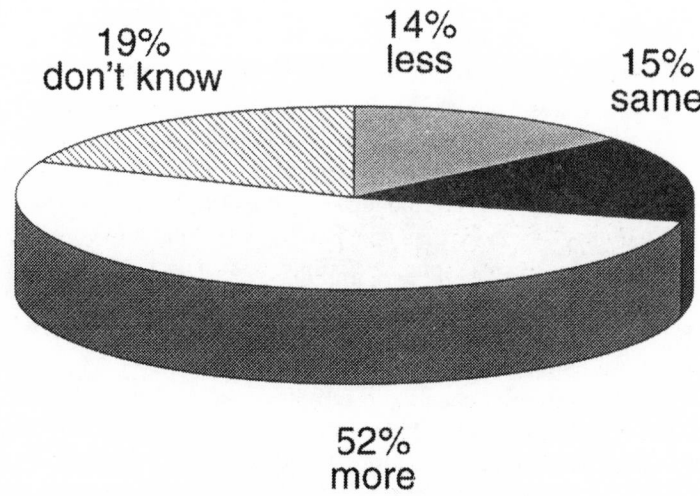

19% don't know

14% less

15% same

52% more

Figure 14. Survey Results:
Barter before 1991 and Today
(79 Heads of Households, Avam Tundra, 1997)

ity and kinship) and tradition were the most frequently mentioned reasons for the continuation of delayed reciprocity. Five individuals felt that delayed reciprocity was more important now than before 1991, and one person did not have an opinion.

To get opinions about the barter economy, I asked a similar question: "When you need something, for example, a spare part or groceries, you can trade for something that you have, for example, meat, furs, or alcohol. Does this kind of barter occur more, the same, or less than prior to 1991?" Figure 14 summarizes the results of the survey question on barter. Forty-one respondents (52 %) answered that barter occurred more often than before 1991. The top three reasons why these individuals felt that barter had increased are: life has changed, there is no money now, and barter was not allowed before 1991. Twelve of the 79 household heads (15 %) felt that barter occurred with the same frequency. Surprisingly, 11 respondents (14 %) felt that barter occurred less often. These individuals explained that their products were in higher demand before 1991 (when they still "traded well"). Fifteen respondents (19 %) had no opinion or did not know about barter; I interpret their lack of opinion as implicit recognition of the illegal (during socialism) or tax evasive (after socialism) nature of barter.

To get an idea of how the changes in the larger economy have impacted the population's purchasing power, I asked about balanced exchange through cash purchase: "You buy something with cash, for example, groceries, spare parts, holiday trips. Does this occur more, the same, or less than prior to 1991?" Figure 15 shows the survey results for the question on cash purchasing. The overwhelming majority of respondents, 64 of 79 heads of households (81 %), felt that they purchase less with money now than they did before 1991. Lack of money (due to delays in paying salaries and welfare) was the most common explanation (45 respondents). Lack of things to buy in the store was the second most common explanation (11 respondents). Twelve of the 79 household heads (15 %) felt that they buy more now than before 1991. The most common explanation was that things can be purchased only with money now. Before 1991, connections were more important than money in purchasing certain consumer goods. Three household heads (4 %) felt that that money purchasing was about the same as it was before.

Lastly, to get a picture of changes in self-interested egoistic behavior, I asked about negative reciprocity: "It happens that someone borrows something and does not return it. Does this occur more, the same, or less frequently than prior to 1991?" Figure 16 shows the results. Forty-one (52 %) of the 79 household heads felt that people were defecting on social exchanges more now than before the break-up of the Soviet Union. The informants mentioned the lack of salaries and changes in people (i.e., becoming less trustworthy) as the reasons for their perceived increase in defections. Eleven informants (14 %) felt that negative reciprocity was the same as it was before 1991. Another eleven (14 %) felt that negative reciprocity had actually decreased since 1991; most of them explained that they have nothing left to take. Sixteen informants (20 %) did not know or had no opinion. This question was intended to get at defections on social exchanges

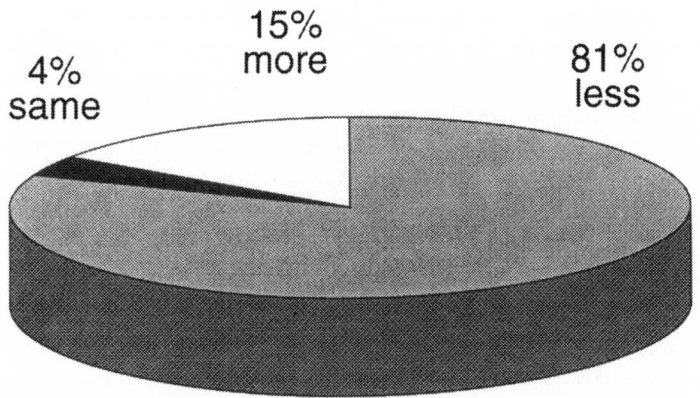

Figure 15.   Survey Results:
Money Purchasing before 1991 and Today
(79 Heads of Households, Avam Tundra, 1997)

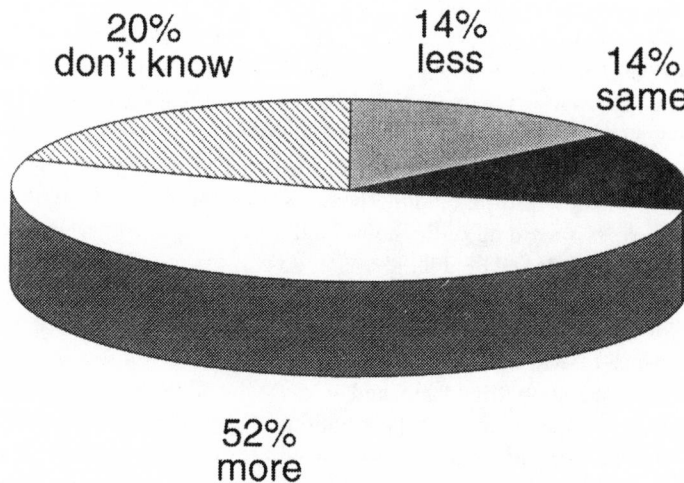

20%
don't know

14%
less

14%
same

52%
more

Figure 16. Survey Results:
Negative Reciprocity before 1991 and Today
(79 Heads of Households, Avam Tundra, 1997)

(borrowing items). My impression from answers to the follow-up question of why they felt negative reciprocity had changed was that people in Ust Avam are being more careful in lending their things.

As Figures 12-16 show, while approximately half of the respondents feel that generalized and delayed reciprocity are less often practiced than before, the other half feels that they occur as frequently or more often than prior to the fall of the USSR. Over half of the respondents feel that the incidence of barter is the same or has increased. Not surprisingly, respondents were almost unanimous on the decrease of their purchasing power. Finally, half of respondents agreed that defection on exchanges (negative reciprocity) has increased. These heads of households claim to be more careful about lending out their things or that they do not have anything else to lend out.

KINSHIP AND EXCHANGE

In the section on distribution of locally produced protein, I found that "relatives" were important recipients and sources, according to the 79 heads of households interviewed in Ust Avam and the surrounding tundra. Here, I present sociodemographic information on the density of genealogical relatedness in the Avam community and survey data on the role of kin. These data could falsify predictions about the role of kinship in altruistic resource transfer, discussed above.

At the time of my village census (1997), there were 673 living individuals[5] in Ust Avam. Only 8 of them were not related to anyone else in the village. The population is settled and most households are small. Average household size is four.

Following J.A. Barnes' methodological suggestions (Pelto & Pelto 1978), prior to asking questions about genealogical relatedness I asked about the role relatives (*rodstvenniki*) play. This question was the first asked during interviews of 79 household heads in the Avam tundra. The answers to this question give us an idea of relatives' roles according to the household heads. These characterizations are presented in rank-order in Table 5.

The answers can be divided roughly into two sets: concepts about kinship (such as close/distant relatives, old/young relatives, number of relatives) and various roles of relatives. Most of the explicit roles imply an enduring social relationship (such as communication, friendship, and help). Many of these concepts also imply some kind of sacrifice of time, energy, emotions, and protein. Two answers, "land" and "origin," were not as frequent as one would expect for an aboriginal population involved with land claims against the government. The answers "big role," "normal role," "positive role," and "little role" are frequent and hard to breakdown further. The relatives who play big, normal, or positive roles are likely to connote an enduring, personally remembered, social relationship. These answers cannot falsify the expectations of altruistic resource transfer and generalized reciprocity. The material exchange depends on the social relationship.

To falsify the hypothesis that kin selection is operating to produce or maintain adaptations for altruistic resource transfer, we would need to observe altruistic resource transfer to non-relatives. With kin selection, we expect the intensity of altruistic behavior to correlate with genealogical relatedness. From the section on distribution of locally produced protein, above, we know that the distribution of meat and fish in Ust Avam is not a random process. Relatives were mentioned as regular recipients.

If the distribution of protein in the community was a random process, the ultimate-level kin selection hypothesis could be falsified if average genealogical relatedness was low enough. The average relatedness of each individual to every other individual in the community (FgAll) is 0.007 for Ust Avam.[6] This figure is slightly lower than the relatedness coefficient for third cousins; in other words, any two individuals chosen at random in Ust Avam will be, on average, related to one another a bit less than third cousins. While this level of genealogical relatedness is high in comparison to a large, undergraduate lecture hall, it is low in comparison to some traditional societies (Chagnon 1983:143, Irwin 1987:144) and might not be sufficient for kin selection, depending on the costs of the altruistic act (Hamilton 1964).

If the distribution of locally produced protein favored consanguineal relatives over affinal relatives and non-relatives, the conditions for kin selection could be shown. In Ust Avam, each individual has 35 genealogical relatives on average, approximately 5 percent of the population. Again, this is low compared to some documented traditional societies (Chagnon 1983). The average relatedness of each

Table 5. Rank-Ordering of Responses by 79 Heads of
Households of the Avam Tundra to the Question,
"What Role Do Relatives Play in Your Life?"

Roles Relatives Play	Order Mentioned			
	1st	*2nd*	*3rd*	*4th*
Big Role	15	5	0	0
Close/Distant Relatives	4	8	2	0
Communication	3	1	2	0
Dependence	2	2	0	0
Don't Know	3	0	0	0
Fight	0	0	1	0
Friendship	1	1	2	0
Future	1	0	0	0
Help	13	14	3	1
Interconnectedness	1	0	0	0
Kinship or Parenting	1	2	0	1
Land	1	1	0	1
Little Role	3	0	0	0
Not Specified	3	0	0	0
Normal Role	11	0	0	0
Notoriety	0	0	1	0
Number of Relatives	10	0	0	0
Old/Young Relatives	2	3	0	0
Origin	1	1	0	0
Positive Role	2	2	0	0
Respect and Love	0	0	1	0
Sharing	0	2	1	1
Sincerity	1	0	0	0
Work	1	1	1	0

individual in the Avam community to consanguineal relatives (FgCon) is 0.213, less than that of an aunt, uncle, or half sibling, but more than that of a first cousin. This level is sufficient for kin selection.

As mentioned above, individuals stated to me repeatedly that half of the other villagers were their relatives (*rodnya*). Obviously, the average proportion of individuals' genealogical relatives is much less than 50 percent. Both Dolgans and Nganasans repeated to me quite often the statement that half of the other villagers were their relatives. Informant accounts of genealogies and official genealogies do not support the statement, if one limits *rodnya* to consanguineal relatives. It is likely that heads of households included not only their consanguineal relatives, but also their own affinal relatives and the affinal relatives of their consanguineal relatives. A bit of information that led me to conclude that affinal relatives of informants' consanguineal relatives are included in the *rodnya* concept is that I was told that it is a sin to marry them.

Specific affinal relatives were mentioned as the source or recipient in exchanges of meat and fish (summarized in Tables 3 and 4) but not as commonly as the more general "relatives" category. The survey did not force individuals to distinguish between affinal and consanguineal relatives in the distribution of meat and fish. Also, affinal relatives often have common consanguineal relatives in the next descending generation. For these reasons, it is hard to falsify the ultimate-level kin selection hypothesis selecting for altruistic resource transfer. On the proximate level, generalized reciprocity appears to account for the bulk of sharing among Ust Avam's population.

CONCLUSION

This paper has documented the transformation of Ust Avam's economy from socialism. The majority of the Avam tundra native population has experienced reductions in external capital and energy inputs since the collapse of the socialist economy. Despite this reduction, hunting, fishing, and trapping are being maintained for family subsistence purposes as well as to support non-hunting families. After the collapse of the Soviet Union, Ust Avam's population has moved from a state-financed industrial economy of scale to an economy of survival (subsistence and sharing with reduced levels of exchange in the larger economy). While the end result is similar to the result of the neotraditionalism model (Pika & Prokhorov 1994), introduced earlier, the mechanism is slightly different. There has been a decrease in access to new technology and information infrastructure in Ust Avam. Distance from the regional industrial center and high costs of transportation have made economies of scale unprofitable. With the economy of survival, there was little opportunity to revive traditional ethnicity.

It appears that Avam tundra hunter-gatherers are not trying to maximize energy or gain in most of the local sharing economy. Motivations related to kinship—such as helping, sharing, or playing a big role in someone's life—appear to reinforce the apparently generalized reciprocity employed by the producing individuals. Crosscutting the generalized reciprocity practiced mostly with relatives are delayed reciprocal exchanges based on the "give it if you have it" code. These delayed exchanges appear to reduce daily consumption variance among non-protein-producing households as well as between producing households in partnership.

The interview data on the role of relatives indicates that relatives help in a number of ways and that, for most people, relatives play an important role. The stated roles of relatives appear to confirm the proximate mechanism for altruistic resource transfer, generalized reciprocity. Relatives (*rodnya*) are claimed to be favored. The ultimate-level explanation of kin selection may also be operative. Average genealogical relatedness in the community is too low for kin selection if the costs of the altruistic act are high, such as death. However, distribution of meat and fish (and, likely, other forms of energetic sacrifice) is conducted on a non-random basis in the community and the costs are low.

Exchange with friends, non-related single mothers and "other people who ask" is not fully explainable by generalized reciprocity/kin selection (Hill's & Kaplan's [1993] first hypothesis). My modified version of Hill's & Kaplan's (1993) second hypothesis, that balanced reciprocity (selected through reciprocal altruism) favors food sharing in order to decrease daily intake variance, seems to work for hunting partners and non-producing households.

There is some direct evidence that food is exchanged for another currency (resource or service) worth more to the acquirer than the food given up. Meat and fish are exchanged for alcohol with transient speculators and a few resident non-natives. However, since transportation is very expensive now and the local "market" is saturated with meat and fish, the "cost" of alcohol in terms of meat and fish is very high. In the winter of 1996, one bottle (1 liter) of 96 percent ethanol could be exchanged for one to two caribou. In previous years, two liters of alcohol could be exchanged for one caribou carcass. These speculative and disadvantageous exchanges are rare (1 or 2 times in the winter, depending on transportation) and are clearly negative reciprocity. Most speculators now want cash instead of meat and fish. This was particularly the case during the summer 1997, when cutters with supply barges came to Ust Avam.

That meat and fish may be given away as charity appears to uphold the moral code of mutual aid, a long-term currency. The investment is made to non-related single mothers, pensioners, and "other people who ask." The moral code of "give it if you have it" (thusly stated in Ust Avam) is obviously an important group norm for community members with few close relatives. Since individuals cannot count on the state for support, and because anyone can become a marginal member of the community owing to the harsh environment, the local welfare system has been a viable, long-term investment, especially for middle-aged producers.

The "tolerated theft" hypothesis (Hawkes 1993) implies that the cost of defending the food from another individual is greater than its fitness value to the acquirer. This hypothesis is supported in a few instances where informants reported that certain individuals regularly took meat or fish without asking. Some measures against theft have been instituted in the last 10 years, such as the attachment of padlocks to apartment and garage doors. In the mid-1980s, a piece of wood or a bucket with coal in front of the door was enough to prevent non-residents from entering a household.

Another potential cost, mentioned above, of defending food is the accusation of being greedy. Although most individuals differentiate between true and untrue accusations, no one wants to be known as greedy, since it threatens short- and long-term reciprocal cooperation. Thus, it is prudent to give meat and fish liberally, if one has it. The "give it if you have it" code fits with the tolerated theft model in that the marginal value of a kilogram of meat to one that has it is low, and the value of that kilogram of meat to the one that does not have it is high. In constast to the tolerated theft scenario, the Dolgan and Nganasan view the "give it if you have it" code as a positive-sum game, since they or their relatives may be in the asking position at some point in the future.

With all of the strategies reviewed above, economic choices are deliberative and rational, based on preferences among consequences. Decisions are made to satisfy group-determined aspiration levels (having enough meat and fish to eat every day) rather than to maximize specific utilities (money or calories). Exchange with the larger economy has attenuated with the decrease in capital supply and the unpredictability of salaries. A certain amount of such exchange occurs through barter, but equivalencies have become more disadvantageous for the native producers in recent years.

With regard to opinions on changes in the types of exchange in Ust Avam, approximately half of the heads of households interviewed felt that the level of the giving of meat and fish was the same or greater than it had been prior to the break-up of the Soviet Union. The other half felt that this practice had abated. Similarly, half of the respondents stated that delayed exchange had abated, while the other half felt it had remained the same or increased. These differences might be related to age differences in the heads of households interviewed. Many elderly informants stated that generalized and delayed exchange had decreased since the break-up of the Soviet Union. Younger producers typically answered that they give more.

Two individuals with family/clan holdings were heavily involved with external sources of capital and energy in recent years. These holdings were located on the Pyasina River with good access to the industrial city of Norilsk. Both holdings had contracts with organizations in Norilsk. Nevertheless, these households shared a considerable amount of their production, trading the remainder through barter for capital goods, such as fishnets, spare parts, and gasoline. Initial capital was provided through low-interest government loans. Family/clan holdings appear to be oriented towards making money in the newly developing market in the Taimyr Region.

The remaining 26 hunters interviewed were officially working for the government hunting enterprise, which has significantly attenuated its relationship with them in terms of capital invested and goods accepted (quantity, variety, and value). The producing households and others interviewed were making ends meet with old equipment and improvised spare parts. The regional government was maintaining energy inputs for the settlement, but not at their pre-1991 levels. For example, diesel fuel shipments were half of the expected amount in 1997. A moderate level of exchange for consumer goods continued to occur but at much lower levels than prior to 1991. Generalized reciprocity, group-determined leveling mechanisms, and investment in the local moral system are being maintained.

ACKNOWLDEGMENTS

This research was supported in part by a grant from the National Science Foundation's Arctic Social Science Program (Doctoral Dissertation Research Award No. 9528936; N.A. Chagnon, Principal Investigator). In addition, my 1997 research was supported by a grant from the International Research & Exchanges Board (IREX), with funds provided by the National Endowment for the Humanities and the U.S. Department of State, Program for Scientific Research in Russia, Eurasia, and Eastern Europe (Title VIII). The research I conducted in 1996 was supported in part by a grant from the American Council of Teachers of Russian (ACTR), with funds provided by the U.S. Department of State, Program for Research and Training on Eastern Europe and the Independent States of the Former Soviet Union (Title VIII). Field research conducted in 1995 and 1996 was also supported in part by a Humanities/Social Science Research Grant from the Graduate Division, University of California, Santa Barbara. None of these organizations is responsible for the views expressed. During my field research, I was affiliated with Moscow State University's Ethnography Department, Moscow State Linguistics University, the Institute of Philosophy (Russian Academy of Sciences), and the Institute of Ethnology and Anthropology (Russian Academy of Sciences); I thank these organizations. I am grateful to Wayne E. Allen, Annegret Staiger, Melody Knutson, Will Palmer, and Ed Hagen for their comments and to Dirk Brandts, UCSB Anthropology, for graphics assistance. Only I, however, am responsible for the views presented.

APPENDIX A: CAPITAL SUPPLY AND WORK PRODUCTS TURNED IN (1979-1995) TO *GOSPROMKHOZ* "TAIMYRSKII"

Below is a chronological summary of receipts documenting goods turned in and supplies received at one hunting brigade of the government hunting enterprise (*gospromkhoz*), "Taimyrskii." The hunters of this brigade received money for products turned in (e.g., 40 rubles for a first-sort Arctic fox pelt). The supplies received from the government hunting enterprise were part of the plan. Each brigade had a plan specified by the *gospromkhoz*. Fulfillment of plans was not compulsory, but their over-fulfillment was rewarded with large salaries, regular supply of fuel and instruments of labor, and prizes—gifts of capital equipment, such as snowmobiles and shotguns.

Date	Products Turned in to the Gospromkhoz	Supplies Received for the Brigade
1/1/79		2.5 tons coal, 50 boxes
2/12/80	17 Arctic fox pelts	
2/15/80	5 Arctic fox and ermine pelts	
2/18/80	36 Arctic fox pelts	
2/19/80	11 Arctic fox pelts	
1/10/81	26 Arctic fox pelts	
1/10/81	11 Arctic fox pelts	

Date	Products Turned in to the Gospromkhoz	Supplies Received for the Brigade
2/3/81	21 Arctic fox pelts	
2/11/81	10 Arctic fox pelts	
2/23/81	10 Arctic fox pelts	
3/6/81		Radio station "karat"
4/12/81	15 Arctic fox pelts	
4/13/81	11 Arctic fox pelts	
4/20/81	19 Arctic fox pelts	
12/31/82	1 snowmobile	
1/1/82		"rubberoid" building material (20 rolls)
1/29/82	5 Arctic fox pelts	
4/29/82	30 kg fresh frozen hare, 8 fresh frozen rock ptarmigan, 14 hare pelts	
9/13/82		boards (4 cu. m), door jam (2) window jam (3)
9/15/82		10 barrels gasoline, 1 barrel kerosene
9/17/82		stove top, grill, doors (2), flue
12/30/83	15 Arctic fox pelts	
1/5/83	21 Arctic fox pelts	
2/7/83		3 sets of two-layer outfit, quilted mittens, fur hats, pressed felt boots, mitten covers, cotton outfits.
4/13/83	13 Arctic fox pelts	
4/13/83	40 Arctic fox pelts	
10/25/8		100 steel leghold traps
10/31/83		Glass 5 sq. m.
1/26/84	51 Arctic fox, hare, and ermine pelts	
2/3/84	44 Arctic fox pelts	
2/3/84	34 frozen rock ptarmigan	
2/7/84		1 barrel gasoline
2/7/84		3 sets of two-layer clothing, quilted mittens, fur hats, pressed felt boots, cotton work clothes
3/5/84	57 Arctic fox and hare pelts	
3/15/84		life jacket (1), hard hat (1), mittens (4 pair), mitten covers (4)
3/24/84	22 Arctic fox pelts	
3/24/84	41 fresh frozen rock ptarmigan	
8/18/84		1 ton salt, 20 sacks
11/1/84		5 kg nylon cord
1/28/85	727 kg frozen whitefish	
8/13/85		25 D batteries

Date	Products Turned in to the Gospromkhoz	Supplies Received for the Brigade
10/4/85		Radio station "karat"
10/4/85		Nails (200 kg), no. 2 steel traps (200)
10/9/85		1.5 cu. m lumber
10/25/85		1 barrel gasoline
11/11/85		Coal (12 t.), salt (1 t.), boards (3.5 cu. m.), cement (1 t.), burlap bags (336)
11/11/85		Gasoline, A-76 (3 t.), barrels (17), Oil M8A (0.2 t)
11/16/85		2 sets of two-layer outfit, fur mittens, fur hats, pressed felt boots
12/30/85	7 Arctic fox pelts	
12/30/85	7 Arctic fox pelts	
1/1/86		2 rolls of net material, 10 kg of fine net
1/5/86	30 fresh frozen rock ptarmigan	
1/29/86	18 hare pelts	
1/29/86	23 ermine, Arctic fox pelts	
1/29/86	48 fresh frozen rock ptarmigan	
2/4/86		47 burlap sacks
4/1/86		1 barrel gasoline
4/15/86	43 Arctic fox and ermine pelts	
4/15/86	64 Arctic fox pelts	
10/3/86		1 snowmobile
10/9/86		12 tons coal, 300 burlap bags
10/9/86		10 barrels gasoline
2/9/87	20 Arctic fox pelts	
2/9/87	7 Arctic fox pelts	
2/22/87	5 Arctic fox pelts	
2/22/87	11 Arctic fox pelts	
4/23/87		1 snowmobile and sleigh
5/26/87		2 sets of fur socks, rubber boots, cotton costumes, fur mittens, forest-cutting costumes, fisherman's costumes
8/19/87	1.5 tons of fish (various sorts)	
9/19/87		60 sacks
9/29/87		SKS bullets (30), signal rockets (30), shot (10 kg), capsules (2000), Styrofoam (10 kg), nylon cord for nets (10 kg)
10/16/87		1 snowmobile
12/23/87	5 Arctic fox and hare pelts	
3/18/88	829 kg frozen whitefish	
5/10/88	121 fresh frozen rock ptarmigan	

Date	Products Turned in to the Gospromkhoz	Supplies Received for the Brigade
12/26/88	20 Arctic fox pelts	
1/20/89	20 Arctic fox pelts	
3/17/89	134 fresh frozen rock ptarmigans	
3/17/89	1 wolverine pelt	
3/17/89	8 ermine and Arctic fox pelts	
4/2/89	7 Arctic fox and ermine pelts	
4/17/89	222 fresh frozen rock ptarmigans	
4/18/89	26 Arctic fox pelts	
4/20/89	160 fresh frozen rock ptarmigans	
4/25/89		electric generator
8/1/89		100 burlap sacks
8/21/89	800 kg fresh frozen whitefish, 280 kg frozen lake trout	
10/2/89		bullets for SKS
10/3/89		1.2 kg nylon cord
10/14/89		1 set pressed felt boots, fur mittens, cotton work jacket
10/14/89		1 set fur coat, pressed felt boots, fur mittens, cotton work jacket
2/2/90	31 Arctic fox pelts	
2/2/90	45 Arctic fox pelts	
2/13/90		nets 50x50 (1), nylon cord (300 g)
9/10/90		15 barrels gasoline, 1 barrel oil
9/11/90		10 tons coal, 1 ton salt, 7 barrels gasoline, 1 barrel oil, 200 burlap sacks
9/12/90		7 barrels of gasoline
9/12/90		7 barrels gasoline
9/24/90		1 snowmobile
9/26/90		1 quilted outfit, 1 set mittens
1/14/91		1 set pressed felt boots, fur mittens, cotton work jacket
3/7/91		30 horsepower boat motor
4/8/91	6 Arctic fox pelts	
4/8/91	50 Arctic fox pelts	
4/8/91	25 Arctic fox and hare pelts	
9/16/91		optical sight
9/16/91		bullets for "SKS," 7.62 mm
9/16/91		bullets for "Toz," 5.62 mm
9/16/91		5 tons coal, 110 sacks
9/16/91		9 barrels gasoline, 1.5 tons coal, 30 sacks
9/18/91		1 windmill and generator

Date	Products Turned in to the Gospromkhoz	Supplies Received for the Brigade
10/15/91		10 barrels of gasoline, 1 barrel of oil
3/23/92	2 tons frozen whitefish	
3/20/95	54 Arctic Fox pelts	
4/13/95	48 Arctic fox pelts	
10/20/95		5 barrels of gasoline
10/20/95		5 barrels of gasoline
[illegible]		7 barrels of gasoline
[illegible]		50 kg nails
[illegibl]e		net 38x38 (1) net 55x55 (1), block of shotgun shells (100 shells)
[illegible]		leaf springs (2), springs for snowmobile caterpillar (12),
[illegible]		1 snowmobile
[illegible]		building materials
[illegible]		8 barrels gasoline
[illegible]		boards (6 cu. m)
[illegible]		2 barrels gasoline
[illegible]		bullets SKS (80), signaling rockets (30)
[illegible]		1 barrel gasoline

NOTES

1. Russian researchers have debated whether Dolgan is a separate language or a dialect of Yakut (see Dolgikh 1963, Anderson 1995). A Yakut ethnographer visiting Ust Avam was able to freely converse with Dolgans there. They later reported to me that they understood most of what he said. However, when I took a Yakut grammar book to Ust Avam, several women fluent in Dolgan could not understand Yakut passages. To make matters more complicated, the Dolgans in the Avam tundra call themselves *tehlar* (people of nature) and their language, *tehli*. The Dolgans in Khatanga District, the *hakhalar*, speak a dialect (*hakhali*) much closer to standard Yakut.

2. The coefficient of relatedness is a measure of genealogical similarity varying from 0.0 (unrelated) to 1.0 (genealogically identical), representing the probability that a focal allele is identical in two individuals by descent from a common ancestor.

3. Reciprocity in game theory and evolutionary ecological models is at odds with Polanyi's (1944) definition of reciprocity (Halperin 1994:95). Halperin (1994:95) states that equivalency ratios are more or less equal in both generalized sharing and formalized exchanges between symmetrically related kin groupings.

4. New migration patterns are blamed on intensive slaughter on the Pyasina River during the 1970s and 1980s. Up to 50,000 caribou per season were killed at 25 sites.

5. In the interim between the first and second phases of my dissertation research, I discovered that the native villages of the Siberian north, like other rural places of residence in Russia, maintain a registration book (*pokhozyaistvennaya kniga*). The registration book lists people by household and describes their date of birth, date of death, adoption, education, and place of work. In Ust Avam, I went through the registration book with the mayor and/or assistant mayor. As I entered the sociodemographic and genealogical information for each individual into a database, I checked with the administration representative about the individual. If the individual was a married woman, I asked for the

maiden name. Many times the father was not listed, especially with younger children. I checked to determine whether the father was known or not. If known, I made a note and entered the father's ID number when I came across his name in the registration book. In addition, when entering names into the database I came across individuals with the same last name and patronymic. Even though the people I worked with were not of Russian ancestry, they have adopted the Russian tradition of assigning patronymics. The patronymic serves as a kind of middle name. When individuals are addressed in a formal way in Russia, the individual is addressed with the first name and patronymic. Thus, the Russian President is addressed Boris Nikolaievich. From the patronymic, one can infer that the Russian President's father was named Nikolai. When I came across individuals with the same last name and patronymic in the registration book, I asked whether they were full siblings and inquired about the full name of the mother and father. In this way, I was able to extend the genealogical information back a generation in many cases. I used the data filter function on my database to create lists of individuals with same last names and patronymics. I then asked the assistant mayor if there was a genealogical relationship between these individuals. Many times I found sets of full siblings. I took notes on genealogies of extended families and at a later time entered additional mothers and fathers into the database. Later, during the structured interviews of heads of households, I asked participants about the names of mothers and fathers, as well as mother's parents and father's parents. The assistant mayor's information was accurate. I found no mistakes based on the information from interviews. As a result of the interviews, however, I was able to add some mothers and fathers to previous data base entries.

6.   I analyzed the genealogical information using the KINDEMCOM program (Chagnon & Bryants n.d.). KINDEMCOM gives several useful benchmarks allowing comparison of the kinship structure and dynamics cross-culturally.

7.   Some younger members of households have recently put money together from relatives to purchase apartments in the regional capital. These apartments are used by members of the extended family on rare trips to the capital. The sharing of apartments is another example of a mixed strategy solution.

REFERENCES

Abrosimova, V. (1992) "Vozmushcheny!" ["We Are Indignant!"] *Sovietskii Taimyr* 84:1.

Anderson, David (1995) *The Evenki and Dolgan of Khantaiskoye Ozero*. Ph.D. dissertation, Cambridge University.

Axelrod, Robert (1984) *The Evolution of Cooperation*. New York: Basic Books, Inc.

Axelrod, Robert, and William D. Hamilton (1981) "The Evolution of Cooperation." *Science* 211:1390-96.

Bobrick, Benson (1992) *East of the Sun: The Epic Conquest and Tragic History of Siberia*. New York: Henry Holt & Co.

Bodley, John H. (1990) *Victims of Progress* (3rd ed.). Mountain View, CA: Mayfield Publishing.

Chagnon, Napoleon A. (1983) *Yanomamo: The Fierce People* (3rd ed.). New York: Holt, Rinehart & Winston.

Chagnon, N.A., and J. Bryant (n.d.) KINDEMCOM: The Fourth Style in the Study of Human Kinship Relations. Mimeographed, Department of Anthropology, University of California, Santa Barbara, CA, 1985.

Cosmides, Leda (1989) "The Logic of Social Exchange: Has Natural Selection Shaped How Humans Reason? Studies with the Wason Selection Task." *Cognition* 31:187-276.

Cosmides, Leda, and John Tooby (1992) "Cognitive Adaptations for Social Exchange." Pp. 163-228 in Jerome H. Barkow, Leda Cosmides & John Tooby (eds.) *The Adapted Mind*. New York: Oxford University Press.

Dolgikh, B.O. (1963) Proiskhozhdeniye Dolgan [Origin of the Dolgan]. Pp. 92- 141 in *Sibirskii Etnograficheskii Sbornik V, Trudy Instituta Etnografii im. N.N. Miklukho-Maklaya, Novaya Seriya, Tom 84*. Moscow: USSR Academy of Sciences Publishers.

Dudwick, Nora C. (n.d.) "Democratization and Its Discontents: Poverty, Patronage and Protection in the Post-Soviet States." Paper presented to the American Anthropological Association, Washington, DC, 1997.

Engels, Frederick (1972) The Origin of the Family, Private Property and the State. New York: Pathfinder Press.

Fisher, Raymond.H. (1943) *The Russian Fur Trade 1550-1700.* Berkeley: University of California Press.

Forsyth, James (1989) "The Indigenous Peoples of Siberia in the Twentieth Century." Pp. 72-95 in Alan Wood & R.A. French (eds.) *The Development of Siberia.* New York: St. Martin's Press.

_____ (1992) *A History of the Peoples of Siberia: Russia's North Asian Colony, 1581-1990.* Cambridge, ENG: Cambridge University Press.

Halperin, Rhoda H. (1994) *Cultural Economies: Past and Present.* Austin: University of Texas Press.

Halstead, Paul, and John O'Shea (1989) "Introduction." Pp. 1-7 in Paul Halstead & John O'Shea (eds.) *Bad Year Economics: Cultural Responses to Risk and Uncertainty.* New York: Cambridge University Press.

Hamilton, William D. (1964) "The Genetical Evolution of Social Behavior (I and II)." *Journal of Theoretical Biology* 7:1-16, 17-52.

Hawkes, Kristen (1993) "Why Hunter-Gatherers Work: An Ancient Version of the Problem of Public Goods." *Current Anthropology* 34:341-361.

Hill, Kim, and Hillard Kaplin (1993) "On Why Male Foragers Hunt and Share Food." *Current Anthropology* 34:701-710.

Ingold, Tim (1980) *Hunters, Pastoralists and Ranchers: Reindeer Economics and Their Transformation.* New York: Cambridge University Press.

Irwin, Colin J. (1987) "A Study in the Evolution of Ethnocentrism." Pp.131-156 in Vernon Reynolds, Vincent Falger & Ian Vine (eds.) *The Sociobiology of Ethnocentrism: Evolutionary Dimensions of Xenophobia, Discrimination, Racism and Nationalism.* London, ENG: Croom Helm.

Jochim, Michael A. (1976) *Hunter-gatherer Subsistence and Settlement: A Predictive Model.* New York: Academic Press.

Krebs, J.R., and N.B. Davies (1993) *An Introduction to Behavioral Ecology* (3rd ed.). Oxford, ENG: Blackwell Scientific Publications.

Kuehnast, Kathleen R. (n.d.) "Children and the Burden of Poverty in Kyrgyzstan." Paper presented to the American Anthropological Association, Washington, DC, 1997.

Lee, Richard B. (1984) *The Dobe !Kung.* Fort Worth, TX: Harcourt Brace Jovanovich College Publishers.

Levin, M.B., and L.P. Potapov, eds. (1964) *The Peoples of Siberia.* Chicago: The University of Chicago Press.

Marx, Karl (1994) *Selected Writings.* Indianapolis, IN: Hackett.

Maynard Smith, J. (1964) "Group Selection and Kin Selection." *Nature* 201:1145-1147.

McNamara, J.M., and A.I. Houston (1992) "Risk-Sensitive Foraging: A Review of the Theory." *Bulletin of Mathematical Biology* 54:355-378.

McNamara, J.M., S. Merad, and A.I. Houston (1991) "A Model of Risk-Sensitive Foraging for a Reproducing Animal." *Animal Behaviour* 41:787-792.

Milovskii, A.S. (1992) "Tubiakou's Spirit Flight: A Siberian Shaman Adapts His Ancient Profession to Modern Times." *Natural History* 7:35-41.

Polanyi, Karl (1944) *The Great Transformation.* New York: Holt, Rinehart, and Winston.

Pelto, Pertti J. (1987) *The Snowmobile Revolution: Technology and Social Change in the Arctic.* Prospect Heights, IL: Waveland Press.

Pelto, Pertti J., and Gretel H. Pelto (1978) *Anthropological Research: The Structure of Inquiry* (2nd ed.). New York: Cambridge University Press.

Pika, A.I., and V.V. Prokhorov (1994) *Neotraditsionalism na Rossiiskom Severe [Neotraditionalism in the Russian North]*. Moscow: Institute of National Prognosis, Center for Human Demography and Ecology, Russian Academy of Sciences.

Plattner, Stuart (1989) "Introduction." Pp. 1-20 in Stuart Plattner (ed.) *Economic Anthropology*. Stanford: Stanford University Press.

Popov, A.A. (1966) *The Nganasan: The Material Culture of the Tavgi Samoyeds*. Bloomington: Indiana University Press.

Sahlins, Marshall D. (1968) *Tribesmen*. Englewood Cliffs, NJ: Prentice-Hall.

_____ (1972) *Stone Age Economics*. Chicago: Aldine Atherton, Inc.

Service, Elman R. (1979) *The Hunters*. Englewood Cliffs, NJ: Prentice-Hall.

Slezkine, Yuri (1994) *Arctic Mirrors: Russia and the Small Peoples of the North*. Ithaca, NY: Cornell University Press.

Smith, E.A. (1991) *Inujjuamiut Foraging Strategies: Evolutionary Ecology of an Arctic Hunting Economy*. New York: Aldine de Gruyter.

Ssorin-Chaikov, Nikolai (n.d.) "Back to the Forest: Poverty and Re-Invention of Evenki Clan-Based Communities in Central Siberia." Paper presented to the American Anthropological Association, Washington, DC, 1997.

Tonkinson, Robert (1978) *The Mardudjara Aborigines: Living the Dream in Australia's Desert*. New York: Holt, Rinehart and Winston.

Trivers, Robert L. (1971) "The Evolution of Reciprocal Altruism." *Quarterly Review of Biology* 46: 35-57.

Weissner, Pauline (1977) *Hxaro: A Regional System of Reciprocity for the !Kung San*. Ph.D. dissertation, University of Michigan, Ann Arbor.

Wilk, Richard R. (1996) *Economies and Cultures: Foundations of Economic Anthropology*. Boulder, CO: Westview Press.

Woodburn, James (1982) "Egalitarian Societies." *Man* (n.s.) 17:431-451.

THE POLITICAL ECONOMY OF COFFEE IN THE SIERRA JUÁREZ OF OAXACA, MEXICO

Roberto J. González

INTRODUCTION

This essay is about a global commodity, coffee, and its history in Talea de Castro, a Zapotec village located in the Sierra Juárez of Oaxaca, Mexico. It is based on 18 months of field work conducted between 1994 and 1997. The paper is an effort to link global processes with local history, to consider the ways in which recently-introduced commodities can rapidly become "traditional," and to compare the hegemonic and counter-hegemonic uses of such crops. Increasingly, scholars (including anthropologists) have written about commodities and their social histories (Ortiz 1947, Salaman 1949, Braudel 1967, Hanks 1972, Crosby 1972, Douglas & Isherwood 1981, Wolf 1982, Mintz 1985, Appadurai 1986, Ferguson 1988, Goodman 1992, Marcus 1995). The social implications of coffee have been researched by historians and anthropologists of Latin America (Dean 1976, Bergad 1982, Roseberry 1983,

Research in Economic Anthropology, Volume 19, pages 239-266.
Copyright © 1998 by JAI Press Inc.
All rights of reproduction in any form reserved.
ISBN: 0-7623-0446-4

Nolasco 1985, McCreery 1994), and similar topics have been covered by scholars focusing on other areas, including New Guinea (Stewart 1992) and Africa (Hedlund 1992).

Coffee, like other tropical commodities (e.g., sugar; see Mintz 1985), has historically been wielded as a hegemonic tool by plantation owners, regional strongmen, and transnational corporations. Frequently, it is described in negative terms by social scientists, perhaps because, symbolically, coffee and other cash crops represent exploitative economic relationships and the contamination of pristine "natives" and "virgin" lands by the contagion of the modern capitalist world-system. A key point of this essay is that, to the contrary, in some regions coffee holds the potential of making a positive impact. In fact, a growing body of evidence from southern Mexico indicates that coffee can form the basis for *counter-hegemonic* impulses by serving as a central component in the historical transformation of ethnic identities and in environmentally sustainable economic projects. At the microlevel, this essay also examines the way in which *campesinos* (smallholder farmers) in one Sierra Zapotec village have gradually incorporated coffee into their "traditional" agricultural repertoire and into their village's distinctive identity.

Coffee is the world's second most valuable traded commodity (after petroleum), accounting for U.S. $7 billion a year in international trade (Lack 1998). The U.S. consumes one-fourth of the world's coffee (more than 23 gallons per capita each year), more than any other country. Mexico ranks fourth among the world's coffee-producing countries (after Brazil, Colombia, and Indonesia), and no other country supplies more coffee to the U.S. (Wilkinson 1994). Coffee exports are Mexico's third largest source of foreign exchange, after petroleum and tourism, and approximately two million Mexicans rely on income derived from coffee (Hernández Navarro 1992). The commodity is of remarkable significance economically and culturally.

This paper begins by looking at coffee in broad historical terms, from its legendary discovery in East Africa more than 1,000 years ago to its arrival in Latin America and Oaxaca. Our anthropological lens then zooms in on the Rincón of the Sierra Juárez and its largest community, Talea de Castro, to examine the critical role that coffee has played in the recent history of the region. Specifically, we will consider how the Taleans have gradually incorporated coffee into their "traditional" agriculture and adopted the crop as a part of village identity. The essay then zooms out to the region, the state and, finally, southern Mexico in general to analyze the emergence of indigenous peoples' organic coffee cooperatives in the 1980s and 1990s. The conclusion focuses on the counter-hegemonic uses of the cooperatives, their ties to new global markets for organic coffee, and their role in the transformation of indigenous identities.

COFFEE THROUGH TIME: THE SOCIAL HISTORY OF A GLOBAL COMMODITY

The Diffusion of Coffee from the Old World to the New World

Coffee, according to one popular account, was discovered in the 9th century by Islamic shepherds caring for goats near the Red Sea in present-day Ethiopia. They were concerned that their goats suffered insomnia and soon discovered that the animals' restlessness was caused by their feeding upon the sweet, red fruit of a mysterious shrub. The stimulating coffee bean was a rapid success. In spite of prohibitions on its consumption, it became popular throughout the Ottoman Empire during the 1500s and covered nearly the entire Islamic world by the end of that century. Coffee cultivation shifted to sites in and around the Arabian city of Mocha, where it was grown on a limited scale. Thus, early on, coffee cultivation, processing, and consumption was an exclusively Moslem possesion.

Coffee beans reached Europe through contacts with the Near East by the late 1600s. Its European success was secured in Paris, where the coffeehouse was imported as well as the beverage. Similar patterns followed in Germany, Italy, and Portugal (Ukers 1935, Wolf 1982:336-337).

Historian Fernand Braudel (1967:186) notes that "if there was such an increase in consumption—and not only in Paris and France [but across Europe]—from the middle of the eighteenth century it was because Europe had organized production itself." For many years the world market depended exclusively on supplies from the Islamic world, particularly from Mocha. However, the Dutch appropriated the crop and, by 1712, had begun growing coffee on large Indonesian plantations. Production began booming and prices began dropping, and within 100 years coffee became the Dutch East Indies Corporation's major export crop.

The significance of this event should not be understated. The Dutch transformed the way in which coffee cultivation was done, because they not only imported coffee seeds but also imported an entire mode of production: plantation-based capitalism. Coffee became a pawn in a global "botanical chess game," described by Jack Kloppenburg (1988:154):

> Plant germplasm was appropriated and shifted across the continents and archipelagos of what is now the Third World as the European powers sought commercial hegemony....Because most of these plantation crops were of tropical or subtropical origin, the movement of germplasm tended to be lateral, among colonial possessions, rather than between the colonies and the metropolitan center.

If the initial move in this "chess game" was coffee's transplantation from the Near East to Southeast Asia, the second move was across the Pacific, to the Americas. The plant was brought to the Americas in the early 1700s, reaching Guayana in 1714 and Haiti, Santo Domingo, Brazil, and other colonies shortly thereafter. When the Indonesian plantations suffered a blight in the 1880s and 1890s, Brazil

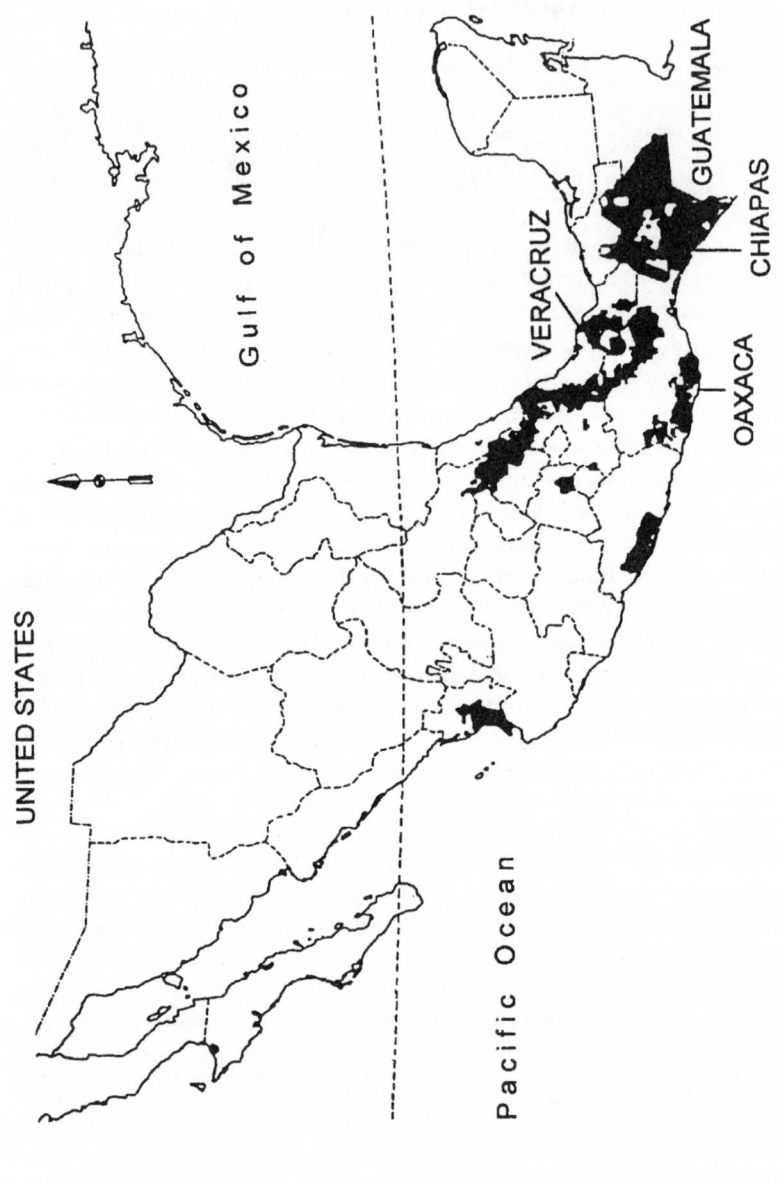

Figure 1. Coffee-producing Regions of Mexico

242

was poised to dominate the world market and, by 1900, it supplied three-quarters of the world's coffee (Wolf 1982:337, Paredes et al. 1997).

In Mexico, coffee cultivation was concentrated in the gulf coastal state of Veracruz. From there it spread to Chiapas, Oaxaca, and other states in the 1800s, though Veracruz was the most important coffee producing state through the 1880s. To this day, much of the country's coffee cultivation is concentrated in these states (see Figure 1). Between 1890 and 1920, however, the Soconusco region of southwestern Chiapas emerged as the most important Mexican coffee zone, in part because legislation passed in 1856 prevented indigenous communities from retaining rights over territories granted to them in the Spanish colonial period. Mexican and foreign investors began establishing large coffee plantations in the zone during the dictatorship of Porfirio Díaz (1876-1911). German, English, and U.S. firms were given concessions to convert millions of hectares of virgin forest into *cafetales* (coffee groves), sometimes for as little as a few cents per hectare. According to one estimate, one-fourth of the land that passed into the hands of the investors in the Soconusco region once pertained to indigenous communities. Mayan workers were coerced into working on the plantations through a system of debt peonage, and conditions were hellish. (A quick glance at the modern classic *I, Rigoberta Menchú* [Burgos-Debray 1984] reveals how little the situation has changed in some parts of Mesoamerica.) Men, women, and children were rounded up and taken to plantations where they were forced to work seven days a week. Similar processes occured in various parts of the country (including the Pacific coast of Oaxaca), and the situation did not change significantly until president Lázaro Cárdenas (1934-1940) instituted land and property reforms (Paredes et al. 1997:33-35, Wolf 1982:337, Esparza 1988:326).

The Introduction of Coffee in the Sierra Juárez of Oaxaca

From 1890 to 1900, Mexico quadrupled its production of coffee and emerged as an important international exporter of the crop (Nolasco 1985:169-170). The pattern in Oaxaca paralleled that of the country. Driven by a soaring demand in the U.S. in the late 1800s, Mexicans in various parts of the country began cultivating coffee during these years. There are various versions of the story of how coffee arrived in Oaxaca; given the 19th-century importance of Veracruz as a coffee-producing center, it seems likely that the crop came from the north, through either the districts of Tuxtepec or Santiago Choapam (see Figure 2). According to one source, coffee entered the Sierra Juárez via Choapam in 1883 before diffusing southward to Villa Alta, Yalalag, and the Mixe zone (Berg 1968:70-71).

A more colorful account relates how coffee was introduced in a region of the Sierra Juárez known as the Rincón in the 1870s in nine villages situated along the border of the Ixtlán and Villa Alta districts: Tepanzacoalco, Cacalotepec, Yaneri,

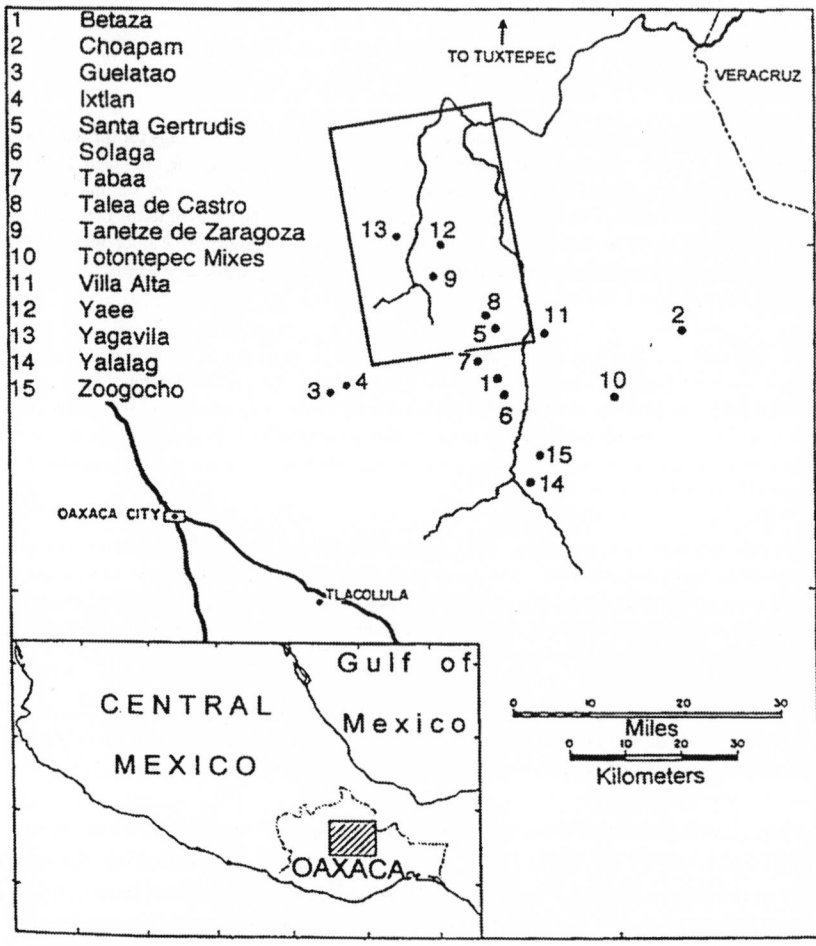

Figure 2.   The Sierra Juárez of Oaxaca, Mexico (Rincón Region Located within Rectangle)

Zoogochi, Yotao, Yagavila, Teotlaxco, Yagila, and Josaa. It is worth translating in full, despite its patent ethnocentrism (Pérez García 1956:273-274):

> Before the middle of the 19th century the inhabitants of these villages were the most backward in all senses of the term: they retained primitive customs, were malicious, untrustworthy, disobedient, and idolatrous. Because of the nature of their lands, they were only able to cultivate limited quantities of maize, enough for only four or five months annually...The rest of the year they relied on a diet of fruits, which they really only half-cultivated due to their indolence...Conscious of this situation, the activists ["men of action"] of that era, known as the Lib-

erals, among them General Fidencio Hernández, who in that period made frequent trips between Oaxaca and Veracruz, observed that the weather in these villages was identical to that of Córdoba and Orizaba, and they began collecting coffee seeds from the Veracruz plantations for cultivating the crop in the Rincón region.

Because the seeds were planted out of season, they then tried to bring saplings for the Rincón plantations, but since the locals were unintelligent people [*gente inculta*], the trees died. In the meantime, General Hernández acquired more preeminence throughout the region and in his capacity as political chief and military commander of the district he decided to treat the affair as a legal one so that the cultivation of coffee might be realized in spite of the stubbornness of the Rinconeros: General Hernández decreed that whoever did not present 25 coffee trees within a year was to be fined 100 pesos per family.

The argument was a convincing one, and left the villagers with no option but to obey....Within a few years the Rinconeros began to collect the first harvests....The rapid economic change surprised them, above all because the coffee buyer came up to the villages looking for the crop, so to speak, and not paying them in cash but rather with merchandise. During the harvest season, the coffee buyer exchanged maize, bread, salt, cotton cloth, thread, and *aguardiente* [sugarcane liquor] for the Rinconeros' coffee.

They say that in that era, the people of the villages realized that they were indebted to General Hernández for their newfound economic success, and that upon waking up every morning and after each of their three meals, they would religiously pronounce the following Zapotec words: *Schalenu diuci schalenu Fidenciu Hernández, va gutagutu!* ("Thanks be to God and thanks be to Fidencio Hernández that now we eat!")

In the corridor of the municipal palace of San Pedro Yaneri the following inscription was preserved until 1908: "To the unconquerable General Fidencio Hernández, who was a benefactor of these villages and introduced them to coffee."

The passage is remarkable for a number of reasons.[1] It appears in a two-volume study conducted by Rosendo Pérez García, who was a schoolteacher for many years in the Sierra Juárez. He claims to have collected his material between 1917 and 1949 and to have gained fluency in Sierra Zapotec and Cajonos Zapotec (Pérez García 1956:9). His own background and status as a "civilized" *mestizo* (literally, "half-breed," or in this context, non-Indian) in a region of *indios—gente inculta*, in his own words—undoubtedly had much to do with his unflattering description of the Rinconeros.

Although the account describes the introduction of coffee into the region as the result of a kind of "white man's burden" borne by General Hernández, there may well have been other motives. It is possible that Hernández and other political strongmen were in cahoots with the Rincón's sole coffee buyer during this period, for all stood to benefit "from the large profits that could be made by procuring underpriced coffee beans for overpriced goods—as well as from the state subsidies on coffee production, trade, and export" that existed at the time (Young 1978:136). If Hernández was indeed playing the role of strongman—and it seems that he was rather dishonest in his dealings with other Sierra villages, as well (Ruiz

Cervantes 1988:370)—then initially, at least, coffee functioned as a hegemonic mechanism of control in the Rincón.

In spite of its ethnocentrism, Pérez García's account matches the versions presented by Rincón Zapotec informants today. Taleans in particular claim that coffee saplings were first brought to Talea from the villages of Yagavila and Teotlaxco, northwest of Talea. Yagavilans report that their grandfathers planted coffee in abundance—"as if it were maize" (Tyrtania 1992:215).

The Arrival of Coffee in Talea de Castro (1905-1945)

The earliest ethnography of a Rincón village reports that coffee was first planted in Talea in about 1905 (Nader 1964). After its introduction, coffee was probably accepted quickly there because of the locale's small land base and large population. Talea, one of the few towns in the Sierra Juárez founded after the Spanish conquest, slowly acquired what little land it could from neighboring villages, and most of it became private property. Between 1902 and 1905, when an important silver mine near the village was abandoned, hundreds of mine workers and their families were left unemployed, and many of them turned to agriculture. Coffee was an especially attractive option for many of these families attempting to survive on small plots of land (less than 5 ha). Throughout the first decade of the century, villagers could use coffee to purchase maize, beans, and merchandise from travelling merchants. From the beginning, coffee helped Taleans survive difficult economic circumstances.

Much of the growth in coffee production was stimulated by a rise in global consumption led by a rapid increase in U.S. coffee drinking at the turn of the century, when coffee was transformed from an expensive and exotic beverage enjoyed only by elite groups to an inexpensive drink consumed by the middle class and the working class. In this period, per capita annual consumption in the U.S. increased from 3 lb to more than 12 lb (Jiménez 1995).[2]

In the decades following its introduction, coffee was traded directly for products from outside the Sierra. Maize, bread, salt, cotton cloth, and thread were among the most popular items in the late 1800s. In the 1920s and 1930s, muleteers from Talea, Betaza, Solaga, Yalalag, Zoogocho, and other villages transported the region's coffee to Tlacolula—the economic link between the Valley of Oaxaca and the Sierra Juárez—via Zoogocho. Others, particularly Mixes, used tumplines to carry as much as five *arrobas* (nearly 60 kg) of the precious cargo from Zoogocho to Tlacolula—a distance of more than 50 km over extremely rugged terrain. They returned with merchandise from the Valley of Oaxaca and other parts of the state and, in this way, factory-produced goods began to circulate through the region (see Berg 1968).

According to informants, Taleans were reluctant to dedicate much land to coffee cultivation in the early years. Coffee was planted in the most marginal areas—on slopes too steep for planting maize, for example, or within the village itself, where plowing was not possible. Choice land was too precious to dedicate to coffee, and it seems likely that a decade-long price crash during the Great Depression convinced growers to be cautious about placing too much faith in the new crop. Throughout this period, relatively little currency changed hands; instead, coffee was bartered directly for merchandise or maize. However, as demand for coffee (and its price) skyrocketed in the post-World War II period, the Rincón's coffee began to exceed the value of the merchandise shipped into the region, leading to the accumulation and circulation of currency.

The Postwar Coffee Boom (1946-1959)

After World War II, record levels of coffee consumption were reached in the U.S. and several European countries. The reasons, according to one survey, were "a pent-up demand resulting from wartime scarcity, an increased number of newly founded homes, [and] a more active social life" on the part of Americans (U.S. Department of Commerce 1961:7). However, perhaps the most significant factor of all was the institution of the "coffee break," which allowed millions of U.S. workers to consume several cups daily, in the workplace, at little or no cost. The coffee break permitted blue-collar (and white-collar) workers to consume a physiologically stimulating "nerve food" to help deal with "the pressures of the machinery of civilized life" (quoted in Jiménez 1995). Like sugar (and frequently together with it in the same cup), coffee served as a "proletarian hunger killer" (Mintz 1979). On the other hand, there was something intensely pleasurable about the coffee break, as well. For a few minutes each day, it gave workers a release, an opportunity to step away from the assembly line (or the shop floor, the news room, etc.), engage others in conversation, and enjoy the simple pleasures of a steaming beverage and a cigarette. Coffee breaks, which had originated before World War II, became even more popular during the war (both in the Armed Services and in industry) and in the postwar decade. By 1959, more than three-quarters of all American workers had coffee available at their place of work (U.S. Department of Commerce 1961:23).

The effects of the boom in the Sierra Juárez were extensive. Rapidly rising coffee prices led to an influx of money into the region, especially from 1946 to 1950. Consequently, more consumer goods were in demand: tools, kerosene lamps, hand grinders, cloth, soap, beer, and biscuits (Berg 1968:79-80, 289). In Talea, as in coffee-producing regions worldwide, many people began planting more coffee trees, hoping that prices would stay up for at least a few years. This would have a profound effect later.

Roads for shipping coffee out of the Sierra Juárez became a high priority in the wake of the price boom. In 1953, a road to Zoogocho was completed, making it easier to transport large quantities of the crop to Oaxaca City. Up until the end of the 1950s, Zoogocho was the most important coffee trading center in the Sierra Juárez. In 1959, the situation changed radically following a sustained lobbying

effort, on the part of several Taleans with coffee interests, to complete a road to
Talea de Castro (Hirabayashi 1993:55-57). Almost overnight, Talea surpassed
Zoogocho as the most important coffee outpost in the Sierra Juárez. Many Taleans
remember the period as one of cultural fluorescence, a glorious time in which their
village emerged as the jewel of the Sierra Juárez.

The Influence of the Mexican Government and Transnational Firms

Although more people were drinking coffee than ever before (with U.S. consumption exceeding *three cups a day* per capita in 1962; see Mathews 1994), the
early 1960s was a time of lower coffee prices due to the fact that, worldwide, trees
planted in the late 1940s were now bearing fruit. World production of coffee
reached record levels, and the cumulative effect was a flooding of the market with
coffee beans and a sharp decline in prices. Figure 3 illustrates the rapid rise in production in the state of Oaxaca. In response to the crisis, the most important cof-
fee-exporting and -importing nations crafted the International Coffee Agreement
(ICA) in 1959, which established export quotas in order to limit world supplies.
The Mexican government played an active role in the ICA, and within five years,

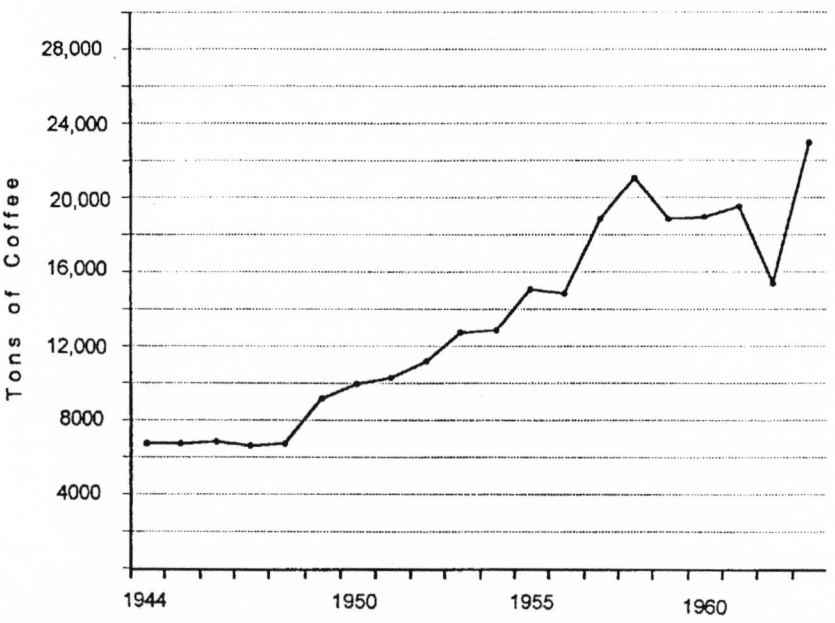

Figure 3.   Coffee Production in Oaxaca State, 1944-1963

prices began to rise again. Versions of the ICA would be renewed for the next 30 years.

Individual countries took a number of additional measures. In Mexico, for example, the Mexican Coffee Institute (INMECAFE) was founded to improve the cultivation, processing, and marketing of Mexican coffee for export and to stimulate the internal market (Nolasco 1985). Later, the INMECAFE would assume an even broader role.

As prices rebounded in the late 1960s and 1970s, more land was converted from subsistence cropping to coffee cultivation across the Sierra Juárez. Informants note that, in the 1970s, the pace of conversion accelerated especially rapidly—though, as a rule, maize farming was not abandoned. Chemical fertilizers, first used in 1967 or 1968, quickly doubled maize yields, easing land pressure and freeing up land for coffee. The cost of fertilizer also required that campesinos plant more coffee, which in turn led to a need to convert more maize fields to cafetales, which in turn required more fertilizer—and so on. A boom in world coffee prices in 1974 was also a factor, as was migration out of the region.

Government initiatives helped expand production, as well. As early as the 1950s, engineers from the Papaloapan Commission, a federal development project, promoted new coffee varieties and techniques (Nader 1964). In 1973, the INMECAFE assumed important functions in the Mexican coffee sector, including credit extension and purchasing, marketing, and exporting the crop. Furthermore, government-subsidized maize and beans were sold at state-owned stores (known as CONASUPO outlets) beginning in the 1970s, and some *campesinos* (smallholder farmers) converted more land to coffee production, confident that income derived from coffee production could be used to purchase cheap maize. All of these efforts can be seen as attempts on the part of the Mexican government to promote economic "development" in largely indigenous regions through the cultivation and "improvement" of export crops.

Government initiatives were only part of the evolution of Mexico's coffee sector. The other was the unprecedented rise of transnational corporations. Anthropologist Margarita Nolasco (1985:222), in a detailed analysis of the Mexican coffee sector, reported in 1985:

> At first glance, the exportation of coffee appears to be primarily in Mexican hands, both in the private sector and in the public (through INMECAFE). But a careful analysis of the 13 principal export companies reveals dependent links to a large North American corporation, General Foods (specifically, its Maxwell House division), and a Swiss corporation, Nestlé....At least 11 of the biggest exporters are effectively subsidiaries of General Foods and another 4 are subsidiaries of the German-based Volkhart Brothers, and between the two they control one-third of the coffee exported from Mexico.

The mechanisms of control over purchasing were realized with the cooperation of Mexican middlemen acting as agents of the transnationals (Nolasco 1985: 245-246):

Out of 186 Mexican exporters (responsible for 70 percent of all exports), seven are based in the Mexican offices of the Volkhart Brothers corporation, who buys 14 percent of all Mexican exports. In other words, a small number of transnational firms operate through Mexican export agents who buy coffee in their own names (as if they had no affiliation to the firms) and then ship it abroad from key points in the coffee-producing regions.

According to Nolasco's calculations, in the late 1970s, six firms purchased nearly 60 percent of all private sector (non-INMECAFE) exports, and 20 purchased nearly 80 percent. The coffee sector, she concluded, could be described as an transnational oligopolgy held in check only by the efforts of the INMECAFE.

Today's global coffee market is controlled by the speculative strategies of trans-national trading corporations on commodities futures markets in New York, Manila, Singapore, and London. The market is dominated by a small number of transnationals that process and package coffee for retail sale. In the U.S., where one-fourth of the world's coffee is consumed (more than 23 gallons per person each year), three firms account for more than 80 percent of retail sales: Nestlé, General Foods, and Procter & Gamble (Samuelson 1989). Worldwide, six transna-tionals based in the European Community and the U.S. control 55-60 percent of world sales (Llambi 1994:189). They take a lion's share of the profits. For exam-ple, a pound of green coffee sold by a Talean campesino for U.S. $1.20 is worth approximately U.S. $2.00 on international commodity markets; by the time it is roasted, packaged, and shelved in U.S. supermarkets, it sells for at least U.S. $8.00 (Erlich 1994).

COFFEE AND "TRADITION" IN TALEA DE CASTRO

In spite of these grim economic statistics, a surprising fact stands out. Over the course of the 20th century, many Taleans have embraced coffee and have even come to view it proudly as a part of their village's "tradition." How did this occur? It is a fair question to ask, for a great deal of research emphasizes the destructive tendencies of cash cropping in general and coffee cultivation in particular. Coffee has been described as a crop that can lead to social stratification in egalitarian communities (Hernández Díaz 1989), to land conflicts, increased violence, and homicide (J. Greenberg 1989), to the deterioration of biodiversity (MacVean 1996), to environmental degradation (Borgstrom 1967), to a dependency on far-flung markets and transnational conglomerates (Early 1982), and to the weak-ening of indigenous peoples' self-sufficiency (Paredes et al. 1997). Anthropolo-gists, historians, economists, and sociologists are nearly unanimous in their assessment of the crop (two notable exceptions being Ruiz Lombardo [1991] and Stolcke [1996]).

Yet, most villagers see coffee in a favorable light and, over the course of this century, coffee has become a vital part of what it means to be Talean. It has become normalized, a part of the local scene. Villagers refer to the *arabica* variety—first introduced at the beginning of this century—as "creole" or "native," as if it were indigenous to the area. Bumper stickers, T-shirts, and video cassettes sold in the village feature images of coffee trees and ripe red beans. The standard invitation to eat is, "Let's go drink coffee." The heavily sweetened beverage is consumed with every meal, and it is more common to wean infants with bottles of warm coffee than with bottles of milk. Intricate rules of thumb—scientific laws, really—about how to grow coffee and when to predict its rising and falling prices have evolved through a trial and error process. And it is now just as common for visitors to be given a gift of ground coffee as a gift of black beans or *panela* (unrefined brown sugar). It appears that coffee, an addictive, globally-traded commodity, has been appropriated by the Taleans.

But why would anyone would want to grow such a crop, much less appropriate it as their own? Can this be passed off as a simple case of false consciousness?

The Meanings of Coffee in a Zapotec Village

We have already discussed how coffee helped some Taleans survive when their means of livelihood, mining, came to an end in 1905. Income derived from coffee has helped them obtain staple foods that would likely have been impossible to cultivate on a small land base.

Taleans also like coffee because, relatively speaking, it is an easy crop to deal with. One need not stoop over all day (as when weeding a maize field) or be out in the scorching sun all day (as when planting beans), and one's hands do not get stuck with the painful, hairlike thorns that cover sugarcane stalks. When the mosquitos are in full force, picking coffee can be inconvenient, but it is not exhausting and certainly not dangerous. Once the trees begin growing, they are nearly maintenance-free, for little weeding is necessary and branches only occasionally need pruning. Arabica trees, if cared for, can last 50 years or more. Picking coffee is one of the few jobs that even small children can do, and the harvest is a rare opportunity for entire families to spend time working together. Very young children occasionally work, and it is considered neither exploitation nor "superexploitation." One informant stated:

> My Joaquina is one clever little girl. She went with her mother yesterday to pick coffee in Victoria's cafetal, and she strapped a tiny little straw basket around her waist and started picking beans...and she's a good worker, too! Of course, she could only reach the lowest branches, but she knew to pick only the red berries and she filled up her basket several times! Other kids spend all day playing in the cafetales, making trouble, but my daughter is a worker. And she's only four!

For men, the harvest is a nice change from the relative solitude that often characterizes the rest of the farming cycle. For women, it is an opportunity to be outdoors, away from the monotony of daily household chores. Much gossip, joking, singing, and flirting goes on in the *cafetales* (coffee groves). The harvest months of December, January, and February are a merry time.

Campesinos often talk about coffee trees as if they were savings accounts. Having the vision to plant coffee trees after getting married insures that one will have cash for the expenses that come with children:

> Thank God that I woke up once I got married and planted my *almud*-and-a-half [approximately one-third hectare] of coffee. As soon as the trees started giving fruit, Rita, my oldest child, entered school. Where would I have gotten the money for her uniform? For notebooks? For pencils? Then the trees started giving more fruit, and Elvira and Poncho entered school. More uniforms, notebooks, pencils, materials for science projects, and everything else. And luckily by the time Rita comes of age the trees will be at their peak, so we'll have the two or three thousand pesos [approximately U.S. $350-$500] necessary to buy the chickens and the ingredients for the *mole* [chile-chocolate sauce] and the *mezcal* [distilled liquor] and cigarettes for the wedding party. If it weren't for my *cafetal*, a single wedding could put me in debt.

Thus, coffee helps pay for life cycle events such as births, weddings, and funerals, and for school and medical expenses. Coffee trees, in fact, are intimately bound to the life cycle of individual farmers and their children, and at times the growers talk about the struggle to successfully cultivate a *cafetal* as if it *were* a child:

> It took me a hell of a lot of work and sacrifice to raise that little *cafetal*. Cleaning [weeding] it, pruning it, replanting saplings that didn't 'take off,' fertilizing it with rotting pulps. But it developed well, and my trouble paid off—now it hardly needs any care at all.

The striking thing is that the time needed for an arabica tree to mature and the time needed for a child to mature are almost perfectly synchonized. This fact is not lost on the *campesinos* and perhaps makes the *cafetal* seem almost as precious as a child (and vice versa).

Many *campesinos* have fond memories of working as children alongside their parents in young *cafetales* that they would later inherit. Thus, *cafetales* and nearby ranch houses often hold sentimental value and priceless memories. Another informant commented on the interrelatedness of children and *cafetales*:

> It's hard to have children without a *cafetal*, and it's hard to have a *cafetal* without children. These days, school is obligatory; it's not like the old days when nearly everyone, including wives and children, would live out on the ranches. So your kids are in school and you have to have the money for that. Even births cost money now that everyone calls on the doctor or Nati [the registered nurse] to deliver the baby! Abigail's birth cost me 700 pesos [U.S. $100] last year! But during the school break at the end of the year—and once they are done with school—you need your kids to help you out with the harvesting or your coffee trees won't get picked.

It is not uncommon for a young person to be given a small *cafetal* as an advance inheritance after getting married, and single men or women likely to inherit significant amounts of coffee land are considerably more eligible than those who will not. On one occasion, a young woman was discussed by some male friends in

these terms: *"No es tan bonita, pero es muy trabajadora—¡y hasta tiene cafetal!"*
("She's not very pretty, but she's a hard worker—and she even has a *cafetal!*")

Some campesinos stated that planting coffee trees is a much sounder investment than putting money in the bank. Even with its occasional price swings, coffee is still a safer bet than the Mexican peso. Coffee may rise and fall, but the peso just keeps sliding down.[3]

Most *campesinos* refuse to sell all of their coffee at once (even if the price is high) because cash, it turns out, is a much more liquid substance than coffee. Once within the household, money is difficult to monitor and tends to slip away quickly. A 60 kg sack of coffee is easier to keep track of, and selling it usually requires a short conference between husband and wife. Selling coffee in Talea is not like trading stocks and bonds. It's much more like withdrawing money from a bank account.

Low coffee prices, like poor harvests, can be disasterous under certain circumstances. An ill child can drain cash resources very quickly:

> My poor daughter. She wouldn't take milk from my breast, you see I was suffering from *susto* [literally, "fright; see Rubel 1964] and she wouldn't take my breast because my milk was bad, but she would drink powdered milk—NIDO [Nestlé's Mexican brand]. The problem was the price of coffee was so low [in 1993] that we had to exchange one and a half *arrobas* [17.3 kg] of coffee for one can [4 liters] of powdered milk. Thank God she developed well and she's healthy now, rosy cheeks and pretty and clever, but *¡jesús!*—she was an *expensive* little girl!

When asked about possible alternatives to coffee, informants said that, long ago, they sold *panela* (unrefined sugar) to earn cash. The problem with *panela* is that it doesn't always sell—and rarely sells in large quantities. Besides, the market is typically saturated by people from nearby villages who sell the same product. With coffee, one doesn't always get the price one would like, but at least large quantities can be sold. The alternative to coffee, it seems, is not *panela*. It's Los Angeles.

Most campesinos who grow coffee are very proud of its quality. If the coffee growers of the Sierra have a reputation for producing dirty coffee, I was told, it is unjustified. It is the *coyotes* (middlemen) who mix the trash in later to skim off a higher profit. Rumors circulate about the dishonest practices of certain coffee buyers in the Rincón who are said to add dried pulp or water or both to green coffee to increase the weight before shipping it to Oaxaca City. The *campesinos'* opinion of retail coffees is summed up concisely in one phrase: "Nescafé no es café." They are correct. The retail coffee sold by Nestlé in Mexico consists of up to 30 percent additives (Hernández Navarro 1992).

How Coffee Became "Traditional" in Talea de Castro

Taking these *campesino* perspectives into account, it is easier to see why coffee has been embraced in Talea. Coffee, though still valued for its economic worth, is important for other reasons, as well. We have seen that coffee cultivation in the village has occurred in a more or less egalitarian manner, on small plots distributed among many households. This decentralized model replicates a pattern that has existed in the Sierra Juárez for many years.

In most Talean households, coffee has not replaced maize farming—it has *supplemented* it. The saying, "You can eat maize, but you can't eat coffee," has guided most of the Sierra's farmers, including the Taleans. Out of more than 300 households describing themselves as *"campesino"* (smallholder farmer, or "peasant"), more than three-quarters reported planting maize in 1995, and most of them planted more than half of what their households consumed. Most growers were cautious enough to continue planting maize through the coffee boom and were prepared when the bottom dropped out of the market.

This point deserves emphasis. Household "maintenance" (the Spanish term *mantenimiento* is more appropriate) in Talea has been reinforced because coffee can provide insurance in case of a failed maize harvest. Though coffee has contributed to the transformation of the village—leading to the construction of a road, cinder block buildings, and a certain level of migration out of the village in years past—it has also allowed many villagers to more easily provide food for their households, not unlike the case of Totonac communities in the Sierra Juárez of Puebla state described by Ruiz Lombardo (1991:17):

> Coffee cultivation has reinforced the domestic mode of production because the two principal crops—maize and coffee—exist in a complementary relationship with respect to the agricultural cycle....Coffee cultivation has effectively countered the capitalist process of the proletarianization of the *campesinado* [peasantry]....In the Sierra Juárez of Puebla, a contrary process exists, that of *recampesinización* [a return to smallholder peasant farming].

Recampesinización—the return to peasantry—is especially relevant in Talea today. Mexico's current economic crisis is so severe that, from 1995 to mid-1997, more than twice as many people moved to Talea than moved away. Most of these people were villagers returning from Mexican cities, and many are returned to work in the fields. The recent boom in coffee prices is a magnet; when I left the field in June 1997, one could earn up to 60 pesos (almost U.S. $9) a day picking coffee in Talea, compared to 25 pesos (U.S. $3.50) working as an unskilled laborer in Mexico City. Anything that draws people so strongly from Mexico City to work in the fields of one of the remotest parts of Oaxaca can only be seen as "traditional" from the perspective of the villagers.

Finally, it appears that Talea's *campesinos* think of coffee as "traditional" in another sense. Over the course of the century, the *campesinos* have developed highly effective methods for growing coffee through trial and error. This became especially clear in the 1960s and 1970s, when state engineers from the Papaloapan Commission and Mexican Coffee Institute (INMECAFE) came to promote new techniques and high-yielding varieties through projects that were often impractical and ineffective. Even today, various officials from the government and NGOs arrive with plans to improve coffee but are politely ignored by most *campesinos*. After one such visit, an informant confided:

> Those kids come from Oaxaca City or Veracruz. *They don't know our lands.* We have poor soil. Our fields have only a thin layer of earth, and below that there is rock. They come from lands with rich soil, and they have a different way of doing things. *Pura teoría, nada de práctica* [Pure theory, no practical experience].

An example of the Taleans' skill in cultivating coffee using "traditional" methods is their exclusive reliance on shade coffee, in which shade trees are planted between the coffee plants. Shade *cafetales* mimic the structure of natural forests: *guajinicuil* (scientific name: *Inga guinicuil*) shade trees form an upper layer of foliage, the coffee trees form a secondary layer, and smaller food plants and vines (such as *chayote* vines, chile plants, *cebollina* or green onion plants, and the vines of a species of tiny tomato known as the *tomate silvestre*) are grown at the lowest levels. The shade trees offer protection from unfavorable weather such as high winds and freezes, and they shed their abundant leaves every six months. The leaves cover the floor of the *cafetal*, providing a natural compost, inhibiting the growth of weeds and grasses, and serving to keep the soil humid. Like other pod-producing plants, the *guajinicuil* also fixes nitrogen in the soil and offers a number of other benefits: a smoother-tasting coffee, protection from harmful fungi and diseases, soil conservation, and a high degree of biodiversity (Nolasco 1985:113). Indeed, the techniques used to grow shade coffee are strikingly similar to cacao cultivation methods developed long before the arrival of Columbus. Some have gone so far as to suggest that, a century ago, indigenous people may have modeled "traditional" coffee growing techniques after ancient cacao-growing methods (R. Greenberg 1994, West 1992).[4]

The *campesinos* use many rules of thumb such as these to guide them in their cultivation of coffee, just as they have for maize, beans, and sugarcane. Taleans have become the scientific experts in the cultivation of this new crop, for they have highly effective "traditional" techniques for growing coffee on land that they and their ancestors have worked for centuries.

CONCLUSION: THE RAPIDLY EVOLVING POLITICS OF COFFEE IN THE SIERRA JUÁREZ

We have seen that the Taleans have created a "tradition" of coffee cultivation by adopting a new crop and learning to grow it successfully in a region they intimately understand, basing their knowledge on the concept of *mantenimiento*, or household maintenance. They have even incorporated the crop into their very identity. We should now ask about coffee and power: Is it possible that, at a broader level, coffee cultivation—conceived as a set of practices embodied in social arrangements and institutions—might form a basis for wider movements that hold the potential of challenging the economic and political power of state and corporate entities? In short, can coffee cultivation form the basis of new cultural identities that might ultimately serve to promote political, economic, and social transformations in southern Mexico (Hernández Castillo & Nigh 1998)?

One thing is very clear, namely, that coffee has strong political implications. At least part of the discontent fueling the 1994 Zapatista uprising in Chiapas was about low coffee prices, the unscrupulous credit and purchasing practices of middlemen, abysmal labor conditions, and the hopelessness of landless workers employed on large coffee plantations (Hernández Navarro 1994). Historically, coffee cultivation was used as a hegemonic tool by the Dutch in Indonesia, by German, North American, and Mexican plantation owners in Chiapas, and by strongmen such as Fidencio Hernández in the Sierra Juárez, but is it possible that coffee cultivation can be used *counter*-hegemonically today?

The 1989 Price Crash and the End of INMECAFE

The INMECAFE (Mexican Coffee Institute) reached its apogee from 1973 to 1989, when it financed, purchased, stored, and exported coffee and played a vital role in guaranteeing a minimum price for small growers who might otherwise have been cheated by intermediaries. By 1982 the INMECAFE purchased nearly 50 percent of the country's product, increasing from less than 7 percent in 1971 and nearly 20 percent in 1973 (Nolasco 1985:186). In the Sierra Juárez, one anthropologist reports that approximately 75 percent of the coffee sold in the region in the early 1980s was collected by the INMECAFE (Tyrtania 1992:218).

In 1982, however, small coffee growers began mobilizing against the INME-CAFE, which was accused of offering low prices, delivering credit too late in the season, weighing coffee unfairly, downgrading the product and, in some regions, conspiring with strongmen. In the early 1980s, small growers began building grassroots cooperatives aimed at issuing credit and purchasing, processing, and marketing the crop (Hernández Navarro & Célis Calleja 1994:220-221). One of the earliest cooperatives was the Union of Indigenous Communities of the Isthmus Region (UCIRI), formed in 1981 with the help of priests affiliated with the progressive wing of the Catholic church. The UCIRI specialized in organic coffee for the European market (Vásquez y de los Santos & Villagómez Velázquez 1993). Other regional cooperatives founded in Oaxaca during the 1980s included the multi-ethnic Union of Indigenous Communities of the Northern Isthmus Zone (UCIZONI) and the Union of Indigenous Communities—"One Hundred Years of Solitude" (UCI-100).

In 1989, a series of events occurred which profoundly changed the roles of the INMECAFE and the new coffee cooperatives. President Carlos Salinas de Gortari announced the restructuring of the Institute, relieving it of its most important functions. A few months later, the International Coffee Organization (ICO)—a global coffee cartel—announced the failure of member nations to renew an agreement on export limits, which flooded the world market with coffee and led to a sharp drop in prices. This situation, coupled with the severe effects of Mexico's economic liberalization policies, led to the worst crisis in the coffee sector in nearly 30 years (Hernández Navarro & Célis Calleja 1994:217).

The regional coffee cooperatives mobilized rapidly. During the summer of 1989, 26 organizations formed the National Network of Coffee Producers, or CNOC (Hernández Navarro 1992, Moguel & Aranda 1992). By 1997, the CNOC included 107 organizations representing 70,000 small growers (Morales 1997), and eventually it was able to secure contracts with European and North American buyers, including the English company Twin Trading, the Dutch company Max Havellar, and Aztec Harvests and Thanksgiving Coffee, these latter both based in northern California (Hernández Navarro 1992:93, Moguel & Aranda1992:105).

The Rise of Oaxacan Coffee Cooperatives

Oaxacan growers affiliated themselves with the CNOC through a statewide network called the State Network of Coffee Producers of Oaxaca, or CEPCO (Moguel & Aranda 1992:181-182). The CEPCO was founded in the summer of 1989 by a number of grassroots organizations, including the UCIRI, the UCI-ZONI, UCI-100, and the Pueblos Unidos of the Rincón of the Sierra Juárez (or Pueblos Unidos).[5] Pueblos Unidos was formed by approximately ten mountain Zapotec villages in the early 1980s for the purpose of pressuring the state government to construct a road connecting the Rincón villages of Juquila, Tanetze, and Yaee. The CEPCO grew quickly. By 1994, more than 20,000 growers were members of the organization, and by the early 1990s, the "CEPCO was the most consolidated, autonomous grassroots economic network in Oaxaca" (Moguel & Aranda 1992:187-188, Fox 1994:207).

In 1992, organizations from across the Sierra Juárez formed the Union of Organizations of the Sierra Juárez of Oaxaca (UNOSJO), which soon became the most important regional grassroots alliance in the area. Within four years the UNOSJO, based in Guelatao de Juárez, included 23 organizations representing 60 communities and was involved in such diverse activities as road construction, forestry, staple foods production, and coffee (Pascual López & Ortiz Medrano 1996). In 1997, the UNOSJO was in its second year of promoting its *"Café del Bosque Nublado"* ("Coffee of the Cloudy Forest") organic coffee project with the support of various international NGOs. Another organic coffee organization, the Mixe-Chinantec-Zapotec Organization (MICHIZA), also has affiliates across the Sierra Juárez. MICHIZA was started by progressive-minded Catholic missionary priests and includes approximately 300 members in the Rincón.

The Perils of Organizing Cooperatives

Although this effervescence in Mexico's coffee sector is an exciting event with broad implications for grassroots development, it has progressed unevenly and is far from complete. For example, in 1991 the CEPCO estimated that it purchased only 8 percent of the coffee produced in the state of Oaxaca (Fox 1994). This is not to underestimate the impact of the CEPCO; indeed, the organization has played a key role in establishing minimum prices since the collapse of the INME-CAFE. Perhaps more importantly, the CEPCO has sensitized indigenous people to the possibilities of interregional alliances.

In spite of the innocuous appearance of the UNOSJO, several of the group's founding members have been subjected to intimidation, albeit anonyously. As the UNOSJO—one of the few Sierra-wide organizations in the history of the region—was being organized in 1991 and 1992, a number of mysterious events took place which, according to some, were meant to snuff out the multi-ethnic organization in the Sierra Juárez. A number of key organizers received anonymous death threats through the mail. Then, in May 1991, a Zapotec engineer was mysteriously hit by an unidentified truck outside the Rincón village of Otatitlán one night. Once he was knocked down, the truck ran over him a number of times. The engineer, who narrowly survived the incident and has sinced moved out of the state, was an outspoken supporter of the then-embryonic UNOSJO and the Pueblos Unidos. During the same year, Rosendo García Miguel, the director of the Pueblos Unidos, was assassinated under mysterious circumstances. Apparently, the murderers were also from the Rincón, but it is not entirely clear whether they were influenced by actors from the "outside." Demonstrations calling for an investigation were largely ignored by state officials (Manzano 1993). More recently, anonymous and unfounded accusations have been made linking the UNOSJO to the Popular Revolutionary Army (EPR), a guerrilla army that has been active in Oaxaca and Guerrero since 1996 (Gaspar González 1997).

The new grassroots organizations appear to threaten at least some established interests and, in the case of the UNOSJO, it may well be that regional- or state-level political figures are fearful of the potential political power that a united Sierra Juárez might exercise. Historically the region has been characterized by strong opposition to penetration from outside forces (whether Aztec, Spanish, or Mexican) and fearless ferocity in battle (both in the Conquest period and during the 1910 revolution; see Chance 1989, Ruiz Cervantes 1988, Garner 1988). As recently as the 1990s, Sierra villages have "kidnapped" visiting state officials (including the governor) when demands were not met or when political promises were not kept, and government functionaries are often reluctant to enter the region (Fox & Aranda 1996:59-60). This unwavering political will, coupled with the remarkable ability to provide for themselves economically and the long tradition of village democracy in the Sierra Juárez, may make some members of the ruling PRI party uneasy in Oaxaca.[6] The fact that some cooperatives are drawing together ethnolinguistic groups that have had antagonistic relations since the pre-Columbian era—as in the case of the Mixes and the Sierra Zapotecs—might be especially troubling for some government and military officials. In the context of nationwide demands for regional autonomy for Mexico's indigenous peoples (Díaz Polanco 1997), the implications of the new cooperatives (many of which are explicitly devoted to the social and cultural invigoration of their communities) may be enough to concern the current political establishment. Self-sufficiency and self-determination, it seems, are increasingly seen as acts of subversion (Guada-rrama Olivera 1996).

Much of the new literature on coffee in Mexico focuses optimistically on the impressive gains made by grassroots cooperatives and regional networks, but a realistic picture of the contemporary coffee scene can quickly temper things. The dismantling of the INMECAFE did, on the one hand, open up a space for independent groups like the CNOC and the CEPCO. On the other hand, international forces—specifically, the transnational corporations alluded to earlier—have also been able to amplify their already extensive presence in the Mexican coffee sector. As stated earlier, in 1991 the CEPCO estimated that it purchased only 8 percent of the coffee produced in the state of Oaxaca (Fox 1994). We can probably safely assume that the remaining 92 percent went into the hands of middlemen who delivered it to Mexican exporters affiliated with transnationals. Indeed, two of the most vocal proponents of the new coffee organizations have offered this assessment of the changes following the 1989 withdrawal of the INMECAFE: "The largest portion [of the purchasing, storing, and marketing of coffee]...has been taken over by reemerging middlemen and by large transnational corporations which now operate directly in this area they once relegated to intermediaries." The cooperatives now find themselves "swimming with the sharks" (Hernández Navarro & Célis Calleja 1994:222).

Still, the importance of the new grassroots organizations should not be underestimated. Organic coffee programs in particular may represent the best hope for an ecologically sound strategy in Mexico's indigenous communities, especially since the global market for such products is rapidly expanding (Jonathan Fox, pers. comm.). Coffee is a crop that can profitably be grown on small holdings and produced in conjunction with subsistence crops, as the Talean *campesinos* have demonstrated for nearly a century. It appears to offer a way for indigenous villages and regions to retain a base of economic self-sufficiency by benefitting from the growing world market for organic coffee.

Organic Coffee and Imperialist Nostalgia

The organic coffee market has not occurred in a vacuum. It has been driven in part by shifts in consumption patterns. Beginning in 1962, coffee consumption in the U.S. began declining for a number of reasons (see Figure 4). High prices were certainly a factor, as prices tripled between 1945 and 1955, rose more or less

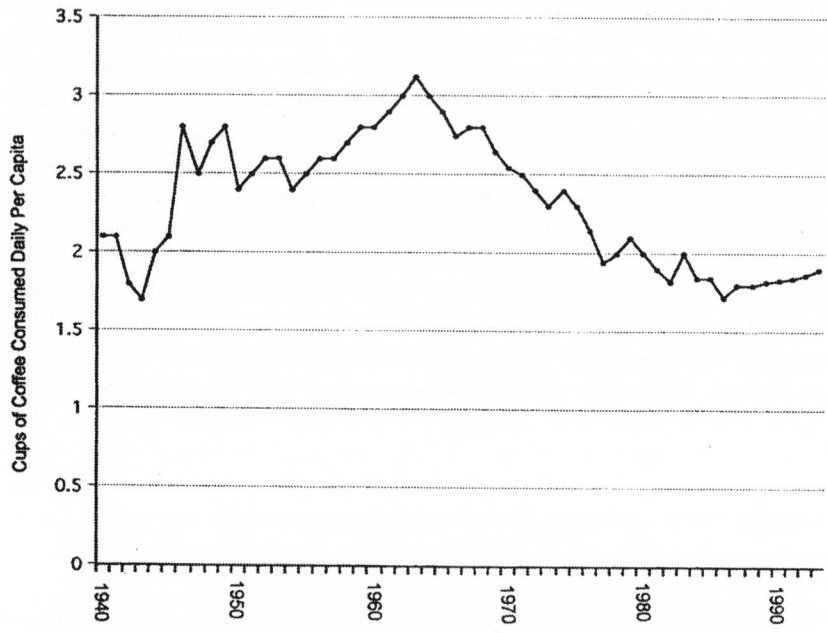

Figure 4.   Coffee Consumption in the United States, 1940-1993

steadily through the 1960s, and then spiralled upwards in the mid-1970s. A decline in the quality of mass-produced coffees—due largely to the introduction of bitter *robusta* coffees—also negatively affected sales. During this period, soft drinks became popular, particularly among young people, and per capita consumption quadrupled from 1946 to 1976. Finally, a number of studies appeared in the late 1970s and early 1980s linking caffeine to reproductive problems, including reduced fertility, miscarriages, and stillbirths. A second wave of studies linked caffeine to certain kinds of cancers and heart disease (Brewster & Jacobson 1983:18, Mathews 1994). In the early 1960s, the U.S. imported more than half of the world's coffee exports; by 1995, its share had decreased to one-fourth as Europe and Japan increased their relative consumption. Overall world consumption continued to increase until the early 1990s and then reached a plateau. According to one analysis, "world coffee consumption has been basically flat in recent years in importing nations owing largely to strong competition from other beverages" (Commodity Research Bureau 1996:41). Coca-Cola, it seems, is indeed conquering the world—and, along the way, its competitors.

Even so, new consumption trends have begun boosting coffee drinking among at least some Americans. In an important essay, William Roseberry (1996:773) argues that, in the new world economic order of flexible production and flexible workers, "yuppie coffees"—gourmet or specialty coffees that offer an alternative to mass-market brands—have emerged as the beverage of choice among members of a certain class of "urban, urbane, professional men and women who distinguish themselves through consumption." Roseberry's essay is about the shaping of tastes and the creation of market niches in the wake of structural transformations in the U.S. and global economies. Relying on trade journals as sources, he outlines the trajectory of specialty coffees that began booming in the 1990s as "coffeemen" (industry people) and advertisers successfully targeted two groups with spending power: "Yuppies" and "Generation Xers." As in the case of the coffee break, there is of course a pleasurable side, as well. Consuming the gourmet blends is a statement of class status and distinction; some companies are affiliated with grassroots cooperatives, which grow organic coffees, so one can ostensibly support indigenous peoples and save the environment while sipping a cup of Mexico's best;[7] and, of course, the coffees usually taste much better than the mass-market brands.

On the psychological side, there is perhaps a subtler process (Roseberry 1996:773-774) occurring in which the consumer

> may connect with the commodities' 'prehistory' as it were, representing a kind of preindustrial nostalgia. . .[for] expensive goods from exotic locales, affordable and consumable only by a privileged few...The class and cultural identification of this yuppie segment could be seen to represent an attempt to re-create, through consumption, a time before mass society and mass consumption.

This phenomenon has been called "imperialist nostalgia" by Renato Rosaldo (1989) and is clearly present in mail-order catalogs and paraphenalia distributed by certain specialty coffee companies. Indeed, Starbucks customers are given the opportunity of taking a culinary safari by consuming bits of Asia, Latin America, and Africa sold in attractive "retro"-styled packages under brand names such as "Arabian Mocha," "Guatemala Antigua," "Mexico Altura," "New Guinea Peaberry," "Estate Java," and "Ethiopia Sidamo." The world, it seems, is not so much an oyster as it is a Starbucks Coffee "Sampler" that can be delivered to one's door for $19.95 plus shipping and handling.

Not surprisingly, the new coffee cooperatives are related to shifts in global capitalism and consumption in the "First World." This paper began by discussing the various networks of power in which coffee cultivation has been embedded over time—European imperialism, state-owned institutes such as the INMECAFE (Mexican Coffee Institute), and the webs of transnational corporations—each having played its part in the structuring of world consumption. Today's situation is characterized by so-called "free" markets that are not always free, the further expansion of transnationals and, at the same time, a contrary trend towards grassroots cooperatives operating independently of the state. At a different level, indigenous peoples (not only the Zapotec but also the Mam Mayans of Chiapas and many other groups) increasingly assert themselves as subjects in the process of historical change rather than as passive objects to be studied by anthropologists. In the meantime, many anthropologists find themselves actively participating in the history-making process as well, playing the role of "cultural brokers" (Wolf 1956) between indigenous communities and NGOs in an emerging and rapidly changing global economic order.

ACKNOWLEDGMENTS

A shorter version of this paper was presented at the annual meetings of the American Anthropological Association in Washington, DC, in November 1997. Field research was made possible through funding from a National Science Foundation Dissertation Research Fellowship. The author thanks Professors Laura Nader (University of California, Berkeley) and Manuela da Cunha (University of Chicago) for critical comments and suggestions on earlier drafts of the paper.

NOTES

1. General Fidencio Hernández, according to Pérez García, was born in Ixtlán, Oaxaca in 1832. He received some formal schooling and then, at a young age, was given an important position by Don Miguel Castro, then owner of the Santa Gertrudis mines near Talea. He affiliated himself with the Liberal party at the age of 23 and, by 1860, was a soldier in the Reform Wars. He participated in the War of the French Intervention, and afterwards dedicated himself to agriculture and small-scale commercial activities. He corresponded with President Benito Juárez and was occasionally called upon to act as "political chief and commander of the National Guard of the District because he was considered *the* public official of the region." It was during this time that he is said to have introduced coffee in the Rincón. Archival sources indicate that Hernández's "coffee decree" was issued in January 1875 (Esparza 1988:301). Hernández died in 1881 of hepatitis (Pérez García 1956:131-133).

2. Jiménez (1995) convincingly argues that such changes—which profoundly affected life in the U.S. but also in Latin American "coffee republics" and coffee producing villages like Talea de Castro—were intimately related to the myriad effects of the rise of American industrial capitalism. The creation of an urbanized, more homogeneous working class meant a standardized market; new mass marketing channels (especially supermarkets) led to more efficient distribution; emergent food conglomorates began standardizing tastes and coffee blends for mass consumption; and consumer tastes were shaped by novel advertising techniques and events promoted by an assertive trade group, National Coffee Association (formed in 1910 as the National Coffee Roasters Association). Technological developments also played an important role: improved transportation systems led to better and cheaper access to coffee in the nation's interior, while new food production and processing techniques (such as vacuum packing) made mass marketing possible.

3. From mid-1994 to mid-1997 the value of the peso with respect to the dollar was cut in half.

4. I have not yet been able to determine whether the suggestion is a plausible one, because of the scarcity of material regarding the technical aspects of Mexican coffee growing in the 1800s. In any event, what is clear is that many plantation owners tend to follow an "agribusiness" monocrop approach by planting coffee in direct sunlight. These "sun coffee" plantations have serious environmental consequences, however: they require heavy fertilization and fumigation, are harder on long-term soil productivity, and decrease the biodiversity characteristic of shade coffee plantations. As a result, several species of migratory birds have all but disappeared from some regions of Mexico (R. Greenberg 1994).

5. Among the most important members were the UCIRI, the Coalition of Ejidos of the Costa Grande of Guerrero, the Union of Unions of Chiapas (Harvey 1992), and the Union of Coffee Producers of Veracruz. Other links in the network included individuals affiliated with the Community Food Councils of the Mexican Food System, an ambitious but highly problematic project instituted to help Mexico achieve food self-sufficiency, community groups formerly affiliated with the INMECAFE, and technical support groups like the Center for Assistance to the Oaxacan Campesino Movement (CAMPO).

6. See Nader (1991) and Fox and Aranda (1996) for descriptions of Oaxaca's municipal tradition based on the *cargo* system and the extensive use of municipal committees, which is remarkably democratic in comparison to other Mexican states. According to one of Fox and Aranda's (1996) sources, less than ten percent of Oaxaca's 470 municipalities are controlled by political bosses. It remains to be seen whether this system of autonomous municipal government will be sustained in the wake of the Popular Revolutionary Army (EPR) guerrillas and the subsequent militarization of the state. It is important to note that the Mexican government is not monolithic, nor is the ruling PRI party. Certain governmental agencies and PRI officials have had members who have provided support—moral, technical, and economic—to independent organizations, including indigenous cooperatives. See Fox (1994) for an analysis of the "thickening of civil society" and the role of government actors in the process.

7. Some companies do indeed sell coffees that are "fairly traded" and certified as organic. In the San Francisco Bay Area, for example, Equal Exchange, Thanksgiving Coffee, and Royal Coffee feature coffees from Africa, Latin America, and Indonesia that meet these criteria. Other companies—for example, Starbucks Coffee—do not sell certified organic coffee or provide information about their suppliers or labor practices to their customers or the media (Lack 1998). The Seattle-based Starbucks Corporation, the most aggressive and rapidly-growing gourmet coffee franchise, was recently embroiled in a scandal when it was alleged that some of their Guatemalan coffees were produced under exploitative labor conditions. The incident was an embarassment for the company which, like the Ben & Jerry's Ice Cream Company, has tried to maintain a progressive pro-environment, socially-conscious image.

REFERENCES

Appadurai, Arjun, ed. (1986) *The Social Life of Things: Commodities in Cultural Perspective*. Cambridge, ENG: Cambridge University Press

Berg, Richard L. (1968) *The Impact of the Modern Economy on the Traditional Economy in Zoogocho, Oaxaca, Mexico and Its Surrounding Area*. Ph.D. dissertation, University of California, Los Angeles.

Bergad, Laird (1982) *Coffee and the Growth of Agrarian Capitalism in Nineteenth Century Puerto Rico*. Princeton, NJ: Princeton University Press.

Braudel, Fernand (1967) *Capitalism and Material Life, 1400-1800* (trans. Miriam Kochan). New York: Harper Colophon Books.

Borgstrom, Georg (1967) *The Hungry Planet*. New York: Collier.

Brewster, Letitia, and Michael F. Jacobson (1983) *The Changing American Diet*. Washington, DC: Center for Science in the Public Interest.

Burgos-Debray, Elisabeth, ed. (1984) *I, Rigoberta Menchú: An Indian Woman in Guatemala* (trans. Ann Wright). London & New York: Verso.

Chance, John (1989) *Conquest of the Sierra: Indians and Spaniards in Colonial Oaxaca*. Norman: University of Oklahoma Press.

Commodity Research Bureau (1996) *Commodity Year Book*. New York: Commodity Research Bureau.

Crosby, Alfred W. (1972) *The Columbian Exchange: Biological and Cultural Consequences of 1492*. Westport, CT: Greenwood Press.

Dean, Warren (1976) *Rio Claro: A Brazilian Plantation System, 1820-1920*. Stanford, CA: Stanford University Press.

Díaz Polanco, Hector (1997) *Indigenous Peoples in Latin America: The Quest for Self-Determination* (trans. Lucía Rayas). Boulder, CO: Westview Press.

Douglas, Mary, and Baron Isherwood (1981) *The World of Goods*. New York: Basic Books.

Early, Daniel K. (1982) *Café: Dependencia y Efectos (Coffee: Dependency and Effects)*. Mexico, DF: Instituto Nacional Indigenista.

Erlich, Reese (1994) "Heavy Frosts Hurt Brazil's Smaller Coffee Farmers." *The Christian Science Monitor*, August 19, p. 8.

Esparza, Manuel (1988) "Los Proyectos de los Liberales en Oaxaca (1856-1910)" ("The Projects of the Liberals in Oaxaca [1856-1919]"). Pp. 269-330 in Leticia Reina (ed.) *Historia de la Cuestión Agraria Mexicana--Estado de Oaxaca (Prehispánico-1925) (History of the Mexican Agrarian Question--Oaxaca State [Prehispanic to 1925])*. Mexico, DF: Juan Pablos Editor.

Ferguson, James (1988) "Cultural Exchange: New Developments in the Anthropology of Commodities." *Cultural Anthropology* 3(4):488-513.

Fox, Jonathan (1994) "Targeting the Poorest: The Role of the National Indigenous Institute in Mexico's Solidarity Program." Pp. 179-216 in Wayne A. Cornelius, Ann L. Craig & Jonathan Fox (eds.) *Transforming State-Society Relations in Mexico: The National Solidarity Strategy*. San Diego: University of California at San Diego, Center for U.S.-Mexican Studies.

Fox, Jonathan, and Josefina Aranda, eds. (1996) *Decentralization and Rural Development in Mexico: Community Participation in Oaxaca's Municipal Funds Program*. San Diego: University of California at San Diego, Center for U.S.-Mexican Studies.

Garner, Paul H. (1988) *La Revolución en la Provincia: Soberanía Estatal y Caudillismo en las Montañas de Oaxaca (1910-1920) (The Revolution in the Province: State Sovereignty and Bossism in the Mountains of Oaxaca 1910-1920)*. Mexico, DF: Fondo de Cultura Económica.

Gaspar González, Aleyda (1997) "Persiste el Hostigamiento a UNOSJO" ("The Harrassment of UNOSJO Continues"). *Contrapunto* (Oaxaca City, Mexico) 2(63), March 1, p.5.

Goodman, Jordan (1992) *Tobacco in History*. New York & London: Routledge.

Greenberg, James B. (1989) *Blood Ties: Life and Violence in Rural Mexico*. Tucson: University of Arizona Press.

Greenberg, Russell (1994) "Phenomena, Comment and Notes." *Smithsonian* 25(8):24-26.

Guadarrama Olivera, Fernando (1996) "La Autosuficiencia Subversiva" ("Subversive Self-Sufficiency"). *La Hora* (Oaxaca City, Mexico) 236:5-6.

Hanks, Lucien M. (1972) *Rice and Man: Agricultural Ecology in Southeast Asia*. Honolulu: University of Hawaii Press.

Harvey, Neil (1992) "La Unión de Uniones de Chiapas y los Retos Políticos del Desarrollo de Base" ("The Union of Unions of Chiapas and the Political Challenges of Developing the Base"). Pp. 219-234 in Julio Moguel, Carlota Botey & Luís Hernández (eds.) *Autonomía y Nuevos Sujetos Sociales en el Desarrollo Rural (Autonomy and New Social Subjects in Rural Development)*. Mexico, DF: Siglo XXI.

Hedlund, Hans (1992) *Coffee, Cooperatives, and Culture: An Anthropological Study of a Coffee Cooperative in Kenya*. Nairobi: Oxford University Press.

Hernández Castillo, R. Aida, and Ronald Nigh (1998) "Global Processes and Local Identity: Indians of the Sierra Madre of Chiapas and the International Organic Coffee Market." *American Anthropologist* 100: In press.

Hernández Navarro, Luís (1992) "Cafetaleros: Del Adelgazamiento Estatal a la Guerra del Mercado" ("Coffee Growers: From State Downsizing to the War of the Marketplace"). Pp. 78-97 in Julio Moguel, Carlota Botey & Luís Hernández (eds.) *Autonomía y Nuevos Sujetos Sociales en el Desarrollo Rural (Autonomy and New Social Subjects in Rural Development)*. Mexico, DF: Siglo XXI.

_____ (1994) "El Café y la Guerra" ("Coffee and War"). *La Jornada* (Mexico City), January 30, p. 48.

Hernández Navarro, Luís, and Fernando Célis Callejas (1994) "Solidarity and the New Campesino Movements: The Case of Coffee Production." Pp. 217-231 in Wayne A. Cornelius, Ann L. Craig & Jonathan Fox (eds.) *Transforming State-Society Relations in Mexico: The National Solidarity Strategy.* San Diego: University of California at San Diego, Center for U.S.-Mexican Studies.

Hernández Díaz, Jorge (1987) *El Café Amargo: Los Procesos de Diferenciación y Cambio Social entre los Chatinos (Bitter Coffee: Processes of Differentiation and Social Change among the Chatinos).* Oaxaca: Universidad Autónoma de Benito Juárez de Oaxaca.

Hirabayashi, Lane Ryo (1993) *Cultural Capital: Mountain Zapotec Migrant Associations in Mexico City.* Tucson: University of Arizona Press.

Jiménez, Michael (1995) "From Plantation to Cup: Coffee and Capitalism in the United States, 1830-1930." Pp. 8-64 in William Roseberry, Lowell Gudmundson & Mario Samper Kutschback (eds.) *Coffee, Society, and Power in Latin America.* Baltimore, MD: Johns Hopkins University Press.

Kloppenburg, Jack (1988) *First the Seed: The Political Economy of Plant Biotechnology, 1492-2000.* Cambridge, ENG: Cambridge University Press.

Lack, Larrry (1998) "Green Beans." *The Monthly* (Emeryville, California) 28(5), pp. 13-15.

Llambi, Luis (1994) "Opening Economies and Closing Markets: Latin American Agriculture's Difficult Search for a Place in the Emerging Global Order." Pp. 184-209 in Alessandro Bonanno et al. (eds.) *From Columbus to ConAgra: The Globalization of Agriculture and Food.* Lawrence, KS: University Press of Kansas.

MacVean, Charles (1996) "The Case of the Missing Migrants." *Science* 274:1299-1301.

Manzano, Crisanto (1993) *Don Chendo* (video). Oaxaca: Instituto Nacional Indigenista, Centro de Video y Posproducción.

Marcus, George (1995) "Ethnography in/of the World System: The Emergence of Multi-sited Ethnography." *Annual Reviews in Anthropology* 24:95-117.

Mathews, Jay (1994) "Increasingly, Coffee Isn't Our Cup of Tea." *The Washington Post*, November 4, p. C1.

McCreery, David (1994) *Rural Guatemala, 1760-1940.* Stanford: Stanford University Press.

Mintz, Sidney W. (1979) "Time, Sugar, and Sweetness." *Marxist Perspectives* 2:56-73.

_____ (1985) *Sweetness and Power: The Place of Sugar in Modern History.* New York: Penguin Books.

Moguel, Julio, and Josefina Aranda (1992) "Los Nuevos Caminos en la Construcción de la Autonomía: La Experiencia de la Coordinadora Estatal de Productores de Café de Oaxaca" ("The New Roads in the Construction of Autonomy"). Pp. 167-193 in Julio Moguel, Carlota Botey & Luís Hernández (eds.) *Autonomía y Nuevos Sujetos Sociales en el Desarrollo Rural (Autonomy and New Social Subjects in Rural Development).* Mexico, DF: Siglo XXI.

Morales, Fidel (1997) "Propuestas para Todos" ("Proposals for All"). *Ojarasca* 47-48 (Mexico City), pp. 50-57.

Nader, Laura (1964) *Talea and Juquila: A Comparison of Zapotec Social Organization.* Berkeley: University of California Press.

_____ (1991) *Harmony Ideology: Justice and Control in a Mountain Zapotec Village.* Stanford: Stanford University Press.

Nolasco, Margarita (1985) *Café y Sociedad en México (Coffee and Society in Mexico).* Mexico, DF: Centro de Ecodesarrollo.

Ortíz, Fernando (1947) *Cuban Counterpoint: Tobacco and Sugar.* New York: Knopf.

Paredes, Lorena Paz, Remedio Cobo, and Armando Bartra (1997) "La Hora del Café" ("The Coffee Hour"). *Ojarasca* (Mexico City) 46, pp. 27-49.

Pascual López, Prócoro, and Neftalí Ortiz Medrano (1996) "UNOSJO: La Escarpada Producción" ("UNOSJO: Rising Production"). *Ojarasca* (Mexico City) 35-36, pp.42-43.

Pérez García, Rosendo (1956) *La Sierra Juárez*. Mexico, DF: Gráfica Cervantina.

Roseberry, William (1983) *Coffee and Capitalism in the Venezuelan Andes*. Austin: University of Texas Press.

_____ (1996) "The Rise of Yuppie Coffees and the Reimagination of Class in the United States." *American Anthropologist* 98:762-775.

Rosaldo, Renato (1989) *Culture and Truth: The Remaking of Social Analysis*. Boston: Beacon Press.

Rubel, Arthur J. (1964) "The Epidemiology of a Folk Illness: Susto in Hispanic America." *Ethnology* 3:268-283.

Ruiz Cervantes, Francisco José (1988) "De la Bola a los Primeros Repartos" ("From the Haciendas to the First Redistribution"). Pp. 331-424 in Leticia Reyna (ed.) *Historia de la Cuestión Agraria Mexicana—Estado de Oaxaca (Prehispanico-1925)*. Mexico, DF: Juan Pablos Editor.

Ruiz Lombardo, Andrés (1991) *Cafeticultura y Economía en una Comunidad Totonaca (Coffee Cultivation and Economy in a Totonac Community)*. Mexico, DF: Instituto Nacional Indigenista.

Salaman, R.N. (1949) *The History and Social Influence of the Potato*. Cambridge, ENG: Cambridge University Press.

Samuelson, Robert J. (1989) "The Coffee Cartel: Brewing Up Trouble." *The Washington Post*, July 26, p. A25.

Stewart, Randal G. (1992) *Coffee: The Political Economy of an Export Industry in Papua New Guinea*. Boulder, CO: Westview Press.

Stolcke, Verena (1996) "The Labors of Coffee in Latin America: The Hidden Charm of Family Labor and Self-Provisioning." Pp. 65-93 in William Roseberry, Lowell Gudmundson & Mario Samper Kutschbach (eds.) *Coffee, Society, and Power in Latin America*. Baltimore, MD: Johns Hopkins University Press.

Tyrtania, Leonardo (1992) *Yagavila: Un Ensayo en Ecología Cultural (Yagavila: An Essay on Cultural Ecology)*. Mexico, DF: Universidad Autónoma Metropolitana-Iztapalapa.

Ukers, William H. (1935) *All About Coffee* (2nd ed.). New York: The Tea and Coffee Trade Journal Company.

United States Department of Commerce (1961) *Coffee Consumption in the United States, 1920-1965*. Washington, DC: United States Government Printing Office.

Vásquez y de los Santos, Elena, and Yanga Villagómez Velázquez (1993) "La UCIRI, el Café Orgánico, y la Experiencia de un Proyecto Campesino Autosugestivo en la Producción" ("The UCIRI, Organic Coffee, and the Experience of a Self-Stated Peasant Production Project"). *Cuadernos del Sur* (Oaxaca City, Mexico) 2(5), pp. 121-137.

West, John A. (1992) "A Brief History and Botany of Cacao." Pp. 105-122 in Nelson Foster & Linda S. Cordell (eds.) *Chilies to Chocolate: Food the Americas Gave the World*. Tucson: University of Arizona Press.

Wilkinson, Tracy (1994) "Organic Business Brews in El Salvador." *The Los Angeles Times*, December 6, p. H3.

Wolf, Eric R. (1956) "Aspects of Group Relations in a Complex Society: Mexico." *American Anthropologist* 58: 1065-1078.

_____ (1982) *Europe and the People without History*. Berkeley & Los Angeles: University of California Press.

Young, Kate (1978) "Modes of Appropriation and the Sexual Division of Labour: A Case Study from Oaxaca, Mexico." Pp. 124-154 in Annette Kuhn & AnnMarie Wolpe (eds.) *Feminism and Materialism: Women and Modes of Production*. London: Routledge & Kegan Paul.

WHY THE MENDE BECAME TREE-CROPPERS

Barry L. Isaac

INTRODUCTION

The paper by Roberto González in this volume raises the question of why—and with what effect—subsistence-oriented cultivators abandon or modify that adaptation to take up market-oriented production of non-edible crops. The question is of sufficient interest, in both the practical and theoretical senses, to prompt me to resurrect a data set that I gathered 30 years ago (1967-68) in Upper Bambara Chiefdom, Kailahun District, Eastern Province, Sierra Leone (West Africa). My field study concerned economic change that had occurred since the terminus of West Africa's first long-distance railroad was established in Pendembu, the chiefdom's capital town, in 1908. In 1967-68, Upper Bambara Chiefdom, with an area of some 100 sq mi, had a population of around 10,000, of whom 3,300 lived in Pendembu (see Figure 1). Kailahun District then had around 550,000 people living in its 1,548 sq mi (see Clarke 1966).

The dominant ethnicity of Upper Bambara Chiefdom is Mende, also a major component of Sierra Leone as a whole (nearly 40% in the 1960s). Until mid-century, the Mende were overwhelmingly subsistence cultivators, mainly of upland rice, and

Research in Economic Anthropology, Volume 19, pages 267-288.
Copyright © 1998 by JAI Press Inc.
All rights of reproduction in any form reserved.
ISBN: 0-7623-0446-4

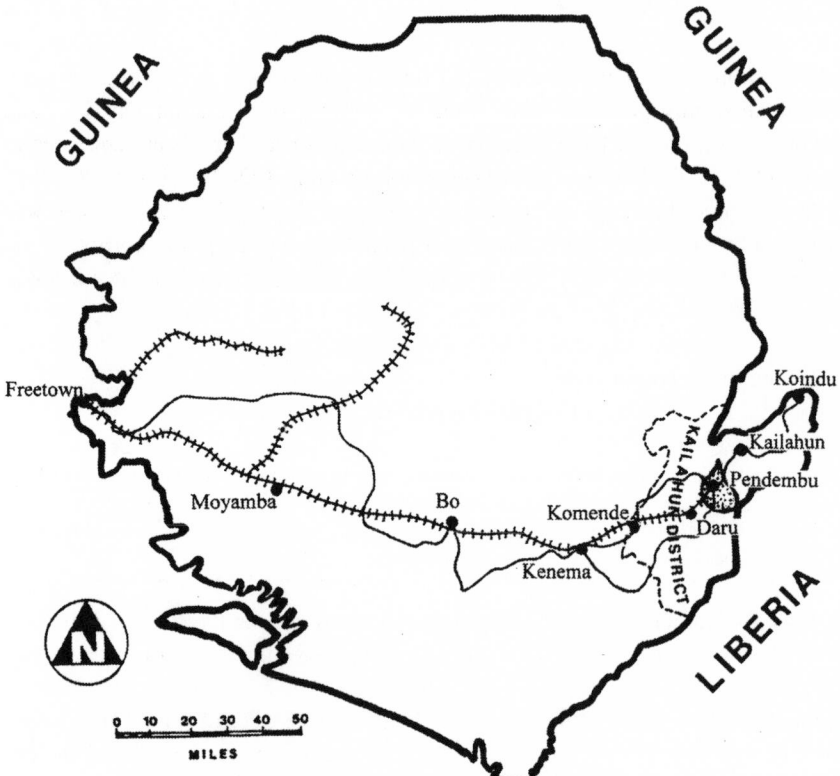

Figure 1. Map of Sierra Leone, Showing the Railway, the
Freetown-Koindu Highway, Kailahun District, Upper Bambara
Chiefdom (stippled area), and Selected Citites and Towns

the great majority remained on the land 30 years ago. Since the 1950s, though, rice
production had fallen dramatically; Upper Bambara Chiefdom was still a substantial exporter of rice in 1950 but had become a large and consistent importer by the
mid-1960s, and many rural households no longer produced enough of this staple
to meet their annual consumption. Increasingly, the rural Mende produced coffee,
cocoa, and palm kernels for cash with which to purchase rice during much of the
year. As we shall see, these changes occurred because Mende agrarian households
became too labor-short for self-sufficiency in rice but still had sufficient labor to
produce commercial tree crops.

Oil Palms and Rice

Palm kernels were the traditional Mende tree crop (see Hofstra 1937, Little
1967)—and the first to be commoditized. In 1918, ten years after the railhead was

established at Pendembu, that station shipped 3,814 tons of palm kernels and 168 tons of palm oil to Freetown; by 1928, only ten years later, the figures for *the first quarter alone* were 4,107 tons and 111 tons, respectively. It is important to note, though, that this produce came from the entirety of Kailahun District—and beyond: "At present a large quantity of French [Guinea] kernels are entrained at Pendembu...," the District Commissioner observed in 1928 (see Isaac 1969:38).

At that time, however, the production of palm "kernels" for export sale was largely a by-product of the rendering of palm oil, from the pulpy portion of the same fruit, mainly for local consumption. More importantly, subsistence farming remained the backbone of the District's economy. Indeed, rice production was a defining Mende lifeway, in the fullest sense, as well as a means of subsistence provisioning in the countryside.

Sjoerd Hofstra (1937:117-118) observed for this period:

> The [cash] income of the people is thus connected with the sale of kernels. They would be able to live an economically self-contained life, as their rice farms provide the necessary food, and the indigenous cotton is sufficient for their clothes; every commodity above this level must, however, be obtained from the export of kernels.

At least for Kailahun District, Hofstra somewhat overstated the case for palm kernels. Besides kernels, local foodstuffs were sold commercially to some extent. One trader whom I interviewed in Pendembu in 1967 recalled of the 1940s that he annually bulked 1,000 or slightly more large bags of rice. He claimed he could have bought upwards of 100 four-gallon tins of palm oil per day during the dry season, had his capital been adequate, and that sweet potatoes, coco-yams (taro), and cassava were available for commercial bulking, as well. Furthermore, the Kailahun District Annual Report for 1950 notes that 134 tons of rice were shipped from the district that year, including 75 tons sent from Pendembu Station; in 1951, 669 tons (253 from Pendembu Station) were exported (see Isaac 1969:41, n.16).

By the late 1960s, the local cash-cropping situation had changed dramatically. Virtually no local rice was offered for sale (ibid.:41, n. 17). Furthermore, my intensive interviews in 1967 with a sample of 41 of Pendembu's 182 market-women (traders in the daily marketplace) revealed that only 18 (43.9%) of them obtained all of their trading stock locally. Eleven (26.8%) others bought part of their stock in Koindu, 8 (19.5%) in Kailahun, and 4 (9.75%)—all dried-fish sellers—bought most of their stock in Freetown; these sites of restocking are 50, 16, and 227 miles away (Isaac 1969:193-194). Finally, I should note that my census of Pendembu's daily marketplace vendors on three different weeks (Saturday through Thursday) in 1967 showed that sellers who dealt exclusively in imported (Burma) rice accounted for an average of 4.5 percent of all morning (peak-period) vendors in January (dry season), 19.5 percent in late June (early-heavy rains), and 15.2 percent in mid-August (heaviest rains) (see Isaac 1969:173-177).

Cocoa and Coffee

Given the ubiquity of cocoa and coffee as cash crops in Upper Bambara Chiefdom in the late 1960s, one could not have guessed that the cultivation of cocoa—the first of these crops to be introduced—was initially met with determined resistance, albeit of the passive kind typical of the defeated (see Scott 1985). The Native Administration Minute Papers for 1927 (see Isaac 1969:46-47) contain the frustrated pleas of a government Cocoa Instructor, who had been sent on trek with seedlings and the equipment to plant demonstration fields:

> Sir,
>   I beg to inform you that the Sub-Chief [Name] has driven me away from his town saying that he don't want cocoa instructor to stay in his town because he [Cocoa Instructor] is not a Mende man and he [Sub-Chief] only knows about rice as their staple food.
>   Moreover, he told his men to carry my loads in another direction and from yesterday until this day I have not seen my things and the Government Tools. Therefore I beg to say that you should kindly send two persons to come and see about it....

Some three weeks later, this harried Cocoa Instructor was still distressed:

> But the man [the Sub-Chief] still disgraced me by giving me the sum of 5 shillings as the payment of my things lost, namely 1 pair black shoes, 3 loaves of bread, 1½ packet of sugar, and laundry soap.

The next day, the District Commissioner sent a firm missive to the Paramount Chief, the offending Sub-Chief's superior:

> My Good Friend,
>   I cannot understand how Sub-Chief [Name] came to refuse the cocoa instructor permission to plant or to give him carriers.
>   2. He has now 'begged' with 10 shillings and has given five shillings compensation for the loss of articles sustained by [the Cocoa Instructor]. I want, however, a full explanation of all this and unless it is forthcoming I shall call all concerned into Pendembu.
>
>   [sgn] Your Good Friend,
>   District Commissioner

We can see that Paramount Chiefs were held responsible for the introduction of cocoa in their administrative units, working through their Sub-Chiefs. In fact, these officeholders and other nobles were the first to plant the new crop. The British Empire's never-setting sun shown benevolently upon cooperative chiefs, such as the man in Kailahun District who received the "King's Medal for Paramount Chiefs" in 1939 "in recognition of the efficient manner in which he has administered his Chiefdom....He has materially increased the wealth of his Chiefdom by encouraging his people to grow economic crops" (Kailahun District Archives; see Isaac 1969:46). Generally speaking, farmers in the district's major towns, such as

Pendembu, were the first to imitate their chiefs. From these centers, cocoa and coffee spread gradually to smaller settlements. This process was still unfolding in Upper Bambara Chiefdom in the late 1960s, when rural villagers were planting new areas on a large scale and increasing their existing holdings.

Explaining Change

We can now turn directly to the two basic questions that motivate this article: (1) Why did the ordinary Mende agrarian household come to plant more and more of these foreign trees? and, (2) Was this increase in arboricultural commitment responsible for the decrease in subsistence rice production?

We have seen that the British colonial government worked through Paramount Chiefs—respected, traditional "indigenous sovereigns"—to introduce commercial cocoa farming to subsistence-oriented Mende cultivators. The question naturally arises of whether colonial coercion was responsible for the great economic changes observed between about 1930 and 1960, namely, a sharp increased in cocoa/coffee production and a sharp decline in rice farming. The answer is unequivocally negative in reference to the big picture of long-term changes. Although the British clearly used both the carrot and the stick, as we have seen, to introduce these commercial trees in Mendeland, there is no evidence to suggest that sustained pressure was exerted upon the ordinary Mende farmer sufficiently to account for the two major trends of change in question. It is important to remember in this regard that we are not dealing with just a few farmers or a minority of the rural population; to the contrary, cocoa/coffee production was embraced by virtually the entirety of the agrarian population, who concomitantly reduced their scale of rice production. Accomplishing this result through coercion would be a Herculean effort that would generate a voluminous archival record and a vivid oral tradition to that effect—neither of which exists.

Furthermore, even if we were to argue that ordinary Mende cultivators were lured deeply into commercial farming by the enticement of imported trade goods, or forced deeper into the commercial sector by taxation after 1895 (see Isaac 1969:Ch.2; cf. Ford 1995), we still could not explain the mass (and massive) adoption of cocoa and coffee production. After all, a great variety of local foodstuffs in addition to rice and palm oil were sold in large quantities for cash well into the 20th century, as we have seen. Furthermore, these other crops are intercropped with rice in the traditional Mende upland rice farm. By way of illustration, Johnny et al. (1981:610-612) recorded for the Moyamba area (see Figure 1) up to 20 other food crops still being grown simultaneously with rice in the Mende upland fields, accounting for 68 percent of the yield by weight and 53 percent of the caloric yield (also see Njoku 1979:107).

We could not argue that the Mende willy-nilly, i.e., for no sound economic reason, gave up their intercropped fields that provided not only subsistence but also produce for cash sale. It is well to remember that the agrarian Mende defined themselves as rice farmers and that rice is still regarded as *the* proper main course at every meal. The agrarian Mende loudly lament their inability to grow enough rice to provision themselves. They dislike the imported Southeast Asian rice but consume it anyway, just because rice is still the proper staple and the marketplace offers virtually none of the preferred local varieties.

Nor can any reasonable case be made that the "necessity" for cash through tree-crop production resulted in a land scarcity for rice production, crowding it out. There is no evidence of land shortage over most (perhaps all) of rural Mende-land, including Upper Bambara Chiefdom, during the time when tree crop production skyrocketed and rice production plummeted. Indeed, the assumption of land scarcity or competition, commonly invoked by economic planners, often rests upon nothing but ethnocentric projection of the European or American situation upon the West African countryside.[1] In the case of the Mende, the best corrective to that view is Njoku's (1979) meticulous study, which demonstrates that labor, not land, is the production in-put in scarce supply in the hinterland of Bo, in the heart of Mendeland, some 70 linear miles from Pendembu, the political center of my own research area (also see Johnny et al. 1981; Richards 1983: 30f).

Even where we find a shortening of the fallow cycle, we cannot automatically attribute it to land scarcity (or to population pressure as its proxy measure). Gleave's (1996:21-23) careful study of the evidence on fallowing in Sierra Leone points to the following intriguing conclusions: (1) fallowing practices are "far more complex than the impression given of them in…the literature…."; (2) "the natural environment, whilst affecting fallowing practices, is not directly a major influence"; (3) "Sierra Leone with a national overall population density…in 1985 of 127 per square mile…is at the lower end of the density range of the Boserupian transition…"; and (4) "farmers do not consider the returns in clearing heavy bush worth the effort, so that younger, less dense fallow is cleared whilst older bush is left to revert to forest" in much of Sierra Leone today—a practice we would expect to find where the significant production bottleneck is labor shortage.

Household Labor Requirements

My agrarian survey in rural Upper Bambara Chiefdom, as laid out below, strongly supports the foregoing assessments. In short, this paper argues that declining rice production in Upper Bambara Chiefdom is to be explained primarily in terms of changes in size and composition of the Mende agrarian household as the result of increasing monetization and commercialization of the general economy from the 1920s onward. The resulting labor shortage—even in the face of rural population increase—redounded not only in an absolute reduction in the area devoted to rice production but also a dramatic decline in food productivity rates, whether measured per worker or per unit of land under cultivation (see Njoku 1979; cf. Handwerker 1981). Concomitantly, commercial tree-cropping was intensified, as it required less labor.

Upland rice production is a laborious undertaking by traditional Mende means, i.e., using only hand tools, mainly the hoe. Njoku (1979) reports a mean of 104 workdays (@ 7 hours) per acre in the Bo area (cf. Currens 1979, Johnny et al. 1981). Field preparation is done by men and requires an average of 32 workdays. Women prepare the seed and contribute about equally with men to planting, which requires some 10 workdays. Women are responsible for weeding, which requires another 20 workdays, on average. Men do the fencing, an operation for which we lack labor data. Female children assist with harrowing and weeding. Male children assist with field preparation and harrowing and, more importantly, are the persons mainly responsible for scaring birds away from the ripening grain; this last operation requires about 21 workdays per acre and can be performed effectively only by several children working cooperative. All hands turn out for harvesting, which requires another 20 workdays per acre. All of these operations must be exactly timed for optimum yield, and they require labor concentration over relatively brief work periods, especially for field preparation and harvesting (Little 1951, Njoku 1979). Thus, even though the agrarian Mende appear to be underemployed during as much as half of the year, a severe labor shortage exists at times of peak agricultural input.

Furthermore, it is evident from the foregoing that a particular balance of male and female labor skills is required. It is important to emphasize *skills*, and not simply raw labor energy, as the following passage from Johnny et al. (1981:606-607) makes clear from their field study in the Moyamba area:

[Mende] men supply the bulk of the labour in the early part of the sowing season, from brushing to planting, but women take over much of the work from weeding to harvest. In most households the number of work days per year supplied by men and women is roughly 60% and 40%, respectively. The various tasks reflect the accumulation of distinct skills and experience, e.g., the specialised knowledge involved in felling a farm so that little additional work is needed to ensure the best possible burn, or the skilled eye essential to distinguish between grassy weed shoots and recently germinated rice....The outside economist is apt to consider all types of labour on upland rice farms as the exercise of undifferentiated brute force....Yet no Mende man would envisage it being easy to replace a woman weeding. Similarly, children...are extremely skilled and effective in pre-harvest bird-scaring, using sling and mud pellets, work which most adults tend to find tedious in the extreme. Thus...the farming-system is family based, in the sense of requiring specialized inputs from a working unit comprising men, women and children.

HISTORICAL PERSPECTIVE

Against this background, we can examine the changes that have occurred in the composition and organization of the Mende agrarian household during the past 100 years. We are fortunate to have comparative data from three time periods. The first is the late 19th century, about which Kenneth Little (1948a-b, 1951, 1967) was able to collect high-quality retrospective data from living memory in the mid-1940s. The second period is the mid-1940s, during which Kenneth Little (1948a, 1951) conducted meticulous field research on Mende agriculture. The third period is the late 1960s, when I studied the Pendembu area (Isaac 1969). These Mende household-focussed studies are complemented by two other intensive field studies of Mende upland rice farming: Athanasius Njoku's (1979) research in several villages within 50 miles of Bo in 1969-70 and Michael Johnny et al.'s (1981) research in two Mende villages south of Moyamba in 1978 (see Figure 1).

Admittedly, there are some hazards to using data collected at different times and in different places by different researchers—even within the same ethnic unit. Ideally, secular change would be documented by the same researcher(s) investigating the same research question(s) in the very same area either continuously or at timed intervals. Of course, that condition is not met here. Nevertheless, the existing data sets show a clear trend that is worth pointing out and attempting to explain.

Late 19th Century

The traditional Mende farming unit was the *mawe*, a three-generational household consisting of a male head with a least four wives, their unmarried children, their married sons and these latters' wives and children, sometimes married daughters with their husbands and children, often some other consanguineal or affinal kin, and an undetermined number of slaves of both sexes (Little 1948a:37-55, 1967:96-98; also see Abraham 1976:31-41). A *mawe* sometimes constituted a village with as many as 40 dwellings containing up to 120 people. Together, the *mawe* worked the *kpaa wa* (family farm), although many of its nuclear-family or other units also made a *bulei* (individual farm) to provision their own wants. A man did not attempt to establish his own *mawe* until he had at least four wives and some slaves, and he was greatly dependent upon his father in acquiring both (Little 1948a:42-43, 1967:97).

The Mid-1940s

In 1945-46, Kenneth Little carried out intensive studies of rice farming in Mendeland. By that time, the Mende agrarian household had undergone profound modifications as the result of two general economic forces. First, the slave trade had been outlawed by the British in 1896, and slavery itself was abolished in 1926 (see Abraham 1976:31-41). Some Mende chiefs and other traditional elders retained a few "servants" (i.e., hereditary slaves) up to the time of my research, but their agricultural labor input was inconsequential. Second, the increasing opportunities for earning money through petty trade, wage labor, and the sale of palm kernels lessened elders' control over young adults of both sexes (see Little 1948a:45). Although the *mawe* ranged up to 50 adults and children in the

Table 1. Kenneth Little's (1948a, 1951) Mende
Farming Household (Mawesia) Samples, Mid-1940s

		Household Composition[b]			
Region[a]	Number of Households (mawesia)	Men ($\overline{X}$)	Women ($\overline{X}$)	Children ($\overline{X}$)	Bushels of Rice Seed Planted ($\overline{X}$)
Bo	180	2.0	2.0	?	?
Bo	28	2.3	2.0	2.4	4.4
Kenema/ Komende	17	8.8	10.3	4.6	5.0
Daru	6	5.3	4.3	4.7	4.0

Notes: [a]These regions are the following (approximate) linear distances from Pendembu, the capital town of Upper Bambara Chiefdom, where I gathered the data reported later in this paper: Bo = about 70 miles, Kenema/Komende = about 40 miles, Daru = 13 miles.

[b]"Men" and "Women" are over 15 years of age. "Children" are about 15 years and younger, but Little typically excluded from his counts all individuals under 6 or 7 years, because they would not have contributed labor to farming.

mid-1940s (Little 1948a:39-40), the average size was much smaller. The *kpaa wa* (family farm) worked by the *mawe* ranged from 5 to 50 acres (Little 1948b:28).

Little's survey data are difficult to use, because he took several "samples" of varying sizes and in different areas (see Table 1). His largest sample includes 180 *mawesia* near Bo, the most urbanized part of Mendeland. This survey revealed an average of 2 men and 2 women per *mawe*, exclusive of persons under 15 years of age (Little 1948a:46). Little's more intensive study of 28 households near Bo revealed 2.3 adult (age 15 and over) men, 2.0 adult women, and 1.4 children aged roughly 6 to 15 per *mawe* (Little 1951:258, 1948a:46n). These *mawesia* were planting a mean of 4.4 bushels of rice seed, or 4 to 5 acres of ground, although the modal seeding was around two bushels (Little 1948a:53).

Little (1951:244) estimated that 1 bu of seed sufficed for 2 acres in the vicinity of Bo but for only 1 acre outside the Bo area. The reason for this variation is not clear. Njoku (1979:109) states that "about 60 lbs. of paddy is sown per acre," that is, about 1 bu of seed per acre, in the Bo area. I shall follow Njoku's estimate in the rest of this article.

Little's surveys of the more rural areas of Mendeland consistently revealed larger *mawesia* and field sizes than in the immediate vicinity of Bo. His samples from locations between Bo and Pendembu (the capital of Upper Bambara Chiefdom, my research site) are of special interest. In the vicinity of Kenema and Komende, some 40 linear miles east of Bo and about the same distance southwest of Pendembu, a sample of 17 *mawesia* had a mean average of 8.8 adult (age 15 and over) men, 10.3 adult women, and 4.6 children; it is unclear whether "children" in this case included all persons under age 15 or only those aged 6 to 15 (cf. Little

1948a:46, 1958:258, 381). The average *kpaa wa* (family farm) in the Ken-ema-Komende area was seeded with 5 bu of rice, that is, it covered about 5 acres. Around Daru, which is only some 13 linear miles from Pendembu, Little sampled six *mawesia*, which averaged 5.3 adult men, 4.3 adult women, and 4.7 children aged roughly 6-15; the average *kpaa wa* was seeded with 4 bu.

Two other aspects of Little's survey data from the mid-1940s are interesting in the present context. First, he noted an "increasing tendency...to regard rice as a commercial crop" (1951:378). Around Daru, the closest location to Upper Bambara Chiefdom, "income was derived mainly from the sale of palm kernels and rice...." (Little 1951:382). Traders whom I interviewed in Upper Bambara Chiefdom in 1966-68 stated that large quantities of local rice had been commercially available for bulking by middlemen as recently as the early 1950s, whereas virtually no local rice entered the market by the late 1960s (Isaac 1969). Second, the *bulei* (individual farm) in the Daru area in the mid-1940s averaged about 2 bu of seed sown, and the mean size of the *bulei* working group was 3 men, 2 women, and 2.5 children (Little 1951:378). These last figures will become significant when we examine my 1967-68 data from Upper Bambara Chiefdom.

THE UPPER BAMBARA CHIEFDOM SURVEY, 1967-68

I collected the 1967-68 data analyzed here in 9 rural villages (Gingima, Kitehun, Tigbena, Kimbuyama, Tambeya, Giema, Semabu, Old Garama, and New Garama) within a 5-mile radius of Pendembu (population about 3,300), the capital of Upper Bambara Chiefdom. The chiefdom's roughly 10,000 people were still mainly rural and agrarian. The population of the 9 study villages was 762, of whom 93.7 percent were Mende. The 9 villages contained 119 households ranging in size from 1 to 18 persons, plus 6 *pewesia* (Women's Houses) maintained by Village Headmen to shelter nursing, disabled, and indigent women (see Little 1967:99). In all, 104 (87.4%) of the 119 households were headed by Mende (99 by men, 5 by women). Two of the 5 female heads and 60 (60.6%) of the 99 male heads stated farming as their only occupation.[2]

This article analyzes only these 60 male-headed farming households. Their structure and composition are analyzed, first, by means of a household typology derived from one used by V. R. Dorjahn (1977) for the neighboring Temne. While typologies fail to portray the developmental cycle of household and family development, they have heuristic value. In the present case, the typology separates conjugal from non-conjugal households and also allows comparison between extended and non-extended households in terms of size and composition.

Tables 2 and 3 show that the mean size of the 60 households was 6.4, with the non-extended cases averaging 5.8 inhabitants and the extended cases, 9.3. By far the most prevalent type was the Monogamous Household (Type A), which consti-

Table 2. Male-Headed Agrarian Households, by
Type and Size, in Upper Bambara Chiefdom, 1967-68

	Households		*Inhabitants*		
Household Type [a]	*N*	*%*	*N*	*%*	*X̄*
I. CONJUGAL(one or more marital unions)	56	93.3	377	98.2	6.7
Type A: Monogamous Non-Extended	25	41.7	115	29.9	4.6
Type B: Polygynous Non-Extended	16	26.7	123	32.0	7.7
TOTAL Types A and B	41	68.3	238	62.0	5.8
Type C: Lineally-Extended	0	0.0	0	0.0	—
Type D: Collaterally-Extended	8	13.3	69	18.0	8.6
Type E: Other Consanguineally Extended	2	3.3	27	7.0	13.5
Type F: Non-Consanguineal Extended	5	8.3	43	11.2	8.6
TOTAL Types C-F	15	25.0	139	36.2	9.3
II. NON-CONJUGAL (no marital union)	4	6.7	7	1.8	1.8
Simple (man living alone)	2	3.3	2	0.5	1.0
Complex (unmarried man and other person[s]					
without resident spouse)	2	3.3	5	1.3	2.5
TOTAL (I and II)	60	100.0	384	100.0	6.4

Notes: [a]The household typology is derived from Dorjahn (1977). The composition is as follows:

Type A = One monogamous union, with or without other person(s) lacking resident spouse(s).

Type B = One polygynous union, with or without other person(s) lacking resident spouse(s).

Type C = Two or more married men related as father and son(s), together with their wives, with or without other person(s) lacking resident spouse(s).

Type D = Two or more married men related as brothers (or half-brothers), together with their wives, with or without other person(s) lacking resident spouse(s).

Type E = Two or more married men related consanguineally but not as father-son or brothers/half-brothers, together with their wives, with or without other person(s) lacking resident spouse(s).

Type F = Two or more married men who are not related consanguineally, together with their wives and any other person(s).

tuted 41.7 percent of the 22 households and contained 29.9 percent of the population. All told, 68.3 percent of the 60 households were of the non-extended forms (Types A and B), which contained 62.0 percent of their total population. This finding is striking, given Kenneth Little's information on the late 19th-century farming household—about three generations earlier. Furthermore, the Lineally-Extended Household (Type C)—the very model of the traditional *mawe*—was completely absent.

Extended and non-extended households had nearly identical proportions of adult women (39.6% vs. 37.0%), adult men (28.8% vs. 29.8%), and children (31.7% vs. 33.2%). However, the mean non-extended household had 3.5 fewer members than did the mean extended case. Surprisingly, the deficiency was spread fairly equally among the three major household components: −1.5, −1.0, and −1.0 adult women, adult men, and children, respectively.

Table 3.   Household Composition, by Sex and Age-Status
(Adult = 15 years and older, Child = under 15 years)

Household Types [a]	Adult Women			Adult Men			Total Adults			Children		
	N	%	$\overline{X}$	N	%	$\overline{X}$	N	%	$\overline{X}$	N	%	$\overline{X}$
CONJUGAL NON-EXTENDED	88	37.0	2.2	71	29.8	1.7	159	66.8	3.9	79	33.2	1.9
Type A	34	29.6	1.4	41	35.7	1.6	75	65.2	3.0	40	34.8	1.6
Type B	54	43.9	3.4	30	24.4	1.9	84	68.3	5.3	39	31.7	2.4
CONJUGAL EXTENDED	55	39.6	3.7	40	28.8	2.7	95	68.3	6.3	44	31.7	2.9
Type C	0	0.0	—	0	0.0	—	0	0.0	—	0	0.0	—
Type D	26	37.7	3.3	21	30.4	2.6	47	68.1	5.9	22	31.9	2.8
Type E	11	40.7	5.5	7	25.9	3.5	18	66.7	9.0	9	33.3	4.5
Type F	18	41.9	3.6	12	27.9	2.4	30	69.8	6.0	13	30.2	2.6
NON-CONJUGAL	2	28.6	0.5	5	71.4	1.3	7	100.0	1.8	0	0.0	—
Simple	0	0.0	—	2	100.0	1.0	2	100.0	1.0	0	0.0	—
Complex	2	40.0	1.0	3	60.0	1.5	5	100.0	1.3	0	0.0	—
ALL HOUSEHOLDS	145	37.8	2.4	116	30.2	1.9	261	68.0	4.4	123	32.0	2.1

Note: [a] For definitions of household types, see Table 1.

THE HOUSEHOLD FARM AND LABOR FORCE

Adult Female Labor

Of the mid-1940s, Kenneth Little (1967:141) observed that "no one can make a proper farm (*kpaa wa*) unless he has at least four wives, and smaller conjugal units are sometimes denied full status as *mawesia*, or farming households." In striking contrast, the Upper Bambara Chiefdom data show that the traditional *mawe* is nearly absent there. Only Type E households exceeded a mean of 4 wives per household, and even within this type the mean number of wives per husband was only 2.2 (Table 4). Furthermore, Table 3 shows that, even when we include all adult women (and not just wives), only Type E households exceeded a mean of 4.0, although Type F closely approached this figure. No Type A household had 4 adult women, and only 7 of the 16 Type B households had 4 or more. In all, only 7 (17.1%) of the 41 non-extended households (Types A and B)—which constituted 68.3 percent of all households and 62.0 percent of their inhabitants—contained 4 or more adult women. More generally speaking, only 15 (25.0%) of the 60 farming households had adequate womanpower for rice farming by mid-1940s standards, when 4 adult women was the measure of household labor adequacy.

Table 4. Conjugal Households (N = 56), by Marital Composition

Household Type[a]	Husbands (N)	Husbands per Household ($\overline{X}$)	Wives (N)	Wives per Husband ($\overline{X}$)	Wives per Household ($\overline{X}$)
A	25	1.0	25	1.0	1.0
B	16	1.0	44	2.8	2.8
C	0	—	0	—	—
D	17	2.1	20	1.2	2.5
E	5	2.5	11	2.2	5.5
F	10	2.0	13	1.3	2.6
TOTAL	73	1.3	113	1.5	2.0

Note: [a]For definitions of household types, see Table 1.

Adult Male Labor

For the 1940s, Kenneth Little (1951:249) observed that "about 6 men are required to control the burning of an acre of ground" and that "in many cases the household itself attends to the burning without outside help...." In my survey, none of the households had more than 5 males aged 15 and over, and only 2 (1 each in Types D and E) had even that many. None of the other 58 households had 4 adult men, 14 (23.3%) had 3 each, 20 (33.3%) had 2 each, and the other 24 (40.0%) had only 1 adult man each. As Table 3 shows, the mean conjugal non-extended household had only 1.7 adult men, and the mean conjugal extended form had 2.7, while the mean for all 60 households was 1.9 adult men.

Child Labor

Many of these households were also deficient in child labor (most critically, for keeping birds and other pests away from the ripening grain). Conjugal households had a mean of 2.2 children (1.9 in the non-extended, 2.9 in the extended form). Indeed, 11 (18.3%) of the 60 households had no resident children at all; 16 (26.7%) had only 1 each, 13 (21.7%) had 2, and 9 (15.0%) had 3 each. Only 11 (18.3%) of the 60 households had 4-8 children each.

Field Size and Household Labor Force

The mean figures for men, women, and children in conjugal households (Table 3) in Upper Bambara Chiefdom in 1967-68 are roughly comparable to Kenneth Little's figures from the mid-1940s for the vicinity of Bo, then and now the most urbanized portion of Mendeland: a mean of 2.3 adult men, 2.0 adult women, and

Table 5.   Amount of Rice Seed Planted,
by Number of Adults per Household, 1967[a]

Number of Adults per Household (by Sex)	Rice Seed Planted per Household (N = 24), in Bushels		Total Households
	Less than 1 bu (N = 7)	1 bu or more (N = 17)	
Women			
1	5	5	10
1-2	5	9	14
3 or fewer	6	11	17
4 or more	1	6	7
5 or more	1	4	7
Men			
1	3	4	7
1-2	6	11	17
3 or fewer	7	16	23
4 or more	0	1	1
5 or more	0	1	1
Both Sexes			
2	2	2	4
2-3	4	3	7
4 or more	3	14	17
5 or more	1	9	10

Note: [a]The question about amount of rice seeded was not included until the census was over half-completed. Thus, the data on seeding presented below are drawn from only 24 of the 60 households surveyed.

1.4 children aged 6-15 (Little 1951:258; cf. Little 1948a:46). These small house-holds around Bo were then planting an average of 4.4 bu of rice seed, or some 4-5 acres of ground, each year (Little 1951:244). In this latter regard, they are very dif-ferent from the similarly-sized households in Upper Bambara Chiefdom in 1967-68.

Data on seeding were gathered in only 24 cases (Table 5)—in the villages of Semabu, Old Garama, New Garama, and part of Giema—as the question was not included until the survey was more than half completed. Seven (29.2%) of the 24 households seeded less than 1 bu in 1967; in fact, 6 of them seeded only ½ bu each, while the other seeded ¾ bu. Seventeen (70.8%) planted 1 bu or more: 8 planted 1 bu each, 4 planted 1½ bu, 4 planted 2 bu, and 1 planted 3 bu. There is some extent of correlation between size of household labor force and amount of rice seeded (cf. Little 1948a:52), at least with respect to female labor. Five (71.4%) of the 7 households planting under 1 bu had only 1 adult woman,

Table 6. Participation in Reciprocal Labor by Heads of
Conjugal Households, by Number of Adult Men per Household, 1967a

Participation in Reciprocal Labor	Number of Adult Men per Household					Total Households
	5	*4*	*3*	*2*	*1*	
Yes	1	0	7	6	4	18
No	1	0	7	9	14	31
TOTAL HOUSEHOLDS	2	0	14	15	18	49

Note: [a]Not inlcuded here are the seven (out of 56) conjugal households (see Table 1) that did not make a rice farm in 1967.

Table 7. Place of Residence of Offspring Aged 15
and Over of Wives of Heads of Conjugal Households

Age [a]	Sex	Parental Household		Elsewhere in Parental Village		Elsewhere in the Chiefdom		Elsewhere in Sierra Leone		Total
		N	*%*	*N*	*%*	*N*	*%*	*N*	*%*	
15-19	male	1	14.3	2	28.6	0	0.0	4	57.1	7
	female	1	9.1	2	18.2	3	27.3	5	45.5	11
	both	2	11.1	4	22.2	3	16.7	9	50.0	18
20-29	male	5	26.3	3	15.8	4	21.1	7	36.8	19
	female	2	10.0	2	10.0	8	40.0	8	40.0	20
	both	7	17.9	5	12.8	12	30.8	15	38.5	39
30-49	male	0	0.0	5	45.5	2	18.2	4	36.4	11
	female	0	0.0	3	30.0	4	40.0	3	30.0	10
	both	0	0.0	8	38.1	6	28.6	7	33.3	21
TOTAL	male	6	16.2	10	27.0	6	16.2	15	40.5	37
	female	3	7.3	7	17.1	15	36.6	16	39.0	41
	both	9	11.5	17	21.8	21	26.9	31	39.7	78

Note: [a]Note that the third grouping includes a 19-year span instead of the 10-year span of the first two groupings. I lumped the entire 30-49 cohort together because there were only 2 (1 male, 1 female) individuals in the 40-49 age range, and both of them lived "Elsewhere in Parental Village."

whereas 12 (85.7%) of the 14 households with 2 or more adult women planted 1 bu or more (p = 0.08 by Fisher's Exact Test). No significant relationship emerges, however, when we contrast households containing 1-2 women with those containing 3 or more (p = 0.36 by Fisher's Exact Test), or households containing 4 or more women with those containing fewer than 4 (p = 0.31).

There appears to be no significant relationship between residential male labor and rice production. Although 13 (76.5%) of the 17 households containing 2 or more adult men seeded 1 bu or more of rice, so did 4 (57.1%) of the 7 containing only 1 adult man, yielding a chance probability of 0.92 by Fisher's Exact Test. The result is not improved by contrasting households containing 1-2 men with those having 3 or more (p = 0.31), or those with 4 or more and those with 3 or more, or fewer (p. 0.71). I believe the best interpretation of these results is that nearly all of the sample households were deficient in male labor and that, accordingly, the ability to cultivate more or less than 1 acre of rice was determined by factors other than resident male labor.

A significant difference does emerge, though, between the 17 households with 4 or more adults and the 7 with fewer than 4 adults; 14 (82.4%) of the former but only 3 (42.9%) of the latter planted 1 bu or more of rice seed (p = 0.08 by Fisher's Exact Test). Neither the contrast between households containing only 2 adults and those with 2 or more (p = 0.91), nor that between households with more or fewer than 5 adults (p = 0.42), showed significant differences in rice production.

Extra-Household Labor Recruitment

At the time of Kenneth Little's surveys in the mid-1940s, most Mende farming households apparently depended upon extra-household male labor for some farming operations. This dependence was present in Upper Bambara Chiefdom in 1967, but to a lesser extent. Table 6 shows that 18 (36.7%) of the 49 conjugal households that made independent rice farms in 1967 participated in reciprocal labor arrangements with other households, while 31 (63.3%) did not do so. To some extent, participation in these inter-household labor exchanges was correlated with size of household male labor force: only 4 (22.2%) of the 18 households with only 1 adult man participated in exchange labor, whereas 14 (45.2%) of those containing 2 or more adult men did so (p = 0.10). No significant relationship emerges from contrasting households with 3 men and those with fewer than 3 (p = 0.95), or those containing 2 men and those with more than 2 (p = 0.42). All we can say, then, is that households with only 1 adult man—i.e., 20 (35.7%) of the 56 conjugal households and 24 (40.0%) of the total of 60 households (see Table 3)—were at a disadvantage in recruiting extra-household labor on the basis of reciprocal exchanges. Let me add that a comparable table could be constructed for women per household but that it would show no correlations; besides, extra-household labor exchange was apparently mainly a male activity.

Furthermore, households with only 1 adult man—the very units in most need of outside labor—were less able to hire extra-household male workers. These household heads had a median cash income of less than half that of heads of 2-man households. It is important to remember that a household's ability to utilize female and child labor depends upon its having access to sufficient male labor for field preparation (clearing, burning, removing debris, hoe plowing). Similarly, male labor is marginally useful only if it is complemented by female labor. Thus, any reduction in the household's ability to recruit laborers of one sex necessarily reduces the utility of laborers of the opposite sex (see Johnny et al. 1981:606-607).

Out-Migration

Apart from slavery, extra-household labor traditionally was recruited on the basis of kinship. A household head depended upon labor contributions from his sons, sons' wives, daughters, daughters' husbands, and sisters' sons and their wives (Little 1948a:47, 48; 1948b:30). By 1967, this traditional base of labor recruitment had been heavily eroded by out-migration. Table 7 shows that fully two-thirds (52 of 78) of the adult (aged 15 and above) offspring of the Upper Bambara Chiefdom households surveyed were living outside of the nine study villages, and that 39.7 percent were living outside of the chiefdom. Surprisingly, the extent of removal of offspring from the chiefdom, largely in pursuit of formal education and work, shows little sex difference except in the youngest age cohort (ages 15-19), in which 57.1 percent of males but only 45.5 percent of females were living elsewhere in Sierra Leone. Furthermore, comparison of the three age cohorts suggests that many of those absent from the chiefdom in the 15-19 age grouping were not destined to return: 38.5 percent of the 20-29 cohort and 33.3 percent of the 30-49 cohort were also living outside of the chiefdom.

Two additional observations should be made about out-migration. First, the out-migration of adult offspring also removes their spouses and children from the kindred's available labor pool. Second, the remaining male and female labor in these villages was, by 1967-68, fragmented among a multiplicity of independent households with separate farms and was, therefore, difficult to aggregate for cooperative work. Mende farmers are articulate about the effects of out-migration on their agricultural production: "The plight of urban workers evoked little sympathy. Several times it was suggested that if food in Freetown was short, arrangements might be made to ship some of the labour back to the countryside" (Johnny et al. 1981:603). As Handwerker (1981:34) noted for Liberia, though, the return of absentees for specific farm tasks would only partially compensate for their prolonged absences; it would not overcome the uncertainty of labor supply, as "it [is] difficult to mesh farm tasks efficiently with the temporal requirements of the farm cycle" given the uncertainty of timely return.

Earlier, we saw that the households surveyed by Kenneth Little in the mid-1940s in the most urbanized area of Mendeland were roughly similar in size and sex-age composition to the rural households I surveyed in Upper Bambara Chiefdom in 1967-68. Yet, the mid-1940s peri-urban households planted an average of 4.4 bu of rice seed each year, whereas the Upper Bambara households planted a mean of only 1.2 bu in 1967. I think that out-migration from Upper Bambara Chiefdom goes a long way toward explaining this difference in field size. The fabric of kinship—the basis for recruiting both remunerated and exchange labor—was badly rent by the late 1960s in rural Upper Bambara Chiefdom, whereas it would have been largely intact even in Little's peri-urban survey area a generation earlier. Thus, households of similar size and internal composition in the late 1960s planted only one-fourth as much rice—while bitterly complaining of their inability to provision themselves with this staple food.

MONETIZATION, COMMERCIALIZATION, AND FREEDOM

The *mawe*, the traditional three-generational agrarian household, had virtually disappeared from rural Upper Bambara Chiefdom by 1967. To a great extent, we can say that it fell victim to freedom—first, freedom for slaves and their descendants in 1926; second, increasing freedom of the young from parental autarchy. The first was a simple matter of colonial politics and requires no further discussion. The second is more complex, as it involves the gradual erosion of parental control as the result of the increasingly pervasive monetization and commercialization of the general economy during this century.

In the early part of the 20th century, a young man needed his elders' help to accumulate the stuffs of bridewealth; indeed, the kinship system was almost the only avenue through which these goods were available. Thus, a young man was subordinate to his male elders. The colonial period (which effectively began in 1896 in the Sierra Leone hinterland) brought not only European money as such but also the necessity for men to sell goods or labor to earn that money, which was the only form of payment of the colonial poll tax (see Isaac 1969:24-28; also see Ford 1995). Of course, certain imported goods available only for colonial money also had an allure for Mende consumers. Elliot Berg's (1965:401) classic statement about machine-made cotton cloth in this regard is still worth quoting:

> [G]oods which could be fitted into traditional patterns of production and consumption were everywhere the early object of African money-earning activity. One commodity, however, deserves to be singled out for special mention: textiles. The possibility of buying European cloth...seems to have been the single greatest incentive to money earning in the early [colonial] years in most parts of Africa....[Previously] cloth was, in most places, a rare and expensive commodity. In some places its ownership and use was restricted to chiefs and members of the nobility....Even where...customs did not limit the possession of cloth to the upper classes, economic factors worked to do so; cloths were woven in limited numbers by village handicrafters, and their price was beyond the reach of the ordinary man.
> [Thus]...European textiles had immediate and enormous appeal to Africans. They were comfortable and durable and so had great utilitarian value. And because of their traditional association with the rich and the powerful, they were prestigious goods. Most important, they were cheap, far cheaper than the local product; any man could earn enough money to dress himself and his wife [well].

One important effect of the increased commercialization of the general economy was the monetization of the components of traditional life, including those of bridewealth (e.g., cloths). Eventually—although I cannot provide a precise date—bridewealth as such became payable mainly or entirely in British colonial currency rather than in homemade "countrycloth" and other traditional items. Already by the mid-1940s, Kenneth Little (1948a:45) observed the impact of these changes:

> A young man has no longer to depend upon the goodwill of the elders, if he wants a wife preparatory to making his own farm. He can gain the money for bride wealth in other ways, and can often please himself as to whether he should remain a member of his father's household or strike out on his own, helped, perhaps, by a younger brother or a relative of his wife.

The 20 years following Little's field work saw an ever increasing independence for young people of both sexes, but especially for males, in the more rural parts of Sierra Leone (cf. Donald 1979) and neighboring Liberia (cf. Bledsoe 1979). One notable result was increased geographical mobility in the rural population, especially by men and women in their prime working years. Another result was earlier household independence—noted by Little (1948a:45) even in the 1940s—which gave rise to a multiplicity of essentially independent farming operations, each with insufficient labor to achieve the traditional economies of scale in rice production (Njoku 1979) and insufficient labor flexibility to participate meaningfully in communal or reciprocal labor arrangements. Thus, as Handwerker (1981:34) noted for neighboring Liberia, "food production activities increasingly were drawn into household units which themselves...have declined in size...." By the late 1960s, most of those household units in Upper Bambara Chiefdom had become unable to plant rice farms even as large as the *bulei* (individual farms) made by the constituent units of the *mawe* in the near-by Daru area a generation earlier!

CONCLUSION

By mid-20th century, the rural Mende had become unable to provision themselves in their preferred staple food and, in response, had increased their commitment to commercial tree crops, which have much lower labor requirements. This cause-and-effect sequence is contrary to textbook expectations, which typically portray the decline in subsistence production as resulting from an increased commitment to commercial crops. The motive force behind the change is also contrary to our Western expectations, which lead us to assume land shortage as the independent variable in agrarian change. For the Mende, it was a shortage of (household) labor—not of land—that initiated the mass adoption of commercial tree crops. Furthermore, this household labor shortage is reflected in a shortening of the fallow period, a phenomenon that economists and anthropologists typically assume to reflect a land shortage (see Gleave 1996:21-23). We are able to perceive and assess the role of the household labor shortage because we have two bodies of detailed ethnographic data—unusual in their depth and co-availability—for the Mende: long-term data showing the decline in household labor supply and detailed data on the labor requirements of upland rice farming.

A salient aspect of the larger picture of socioeconomic change in the century since the British annexation of Mendeland in 1985 should also be addressed briefly here, namely, the effects of pervasive monetization. Neither commercial trade nor money per se was new to the Sierra Leone hinterland in the late 19th century (see Howard 1979). Rather, what changed was their ubiquity; largely as the result of colonial taxation in British money (cf. Ford 1995), commoditization (of crops or labor) and commercialization came to involve *ordinary people* (especially males at first) on an unprecedented scale and frequency. As imported (monetized) substitutes for local wares became widely available, local products themselves increasingly became monetized. A good example is cloth, which was a traditional component of Mende bridewealth. In turn, the monetization of the components of bridewealth led increasingly to their displacement by commoditized substitutes and, eventually, to the monetization of bridewealth itself. Thus, it became possible for a young man to accumulate his own bridewealth through wage employment. Once that point was reached, the traditional large agrarian household was doomed by a combination of wage-seeking out-migration and the liberating (for the young) effects of self-generated bridewealth.

For nearly 50 years, the impact of monetization and commoditization upon non-Western cultures has been the subject of intense interest among anthropologists. Initially, it seemed that the penetration of "general-purpose money"—i.e., a single currency that serves most or all of the *non*-commercial as well as commercial purposes—inevitably and fundamentally transformed non-Western/non-capitalist cultures (see, e.g., Bohannan 1959). The implication was that the whole culture, not just the economic portion thereof, was thereby radically altered. More recently, a contrary trend has emerged in anthropological thinking, one that stresses adjustment (i.e., partial change) rather than wholesale transformation (see Hutchinson 1992, Schaniel 1994; cf. Moran 1997).

Like most shifts in anthropological thinking, this one doubtless deserves much more critical scrutiny than it is likely to receive. Is it that we are becoming better (more culturally sensitive) ethnographers and/or less linear (more flexible or context-sensitive) in our assumptions about change? Or did the ethnographers of olde witness sharp and revolutionizing transformations that then levelled off, to be observed today as slow adaptation or even as local resistance? Alternatively, were certain ethnographers' reports of time-and-place-bound field conditions prematurely generalized into vacuous anthropological theory?

There almost certainly exists a continuum of responses—from radical transformation to only narrow change—to the introduction of general-purpose money or its radically increased penetration of local economies. Furthermore, the pace of change need not be constant in cases falling initially at any point along the continuum; rather, the pace might oscillate—but we would never detect these oscillations in the absence of historical controls, which are lacking (or not brought to bear) in most ethnographic studies. There might also exist a threshold of transformation, specific to each culture or aspect thereof; short of the threshold, change would be slow and quantitative (adaptational), but above it, rapid and qualitative (transformational). For instance, the introduction or increased ubiquity of general-purpose money might initially reinforce some important aspect of local culture—as happened time and again with the fiesta system among Latin American peasants—but, over the long run, cause its demise. Neither the initial nor the end point in such a sequence alone would suffice for comparative work aimed at building sound theory.

ACKNOWLEDGMENTS

Data collection for this article was made possible by a U.S. Public Health Service grant in 1966-68. I thank Paramount Chief Madam Konor Jajua and Speaker Chief Cieku Kutubu for facilitating research in Upper Bambara Chiefdom. It is my pleasure to also acknowledge the wise counsel of Professor Vernon R. Dorjahn—before, during, and since the field period. My colleague at the University of Cincinnati, Dr. Joseph Foster, helped with the measures of statistical significance.

NOTES

1. Lest I seem to be waggling my finger too accusatorially at others, I hasten to point out that I, too, was initially guilty of this ethnocentric projection. Njoku's (1979) essay provided my initial awakening in this regard.

2. Of the others, 15 (15.2%) were engaged full- or part-time in traditional non-farming occupations (e.g., carpentry, smithing), eight (8.1%) were Village Headmen, six (6.1%) were laborers, one (1.0%) was a schoolteacher, one (1.0%) was a schoolteacher, one (1.0%) was a chiefdom Section Chief, and eight (8.1%) were idled by illness or old age.

REFERENCES

Abraham, Arthur (1976) *Topics in Sierra Leone History: A Counter-Colonial Interpretation.* Freetown: Leone Publishers.

Berg, Elliot J. (1965) "The Development of a Labor Force in Sub-Saharan Africa." *Economic Development and Cultural Change* 13:394-412.

Bledsoe, C. (1976) "Women's Marital Strategies among the Kpelle of Liberia." *Journal of Anthropological Research* 32:372-389.

Bohannan, Paul (1959) "The Impact of Money on an African Subsistence Economy." *The Journal of Economic History* 19:491-503.

Clarke, J. I. (1966) *Sierra Leone in Maps.* London: University of London Press.

Currens, Gerald E. (1979) "Land, Labor, and Capital in Loma Agriculture." Pp. 79-102 in V. R. Dorjahn & B. L. Isaac (eds.), *infra*.

Donald, Leland (1979) "Ethnicity and the Occupational Structure of a Yalunka Town." Pp. 157-172 in V. R. Dorjahn & B. L. Isaac (eds.), *infra.*

Dorjahn, Vernon R. (1977) "Temne Household Size and Composition: Rural Changes over Time and Rural-Urban Differences." *Ethnology* 16:105-127.

Dorjahn, Vernon R., and Barry L. Isaac, eds. (1979) *Essays on the Economic Anthropology of Liberia and Sierra Leone.* Philadelphia: Institute for Liberian Studies, Monograph 6.

Ford, Martin (1995) "The Political Economy of Taxation in Liberia, ca. 1830-1930." Pp. 397-419 in B. L. Isaac (ed.) *Research in Economic Anthropology, Vol. 16.* Greenwich, CT: JAI Press, Inc.

Gleave, M. B. (1996) "The Length of the Fallow Period in Tropical Fallow Farming Systems: A Discussion with Evidence from Sierra Leone." *The Geographical Journal* 162:14-24.

Handwerker, W. Penn (1981) "Productivity, Marketing Efficiency, and Price-Support Programs: Alternative Paths to Rural Development in Liberia." *Human Organization* 40:2739.

Hofstra, Sjoerd (1937) "The Social Significance of the Oil Palm in the Life of the Mendi." *Internationales Archiv für Ethnographie* 34:105-118.

Howard, Allen M. (1979) "Production, Exchange, and Society in Northern Coastal Sierra Leone during the 19th Century." Pp. 45-61 in V. R. Dorjahn & B. L. Isaac (eds.), *supra.*

Hutchinson, Sharon (1992) "The Cattle of Money and the Cattle of Girls among the Nuer, 1930-83." *American Ethnologist* 19:294-316.

Isaac, Barry L. (1969) *Traders in Pendembu, Sierra Leone.* Ph.D. dissertation, University of Oregon.

Johnny, Michael, John Marimu, and Paul Richards (1981) "Upland and Swamp Rice Farming Systems in Sierra Leone: The Social Context of Technological Change." *Africa* 51:596-620.

Little, Kenneth (1948a) "The Mende Farming Household." *The Sociological Review* 40:37-55.

_____. (1948b) "Land and Labour among the Mende." *African Affairs* 47:23-31.

_____. (1951) "The Mende Rice Farm and Its Costs." *Zaire: Revue Congolaise* 5:227-273, 371-389.

_____. (1967) *The Mende of Sierra Leone.* London: Routledge & Kegan Paul.

Moran, Mary H. (1997) Review: *Money Matters,* by Jane I. Guyer (ed.). *American Anthropologist* 99:213-214.

Njoku, Athanasius O. (1979) "The Economics of Mende Upland Rice Farming." Pp. 103-120 in V. R. Dorjahn & B. L. Isaac (eds.), *supra.*

Richards, Paul (1983) "Ecological Change and the Politics of African Land Use." *The African Studies Review* 26:1-72.

Schaniel, William C. (1994) "Potatoes, Muskets, and a Changing Community: Economic Roles of Women and Slaves in Maori Society, 1769-1839." Pp. 133-148 in Colin M. Duncan & David W. Tandy (eds.) *From Political Economy to Anthropology: Situating Economic Life in Past Societies.* Montreal: Black Rose Books.

Scott, James C. (1985) *Weapons of the Weak: Everyday Forms of Peasant Resistance.* New Haven, CT: Yale University Press.

PART V

COMPLEX PREHISTORIC ECONOMIES: POVERTY POINT (LOUISIANA) AND AMERICAN BOTTOM (ILLINOIS)

ELEMENTS AND ORGANIZATION OF POVERTY POINT POLITICAL ECONOMY:
HIGH-WATER FISH, EXOTIC ROCKS, AND SACRED EARTH

Jon L. Gibson

Some 17 centuries before the birth of Christ, one Lower Mississippi Archaic community separated from the cultural mainstream. The nonconforming community was Poverty Point. It spread across a 1,800 km² section of high ground and swamp in the Mississippi River floodplain in far northeastern Louisiana (Figure 1). The name Poverty Point belies the community's real nature, which had nothing to do with being poor or destitute. The name comes from the back-country antebellum plantation on which the ruins of its principal settlement are located.

These ruins are still impressive today. Spread over about 3 km², they are the largest known Archaic earthworks in the United States. They are dominated by an extensive ridged enclosure and several mounds, two of which are thought to be shaped like birds. Occupational debris occurs on, in, and under the six

Research in Economic Anthropology, Volume 19, pages 291-340.
Copyright © 1998 by JAI Press Inc.
All rights of reproduction in any form reserved.
ISBN: 0-7623-0446-4

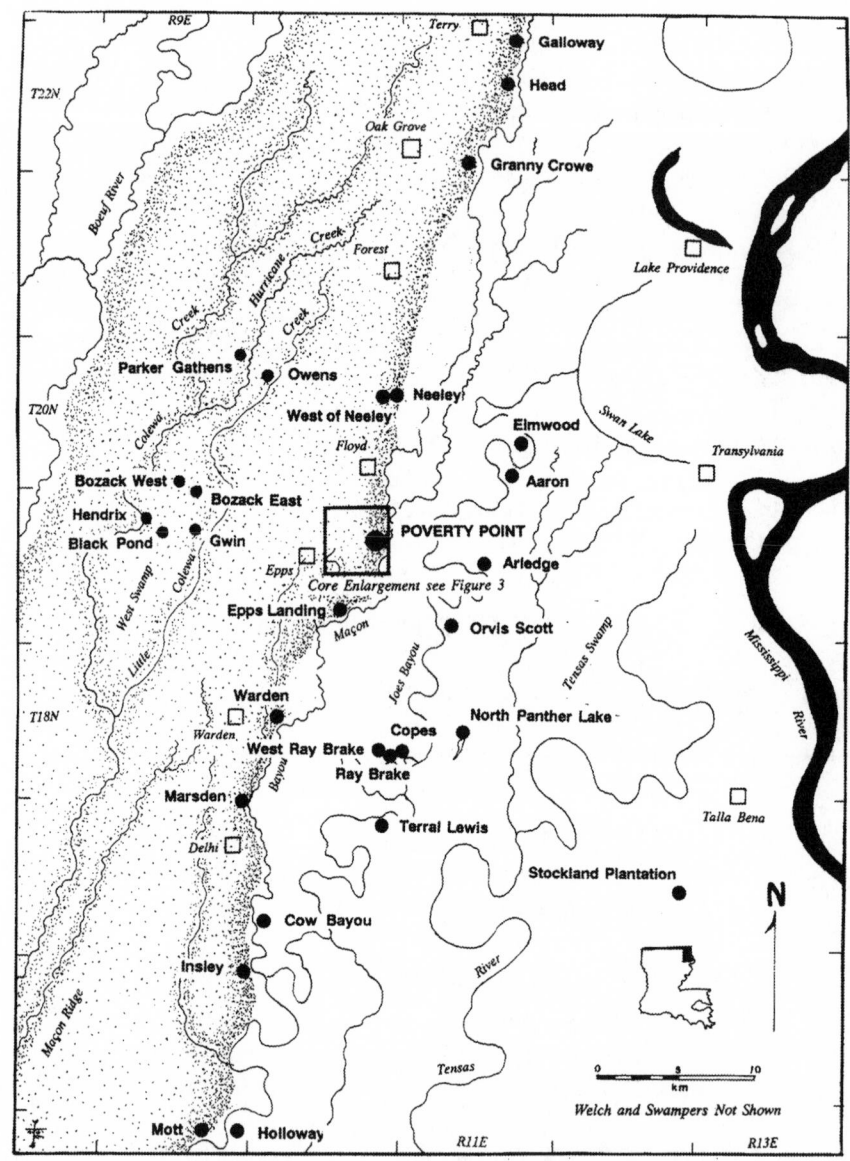

Figure 1.   The Realm of Poverty Point

made-dirt rings that make up the enclosure and also forms discrete middens outside of it.

Poverty Point's earthworks have been investigated on and off for more than a century, but off-earthwork middens have received very little attention. Although research concentrated on the Poverty Point site, archaeologists soon discovered that its diagnostic artifacts, such as löess cooking balls, hematite and magnetite plummets, and Motley, Epps, and Delhi points made of exotic gray flint, were not confined there but occurred also at surrounding sites. Dozens of these nearby sites have been surface-collected, and 18 have been tested.

Although I would like to have more data, particularily on subsistence—a familiar refrain, *n'est pas?*—I think we have reached a point where we can at least take a stab at putting existing data together to see where they lead us. Thus, when the editors afforded me the opportunity to discuss the *political* and *economic* relationships between Poverty Point's core and periphery occupations, I seized it. With any more data, I wouldn't have been as eager; any fewer would have made me cautious, too. So, I guess we can say the data are just right.

This inquiry into Poverty Point's core-periphery relationships turns on three points. First, it examines raw data on sites, their physical aspects and contents. Second, it examines the articulation of components from chronological, functional, and organization points of view. Third, it considers how the cultural system started and developed.

CORE COMPONENTS

By core components, I mean those that occur within 4 km of the largest mound at Poverty Point. That distance is heuristic. It circumscribes the extent of surveyed ground (Gibson n.d.c, Thomas & Campbell 1978), but it may be more than an analytical expedient. Strip surveys across this tract reveal that activity intensity falls off from the center outward, just as we would expect around the fringes of any nucleated settlement.

Poverty Point: The Central Earthworks

1. *Architecture*   The main core occupation is associated with Poverty Point's earthen enclosure. Architecturally, the enclosure consists of six concentrically arranged earthen rings (Figure 2). The figure is crescent-shaped, or more precisely, semi-elliptical (Stielper 1983), and its component rings terminate along a 10m high bluff overlooking Bayou Maçon. Opposing ends of the outermost ring are about 1,200m apart, and the ends of the innermost one, a little over 600m. A 14 ha open area, or plaza, is enclosed by the inner ring and bluff. The rings stand 1.0-1.5m high, and the elevation on the crest of the inner one is 0.5-1.0m above the other five. Crest-to-crest spacing varies between 46m and 56m, and averages 51m. The rings have plano-convex cross sections with gentle side slopes and rounded crests. Wide, shallow swales up to 1m or so deep separate the rings. Fill for the rings came from these ditches.

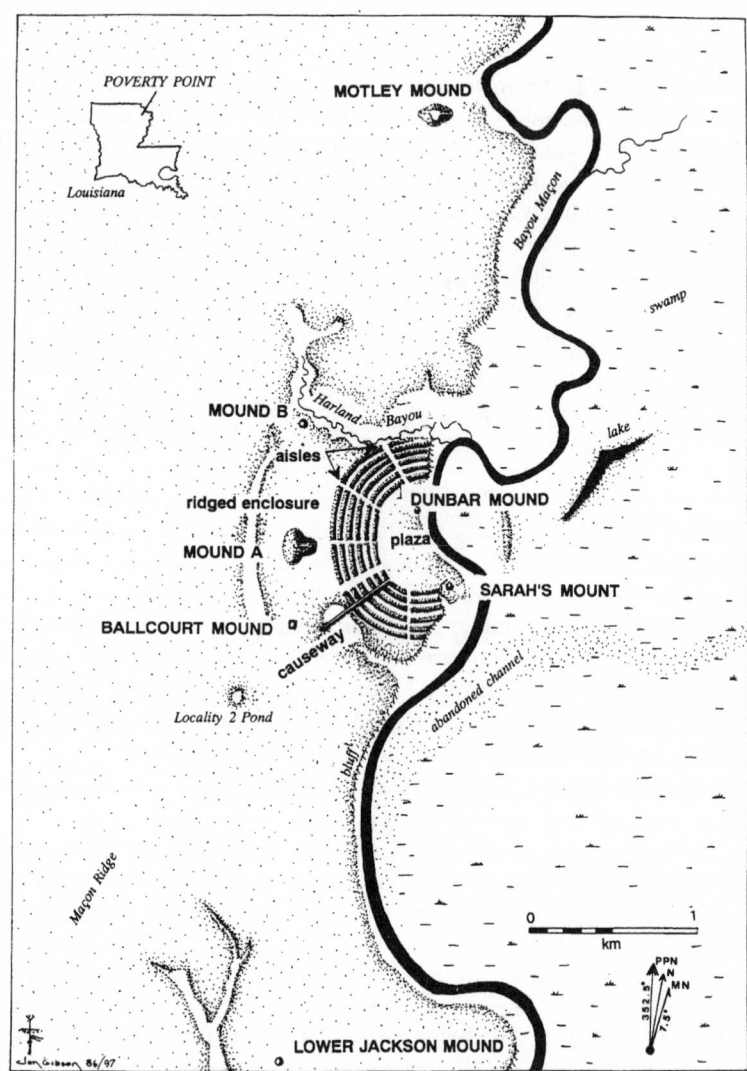

Figure 2.   Mounds and Rings at the Poverty Point Site

Five aisles radiate through the concentric rings, like spokes of a giant wheel (Figure 2). The western aisle divides the rings in half and links the plaza with the large bird mound. The other four aisles split the northern and southern arc segments into compartments. All aisles—except the middle, or western, one—fall along convergence planes of the long and short arc segments of the elliptical rings

(Gibson 1990a:227). Altogether, the aisles create six separate compartments, the same as the number of ridges.

An artificial ridge runs across all six rings, roughly parallel to the southwestern aisle. It continues beyond the rings for another 90m across a natural depression and points in the general direction of two isolated, off-earthwork components, Ballcourt Field (Gibson n.d.c:32, 35, Table 8, Figure 11) and Locality 2 (Thomas & Campbell 1978:69-78), respectively located 450m and 800m southwest of the outer ring.

An 80m long and 20m wide pad of made-dirt augments the lip of the bluff in the southeastern corner of the plaza, providing a sort of "false face" when viewed from downslope. Elsewhere along the bluff, both inside the plaza and along ringed sections, basket-loaded dirt fills old gullies and low places. Some land-filled depressions show signs of having been repaired repeatedly (Greene 1990), evidently to "save face." Löess is notoriously susceptible to gullying and sluffing, especially when runoff is channelized by artificial features such as the inter-ring swales.

Six mounds go along with the six rings and six compartments (Figure 2). The mounds are *assumed* to be Poverty Point buildings, but only Mound B has been dated (Ford & Webb 1956:Table 9). The two largest mounds are identified as bird effigies (Ford & Webb 1956:33). The larger of the two, Mound A, is 21.5m high and contains around 180,000m³ of fill. It is "flying" toward the west, its "wings" stretched north and south and its "tail" pointed east, toward the entrance of western aisle in the enclosure. The smaller Motley Mound is 15.5m high and contains around 100,000m³ of fill. Its "tail" section is missing, and its "wings" extend east-west, perpendicular to the axis of Mound A. Motley lies more than 1.5 km north of the enclosure and 2.5 km north-northeast of Mound A.

Two other mounds lie outside the enclosure. Mound B is a conical structure, reaching over 6m high and containing nearly 5,000m³ of fill (Ford & Webb 1956:33-34, Figure 11; Shenkel 1986:Table 1). It stands about 360m in a north-westerly direction from the closest ring segment and 520m north of Mound A. Ford discovered an ash bed at the base of Mound B and in it, some fragments of burned bone, including the end of a human femur (Ford & Webb 1956:33). Five radiocarbon samples, taken from the ash bed and assayed by the dry carbon method in the 1950s, give dates of cal B.C. 893-A.D. 76, cal B.C. 1394-370, cal B.C. 1046-558, cal B.C. 1626-397, and cal B.C. 1680-1062 (see Ford & Webb 1956:Table 9; two sigma range, calibration by Radiocarbon Calibration Program Rev 3.0.3A, see Stuiver & Reimer 1993). The second mound is called the Ballcourt. It is a 30m square, 2.7m tall, flat-topped mound located 210m southwest of the nearest ring segment and 190m south of the southern "wing tip" of Mound A. The name is a vernacular reference only and lacks functional meaning. Initially, the Ballcourt was thought to be natural (Haag 1990:27), but exotic clay peds incorporated in its artifactually sterile, weathered mass testify to its artificiality (Gibson 1994a:36-37).

Mound A, Mound B, and Ballcourt are in precise alignment. They all fall along the 352.5° azimuth, and what is even more enlightening is the fact that this line, carried some 3.85 km southward from Mound B (or 2.7 km from the "wing tip" of Mound A), runs squarely into the Lower Jackson mound, a late Middle Archaic structure built some 1,500 to 2,000 years before the others. The likelihood of four mounds falling in line over such a long distance is so remote as to rival my chances of winning the Powerball Lottery.

The final two mounds are located inside the ringed enclosure, along the bluff edge. Dunbar Mound, or Moore's (1913) Mound E, is a badly mutilated remnant of what may have been a "double-decker" structure, perhaps originally rectangular or oval in outline (Gibson 1990a:217-219). Its base seems to have been a low platform about 70m long (north-south), and its upper "deck" appears to have been a small dome that did not extend all the way to the edges of the basal platform. Bluff erosion has claimed the eastern side of the structure, and the remnant stands 2m high. Postmolds and hearths dot the floors of at least three of the many stages in the basal platform (Gibson 1984:130-133, Figure 21). They seem to form both straight and curving linear patterns, but no complete structural outlines are revealed. The other mound, Sarah's Mount (Moore's [1913] Mound D), actually sits upon the eastern end of the innermost ring, flush with the bluff (Gibson 1990a:215). It is a rectangular or oval platform with a flattish summit, measuring 18m by 30m (north-south) at the base. It stands only 1.1m higher than the elevated ring it sits on but more than 8m above the foot of the bluff, the slope of which coincides with its eastern face.

Long, narrow middens line the crests and bottom edges of the artificial rings, while preconstruction midden underlies the rings in a number of places. Midden dates range between cal B.C. 1710 and 1140, and fill dates between cal B.C. 1540 and 980 (general spans of two standard-deviation range of two dozen assays). Not only do most dates fall within two standard deviations of each other, but comparison of relative stratigraphic positions indicates that we are dealing with a short time interval between preconstruction midden and ring construction on any given part of the site. I like the span from B.C. 1700-1600 to 1500-1350 best, but others prefer a longer span. Extended time, of course, reduces the scale of building and brings it more in line with our ideas about hunter-gatherer labor capabilities. In my view, it's time we changed some of those ideas.

Occupational debris is incorporated in ridge fill and strewn across the once temporarily exposed surfaces of some inner construction modules (Ford & Webb 1956; Gibson 1984, 1987, 1989, 1990a-b, 1993, 1994a; Haag 1990, Kuttruff 1975, Exnicios & Woodiel 1990). Midden dirt infills ancient gullies and other low places inside the plaza, as well as along the bluff between opposite ends of the outer ring (Greene 1990, Hillman 1990, Woodiel 1981). Two gully-filling episodes are dated; one from the south end of the plaza, cal B.C. 1517-1014 (Woodiel 1981:11), and another from underneath the third ring in the north sector, cal B.C. 1885-831 and 1746-1501 (Gibson 1984:112). A third repair job from beneath the eroding end of the innermost ring in the north sector dates sometime after cal B.C. 1937-1442 and 1525-1119 (Greene 1990:Table 1).

2. *Assemblage* Artifacts occur by the millions. Densities vary greatly, from highs of around one artifact per 12 cm³ in the crest and bottom-edge middens to lows of one artifact per 16,667 cm³ in some almost-sterile lenses of ring fill. Composition across the ringed enclosure also varies considerably, both vertically and horizontally; intrasite differences are so pronounced as to resist any attempt to generalize about the site assemblage as a whole. In fact, these distributional differences are the primary focus of Poverty Point studies done during the 1970s (Gibson 1970, 1972, 1973, 1974, n.d.a; Webb 1970a, 1982:65-67; Webb & Gibson 1981).

We are safe in saying one thing about Poverty Point's artifact assemblage: it is dominated by löess cooking balls and fragments of them, commonly called Poverty Point objects (PPOs). Eighty-five to more than 95 percent of the artifacts from any given section of the rings are PPOs (e.g., Gibson 1993:71). They come in many shapes: grooved cylinders, grooved melons, cross-grooved melons, bicones, and several others (Ford & Webb 1956:39-49; Webb 1968:308, 1982:37-40; Webb et al. n.d.:1-64).

The forms may be stylistic or otherwise nonfunctional, a conclusion Pierce (n.d.) draws from analyzing their engineering properties. He finds that size and shape do not affect their heat storage or transfer capacities. I conclude the opposite. After cooking with PPOs dozens of times under controlled conditions, modeled after excavated ovens (see Webb et al. n.d.:68-72), I find that form does have a lot to do with how hot ovens get and how long they stay hot (Gibson 1975:214-215). If you hold the number of objects constant but change the shape of the PPOs used in the pit, you change the pit oven's temperature. If Pierce is right, and size and shape are not directly responsible for temperature variations, then it's obvious we are missing something here, something having to do with the interaction between cooking balls and the cooking pits, or else $E \neq MC^2$.

Chipped stone furnishes the next most common class of artifacts, usually making up somewhere between 2 and 6 percent of the materials on any large ring segment. Percentages may vary wildly on smaller segments. Debitage and debris, resulting from bifacial toolmaking and blade manufacture, comprise the dominant share of chipped stone, but formal and nonformal tools occur in large numbers. In his study of nearly 100,000 artifacts from 18 surface collections, Clarence Webb (1982:Table 6) tabulated over 3,800 bifacial cores and bifaces, over 11,700 points, 650 formal bifacial tools (including adzes, celts, hoes, and drills), and nearly 10,000 formal and expedient flake and blade tools. Although impressive, these numbers reflect selective collecting. Excavations from adjoining sections of three rings in the upper western compartment of the ringed enclosure give more typical tool-to-total chipped stone ratios, e.g., one point or point fragment for every 29 chipped stone artifacts on the third ring, one per 103 on the fourth ring, and one per 65 on the fifth ring (Gibson 1993:71).

One thing that's become more apparent in recent years is just how many chipped stone tools from ring fill have signs of repair and recycling or of having been used for multiple purposes (Gibson 1996a). Although data are inconsistently reported, it appears that reworked and multiple-use tools are not as common in collections made from ring surfaces. If this is the case, it means that proportionally more tools were being curated while construction was ongoing than either before or after, and this implies that rocks were in short supply during construction (see Andrefsky 1994:22), forcing people to reuse what they already on hand (Gibson 1996a:41-43).

After chipped stone, the next most common class of cultural material is unmodified or incidentially modifed stone, which usually comprises 1-3 percent of collections from a given spot (Gibson 1993:71). This material includes fire-cracked rock (chert, sandstone, and quartzite), angular (probably fire-cracked) sandstone chunks, pieces of gravel, and small pieces of other rocks and minerals. The least common class of artifacts is ground and polished stone, which makes up less than one percent of the collections from everywhere within the ringed enclosure. This class includes stone vessel fragments, celts, plummets, gorgets, pendants, beads, and other lapidary items (Webb 1982:Tables 10-11, 13).

Poverty Point's stone assemblage is notable for its large quantities of exotic material, that is, material that comes from several locales hundreds of kilometers away, including the Ouachita Mountains in central Arkansas, the Ozark Plateau in eastern Missouri, the Shawnee Hills in southern Illinois, the Knobs in western Kentucky and southern Indiana, the Tennessee River Valley in western Tennessee and eastern Mississippi, and the Appalachian Piedmont in eastern Alabama and western Georgia, as well as other places (Conn 1976, Ford & Webb 1956:125-127; Gibson 1994b:256-261, 1994c:158-159; Lasley 1983, Smith 1976, Walthall et al. 1982). Getting a handle on just how much foreign material was used at Poverty Point is hard because of uneven data reporting, but at least half the flint/chert and most other rock are foreign (Gibson 1994b:Table 1, Gibson & Griffing 1994:Table 2). These materials are thought to have been delivered through exchange (Brasher 1973, Ford & Webb 1956:125-127, Gibson 1994b-c, Gibson & Griffing 1994, Jackson 1991a).

Outer Core Components

Discrete concentrations of Poverty Point artifacts also occur outside but close to the rings (Figure 3). We've known about some of these spots for years (Altschul 1990, Ford 1936:213-216, Greengo 1964:100, Moore 1913:64-66, Thomas & Campbell 1978:79-92, Webb 1944), and others have turned up recently (Gibson n.d.c). Until now, they have been ignored or simply glossed over as undistinguished parts of the Poverty Point site, but they have to be examined separately if we hope to grasp how they mesh behaviorally and organizationally with the main occupation at the central rings. They are crucial to picturing overall core-community patterning.

Seventeen isolated components, or refuse concentrations, and nine other spots yielding an artifact or two are known within easy walking distance (3.5 km) of the rings (Figure 3), and others are rumored to lie in the thick woods west of the rings and on inaccessible private property north and south of the enclosure. All but one of these core components are up on the Maçon Ridge, either along its bluff-demarcated eastern margin or on the undulating terraceland west of the bluff. The other component lies down in the swamp directly across Bayou Maçon from the ringed enclosure.

1. *Bluff Components* Three components—Alexander Point, Motley East, and Motley North—line the Maçon Ridge bluff, north of the enclosure. Three—Jackson, or Neal, Carl's Old Barn, and Morrow-Lower Jackson—lie south of it.

(a) *Alexander Point* Alexander Point is located a few hundred meters across Harland Bayou from the outer ring and about 1.3 km south of Motley Mound (Figure 3). Artifacts are scattered over a 4.5 ha area but are concentrated along the immediate edge of the terrace, where patches of dark midden and aboriginally filled-in gullies occur (Dennis LaBatt, pers. comm. 1991, Thomas & Campbell 1978:96-116).

Formal tool classes represented among artifacts recovered by Thomas and Campbell (1978:Tables 3, 8; Sires 1978:Table 10; Swanson 1978a:215-217, Swanson 1978b:Table 14) include: 177 PPOs (identifiable objects, 3.9 kg total weight), 55 microliths, 27 projectile points, 17 ground celts/adzes, 12 sandstone and soapstone vessel sherds, 3 gorgets, and 1 plummets. A separate surface collection of 1,119 stone artifacts, made by Dennis LaBatt, contains several kinds of raw materials: 522 pieces of northern gray flint, 336 of local pebble chert, 154 of white chert, 50 of novaculite, 27 of other exotic chert (Gibson & Griffing 1994:Table 2).

Eleven circular and shallow basin-shaped pits are recorded (Thomas & Campbell (1978:111). Carbonized plant food remains recovered from these pits include hickory nuts, acorns, walnuts, and pecans, as well as various seeds (persimmon, grape, chenopod, doveweed, and knotweed), wild beans, and possibly squash (Shea 1978:247-251, Tables 27-28). The identify of the squash is not in question. Its context is. Five plain sherds, similar to Coles Creek pottery, are reported from the same pit (Thomas & Campbell 1978:273). The pits also produced fish, turtle, snake, and squirrel bones, with freshwater drum being prevalent (Byrd 1978:Table 17).

(b) *Motley East* Motley East, or Thomas and Campbell's (1978) Locality 6 (northeastern section only), is a 1 ha concentration of Poverty Point artifacts, located along the immediate terrace edge about 400m east-southeast of the eastern "wing tip" of Motley Mound and about 1,100m north of the northern edge of Alexander Point (Figure 3). Extensive pockets of dark midden remain below the plow zone, but basket-loaded fill is not recorded (Thomas & Campbell 1978:121-133).

PPOs dominate the assemblage: 163 classifiable objects are included and, together with unclassifiable baked clay scrap, weigh nearly 2.8 kg (Thomas & Campbell 1978:Table 3). A total of 549 pieces of chipped stone are inventoried. Debitage and debris predominate and derive mainly from biface reduction (Sires 1978:Table 12). Only 13 projectile points and three microliths are included (Sires 1978:Table 12). Three soapstone vessel fragments complete the collection (Swanson 1978b:Table 14). Other formal tools, such as chipped hoes, plummets, gorgets, celts/adzes, and beads, are not represented in the existing collection.

A little over half of the Motley East chipped stonework is made of exotic raw material. Sires (1978:Table 10) lists gray flints (n = 133, 32.4%), white cherts (including novaculite; n = 88, 21.4%), and local pebble chert (n = 190, 46.2%), among others.

Six features, including circular pits and shallow basins, are recorded (Thomas & Campbell 1978:129-131). Contents include ash, PPOs, stone artifacts, and charred animal and plant remains. Fish dominate, but turtles, small mammals, and snakes also occur (Byrd 1978:Table 22). Bones of catfish and freshwater drum are most abundant, followed by bowfin and gar. The most common turtle remains are from mud-musk species, but at least one softshell is included. None of the snake or mammal remains are specifically indentified. Charred plant remains include abundant hickory nuts and acorns, as well as walnuts, pecans, persimmon seeds, doveweed seeds, a fruithead from one of the Composites (Asteraceae), and varied wood charcoal (Shea 1978:252-255, Table 29).

(c) *Motley North*   Motley North is an exposure of Poverty Point materials, beginning about 300m north of Motley Mound (Figure 3). Artifacts are concentrated along a 1 ha section of terrace edge and are strewn over another 6.5 ha. Our data are limited to the section with scattered artifacts, not including the richer eastern section (Thomas & Campbell 1978:117-121). Thomas and Campbell (1978:121) note that artifacts were confined to the surface and plow zone and that in situ midden was lacking in their tests.

Artifacts are scarce. No identifiable PPOs are inventoried, and PPO scrap weighs only 16g (Thomas & Campbell 1978:Table 3). Chipped stone dominates the collection, and debris and debitage from biface reduction comprise the majority of the 362 stone artifacts recovered (Sires 1978:Table 11). The collection also contains 9 microliths, 18 points, and 2 ground celts (Sires 1978:Table 10, Swanson 1978a:215). Of the three major raw materials, local pebble chert (n = 148, 60.7%) is predominant, followed by exotic white chert (n = 55, 22.5%) and exotic gray flints (n = 41, 16.8%) (Sires 1978:Table 11).

One feature is described, a shallow basin-shaped pit with fired walls and ash in the bottom (Thomas & Campbell 1978:120). No data on faunal or floral remains are available.

I reiterate that our data on Motley North come from the periphery of the site, not its main occupation area, and you can't always judge the center by looking at the edges.

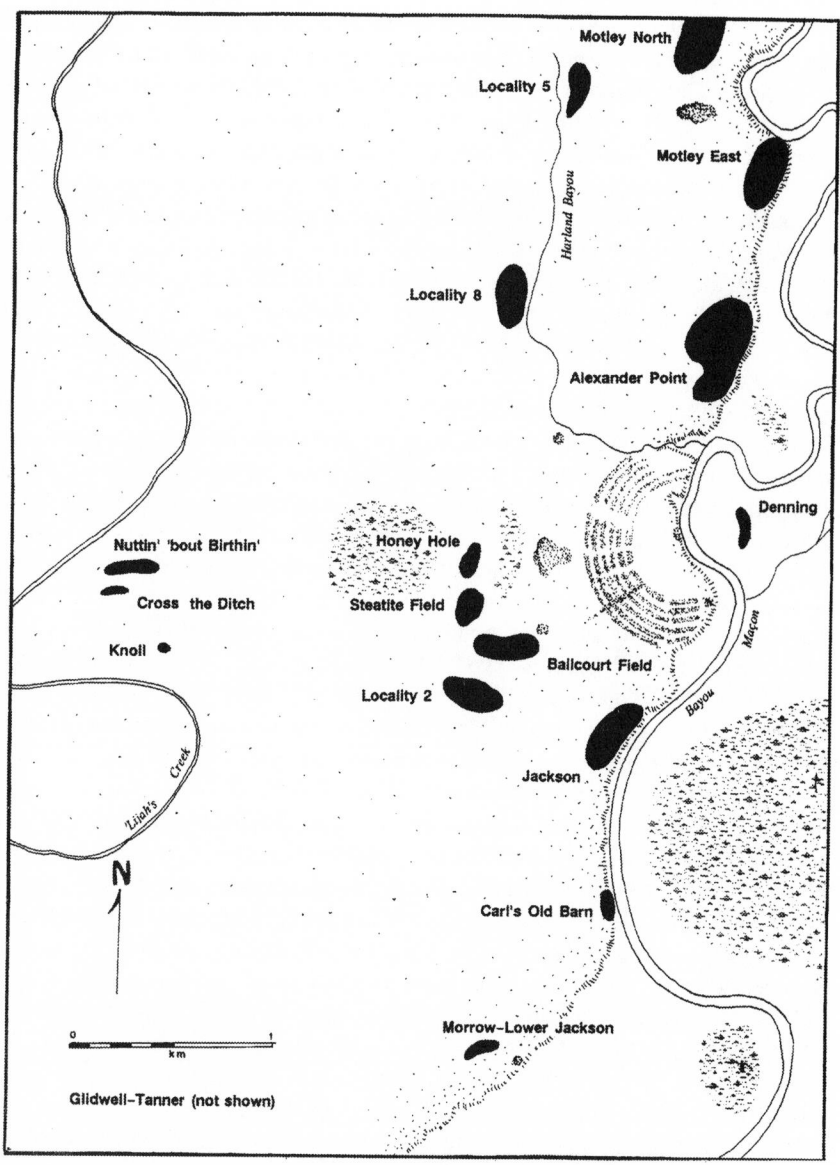

Figure 3. Core Components

(d) *Jackson, or Neal* Early descriptions indicate that six mounds and a curving embankment once stood at the Jackson, or Neal, site (Ford 1936:213-216, Ford & Webb 1956:13-14, Greengo 1964:100, Moore 1913:64-66). Except for a small slice of the northernmost structure, they are all gone now—land-leveled in early 1960s. The mounds are widely presumed to have been post-Poverty Point constructions, probably built during Coles Creek times, some 1,500-2,000 years after Poverty Point's central enclosure was put up (e.g., Greengo 1964:100).

We have it on good authority that a substantial Poverty Point component existed at Jackson and that it seems to have been associated with the artificial embankment (Greengo 1964:100), especially its northern, mound-punctuated end. That places its location along the immediate terrace edge, around 300-350m south-southwest of the nearest ring of the Poverty Point enclosure (Figure 3).

All we know about Jackson's Poverty Point materials is that they include PPOs, plummets, and microliths (Ford 1936:213, Greengo 1964:100, Moore 1913: 64-66). No further details are available.

Moore's (1913:Figure 28) sketch map of Jackson's earthworks shows the embankment as a comma-shaped ridge with two broad, low platform mounds incorporated into its center and northern end. Color infrared imagery reveals that the ridge actually has a squat U-shape and three incorporated mounds—the middle one, the one at the north end, and a third one at the south end. Concentrations of Poverty Point materials are not reported elsewhere along the embankment or around its two other embedded mounds, lessening the chance that it was a Poverty Point construction (cf. Greengo 1964:100).

(e) *Carl's Old Barn* Carl Alexander (pers. comm. 1970) often spoke of finding cooking balls around his barn located on the terrace edge about 1,500m south of Poverty Point's rings and 750m below the lower mound at Neal. I have no other information on this component (Figure 3).

(f) *Morrow-Lower Jackson* For a while, archaeologists regarded the Lower Jackson Mound as the southernmost structure of the Poverty Point earthwork complex (Gibson 1990a:211, Webb 1970b:9). Two reasons lay behind that conclusion: first, the mound lined up with the three mounds at the main enclosure; and second, the fields surrounding the mound produced Poverty Point artifacts. The advanced degree of pedogensis in the mound fill and other circumstances now favor a late Middle Archaic origin for Lower Jackson Mound (Gibson & Saunders n.d.).

Nevertheless, Lower Jackson does have a Poverty Point component. Dennis LaBatt (pers. comm. 1991, 1996), who plowed this area for years, tells me that Poverty Point artifacts come mainly from a small, 400-500m² area on a low ridge a couple of hundred meters west-northwest of the mound, a spot I refer to as the Morrow-Lower Jackson component so as to distinguish it from the older Lower Jackson Mound component (Figure 3). Morrow-Lower Jackson collections have not been analyzed, but LaBatt (pers. comm. 1996) reports finding PPOs, hematite plummets, soapstone vessel fragments, red jasper beads, projectile points (including Motleys), and exotic materials, especially white cherts and gray flints.

2. *Components Back from the Bluff, Northwest of the Rings* Thomas and Campbell (1978) record two components northwest of the rings and away from the bluff, Locality 5 and Locality 8. Both are located within 100m of an arm of Harland Bayou, which is actually little more than a steep-walled, rain-activated drainageway that may not have existed until sometime after 1848, when the congressional land survey was completed (Figure 3). The survey plat (T19N R10E, District North of Red River, LA) shows Harland (Harlin) Bayou's head lying between the rings and Mound B and not running off in a northwesterly direction as it does today.

(a) *Locality 8* Of the two components, Locality 8 is closest to Poverty Point's rings, some 600m distant in a northwesterly direction (Figure 3). It begins about 1,200m west of the bluff. Thomas and Campbell (1978:141-146, Figure 47) report that artifacts were lightly scattered over a 3 ha area, with most coming from a 1 ha spot on the end of a low rise.

The Poverty Point affiliation of Locality 8 is revealed by the presence of exotic lithic materials, as the few formal artifacts are not really diagnostic. Sires (1978:Table 12) tabulates only 70 artifacts, and of those, 10 are made of white chert, 17 of gray flint, and 21 of local pebble chert. The dominance of exotics follows the pattern at other off-earthwork components. Formal tools include three dart points and one microlith, and incidental tools include three pebble hammerstones and an abrader (Sires 1978:Table 12, Swanson 1978a:213-215). Thomas and Campbell's (1978) excavations turned up no midden, no pits, and no relevant faunal or floral remains.

(b) *Locality 5* Locality 5 is a light artifact scatter covering about 3 ha of gently sloping land along the east side of Harland Bayou, about 2.5 km due north of Poverty Point's bird mound and 0.5 km northwest of Motley Mound (Figure 3; see Thomas & Campbell 1978:141). Excavations revealed no midden, features, or biological residues.

Only 21 nondiagnostic artifacts are reported (Sires 1978:Table 12). Among them are 6 bifaces (including 4 points) and 4 flakes; the remainder are unmodified rocks. Poverty Point affiliation is determined on the basis of exotic raw materials, which include five pieces of gray chert and one piece of white chert; nine artifacts were of local pebble chert (Sires 1978:Table 12).

3. *Components Back from Bluff, West and Southwest of the Rings* Eight Poverty Point components—Steatite Field, Honey Hole, Ballcourt Field, Locality Two, Nuttin' 'bout Birthin', Across the Ditch, Knoll, and Glidwell-Tanner (16WC40)—as well as nine isolated finds are located west and west-southwest of the rings at distances ranging from 500m to about 4 km.

(a) *Steatite Field* Steatite Field is located about 400-500m west-southwest of the rings (Figure 3). An extensive, north-south-running slough separates the area from the rings and the large bird mound. This is the spot where Clarence Webb (1944) excavated a cache of soapstone and sandstone vessel fragments in 1935. Stone vessel fragments still litter the ground today, and Thomas and Campbell (1978:91), who conducted the most recent work in the locality, suspect additional soapstone caches are present. We're uncertain how large Steatite Field really is. Thomas and Campbell's (1978:Figure 22) investigations show artifacts spread over 0.75 ha, but they carry beyond those contract-imposed study boundaries.

The cache of stone vessel fragments is the most widely reported find at Steatite Field. Webb (1944) says it was an oval, vertical-walled pit 2.5m long, 2m wide, and 0.6m deep, containing over 2,200 stone vessel fragments—with more being scattered on the ground around the pit where carried by plowing. He also notes that the pit floor was fire-blackened in four spots, one of which retained a bed of ashes and charcoal. Thomas and Campbell's (1978) work located 727 additional vessel fragments, 718 soapstone and 9 sandstone, but no more caches (Swanson 1978b:Table 14). No vessels could be reconstructed, and some fragments from the Webb cache matched pieces found on different segments of the rings, more than 1 km away (Mitchell Hillman, pers. comm. 1986), suggesting that the cache was a collection of fragments picked up across the site rather than a deposit of vessels intentionally smashed, or "killed," for ritual burial.

But Steatite Field is more than a steatite deposit. It is an occupational area. PPOs are the most common artifacts, more than 4.8 kg by weight, including 293 identifiable objects (Thomas & Campbell 1978:Table 3). Core and blade residue makes up a majority share of the stonework (n = 423), but microlithic blade tools are underrepresented (n = 6), as are microlithic flake tools (n = 12) (Sires 1978:Table 11). Materials resulting from biface reduction are not very numerous, either: 26 chipped pebbles, 4 cores, 111 flakes, 127 pieces of debris, and 28 bifacial tools, including 11 points (Sires 1978:Table 11). Ground and polished stone artifacts include a mano, a pebble hammerstone, an abrader, a ground adze, and a plummet fragment (Swanson 1978a:211, 213, 215-216). Exotic materials once more outnumber local cherts, but not by much. Sires (1978:Table 11) lists local pebble chert (n = 168, 49.4%), gray flint (n = 115, 33.8%), and white chert (n = 57, 16.8%), as well as other materials.

Thomas and Campbell (1978:82, Figure 22) note that soapstone vessel fragments were concentrated west of the spots bearing the highest densities of PPOs and chipped stone artifacts. Two separate concentrations of PPOs are reported, also. These concentrations indicate that activities involving stone vessels were largely segregated from those involving PPOs and chipped stone. It also suggests that two cooking areas were present.

Several features are described (Thomas & Campbell 1978:85, 87-91, Figure 24). One is a short trench with a circular pit at one end. There are two clusters of postmolds, one containing six molds and the other, four, but neither cluster forms recognizable patterns. Four pits, large and small, hold PPOs, but only two have ashy bottoms indicating their use as fire pits. All of the features are relatively close to the southernmost PPO concentration.

Faunal remains from the pits are rare and unidentifable. Byrd (1978:Table 21) recognizes only softshell turtle. Charred floral remains, recovered from pits and postmolds, include hickory nut shell (n = 522), acorn meat and shell (n = 16), persimmon seeds (n = 70), Asteraceae fruitheads (n = 6), hackberry seed coat (n = 1), blackgum fruit (n = 1), and unidentified fruit (n = 9) (Shea 1978:Table 32).

(b) *Honey Hole* This artifact concentration is located about 200m north of Steatite Field and 400-500m west of the rings (Figure 3). Dennis LaBatt (pers. comm. 1991, 1996) tells me that Poverty Point material occurs in profusion over a half-hectare area that is darker than the surrounding area. His collection has not been analyzed, but it contains PPOs, projectile points, hematite plummets, red jasper beads, and exotic materials, among other items.

(c) *Ballcourt Field* Poverty Point artifacts are lightly scattered across a gently sloping, 10 ha area immediately south and west of Ballcourt Mound but are concentrated in a 1.6 ha spot off the end of the mound, where a small, round pond once stood (Gibson n.d.c:32, 35, Figure 11, Table 8). Locality Two lies about 200m southwest of the southern margin of Ballcourt Field (Figure 3).

A small collection, made during a single walkover of the site, consists primarily of chipped stone materials and a few PPOs (Gibson n.d.c:Table 8). Debitage predominates (n = 57), but microlithic tools (n = 8), points (n = 7), and cores (n = 5) occur. Single lumps of hematite, ironstone, red slate, red ochre, greenstone, and basalt are present, and so are fire-cracked rock (n = 4) and sandstone (n = 4). One plummet fragment and one gorget fragment round out the lithic fraction of the collection. The plummet is made of magnetite. The remainder of the collection consists of 30 PPO fragments. Debitage includes local pebble chert (n = 23, 40.4%), northern gray flint (n = 15, 26.3%), exotic white chert (n = 12, 21.1%), novaculite (n = 4, 7.0%), and other exotic rocks (n = 3, 5.3%). As in other off-earthwork components, exotic materials outnumber local ones. Observations made during land-leveling operations in 1993 reveal that patches of dark midden containing PPO rubble and other artifacts occur beneath the plow zone in the area of heaviest occupation (Gibson 1994a:44-48, Gibson & Saunders 1993).

(d) *Locality 2* Locality 2 begins around 200m southwest of Ballcourt Field (Figure 3). Poverty Point materials are densest over the half-hectare summit of a low ridge and are moderately and lightly scattered across along the ridge for about 11 ha (Thomas & Campbell 1978:Figure 19). The ridge, one of several in the area, skirts a swale that contains a pond. The rectangular pond is assumed to be a modern construction (Thomas & Campbell 1978:69), but I can't help wondering if it didn't have a natural precursor. The dark gray, silty clay around its margins looks to me like old pond-bottom mud, and small, natural ponds dot the surrounding landscape.

Locality 2 is the most productive off-earthwork component. Thomas and Campbell's (1978) collection contains over 11,000 stone artifacts and more than 6.4 kg of PPO residue. Included among the mass of PPO residue are 199 identifiable objects (Thomas & Campbell 1978:Table 3). Sire's (1978:Table 11) list of stonework includes: 267 unmodified rocks, 53 modified rocks, 160 fire-cracked rocks, 173 nonblade cores, 3,457 pieces of debitage, 5,692 pieces of debris, 735 core and blade elements excluding microlithic tools, 214 microlithic flake tools, 85 microlithic blade tools, and 263 bifaces. Sixty-eight dart points are among the bifaces (Sires 1978:Table 11), and the absence of any other formal tool classes among the remaining bifaces suggests they are varied projectile point reduction stages. Swanson (1978a:213-218) identifies 10 pebble hammerstones and three abraders, along with various ground and polished stone objects: 11 plummets, 6 adzes, 5 gorgets, 3 beads (including two drilled fossils), 2 bannerstones, 1 celt, 1 tube, and 2 other objects. He also records 335 soapstone and 42 sandstone vessel fragments (Swanson 1978b:Table 14). Exotic raw materials dominate chipped stonework (Thomas & Campbell 1978:71); a breakdown of 9,496 artifacts reveals that white chert (n = 5,442, 57.3%) and gray flint (n = 2,348, 24.7%) prevail. Artifacts of local pebble chert number 1,706 (only 18.0% of the collection).

Patches of dark midden are preserved under the plow zone, and two pits are described (Thomas & Campbell 1978:73-75). One pit is a shallow, irregular basin containing PPOs, a few flakes, and charcoal and other charred plant materials. The other is a small, deep earth oven. The few pieces of animal bones recovered are unidentified (Byrd 1978:Table 20), and Shea's floral analysis discloses only charred hickory nutshell and wood charcoal from the earth oven (Shea 1978:255, Table 31).

(e) *Nuttin' 'bout Birthin' (16WC5-Loc. 15)*   This component is a small lithic scatter along the crest of one of the many accretion-belt ridges that comprise the gently undulating landscape west of Poverty Point's rings (Gibson n.d.c:27). The scatter covers less than 0.2 ha and lies about 2.4 km due west of Poverty Point's outer ring (Figure 3). Alligator Bayou, called 'Lijah's Creek by local residents, flows less than 500m to the west. Two other Poverty Point components are nearby; Cross the Ditch is located on an adjacent ridge, only 120m to the south, and Knoll is 400m to the southeast on still another ridge. In addition, several isolated finds of Poverty Point artifacts occur in the vicinity.

Only 10 artifacts are reported from Nuttin' 'bout Birthin', and they consist of debitage, debris, a microlithic tool, and two projectile points (Gibson n.d.c:Table 3). Artifact forms are consistent with but not especially diagnostic of Poverty Point materials, leaving Poverty Point cultural affinity to be judged by the presence of exotic materials, which include novaculite (n = 2) and white chert (n = 1).

(f) *Cross the Ditch (16WC5-Loc.17)*   This component is a companion to the Nuttin' 'bout Birthin' site and is located on a segment of a paralleling ridge directly across (south) from it (Figure 3). The exposure is tiny, covering only about 200 m². Seven stone artifacts are reported, including a hammerstone, a unifacially chipped rock, and five flakes (Gibson n.d.c:Table 2). As with its companion, Poverty Point affinity is based on the presence of exotic materials; three flakes are of white chert.

(g) *Knoll*   The other nearby site is Knoll (Figure 3). It occupies the highest spot in the vicinity, an isolated prominence located just off the end of a curving ridge. No evidence of occupation is reported from nearby sections of the adjoining ridge, which is one of several that scroll through the area east of 'Lijah's Creek. But Nuttin' 'bout Birthin' and Cross the Ditch are located on the first two ridges to the north, and a Dalton component is found on the first ridge to the south, less than 50m from Knoll (Gibson n.d.c:Figure 8).

Knoll's collection consists of only three stone artifacts, all made of local pebble chert (Gibson n.d.c:Table 4). The two biface thinning flakes are nondiagnostic, and Poverty Point affinity rests solely on the third object, an opposing double-platform (lisse) blade core.

(h) *Glidwell-Tanner (16WC40)* This site is located 4 km west of the big mound at Poverty Point, alongside an ephemeral streamlet that cuts through a 1.5m high ridge (Figure 3). It sits upon the highest part of the ridge. The ridge rises out of a poorly drained area of ridge and swale topography, which drains into Alligator Bayou (or 'Lijah's Creek). Thomas and Campbell (1978:147-152) tested Glidwell-Tanner in 1978 and found cultural materials confined to the surface. Fifty artifacts were recovered, primarily lithics, and Poverty Point occupation is judged solely by the presence of northern gray flint and Crescent Hills chert.

(i) *Isolated Finds* Other evidence of Poverty Point occupation is widely scattered over a 14 ha area, lying inside a sweeping meander of 'Lijah's Creek and west of the Nuttin' 'bout Birthin', Cross the Ditch, and Knoll sites (Gibson n.d.c:28). The six concentric crescent-shaped accretion ridges that sweep across the area look so much like Poverty Point's rings that they could have been inspirational (Gibson n.d.c:28). The ridged terrain lies between 2.6 and 3.2 km slightly south of west of Poverty Point's ridged enclosure (Figure 3).

Several isolated prehistoric artifacts or small groups of artifacts are recorded, all from ridge crests (Gibson n.d.c:28). Seven are probably of Poverty Point origin: (a) a white biface thinning flake, (b) a blade tool, (c) a projectile point preform of exotic white chert, (d) a novaculite chip, (e) a Gary projectile point, (f) a laterally recycled projectile point of novaculite, and (g) a single platform (lisse) blade core, a point fragment (distal) of local pebble chert, and a sandstone lump (Gibson n.d.c:Table 6). Two additional isolated finds include an edge-battered and denticulated Edgewood point of white chert from a high ridge west of 'Lijah's Creek and a broken Maçon point of exotic gray flint from a ridge lying between Knoll and Ballcourt Field (Gibson n.d.c:32, 42).

4. *Component in Front of Bluff, Opposite the Rings (Denning Site)* For years, no evidence of Poverty Point occupation turned up in the swamp directly across Bayou Maçon from the ringed enclosure. Lots of artifacts showed up in spoil dredged from the bayou in the 1960s but not in the low ground opposite the rings and east of the bayou, where we would expect the wee lad to have thrown a PPO at least now and then. The combination of thick woods, which weren't cleared until sometime between 1946 and 1964, and Ford and Webb's (1956) pronouncement that the area once was part of the Maçon Ridge, which was washed away by the Arkansas River carrying half the ringed enclosure with it, discouraged local enthusiasts and archaeologists from looking.

It was not until Mitchell Hillman and Thurman Allen cored a low ridge, searching for the eastern shoreline of a hypothetical reservoir, that the Denning site was discovered (Figure 3; see Hillman 1990:143). Artifacts have not been inventoried but include PPOs, microliths, and large, mostly plain hematite plummets (Dennis LaBatt, pers. comm. 1997). The biggest surprise came from the discovery that part of the low ridge where artifacts were recovered was made of artificial fill (Hillman 1990:143). Hillman concluded that a scallop-like indention in the bluff had been plugged with a dam, forming a 150-200 ha pond directly abutting the bluff opposite the ringed enclosure.

PERIPHERY COMPONENTS

Core components are defined as those lying within 4 km of Poverty Point's central rings. Periphery components lie outside this circle, up to distances of nearly 40 km. Like the 4 km radius, the 40 km radius is heuristic but has culturally significant overtones. It circumscribes the known extent of Poverty Point phase components, or those having assemblages bearing the greatest technological and stylistic similarities with materials from the Poverty Point site (Gibson & Griffing 1994). Beyond the 40 km circle are sites having only attenuated similarities or none at all (Jeter & Jackson 1994, Kidder 1991; Webb 1968:Table 2, 1982:18).

I am aware of 29 periphery components within a 4-40 km or so distance of Poverty Point's ringed enclosure (see Figure 1). Ten occur on the Maçon Ridge bluff, north and south of the ringed enclosure; two are in the swamp just east of the bluff; seven are in the West Swamp, a poorly drained section of the Maçon Ridge lying several kilometers west of the rings; nine are located along Joes Bayou, which parallels the bluff to the east at distances ranging up to 10 km; and one is out in the Tensas swamp on an old Mississippi River meander-belt ridge 24 km east of the ringed enclosure.

Maçon Ridge Sites

1. *Bluff Components*   The eastern edge of the Maçon Ridge is lined by an 8-10m high bluff for almost its entire 160 km length. Ten periphery components are reported along the bluff, half of them—Galloway, Head, Granny Crowe, Neeley, and West of Neeley—north of the ringed enclosure and the other five—Epps Landing, Warden, Marsden, Insley, and Mott—south of it (see Figure 1). Two possible components, Welch and Swampers, lie even further south. Bluff components are not well known. We have little or no detailed information on Galloway, Epps Landing, and Warden and only limited data from Granny Crowe, Head, Neeley, West of Neeley, Marsden, Insley, Mott, Welch, and Swampers (see Figure 1).

(a)   *Head*   The Head site is located on the Maçon Ridge bluff nearly 20 km north of the ringed enclosure (see Figure 1). We don't know if the single conical mound at Head is of Poverty Point or later origin. Harvard University's excavations in 1964 focused on later ceramic-bearing sections of the site, but a surface collection made from Poverty Point areas produced "a dozen or so Poverty Point objects, a projectile point base, a blade, and an ovate biface made on a dark grey-brown non-local chert" (Kidder 1991:30).

(b) *Granny Crowe* Granny Crowe is located 11 km north of Poverty Point's ringed enclosure (Figure 1). Poverty Point artifacts occur in three spots— a large ridge, a small one, and a low knoll—the highest elevations encircling a low area (Stanley Morgan, pers. comm. 1989, 1997). Altogether, artifacts are scattered over approximately 4 ha.

Stanley Morgan's surface collection from Granny Crowe has not been inventoried fully, but it includes projectile points, five northern gray flint bifaces with sickle sheen, some flake tools, and chipping debris and debitage. Among the formal tools are a triangular siltstone pendant, a bannerstone fragment, two stone beads, a fat siltstone plummet made without perforation or groove, an unfinished hematite plummet, and a grooved hematite plummet (Stanley Morgan, pers. comm. 1989, 1997).

(c) *Neeley* Neeley is about 9 km north of Poverty Point's large bird mound (see Figure 1). Neeley has two conical mounds of uncertain affiliation. Harvard's 1964 tests failed to detect intact Poverty Point midden, but Poverty Point materials collected from the surface included some PPO fragments, a gorget fragment, a lug-bearing soapstone vessel fragment, blades, a possible Motley point on northern gray flint, and nonlocal chert residue (Stanley Morgan, pers. comm. 1997; Kidder 1991:30).

(d) *West of Neeley* This Poverty Point component lies about 0.5 km slightly south of west from the Neeley site and about 8.8 km north of Poverty Point's big bird mound (see Figure 1). Neeley sits directly upon the bluff, but West of Neeley rests on a low ridge skirting a shallow pond back away from the bluff. Poverty Point artifacts are spread over 0.5 ha on the north side of the pond and are concentrated in a 600 m² spot close to the water. Paleoindian and Coles Creek components ring the eastern and southern sides of the brake.

Surface collections made by Stanley Morgan include a grooved PPO fragment, 47 projectile points and 22 other bifaces, 1 biface (hoe/adze) with sheen, 2 hardstone celts, a pseudocelt of soft greenstone, a hematite plummet, flake tools, chipping debris and debitage, and other materials. Exotic materials include quartz crystal, hematite, and red ochre, as well as various fine-grained rocks. Local chert dominates chipped stone (n = 340/455, or 74.7%), but exotic materials are well represented: novaculite (n = 71, 15.6%), northern gray flint (n = 11, 2.4%), Crescent Hills chert (n = 8, 1.8%), and other cherts (n = 25, 5.5%) (Gibson & Griffing 1994:Table 2).

(e) *Marsden, or Marston* The Marsden site sits on the Maçon Ridge bluff at the junction of Alligator Bayou and Bayou Maçon about 18.5 km south of Poverty Point's big bird mound (see Figure 1). We don't know how extensive the

Poverty Point component is, because it is covered by later Baytown midden and earthworks (Bitgood 1989:50-75). Poverty Point diagnostics include three Poverty Point objects and some pieces of galena (Bitgood 1989:74). The plummet, bannerstone, boatstone, and tubular clay pipe fragments recovered during Harvard's excavations there in 1964 may also be Poverty Point materials, and so may some of the abundant amorphous pieces of baked clay (Bitgood 1989:Tables 6b-6b, 7c-7f, 8b). Poverty Point occupation zones line the immediate edge of the bluff, but the four or five mounds postdate Poverty Point (Kidder 1991:33).

(f) *Insley* Further south along the bluff, near the junction of Bayou Maçon and Joes Bayou approximately 29 km south of Poverty Point's big bird mound, is the Insley site (see Figure 1). Clarence B. Moore (1913:60-61) dug in several of the mounds in the winter of 1912-1913. James Ford made surface collections in the 1930s (Ford 1936:Figure 1), as did Philip Phillips in 1954 (see Bitgood 1989:77). Harvard dug several test pits in 1964 (Bitgood 1989:75-91, Kidder 1991:33-35). David Griffing (1990) collected Insley for years and was there during land-leveling.

A sketch map of Insley (see Kidder 1991:Figure 4) shows 12 mounds; some, especially those in the western section of the rude circle of mounds, are probably Poverty Point constructions, but others are later, probably Baytown constructions (cf. Bitgood 1989:91). Griffing (1990:220) could not find the small domed mounds in the western part of the site, and it is conceivable that they were destroyed sometime between Harvard's 1964 work and his visits in the 1980s.

Poverty Point artifacts recovered from Insley include: 212 identifiable PPOs, 3 pieces of untempered and fiber tempered pottery, a tubular pipe, 86 microliths (including Jaketown perforators), 142 projectile points, 2 hoes/adzes, 15 hematite and magnetite plummets, a hardstone celt, 6 slate and limonite gorgets, 2 red stone beads, 19 soapstone vessel fragments (n = 19), and chipped debris and debitage (Gibson & Griffing 1994:Table 1; Griffing 1990:Tables 1-4, David Griffing, pers. comm. 1994 [updated inventory]). Quartz crystal, soft greenstone, hematite, and other exotic rocks are present, and several kinds of foreign cherts are represented among chipped-stone artifacts: novaculite (192 out of a total sample of 880 pieces, or 14.7%), northern gray flint (n = 182, 13.9%), Crescent Hills chert (n = 30, 2.3%), and other exotics (n = 24, 1.8%) (Gibson & Griffing 1994:Table 2). All together, exotic materials make up 32.7 percent of the chipped stone; local pebble chert makes up the rest.

(g) *Mott* The Mott site is some 38 km south of Poverty Point's bird mound (see Figure 1). Mott's major occupation and 14 mounds date to the late Coles Creek period (Gibson 1996b:64), but Poverty Point materials occur along the bluff edge overlooking Bayou Maçon (Kidder 1991:33). Harvard's tests at Mott in 1964 produced several PPO fragments, some typical projectile points, and a hoe with sickle sheen, as well as nonlocal cherts, including black flint and northern gray flint (Kidder 1991:33).

(h) *Possible Components* Kidder (1991:35) reports two more possible Poverty Point components, Welch and Swampers, on the bluff more than 40 km south of Poverty Point. Without additional information, we cannot confirm either site as a Poverty Point component. The biconical PPOs from Welch and the blade-lets, novaculite point, and green talc bead from Swampers could date after and before the Poverty Point period (Kidder 1991:35).

2. *Components in West Swamp* West Swamp is the vernacular name for a poorly drained expanse of the Maçon Ridge lying west of Poverty Point. It is bordered by Hurricane and Little Bogzack creeks on the east and Colewa Creek on the west. A 2-3m scarp delimits the eastern edge of West Swamp, while the western margin is gradually sloped. At the closest point, West Swamp lies a little over 6 km west of Poverty Point's big bird mound.

Seven Poverty Point components are reported from West Swamp: Parker Gathens, Owens, Gwin (16WC28), Hendrix (16WC55), Black Pond, Little Bogzack East, and Little Bogzack West (see Figure 1). The Bogzack sites are listed on Mitchell Hillman's (pers. comm. 1985) authority. I have no detailed information about them.

(a) *Parker Gathens* The Parker Gathens site is located 15 km northwest of the big bird mound. Several low ridges and knolls surround a water-filled depression, and Poverty Point materials are scattered across the largest east-west ridge and an adjacent knoll, an area of around 1.5 km (Stanley Morgan, pers. comm. 1997).

My information comes from a surface collection made by Stanley Morgan and inventoried by David Griffing (Dennis LaBatt, pers. comm. 1997). Artifacts consist of 2 identifiable PPOs, 1 soft greenstone plummet, 4 gorgets (2 of gray shale, 1 decorated specimen of pink slate, and 1 cross-hatched object of limonite), 4 projectile points (1 each of novaculite and local pebble chert and 2 of northern gray flint), 1 northern gray flint Gary point recycled into a drill, 1 chipped celt with heavy bit wear, 1 biface fragment of gray northern flint, 1 thick biface thinning flake of gray northern flint, and 1 chunk of Pickwick chert.

(b) *Owens* The Owens site is located on two low ridges lying between Indian and Boggy bayous, immediately west of a scarp-delimited lobe of higher ground that juts out into West Swamp. It is 12.4 km northwest of Poverty Point's big bird mound and 6.7 km slightly north of west from the West of Neeley site (see Figure 1). Artifacts are scattered for about 1.8 ha across the crests of a large Y-shaped ridge, which runs parallel to the Indian Bayou, and a smaller, perpendicular ridge (Stanley Morgan, pers. comm. 1988, 1997).

Stanley Morgan's surface collection consists of 2 PPOs (unidentified fragments), 81 projectile points, 52 rough bifaces, 2 chipped celts, 2 hoes, 22 microliths, 5 slate and red stone gorgets (including 1 notched and cross-hatched object), 2 hardstone and greenstone celts, 1 notched and crosshatched pendant fragment, 1 soapstone vessel fragment, 1 flattish fat-bellied owl pendant of red jasper, and 1 helmented red jasper button with two pairs of hidden perforations (one pair broken through the septum). Pieces of debris and debitage number 1,012, including 25 hoe sharpening flakes of northern gray flint. Other materials include 5 local chert pebbles, 1 chunk of quartzite, 1 sheet of slate, 1 lump of granite, 1 piece of calcite, and 1 clinker.

Materials represented among debris and debitage include local pebble chert (n = 710, 62.2%), novaculite (n = 245, 21.5%), northern gray flint (n = 136, 11.5%), white chert (n = 26, 2.3%, including at least 16 Crescent Hills flakes), and other exotic flints (n = 12, 2.1%, including black flint) (see Gibson & Griffing 1994:Table 2).

(c) *Hendrix (16WC55)*   The Hendrix site sits on a low rise on the east bank of Colewa Creek, about 14.5 km west-northwest of the big mound at Poverty Point and 11 km southwest of Owens (see Figure 1). The site is compact, covering about 0.4 ha. Its relatively small size, coupled with its long succession of occupations, especially a heavy Paleoindian one, complicates the task of factoring out some Poverty Point elements. The data reported herein derive from a surface collection made by the Henry Hendrix family and tabulated by David Griffing (see Gibson & Griffing 1994:Table 3).

Projectile points dominate. Eliminating all Paleoindian and Woodland points leaves a total of 588 that could belong to the Poverty Point (or other Late Archaic) component. PPOs are comparatively inconsequential, numbering only 187 (69 identifiable and 118 unidentifiable fragments). Other chipped stone artifacts include 120 bifaces and bifacial foliates (some of which probably belong to earlier or later components), 4 hoes, 6 drills, and a celt. Microliths, or small flake and blade tools, are not listed because it's hard to separate Poverty Point and Paleoindian tools. The same can be said of debris and debitage, except for the novaculite (n = 348) and northern gray flint (n = 57) flakes, which can be attributed to the Poverty Point occupation. Rough groundstone objects of possible Poverty Point (or Late Archaic) association include 29 hammerstones, 10 grinding stones, 2 pitted stones, an anvil, a faceted stone, and 3 battered rocks. The polished stone fraction consists of 19 hardstone and soft greenstone celts, 6 plummets, 6 gorgets, a soapstone vessel fragment, and a grooved quartz crystal pendant. Unmodified materials include 5 quartz crystals and a lump of galena.

(d) *Gwin (16WC28)*   The Gwin site consists of a light scatter of artifacts atop 11 neighboring ridges, located about 15.5 km west of Poverty Point's big bird mound (see Figure 1). Runoff from the area drains into Little Colewa Bayou. Thomas and Campbell (1978:152-162) investigated the site in 1978, using controlled surface collecting, subsurface boring, and test pitting, but detected no intact Poverty Point midden or features. Artifacts attributable to Poverty Point activity consist of a few PPO fragments, four microliths, some projectile points, and unidentified exotic cherts (Thomas & Campbell 1978:160).

(e) *Black Pond*   Better known for its Paleoindian component (Griffing 1996), the Black Pond site is located on the crest and side slope of a ridge, one of several that jut into a poorly drained area on the west side of Colewa Creek, about

15 km west-southwest of the big mound at Poverty Point (see Figure 1). Poverty Point materials are spread thinly over a 0.4 ha area, amongst more plentiful Dalton and San Patrice artifacts. Mark Fox's surface collection contains flakes, bifaces/bifacial foliates, and projectile points of northern gray flint, Crescent Hills chert, and novaculite.

Lowland Sites

1. *Swamp Sites Just East of the Bluff* Two Poverty Point components have been reported out in the swamp within sight of the Maçon Ridge bluff.

(a) *Cow Bayou, or Weatherly* The Cow Bayou, or Weatherly, site sits upon a terrace inlier, a cut-off section of the Maçon Ridge, east of Bayou Maçon and about 25 km south of Poverty Point's bird mound (see Figure 1). Little is known about Cow Bayou, except that it has PPOs, Motley points, and exotic flints (Gibson 1991:36; David Griffing, pers. comm. 1989).

(b) *Holloway* Stanley Morgan (pers. comm. 1990, 1997) informs me of another site, Holloway, located on the east side of Bayou Maçon, just across from Mott, about 38 km south of Poverty Point's big mound (see Figure 1). PPO fragments, two hoe flakes of northern gray flint, a Jaketown perforator, novaculite projectile points, a minature cup-shaped object of polished magnetic greenstone, and debitage of Crescent Hills and other exotic flints were recovered (Stanley Morgan, pers. comm. 1990, 1997). Two cooking pits filled with PPOs were also noted.

2. *Joes Bayou Components* Joes Bayou winds through the swamp east of the Maçon Ridge bluff. For about 40 km, it parallels the bluff at distances of up to 10 km. Near Insley, it enters Bayou Maçon, and from that point, the enlarged bayou hugs the bluff until uniting with the Tensas River. Joes Bayou is an underfit stream, which flows through an abandoned meander belt of the Arkansas River (Lenzer 1978:43, Saucier 1994:Plate 9) or possibly a major Mississippi distributary.

Nine Poverty Point components are reported from Joes Bayou (see Figure 1). We have no data on three of them—Elmwood, North Panther Lake, and West Ray Brake—and include them strictly on Mitchell Hillman's authority (Mitchell Hillman, pers. comm. 1983). Hillman recognized Poverty Point components only if they yielded finger-grooved PPOs and exotic lithics, in addition to the usual point styles and other typical artifacts. Three components—Terral Lewis, J.W. Copes, and Orvis Scott—have been excavated (Gibson 1996a, Gregory et al. 1970, Jackson 1986). Two others, Aaron and Arledge, have been comprehensively surface collected (Irving Arledge, pers. comm. 1985; Webb 1982:29-30), while the remaining component, Ray Brake, has been only cursorily collected (Webb 1982:25-26).

(a) *Aaron* The Aaron site is 11 km northeast of Poverty Point's bird mound (see Figure 1). It covers about 3 ha along the outside bank of an old oxbow lake (Webb 1982:29), a setting common to several Joes Bayou Poverty Point components. Patches of dark soil were scattered across the artifact-bearing area, but no concentrated midden was observed. Clarence Webb (1982:29-30, Table 3) inventoried surface collections made by the site's owner, and Edith Cary Hallmark, Edwin Jackson, and I tabulated another collection made by local resident Irving Arledge (Gibson & Griffing 1994:Tables 1-2).

PPOs were present but were not always collected, thus making quantitative comparisons with other components more tenuous than usual. The combined collections include: 480 projectile points, 16 hoes/adzes, 23 hematite and magnetite plummets, 30 hardstone and soft greenstone celts, 427 microliths, 23 gorgets, and 6 hardstone beads (Gibson & Griffing 1994:Table 1, Webb 1982:29-30, Table 3). Other chipped stone items include 26 unrefined bifaces, 6 pencil drills, and 1,030 pieces of debris and debitage. Ninety-three biface thinning flakes bear sickle sheen. Polished stone artifacts include 5 narrow-ended rectangular and other unspecified tablets, 3 flourite, quartz crystal, and diorite pendants, a limonite button with hidden perforation, and a pot-bellied owl pendant of red jasper. Among the incidental artifacts are a polished pebble, a pebble hammerstone, a sandstone mano, a sandstone reamer, and a sandstone saw (Webb 1982:Table 3). There are 14 soapstone vessel fragments (Webb 1982:Table 3).

Imported exotic flints make up more than three-quarters of Aaron's chipped-stone artifacts (81.4%, or 1,421 out of 1,745 items) (Gibson & Griffing 1994:Table 4). Northern gray flint dominates (70.1%, n = 1223), followed by other exotics (8.7%, n = 151), Crescent Hills chert (2.4%, n = 42), and novaculite (0.2%, n = 5). In addition to exotic-stone artifacts, there are three quartz crystals and a lump of galena (Webb 1982:Table 3).

(b) *Arledge* Like Aaron, Arledge sits on the outside bank of an old, cut off meander loop about 7 km slightly south of east from Poverty Point's bird mound and 6 km south of Aaron (see Figure 1). Artifacts are scattered lightly over a crescent-shaped area of about 22 ha, making Arledge the largest known periphery component. Concentrations of materials occur hither and yon, marking spots of intensive or repeated activities, but stained-earth midden seems to be lacking.

Irving Arledge's surface collection contains 11 identifiable PPOs, 31 chipped hoes, 41 plummets (hematite, magnetite, and limonite), 25 hardstone and soft greenstone celts, 172 projectile points, 103 microliths, 24 gorgets, and 5 hardstone beads (Gibson & Griffing 1994:Table 1). Pieces of debris and debitage, including core and bladelets, number 270. Among the biface thinning flakes are 30 with sickle sheen, all of blue-gray Dover flint. There are 20 other bifaces and bifacial foliates and two drills, one pencil-shaped and the other key-shaped. Fire-cracked rock (n = 5), unmodified red jasper pebbles (n = 2), and cobble and pebble hammerstones (n = 9) are present. The collection also includes a headless, pregnant-female figurine of baked löess, a baked clay bead, 5 soapstone vessel fragments, 2 faceted lumps of polished hematite, 3 ground and polished galena lumps, 3 narrow-ended rectangular tablets, a red hardstone pendant, and a red jasper owl pendant.

In addition to exotics used to make artifacts, foreign raw materials include quartz crystals (n = 7), hard gray greenstone (n = 1), soft greenstone (n = 5), and gray slate (n = 1). Exotic flints make up 56.4 percent (n = 318) of a sample of 564 chipped-stone artifacts; they include northern gray flint (n = 212, 37.6%), Crescent Hills chert (n = 62, 11%), other exotic (n = 27, 4.8%), and novaculite (n = 17, 3%) (Gibson & Griffing 1994:Table 2). The remainder are local pebble chert (n = 246, 43.6%).

(c)   *Orvis Scott*   On down Joes Bayou, about 4 km as the crow flies from Arledge, is the Orvis Scott site. Orvis Scott is a little over 8 km southeast of the bird mound at Poverty Point and is located on a barely perceptible rise between two meander loops of Joes Bayou, not on the banks of an oxbow lake (see Figure 1). Artifacts are scattered over 2 ha, but the main concentration covers less than 0.6 ha, and the really heavy concentration is limited to an area of only a little more than 0.1 ha. Patches of dark earth are scattered about, but cultural materials are confined to the plow zone. I tested the site in 1992 (Gibson 1996a).

Combined excavated collections and surface collections made by Orvis Scott, the landowner, include 6,873 PPOs (37 identifiable and 6,836 unidentifiable fragments, or the equivalent of 130 whole PPOs), 156 pieces of pottery (Tchefuncte-like), 22 hematite plummets, 5 limonite and cannel coal gorgets, 20 hardstone and soft greenstone celts, 26 soapstone vessel fragments, 14 hoes, 243 points, 178 microlithic tools (including 11 blade tools), a narrow-ended rectangular tablet, and a boatstone (Gibson 1996a:7-25). There are 36 unspecified bifaces. Incidental tools include 15 pebble hammerstones, 2 abraders, and a hone. Cores, flakes, and chipped debris number 479, inclusive of the 178 microliths. Seven flakes exhibit sickle sheen. There are 350 pieces of fire-cracked rock—local gravel and sandstone.

Unmodified raw material lumps and fragments include: chert pebbles (n = 195), brown sandstone (n = 83), Catahoula sandstone (n = 4), basalt (n = 4), and one lump each of limestone, granite, limonite, gray slate, black and gray slate, light gray shale, red ochre, quartz crystal, hard grayish greenstone, and soft greenstone (Gibson 1996a:15). The chert pebbles, sandstones, limestone, limonite, and red ochre could all be local materials, *although the nearest potential sources are 45 to 80 km or more distant*. Materials represented among chipped stone artifacts are: local chert gravel (n = 168, 36.2%), northern gray flint (n = 157, 33.9%), Crescent Hills chert (n = 88, 19.1%), Pickwick chert (n = 8, 1.7%), black flint (n = 6, 1.2%), and other exotic (n = 14, 3.1%) (Gibson 1996a:26-31).

(d)   *J.W. Copes*   The J.W. Copes site is located on the outer northeastern bank of Bream Brier Brake, an old, largely filled-in oxbow lake. Copes is 11.5 km south of Poverty Point's bird mound, 7.3 km southeast of Orvis Scott, and 1.5 km northeast of Ray Brake site (see Figure 1). Mitchell Hillman tested the site in 1975 (see Webb 1982:26), and Edwin Jackson carried out extensive testing in 1982

(Jackson 1982, 1986). Artifacts cover about 0.5-0.75 ha and are concentrated in a 2,000m² central area of black-earth midden. The midden is about 1m thick at thickest and is shot through by sterile silt lenses or layers, which Jackson (1991b:132) interprets as "prepared structure floors." He found 48 features, mainly cooking and trash pits, baked-clay hearth platforms, unprepared hearths and ash-charcoal concentrations, and post molds.

Artifacts from Copes (Jackson 1986:314-375, Tables 35, 40-41, 45-46, 48; Webb 1982:29-30, Table 2) include 2,483 PPOs (78 identifiable, 2,405 unidentifiable fragments, or the equivalent of around 396 whole objects), 34 clay pipe fragments, 5 clay figurine fragments, 120 projectile points (or hafted bifaces), a hafted biface reworked into a drill, an incomplete biface, 9 hoes, 13 microlithic blade tools, and 144 microlithic flake tools. Chipped debris and debitage total 436. In addition, there are 34 flake cores, 10 blade cores, and 32 unmodified blades. Rough ground and polished stone artifacts include an abrader, a pebble hammerstone, a gorget, 31 smoothed tabular pieces of sandstone, 10 hematite and magnetite plummets, 12 celt/adzes, 26 soapstone vessel fragments, 2 red jasper beads, a crinoid bead, and a slate zoomorphic pendant. Nine large socketed antler points, 3 polished split bone points, 9 awls, 12 pins, 5 degorgers, 2 flakers, 2 socketed handles, a scoop, a needle, a reamer, a turtle carapace bowl, 3 drilled carapace fragments, 2 carapace cutouts, 5 snake vertebra beads, and a drilled alligator-tooth pendant testify to the good organic preservation conditions in the central midden.

Local and exotic rocks are represented among chipped stone artifacts (Gibson & Griffing 1994:Table 2, Jackson 1986:Tables 38, 42, 44-45): local gravel cherts (n = 288/639, 45%), northern gray flint (n = 235/639, 36.8%), novaculite (n = 39/639, 6.1%), Crescent Hills chert (28/639, 4.4%), and other exotic cherts (49/639, 7.7%). Unmodified raw materials include sandstone (n = 283), galena (n = 18), quartz crystal (n = 5), hematite (n = 4), slate (n = 2), petrified wood (n = 2), local chert pebbles (n = 2), and a piece of flourite. Jackson admits to being cautious in identifying foreign materials, so his breakdown may understate the amount of exotic exchange materials. Understated or not, they still make up over half of the rocks at Copes.

Although squash occurs, wild plants form the bulk of the floral remains. Sweet pecan/hickory nutshell and meat dominates, occuring in 74 percent of the flotation samples, followed by acorn shell (54%), squash rind and seeds (24%), grass seeds (21%), and persimmon seeds (7%) (Jackson (1991b:133-134, Table 1). Seeds of honeylocust, goosefoot, marshelder, portulaca, wild bean, *Sporobolus* sp., and *Lithspermum* sp. occur in minor amounts (each present in a little over 2% of the samples).

Fish and deer comprise 85 percent of the identified faunal remains. Small mammals, birds, reptiles, and amphibians make up the remainder (Jackson 1991b:Table 2). Jackson identified 1,935 deer bones and 24,909 fishbones. Major fish groups are catfish (n = 11,173), bass/sunfish/drum/shad (n = 2,592), bowfin (n = 1,697), gar (n = 1,634), and sucker (n = 1,058). Squirrel (n = 316), rabbit (n = 288), and raccoon (n = 106) are the leading small mammals; ducks (n = 74), large wading birds (n = 31), and turkey (n = 13), the primary birds; snakes (n = 1,484) and turtles (n = 1,112), the main reptiles; and frogs (n = 152), the primary amphibians. Fish counts may be underrepresented because quarter-inch recovery screens were used.

Three radiocarbon dates run on samples from lower, middle, and upper midden zones reveal that Copes was occupied ca. B.C. 1500 (Jackson 1986:308-310): upper midden, cal B.C. 1496 (1292, 1278, 1261) 944; middle midden, cal B.C. 2008 (1734, 1707, 1693) 1498; lower midden, cal B.C. 1682 (1431, 1418, 1413) 1131. The oldest date is from the middle midden, but all three dates are within two standard deviations. They show that Copes was occupied at the same time as Poverty Point, very likely about the time that ring construction was getting underway.

(e) *Ray Brake* According to Webb (1982:25-26), the Ray Brake site extends for 100m along the outside (eastern) bank of an old, partly filled-in oxbow lake called Ray Brake. It is 11.8 km south of Poverty Point's bird mound, 1.5 km southwest of the J.W. Copes site, and 0.8 km east of the West Ray Brake site, which is located on the other end of the same oxbow (see Figure 1).

Webb visited the site in 1967, finding a compact black-earth midden and numerous PPOs, including bicones, plain and finger-grooved, and melons with finger grooves (Webb 1982:26). Lumps of sandstone, deer bones, and Tchefuncte-like and later pottery were also observed. A small, conical mound of unknown affiliation stands 400m south of the Poverty Point midden.

(f) *Terral Lewis* The Terral Lewis site is on the south (left descending) side of Joes Bayou, some 200m back from the bank. Infared imagery shows a low, mostly filled-in section of old ridge and swale topography south and west of the slight rise where the site sits. Terral Lewis is 17.6 km south of Poverty Point's bird mound and 6.2 km south of J.W. Copes (see Figure 1). It was tested in 1966 and 1967 by Hiram Gregory, Lester Davis, Manning Durham, Clarence Webb, Northeast Louisiana Archaeological Society members, and students from Northwestern State University (Gregory 1991, Gregory et al. 1970, Webb 1982:24-25).

The site is compact. Artifacts are spread over about 0.5-0.75 ha (Webb 1982:24). Dark midden reaches nearly 1m thick in places. Excavations uncovered six clay ball-filled pits, two clay ball accumulations, and a few post molds (Gregory et al. 1970:37, Webb 1982:25).

Collections from the excavations, as well those made from the surface by the Tate and Lewis families and by the excavators, contain: 381 PPOs and other baked clay fragments (381 identifiable, plus 103.2 kg of unidentifiable scrap—or the equivalent of around 1,375 objects, if all were PPOs), 3 untempered potsherds (including one Tchefuncte Incised sherd), 5 hematite and magnetite plummets, 5 slate and limonite gorgets, a soft greenstone celt, 4 soapstone vessel fragments, 4 hoes with sickle sheen, 110 projectile points, 2 microlithic blade tools (both Jaketown perforators), an unspecified biface, a sandstone hone, a polished bar weight, a pendant, and a stone bead (Gregory 1991:122-126, Table 4; Webb 1982:25).

Core and blade technology is indicated by a single core and seven unused blade-lets, in addition to Jaketown perforators. Five hundred fifty-one pieces of debris and debitage are recorded, including 243 biface thinning flakes (Gregory 1991:124). Webb (1982:25) also lists unspecified numbers of retouched and used flakes, bifacial tools, hammerstones, and sandstone saws.

Gregory (1991:Table 3) recognizes northern gray flint (n = 228) and exotic tan chert (n = 24) among a sample of 325 chipped stone artifacts, excluding projectile points. He breaks down the remaining 73 pieces by color: 22 white, 11 pink, 11 red-gray, 5 "burned" red, and 4 red-yellow, as well as 11 local red and 9 local tan (Gregory 1991:Table 3). Webb also identified novaculite in private collections. Other raw materials include two quartz crystals and a lump of flourite.

No faunal or floral remains were recovered, and pollen analyses proved negative (Webb 1982:24-25).

3. *Tensas Swamp Component (Stockland Plantation)*   The extensive back-water lowland lying east of the Maçon Ridge and west of the Mississippi River is called the Tensas Basin, or Swamp (Fisk 1944:28-29). The Joes Bayou meander belt ridge runs through the swamp in the Poverty Point vicinity and generally cir-cumscribes the eastern extent of periphery components (see Figure 1). I am aware of only one component out in the swamp east of Joes Bayou ridge, and it is on an old Mississippi River levee sticking above the alluvially drowned terrain. Any sites lying between the two meander belts are probably buried under meters-thick sediments (e.g., Hillman Mound; see Saunders et al. 1994:148-151).

Stockland Plantation is located on the south side of Bull Bayou on a relict Mis-sissippi River levee, about 24 km southeast of the bird mound at Poverty Point (see Figure 1). It is the most easterly Poverty Point component known in the Poverty Point site vicinity. Stanley Morgan (pers. comm. 1988), who found the site, reports that artifacts are scattered over 4 ha but that PPO residues are concentrated in two locations. Remains of cooking pits were found in the easternmost location (Stan-ley Morgan, pers. comm.1988), and Morgan suspects that midden is buried beneath recent alluvium.

Morgan's surface collection includes: 203 PPOs (17 identifiable, 186 unidenti-fiable fragments), 2 pieces of daub (one with cane impressions), a figurine head, 63 potsherds (including Wheeler Plain, unidentified plain, Tammany Punctated, and single-line incised, as well as post-Tchefuncte decorated varieties), a limonite gorget, 7 soft greenstone and hardstone celts, 43 projectile points, 4 soapstone ves-sel fragments, 2 hoes, 17 microliths, a hematite plummet, a red jasper bead, a notched red jasper pendant, and 9 small fragments of unidentified polished stone objects (including three of granite)(see Gibson & Griffing 1994:Table 1). Two blades and 12 cores are inventoried, as are nine bifaces/bifacial foliates. A scaled piece and a small, snub-nosed scraper round out the bifacial tools. Other artifacts include debris and debitage (n = 295) and a pebble hammerstone. Eighteen biface thinning flakes exhibit sickle sheen. There are 38 pieces of sandstone and four lumps of sandy red ochre.

Unmodified raw materials include local chert and quartzite pebbles (n = 55), greenstone (n = 5), a lump of petrified wood, a graystone pebble, a chunk of white stone, a piece of greenish hard stone, a quartz crystal, and clinkers (n = 5). Materials represented among chipped stone artifacts are: local pebble chert (n = 290, 71.4%), northern gray flint (n = 58, 14.3%), Crescent Hills chert (n = 43, 10.6%), novaculite (n = 13, 3.2%), and other exotic cherts (n = 2, 0.5%) (Gibson & Griffing 1994:Table 2).

ARTICULATION OF COMPONENTS

To constuct a picture of occupation at and around the Poverty Point site, we have to account for the variability among components in a coherent fashion. Figuring out how the components all fit together, if they do, depends on synthesizing chronological, functional, and organizational details and looking at the result in terms of what we know or think about hunter-gatherers.

Chronology

Poverty Point chronology is inadequate. We have over three dozen radiocarbon dates from the Poverty Point site, not counting five lignite-contaminated assays taken from the bayou bank (Greene 1990:Table 1). The two sigma range of dates runs from cal B.C. 3986 to cal A.D. 961, but the cal B.C. 1730-1350 span encompasses the major activity, including earthwork construction (Gibson n.d.b). The dates are inadequate for resolving questions about site growth, as hypothesis testing fails to support any successional model with confidence (Gibson n.d.b). Stratigraphically, we recognize pre-construction occupation, land-filling, embankment construction, and post-construction occupation, but we can't tell for sure if any or all of these "events" in one part of the site predated or postdated those in any other part (Gibson 1995). Standard errors overlap, suggesting (but not proving) that Poverty Point was relatively short-lived and that earthwork building took place rapidly (Gibson 1996b). Occupation spanned generations or a few centuries at most, not thousands of years.

Copes and Terral Lewis are the only other dated components (Huxtable et al. 1972:Table 2, Jackson 1986:308-310). Copes' three radiocarbon dates suggest a short occupation sometime between cal B.C. 1500 and 1400, showing that it was contemporary with Poverty Point, probably with the onset of construction there. Terral Lewis dates to about the same time or maybe a tad later. Four PPOs produced an average thermoluminscence age of 3040±230 B.P. (cal B.C. 1869 [1294, 1284, 1268] 792).

Lack of adequate chronology is a serious but not fatal problem. Stylistic and assemblage similarities are close enough to let us assume that components are fairly close in time, if we don't ask for particulars about contemporaniety or succession. Because components all have substantial quantities of exotic exchange materials, I assume they were occupied sometime during the time that Poverty Point, the trade center, was flourishing. There is no evidence for intensive exchange in the vicinity before Poverty Point (Gibson 1994c, 1996c). A trickle of Ouachita Mountain rocks reached the area before Poverty Point got involved in trade, but not the Midwestern rocks that figure so prominently after its involvement.

Function

In an earlier attempt to assess functional variability, David Griffing and I quantitatively compared assemblages from 10 components: Poverty Point, Owens, and Hendrix from the West Swamp; West of Neeley and Insley from the bluff; and Aaron, Arledge, Copes, Terral Lewis, and Stockland Plantation from the swamp (Gibson & Griffing 1994). Cumulative graphing produced two groups. The SCOT group consisted of Stockland Plantation, Copes, and Terral Lewis. These swamp sites were characterized by large percentages of PPOs and small percentages of points and microlithic tools. The WHOAA group included West of Neeley, Hendrix, Owens, Arledge, and Aaron. These sites were characterized by small percentages of PPOs and large percentages of points and microlithic tools. Unlike SCOT components, they were found in different environments: Maçon Ridge bluff, West Swamp, and Joes Bayou meander belt. Insley graphed midway between the two groups (Gibson & Griffing 1994:Figure 6). We used Webb's (1982:Tables 4, 6, 8, 10-11, 12) data on Poverty Point and produced a WHOAA ogive, but we cautioned that, if the great uncollected volume of PPOs had been taken into account, a SCOT ogive would have resulted. We should have taken the extra PPOs into account. Poverty Point is a SCOT component; PPOs make up some 85-95 percent of the artifacts from any given 1m test unit dug anywhere within the ringed enclosure.

I know that graphing obscures variability. No archaeological assemblage can be represented truly by one graph line unless it resulted from a singular and temporally limited activity. Nevertheless, graphing at least enables us to conceptualize inherent variablity and see which classes of artifacts are most responsible for the differences.

Figure 4 presents an updated comparison of Poverty Point components. I have adjusted PPO numbers to countermand the effects of breakage and have added six core components (Alexander Point, Motley East, Motley North, Steatite Field, Ballcourt Field, and Locality 2) and a periphery component (Orvis Scott). The other components are essentially the same bunch that figured in our earlier analysis (Gibson & Griffing 1994).

Reanalysis upholds the two assemblage groups. The SCOT group includes Stockland Plantation, J.W. Copes, Terral Lewis, Motley East, Alexander Point, Steatite Field, Ballcourt Field, and Locality 2 (Figure 4), as well as Poverty Point.

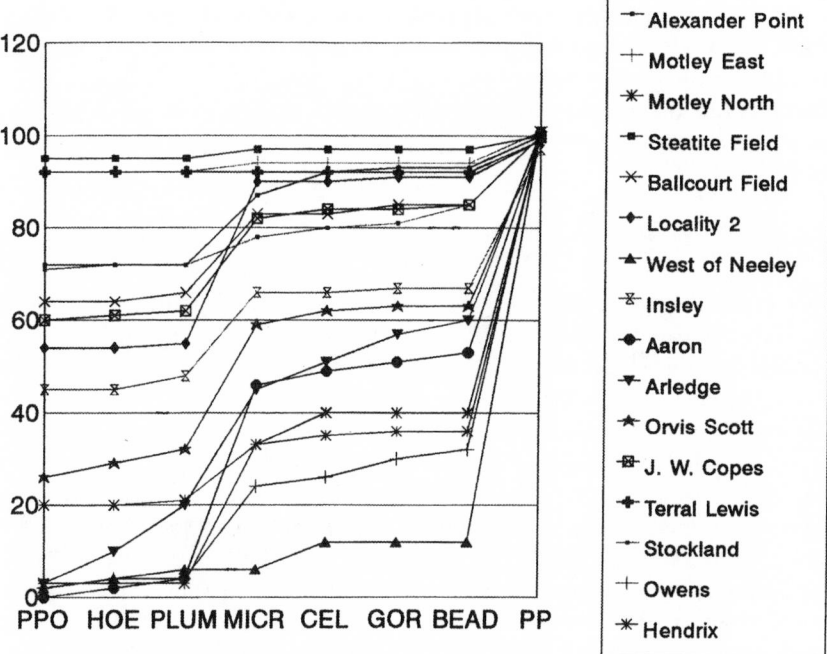

Figure 4. Quantitative Comparison of Poverty Point Components
(PPO = Poverty Point Objects [löess cooking balls], PLUM = Plummets, MICR =
Microliths, CEL = Celts, GOR = Gorgets, PP = Projectile Points)

The WHOAA group includes West of Neeley, Hendrix, Owens, Aaron, Arledge,
and Motley North. PPOs dominate SCOT assemblages and are minor occurrences
in WHOAA assemblages. Projectile points dominate WHOAA assemblages and
are minor in SCOT collections. Microliths run a close second to points at
WHOAA sites and are variable at SCOT sites, ranging from unimportant to moderately important (Table 1). Other artifact classes—plummets, hoes, gorgets, celts,
and lapidary—are rare or absent everywhere, but groundstone celts and hoes occur
more consistently on WHOAA components (Table 1). Hoes are limited to sites in
or around swamps.

SCOT sites have either thick, black-earth middens or scattered pockets of midden (Table 1). Stained-earth midden is lacking or limited at WHOAA sites. Pits
and other features are common at SCOT components, rare or nonexistent at
WHOAA sites (Table 1). SCOT site extent ranges from about 0.5 to 4.5 ha, over-
lapping but generally smaller than WHOAA components, which range from 0.5 ha
up to 22 ha.

Table 1.   Relative Occurrence of Selected Artifacts and
Features in SCOT and WHOAA Assemblage Groups

	Occurrence, by Assemblage Group[a]	
Artifact and Feature	SCOT	WHOAA
Artifact and Feature	SCOT	WHOAA
PPOs[b]	very prevalent (75)[c]	uncommon (5)
Projectile points	common (10)	very prevalent (62)
Plummets	very rare (≤1)	rare (≤3)
Hoes	very rare (≤1)	rare (≤2)
Gorgets	very rare (≤1)	rare (≤2)
Microliths	common (12)	common (22)
Celts	rare (≤2)	uncommon (≤4)
Lapidary	very rare (≤1)	very rare (≤1)
Stained-earth midden	concentrated	sparse/absent
Pits	concentrated	sparse/absent

Notes: [a]The SCOT group includes Stockland Plantation, J.W. Copes, Terral Lewis, Motley East, Alexander Point,
Steatite Field, and Locality 2 sites. The WHOAA group includes West of Neeley, Hendrix, Owens, Aaron,
Arledge, and Motley North sites (see Figure 1).
[b]PPOs, or Poverty Point objects, are löess cooking balls.
[c]Numbers in parentheses are assemblage-group averages.

Except for Stockland Plantation, exotic flints make up a little more than half
of the chipped stone tools and debitage at SCOT sites, and at Terral Lewis and
Locality 2, more than eight out of ten artifacts are made of exotic cherts.
Exotic cherts at WHOAA sites make up 25-80 percent or more of chipped
stone artifacts. Generally, exotic rock is more plentiful on sites close to Poverty Point, no matter which group they belong to, but there are exceptions, and
function was probably responsible for them (Gibson 1996c, Gibson & Griffing
1994). For example, on sites where hoes and/or hoe resharpening flakes are relatively common, such as the Joes Bayou sites, so is exotic chert. Why?
Because hoes are large tools made almost exclusively out of northern gray
flint. That doesn't explain, however, why Locality 2 had so much exotic rock,
especially Crescent Hills chert. No hoes are found at Locality 2, and other formal artifacts aren't made disproportionally of Crescent Hills (Thomas & Campbell 1978). Thus, circulation of exotic stone throughout Poverty Point's
immediate hinterland was a complicated affair, not subject wholly to dis-
tance-related falloff.

What does all this mean functionally? For one thing, it means that a whole lot
of cooking and nut-acorn processing was going on at SCOT sites. The use of
löess-cooking balls, earth ovens, hearths, and other pits would have saved cooks
time and energy over the long term. These objects and appliances suggest a degree

of residential permanence, as does the sheer quantity of PPO residue. Mobile field campers, especially those working out in the swamp a long way away from the Maçon Ridge, where löess occurs, surely wouldn't have hauled around bags full of heavy PPOs. A few, yes—enough to fix meals for a couple of days or maybe even a fortnight or two—whereas large quantities of PPOs evince prolonged occupancy or frequent reuse. Resupply was assurred at long-occupied places and, after a while, stockpiles of usable cooking balls and piles of their spent remains would have accumulated.

I'm not sure why and how black-earth middens formed at SCOT sites (cf. Gibson 1996a), but I have little doubt that they, too, indicate extended occupancy. Their nature remains hidden in their chemistry, but we can be sure that it took more one campfire or a few rotten fish guts to stain dirt as black as these middens. Our efforts to detect phosphorous in a black spot at Orvis Scott were to no avail, but that's probably because phosphorous was encapsulated and impossible to detect in the poorly drained soil (Gibson 1996a:33). Some of the blackest middens I've ever seen formed where fish were a major constituent. Without marshalling argument, I simply assert that fishing hobbles mobility and that, where fish were a major food, we can expect to find residentially tethered, even sedentary, populations. Jackson (1986, 1991b) makes a strong case for J.W. Copes being permanent.

The generally compact size of SCOT components reflects concentrated living activities, such as we expect at a main residence, rather than dispersed activities, such as we expect at fishing or foraging locations. Although some WHOAA sites are as compact as SCOT sites (e.g., Orvis Scott), others are extensive. Aside from Poverty Point, Arledge—at 22 ha—is the most extensive site, and it is a WHOAA component.

Were WHOAA components repeatedly used field camps or locations where some kind of exploitation transpired, which would account for artifacts being so widely dispersed? Or were they more temporary campsites successively occupied over the course of many seasons or during a particular season year after year (see Binford 1982)? At Orvis Scott, intrasite analysis disclosed that all classes of artifacts focused on one small area (Gibson 1996a:33-37). I think it unlikely that temporary campers repeatedly reoccupying the same campgrounds would have managed to stay on exactly the same small spot every time, leading me to suspect that Orvis Scott and other small WHOAA components were used once or only a few times.

Lack of concentrated midden rules out prolonged occupation, but artifact associations and the considerable range in site size reveal that WHOAA components were a varied lot with distinctive work emphases. The biggest differences are between swamp and upland components, although those differences are smoothed out somewhat because points and microliths are major tool classes in both groups of components (Table 1). Because points and microliths are multi-purpose tools, they merely show that folks everywhere primarily busied themselves with maintenance chores, but the higher proportion of points suggests that more emphasis was put on hunting at upland WHOAA components than at swamp components. This makes good sense, especially if upland WHOAA components experienced concerted activity during fall and winter, when nuts and acorns ripened and when deer and small game, preoccupied with feeding and breeding, were concentrated in mast woods.

Lowland WHOAA components emphasized fishing (plummets) and digging (hoes). Opal glazes coat hoe bits (Peter Gendel, pers. comm. 1984), and glazed resharpening flakes make up 2-11 percent of the debitage at swamp WHOAA components. We don't know what swampers were digging for, but they weren't gardening—or at least, the sparse occurrence of squash and starchy seeds suggests that these plants, widely domesticated in midwestern North America, weren't very important. Those recovered from Poverty Point middens probably weren't domesticated varieties, either (Jackson 1986, 1991b). Without any direct evidence, I can only speculate that swampers were grubbing for rhizomes and roots—Greenbriar, perhaps, or maybe Bulltongue, Ground Nut, or Chufa. Tubers of these plants were important foods among some historic tribes in the Lower Mississippi Valley, even after maize horticulture was adopted (Swanton 1911). I imagine Poverty Point swampers found favor in these ubiquitous foods, too.

SCOT and WHOAA assemblages are different, and I attribute much of the difference to occupational stability-instability. SCOT components have the look of prolonged residence. WHOAA components look temporary. Of course, more is involved than simply how long people continuously lived at a place. WHOAA assemblages differ among themselves, especially between swamp and ridge settings. They all have similar tools but in varying combinations and relative frequencies. Even swamp WHOAA assemblages are not alike.

Technological Organization

SCOT components are interpreted as residences; WHOAA components, as field camps or other short-term encampments. Together, they indicate that Poverty Point's basic adaptational strategy operated by moving food and other resources to consumers rather than moving consumers to resources, a strategy known as logistical mobility (Binford 1979). If such was the case, then we would expect WHOAA components to show more signs of temporariness than SCOT components. The organization of technology should bear witness.

We are concerned here with detecting economizing behavior, or technological ways of saving time, energy, and material, all paramount concerns to people working away from home temporarily. Odell (1996) identifies several economizing measures—transport cost, multiple-use tool design, tool recycling, and tool maintenance.

1. *Transport Cost*   Poverty Point's 1,800 sq km homeland is rockless, yet Poverty Point people consumed large amounts of rock. Getting rock supplies into the hands of the needy was costly. Most utilized rock was exotic, brought in from

up to 1,600 km away via interregional exchange, but local gravel and sandstone were also used. Because foreign exchange materials had higher initial transport costs, I assumed they would show signs of more intensive conservation than local materials. And they did, in a general way. Most exotic flints and cherts arrived in the land of Poverty Point as bifaces (Gibson & Griffing 1994:242, Jeter & Jackson 1994:164); most local chert, as gravel. Any cost savings earned by trading bifaces rather than cobbles or outcrop scree were realized by middlemen living along trade routes. Once materials reached the Poverty Point area, though, transport costs for exotic and local rock equalled out.

Why? Two reasons. First, "local" gravels had to be brought in from outside, too. The nearest gravel deposits lay in the hills south and west of Poverty Point territory, 65-90 km away (Bass 1981). Bedrock exposures of sandstone were even further away. In short, local materials were beyond foraging reach of any component, although they were within logistical reach of components on the far southern and western peripheries. Thus, local materials entered Poverty Point territory bearing a transport surcharge, just like exotic ones. Second, I expect these surcharges had to be paid or guaranteed *before these local rocks were exchanged locally*. What was "paid" is unknown, but guesses usually evoke food or other kinds of perishables or promises of assistance during times of need. These costs of doing business undoubtedly were passed on to consumers in some manner. No matter the price, the bottom line is that need and function, not transport costs, dictated who got what and how much they got (Gibson & Griffing 1994). Exotic flint and local chert would have wound up costing about the same.

Based on debitage, Aaron, a periphery WHOAA component, has the highest percentage of exotic flint, a little over 81 percent (Gibson & Griffing 1994:Table 4). Alexander Point, a core SCOT component, is next, with almost 72 percent; then comes Orvis Scott, a periphery WHOAA component, with close to 64 percent; Terral Lewis, a periphery SCOT site, with nearly 62 percent; and Arledge, a periphery WHOAA site, with around 61 percent. Percentages drop off at other components, but percentages of exotic rock vary independently of site class, indicating than temporariness (WHOAA components) did not dictate how much exotic material was consumed to an appreciable extent.

Location did, though, and location was closely tied to function. Thus, function (type of activity) determined the kinds of materials that wound up at various components. For example, if a lot of hoeing or hoe maintenance was done, then a lot of exotic northern gray flint was present, *proportionally*. Why? Because hoes were large tools made invariably of northern gray flint, usually the Dover variety (Gibson & Griffing 1994:238-239). Distance from Poverty Point, the presumed central supplier of both exotic and local stone, also influenced the total *amount* of exotic rock that reached distant peripheries. Again, however, there were strong functional conditions on distance; by itself, distance was a weak to neutral indicator of exotic vs. local material proportionality.

Does this mean that rock use within Poverty Point's hinterland was unaffected by transport costs? Not exactly. Exchange of bifaces and small, light gravel are indicators of economizing behavior, although most of the savings they promoted were realized outside the local exchange sphere. Still, because those savings were inherent in shape and size, they preferred savings for local consumers. Since conservation was already set in stone, I suggest that function was the main determinant of material appropriations within Poverty Point's primary supply zone.

Temporariness simply had little effect on how much exotic vs. local rock was consumed. Field camps were just as likely as residences to have large amounts of exotic rock, especially when they were out in the swamp close to Poverty Point. This suggests that an economizing ethic pervaded the entire locality, from Poverty Point down to the smallest component, from the core out into the periphery. After-all, when a supply zone as large as Poverty Point's had absolutely no rock sources, it made good sense for all users to be frugal with rock supplies.

2. *Multiple-Use Tool Design* Bifaces are held to be the ultimate economy-model tool. Their generalized design makes them multipurposive, suitable for use in a variety for tasks, for transformation into other shaped tools, and for conversion into cores from whence came the debitage needed to make unifacial or expedient tools (Jackson 1986, Kelly 1988, Odell 1996:57). Bifaces were a major component of Poverty Point technology, and so were unifacial tools made from biface-reduction flakes.

My major problem with employing bifaces to indicate economizing behavior is that they were functional tools, first and foremost. Any other purpose they served was incidental or secondary. Hoers didn't use large bifaces because they had long-use lives or made good cores when they broke. They used hoes because hoes were made for hoeing. The distribution of hoes or of any specialized tool, for that matter, reflected location where activities requiring those tools were conducted. Using the right tool for the job was far more economical than trying to make a tool do a job for which it was not intended. Multifunctional utility may have been incorporated in biface design from the moment the first flake was struck, but we may rest assured that work organization was the driving force behind biface distribution.

Bifaces were major stone tools at *every* Poverty Point site, not just the temporary ones, and thin, hafted bifaces ("projectile points") made up the majority of those bifaces. WHOAA components had proportionally more bifaces than SCOT components, by a wide margin—an average of about 6 to 1 (Gibson & Griffing 1994:Table 1)—but that only means that biface-requiring jobs were more common, precisely what we expect out in the field camps. Using bifaces, the ultimate utility tools, Poverty Point's version of the "Swiss Knife," ensured savings by enabling campers to travel lightly while remaining fairly efficient.

3. *Tool Maintenance and Recycling* Modification of finished bifaces evinces economizing behavior. At Orvis Scott, for example, more than 1 in 10 projectile points bears conspicuous signs of alteration, either for secondary or alter-

native use or for outright recycling, not merely resharpening (Gibson 1996a:24). Complete points sometimes have battered or polished edges and distal ends; others, denticulated or notched margins. Point fragments are also recycled. Although metrical study is lacking, other Orvis Scott points look like they were resharpened; short Garys and Carrolltons from long Garys, short and narrow-bodied Motleys and Delhis from initial-stage points of similar form.

Hoes were nearly always resharpened, too, but that simply came with the ground. Digging created opaline glazes on hoe bits. Glazed hoes were dull hoes, next to useless until the glaze was removed. WHOAA sites, such as Aaron and Arledge, had lots of hoe flakes, and the thrifty hoers who worked the swamp didn't let that useful debitage go to waste. More than 1 in 3 hoe resharpening flakes at Arledge were used in ways that left altered margins; at Aaron, the number rose to almost 1 in 2. Using hoe resharpening flakes as expedient tools is a good example of economizing behavior; it made a finite amount of rock go further, last longer, do more things—little things that didn't require taking a cut out of fresh rock supplies.

Maintenance and recycling were carried out at other sites. Just how much, we can't say, because of uneven data recording. Thus, we are prevented from seeing if temporary components had higher incidences overall than residential components, as we anticipate. Nevertheless, I don't think the picture can be explained simply by evoking mobility alone. At Poverty Point, most bifaces recovered from construction fill were reworked in some fashion, whereas bifaces from midden formed in top of the constructed rings weren't (Gibson 1996a:42). When coupled with the overall scarcity of bifaces in the construction fill, tool recycling hints of technological stress, which could be explained as a result of rock-supply shortages during all-out building episodes (Gibson 1996a:42-43; also see Andrefsky 1994:22, Bamforth 1986:40) or, maybe, time constraints (Carr 1994:36, Torrance 1983). Perhaps people who were busy moving dirt didn't take time to replenish rock supplies or make many new bifaces but used their old ones long and hard. We find some worn-out or broken bifaces bearing resharpened edges. We sometimes even find worn-out or broken reworked tools bearing a second round of resharpening or being modified into smaller tools.

Flake tools may be thought of as another economizing measure. Maintaining and recycling bifaces produced debitage, and where austerity dictated, substantial amounts of debitage were used for tools. Kind of rock made little difference, indicating that one flake made as good a tool as the next. We find that flake tools were made of local gravel chert just as often as they were of "high-quality" Dover flint. At Orvis Scott, 45 percent were made out of local pebble chert and 41 percent, of Dover; at Aaron, 41 percent were local chert, 24 percent Dover; at Arledge, 33 percent were local, 38 percent Dover; at Alexander Point, 15 percent were local, 20 percent were Dover; and at Stockland Plantation, 16 percent were local, 13 percent were Dover. The pervasive randomness suggests serendipity and expediency, conditions sometimes considered the opposite of those prompting curation (Carr 1994:36).

Around Poverty Point, though, the heaviest use of flake tools occurred at WHOAA components and the lightest, at SCOT components—linking expedient tools more closely with temporary camps than with residences (see Carr 1994:36). Thus, expediency and curation weren't alternative strategies at all. They were merely different means of contending with the same problem—providing tools in a land without native rock, a land where all rock supplies had to be brought in from outside.

4. *Conclusion* Function drove technological organization. The SCOT and WHOAA groups are essentially functional groups—SCOT, places of residence; WHOAA, places of temporary activity. And then there is Poverty Point itself, the sociocultural center. My crude analysis reveals that components articulate best when viewed as nodes in a pattern of logistical mobility.

WHOAA and SCOT components shared a common array of lithic materials. Materials were provided by exchange. Direct exchange was probably limited to SCOT sites, since they were where people lived. Since WHOAA sites were probably where people worked and camped for short spells, materials that wound up there probably were brought from nearby residences. Poverty Point probably provided rock for the entire community and likely did so in a direct manner.

Technological signs of economizing behavior are evident. Bifaces and flake tools dominate WHOAA assemblages. Thus, temporary sites have the most economical tools, just as we would expect. They also have high percentages of resharpened and recycled tools; even resharpening debitage is utilized, just as we would expect. Yet, material conservation measures like these are not confined to temporary sites. At Poverty Point, bifacial tools dating to moments of construction are also characterized by signs of multiple use and reworking, leading me to conclude that temporariness per se isn't directly responsible for economizing behavior. Material scarcity is the real culprit. Thus, when jobs take people away from tool supplies or keep them from replenishing supplies, thrifty folks respond by making a few tools do the work of many for as long as they can. And that can happen anywhere—at home or in camps down in the swamp or deep in the woods.

THE CORPORATE CHARACTER OF POLITICAL ECONOMY

Poverty Point's realm covered some 1,800 km², about 70 km north-south and 10-40 km east-west. I don't believe political power or sovereignty defined the realm. I'm not sure how much common language and ethnicity contributed to its bounding, but this much I do know: Poverty Point's realm was an area confirmed by "high styles" and by exchange of a common array of technological materials.

Exchange meant economics and politics. Anytime more than a handful of people become involved in anything, especially in something economically vital, interaction inevitably becomes politically infused. Poverty Point's political economy focused on getting vital technological raw materials into as many needy hands as possible. Actually, our focus may be a little out of focus because of the high visibility of rock. Other things were circulated, too. Edwin Jackson (1986:451, 511-513) found that the inhabitants of J.W. Copes, a permanent residence, ate more venison stew than roast, suggesting that roast was sent off to some distant table. He also found fewer vertebra of large fish than expected, suggesting that bone-in fillets found their way to other places (Jackson 1986: 513-516). Still, it is rock that provides the hard evidence for Poverty Point's political economy.

Poverty Point's political economy was many faceted. One facet involved the community core; another, the periphery; a third, the relationships between core and periphery; and a fourth, the external relationships. Unfortunately, available data limit the depth and breadth of inquiry.

Our data suggest that these relationships, at least those involving the core and periphery, were dominated by corporate behavior (see Blanton et al. 1996). Corporate behavior, as political strategy, keeps prominent individuals or special subgroups from amassing disproportionate authority by compelling them to adhere to a group-first, or team, mentality. Ambition is channeled into actions approved by wide consensus. With corporate-based actions, what benefits the group also benefits the individual, and vice versa.

Earthworks as Corporate Strategy

Poverty Point's massive earthworks and seemingly unrestricted, equal-opportunity system of exchange are testimonials to political-economic corporateness. Poverty Point's mounds were not tombs, nor were they temples, though they undoubtedly served as stages for all kinds of ritual. People lived on the rings and dropped their trash underfoot and threw it downslope, but the rings were not built just so people could live astraddle them. They could have lived on the flood-free natural ground and saved themselves a whole lot of trouble. What earthworks represented and what people did on them are separate things.

I contend that Poverty Point's earthworks are symbols of origin and cosmos (Gibson 1994d:179, 1996c:295-296, 1998a, n.d.d). As such, they make ideal landmarks, conspicuous expressions of ties to the land, constant reminders of communal identity and pride. In addition, when widespread native oral texts dealing with numbers, spatial layout, and directional orientation are taken into account, Poverty Point's earthworks assume larger meaning as magical shields protecting everyone—the *corporate* body inside the sacred inner sanctum—from evil spirits and forces (Gibson 1998a). As cosmic metaphors and magical safeguards, Poverty Point earthworks issue the ultimate corporate statement.

Earthworks were good for the whole group. That's why people were willing to work on them. Actually, they were better than good, because people invested some seven million workhours building them. That's a lot of labor and good will, considering that work probably was not coerced. I think people gave their labor willingly, because earthworks embodied their deepest feelings and beliefs and protected each and every one of them from dark spirits and forces lurking outside. If the earthworks had been monuments commissioned strictly by and for ingratiatory individuals, I doubt that people would have been as generous with their labor and loyalty. I construe the earthworks' symbolic meaning as being both primal and group-serving, not individualistic and egoistic (Gibson 1998a).

Exchange as Corporate Strategy

Corporateness seems to have permeated local exchange, too. Exchange materials were not channeled into the hands of a priviledged few or made exclusively into prestige objects or icons. On the contrary, Poverty Point exchange appears to have been quite open and unrestricted (Gibson 1994e, 1998b). No correlation was found between distance hauled and attached value or between distance hauled and material availability (Gibson 1994c, 1998b, Gibson & Griffing 1994). What we found was that exotic materials, some from as far away as 1,600 km, were transformed into utilitarian equipment that was used in all sorts of places, from temporary camps to permanent residences. We found that local materials, collected much closer to home, were treated essentially the same way. From this, we conclude that a material's value was measured in terms of its suitability (or desirability) for making certain tools and that suitability was gauged by job performance.

Exotic materials dominate assemblages at many sites, including both field camps and residences. As a matter of fact, Aaron, a field camp, has the highest percentage of northern gray flint of any known site (Gibson & Griffing 1994:Table 2), nearly three times higher than Poverty Point and around twice as high as its nearest "competitors"—Terral Lewis, Alexander Point, and Copes—which are SCOT components, or residences (Figure 4). Why? Because a lot of hoeing and hoe maintenance went on at Aaron. Hoes were large, hand-sized bifaces, and they were made predominantly out of exotic northern gray flint. What was important was that northern gray flint made an ideal hoe material. Just because it was imported from so far away didn't make it too "expensive" to be used for grubbing. Particle-induced x-ray emission (PIXE) analysis confirms that at least one hoe from Poverty Point was made out of Dover flint, indistinguishable from that found at the Dover quarry in Stewart County, Tennessee. Thus, how far away a material originated doesn't seem to have mattered greatly in terms of how, where, or by whom it was used. Distance and a material's value probably are directly correlated, but not in the sense of high value being ascribed materials slated for social or sacred contexts rather than secular ones. Obviously, northern gray flint was considered quite valuable. Poverty Point traders did, after all, go to considerable lengths to get it, but its importance lay in its common, everyday usefulness.

Despite the egalitarian, practical, and work-oriented character of local exchange, it would be wrong to assume that local distribution was politically unfettered and that distributors lacked ingratiatory motive. Obligation and payback, as well as influence, if not outright power, probably reverberated throughout exchange dealings. Patronage curries debt and conveys prestige. In corporate-based exchange, what is good for the group is also good for the individual promoter, but promoters truly concerned with helping people would have been careful about showing just how good. I can envision them flashing a crystal pendant around at feasts or puffing on a stone pipe instead of a clay one at rituals, but showing off too much likely would have compromised their ability to collect on obligations created by their sincere or calculated benevolence.

Poverty Point's political economy seems steeped with group consciousness and communal welfare. Poverty Point people lived in a land where food abounded and rocks didn't. To balance plenty with scarcity, they developed new and ingenious technological and economic strategies, while continuing to hold to proven ways and means. Assuredly, one time-honored strategy was keeping up those familiar relationships that ensured economic security, those relationships that defined and serviced a core of people—loyal kin, friend, and neighbor—who could be counted on during hard times. Maintaining mutual trust and reliance, of course, meant having to maintain fair and amicable relationships during good times, too. In my judgment, Poverty Point's political economy rings of familiarity and is flush with corporate ethics and responsibilities.

GROWING THE POLITICAL ECONOMY: A HYPOTHETICAL SAGA

People lived on the grounds at Poverty Point before the ringed enclosure and big mounds were built (Webb 1982). They erected at least one mound, Lower Jackson, on the far southern end of what would become Poverty Point's core area (see Figure 1). Lower Jackson mound may predate the rings by two or three thousand years, maybe more. The well-developed argillic horizon in the Ballcourt, some 2.5 km north of Lower Jackson, suggests that the Ballcourt, too, was an early construction. These are critical points, for they show, first, that the site was occupied *before* Poverty Point culture emerged there and, second, that the early occupants were mound builders. But, then, mounds had been built in the general vicinity at least 2,500 years before Poverty Point culture emerged, so the act of mound building was not unprecedented or unusual. That people were living on the site before Poverty Point culture evolved vouches for the economic attractiveness of the land, and I suspect that fishing conditions are what made it attractive (Gibson n.d.d, Gibson & Saunders n.d.).

Around cal B.C. 1730, residents consolidated their living quarters into a large half-circle. The black-earth midden that formed underfoot was laden with exotic rock, revealing that long-distance exchange was already in full swing. Although this is the first occupation we identify as Poverty Point culture, I'm confident it was merely a phase of a longer in situ development, one merely punctuated by accelerated exchange and related socioeconomic activities.

What is new is that, now, we have three basic conditions of Poverty Point culture—successful subsistence, mound-building, and exchange—together at the site. The mixture is potent; the result, a unique political economy that seemingly grows itself first into unparalleled and then into unsustainable proportions. Without making ado over data deficiency and paradigm prejudice, herewith is a hypothetical view of how Poverty Point's political economy developed.

Fishing, Mound Building, and Exchange in Developmental Perspective: A Model

I contend that a productive warm-water fishery provided a key but not the kick for Poverty Point development. Lower Mississippi rivers, lakes, and swamps teemed with fish, and annual overflows kept them teeming year after year, but nutrient and cover differences and other factors caused fish to congregate in some spots and avoid others. Thus, there were good fishing holes and not-so-good ones. Along with this, some people simply were good fishers and others, not so good. I'll not go into why this is so; the point is that groups or individuals who claimed the best fishing holes or who were the best fishers were, in my view, able to seize opportunity, which others couldn't.

I envision good fishers often catching more fish than they can eat. Like good kinsfolk and neighbors, they pass on the surplus to those of empty net. They may have even thrown in a spare turtle or snake or raccoon, too. Although give-aways, like these, manifest help-thy-neighbor mentality, they also forge an informal patron-client interdependency. Such relationships not only generate bottom-up respect and loyality, they have political economic consequences. Largess inures obligation, and the continued provisioning of the same people by the same people deepens obligation (see Arnold 1996). I doubt that patronizing fishers are interested in getting paid back with fish, but physical labor is welcomed.

The idea of building earthworks is a timely stroke of genius. Mounds offer something for each individual and for the group as a whole. Patrons get a landmark and a public monument to their generosity. The group gets to tell the story of its genesis by means of earthen metaphor, as well as issue a bold statement about its unity and capacity for concerted action. Earthworks also provide a salve for deepening inequalities in social station. They don't cancel inequalities, but they make everyone proud to be a member of the same "team." Some people get to carry dirt, and others get to tell them where to dump it. But even such fledgling labor "control" is accepted because mounds are good for the community; no, they are more—they are the community. Everyone, little people and big people, wins with mounds.

I construe gifting and payback and mound building cycling though small-scale, pre-Poverty Point Archaic societies for centuries, but usually within contexts emphasizing the group over the individual. I contend that Poverty Point was spawned in corporate context, too, and that corporate strategy prevailed during its entire development, absorbing individualizing flourishes like soft rain on bone-dry löess.

But we're not talking about sociocultural status quo or business as usual. A couple of conditions got political economy untracked and headed toward organizational complexity. Climate turned cooler and wetter during Poverty Point times (Gunn 1996:Figure 21.1). There was more water. It stayed up longer, meaning that fishers had to "fish the woods," the swamps and flats lying between streams, which now remained flooded for long periods. Weighted nets were required to fish the woods. Unweighted nets would have rolled up in the swift waters, leaving them tangled and useless. Poverty Point fishers came up with a perfectly designed net weight—a streamlined, thumb-length, teardrop-shaped plummet with a suspension groove or hole cut in the narrow end. Good weight-to-size ratio was effected by using hematite and magnetite, iron ores from the Ouachita Mountains in central Arkansas.

Being able to fish during high water has resounding implications for political economy. I regard this technological coup as a major turning point in Lower Mississippi fisheries. It means people could fish year-round. There is no flood-imposed downtime or need for storage technology. It is like having a stocked pantry to fall back on, especially during the dead of winter and early spring when other foods are scarce. When year-round fishing is added to all other food pursuits, I think food supply is rendered capable of supporting a substantial number of sedentary people and providing the surplus that makes economy ever more political. Thus, in this model, weather, long-lasting high water, netting technology, and acquisition of iron ore all come together under favorable logistical, piscatorial, sociocultural, and historical circumstances to bring about revisions of the political economic olio.

Weighted-net technology helps grow the economy, and that means demographic and areal expansion of the local community. But an entrepreneurial enterprise—long-distance exchange—helps separate Poverty Point from contemporary and preexisting political economies. While net-weight materials may get the cross-country enterprise started, it is other Ouachita materials that really open up exchange and keep it from specializing in just one or two materials.

Traders quickly realize that, if they are going to deal with mountain communities for magnetite and hematite, they might as well deal with them for all kinds of handy rocks, and those include novaculite, quartz crystal, slate, shale, calcite, and others (see Ericson & Blade 1963). Ensuring delivery of basic technological materials creates another niche in political economy, another level of organization—

one that, like fishing, carries the potential for social unequalization, informal dis-enfranchizing of various consumer segments. I see little evidence of socially con-trolled access to rock supplies, but we can be sure that local distributors gain prestige and "IOUs" in the process. Rock dealers and big fishers may have been one and the same or they may have been different people. We'll never know, but what really matters is that it doesn't matter in terms of the probable political eco-nomic consequences. If the same individuals are responsible for both fish and rock giveaways, then their status compared to everyone else's is bound to have been elevated, because they have two means, not just one, of becoming importance and gaining prestige. If different people are reponsible for the giveaways—some for rocks and others for fish—then we can expect there to have been competition and perhaps even formal rivalries. Again, exaggerated social inequalities are a likely outcome. Regardless of whether patrons are the same or different or whether one or two separate delivery systems—one for surplus food and the other for techno-logical materials—are employed, I think only a few personages ever become deeply involved on the promotional end. Still, that's enough to produce social ine-qualities, no matter how the process really worked.

I can see either competition for or monopolization of prestige pushing stone dealing onto new levels and into new lands. Traders add Midwestern and Interior Southeastern materials to those from the Ouachitas, giving them entirely new lines of rock to "trade," or rather, give away. I see indebtedness growing by leaps and bounds; payback becoming more demanding, more time-consuming, subject to greater manipulation and perhaps outright control by competing factions or a few strong personalities. If not for local and long-distance exchange, I suspect Poverty Point would have been just another petty polity, perhaps larger than most but not really different. Exchange changes all that.

Meaning of the Mounds and Rings

I consider the foregoing conditions to be the probable state of political economy immediately prior to the construction boom. With so many things happening, especially dealings involving outsiders, fears of unfamiliar faces and places and powers undoubtedly surface and are blamed for things that go wrong. Some kind of protection is needed, and the need is felt most strongly by those who have the most to lose when things go wrong—the patrons. I can understand patrons calling in markers and pledging them to erecting colossal earthworks.

But why earthworks and why so big? I believe the answer lies in their metaphor-ical nature, in their evocation, embodiment, and clear conveyance of sacred beliefs concerning protection and group-preservation (Gibson 1998a). I suggest that Pov-erty Point's earthworks are a safety net, a magical shield against omnipresent dark forces and evil spirits bent on causing harm to everyone and wrecking the good life. The bigger and more involved political economy becomes, the more people stand to lose, personally and collectively. Organization grows more vulnerable, as individualizing opportunism threatens the prevailing esprit d'corps. I see the grandiosity and redundancy of architectural protection elements as measures of the importance that everyone, from trade emmissary and food distributor down to novice knapper and mediocre fisher, place in the salvation conveyed by the earthworks. Corporateness asserts itself one more time.

Despite their magnificence, the earthworks are the cry of a lost cause. By acknowledging the need for protection—and on such a massive scale—people already are feeling the downside of a political economy that has no way to grow without radical technological or economic infusion. True, a period of relative stability and prosperity follows earthwork construction, but it is borrowed time.

REFLECTION

Poverty Point's political economy affected an area of some 1,800 km² and more than five dozen known components. Fishing was the primary activity in a collector-subsistence economy. Of this, we are confident. The rest is speculative.

The interplay of a year-round productive fishery, mound-building tradition, and long-distance exchange is socially manipulated by talented or ambitious individuals or factions. Surplus giveaways create prestige for givers and indebtedness for receivers, giving rise to inequality and informal power. But corporate strategies surpress the socially destablizing potential of inequality and power. As long as everyone has plenty of food, adequate material for tools, and protection from evil, Poverty Point prospers. But when no new corporate strategy appears to accomodate upwelling prosperity and make room for a new generation of want-to-be manipulators, the political economy runs into trouble. Poverty Point no longer provides a place of unbounded opportunity. The protective magic of its grand earthworks no longer works. The place with the broken rings becomes a victim of its success.

ACKNOWLEDGMENTS

For a good many years now, Poverty Point data-gathering efforts have been sustained by several people. For ushering data through bouts of land leveling and recording nadirs, as well as zeniths, the following individuals have my enduring thanks: Carl Alexander (deceased), Irving Arledge, Mark Fox, Peter Gendel, David Griffing, Edith Cary Hallmark, Mitchell Hillman (deceased), Edwin Jackson, Dennis LaBatt, Stanley Morgan, Orvis Scott, and Clarence Webb (deceased). Kelly Kimball crafted Figure 4.

REFERENCES

Arnold, Jeanne E. (1996) "The Archaeology of Complex Hunter-Gatherers." *Journal of Archaeological Method and Theory* 3:77-126.

Altschul, Jeffrey H. (1990) "A View from the Outside: A New Look at Areas Adjoining the Poverty Point Site." Pp. 101-112 in Kathleen M. Byrd (ed.), *infra*.

Andrefsky, William, Jr. (1994) "Raw-Material Availability and the Organization of Technology." *American Antiquity* 59:21-34.

Bamforth, Douglas B. (1986) "Technological Efficiency and Tool Curation." *American Antiquity* 51:38-50.

Bass, Sandra A. (1981) *A Closer Examination of Local Lithic Sources for Tool Manufacture at the Poverty Point Site*. M.A. thesis, Louisiana State University, Baton Rouge.

Binford, Lewis R. (1979) "Organization and Formation Processes: Looking at Curated Technologies." *Journal of Anthropological Research* 35:255-273.

_____. (1982) "The Archaeology of Place." *Journal of Anthropological Archaeology* 1:5-31.

Bitgood, Mark J. (1989) *The Baytown Period in the Upper Tensas Basin*. Cambridge, MA: Harvard University, Peabody Museum, Lower Mississippi Survey, Bulletin No. 12.

Blanton, Richard E., Gary M. Feinman, Stephen A. Kowalewski, and Peter N. Peregrine (1996) "A Dual-Processual Theory for the Evolution of Mesoamerican Civilization." *Current Anthropology* 37:1-14.

Brasher, Ted J. (1973) *An Investigation of Some Central Functions of Poverty Point*. M.A. thesis, Northwestern State University, Natchitoches, LA.

Byrd, Kathleen M. (1978) "Zooarchaeological Remains." Pp. 238-244 in Prentice M. Thomas, Jr. & L. Janice Campbell (eds.), *infra*.

_____., ed. (1990) *Recent Research at the Poverty Point Site*. Lafayette: Louisiana Archaeological Society, *Louisiana Archaeology*, No. 13.

_____., ed. (1991) *The Poverty Point Culture, Local Manifestations, Subsistence Practices, and Trade Networks*. Baton Rouge; Louisiana State University, *Geoscience and Man*, Vol. 29.

Carr, Philip J. (1994) "Technological Organization and Prehistoric Hunter-Gatherer Mobility: Examination of the Hayes Site." Pp. 35-44 in Philip J. Carr (ed.) *The Organization of North American Prehistoric Chipped Stone Tool Technologies*. Ann Arbor: University of Michigan, International Monographs in Prehistory, Archaeological Series, No. 7.

Conn, Thomas L. (1976) *The Utilization of Chert at the Poverty Point Site*. M.A. thesis, Louisiana State University, Baton Rouge.

Ericson, R.L., and L.V. Blade (1963) *Geochemistry and Petrology of the Alkalic Igneous Complex at Magnet Cove, Arkansas*. Washington, DC: U.S. Geological Survey, Professional Papers No. 425.

Exnicios, Joan, and Deborah Woodiel (1990) "Poverty Point Excavations, 1980-1982." Pp. 73-93 in Kathleen M. Byrd (ed.), *supra*.

Fisk, Harold N. (1944) *Geological Investigations of the Alluvial Valley of the Lower Mississippi River*. Vicksburg, MS: United States Army Corps of Engineers, Waterways Experiment Station, Mississippi River Commission.

Ford, James A. (1936) *Analysis of Indian Village Site Collections from Louisiana and Mississippi*. Baton Rouge: Louisiana Geological Survey, Anthropological Study, No. 2.

Ford, James A., and Clarence H. Webb (1956) *Poverty Point, a Late Archaic Site in Louisiana*. New York: American Museum of Natural History, Anthropological Papers, No. 45(1).

Gibson, Jon L. (1970) "Intrasite Variability at Poverty Point: Some Preliminary Considerations on Lapidary." Pp. 13-20 in Bettye J. Broyles & Clarence H. Webb (eds.) *The Poverty Point Culture*. Morgantown, WV: Southeastern Archaeological Conference, Bulletin, No. 12.

_____. (1972) "Patterns at Poverty Point: Empirical and Social Structures." *Bulletin of the Southeastern Archaeological Conference* 15:119-125.

_____. (1973) *Social Systems at Poverty Point, an Analysis of Intersite and Intrasite Variability.* Ph.D. dissertation, Southern Methodist University.

_____. (1974) "Poverty Point, the First North American Chiefdom." *Archaeology* 27:96-105.

_____. (1975) "Fire Pits at Mount Bayou (16CT35), Catahoula Parish, Louisiana." *Louisiana Archaeology* 2:201-218.

_____. (1984) *The Earthen Face of Civilization: Mapping and Testing at Poverty Point, 1983.* Lafayette: University of Southwestern Louisiana, Center for Archaeological Studies.

_____. (1987) *The Ground Truth about Poverty Point: The Second Season, 1985.* Lafayette: University of Southwestern Louisiana, Center for Archaeological Studies, Report, No. 7.

_____. (1989) *Digging on the Dock of the Bay(ou): The 1988 Excavations at Poverty Point.* Lafayette: University of Southwestern Louisiana, Center for Archaeological Studies, Report, No. 8.

_____. (1990a) "Earth Sitting: Architectural Masses at Poverty Point." Pp. 201-237 in Kathleen M Byrd (ed.), *supra.*

_____. (1990b) *Search for the Lost Sixth Ridge: The 1989 Excavations at Poverty Point.* Lafayette: University of Southwestern Louisiana, Center for Archaeological Studies, Report, No. 9.

_____. (1991) *Island in the Past: Archaeological Excavations at the Francis Thompson Site, Madison Parish, Louisiana.* Lafayette: Louisiana Archaeological Society, Louisiana Archaeology, No. 14.

_____. (1993) *In Helona's Shadow: Excavations in the Western Rings at Poverty Point, 1991.* Lafayette: University of Southwestern Louisiana, Center for Archaeological Studies, Report, No. 11.

_____. (1994a) *Cool Dark Woods, Poison Ivy, and Maringoins: The 1993 Excavations at Poverty Point, Louisiana.* Lafayette: University of Southwestern Louisiana, Center for Archaeological Studies, Report, No. 12.

_____. (1994b) "Over the Mountain and Across the Sea: Regional Poverty Point Exchange." Pp. 251-299 in Jon L. Gibson (ed.) *Exchange in the Lower Mississippi Valley and Contiguous Areas at 1100 B.C..* Lafayette: Louisiana Archaeological Society, Louisiana Archaeology, No. 17.

_____. (1994c) "Empirical Characterization of Exchange Systems in Lower Mississippi Valley Prehistory." Pp. 127-175 in Timothy G. Baugh & Jonathon E. Ericson (eds.) *Prehistoric Exchange Systems in North America.* New York: Plenum Press.

_____. (1994d) "Before Their Time? Early Mounds in the Lower Mississippi Valley." *Southeastern Archaeology* 13:162-181.

_____. (1994e) "Lower Mississippi Valley Exchange at 1100 B.C." Pp. 1-11 in Jon L. Gibson (ed.) *Exchange in the Lower Mississippi Valley and Contiguous Areas in 1100 B.C..* Lafayette: Louisiana Archaeological Society, Louisiana Archaeology, No. 17.

_____. (1995) "Things That Count: Mean Vertical Positions and Poverty Point Archaeology." Pp. 61-83 in Jon L. Gibson, Robert W. Neuman & Richard A. Weinstein (eds.) *"An' Stuff Like That There," In Appreciation of William G. Haag.* Lafayette: Louisiana Archaeological Society, Louisiana Archaeology, No. 18.

_____. (1996a) "The Orvis Scott Site: A Poverty Point Component on Joes Bayou, East Carroll Parish, Louisiana." *Midcontinental Journal of Archaeology* 21(1):1-48.

_____. (1996b) *Ancient Earthworks of the Ouachita Valley in Louisiana.* Tallahassee, FL: National Park Service, Southeast Archeological Center, Technical Reports, No. 5.

_____. (1996c) "Poverty Point and Greater Southeastern Prehistory: The Culture That Did Not Fit." Pp. 288-305 in Kenneth E. Sassaman & David G. Anderson (eds.) *Archaeology of the Mid-Holocene Southeast.* Gainesville: University Press of Florida.

_____. (1998a) "Broken Circles, Owl Monsters, and Black Earth Midden: Separating Sacred and Secular at Poverty Point." Pp. 17-30 in Robert C. Mainfort, Jr. & Lynne P. Sullivan (eds.) *Ancient Enclosures of the Eastern Woodlands.* Gainesville: University Press of Florida.

_____. (1998b) "Swamp Exchange and the Walled Mart: Poverty Point's Rock Business." Forthcoming in Evan Peacock & Samuel O. Brookes (eds.) *Materials and Exchange in the Mid-South,*

Proceedings of the 16th Annual Mid-South Archaeological Conference. Jackson: Mississippi Department of Archives and History, Archaeological Report.

_____. (n.d.a) "To Have or Not to Have: Exchange and Redistribution at Poverty Point." Paper presented to the American Anthropological Association, New Orleans, 1973.

_____. (n.d.b) "Poverty Point Chronology: The Long and the Short of It." Paper presented at the 34th Caddo Conference, Bossier City, LA, 1992.

_____. (n.d.c) "Beyond the Peripheries: A Cultural Resources Survey of a Tract of Land Adjoining the Poverty Point Site in West Carroll Parish, Louisiana." Ms prepared for Capital Bank of Delhi, Louisiana (copy on file there and with Farmers Home Administration, Alexandria, LA).

_____ (n.d.d) *Poverty Point, Place of the Rings.* Gainesville: University Press of Florida (forthcoming, schedule for 2001).

Gibson, Jon L., and David L. Griffing (1994) "Only a Stone's Throw Away: Exchange in the Poverty Point Hinterland." Pp 207-250 in Jon L. Gibson (ed.) *Exchange in the Lower Mississippi Valley and Contiguous Areas at 1100 B.C.* Lafayette: Louisiana Archaeological Society, Louisiana Archaeology, No. 21.

Gibson, Jon L., and Joe W. Saunders (1993) "The Death of the South Sixth Ridge at Poverty Point: What Can We Do?" *Society for American Archaeology Bulletin* 11(5):7-9.

_____. (n.d.) "Most Ancient Monuments of the Lower Mississippi Valley." Paper presented to the Society for American Archaeology, New Orleans, 1996.

Greengo, Robert E. (1964) *Issaquena: An Archaeological Phase in the Yazoo Basin of the Lower Mississippi Valley.* Washington, DC: Society for American Archaeology, Memoir No. 18.

Greene, Glen S. (1990) "The Deep Six Paleosol: The Incipient Poverty Point Occupation, 1983 Excavations." Pp. 113-131 in Kathleen M. Byrd (ed.), *supra.*

Gregory, Hiram F., Jr. (1991) "Terral Lewis: Recapitulation." Pp. 121-128 in Kathleen M. Byrd (ed.), *supra.*

Gregory, Hiram F., Jr., Lester C. Davis, and Donald G. Hunter (1970) "The Terral Lewis Site: A Poverty Point Activity Facies in Madison Parish, Louisiana." Pp. 35-46 in Bettye J. Broyles & Clarence H. Webb (eds.) *The Poverty Point Culture.* Morgantown, WV: Southeastern Archaeological Conference, Bulletin No. 12.

Griffing, David L. (1990) "Surface Surveys of the Insley Site, Franklin Parish, Louisiana." *Louisiana Archaeology* 12:219-240.

_____. (1996) "The Baskin Site, An Early Archaic Site in Franklin Parish." *Louisiana Archaeology* 21:103-125.

Gunn, Joel (1996) "A Framework for the Paleoindian/Early Archaic Transition." Pp. 415-420 in David G. Anderson & Kenneth E. Sassman (eds.) *The Paleoindian and Early Archaic Southeast.* Tuscaloosa: University of Alabama Press.

Haag, William G. (1990) "Excavations at the Poverty Point Site: 1972-1975." Pp. 1-36 in Kathleen M. Byrd (ed.), *supra.*

Hillman, Mitchell M. (1990) "The 1985 Test Excavations of the 'Dock' Area of Poverty Point." Pp. 133-149 in Kathleen M. Byrd (ed.), *supra.*

Huxtable, J., M.J. Aitken, and J.C. Weber (1972) "Thermoluminescent Dating of Baked Clay Balls of the Poverty Point Culture." *Archaeometry* 2:269-275.

Jackson, H. Edwin (1982) "Recent Research on Poverty Point Period Subsistence and Settlement Systems: Test Excavations at the J.W. Copes Site in Northeast Louisiana." *Louisiana Archaeology* 8:73-86.

_____. (1986) *Sedentism and Hunter-Gatherer Adaptations in the Lower Mississippi Valley: Subsistence Strategies during the Poverty Point Period.* Ph.D. dissertation, University of Michigan.

_____. (1991a) "The Trade Fair in Hunter-Gatherer Interaction: The Role of Inter-societal Trade in the Evolution of Poverty Point Culture." Pp. 265-286 in Susan A. Gregg (ed.) *Between Bands and States: Sedentism, Subsistence, and Interaction in Small Scale Societies.* Carbondale: Southern Illinois University, Occasional Paper, No. 9.

_____ . (1991b) "Bottomland Resources and Exploitation Strategies during the Poverty Point Period: Implications of the Archaeological Record from the J.W. Copes Site." Pp. 131-157 in Kathleen M Byrd (ed.), *supra.*

Jeter, Marvin D., and H. Edwin Jackson (1994) "Poverty Point Extraction and Exchange: The Arkansas Lithic Connections." Pp. 133-206 in Jon L. Gibson (ed.) *Exchange in the Lower Mississippi Valley in 1100 B.C..* Lafayette: Louisiana Archaeological Society, Louisiana Archaeology, No. 17.

Kelly, R.L. (1988) "The Three Sides of a Biface." *American Antiquity* 53:717-734.

Kidder, Tristram R. (1991) "New Directions in Poverty Point Settlement Archaeology: An Example for Northeast Louisiana." Pp. 27-50 in Kathleen M. Byrd (ed.), *supra.*

Kuttruff, Carl (1975) "The Poverty Point Site: North Sector Test Excavations." *Louisiana Archaeology* 2:129-151.

Lasley, Scott E. (1983) *Particle Induced X-Ray Emissions (PIXE) Analysis of Trade Items from Poverty Point, Louisiana.* Senior Honor's thesis, University of Southwestern Louisiana, Lafayette.

Lenzer, John P. (1978) "Geomorphology." Pp. 24-57 in Prentice M. Thomas, Jr. & L. Janice Campbell (eds.), *infra.*

Moore, Clarence B. (1913) *Some Aboriginal Sites in Louisiana and Arkansas.* Philadelphia: *Journal of the Academy of Natural Sciences of Philadelphia,* Vol. 16, Part 1.

Odell, George H. (1996) "Economizing Behavior and the Concept of Curation." Pp. 51-80 in his (ed.) *Stone Tools, Theoretical Insights into Human Prehistory.* New York: Plenum Press.

Pierce, Christopher (n.d.) "Distinguishing Style and Function in Poverty Point Objects." Paper presented to the Society for American Archaeology, New Orleans, 1991.

Saucier, Roger T. (1994) *Geomorphology and Quaternary Geologic History of the Lower Mississippi Valley, Volume 1.* Vicksburg, MS: U.S. Army Engineer Waterways Experiment Station.

Saunders, Joe W., Thurman E. Allen, and Roger T. Saucier (1994) "Four Archaic? Mound Complexes in Northeast Louisiana." *Southeastern Archaeology* 13:134-153.

Shea, Andrea B. (1978) "Botanical Remains." Pp. 245-260 in Prentice M. Thomas, Jr. & L. Janice Campbell (eds.), *infra.*

Shenkel, J. Richard (1986) "An Additional Comment on Volume Calculations and A Comparison of Formulae Using Several Southeastern Mounds." *Midcontinental Journal of Archaeology* 11:201-220.

Sires, Earl W. (1978) "Lithics." Pp. 179-210 in Prentice M. Thomas, Jr. & L. Janice Campbell (eds.), *infra.*

Smith, Brent D. (1976) "The Late Archaic-Poverty Point Steatite Network in the Lower Mississippi Valley: A Preliminary Report." *Newsletter of the Louisiana Archaeological Society* 3(4):6-10.

Stielper, Mark F. (1983) *Poverty Point Morphology.* Senior Terminus paper, University of Southwestern Louisiana, Lafayette.

Stuiver, M., and P.J. Reimer (1993) *Radiocarbon Calibration Program Rev. 3.0.3c, MAC Test #9.* Seattle: University of Washington, Quaternary Isotope Lab.

Swanson, Mark T. (1978a) "Ground and Polished Stone." Pp. 211-219 in Prentice M. Thomas, Jr. & L. JaniceCampbell (eds.), *infra.*

_____ . (1978b) "Stone Vessel Fragments." Pp. 220-226 in Prentice M. Thomas, Jr. & L. Janice Campbell (eds.), *infra.*

Swanton, John R. (1911) *Indian Tribes of the Lower Mississippi Valley and Adjacent Coasts of the Gulf of Mexico.* Washington, DC: Bureau of American Ethnology, Smithsonian Institution, Bulletin No. 43.

Thomas, Prentice M., Jr., and L. Janice Campbell, eds. (1978) *The Peripheries of Poverty Point.* Pollock, LA: New World Research Inc., Report of Investigations, No. 12.

Torrance, Robin (1983) "Time Budgeting and Hunter-Gatherer Technology." Pp. 11-22 in G. Bailey (ed.) *Pleistocene Hunters and Gatherers in Europe.* New York: Cambridge University Press.

Walthall, John A., Clarence H. Webb, Steven H. Stowe, and Sharon I. Goad (1982) "Galena Analysis and Poverty Point Trade." *Midcontinental Journal of Archaeology* 7:133-148.

Webb, Clarence H. (1944) "Stone Vessels from a Northeast Louisiana Site." *American Antiquity* 9:386-394.

_____. (1968) "The Extent and Content of Poverty Point Culture." *American Antiquity* 33:297-321.

_____. (1970a) "Intrasite Distribution of Artifacts at the Poverty Point Site with Special Reference to Women's and Men's Activities." Pp. 21-34 in Bettye J. Broyles & Clarence H. Webb (eds.) *The Poverty Point Culture*. Morgantown, WV: Southeastern Archaeological Conference, Bulletin No. 12.

_____. (1970b) "Settlement Patterns in the Poverty Point Cultural Complex." Pp. 3-12 in Bettye J. Broyles & Clarence H. Webb (eds.) *The Poverty Point Culture*. Morgantown, WV: Southeastern Archaeological Conference, Bulletin No. 12.

_____. (1982) *The Poverty Point Culture* (2nd ed., rev.). Baton Rouge: Louisiana State University, *Geoscience and Man, Vol. 17*.

Webb, Clarence H., James A. Ford, and Sherwood M. Gagliano (n.d.) "Poverty Point Culture and the American Formative [Part 1]." Ms on file with Louisiana Division of Archaeology, Baton Rouge, 1970.

Webb, Clarence H., and Jon L. Gibson (1981) "Studies of the Microflint Blade Industry at Poverty Point Site." Pp. 85-101 in Frederick Hadleigh West & Robert W. Neuman (eds.) *Traces of Prehistory: Papers in Honor of William G. Haag*. Baton Rouge: Louisiana State University, *Geoscience and Man, Vol. 22*.

Woodiel, Deborah K. (1981) "Survey and Excavation at the Poverty Point Site, 1978." *Bulletin of the Southeastern Archaeological Conference* 24:9-11.

PRE-MISSISSIPPIAN ECONOMIES IN THE AMERICAN BOTTOM OF SOUTHWESTERN ILLINOIS, 3000 B.C.–A.D. 1050

Andrew C. Fortier

INTRODUCTION

Geographically, the American Bottom represents an 80-mile strip of floodplain situated strategically just south of the Mississippi-Missouri-Illinois river confluence (White et al. 1984). It is dominated by numerous oxbow sloughs, lakes, open marshlands, woodlands, and occasional sand prairies, all set within a relatively flat ridge and swale topography (Figure 1). The Bottom is ringed on the east by a loessal bluffline from which exit a series of small and sometimes intermittent creeks. Colluvial and alluvial fans extend out from the bluffs, often burying floodplain features and older cultural resources. The Mississippi River marks the western portion of the Bottom, but its broad meanders evince the fluctuating and occasionally destructive nature of this border. Because of the river's dynamic nature, the floodplain zone

Research in Economic Anthropology, Volume 19, pages 341-392.
Copyright © 1998 by JAI Press Inc.
All rights of reproduction in any form reserved.
ISBN: 0-7623-0446-4

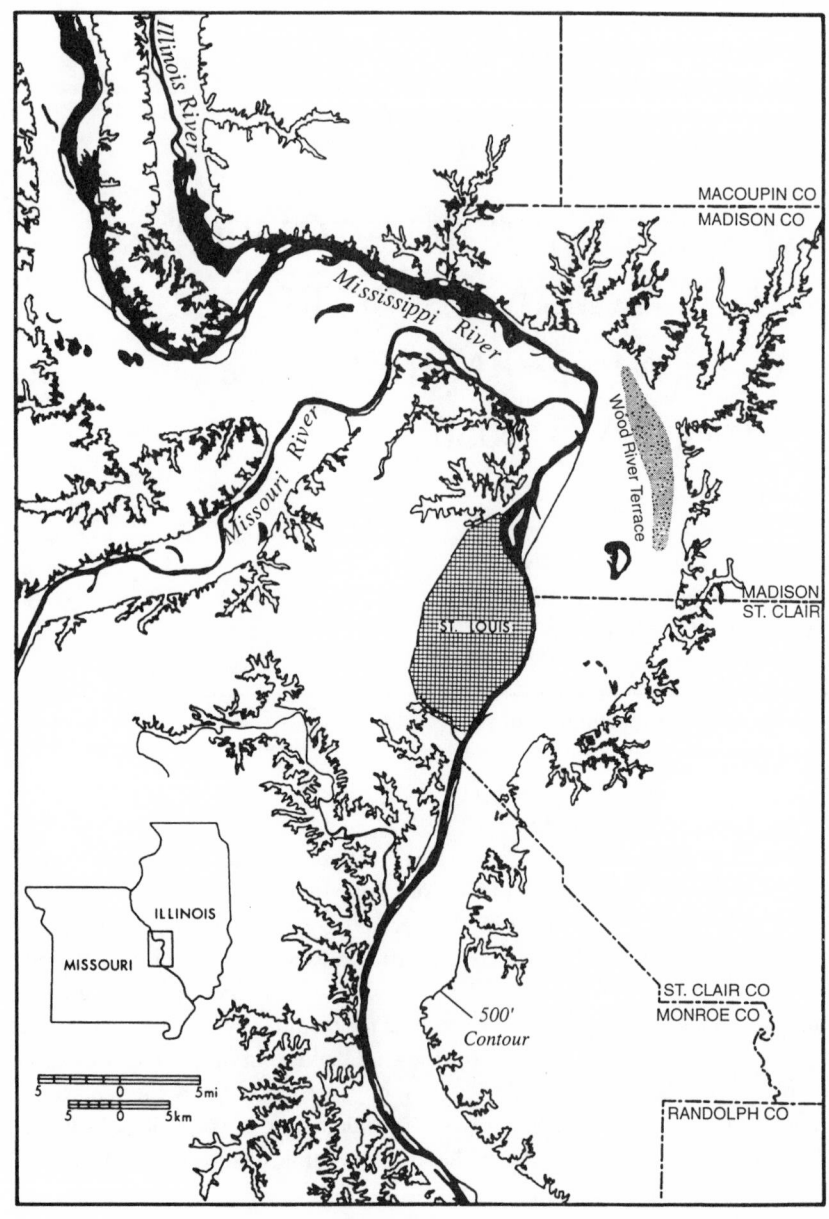

Figure 1. The American Bottom Region

itself has always been abundant in natural aquatic resources, supporting a wide variety of wild plant and animal species (Hus 1908). Additional resources thrive in the surrounding blufftops and uplands, but more importantly, in the past, these areas also served as a refuge during times of flooding. Prior to 1940s levee construction, and certainly prehistorically, the Mississippi River exerted a dramatic effect on the location and duration of settlements in the Bottom. Prehistorically, it is probable that only 25 percent of the land surface was ever available for human occupation at any given time, even in seasonally drier periods. For this reason, higher ridge portions, prominent terraces, and talus bluff base slopes were favored settlement locales in the Mississippi River trench through much of prehistory.

Therefore, despite the great ecological diversity and resource potential available to prehistoric inhabitants in this area, it was essentially an unstable environment. Such consistent instability generally did not constitute a very favorable environment for long-term settlement. This is observed most clearly in the area's early prehistoric record, which is characterized by numerous incursions from outside and by occupations that were mostly temporary. Cultural entities such as Dalton (lower Mississippi River valley), Titterington (central Missouri), Riverton (Wabash River valley), Ledbetter (mid-South), Marion (central prairie and Great Lakes), Black Sand (upper Mississippi River valley?), Florence (lower Mississippi River valley?), Crab Orchard (southern Illinois, Shawnee Hills), and Havana/Hopewell (Illinois River valley and points beyond) are all intrusive and clearly not products of a *local* prehistoric continuum. While the American Bottom occupied a strategic position at the confluence of three rivers, and while its aquatic resources were attractive, its dynamic nature severely constrained the formation of long-lasting land/human relationships for most of prehistory.

ECONOMIC AND CULTURAL DISCONTINUITIES

The American Bottom prehistoric sequence is one of the most refined cultural trajectories in the Midwest. To date, 27 distinct phases and 4 cultural complexes, spanning nearly 7,000 years, have been defined (Figure 2). Over 100 years of archaeological research of various qualities and extents have identified thousands of sites, including many that have been completely excavated and published. Artifacts number in the hundreds of thousands. The FAI-270 Project, initiated in 1978, alone has excavated over 110 sites and 13,000 features (Bareis & Porter 1984). It has also processed millions of liters of soil, forming the basis of one of the most extensive prehistoric floral and faunal assemblages ever recovered in North America.

Also impressive is the work carried out over the past 30 years at Cahokia, the most extensive Mississippian mound center in North America. Results from multiple excavations at this site have ignited debates over general issues concerning cultural complexity, such as the status of Cahokia as a chiefdom or state, the occurrence of class hierarchy and craft specialization, and the emergence and

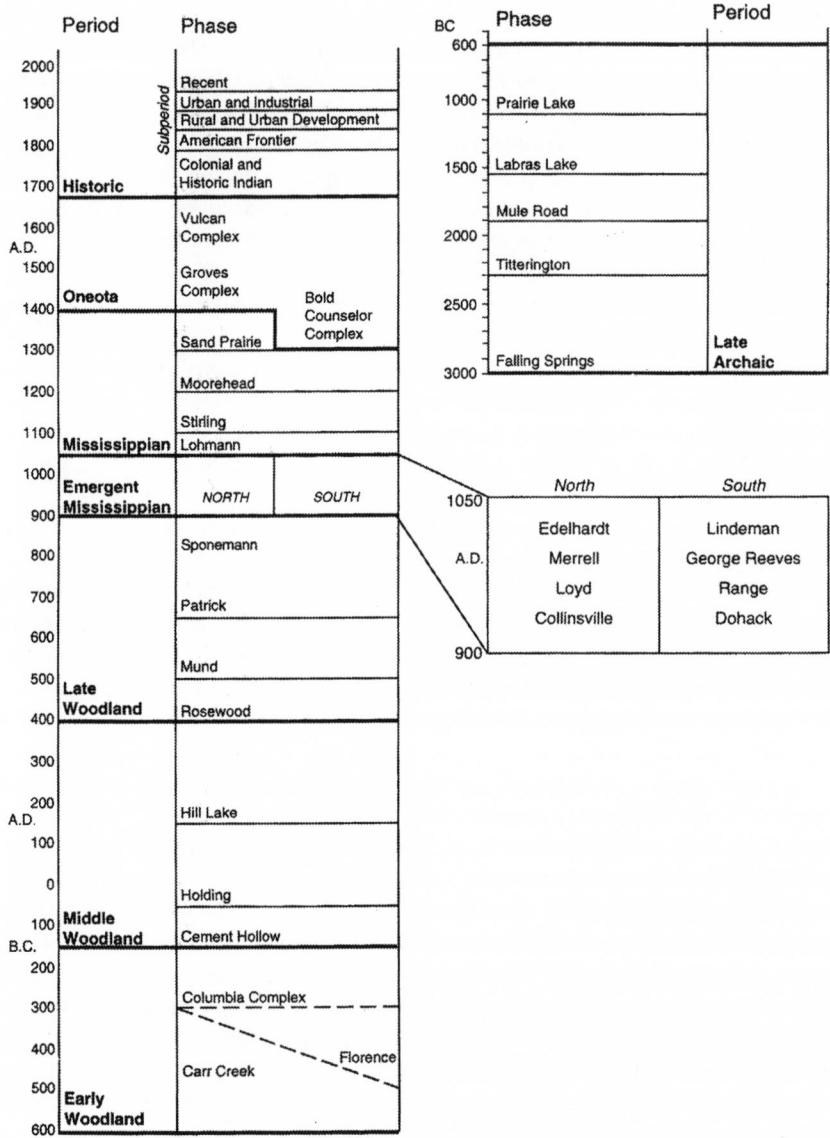

Figure 2. American Bottom Cultural Sequence
(Dates are calibrated for A.D. 400–1050.)

interrelationship of political and religious power (Kelly 1982, Pauketat 1991, Emerson 1995). Research questions at Cahokia have always been central in American Bottom prehistoric studies, and regardless of other goals and perspectives, the study of any one group or phase in the American Bottom, after A.D. 400, is set within the theoretical framework of Cahokia's emergence as a complex society.

The A.D. 400 date represents a dramatic break in the culture history of the American Bottom. It denotes the point at which an initial American Bottom resident population is established. Although there is a continuance of the pattern of outside incursions from this time forward, this population base slowly expands, stabilizes and, ultimately, develops into an American Bottom cultural heartland. The period between A.D. 400 and 1050 is, therefore, of fundamental importance in terms of understanding the processes leading to this technological, economic, and societal transformation.

Prior to A.D. 400, the American Bottom sequence represents a trajectory of cultural discontinuities. Systemic equilibriums were rarely established because of repeated population translocations in this area. For this reason, with a few possible exceptions, it is virtually impossible to argue for a long-term resident population in the American Bottom prior to A.D. 400. While the term "punctuated equilibrium" might best describe the cultural sequence in this area during this period, rarely did any group persist long enough to establish a base-line equilibrium.

This essay rejects the traditional American Bottom evolutionary paradigm that regards the cultural sequence of this area as the result of a series of gradualistic, linked adaptations springing forth from a long-standing resident population (Bareis & Porter 1984). It also rejects the idea that wholesale changes in artifact assemblages are simply the result of cyclical stylistic transformations. Changes in specific artifact styles, for example, more often than not are also coupled with corresponding shifts in settlement patterning, technology and, sometimes, subsistence. In terms of cultural trajectory, the American Bottom has also been affiliated directly with the Illinois River Valley (Seeman 1992). While the two areas certainly had somewhat similar cultural formats at certain times in prehistory, internal population dynamics, settlement strategies, certain subsistence practices, lithic procurement patterns, and processes leading to the emergence of Mississippian culture are dramatically different. Because of its position at the confluence of three major rivers, the American Bottom prehistoric trajectory has clearly been influenced by a number of different cultural traditions originating from many sources in the Midwest and Mid-South.

In the first part of this essay, I emphasize the unstable and discontinuous nature of the American Bottom sequence prior to A.D. 400. Three specific examples of cultural discontinuity are presented: (1) a series of cultural breaks within the Late Archaic period, (2) the abrupt transition from Late Archaic to Early Woodland, and (3) the distinct Middle to Late Woodland transition. This latter discontinuity is particularly enlightening, in that a wholesale transformation of technological, subsistence, and settlement systems is evident, a process that set the stage for the eventual appearance and development of an enduring resident population in the American Bottom. The second part of this essay examines this post-A.D. 400 process and proposes a number of socioeconomic mechanisms underlying the development of complex society in this area. It is during this period, i.e., A.D. 400-1050, that the unique character of the American Bottom emerges and the divergence from other areal sequences, such as in the Illinois River Valley, is most apparent. The development of complex Mississippian societies in this area ca. A.D. 1050, formed essentially in the very heart of an unstable floodplain environment, is remarkable. The eventual emergence of this area as a Mississippian heartland, a process that effectively occurred over four to five centuries, involved a fundamental restructuring of adaptive processes, entailing modifications or transformations of the subsistence, settlement, technological, and sociopolitical systems.

THE LATE ARCHAIC PERIOD: 3000-600 B.C.

The Late Archaic period in the American Bottom is characterized by a series of regionally recognizable cultural entities. Although we can chronologically sequence these groups, cultural phases are by no means *in this area* connected in a genetic or evolutionary sense. The period is subdivided into five phases (Figure 2) of roughly equal duration, with the exception of the first, the Falling Springs phase, which extends for a longer period of time, i.e., 3000-2300 B.C. The characteristics of each phase have been described at length elsewhere (McElrath et al. 1984, Kelly et al. 1979; McElrath 1986, 1993; McElrath & Fortier 1983, Fortier 1984, Emerson 1984, Philips et al. 1980, Emerson & McElrath 1983, Nassaney et al. 1983, Fortier 1996). The dates for these phases, as well as those preceding the A.D. 400 marker, are presented as uncorrected dates.

Falling Springs Phase (3000-2300 B.C.)

The existence of a resident Falling Springs phase population in the American Bottom is possible but has not been substantiated. Only a handful of occupations have been excavated (McElrath 1986, Fortier 1996) from this phase, so little is known about the extent and variety of community types, or about subsistence. As is typical of the Archaic Period in general (Asch et al. 1972), a heavy emphasis on "first-line," energy-efficient foods such as nuts and deer meat is evident. Due to poor preservation and the calcination of bone from open-fire roasting, we lack adequate faunal evidence. Meat procurement is, therefore, only indirectly inferred by the presence of bifacial scrapers, knives, and projectiles. The typical Falling Springs biface assemblage is generally related to the Helton or Hemphill phase materials of the lower and central Illinois River valley (Cook 1976, Conrad 1981, McElrath 1986:106-107).

The Mclean site (see Figure 3) has yielded the only feature (pits) remains from this phase (McElrath 1986) and the only evidence for community organization.

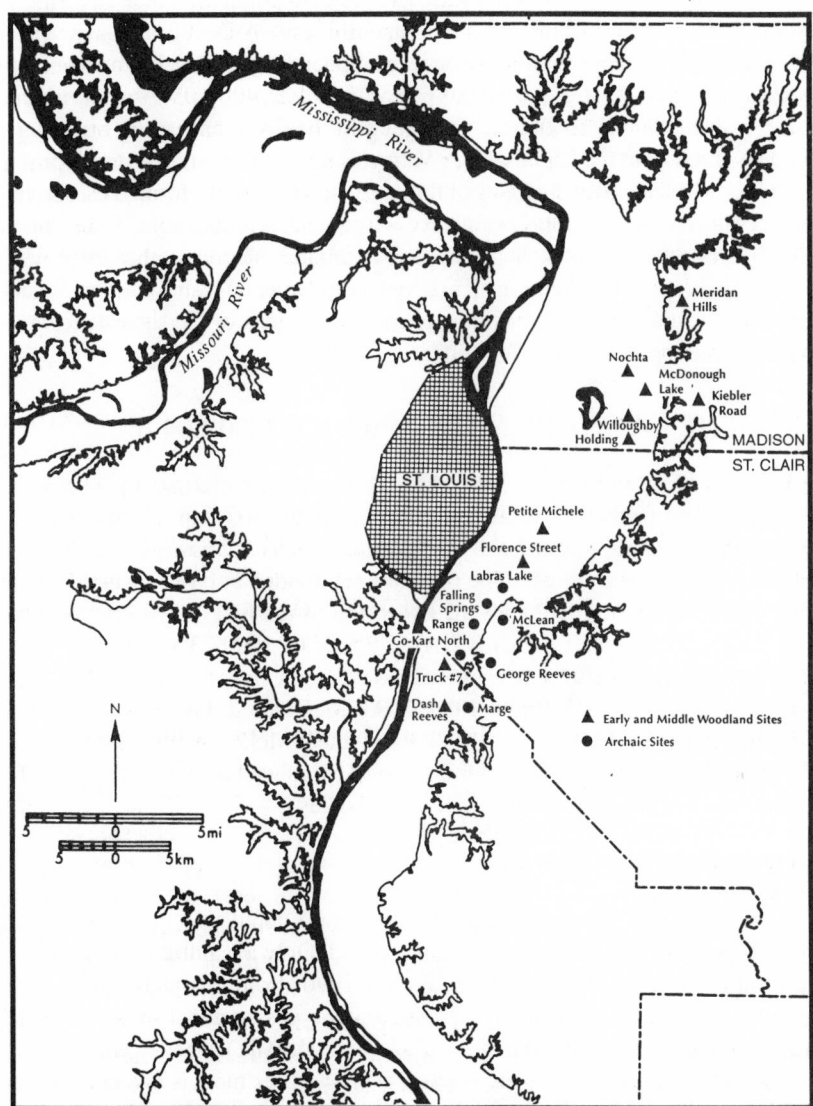

Figure 3. Location of Pre-AD 400 Sites Mentioned in the Text

There are no structures, but just over 160 pits are organized linearly on a bluff ridge overlooking the American Bottom floodplain. Within this linear pattern, McElrath (1986:117) was able to define a northern and southern occupation area, and both of these areas were further subdivided into eastern and western activity clusters. Hence, the overall settlement plan is both linear and quadripartite. He argues, furthermore, that the quadripartite division of the community plan at McLean is indicative of socially segmented, specialized task groups and that the site was occupied during one or more seasons, although probably not continuously. A connection to a possible floodplain base camp (the Falling Springs site itself) from this same time period is proposed. Such a model implies a segmentary settlement system and a relatively mobile economy organized around seasonal extractive loci, such as nut processing camps and/or butchering sites in the uplands, and more permanent base locales in the floodplain (Emerson 1984, Emerson & McElrath 1983).

Titterington Phase (2300-1900 B.C.)

Sometime around 2300 B.C., Falling Springs groups are abruptly replaced by an incursion of Titterington phase hunters and gatherers with a tool kit bearing no resemblance to the previous assemblages in this area. The Titterington phase is characterized by large bifacial knives (Etley, Sedalia, and Wadlow types), Clear Lake scrapers and gouges, Sedalia Diggers (Chapman 1988:203), and hafted bifaces, including Etley, Stone Square Stemmed, and Table Rock Stemmed types. The Titterington assemblage is clearly derived directly from the Western and Central portions of Missouri and, from a technological standpoint, appears to be adapted primarily to big game hunting.

The largest excavated Titterington phase occupation in this area is the Go-Kart North site (Fortier 1983, 1984). The community plan consists of 124 pits organized along a line, adjacent to what was probably an active meander of the Mississippi River. A series of discrete pit clusters indicate specialized cooking and processing areas, perhaps associated with individual families or other socially distinct task groups. The spatial layout of this settlement does not differ appreciably from the aforementioned McLean site plan, although social segmentation is not evidenced at the Go-Kart North site. The linear arrangement of occupations along channel banks and blufftops is a common theme throughout the Archaic period, and it may simply be related to the linear nature of those physiographic features. A poorly preserved but diverse faunal assemblage was recovered from the Go-Kart North site, including fish, bird, mussel shell, turtle, and deer. Plant remains were also diverse, although nuts, as at McLean, were the dominant class of recovered materials (Fortier 1984:166-182).

The Titterington phase was defined first in the St. Louis area on the basis of ten mortuary sites (Titterington 1950). Since that time, a number of habitation sites have also been identified in Missouri (Turner 1965, Klippel 1969, Harl 1995) and Illinois (Houart 1971, Cook 1976, Roper 1978, Fortier 1984, Ahler et al. 1992). As a whole, Titterington lithic assemblages are quite distinct and differ in several respects from preceding Falling Springs and subsequent Mule Road phase assemblages. The technology of big biface production during the Titterington phase is anomalous, as is the pattern of procuring high-quality, non-local cherts. Heat treatment of cherts, a common feature in earlier assemblages, is absent. For the Modoc rockshelter, Ahler et al. (1992:127) argue that, following the Falling Springs phase, there were important changes in "both the range and intensity of site activities," subsistence, and lithic tool inventories during the Titterington phase. While Ahler et al. (1992:128-129) regard these changes as significant, they see the Titterington phase as an *in situ* development, a view that has not generally been adopted by most researchers in the American Bottom (Emerson et al. 1986, Fortier 1984). They believe that the differences between Falling Springs and Titterington lithic assemblages are derived from a settlement system that was highly flexible and adaptive and "capable of rapid adjustment to changes in the physical or social environment" (Ahler et al. 1992:127). Nassaney and Lopinot (1986) have offered a similar view, although it was directed at a broader pattern of cyclic settlement and social organization that they envisioned for the entire Late Archaic period. Based on the number of new artifact types, unique chert reduction technology, and differences in chert type procurement that characterize Titterington phase sites, it is difficult, however, to see American Bottom Titterington assemblages as being derived from previous formats in this area. I would argue that Titterington and Falling Springs assemblages are virtually unrelated and that the only cultural traits they share is the linear patterning of their settlements and their heavy reliance on nuts and deer.

Mule Road Phase (1900-1550 B.C.)

The following phase, Mule Road, has only recently been defined (McElrath 1993). It appears to represent an incursion into the American Bottom, possibly from the Mid-South. Originally, Mule Road assemblages, such as the one excavated at the George Reeves site (see Figure 3), were thought to be denigrated Titterington phase assemblages (McElrath & Finney 1987:101-115). This interpretation was largely based on the co-occurrence of typical Titterington phase artifacts, such as Etley and Sedalia knives and Stone Square Stemmed projectiles, at the George Reeves site and what appeared to be closely related but poorly made Titterington/Ledbetter types. However, the George Reeves assemblage has been re-examined recently (McElrath 1993) and, based on additional Ledbetter excavations in the Mid-South (Bentz 1988), McElrath reassessed the assemblage as being more typical of the Ledbetter culture whose heartland lies in the Kentucky-Tennessee area. Moreover, although they both are characterized as being big biface traditions, he regards the Ledbetter and Titterington artifacts as coming from two separate, historically and regionally distinct—Mid-South versus Upper Midwest—trajectories.

It is difficult to assess the extent or nature of the Mule Road phase community layout. Only 19 pit features could be directly affiliated with the Ledbetter component, and they were dispersed somewhat linearly, although not to the same extent as the McLean or Go-Kart North sites. Pit fills yielded mostly nutshells and small fragments of unidentifiable calcined bone. Given the size and diversity of the lithic assemblage from this site, McElrath and Finney (1987:48-53) have suggested that the Late Archaic component at George Reeves functioned as a permanent base camp. There are very few sites from this phase in the American Bottom, so population levels must have been extremely low.

Labras Lake (1550-1100 B.C.) and Prairie Lake (1100-600 B.C.) Phases

The Labras Lake phase is characterized by a radically different lithic format, including the abandonment of large Titterington/Ledbetter bifacial tool industries and the occurrence of smaller, hafted biface types, such as Trimble Side-Notched and Merom Expanding Stemmed, which are more closely affiliated with the Riverton Culture of eastern Illinois (Winters 1969). The arrival of Riverton cultural traits at this time appears to represent a wholesale replacement of the previous Titterington and Ledbetter big-biface traditions in the American Bottom. The settlement system seems to be mostly focused on the floodplain, and individual sites such as Labras Lake (Philips et al. 1980, Yerkes 1987) and Range (Kelly et al. 1987) are situated along old meander banks of the Mississippi River, close to abundant aquatic resources (see Figure 3).

Several communities such as Labras Lake and Marge (Fortier 1996) have produced evidence of dwellings, perhaps indicating a greater degree of sedentism in some localities. The concept of sedentism here follows that of Emerson et al. (1986:252-253) in their discussion of Late Archaic settlement models in the American Bottom. They (ibid.:252) argue that "sedentism...is a threshhold event rather than a continuum and can be seen as present when a part of the (social group) population remains at the same location throughout the year. Occupation during each season of the year is a requisite to determining sedentism in an archaeological context." They (ibid.:266-267) go on to say that, "while the archaeological record indicates an increasing utilization and occupation of the floodplain during the entire period, there is no good evidence for sedentary settlements until the Prairie Lake phase (although there are hints that the Labras Lake phase peoples may have been fairly sedentary)." In fact, it is during the Labras Lake phase that a relatively permanent resident population can be recognized for the first time in this area. Evidence for increasing population aggregation is even more pronounced during the succeeding Prairie Lake phase (1100-600 B.C.), when extensive floodplain occupations appear throughout the American Bottom (McElrath & Fortier 1983, Nassaney et al. 1983, Emerson 1984).

The concept of base locale was utilized by Emerson (1984:343) to describe the aggregation of terminal Late Archaic populations in resource rich environs. "It was a system of centrally based sedentary occupations from which short-term extractive trips were made for the purpose of exploiting specific resources" (Emerson 1984:344). As Emerson points out, it is similar to Meggars' (1956:138-140) concept of "Central-Based Wandering." In the American Bottom, though, so-called wandering would have been restricted to seasonal and localized, task-specific expeditions. This system was probably initiated during the Labras Lake phase, but archaeologically it is best manifested during the subsequent Prairie Lake phase (Emerson et al. 1986).

Late Archaic Summary

In terms of subsistence and activity organization, the Late Archaic period in the American Bottom is remarkably homogeneous, despite variations in lithic assemblage formats and despite repeated external incursions. Groups followed regional formats that varied only slightly from locality to locality. For a brief period at the end of the Archaic, populations were apparently more sedentary, even though settlement and economic organization continued to be structured around individual families or tasks, as evidenced archaeologically by discrete clusters of cooking/roasting pits. There is no evidence that groups ever developed any form of incipient horticulture or that economies ever developed beyond the bounds of family or immediate lineage relationships. There is no evidence of centralized community activity, for example, in the form of a central place around which multiple activities took place. Status differentiation or social ranking is not apparent, although archaeological evidence for either the presence or the absence of social heirarchy is lacking. Subsistence activities followed a generalized pattern with a continued emphasis on high-energy foods such as nuts and other easily obtainable aquatic resources. By the end of the period, base locale occupations exhibit a greater degree of resource diversity but still exhibit no direct evidence, with the notable exception of curcubits (Fortier 1986), that subsistence systems were involved in horticulture.

Dramatic changes in lithic technology and hafted biface formats characterize the Late Archaic sequence of the American Bottom (Figure 4). For this reason, it is difficult to see any continuity between phases. During the Late Archaic period, the American Bottom appears to have functioned primarily as a crossroads through which passed a series of cultural traditions, none of which had much lasting impact on the overall sequence. Interestingly, all of these traditions, despite various durations of occupation, exclusively utilized American Bottom lithic resources. Each group simply applied its own technological and stylistic formats to these resources. Evidence for regional exchange is extremely restricted. Few if any extra-regional materials have been recovered from terminal Late Archaic sites in the American Bottom. In short, settlement structure at the end of the Archaic period appears to have been moving toward permanent sedentism, and technological accomplishments were certainly sophisticated enough to allow long-term settlement of this area but, sometime around 600 B.C., this process ended abruptly.

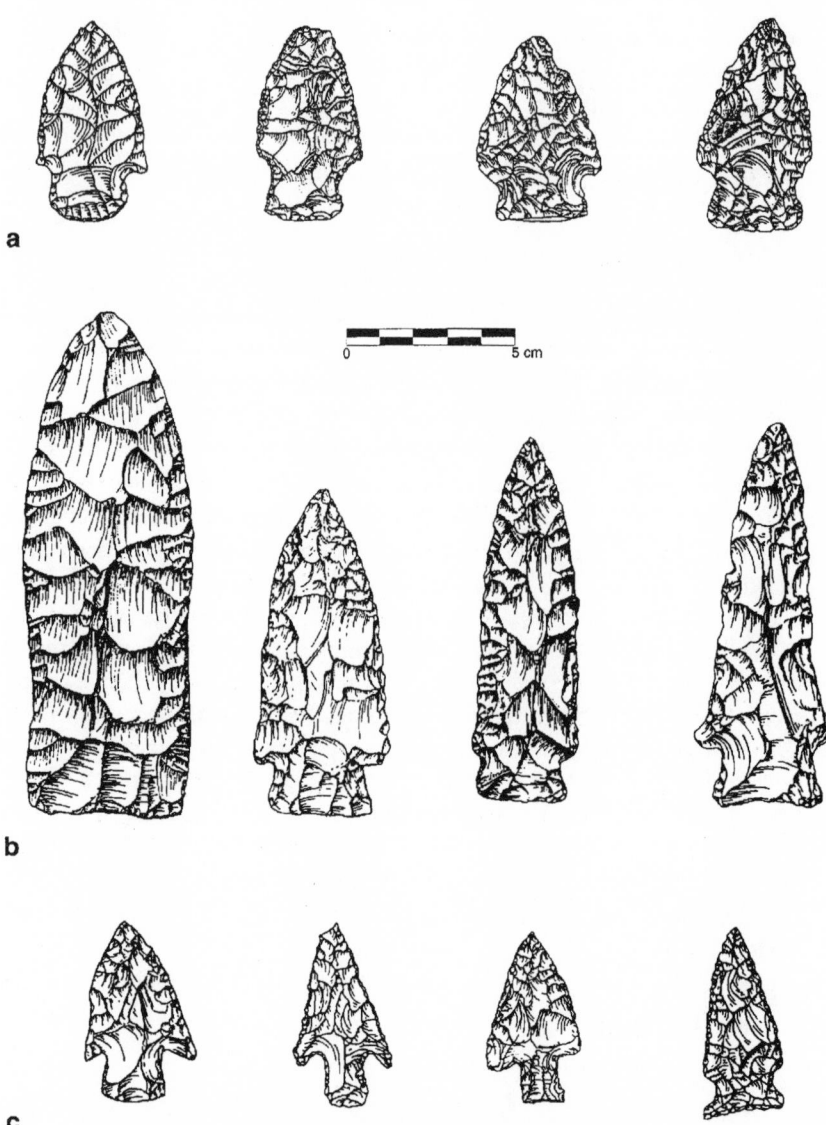

Figure 4. Changes in Late Archaic Hafted Biface Formats:
a, Falling Springs Phase; b, Titterington Phase;
c, Labras Lake and Prairie Lake Phases

THE LATE ARCHAIC-EARLY WOODLAND TRANSITION: 600 B.C.

The course of American Bottom prehistory might have been significantly altered had the terminal Late Archaic pattern been long-lasting. Instead, technological, settlement and, to some extent, subsistence formats were abruptly aborted by the arrival of Early Woodland pottery-bearing groups sometime after 600 B.C. This discontinuity is characterized by the abandonment of highly aggregated settlements and the appearance of much smaller, dispersed, short-term occupations having low artifact densities and limited subsistence remains. Late Archaic sites are found most often on the higher, clay bank meanders in the floodplain, while Early Woodland occupations are often, although not exclusively, found in low inner-channel and low-lying marsh edge environments (Emerson & Fortier 1986). An important exception to this pattern is the Wood River Terrace area of the northern American Bottom, where high sandy knolls contain both Late Archaic and Early Woodland occupations (Evans n.d.). There are also a few sites in the southern and central Bottom and adjacent uplands that have both Late Archaic and Early Woodland (Marion culture) remains, but the more common pattern is that the settlements are mutually exclusive (Fortier et al. 1984a, Emerson & Fortier 1986).

From a technological standpoint, Late Archaic hafted biface styles do not occur at Early Woodland sites. Late Archaic Motley, Dyroff, and Springly types, as well as residual Merom Expanding and Trimble Side-Notched varieties, are replaced by the ubiquitous Kramer point style. Marion Thick pottery in the form of thick-walled, coarse-tempered jars or tubs is a hallmark of the earliest Early Woodland occupation of this area. It is more difficult to characterize a typical Early Woodland (Carr Creek phase) lithic assemblage, since excavations thus far have produced so few artifacts. The assemblages are small and remarkably nondiverse. The occupations are ephemeral and, given the low density of site distribution south of this area, the American Bottom appears to represent the very southern tip of the Marion culture expansion in Illinois.

In short, the Late Archaic-Early Woodland transition in the American Bottom appears to represent population replacement or displacement. After 600 B.C., the area experienced a significant decrease in occupation activity and probably an overall decrease in population. There are no known Early Woodland base locales in the floodplain or uplands. The Late Archaic base locale settlement/subsistence pattern was replaced by a pattern of diffuse and dispersed, small, specialized task-specific extractive loci, mostly oriented to lowlying localities within the floodplain proper but also occurring in some of the upland creek drainages. The contribution that Marion cultures made to subsequent intrusive Early Woodland groups in this area, such as Black Sand, Florence, and Columbia Complex, is problematical.

From 600 to150 B.C., the area continued to experience a series of intrusions by various unrelated Early Woodland groups, with apparent minimal intermixing. It is difficult to accept these changes in ceramic format as simply resulting from a process of stylistic adoption. In addition to design format changes and the use of specific decoration techniques (noding, punctating, incising, etc.), there are major technological differences between these ceramics, for example, in temper types (sand versus grog), vessel wall thicknesses, and rim and lip types.

There are no good explanations at this time for the disappearance of terminal Late Archaic populations in this area. Given their low population levels, it seems highly implausible that Early Woodland groups physically displaced Late Archaic populations. Nor can the initial Early Woodland stage simply be characterized as an Archaic culture with pottery. Settlement types, location, and function were transformed overnight, as were lithic assemblage formats and subsistence practices. The low diversity in subsistence remains from this period suggest that resources may have been more restrictive or limited and perhaps oriented more to aquatic plant species, such as tubers or American lotus, which do not preserve well in the archaeological record. The occupation of previously unoccupied, low-lying floodplain regimes suggests that water levels may have dropped significantly during this period. Perhaps this drop was the driving force that led to the abandonment of this area by Late Archaic groups ca. 600 B.C. Falling water levels may have brought about an associated decrease in resource availability, particularly in the very same areas that had previously supported large Late Archaic population aggregates. In this scenario, Early Woodland groups simply moved into a previously abandoned void, occupying low areas in the floodplain, the only remaining niches containing aquatic resources.

In summary, it is difficult to characterize Early Woodland economies. Initially, they appear to be largely dispersed, opportunistic, and ephemeral. In contrast, although terminal Late Archaic societies had been highly mobile as well, their population levels appear to have been relatively substantial and aggregated in numerous locations in the American Bottom. Late Archaic artifact assemblages are diverse and reflect a wide variety of activities. This is in stark contrast to the absence of such diversity at subsequent Early Woodland, Carr Creek phase occupations. By 500-300 B.C., however, some Early Woodland occupations in this area, such as the Florence site (Florence phase), once again evince much greater stability (Emerson et al. 1983); they have been interpreted as "residential bases" (Binford 1980:9) consisting of "logistically organized collectors exploiting specific resources through a system of specifically organized task groups" (Emerson & Fortier 1986:511). The presence of a large structure, storage pits, and a variety of processing pits and hearths at the Florence site anticipates the themes of task organization and community layout that develope after 150 B.C. in the subsequent Middle Woodland period in this area. It is not clear, however, from which, if any, of the intrusive Early Woodland Florence, Black Sand, Liverpool, or Morton-like cultures such Middle Woodland groups are actually derived.

THE MIDDLE TO LATE WOODLAND
TRANSITION: 150 B.C.-A.D. 350

Without a doubt, the transition from the Middle to Late Woodland periods is one of the most dramatic discontinuities in the archaeological record of the American Bottom. Only in the last 20 years have there been enough excavated data from both periods in this area to allow even a cursory examination of this process. Of course, at the regional level this transition has been closely tied to the so-called collapse of Hopewell—a process, various researchers have argued, that resulted from adaptations to climatic change, cultural fatigue, warfare, over-utilization of resources in preferred riverine niches, forced social integration brought about by the collapse of the Hopewell Interaction Sphere, population increase and concomitant local intensification subsistence-related processes (Braun 1977:35-110), or all of the above. In the American Bottom, the "collapse" of Hopewell appears to have occurred gradually over a several century period. However, for this model we must first summarize what we know about Middle Woodland culture in this area and outline some of the important technological, subsistence, and social phenomena characterizing this period.

Cement Hollow Phase (150 B.C.-50 B.C.)

The first recognizable Middle Woodland groups in the American Bottom date to approximately 150 to 50 B.C. and are referred to as the Cement Hollow phase (Fortier et al. 1984a). Artifacts from this phase are roughly equivalent to the Early Havana phase of the Illinois River Valley. Site density is extremely low. Structures, if even present during this phase, are unknown, and site size is generally small, consisting of scatters of pits. Subsistence was based primarily on deer, nuts, and wild seeds and fruits. Evidence for plant husbandry is lacking. Ceramic vessels consist of large, thick-walled, sand-tempered jars, often with zoned and dentate stamped or plain impressed decorations. Contracting-stemmed points (Dickson-Waubesa types) and large hafted, corner-notched, broad-bladed knives and scrapers (Snyders and Norton types) are the diagnostic lithics from this time. Towards the end of this phase, there is some evidence that exotic materials such as copper, galena, and mica were utilized, e.g., at the Petite Michele site, which I am presently analyzing. In terms of subsistence, settlement patterning, and technology, early Middle Woodland Cement Hollow phase occupations differ imperceptibly from previous Early Woodland settlements in this area. Although some local evolution cannot be ruled out, the American Bottom more likely represents a southern extension of Middle Woodland Havana developments to the north.

Holding Phase (50 B.C.-A.D.150)

During the following two centuries (after 50 B.C.), fundamental changes occurred in technological, subsistence, community, ideological, and settlement systems in this area. This period, referred to locally as the Holding phase (50 B.C.-A.D. 150), represents a significant break with the past, and it is associated and coeval with the emergence of Hopewell or Havana/Hopewell cultures throughout the Eastern Woodlands (Fortier n.d.). Broad regional exchange systems appeared, and horticulturally-oriented village life developed with extraordinary refuse accumulations, elaborate household structures, and a dizzying array of new ceramic and lithic inventories. Although the American Bottom lacks evidence for mortuary behavior, elsewhere in Illinois an elaborate funerary format emerged, including the construction of log-chambered tombs, within which were deposited exotics such as platform effigy pipes, copper artifacts (tinklers, celts and awls), clay human figurines, mica, fluorite, obsidian, drilled bone, chert blades, and elaborately decorated ceramic bowls and jars.

During the early Middle Woodland Cement Hollow phase, sites were generally small and, typically, dispersed throughout the American Bottom floodplain. During the Holding phase, a settlement aggregate, consisting of several large village occupations (Holding, Nochta, McDonough Lake, and Meridian Hills) and smaller extractive loci (Willoughby and Kiebler Road), emerged in the area just east of the Edelhardt Meander Scar, several miles north of the Cahokia Mound Center (see Fortier et al. 1989:562-569). Occupations are mostly situated along the meander bank but also occur on the adjacent blufftops. Although the cultural affiliation of several mounds—Fox Hill, Gertrude Witte, Blue, and Sugar Loaf—on these bluffs has never been established, some mortuary behavior may be associated with this concentration of habitations.

(a) *Fandangos, Big Men, and Exchange*   The emergence of a multi-tiered Middle Woodland settlement system is evidenced sometime after 50 B.C. in this area. Some of the larger sites, such as Holding, have produced exotic materials such as obsidian, mica, copper, and fluorite, indicating that some groups were connected to the outside world through participation in the Hopewell Interaction Sphere. Regional interaction is further evidenced by the presence of nonlocal cherts such as Kaolin, Mill Creek, Cobden, and Dongola and ceramic types such as Crab Orchard from the Southern Illinois area and Marksville from the lower Mississippi River valley.

Just how these exchange systems worked is unclear, although some scholars have suggested that specific exchanges, especially of exotic goods, may have involved the use of transaction centers, major production and exchange nexuses, usually located along major waterways (Struever & Houart 1972:52, Kay 1979:96-97). The Twenhafel site in Southern Illinois, the Mellor site in Central Missouri, the Mann site in southern Indiana, and perhaps sites such as Albany in western Illinois, are possible candidates. There are no comparable sites in the American Bottom.

Transaction centers may have emerged as places where exotic artifacts were exchanged, distributed, consumed, and produced. Such activities were probably conducted within more generalized social contexts, such as scheduled feasts, adoption ceremonies, mound construction and burial, or combinations of all these (Seeman 1979). As Seeman (1992,1995) has cogently argued, such artifacts probably functioned as symbolic forms of communication, and the centers themselves as ceremonial theaters where such communication took place. The distinction between economic and socially-based activities would naturally be blurred, inseparable, and archaeologically invisible in such contexts. Moreover, the relationship between artifacts moved over long distances and the actual producers of such goods is generally complex, even when this process can be observed ethnographically (Helms 1993). Exchanges involving exotics or particularly well-crafted items are often embedded in political-ideological and, sometimes, cosmological contexts that are virtually indecipherable in the archaeological record. I think we can assume that this process was equally complex during the Hopewell period in the central Midwest.

In my opinion, transaction centers did not function primarily as trade centers or gateways (Hall 1967:176, Kelly 1991a:61-80, Burghardt 1971), but served as "rendezvous centers" where people gathered for some of the aforementioned specified occasions, such as fall harvests or hunts. Such centers may have operated in much the same manner as the well-known Great Basin Shoshone pinyon festivals, or *fandangos* (Thomas 1972:146-147), which periodically brought peoples together at designated locations to share excesses in food. According to Steward (1938:237), "the dancing, feasting and general visiting complex is generally considered to have functioned in the promotion of social intercourse, with essentially noneconomic motivation." In this sense, similar large-scale social interactions during the Hopewell period may have functioned more to promote social integration in an area than to acquire exotics. Clay (1988) makes a similar argument for the Peter Village site in Kentucky, which dates to this same time period. It should be noted that, when so-called exotic artifacts have been found at habitations in Illinois, they normally occur in generalized refuse or midden contexts. The vast majority of exotics are, however, found almost exclusively in mortuary contexts, and they are generally thought to be associated with high-status individuals. Within habitations, hoarding of exotic goods in special structures does not occur. If certain individuals were accumulating such items as personal wealth during their lifetimes, archaeological evidence prior to interment has remained invisible.

The trafficking mechanisms for goods within the Hopewell Interaction Sphere has been much discussed in the literature of the Eastern Woodlands and especially so in Illinois, where early excavations into mounds along the Illinois River valley and elsewhere produced spectacular mortuary remains (Deuel 1952, Neumann & Fowler 1952; McGregor 1952, 1958; Wray & McNeish 1961, Griffin et al. 1970).

Cached and exotic mortuary artifacts, often associated with single individuals, seemed to indicate the presence of an elite, presumably in control of the distribution of highly valued goods, even in death. A ranked social system, perhaps based on hereditarially ascribed status, was envisioned. From an economic standpoint, society was thought to operate under a system of hierarchical redistribution, originating from a central individual, "Big Man," or lineage, similar to systems described by Sahlins (1963:285-303,1972) for some groups in Polynesia.

During the 1970s, a number of researchers (Braun 1979, Buikstra 1976) argued that Middle Woodland society was not analogous to such ranked hereditary systems of control, but to one based on achieved status in which a few individuals earned high status positions, achieved by virtue of age or gender or other means of social standing, e.g., ability in hunting, craft production, leadership, curing, or ideological understanding. Moreover, as more and more Middle Woodland village sites were excavated in the Midwest (Freeman 1969, Wiant & McGimsey 1986, Stafford & Sant 1985, Fortier 1985a, Fortier et al. 1989), little evidence for ranking of any kind could be seen at the community level, not even special "Big Man" structures or evidence for hoarding. One could further speculate that Middle Woodland economies were corporate, i.e., that the flow of goods was controlled by community decisions, not individuals. In this sense, elaborate grave goods would not represent personal items possessed by that individual in life, but rather a kind of corporate gift to that individual—in essence, a salutation to some kind of achievement, presumably of some benefit to the corporate group. Exotic goods, therefore, would have represented items of community, not personal, wealth (Seeman 1995).

(b) *Horticultural Revolution*   One achievement that really sets the Holding phase people apart from previous Woodland societies in this area is the development of a subsistence system based on horticulture. If there was a period of experimentation in the American Bottom leading to this horticultural revolution, it is not evident in the archaeological record. Food plants such as maygrass, goosefoot, erect knotweed, little barley, wild bean, American lotus, panicum type 61, cucurbits, blackberry, pawpaw, persimmon, plum, and small-seeded legumes increase dramatically in number in most archaeobotanical assemblages of this period and make up a significant percentage of this new, horticulturally-based economic system (Parker 1989:429-464). Maize occurs for the first time but in small quantities and at only one site, Holding (Riley et al. 1994). Tobacco also appears for the first time but, again, only at one site, Meridian Hills (Williams 1993:197).

The emergence of sedentary population aggregates appears to be closely correlated with broad-scale plant use during this period. Extensive villages probably emerged for the first time as a direct consequence of the need to care for cultivated stands of plants in singular locations. The Holding site is the best excavated example of such a village; it consists of multiple structures and pits organized around a central courtyard (Fortier et al. 1989). The broad diversity of plants and animals procured, as well as the extensive lithic and ceramic assemblage, indicate a long-term settlement history at this site. The presence of midden deposits over this habitation further confirms the sedentary nature of this settlement. It is the only Middle Woodland site in the American Bottom where three Middle Woodland phase occupations occur in the same location.

(c) *A Technological Renaissance* Holding phase communities also exhibit a number of new lithic and ceramic technologies not previously seen in this area. Regarding lithics, the appearance of a lamellar blade technology is most dramatic and enigmatic. There are simply no precedents for this specialized technology in this area or elsewhere in the Midwest. Blade technology had previously surfaced at various times over broad areas of the West, Subarctic, and Arctic regions (Sanger 1970), and it can also be observed in Mesoamerica and in Late Archaic contexts in the Gulf and lower Mississippi River valley regions. The Poverty Point Late Archaic blade traditions of these latter regions (Haag & Webb 1953, Ford et al. 1955) are derived from a long history of blade manufacturing, dating as early as 3600 B.C. (Russo 1994). They may extend up to the Early and Middle Woodland periods in those areas. With the notable exception of the Poverty Point assemblages, most of the aforementioned blade traditions do not resemble Havana/Hopewell blade traditions in the Midwest. The source of this technology in the Midwest, therefore, remains a mystery.

The occurrence of lamellar blades at Middle Woodland sites after 50 B.C. is a hallmark of this culture. They represent an expedient means of mass producing tools for a variety of tasks. They are light and easily portable, and they make efficient use of raw chert material. At one time, it was thought that blade production represented only a minor element of the lithic technology of Hopewellian peoples and served only specialized ceremonial functions, since blades had been found mostly in mortuary contexts. However, recent excavations at some major blade-producing sites in the American Bottom, such as Holding and Dash Reeves, have recovered literally thousands of blades in midden contexts. Moreover, it is also clear that they were used for a variety of purposes, including as knives, side scrapers, end scrapers, denticulates, drills, gravers, and perforators. In most respects, the blade tool industry functionally mirrors the more ubiquitous small, nonblade flake and larger, core tool industries. At Dash Reeves, for example, there are perforators, gravers, denticulates, and scrapers made on cores, blades, and nonlamellar blade flakes, a facet of Middle Woodland lithic technology that has, to date, not been recognized in the literature of the Midwest.

The unique nature of blade technologies at this time has led some scholars to believe that blades or, more probably, blade cores, were a medium of exchange, a "blades for trade" model (J. Williams 1989, Hofman & Morrow 1985, Hofman 1987, Reid 1976). This exchange may have been closely associated with specific chert colors or types found only in specific regions. For example, the red Ste. Genevieve cherts of Monroe County and the high-quality white Crescent Hills quarry cherts from the American Bottom area may have been particularly valued by Southern Illinois or Missouri River peoples (Hofman 1987), while the blue

Dongola and yellow Kaolin types from Southern Illinois may have also been desired by American Bottom inhabitants. If such exchange was based on color, then it would represent a good example of symbolic communication in this area (Seeman 1995). The Dash Reeves site, which I am presently analyzing, is located in Monroe County in close proximity to a rare red chert source, and the settlement may have functioned specifically as a production center for blades. Hundreds of cores and thousands of blades were recovered from this site; about 5 percent of the chert consists of Southern Illinois types, a fact which may support the aforementioned exchange model.

Holding phase lithic assemblages in this area are also characterized by numerous formal tool types, including large disc scrapers, chert hoes and adzes, a micro-tool industry (including needle-like drills and perforators, beks, gravers, denticulates, and end scrapers), a core tool industry (which includes the same formal types, except that they are made on cores), and a variety of hafted biface types. By way of contrast, the earlier Cement Hollow phase assemblages contain fewer artifacts and have fewer formal types. The florescence of lithic technology during the Holding phase is even more apparent if one includes the various technologies that produced exotics such as copper celts, tinklers, earspools, and awls, as well as platform pipes, hematite plummets and cones, and the manipulation of other exotic minerals, such as mica, fluorite, and schist.

Another kind of renaissance occurred in ceramic technology, combining new technologies with an elaboration of earlier style motifs. New vessel forms, such as serving bowls, appear, as do new tempers, such as grog and limestone. The big, thick-walled jars of the Cement Hollow phase are replaced by a variety of thinner-walled and smaller jar forms. There appears to have been a close relationship between vessel diversity at sites and emergent horticultural economies, particularly evidenced by the appearance of food-serving vessels, such as bowls. The Holding phase is also characterized by the appearance of elaborate design motifs, often placed in structured or zoned design fields, including some that display quadrapartite or opposing design symmetry. It is also not uncommon to find multiple motifs on a single vessel, such as cross-hatching, punctating, rocker stamping, trailing, impressing, and brushing (Maher 1989). Rarely, recumbent bird designs appear, perhaps related to mortuary behavior or cosmology.

Hill Lake Phase (A.D. 150-350)

Sometime after A.D. 150, near the beginning of the Hill Lake phase, notable changes in settlement, technology, and subsistence begin to appear in the archaeological record of this area. Interaction Sphere items are no longer present in assemblages; subsistence systems appear to revert to pre-Holding phase levels, especially in terms of the scarcity of cultigens and a decrease in diversity in procured plants; zoned ceramic design fields are replaced by singular, unstructured patterns covering the entire vessel surface; specialized serving bowls drop out of assemblages; the quality of workmanship on lithic artifacts subtly declines. On the other hand, the Hill Lake phase is undeniably Middle Woodland; many ceramic motifs as well as artifact types survive throughout this period; lamellar blade technology occurs at some sites, although not at all; the pattern of selecting colorful cherts continues, although there is an abrupt decline in the number of nonlocal varieties procured; ovate disk scrapers, as well as a variety of woodworking tools, continue to constitute important elements of lithic assemblages; and sites continue to be located in lowlying floodplain areas of the American Bottom. However, a new focus of settlement appears nearly 40 km to the south, in the Hill Lake and Fish Lake localities.

There are to date only two sites excavated from the Hill Lake phase in this area. One site, Dash Reeves, is extensive and has yielded thousands of chert and nonchert artifacts. As mentioned above, this site is interpreted as a specialized lithic production center. The second site, Truck #7, is represented by a single large, circular structure with associated interior and exterior pits. The excavator (Fortier 1985a:275-276) argues that this structure and associated features was a single-family residence occupied over the late fall-winter period. Other Hill Lake phase sites have been identified in this same area from surface remains only. Based on surface densities, they appear to represent small occupations more similar to Truck #7 than to Dash Reeves. There is no evidence for a major reorganization of society during this period and only minimal evidence for a gradualistic transition into Late Woodland.

The Late Woodland Transition

The Hill Lake phase (A.D. 150-350) appears to represent a period of adaptation in the American Bottom that followed a rather dramatic shift away from regional interaction and exchange and from experimentation in technology and subsistence. It is significant that the collapse of the Hopewell Interaction Sphere in this area, a process seen throughout the Midwest, did not terminate the Middle Woodland cultural sequence. Hill Lake people linger for nearly two centuries. Perhaps some ties were maintained during this phase with the north and south, but this is not clear. Sometime between A.D. 300 and 350, the American Bottom is abruptly abandoned (McElrath & Fortier n.d.). Approximately 100 years later, the area is reoccupied by small groups of Late Woodland peoples who are completely distinct from the previous Middle Woodland occupants.

The archaeological record speaks strongly against an evolutionary model in regard to the Middle to Late Woodland transition in the American Bottom. Middle Woodland assemblages differ in several important respects from Late Woodland assemblages. Late Woodland lithic assemblages lack lamellar blades, exotic chert (especially those from Southern Illinois), ovate disk scrapers, chert hoes, and a broad spectrum of small formal tool types, including gravers, spurs, drills, and perforators (Figure 5). A number of Middle Woodland hafted biface types,

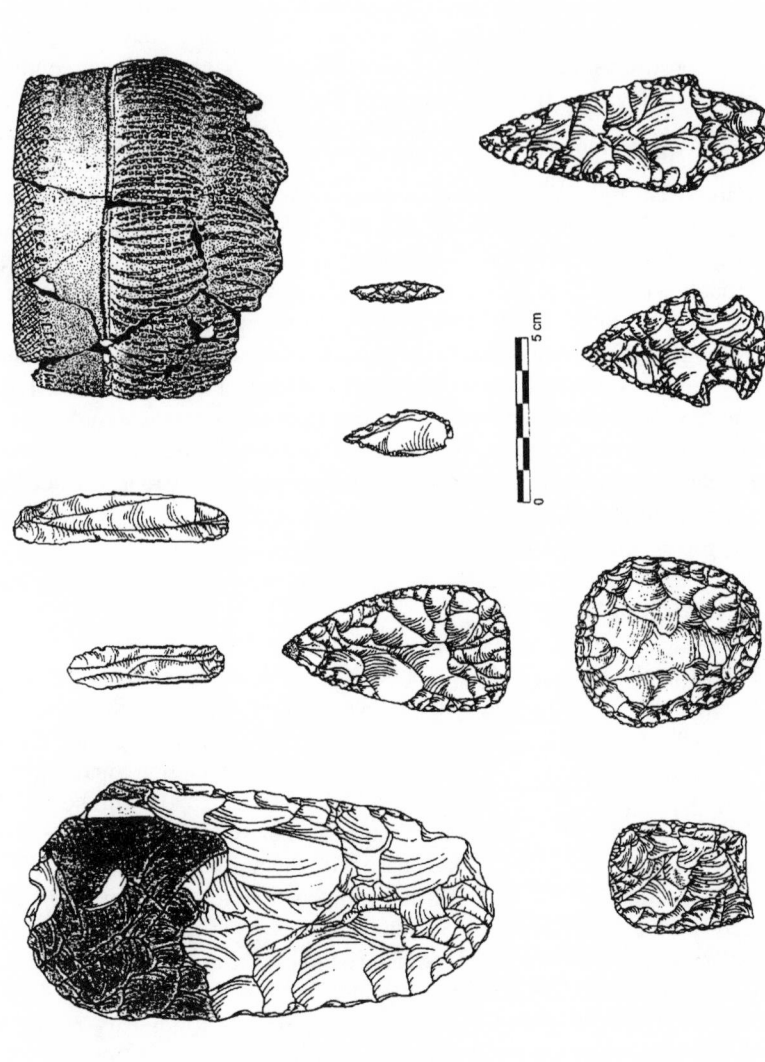

Figure 5. Diagnostic Middle Woodland Artifact Types That Did Not Survive into the Late Woodland Period

such as Manker, Dickson, Snyders, Burkitt, Clear Lake Side Notched, and Mason, are also absent. From a qualitative standpoint, workmanship—particularly pressure flaking and tool symmetry, as well as formal consistency—is greatly diminished during the early Late Woodland period. The elaborate core technologies of the previous period are replaced by simple, nonformal, multi-directional reduction techniques.

Dramatic changes in ceramics also occur, including the abandonment of design traits such as rocker stamping, brushing, incising, cross hatching, punctation, and zoning. Nonlocal ceramics, such as Crab Orchard varieties, no longer occur. The typical Late Woodland vessel, on the other hand, is a cordmarked jar, the only decorative attributes of which are lip notching or impressing and bossing, traits which probably represent some kind of continuance of Middle Woodland traditions.

A significant difference between Middle and Late Woodland settlements is their location on the landscape. During the Middle Woodland Hill Lake phase, settlements are mostly located in floodplain environs; only a few occupations have been found in the uplands. During the subsequent early Late Woodland phase, known locally as the Rosewood phase, settlements are almost exclusively situated in bluff base, bluff top, or upland drainage localities. Perhaps more significantly, Hill Lake and Rosewood phase settlements never co-occur or overlap. Apparently, once they were abandoned, Hill Lake site areas were either not available or not known to subsequent Late Woodland groups. Nor does it appear to be a simple matter of Hill Lake peoples moving out of the floodplain to new locations in the uplands, since there are very few Hill Lake sites in those environmental niches.

There are other attributes that separate Middle and Late Woodland occupations in this area, including: (1) the absence of middens at early Late Woodland sites; (2) the first-time occurrence of deep earth oven pits at Late Woodland sites; (3) an overall increase in pit depths as well as an increase in the diversity of pit types at Late Woodland settlements; (4) a significant increase in the diversity of fauna procured, with a special emphasis on fish; (5) an apparent change in cooking practices, with a focus on *en masse* steaming in earth ovens; and (6) a shift in bone preservation at sites, from small, poorly preserved, calcined bone Middle Woodland assemblages to larger, unburned Late Woodland assemblages.

There can be no doubt that the Middle/Late Woodland transition was abrupt in this area. Late Woodland assemblages, settlement systems, and subsistence practices do not evolve out of a precedent Middle Woodland population here. The reasons for abandonment of the American Bottom at A.D. 350 are not clear and are beyond the scope of this paper. What is important is that the subsequent re-occupation of the American Bottom after this time was not just another temporary incursion, but rather the basis for a much longer land/human relationship, one leading eventually to the formation of an American Bottom cultural heartland.

INCIPIENT HEARTLAND:
THE FIRST ECONOMIC TRANSFORMATION

The first Late Woodland settlements in the American Bottom appear sometime around A.D. 400 and have their closest cultural affinities to the Weaver/White Hall cultures of the lower and central Illinois River valley. In those areas, the Middle to Late Woodland transition is generally less dramatic, and at some sites, early Late Woodland occupations appear to be directly derived from late Middle Woodland settlements. Some scholars have argued that, as populations overreached their carrying capacities at the end of the Middle Woodland period within the river valley regimes, groups readjusted and underwent a fragmentation process, which resulted in the formation of frontier settlements in various upland drainages away from the major river valleys (Braun 1977, Green 1993). It is conceivable, although by no means proven, that this fragmentation process within the Illinois River valley may have led directly to the reoccupation of the American Bottom.

If this model is accepted, these first settlers would presumably have had no prior knowledge of preferred Middle Woodland settlement localities in the American Bottom. The archaeological record indicates that these first Late Woodland inhabitants moved into a variety of niches not previously occupied by Middle Woodland groups. The Mississippi River floodplain, favored by Middle Woodland occupants, was curiously avoided. Settlements are found, instead, exclusively in higher bluff edge, bluff base, and interior upland localities. The early Late Woodland period in this area, which consists of both the Rosewood and Mund phases (A.D. 400-650, corrected), is one of the rare times in American Bottom prehistory that groups did not incorporate the Mississippi floodplain into their settlement system. We do not know whether the avoidance of the floodplain was due to cultural preference, to a higher than normal water regime in the Mississippi River trench at that time, or to other, unknown factors.

There is nearly a ten-fold increase in archaeological sites during the Rosewood-Mund phase over the previous Hill Lake phase and, given the broad spatial range of occupation in the area, this count is probably underestimated (Figure 6). The earliest Late Woodland (Rosewood phase) occupations are mostly small and transitory. Groups probably moved frequently over the landscape during this initial period. They appear over a much broader range of territory than did the previous Hill Lake occupants. However, with a few exceptions, such as the Carbon Dioxide site (Johannessen 1985a:97-102), Rosewood phase sites also exhibit a heavy reliance on starchy seed cultivars, and great diversity of plant use is characteristic. These facts suggests that people in *some* locations may not have strayed too far from tended plant stands. Thus, the observed increase in settlement density at this time may be the result of an actual population increase in the area rather than widespread movements by a few communities. In reality, we have probably not yet identified the larger, more permanent occupations from the earliest phase of occupation, the notable exception being the Rosewood site itself (Bentz n.d.,

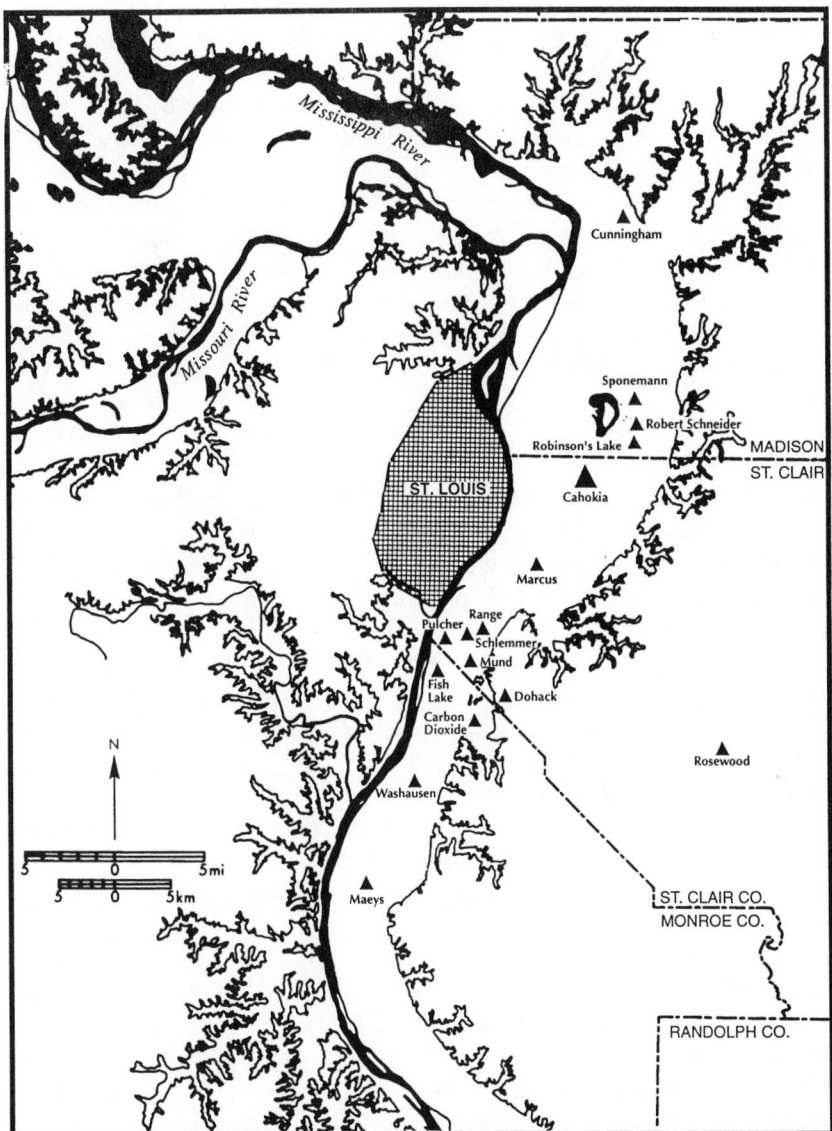

Figure 6. Location of Post-A.D. 400 Sites Mentioned in the Text

Kelly et al. 1984). This large, only partially excavated occupation is located in the uplands and consists of multiple structures and pits arranged in no discernible plan. Whether such sites served as central bases for smaller task groups is not known. At the end of the Rosewood phase and during the Mund phase, additional large village sites such as Cunningham (Meinkoth et al. 1996) and Mund (Fortier et al. 1983) have been identified in bluff base contexts. They indicate that a relatively sedentary settlement system was emerging in the area.

A pattern of increased sedentism was established at the very beginning of the Rosewood phase and was based on a combination of subsistence-related factors, the most important of which were intensification in the use of cultivated plants and transformations in food processing technology, associated with *en masse* fish capture and processing techniques. Archaeological faunal assemblages from early Late Woodland occupations are dominated by fish remains, often concentrated in the fills of pits referred to as earth ovens—indirect heating facilities not previously observed in the archaeological record of this area. Typically, after the excavation of a deep, cylindrical pit, a bed of hot limestone rocks was laid at the base. Meat foods, perhaps covered with plants, were placed over the limestone and covered with thatch. Water was then thrown over the thatch, which was immediately covered with soil, thus sealing the steaming meat below. The narrow confines of the pit helped to capture and hold the heat. Once this indirect cooking process had been completed, the food was removed and, often, soil and/or refuse (including the fish bones) was thrown back into the pit fill. Sometimes a secondary bed of limestone was added above this mixed soil/refuse zone and the cooking process was repeated in the same pit. Occasionally, the sides and bases of pits were lined with thatch prior to the addition of the hot rocks. Archaeologically, the use of thatch or other plants as liners is evidenced by thin, black, greasy-textured zones or by preserved thatch itself (Fortier et al. 1983:120-124, Bentz et al. 1988). In many cases, numerous burned pieces of clay or silt occur in these pits, suggesting that pits may sometimes have been clay-lined, as well.

While the technique of processing large quantities of meat was a significant new contribution to the Late Woodland subsistence system, drying or smoking techniques, allowing the preservation of such foodstuffs, must have been utilized. The appearance of deep, bell-shaped pits at this time represents the only indirect evidence for on-site storage. Similar-shaped storage or cache pits have been documented ethnohistorically for Plains Indians (Wilson 1917), although in those cases only plants were stored in such facilities. Swanton (1946:372-381) describes a number of techniques used by groups in the Historic Southeast to dry and preserve meat, including means to process and preserve large fish captures. Unfortunately, virtually all of the techniques he discusses would produce no direct archaeological evidence. The innovation in *en masse* food processing technology must have represented a significant breakthrough for horticulturally-based groups not wanting to leave particular localities. This is not to say that deer hunts were discontinued or that other kinds of fauna were not procured. It simply meant that certain foodstuffs, such as fish, not normally available or storable during the lean periods of winter and early spring, could now be stored and utilized over a longer period of time.

We do not have many complete community plans from this early Late Woodland period. Most sites are bluff-edge task areas or extractive loci, consisting of dispersed scatters of clustered pits, often with one or more earth ovens and a variety of shallow cooking pits or hearths. Larger communities, such as Mund and Cunningham, appear to be arranged linearly along high points in alluvial fans. At Cunningham, a series of small houses are oriented along a creek extending out from the bluffs on the fan (Meinkoth et al. 1996). Pits are either clustered near the houses or occur 50-100m away from them in distinct clusters. No open community areas are identifiable. At Mund, the community appears to have been laid out perpendicular to the fan but also near a creek (Fortier et al. 1983). In this case, however, at least two open mini-courtyard areas, around which occur a series of pits, were identified. Such open areas may represent community areas, but the settlement plan as a whole was not centric.

Intensification in cultivated plant use cannot be underestimated in terms of its contribution to settlement and subsistence stability throughout this incipient Late Woodland period. While plant use diversity and the use of cultivars had appeared earlier, during the Middle Woodland Holding phase, diverse plant procurement patterns are not typically represented at every site at that time. During the early Late Woodland period, in contrast, cultivated plants are not only present at every site, but often occur in distinct masses and usually dominate the plant use spectrum. It is important to note that maize was not yet a major component of plant use systems in this area, despite its appearance in the Middle Woodland period. Maize remains, in fact, consist of only three minuscule glume and cupule fragments from three features at the Mund site (Johannessen 1983:312) and one cupule and three possible kernel fragments from a single feature at the Cunningham site (Parker 1996:184). Maize remains have not yet been identified at any of the smaller extractive loci from this period. In short, a strong argument can be made that, in the American Bottom, sedentism during the early Late Woodland period was not based on a horticultural or economic system utilizing maize.

Early Late Woodland artifact inventories reflect an increasing focus on local resource acquisition and local adaptation to an increasingly sedentary way of life. Ceramic vessels are simple in form and are repeated over and over again in assemblages. Undecorated cordmarked jars are the dominate vessel form. Some of the larger versions may have been storage jars, perhaps for cultivated seeds and other plant remains. Smaller, incurving, restricted-orifice vessels may have been used for cooking, since burned food residues commonly occur around the upper rims. Curiously, bowls are absent in ceramic assemblages from this period.

The lithic assemblages are even more nondescript, consisting of numerous nonformal, expedient tool types, almost always made on low-quality local cherts. Hafted bifaces are represented by crude, thick fish-tail types (Mund/Schild Types) and a few stemmed types such as Steuben and Lowe Flared (Fortier et al. 1983:252-259). The manufacturing technology appears crude and almost haphazard, and no genetic affiliation can be made between these types and the kinds of well-made hafted bifaces of the preceding Middle Woodland period.

A new artifact type, limestone spade, appears late in this period; it is an artifactual signifier of the emergent horticultural economy. These crudely-made spades bear no resemblance to the better-made chert hoes of the Middle Woodland period, knowledge of which must have been lost or modified during the Middle/Late Woodland transition. Late Woodland limestone spades are elongate and rarely display polish or evidence of hafting but, given the silica polish on some, their use as gardening tools is undeniable.

In the past, it was fashionable to regard this post-Middle Woodland period as a somewhat bland dark age, i.e., "the Good Gray Cultures" (S. Williams 1954), a characterization which masks the fact that a fundamental economic transformation was taking place in some areas that set the stage for an eventual reconfiguration of social and economic organization. It was a period during which populations moved into selected niches in upland and bluff base localities and over time became entrenched, particularly in environments capable of supporting long-term horticultural activity and ones that had ready access to the aquatic resources of the floodplain. We can observe the development of major villages along bluff base environments and particularly on recently formed alluvial and colluvial fans. These locations may have been beneficial because of their proximity to creeks and their position above the paludal environs of the floodplain. It is further possible that the disturbed soils of recently formed fans, such as those at Mund and Cunningham, created an ideal environment for wild stands of potentially cultivable, weedy seed plants. The resulting settlement stability and concomitant population increase over the following centuries are the most significant contributions of this period to the formation of an American Bottom cultural identity.

THE SECOND ECONOMIC
TRANSFORMATION, A.D. 650-850

The Late Woodland period is often regarded as a period of cultural conservatism in the Midwest, a time when people ate well enough but accomplished little of substantial value, especially in terms of advances in material culture. In the American Bottom, after A.D. 650, however, there were actually a number of fundamental technological innovations that contributed to even further entrenchment and stabilization of the residential population (Figure 7). Interestingly enough, none of these changes involved maize agriculture. Innovations during this period, referred to as the Patrick phase, include: the bow and arrow; small but substantial, single-nuclear-family semi-subterranean dwellings; more nucleated community plans with large community structures; ceremonial items such as discoidals and effigy pipes; and an exponential increase in the number of pottery forms, vessel size ranges, and vessel counts in site assemblages. Another primary com-

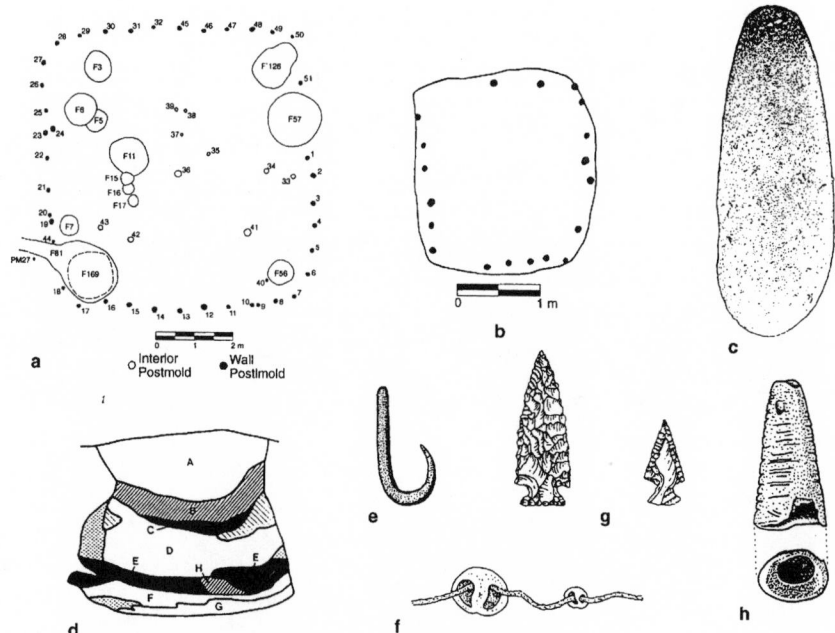

Figure 7. Late Woodland Innovations: a, Community Structure;
b, Household Sleeper; c, Limestone Hoe; d, Earth Oven
(in profile); e, Bone Fishhook; f, *Anculosa* Shell Bead;
g, Arrow Points; h, Cup and Pin Gaming Piece

ponent of this so-called second economic transformation is the expansion of major population aggregates into virtually every niche of the floodplain, as well as uplands. Remarkably, this period of settlement dispersal marks the first permanent occupation of the floodplain since the late Middle Woodland period three centuries before.

The impetus for moving out into the lowlying Mississippi River floodplain at this time is not well understood, but it was probably precipitated by a combination of factors, including an amelioration of aquatic conditions in the floodplain, increasing population along the bluff base, and a concomitant need to expand the food resource base. This was probably not an overnight process, but one that extended over the entire Patrick phase and following Emergent Mississippian period (ca. A.D. 850-1050). Expansion into major and minor upland drainages also occurred at the same time. If the large number of new sites—approximately a hundred-fold increase over the previous Rosewood phase and Mund phase—is any indication, population density in this area must have risen rather dramatically.

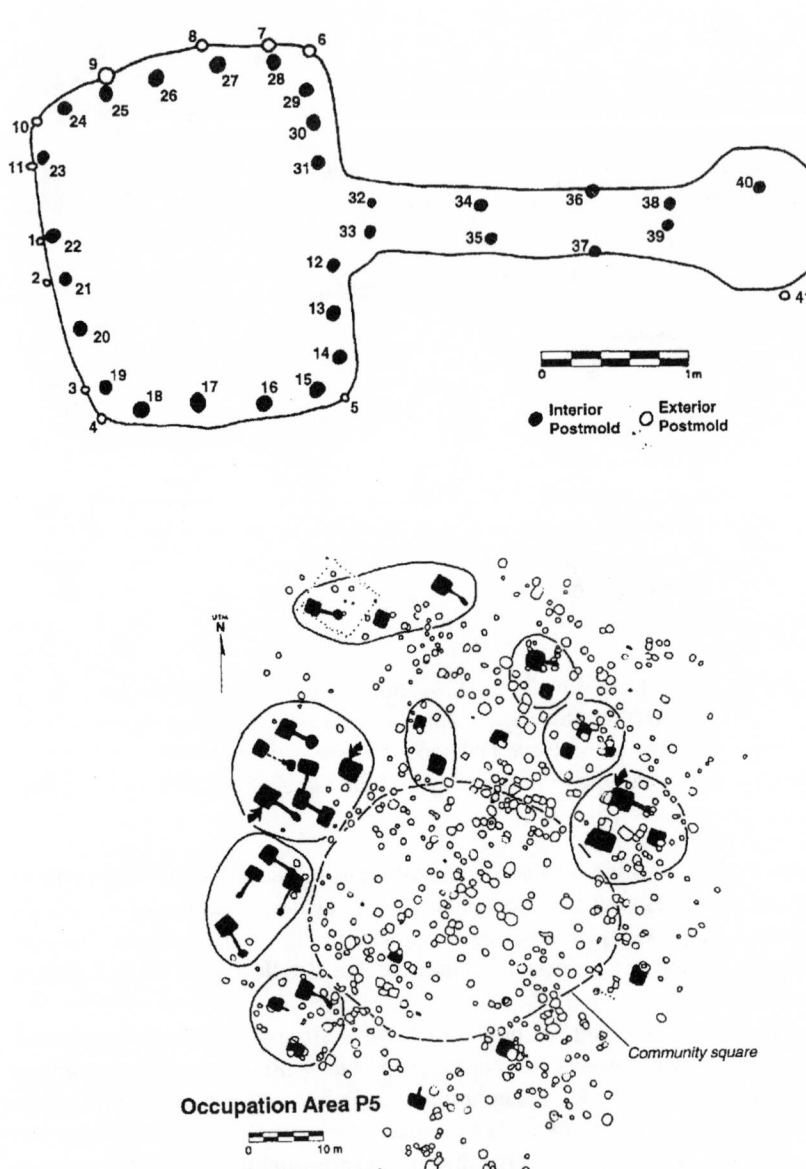

Figure 8. Patrick Phase Courtyard Village from the Range Site (lower) and Keyhole Structure from the Fish Lake Site (upper)

The organization of communities is still not very well known, but settlement configurations were becoming more complex and better organized. At some sites, such as Range (Kelly et al. 1987), three distinct structure types have been identified, including small, rectilinear basin sleeping facilities, specialized keyhole structures (which may represent some kind of winter sleeper; see Fortier et al. 1984b:80-81), and large, square-post structures, which may represent community gathering points. The Fish Lake site (Fortier et al. 1984b) also yielded keyhole structures and one large community structure.

The term keyhole structure was first defined in Illinois by Binford et al. (1970) at the Hatchery West site. Similar structures had previously been identified by Dragoo (1955) in Pennsylvania and described as "ping-pong paddle" or "turtle" structures (Smith 1974, 1976). In the American Bottom, they have been identified at the Sponemann (Fortier 1991:80-90), Wilderman (Wolforth 1989:14-18), Samson (Douglas K. Jackson, pers. comm., 1997), and Duggan (Brad Koldehoff, pers. comm., 1997) sites. Keyhole structures generally include a small, rectilinear basin with interior wall posts, a narrow ramp extending out from one wall, and a shallow pit located at the end of the ramp. They appear to have functioned as specialized winter sleepers, with the ramps serving as heat ducts (Fortier1991:89-90).

Although most Late Woodland Patrick villages appear to be laid out linearally, paralleling old meander banks or bluff top ridges, Kelly et al. (1987:211-216) have identified one circular community plan at Range, the center of which is marked by a central post (Figure 8). The occurrence of community structures and planned villages at this time represents a significant new trend toward increased social integration.

Small, semi-subterranian sleeper dwellings are a hallmark of the Patrick phase, although the use of small-post structures is not new in this area. They date back to the Archaic period (Fortier 1993). Most of these earlier structures have irregular or nonpredictable dimensions, and some of these have small basins. Patrick phase structures, on the other hand, are systematically rectilinear and have remarkably small floor areas, never exceeding 4-6 sq m. The wall post orientations and the absence of interior support posts suggest that roofs consisted of small, arched poles tied at the center and possibly covered with bark, rush mats, or hides. The living areas do not contain hearths or any other interior features, nor is there usually any artifactual evidence of activity. Large, sub-conoidal, cordmarked storage and cooking vessels, which typify this phase, are recovered almost exclusively from pits located outside of these structures. Given the small floor areas and angled nature of the walls, the existence of interior platforms or roof storage is improbable. These units appear to have functioned primarily as family sleepers.

Household activities, including food storage, must have been conducted almost exclusively outside of these facilities. Since we find so little artifactual debris in these dwellings, they may also have been cleaned on a regular basis. At the Range site, Kelly et al. (1987:213-216) has observed that deep storage and processing pits appear to be paired or clustered along the edges of central community areas

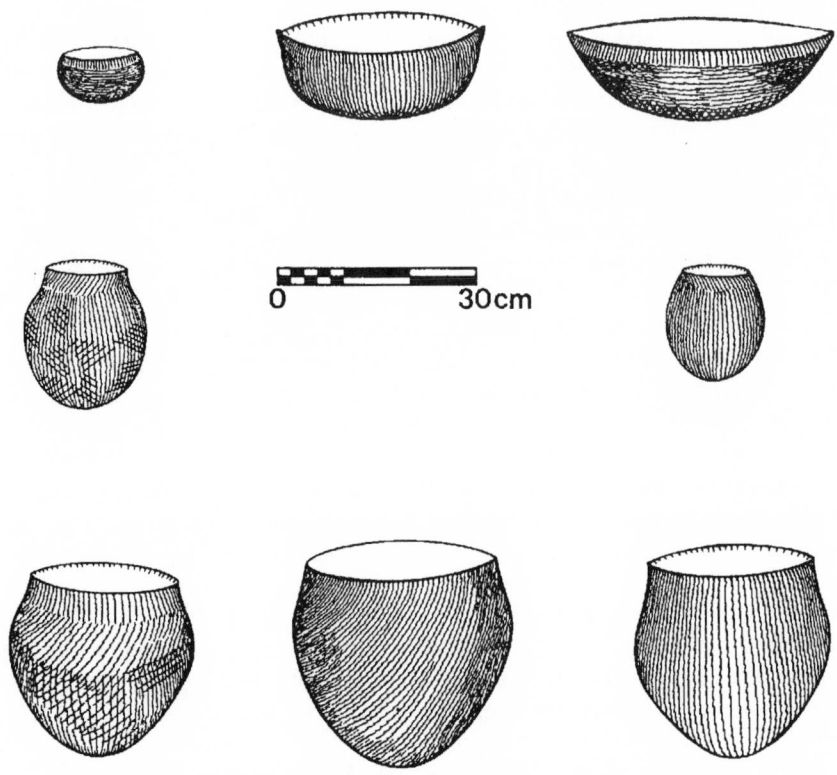

Figure 9. Patrick Phase Bowls (upper),
Cooking Vessels (middle), and Storage Jars (lower)

and are usually associated with specific structure groups. In addition, they argue that similar activities may have been centered in large, square-post structures, which they regard as community facilities. The organization of activities in specified areas within the community and outside the physical limits of individual households argues for a corporate village economy. If there were any high-status individuals controlling storage or distribution, their existence is archaeologically invisible. Of course, documenting storage, especially of perishable foods and goods, is rarely possible in archaeological contexts, and the possible existence of off-site storage, or centralized storage at other settlements, limits interpretation of how such corporate or household economies might have operated.

Subsistence systems were also probably becoming more complex during the Patrick phase. Large, constricted-orifice storage jars, usually measuring 30-50 cm in height, increase in numbers for the first time, as do serving vessels such as bowls. Cooking vessels, normally 20-30 cm in height, vary in shape and capacity and reflect a wide diversity in cooking practices. Kelly et al. (1987:258-277) have identified at least six jar types at the Range site, four of which do not appear in the preceding Mund phase (Figure 9). In general, the quantity of plant and animal remains rises sharply. Large cultivated seed masses in pits occur more frequently, suggesting that husbandry and procurement systems were becoming more productive than in preceding centuries. There is also a continued focus on fish, supplemented by other aquatic and avian fauna. Venison usage remained constant and contributed a significant amount of protein and fat to the diet. There is evidence for some maize use, but this plant apparently did not contribute much to the subsistence system.

For the most part, Patrick phase lithic assemblages continue to follow a typical Late Woodland pattern, that is, a reliance on small, expedient, nonformal tools made from locally procured cherts. One fundamental change occurred in the lithic format, however, and this was the appearance of small, unifacial flake arrow points. The emergence of the bow and arrow occurred almost simultaneously throughout the Eastern Woodlands at this time. A number of formal types appear in the American Bottom, such as Koster, Wanda, and Roxanda, that have no counterparts in the previous Mund and Rosewood phases. Many of these points are poorly made, asymmetrical, and curved in profile. Some exhibit end and lateral edge wear, which may indicate their use as hafted drills or perforators rather than as arrow points.

The effect of bow and arrow technology on Late Woodland economy and society in general is unclear. The bow and arrow may have increased hunting efficiency, but if this occurred, it is not reflected in the subsistence record. For example, no *extraordinary* increase in deer or any other mammalian or avian faunal remains at sites is documented at this time. Schott (1993:425-438) has also questioned the economic importance of the bow and arrow. He has argued that we should not necessarily assume that arrow technology was more efficient than dart or spear technology and that all of these means of hunting should be regarded as complementary. Others (Wray & McNeish 1961:67-68) have argued that arrow points signal the onset of armed strife or warfare in the Midwest, but this is also not directly observable in the archaeological record of the American Bottom. One could also argue that the technical means for carrying on such conflict had previously existed in the form of atalatls, hafted stone knives, celts, axes, or bone and wood spears.

There is, of course, some evidence that arrow points were systematically shot at human beings elsewhere in the state, as indicated by occasional projectiles found embedded in human remains in various mortuary contexts in the Illinois River valley (e.g., Koster Mound 7, Burial 11; Koster Knoll H, Burial 1, Koster Mound 6, Burial 14; Koster Mound 3, Burials 14 and 10; possibly Burials 9 and 12; Koster Mound 1, Burial 13) (Perino 1973: 141-206). With increasing population and emerging competition over decreasing land and/or potential food resources, perhaps it is not surprising that more and more evidence for conflict appears in the

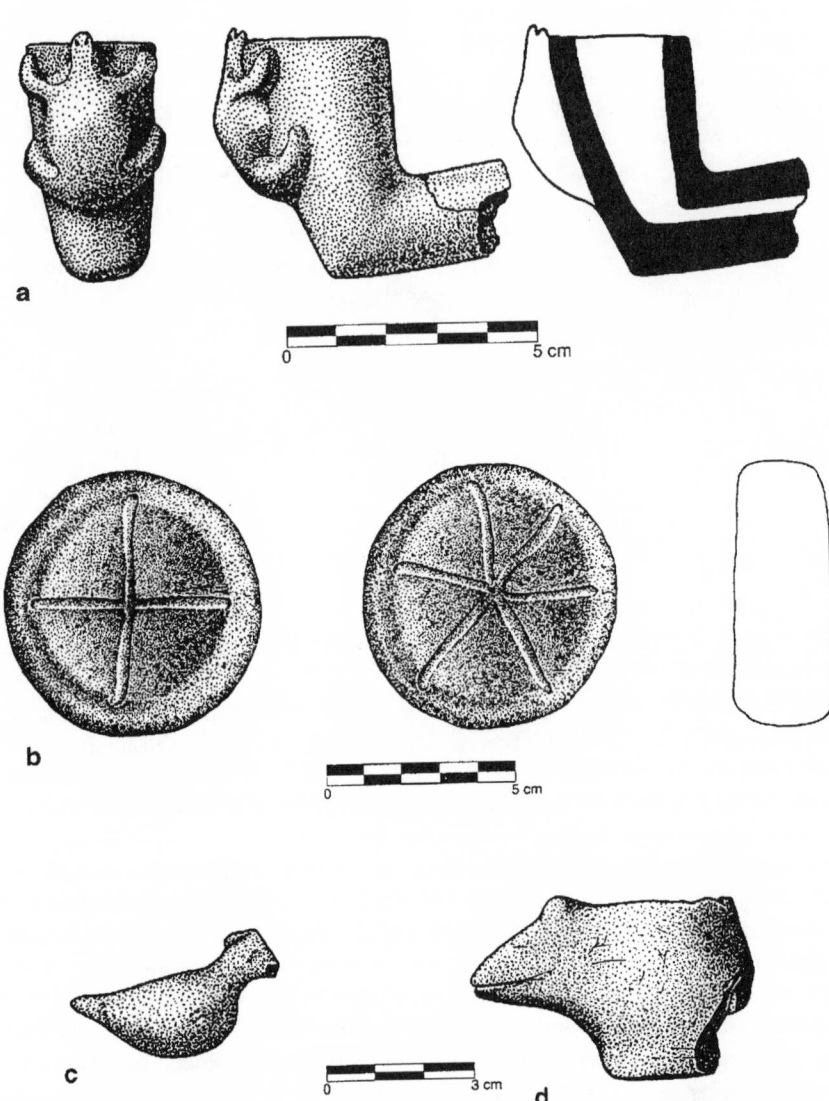

Figure 10. Ceremonially Significant Artifacts, A.D. 650-850: a, Ceramic Turtle Effigy Pipe from the Fish Lake Site; b, Clay Discoidal with Cross and Sunburst Design from the Dohack Site; c, Ceramic Bird Effigy from the Range Site; d, Siltstone Frog Effigy Pipe from the Range Site

archaeological record in the Midwest after A.D. 650. Evidence for such conflict is lacking in the American Bottom, probably because so few burial mounds and associated skeletal material have been excavated from this period. Such strife, if it existed in this area, may have been relatively restricted or incidental, however, since there is no evidence that people in the American Bottom made any attempt to fortify villages, hoard goods, or otherwise take defensive measures for broader-scale conflicts.

Evidence for ceremonial activity at this time comes in the form of ceramic and stone discoidals, clay discs, effigy pipes, and other specially worked clay or stone artifacts (Figure 10). At the Range site, Kelly et al. (1987:423) noted a close correlation between Patrick phase discoidals and the large, square community structures, and they suggested that this association made a possible case for community ceremonialism or interaction between communities, since discoidals (chunky stones) historically were often used as a form of intercommunity competition and recreation (Swanton 1946, Culin 1907, DeBoer 1993). Chunk yards and chunky stones were widely regarded in the Southeast as sacred community property (Swanton 1946:682-684), and chunky contests as well as various ball games were conducted between communities during renewal festivals such as the Green Corn Ceremonial. The gambling that took place during these intercommunity competitions was apparently mostly recreational but, in some instances, particularly during ball games, the contests resulted in the redistribution of a considerable amount of private property (Vennum1994:103-117).

A small but significant number of discoidals and pipes associated with the large community structures are decorated, including discoidals with cross and sunburst designs, a turtle effigy pipe from the Fish Lake site (Fortier et al. 1984b:123-125), and a frog effigy pipe from the Range site (Kelly et al. 1987:336). The cross and sun circle motifs historically are, according to Howard (Howard 1968:19) and Waring (1968), the most commonly utilized motifs in the Southeastern Ceremonial Complex. The cross is thought to be associated with the concept of the sacred fire that occupies the center of the universe, its crossed embers representing the four directions of the universe. The sunburst symbol is the fire itself, which is also the sun. Frogs and turtles are land-water creatures that are often associated with creation myths and renewal ceremonies.

Courtyard communities and structural diversity within settlements (large community structures, sleepers, and keyholes), innovations in ceramic and food processing/storage technology, increasing subsistence diversity, and the existence of ceremonial/recreational artifacts associated with possible public facilities are hallmarks of the Patrick phase in this area. This constellation of traits has not been documented anywhere else in the Midwest. For the first time, we can observe, archaeologically, population growth and cultural adaptations in this area that are not derived from outside incursions. It is from this point that we can also define a relatively stable American Bottom cultural identity and begin to document some of the processes leading up to the development of increasingly more complex socioeconomic formations by A.D. 1050.

EMERGENT MISSISSIPPIAN
CORN CULTURE, A.D. 850-1050

Although the use of maize has been documented prior to A.D. 850 (corrected) in the American Bottom, it is not highly visible in the archaeological record until after that period. It is also true that less than 0.1 percent of several thousand pit features from the Patrick phase have been examined for archaeobotanical remains. Regarding the two largest Patrick phase villages in the floodplain, a sample of only 40 of the 1,872 features at the Range site were analyzed (Kelly et al. 1987:406), and only 13 of 147 features were examined at the Fish Lake site (Fortier et al.1984b:190). Maize was not identified at Fish Lake, and only a few fragments were recovered from the Range site. In this light, the idea of a sudden explosion of maize remains at A.D. 850 probably needs to be tempered somewhat, at least until better sampling methods are employed at pre-A.D. 850 sites in this area. On the other hand, while only 5 percent of the nearly 850 Emergent Mississippian Dohack phase features at the Range site were analyzed for floral remains, over 70 percent of those analyzed yielded maize (Whalley 1990:279). Similar ubiquity is observed at virtually every Emergent Mississippian site dating to this period (Johannessen 1985b:259-265). At the Sponemann site, where a much larger sample of feature fills were examined, maize incidence reached 34 percent (Parker 1991:416). Although sampling problems at earlier sites need to be resolved, it is also clear that, after A.D. 850 (corrected), maize can no longer be regarded as an insignificant or experimental crop.

The initial impact of maize on village life is barely perceptible from an archaeological standpoint. Many of the ceramic traits that distinguish the preceding Patrick phase from either the Emergent Mississippian Sponemann or the Dohack phase are not directly correlated with the presence of maize. Structures are morphologically similar, the general subsistence pattern is not appreciably altered, discoidals and pipes are virtually identical to those of the Patrick phase, and there are no substantial changes in the lithic assemblage, with one exception. At the Range site, polished Mill Creek hoe fragments appear for the first time. The appearance of these hoe fragments signals the first use of chert hoes since the Middle Woodland period, but more importantly, Mill Creek is a Southern Illinois-derived chert. This is the first evidence during this period that American Bottom people were beginning to interact and perhaps form exchange relations with the outside world. Another artifact type probably correlated with increased maize use is the shell hoe, a gardening tool that is prominent at larger sites such as Range (Kelly 1990:262).

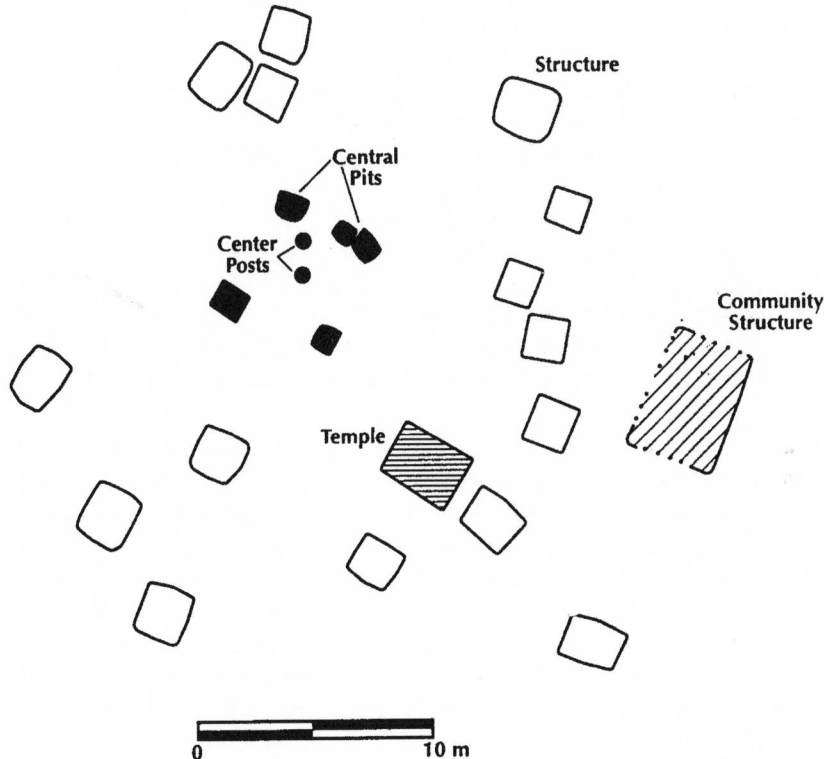

Figure 11. Emergent Mississippian Courtyard Village at the Range Site

A possible relationship between emergent maize agriculture and decreased numbers of deer remains at some Dohack phase (A.D. 800-850) sites such as Range (Kelly 1990:263-264) has been proposed, although it is unclear why such an association should occur. Also, we should note that this relationship has not been observed at all maize-bearing sites of this period. For example, at the Sponemann site, where over 30 percent of the features yielded maize, deer remains comprise the most significant percentage of procured fauna (L. Kelly 1991:425). This is also true of the Dohack site (Cross 1985:283), where deer remains are predominant (Cross 1985:283). It is clear that maize did not replace large mammals or any other major sources of protein; nor is there any evidence that increased agricultural activity had any deleterious effect on the deer population of the American Bottom. Of course, human population levels in the floodplain were steadily increasingly, so the demand for venison may have been greater, particularly at the larger village sites. Competition between villages for larger mammals may have correspondingly increased, perhaps resulting in hunting expeditions that were probably better organized and corporately scheduled. Quite possibly, hunting territories were becoming more and more defined in the floodplain as well as the surrounding uplands, a factor which may have been a primary source of strife between groups, or alternatively, a stimulus for cooperative alliances.

After A.D. 850, community plans increase in complexity as well as diversity. Smaller communities such as Robinson's Lake, Schlemmer, Robert Schneider, and Marcus consist of only a few household structures and associated pit clusters (Milner 1984, Berres 1984, Fortier1985b, Emerson & Jackson 1987). How these smaller occupations were integrated with the larger village sites is unknown. Perhaps they represent seasonally-oriented, caretaker types of occupations, situated near designated agricultural fields that were associated with specific villages or segments of a village. In this sense, they may represent a prototype of the ubiquitous single-family farmstead of the Mississippian period.

The best example of increasing community complexity during the Emergent Mississippian period is the Range site, a large, multiple occupation community which persisted and steadily grew throughout the Emergent Mississippian period (Kelly1990:87-110). The more dispersed, linear village plans of the preceding Patrick phase are replaced by plans consisting of a ring of structures enclosing a courtyard or plaza area, the center of which is marked by four pits arranged in a rectilinear pattern, with a center post placed in the middle (Figure 11). The pits may have been cleaned out from time to time and the post replaced periodically, perhaps indicating that renewal ceremonies such as the Green Corn Ceremonial or busk may have been initiated at this time (Howard 1968, Witthoft 1949). The association of maize and the busk is, of course, significant but the existence of harvest celebrations such as the busk probably predate heavy use of maize. Nevertheless, because of its higher yield and eventual importance as a staple, and because of the year-round care that is required to bring about a successful harvest, maize probably intensified the importance of what might be called the harvest or busk cycle (Howard 1968). Year-round management of maize would have included the storage of seeds during the winter, preliminary germination during the spring, spring planting, protection of the crop from animals during the spring and summer, the fall harvest, and the selection of seeds for the following year.

Kelly (1990) has specifically argued for the existence of busk ceremonialism at Range at this time, and he associates this phenomenon with the use of maize. He also points to the centrally located community pits and center posts as a kind of early circle and cross motif associated with harvest ceremonialism. It should be pointed out that, in historic times, the busk or Green Corn Ceremonial was not a single event but a year-long series of ritual events, closely associated with: (1) the preparation of fields and planting of maize in the spring, (2) the monitoring of the crop throughout the spring and summer, including special celebrations centered around the formation of cobs and the eating of green corn, (3) the fall harvest of mature maize, and (4) storage of the crop and seeds over the winter. Almost all social activities were scheduled according to this yearly cycle (Swanton 1928:473-672, Witthoft 1949, S. Williams 1977:51-64).

With the exception of the large, square-post structures, floor area size differentiation during the Patrick phase shows little variability. However, post-A.D. 850 dwellings vary considerably in size, leading Kelly et al. (1990:285) to postulate that social ranking (by wealth?) within communities may have emerged at this time. They suggest that some of these larger structures, which they believe functioned as family households, may have housed community leaders, although there is little in the way of artifactual data in these houses to indicate wealth differentiation. There are also larger community structures, located in the plaza area or sometimes around the ring, containing large, centralized interior hearths. Kelly et al. (1990:289-296) postulate that some of these structures may have served as early temples, or places in which special community ceremonies were conducted. The concept of keeping an eternal fire is an important aspect of the busk cycle. Kelly regards the use of such structures and the central courtyard as a precursor to the Mississippian temple mound concept.

Interaction with areas outside of the American Bottom, as mentioned above, was relatively minimal and mostly restricted to pre-manufactured chert hoes. There is also evidence for outside exchange in the form of a few copper pendants and Anculosa shell beads from the lower Ohio River valley. Some kind of exchange system may also have existed within the American Bottom. The occurrence of northern Madison County shale paste ceramics at southern and central American Bottom sites and of imported limestone-tempered Pulcher ceramics at northern American Bottom sites speaks for some interaction in the area, perhaps involving commodities carried in those vessels. Red Ste. Genevieve cherts derived from southern American Bottom sources also appear at sites in the north. High-quality Crescent Hills quarry cherts appear throughout the American Bottom and assume dominance by the end of this period (Kelly 1984, Ives 1984). During the Mississippian period, access to such cherts may have been regulated by elites. It is interesting, however, that these cherts were preferred throughout this region nearly 200 years prior to Cahokia's hegemony. This fact would indicate that some kind of distribution system involving chert raw material or, possibly, the completed hoes themselves, was already present by A.D. 850, and certainly by A.D. 900 (Brown et al. 1990:265-270). Such a distribution system may not have involved a controlling authority at first, as the quarry area may have been regarded as common ground but, as elite polities emerged at the end of this period, this situation apparently changed.

To summarize, the Emergent Mississippian period from A.D. 850 to1050 is a time of increasing social integration and growing centralization. At some of the larger sites, there is some indication of social ranking and perhaps the emergence of elites or, at least, of special-interest segments within the community. Some of these segments may have been associated with scheduling the planting/harvest cycle and related social activities. Of course, pre-maize human-plant associations extend far back into the past and may well have included harvest ceremonialism. The emergence of maize as a primary crop, however, appears to have intensified this older plant relationship. Knowledge about when to plant, about curation of seeds over the winter, about above- and below-ground storage, and about the use of lime in processing created a kind of maize culture. The Green Corn Ceremonial cycle, or ritual behavior closely related to it, appears to have developed during the early Emergent Mississippian period in this area, and with it, persons charged with creating, scheduling, and regulating all of the rituals and ceremonies pertinent to maintaining this cycle. Artifacts such as decorated disks and discoidals, pipes, and effigies in ritually significant contexts persist at sites such as Range throughout this period. Some of these artifacts display symbols that anticipate or duplicate design elements associated with post-A.D. 1050 Mississippian period and Southeastern Ceremonial Complex iconography.

Another important trend of the Emergent Mississippian period is an increase in storage facilities. By the end of the period, some communities even possess granaries (Fortier 1996). There is no doubt that such facilities were developed primarily to accommodate maize harvests, but other plant remains are found, as well. It is during this period that we can observe increases in both house size and interior household activity. Dwellings contain interior cooking and storage pits, hearths, and floor-level debris, such as ceramic vessels and stone tools, that are suggestive of activities actually conducted within households. There is a significant decline in the structure to non-structure feature ratio at sites such as Range (Kelly et al. 1990:377, 381, 384), which compliments the pattern of increasing interior household activity. The meaning of this trend is not entirely clear, nor is its relationship, if any, with maize use or harvest ceremonialism. As I pointed out earlier, there is no archaeological evidence in households for wealth differentiation or any indication of hoarding. This is a matter of speculation, but it may represent some kind of archaeologically undetectable shift in social organization, perhaps pertaining to expanding living arrangements or kin relationships. The Emergent Mississippian period is clearly a period of population growth in the American Bottom, as evidenced by a significant increase in settlements, so perhaps what we are seeing is individual households adapting to growing village sizes and associated constraints on land availability.

Mound building activities may have been initiated at the end of the pre-Mississippian period, perhaps at such sites as Pulcher and probably at Cahokia. Such places no doubt were major village centers initially but gradually assumed more and more importance during this period, emerging eventually as regional redistribution centers, seats of religious authority and ceremonialism, and focal points of political decision making. Temple mounds at such centers replaced the smaller, less impressive village community buildings.

Populations literally implode into these centers at the end of this period, as many of the larger villages and isolated households are apparently abandoned. These same people would have supplied the labor necessary to construct the large earthen mounds at such centers. This rapid consolidation of population and expansion of villages into multiple-community town centers is a remarkable event about which we still know very little. Were people conscripted or did they willingly volunteer, as medieval European communities did during the construction of great city churches? These are questions for which we cannot derive ready answers from the archaeological record. The subsequent development of a regional center at Cahokia, the emergence of ranked and stratified elites, the development of an interregional exchange system (Kelly 1991b:65-92, Brown et al. 1990, Hirth 1984), and possible craft specialization are subjects beyond the scope of this paper (see, Emerson 1995, Pauketat 1991, 1994).

CONCLUSIONS

I have argued in this essay that the prehistoric cultural trajectory in the American Bottom from 3000 B.C. to A.D. 1050 can be subdivided into two distinct segments. The first segment covers a period of approximately 3,500 years and is characterized by a pattern of cyclical population incursions and displacements. Compared to the adjacent Illinois River valley, the American Bottom is unique in this regard. To a large extent, the ebb and flow of populations through the American Bottom is due to its unique physiographic position at the confluence of three major rivers, as well as to the periodic hydrological instability created by the merging of these rivers at this point. This situation made the American Bottom an attractive location because of its abundant aquatic resources. Although population aggregates emerge, for this reason, at various times in this area, a long-term, multi-phase residential continuum is rarely evidenced in the archaeological record. The repeated stylistic and technological transformations of entire assemblages, often corresponding to shifts in settlement organization and location, argue against an evolutionary model of cultural development for this segment in the American Bottom.

The second segment covers a period of 650 years, from A.D. 400 to A.D. 1050. It is during this segment that we can observe a sequential process of cultural development in the American Bottom and, as I have argued, the emergence of an identifiable American Bottom resident population and trajectory. This is not to say that changes in settlement patterning, technology, or subsistence were any less dramatic than during the preceding segment of prehistory, or that the area no longer encountered influences—people or ideas—from outside the area. If anything, changes appear to accelerate as one approaches the A.D. 1050 Mississippian marker. The difference between this period and the previous segment is that changes are now *mostly* brought about by an American Bottom population.

The gradual emergence of a residential population in this area was largely based on a trend toward increasing cultivated plant use and the development of new food processing practices that allowed for a substantial increase in year-round protein consumption. As a result, population levels increased dramatically, and virtually every environmental niche in the floodplain and adjacent uplands evidenced some kind of long-term, cyclical occupation record, i.e., a cycle of occupation, abandonment, and reoccupation. The sizes of some villages expanded, especially after A.D. 650, and settlement organizational themes became more complex. In the floodplain, such villages emerged along the highest points of elevation, such as talus slopes, certain prominent meander scar banks, and unique features such as the Lunsford-Pulcher Terrace in the central portion of the American Bottom. Presumably, these locations provided protection for settlements and crops from periodic flooding from the Mississippi River.

The processes leading to centralization and increasing social integration, the results of which are clearly visible in the archaeological record only after A.D. 1050, are initiated during this A.D. 400-1050 period and involve a number of broad themes or economic processes. Economy is generally defined here as an embedded interrelationship consisting of various technological, social, subsistence and, sometimes, cosmologically operative segments of society, which are often indistinguishable one from another (Herskovits 1952, Nash 1966). The reader is directed to Halperin (1994) for a much more sophisticated view of economy, one which borrows heavily from Polanyi's (1957) "generic model of economy." As Halperin (1994:55-63) has aptly pointed out, Polanyi's (1957) distinction between locational ("changes of place") and appropriational ("changes of hands") movements, as instituted economic processes, affords an encompassing and dynamic model of economy, and one which focuses not only on the physical movement of goods or people (locational) but also on the decision making processes involved in such movement (appropriational). The Marxist differentiation between the forces of production and relations of production is nearly identical (Chesnokov 1969:72-92). In a Native American cultural format, the position in space and the transfer of gambled goods at a lacrosse or chunkey game would be an example of locational process or of the forces of production; the decision, which may be instituted, or corporate, as to when or where to hold the games, the establishment of rules, the setting of a value on goods, and the transfer of rights to winners or losers would be an appropriational process, or equivalent in Marxist terms to the relations of production. In my simpler definition of economy, operative segments of economy would be nearly equivalent to Polanyi's appropriational movements.

Locational and appropriational movements as well as associated general economic processes, such as production, distribution, storage, and consumption, may be discernable throughout prehistory in the American Bottom (Dalton 1968, 1977; Hodder 1979, Halperin 1994). The hypothetical Hopewellian *fandangos*, for example, certainly would have involved both appropriational and locational movements. Locational aspects are clearly represented by the trafficking of exotic goods. Appropriational aspects of fandangos can only be conjectured, but they must have underlain the symbolic systems of communication that Seeman (1995) has proposed.

I propose that the most important economic process operating in the American Bottom after A.D. 650 involved the concept of renewal. This process manifests itself on the archaeological landscape in a number of ways and becomes more and more visible through time. The effects of renewal concepts can be seen initially during the Patrick phase and early Emergent Mississippian period in the repositioning and cyclical restoration of community center posts, pits, and special structures, and the reconditioning of hearths in possible temple structures; and later, during the early Mississippian period—in addition to these renewal events—in cyclical mound construction episodes (Pauketat 1991), Green Corn Ceremonial loci (Fortier 1992:340-348), and sun watch complexes (Wittry 1969, Sherrod & Rolingson 1987:85-128). The center post and four pit configurations set within central plazas at the Range site, and the presence within the same contexts of discoidals with cross and sunburst symbols, are analogous to renewal icons found throughout the historic and prehistoric Eastern Woodlands (Howard 1964).

Historically, morning star rituals, mourning/adoption ceremonialism, ball games celebrating creation myths, and Green Corn or harvest cycles are significant aspects of the renewal process (Hall 1987, 1997). All of the constituent processes of an economy, i.e., production, distribution, storage, and consumption, can be found in Eastern Woodlands renewal ceremonials. Many social and intercommunity gatherings were scheduled in accordance with these ceremonials. Ball and chunkey games in the historic Southeast were often scheduled during the harvest period, a time when the redistribution of goods or the discard of "old" properties signaled the beginning of the new year (Vennum 1994, Howard 1968). In this sense, the chunkey game and ball games such as lacrosse not only functioned to cement or renew social relations, but served as a form of economic leveling mechanism, not unlike the potlatch on the Northwest coast (Dalton 1977:204-207), the horse and goods give-aways among the Plains Indians (Weist 1973), the Great Basin *fandangos* (Steward 1938), and the busk feasts of Eastern Woodlands groups (Witthoft 1949). As Nash (1966:35-36) pointed out, "Most small-scale economies have a way of scrambling wealth to inhibit reinvestment in technical advance, and this prevents crystallization of class lines on an economic basis." Perhaps the absence of archaeological evidence for social ranking in pre-Mississippian societies of the American Bottom, which would be based on differential artifact accumulation in households, is an effect of such leveling mechanisms.

The decision-making processes for ceremonial scheduling—"appropriational movements"—can only be conjectured for the four-century period preceding Mississippian culture in the American Bottom. The "locational movements" of this period are observable in that we can see certain artifacts moving around the landscape and can observe changes in community plans and artifact associations. We can also distinguish the final effect of such processes by A.D. 1050 at Cahokia, where we can see the visible mortuary remains of elites and retainers, exotic goods, figurines reflecting a complex cosmology based on underworld and upper-world renewal symbolism (Emerson 1989), large palisaded enclosures, observatories, and evidence for massive earth-moving projects.

The emergence of controlling polities and social ranking at A.D. 1050 appears to have been rapid and, in many respects, unpredictable. While I believe such authority emerged as a result of a longer-term process related to the regulation of renewal ceremonialism, support for this speculation in the archaeological record is ambiguous at best. To determine whether or not such an elite structure existed at the end of the Emergent Mississippian period, we need to conduct archaeological investigations at possibly larger Emergent Mississippian mound centers such as Pulcher, Maeys, or Washausen. Evidence for Emergent Mississippian elite hierarchies at Cahokia is lacking at this time and may be difficult to find, given the extent of construction activities after A.D. 1050. I should point out, however, that even if evidence for pre-Mississippian hierarchically-ranked society were identified at these locations, it would still not provide an *explanation* for the sudden appearance of the kind of cultural complexity evidenced at Cahokia at A.D. 1050. Appropriational decisions, such as the passage of rights and power to an individual or lineage, could be made rapidly and, more importantly, would leave no evidence in the ground.

The structure of political authority and how it came to be empowered are obviously critical issues in understanding the emergence of such a complex social format. The elusive nature of so-called appropriational movements in the archaeological record is noteworthy but should not impede our understanding of political economy during this period or its basis in social relations. We should not regard economic structure as an isolated, tangible entity, simply identified by its subsistence remains or artifacts, but as an integrative component of a given cultural system, virtually inseparable from technological, subsistence, corporate descent, and ideological aspects of culture.

The economic organizing principle of renewal presented above consists of a series of interwoven sociological, political, subsistence-related, technological, and ideological formations. Busk ceremonialism, which I envision originating and becoming instituted during the four centuries prior to the Mississippian period, is a good example of how all these formations are integrated into a yearly cycle of embedded activities. In this sense, a decision to organize a particular community around a central courtyard is not solely economically, ideologically, or politically mandated, but is a product of an integrative, corporate worldview which *simultaneously* takes into consideration questions about a community's symbolic position in the universe (ideology), the placement and organization of food processing and storage tasks (subsistence), the methods of house construction (technology), and the relative positioning of human beings (political sociology) within the community landscape.

ACKNOWLEDGMENTS

This paper would not have been possible without the moral and financial support of Dr. John A. Walthall, Chief Archaeologist at the Illinois Department of Transportation, and Dr. Thomas E. Emerson, Director of the Illinois Transportation Archaeological Research Program (ITARP). I have also benefited immensely from nearly 25 years of interaction with fellow American Bottom prehistorians Thomas E. Emerson, Dale L. McElrath, Charles J. Bareis, John E. Kelly, and Thomas O. Maher. The figures in this essay were generated by ITARP graphic production specialists Michael Lewis and Linda Alexander. These figures are used with permission from ITARP. Finally, I wish to express my appreciation to Barry Isaac and Bob Connolly for their thorough and thought provoking editorial comments and for introducing me to the world of economic anthropology.

REFERENCES

Ahler, S.R.,M.J. Bade, F.B. King, B.W. Styles, and P.J. Thorson (1992) *Late Archaic Components at Modoc Rock Shelter, Randolph County, Illinois.* Springfield: Illinois State Museum, Reports of Investigations, No. 48.

Asch, N. B., R. I. Ford, and D. L. Asch (1972) *Paleoethnobotany of the Koster Site: The Archaic Horizons.* Springfield: Illinois State Museum, Reports of Investigations, No. 24.

Bareis, C. J., and J.W. Porter, eds. (1984) *American Bottom Archaeology: A Summary of the FAI-270 Project Contribution to the Culture History of the Mississippi River Valley.* Urbana: University of Illinois Press.

Bentz, C., ed. (1988) *The Bailey Site (40GL26): Late Archaic, Middle Woodland, and Historic Settlement and Subsistence in the Lower Elk River Drainage of Tennessee.* Knoxville: Tennessee Department of Transportation, Environmental Planning Office, Publications in Archaeology No. 2, and Tennessee Department of Environment and Conservation, Division of Archaeology, Miscellaneous Publication No.2.

_____. (n.d.) "Late Middle Woodland Occupations in the American Bottom Area." Paper presented at the Illinois Archaeological Survey Workshop, Bloomington, 1980.

Bentz, C., D. L. McElrath, F. A. Finney, and R. B. Lacampagne (1988) *Late Woodland Sites in the American Bottom Uplands.* Urbana: University of Illinois Press, American Bottom Archaeology FAI-270 Site Reports, Vol. 18.

Berres, T. E. (1984) *A Formal Analysis of Ceramic Vessels from the Schlemmer Site (11-S-382): A Late Woodland/Mississippian Occupation in St. Clair County, Illinois.* M.A. thesis, Western Michigan University.

Binford, L. R. (1980) "Willow Smoke and Dog's Tails: Hunter-Gatherer Settlement Systems and Archaeological Site Formation." *American Antiquity* 45:4-20.

Binford, L.R., S. R. Binford, R.C. Whallon, and M.A. Hardin (1970) *Archaeology at Hatchery West.* Menasha, WI: Society for American Archaeology, Memoirs 24.

Braun, D.P. (1977) *Middle Woodland-(Early) Late Woodland Social Change in the Prehistoric Central Midwestern U.S.* Ph.D. dissertation, University of Michigan.

_____. (1979) "Illinois Hopewell Burial Practices and Social Organization: A Reexamination of the Klunk-Gibson Mound Group." Pp. 66-79 in D.S. Brose & N. Greber (eds.) *Hopewell Archeology: The Chillicothe Conference.* Kent, OH: The Kent State University Press.

Brown, J. A., R.A. Kerber, and H.D. Winter (1990) "Trade and the Evolution of Exchange Relations at the Beginning of the Mississippian Period." Pp. 251-280 in B.D. Smith (ed.) *The Mississippian Emergence.* Washington, DC: Smithsonian Institution Press.

Buikstra, J. E. (1976) *Hopewell in the Lower Illinois Valley: A Regional Approach to the Study of Human Biological Variability and Prehistoric Behavior.* Evanston, IL: Northwestern University Archeological Program, Scientific Papers, 2.

Burghardt, A. F. (1971) "A Hypothesis about Gateway Cities." *Annals of the Association of American Geographers* 61:269-285.

Chapman, C. H. (1988) *The Archaeology of Missouri, I.* Columbia: University of Missouri Press, Missouri Studies, LXII.

Chesnikov, D. I. (1969) *Historical Materialism.* Moscow: Progress Publishers.

Clay, R.B. (1988) "Peter Village: An Adena Enclosure." Pp. 19-30 in R.C. Mainfort, Jr. (ed.) *Middle Woodland Settlement and Ceremonialism in the Mid-South and Lower Mississippi Valley.* Jackson: Mississippi Department of Archives and History, Archaeological Report No. 22.

Conrad, L. A. (1981) *An Introduction to the Archaeology of Upland West Central Illinois: A Preliminary Archaeological Survey of the Canton to Quincey Corridor for the Proposed FAP 407 Highway Project.* Macomb: Western Illinois University, Archaeological Research Laboratory Reports of Investigations, No. 2.

Cook, T. G. (1976) *Koster. An Artifact Analysis of Two Archaic Phases in Westcentral Illinois.* Evanston, IL: Northwestern University Archaeological Program, Prehistoric Records, No. 1, and Koster Research Reports, No. 3.

Cross, P. G. (1985) "Faunal Remains." Pp. 271-287 in A.B. Stahl, *The Dohack Site (11-S-642),* Urbana: University of Illinois Press, American Bottom Archaeology FAI-270 Site Reports, Vol.12.

Culin, S. (1907) *Games of the North American Indians.* Washington, DC: Smithsonian Institution, 24th Annual Report of the Bureau of American Ethnology.

Dalton, G., ed. (1968) *Primitive, Archaic, and Modern Economies: Essays of Karl Polanyi.* Boston, MA: Beacon Press.

_____ . (1977) "Aboriginal Economies in Stateless Societies." Pp. 191-212 in T.K. Earle & J. E. Ericson (eds.) *Exchange Systems in Prehistory.* New York: Academic Press.

DeBoer, W.R. (1993) "Like a Rolling Stone: The Chunkey Game and Political Organization in Eastern North America." *Southeastern Archaeology* 12(2):83-92.

Deuel, T. (1952) "The Hopewellian Community." Pp. 249-265 in T. Deuel (ed.) *Hopewellian Communities in Illinois.* Springfield: Illinois State Museum, Scientific Papers, 5.

Dragoo, D.W. (1955) "Excavations at the Johnston Site, Indiana County, Pennsylvania." *Pennsylvania Archaeologist* 25(2):85-141.

Emerson, T. E. (1984) "The Dyroff and Levin Sites." Pp. 201-362 in A.C. Fortier, *The Go-Kart North Site,* and T.E. Emerson, *The Dyroff and Levin Sites.* Urbana: University of Illinois Press, American Bottom Archaeology FAI-270 Site Reports, Vol. 9.

_____ . (1989) "Water, Serpents, and the Underworld: An Exploration into Cahokian Symbolism." Pp. 45-92 in P. Galloway (ed.) *The Southeastern Ceremonial Complex: Artifacts and Analysis.* Lincoln: University of Nebraska Press.

_____ . (1995) *Settlement, Symbolism, and Hegemony in the Cahokian Countryside.* Ph.D. dissertation, University of Wisconsin, Madison.

Emerson, T.E., and A.C. Fortier (1986) "Early Woodland Cultural Variation, Subsistence, and Settlement in the American Bottom." Pp. 475-522 in K.B. Farnsworth & T.E. Emerson (eds.) *Early Woodland Archeology,* Kampsville, IL: Center for American Archeology, Kampsville Seminars in Archeology, Vol. 2.

Emerson, T.E., and D.J. Jackson (1987) *Emergent Mississippian and Early Mississippian Homesteads at the Marcus Site (11-S-631).* Urbana: University of Illinois Press, American Bottom Archeology FAI-270 Site Reports, Vol. 17, No.2:305-391.

Emerson, T.E., and D.L. McElrath (1983) "A Settlement-Subsistence Model of the Terminal Late Archaic Adaptation in the American Bottom, Illinois." Pp. 219-242 in J.L. Phillips & J.A.

Brown (eds.) *Archaic Hunters and Gatherers in the American Midwest.* New York: Academic Press.

Emerson, T.E., D.L. McElrath, and J.A. Williams (1986) "Patterns of Hunter-Gatherer Mobility and Sedentism during the Archaic Period in the American Bottom." Pp. 247-273 in S.W. Neusius (ed.) *Foraging, Collecting, and Harvesting: Archaic Period Subsistence and Settlement in the Eastern Woodlands.* Carbondale: Southern Illinois University, Center for Archaeological Investigations, Occasional Papers, No. 6.

Emerson, T.E., G.R. Milner, and D.K. Jackson (1983) *The Florence Street Site (11-S-458).* Urbana: University of Illinois Press, American Bottom Archaeology FAI-270 Site Reports, Vol. 2.

Evans, B.J. (n.d.) "Cultural Discontinuity in the American Bottom During the Late Archaic-Early Woodland Transition." Paper presented to the Society for American Archaeology, Minneapolis, 1995.

Ford, J.A., P. Phillips, and W.G. Haag (1955) *The Jaketown Site in West-Central Mississippi.* New York: Anthropological Papers of the American Museum of Natural History, Vol. 45, Part I.

Fortier, A.C. (1983) "Settlement and Subsistence at the Go-Kart North Site: A Late Archaic Titterington Occupation in the American Bottom, Illinois." Pp. 243-260 in J.L. Phillips & J.A. Brown (eds.) *Archaic Hunters and Gatherers in the American Midwest.* New York: Academic Press.

_____. (1984) "The Go-Kart North Site." Pp. 2-197 in A.C. Fortier, *The Go-Kart North Site,* and T.E. Emerson, *The Dyroff and Levin Sites.* Urbana: University of Illinois Press, American Bottom Archaeology FAI-270 Site Reports, Vol. 9.

_____. (1985a) "Middle Woodland Occupation at the Truck #7 and Go-Kart South Sites." Pp. 163-280 in A.C. Fortier, *Selected Sites in the Hill Lake Locality.* Urbana: University of Illinois Press, American Bottom Archaeology FAI-270 Site Reports, Vol. 13.

_____. (1985b) "The Robert Schneider Site (11-Ms-1177)." Pp.171-313 in F.A. Finney, *The Carbon Dioxide Site (11-Mo-594),* and A.C. Fortier, *The Robert Schneider Site (11-Ms-1177).* Urbana: University of Illinois Press, American Bottom Archaeology FAI-270 Site Reports, Vol. 11.

_____. (1986) *The Meyer Site: A Late Archaic Occupation in the American Bottom.* Urbana: University of Illinois, Department of Anthropology, FAI-270 Archaeological Mitigation Project Report No. 72.

_____. (1991) "Sponemann Phase Features and Community Organization." Pp. 55-156 in A.C. Fortier, T.O. Maher & J.A. Williams, *The Sponemann Site: The Formative Emergent Mississippian Sponemann Phase Occupations (11-Ms-517).* Urbana: University of Illinois Press, American Bottom Archaeology FAI-270 Site Reports, Vol. 23.

_____. (1992) "Interpretation." Pp. 339-348 in D.J. Jackson, A.C. Fortier & J.A. Williams *The Sponemann Site 2: The Mississippian and Oneota Occupations (11-Ms-517).* Urbana: University of Illinois Press, American Bottom Archaeology FAI-270 Site Reports, Vol. 24.

_____. (1993) "American Bottom House Types of the Archaic and Woodland Periods: An Overview." Pp. 260-275 in T.E. Emerson, A.C. Fortier & D.L. McElrath (eds.) *Highways to the Past: Essays in Illinois Archaeology in Honor of Charles J. Bareis. Illinois Archaeology, Vol. 5 (1 & 2)* (whole issue).

_____. (1996) *The Marge Site (11-Mo-99): Late Archaic and Emergent Mississippian Occupations in the Palmer Creek Locality.* Urbana: University of Illinois Press, American Bottom Archaeology FAI-270 Site Reports, Vol. 27.

_____. (n.d.) "Renaissance and Disequilibrium: Middle Woodland Discontinuities in the American Bottom." Paper presented to the Society for American Archaeology, Minneapolis,1995.

Fortier, A.C., et al. [F.A. Finney and R. B. Lacampagne] (1983) *The Mund Site (11-S-435).* Urbana: University of Illinois, American Bottom Archaeology FAI-270 Site Reports, Vol. 5.

_____. [T.E. Emerson and F.A. Finney] (1984a) "Early Woodland and Middle Woodland Periods." Pp. 59-103 in C.J. Bareis & J.W. Porter (eds.), *supra.*

_____. R.B. Lacampagne and F.A. Finney] (1984b) *The Fish Lake Site (11-Mo-608.* Urbana: University of Illinois Press, American Bottom Archaeology FAI-270 Site Reports, Vol. 8.

_____ . [T.O. Maher, J.A. Williams, M.C. Meinkoth, K. E. Parker, and L.S. Kelly] (1989) *The Holding Site: A Hopewell Community in the American Bottom (11-Ms-118)*. Urbana: University of Illinois Press, American Bottom Archaeology FAI-270 Site Reports, Vol. 19.

Freeman, J. E. (1969) "The Millville Site, A Middle Woodland Village in Grant County, Wisconsin." *The Wisconsin Archeologist* (n.s.) 50:37-88.

Green, W. (1993) "A Prehistoric Frontier in the Prairie Peninsula: Late Woodland Upland Settlement and Subsistence Patterns." Pp. 201-214 in T.E. Emerson, A.C. Fortier & D.L. McElrath (eds.) *Highways to the Past: Essays on Illinois Archaeology in Honor of Charles J. Bareis*. Urbana: *Illinois Archaeology, Vol. 5 (1&2)* (whole issue).

Griffin, J.B., R.E. Flanders, and P. F. Titterington (1970) *The Burial Complexes of the Knight and Norton Mounds in Illinois and Michigan*. Ann Arbor: University of Michigan, Museum of Anthropology, Memoirs 2.

Haag, W.G., and C. H. Webb (1953) "Microblades at Poverty Point Sites." *American Antiquity* 18:245-248.

Hall, R. L. (1967) "The Mississippian Heartland and Its Plains Relationships." *Plains Anthropologist* 12:175-183.

_____ . (1987) "Calumet Ceremonialism, Mourning Ritual, and Mechanisms of Inter-Tribal Trade." Pp. 29-43 in D.W. Ingersoll & G. Bronitski (eds.) *Mirror and Metaphor: Material and Social Constructions of Reality*. Lanham, MD: University Press of America.

_____ . (1997) *An Archaeology of the Soul: North American Indian Belief and Ritual*. Urbana: University of Illinois Press.

Halperin, R. H. (1994) *Cultural Economies, Past and Present*. Austin: University of Texas Press.

Harl, J.L. (1995) *Data Recovery Investigations at the Hayden Site (23SL36) and the Rabanus Site (23SL859), Chesterfield, St. Louis County, Missouri: New Insights into the Titterington/Sedalia Phase in East-Central Missouri*. St. Louis: University of Missouri-St. Louis, Archaeological Services, Department of Anthropology, and Division of Continuing Education-Outreach, Research Report No. 182.

Helms, M.W. (1993) *Craft and the Kingly Ideal: Art, Trade, and Power*. Austin: University of Texas Press.

Herskovits, M. J. (1952) *Economic Anthropology*. New York: Alfred A. Knopf.

Hirth, K. G. (1984) "Early Exchange in Mesoamerica: An Introduction." Pp. 1-15 in K. G. Hirth (ed.) *Trade and Exchange in Early Mesoamerica*. Albuquerque: University of New Mexico Press.

Hodder, I. (1979) "Economic and Social Stress and Material Culture Patterning." *American Antiquity* 44:446-454.

Hofman, J.L. (1987) "Hopewell Blades From Twenhafel: Distinguishing Local and Foreign Core Technology." Pp. 87-117 in J.K. Johnson & C.A. Morrow (eds.) *The Organization of Core Technology*. Boulder, CO: Westview Press.

Hofman, J.L., and C. Morrow (1985) "Chipped Stone Technologies at Twenhafel: A Multicomponent Site in Southern Illinois." Pp. 165-182 in S.C. Vehik (ed.) *Lithic Resource-Procurement: Proceedings From the Second Conference on Prehistoric Chert Exploitation*. Carbondale: Southern Illinois University, Center for Archaeological Investigations, Occasional Paper 4.

Houart, G. L. (1971) *Koster: A Stratified Archaic Site in the Illinois Valley*. Springfield: Illinois State Museum Investigations, No. 22, and Illinois Valley Archeology Program, Research Papers, 4.

Howard, J. H. (1968) *The Southeastern Ceremonial Complex and Its Interpretation*. Columbia: Missouri Archaeological Society, Memoir No. 6.

Hus, H. (1908) "An Ecological Cross-Section of the Mississippi River in the Region of St. Louis, Missouri." *Missouri Botanical Garden, Annual Report* 19:127-258.

Ives, D. J. (1984) "The Crescent Hills Prehistoric Quarrying Area: More Than Just Rocks." Pp. 187-195 in B.M. Butler & E. May (eds.) *Prehistoric Chert Exploitation: Studies From the Midcontinent*. Carbondale: Southern Illinois University, Center for Archaeological Investigations, Occasional Paper 2.

Johannessen, S. (1983) "Plant Remains From the Mund Phase." Pp. 299-318 in A.C. Fortier, F.A. Finney & R.B. Lacampagne, *supra*.

_____. (1985a) "Plant Remains." Pp. 97-102 in F.A. Finney, *The Carbon Dioxide Site (11-Mo-594)*, and A.C. Fortier, *The Robert Schneider Site (11-Ms-1177)*. Urbana: University of Illinois Press, American Bottom Archaeology FAI-270 Site Reports, Vol. 11.

_____. (1986b) "Plant Remains." Pp. 249-269 in A.B. Stahl, *The Dohack Site (11-S-642)*. Urbana: University of Illinois Press, American Bottom Archaeology FAI-270 Site Reports, Vol. 12.

Kay, M. (1979) "On the Periphery: Hopewell Settlement of Central Missouri." Pp. 94-99 in D.S. Brose & N. Greber (eds.) *Hopewell Archaeology. The Chillicothe Conference*. Kent, OH: Kent State University Press.

Kelly, J. E. (1982) *Formative Developments at Cahokia and the Adjacent American Bottom: A Merrell Tract Perspective*. Macomb:Western Illinois University Archaeological Research Laboratory.

_____. (1984) "Late Bluff Chert Utilization on the Merrell Tract, Cahokia." Pp. 23-44 in B.M. Butler & E. May (eds.) *Prehistoric Chert Exploitation: Studies From the Midcontinent*. Carbondale: Southern Illinois University, Center for Archaeological Investigations, Occasional Paper 2.

_____. (1990) "Range Site Community Patterns and the Mississippian Emergence." Pp. 67-112 in B.D. Smith (ed.) *The Mississippian Emergence*. Washington, DC: Smithsonian Institution Press.

_____. (1991a) "Cahokia and Its Role as a Gateway Center in Interregional Exchange." Pp. 61-80 in T.E. Emerson & R.B. Lewis (eds.) *Cahokia and the Hinterlands: Middle Mississippian Cultures of the Midwest*. Urbana: University of Illinois Press.

_____. (1991b) "The Evidence for Prehistoric Exchange and Its Implications for the Development of Cahokia." Pp. 65-92 in J.B. Stoltman (ed.) *New Perspectives on Cahokia: Views from the Periphery*. Madison, WI: Prehistory Press, Monographs in World Archaeology, No. 2.

Kelly, J.E., F.A. Finney, D.L. McElrath, and S.J. Ozuk (1984) "Late Woodland Period." Pp. 104-127 in C.J. Bareis & J.W. Porter (eds.), *supra*.

Kelly, J.E., A.C. Fortier, S.J. Ozuk, and J.A. Williams (1987) *The Range Site: Archaic Through Late Woodland Occupations (11-S-47)*. Urbana: University of Illinois Press, American Bottom Archaeology FAI-270 Site Reports, Vol. 16.

Kelly, J.E., J.R. Linder, and T.J. Cartmell (1979) *The Archaeological Intensive Survey of the FAI-270 Alignment in the American Bottom Region of Southern Illinois*. Springfield:Illinois Transportation Archaeology Scientific Reports, No. 1.

Kelly, J.E., S.J. Ozuk, and J.A. Williams (1990) *The Range Site 2: The Emergent Mississippian Dohack and Range Phase Occupations (11-S-47)*. Urbana: University of Illinois Press, American Bottom Archaeology FAI-270 Site Reports, Vol. 20.

Kelly, L.S. (1991) "Sponemann Phase Fauna." Pp. 421-440 in A.C. Fortier, T.O. Maher & J.A. Williams, *The Sponemann Site: The Formative Emergent Mississippian Sponemann Phase Occupations*. Urbana: University of Illinois Press, American Bottom Archaeology FAI-270 Site Reports, Vol. 23.

Klippel, W.E. (1969) *The Booth Site: A Late Archaic Campsite*. Columbia: Missouri Archaeological Society Research Series, No. 6.

Maher, T. O. (1989) "The Middle Woodland Ceramic Assemblage." Pp. 125-318 in A.C. Fortier, T.O. Maher, J.A. Williams, M.C. Meinkoth, K.E. Parker & L.S. Kelly, *supra*.

McElrath, D.L. (1986) *The Mclean Site (11-S-640)*. Urbana: University of Illinois Press, American Bottom Archaeology FAI-270 Site Reports, Vol. 14.

_____. (1993) "Mule Road: A Newly Defined Late Archaic Phase in the American Bottom." Pp. 148-157 in T.E. Emerson, A.C. Fortier & D.L. McElrath (eds.) *Highways to the Past: Essays on Illinois Archaeology in Honor of Charles J. Bareis. Illinois Archaeology, Vol. 5 (1 & 2)* (whole issue).

McElrath, D.L., T.E. Emerson, A.C. Fortier, and J.L. Phillips (1984) "Late Archaic Period." Pp. 34-58 in C.J. Bareis & J.W. Porter (eds.), *supra*.

McElrath, D.L. and F.A. Finney (1987) *The George Reeves Site (11-S-650)*. Urbana: University of Illinois Press, American Bottom Archaeology FAI-270 Site Reports, Vol. 15.

McElrath, D.L. and A.C. Fortier (1983) *The Missouri Pacific #2 Site (11-S-46)*. Urbana: University of Illinois Press, American Bottom Archaeology FAI-270 Site Reports, Vol. 3.

_____. (n.d.) "The Development of Late Woodland Culture in the American Bottom." Paper presented to The Urbana Late Woodland Conference, Urbana, Illinois, 1997.

McGregor, J.C. (1952) "The Havana Site." Pp. 43-91 in T. Deuel (ed.) *Hopewellian Communities in Illinois*. Springfield: Illinois State Museum, Scientific Papers, 5(2).

_____. (1958) *The Pool and Irving Villages: A Study of Hopewell Occupation in the Illinois River Valley*. Urbana: University of Illinois Press.

Meggers, B. J., ed. (1956) "Functional and Evolutionary Implications of Community Patterning." Pp. 129-157 in R. Wauchope (ed.) *Seminars in Archaeology: 1955*. Salt Lake City, UT: Memoirs of the Society for American Archaeology, No. 11.

Meinkoth, M. C., K. Hedman, and D.L. McElrath (1996) *The Cunningham Site: A Late Woodland Occupation in the American Bottom (11-Ms-1353)*. Urbana: University of Illinois, Illinois Transportation Archaeological Research Program Research Reports, No. 41.

Milner, G. R. (1984) *The Robinson's Lake Site (11-Ms-582)*. Urbana: University of Illinois Press, American Bottom Archaeology FAI-270 Site Reports, Vol. 10.

Nash, M. (1966) *Primitive and Peasant Economic Systems*. Scranton, PA: Chandler Publishing Co.

Nassaney, M.S., and N.H. Lopinot (1986) "The Significance of a Short-Term Late Archaic Occupation in the American Bottom." Pp. 201-224 in S.W. Neusius (ed.) *Foraging, Collecting and Harvesting: Archaic Period Subsistence and Settlement in the Eastern Woodlands*. Carbondale: Southern Illinois University, Center for Archaeologcal Investigations, Occasional Paper No. 6.

Nassaney, M.S., N. H. Lopinot, B.M. Butler, and R. W. Jefferies (1983) *The 1982 Excavations at the Cahokia Interpretive Center Tract, St. Clair, Illinois*. Carbondale: Southern Illinois University, Center for Archaeological Investigations, Research Paper No. 37.

Neumann, G.K., and M. L. Fowler (1952) "Hopewellian Sites in the Wabash Valley." Pp. 175-248 in T.Deuel (ed.) *Hopewellian Communities in Illinois*. Springfield: Illinois State Museum, Scientific Papers, 5.

Parker, K.E. (1989) "Archaeobotanical Assemblage." Pp. 429-464 in A.C. Fortier, T.O. Maher, J.A. Williams, M.C. Meinkoth, K.E. Parker & L.S. Kelly, *supra*.

_____. (1991) "Sponemann Phase Archaeobotany." Pp. 377-419 in A.C. Fortier, T.O. Maher & J.A. Williams *The Sponemann Site: The Formative Emergent Mississippian Sponemann Phase Occupations (11-Ms-517)* Urbana: University of Illinois Press, American Bottom Archaeology FAI-270 Site Reports, Vol. 23.

_____. (1996) "Floral Analysis." Pp. 173-186 in M.C. Meinkoth, K. Hedman & D.L. McElrath, *supra*.

Pauketat, T.R. (1987) "Mississippian Domestic Economy and Formation Processes: A Response to Prentice." *Midcontinental Journal of Archaeology* 12:77-88.

_____. (1991) *The Dynamics of Pre-State Political Centralization in the North American Midcontinent*. Ph.D. dissertation, University of Michigan.

_____. (1994) *The Ascent of Chiefs and Mississippian Politics in Native North America*. Tuscaloosa: University of Alabama Press.

Perino, G. (1973) "The Koster Mounds, Greene County, Illinois." Pp. 141-206 in J.A. Brown (ed.) *Late Woodland Site Archaeology in Illinois 1: Investigations in South-Central Illinois*. Urbana: Illinois Archaeological Survey, Bulletin No. 9.

Phillips, J.L., R.L. Hall, and R.W. Yerkes (1980) *Investigations at the Labras Lake Site: Vol. 1, Archaeology*. Chicago: University of Illinois at Chicago, Department of Anthropology, Reports of Investigations, 1.

Polanyi, K. (1957) "The Economy as Instituted Process." Pp. 243-270 in K. Polanyi, C. Arensberg & H.W. Pearson (eds.) *Trade and Market in the Early Empires*. New York: The Free Press.

Reid, K.C. (1976) "Prehistoric Trade in the Lower Missouri River Valley: An Analysis of Middle Woodland Bladelets." Pp. 63-99 in A.E. Jonhson (ed.) *Hopewellian Archaeology in the Lower Missouri Valley.* Lawrence: University of Kansas Publications in Anthropology, 8.

Riley, T.J., G.R. Waltz, C.J. Bareis, A.C. Fortier, and K.E. Parker (1994) "Accelerator Mass Spectrometry (AMS) Dates Confirm Early *Zea Mays* in the Mississippi River Valley." *American Antiquity* 59:490-498.

Roper, D.C. (1978) *The Airport Site. A Multicomponent Site in the Sangamon River Drainage.* Springfield: Illinois State Museum Research Series, Papers in Anthropology, No. 4.

Russo, M. (1994) "A Brief Introduction to the Study of Archaic Mounds in the Southeast." *Southeastern Archaeology* 13(2):89-93.

Sahlins, M.D. (1963) "Poor Man, Rich Man, Big-Man, Chief: Political Types in Melanesia and Polynesia." *Comparative Studies in Society and History* 5:285-303.

_____. (1972) *Stone Age Economics.* New York: Aldine.

Sanger, D. (1970) "Mid-Latitude Core and Blade Traditions." *Arctic Anthropology* 7:106-114.

Seeman, M.F. (1979) "Feasting with the Dead: Ohio Hopewell Charnel House Ritual as a Context for Redistribution." Pp. 39-46 in D.S. Brose & N. Greber (eds.) *Hopewell Archaeology: The Chillicothe Conference.* Kent, OH: Kent State University Press.

_____. (1992) "Woodland Traditions in the Midcontinent: A Comparison of Three Regional Sequences." Pp. 3-46 in D.R. Croes, R.A. Hawkins & B.L. Isaac (eds.) *Long-Term Subsistence Change in Prehistoric North America.* Greenwich, CT: JAI Press, Research in Economic Anthropology, Supplement 6.

_____. (1995) "When Words Are Not Enough: Hopewell Interregionalism and the Use of Material Symbols at the GE Mound." Pp. 122-143 in M.S. Nassaney & K.E. Sassaman (eds.) *Native American Interactions. Multiscalar Analyses and Interpretations in the Eastern Woodlands.* Knoxville: University of Tennessee Press.

Sherrod, P.C., and M.A. Rolingson (1987) *Surveyors of the Ancient Mississippi Valley.* Fayetteville: Arkansas Archeological Survey Research Series, No. 28.

Shott, M.J. (1993) "Spears, Darts and Arrows: Late Woodland Hunting Techniques in the Upper Ohio Valley." *American Antiquity* 58:425-443.

Smith, I.F. (1974) "Keyholes, Ping Pong Paddles or Turtle Pits." *Eastern States Archaeological Federation*, Bulletin 13:15-16.

_____. (1976) "A Functional Interpretation of Keyhole Structures in the Northeast." *Pennsylvania Archaeologist* 46 (1-2):1-12.

Stafford, B. D., and M.B. Sant, eds. (1985) *Smiling Dan: Structure and Function at a Middle Woodland Settlement in the Lower Illinois Valley.* Kampsville, IL: Kampsville Archeological Center, Research Series, Vol. 2.

Steward, J.H. (1938) *Basin-Plateau Aboriginal Sociopolitical Groups.* Washington, DC: Smithsonian Institution, Bureau of American Ethnology, Bulletin No. 120.

Struever, S., and G.L. Houart (1972) "An Analysis of the Hopewell Interaction Sphere." Pp. 47-79 in E.N. Wilmsen (ed.) *Social Exchange and Interaction.* Ann Arbor: University of Michigan, Museum of Anthropology, Anthopological Papers, No. 46.

Swanton, J.R. (1928) *Religious Beliefs and Medical Practices of the Creek Indians.* Washington, DC: Bureau of American Ethnology, 42nd Annual Report, pp. 473-672.

_____. (1946) *The Indians of the Southeastern United States.* Washington, DC: Smithsonian Institution, Bureau of American Ethnology, Bulletin 137.

Thomas, D.H. (1972) "Western Shosone Ecology: Settlement Patterns and Beyond." Pp. 135-153 in D.D. Fowler (ed.) *Great Basin Cultural Ecology:A Symposium.* Reno, NV: Desert Research Institue, Publications in the Social Sciences, No.8.

Titterington, P.F. (1950) "Some Non-Pottery Sites in the St. Louis Area." *Journal of the Illinois State Archaeological Society* 1:18-31.

Turner, R. (1965) *Green Ridge: A Late Archaic Site of the Sedalia Complex in West Central Missouri.* Columbia: Missouri Archaeological Society Research Series, 3.

Vennum, T., Jr. (1994) *American Indian Lacrosse: Little Brother of War.* Washington, DC: Smithsonian Institution Press.

Waring, A. J., Jr. (1968) "The Southern Cult and Muskhogean Ceremonial." Pp. 30-69 in S.Williams (ed.) *The Waring Papers: The Collected Works of Antonio J. Waring, Jr..* Cambridge, MA: Harvard University, Papers of the Peabody Museum of Archaeology and Ethnology, Vol. 58.

Weist, K.M. (1973) "Giving Away: The Ceremonial Distribution of Goods Among the Northern Cheyenne of Southeastern Montana." *Plains Anthropologist* 18:97-103.

Whalley, L. (1990) "Dohack Phase Floral Remains." Pp. 269-280 in J.E. Kelly, S.J. Ozuk & J.A. Williams, *supra.*

White, W.P., S. Johannessen, P.G. Cross, and L.S. Kelly (1984) "Environmental Setting." Pp. 15-33 in C.J. Bareis & J.W. Porter (ed.), *supra.*

Wiant, M.D., and C.R. McGimsey, eds. (1986) *Woodland Period Occupations of the Napoleon Hollow Site in the Lower Illinois Valley.* Kampsville, IL: Kampsville Archeological Center, Research Series, Vol. 6.

Williams, J.A. (1989) "Lithic Assemblage." Pp. 319-428 in A.C. Fortier, T.O. Maher, J.A. Williams, M.C. Meinkoth, K.E. Parker & L.S. Kelly, *supra.*

———. (1993) "Meridian Hills: An Upland Holding Phase Middle Woodland Habitation Site." Pp. 193-200 in T.E. Emerson, A.C. Fortier & D.L. McElrath (eds.) *Highways to the Past: Essays in Illinois Archaeology in Honor of Charles J. Bareis. Illinois Archaeology 5 (1 & 2)* (whole issue).

Williams, S. (1954) *An Archaeological Study of the Mississippian Culture in Southeast Missouri.* Ph.D. dissertation, Yale University.

———., ed. (1977) *The Waring Papers: The Collected Works of Antonio J. Waring, Jr.* Cambridge, MA: Harvard University, Papers of the Peabody Museum of Archaeology and Ethnology, Vol. 58.

Wilson, G. L. (1917) *Agriculture of the Hidatsa Indians: An Indian Interpretation.* Minneapolis: University of Minnesota, Studies in the Social Sciences, No. 9.

Winters, H. D. (1969) *The Riverton Culture: A Second Millenium Occupation in the Central Wabash Valley.* Springfield: Illinois State Museum, Reports of Investigations, No. 13, and Illinois Archeological Survey Monograph, No.1.

Witthoft, J. (1949) *Green Corn Ceremonialism in the Eastern Woodlands.* Ann Arbor: University of Michigan, Museum of Anthropology, Occasional Contributions, No. 13.

Wittry, W.L. (1969) "The American Woodhenge." Pp. 43-48 in M.L. Fowler (ed.) *Explorations into Cahokia Archaeology.* Springfield: Illinois Archaeological Survey, Bulletin No. 7.

Wolforth, T. (1989) *Archaeological Investigations at the Wilderman Site (11-S-729) St. Clair County, Illinois.* Urbana, IL: Resource Investigation Program Research Reports, No. 31.

Wray, D.E., and R.S. MacNeish (1961) *The Hopewellian and Weaver Occupations of the Weaver Site, Fulton County, Illinois.* Springfield: Illinois State Museum, Scientific Papers, 7(2).

Yerkes, R.W. (1987) *Prehistoric Life on the Mississippi Floodplain: Stone Tool Use, Settlement Organization and Subsistence Practices at the Labras Lake Site, Illinois.* Chicago: University of Chicago Press.